Roger Courtney was born and brought up in a Presbyterian family in Belfast. His mother was a daughter of the manse. He was educated at Belfast 'Inst' (Royal Belfast Academical Institution) and Queen's University Belfast, where he studied psychology and philosophy. Having trained as a community and youth worker in Birmingham, he set up the Crescent Arts Centre in south Belfast. For 16 years he was Chief Executive of the Simon Community NI providing accommodation for people who are homeless. For the past 15 years he has been working as a freelance consultant, mentor, trainer and lecturer. He has written extensively on the management of voluntary organisations and fundraising. His main hobby is music and he is the composer of the well-known peace hymn, 'The Pollen of Peace'.

D1354065

2/2208108

The Presbyterian is happiest when he is being a radical.

A.T.Q. STEWART

DISSENTING VOICES

REDISCOVERING THE IRISH PROGRESSIVE PRESBYTERIAN TRADITION

PROFILES OF 300 PROGRESSIVE PRESBYTERIANS OVER FOUR CENTURIES

ROGER COURTNEY

ULSTER HISTORICAL FOUNDATION

This book has received financial support from the Northern Ireland Community
Relations Council which aims to promote a pluralist society characterised by
equity, respect for diversity and recognition of interdependence. The views
expressed do not necessarily reflect those of the Council.

Community Relations Council

Ulster Historical Foundation is pleased to acknowledge support for this publication
provided by the Northern Ireland Community Relations Council
and Atlantic Philanthropies.

BACK COVER IMAGES
From left to right: William Steel Dickson, Henry Joy McCracken
Isabella Tod, Ray Davey and William Neilson

Published 2013
by Ulster Historical Foundation,
49 Malone Road, Belfast BT9 6RY
www.ancestryireland.com
www.booksireland.org.uk

© Roger Courtney
ISBN: 978-1-909556-06-5

DESIGN AND FORMATTING
FPM Publishing

PRINTED BY
Bell & Bain Ltd.

Contents

Foreword

This book is a reminder that all institutions, including churches, are led, or indeed misled, by people like ourselves. The church is like a ship on the sea in all kinds of weather; sometimes all seems calm, sometimes the wind is from behind and progress is steady and at other times the wind is contrary and the seas are rough.

Here is a fascinating book about individuals who have served God within the Presbyterian Churches in Ireland and their Synods for more than 400 years. The historical conditions were constantly changing, the seas were frequently turbulent, the future unpredictable and courage was frequently required.

One of the best ways into history is through the lives of individuals, and here are hundreds of them. Happily, not all of them were, or are, ministers or men. The historical introduction and the timeline enable us to locate the lives of these people in their historical settings and we can then fill out the hinterland of their existence and reflect upon their convictions, the contribution they made to the Kingdom of God and the credibility of their witness to Jesus Christ and the gospel.

This book illustrates that there is and has been a fairly wide spread of opinion within the historic Presbyterian traditions in Ireland. It has not always proved possible to contain that divergence and painful schisms have occurred. It may be that the uncertain political environment in which the church has frequently found itself has encouraged an unhelpful and inhibiting defensiveness, not least with the 'Troubles' of the latter part of the twentieth century. Roger Courtney is correct when he writes that the public image of the church is conservative but behind that exterior there are found radical voices. Perhaps this book will encourage some of us to follow that radical tradition more faithfully.

This book is the end product of widespread research. As I read through parts of it, for it is not a book one can read at one sitting, I kept wondering how the author could have discovered all these people and the details of their lives. This book will add much which is distinctive to the already existing volumes of Presbyterian history. Within and without the walls of many familiar buildings convictions were shaped and lives were lived for which we have every reason to give thanks to God.

VERY REV. DR JOHN DUNLOP

The Irish Progressive Presbyterian Tradition

It is an often neglected fact that the Protestant Reformation of the early sixteenth century was birthed amidst an emergent atmosphere of increasing instability. The mainstream reformers steered a middle course between the stagnant corruption of the old church and the turbulent effervescence of the new radical groupings; they established themselves as *magisterial* reformers. Unable to reform the old church on their own, and wary of the apocalyptic vision of charismatic leaders, Luther and Calvin *et al* consciously co-operated closely with rulers and councils in order to manage mutually beneficial reforms. While the theological watchword of the Protestant Reformation was *sola scriptura*, the reality was a creative working relationship, reformer and magistrate striving together to enact the reality of a godly community.

As an example, Martin Luther would undoubtedly have died as a relatively young man were it not for the protection and active intervention of Elector Friedrich the Wise at key moments in his struggle with the old church ways. It was Friedrich who intervened and ensured that Luther's examination by Cardinal Cajetan in October 1518 was switched from the hostility of Rome to the relative safety of Augsburg. Even more blatantly, in May 1521 Friedrich had Luther 'kidnapped' and transported to the Castle Wartburg following his hearing before Emperor Charles V and the pronouncement of the Edict of Worms by which Luther was declared a convicted heretic.

Indeed the term 'Protestant' was born at a political meeting. At the Diet of Speyer in April 1529 the Emperor demanded the annulment of a previous agreement which allowed local princes freedom to determine the religious allegiance of their subjects. Five princes and fourteen cities entered a *protestatio* and the term 'Protestant' was born and a resultant rift that has never been repaired.

John Calvin, father of Presbyterianism, was the leading expositor of

Protestant theology; his *commentaries* representing the distillation of his intensive study of scripture and his *Institutes of the Christian Religion* the supreme example of a systematic presentation of theological topics. Yet Calvin lived in no ivory tower from which he emerged, Moses-like from the mountain top, to declare the mind of God. As a *magisterial* reformer he struggled in an often stormy relationship with the Genevan city councillors to enact his vision of provision for godly living in the city. His theology, and therefore his influence, spread far beyond the pulpit in St. Pierre, affecting the lives of ordinary Genevans at several levels.

Three examples relating to Geneva will suffice. In order to reflect the dignity of all human beings as the crown of God's creation, a structured programme of poor relief was introduced which included care of the young and disabled, compulsory work for the able-bodied and repression of begging and vagrancy. From December 1541 ministers and elders met as a *Consistory* every Thursday to discuss public morals. This particular representation of the Church-State partnership quickly became a byword for unhealthy surveillance and the focus of an extended power struggle as to what individual freedoms Genevans might enjoy. Eventually the opposition was broken and Calvin's vision won the day. Rather less successful was Calvin's attempt to sanctify the tavern culture of the city. In 1546 drinking and gambling were monitored and bawdy songs forbidden in the taverns. People were not served until they were observed to say grace and a Bible passage was read aloud every hour in hope of stimulating subsequent godly conversation. This regime only lasted three months, proving an unworkable experiment in social behaviour modification.

John Knox was instrumental in bringing Calvin's ideas to Scotland where Presbyterianism was adopted by Parliament in 1560 and the later migration of significant numbers of Scots into Ulster in the early 1600s in turn added a Presbyterian thread to the tapestry of Irish church history. Irish Presbyterianism was formally inaugurated at Carrickfergus on 10 June 1642 by chaplains in Major Robert Munro's Scottish army, though the earliest known Presbyterian minister to work in Ireland was Rev. Edward Brice, in Broadisland (now Ballycarry) in 1611. Never accounting for more than 12 per cent of the population of this island, and always more concentrated in the north and east, Presbyterians have made their mark in Irish history.

Presbyterians first arrived in Ireland in significant numbers during the early seventeenth century by means of private and government sponsored plantation. Due to Irish clerical shortages and Scottish ministerial ejections, prior to 1634 Presbyterian ministers worked in Anglican churches in Ulster in what has become known as the 'Prescopalian' experiment. John Livingstone's ministry in Killinchy is one such example. However, this

Ulster experiment imploded under increasingly ritualistic pressures from Lord Deputy Thomas Wentworth, the English civil war and the 1641 uprising. In the aftermath of the interregnum Anglicanism triumphed over Presbyterianism in the Irish Church and Presbyterians, despite their professed loyalty to Charles and his promise of protection to them, suffered once more. Established Church ministers were responsible for key community functions including probate, marriage, divorce, education and independently minded Dissenter ministers represented, at best, an irritant. Selective biographies in this book illustrate such times, for example John Hart (Taughboyne) who was imprisoned in Lifford for four years for ignoring a summons issued by Robert Leslie, bishop of Raphoe and Patrick Adair (Cairncastle, Belfast) who conducted much of his ministry in secret and authored the first history of the early Irish Presbyterians.

In the early eighteenth century Presbyterians were clearly demarcated as second class citizens by the penal legislation. The Test Act (1704) made participation in the Sacrament of Communion according to the Established Church rite a condition of holding any office, civil or military under the crown. This discriminative act was not abolished until 1780. Perhaps more alarmingly, Presbyterian marriages were not recognised as valid, making Presbyterian couples fornicators and their children illegitimate in the eyes of the law and creating inheritance problems for all concerned. While all Presbyterians were united in their opposition to the draconian political code, they were divided on theological issues.

In 1698, and again in 1705, the Presbyterian Synod ruled that all ministers must subscribe to the Westminster Confession of Faith. A 'Belfast Society' was formed in 1705 of ministers sympathetic to notions of non-subscription; arguing for liberty of conscience. John Abernethy (Antrim) was the leading advocate of such liberty. The Synod judged the non-subscribers to be orthodox in their theological views and in 1726 Abernethy and fifteen supporters were organised as a non-subscribing Presbytery of Antrim. Thomas Nevin (Downpatrick) was another notable member of the Belfast Society and Antrim Presbytery.

The complexion of Irish Presbyterianism was soon complicated by the arrival of the Seceders in 1746 and Reformed Presbyterians in 1763. The former challenged the Synod of Ulster with fresh evangelicalism and the latter refused to recognise the civil government. The apex of denominational division was reached in 1798 when Presbyterian fought against Presbyterian in armed conflict on the respective side of rebels or yeomen. Presbyterians had divided over the pace of reform, especially Catholic emancipation with some like Sinclair Kelburn (Belfast), Thomas Ledlie Birch (Saintfield), Samuel Barber (Rathfriland) and Steel Dickson (Portaferry) advocating immediate votes for Catholics, and others, such as

William Bruce (Belfast), Robert Black (Derry) and James Patterson (Ballee), urging caution. Interestingly, the political divisions were not mirrored in theological positions and recent research has established that of the 30 ministers and 18 probationers who were active in the rebellion they divided equally between 'new light' and 'old light' in their theology.

The descendent of Irish Presbyterian radicalism was spawned in the formation of the Belfast Academical Institution ('Inst') in 1814 which in turn became the battleground for another subscription controversy and the legendary clashes between Henry Cooke (Belfast) and Henry Montgomery (Dunmurry). In 1830 Montgomery led a secession of 17 non-subscribing ministers, which in turn paved the way for a union between Synod of Ulster and Seceders in 1840 to form the General Assembly of the Presbyterian Church in Ireland. Through succeeding episodes of famine, revival and missionary expansion the Presbyterians were active participants. The disestablishment of the Church of Ireland in 1870 and the rise of the Home Rule Movement led to a new Presbyterian and Anglican rapprochement and the replacement of the former Protestant, Dissenter and Catholic divisions with a simple Protestant – Catholic setup.

The twentieth-century saw the partition of Ireland and Presbyterians, despite belonging to an all-Ireland church structure, were now living under two political jurisdictions. Throughout the Home Rule crisis individual ministers adopted opposing stands on this question. While the first page of the Ulster Covenant was signed by Unionist leader Edward Carson and local dignitaries including Presbyterian Moderator Henry Montgomery (Belfast), James Armour (Ballymoney) called Ulster Day 'Protestant Fools Day'! Further internal divisions were exposed by a rise in fundamentalism in opposition to 'modernist' tendencies as evidenced by the heresy trial of Ernest Davey in 1926. Ongoing divisions have emanated from mistrust and division regarding ecumenical overtures in the aftermath of the Second World War and continue to excite Presbyterian debate.

Dissenting Voices offers an overview of the lives of almost 400 Presbyterians, mostly ministers. Such biographies offer a unique insight into the breadth of Irish Presbyterianism. Unsurprisingly, political and theological conflict predominates in many biographies. There are numerous examples in this book of a continuing *magisterial* element within Irish Presbyterianism; individuals who saw injustice and oppression in society and who got involved in righting such cases. Many Presbyterians became deeply involved in the issues of their day: tenant rights, famine relief, Irish language, education, and extension of the franchise, orphans, town mission, alcohol abuse, the disabled and the poor. The Reformers' vision of a godly society equated with Christian involvement in all levels of society. It involved vision, financial investment and hard work and Irish

Presbyterian people have given all three in abundance. This book attempts to shed light on some of their stories and as such it enriches our understanding and appreciation of all that was entailed.

L.S. KIRKPATRICK
Union Theological College

Introduction

This book is very much the result of a personal journey. I was brought up a Presbyterian. My grandfather was a Presbyterian minister who lived with us during my early childhood and so my mother was, what they call, a daughter of the manse. My father had refused to become a church elder because it would have involved signing the Westminster Confession of Faith and he made a protest against an invitation being made to the Rev. Robert Bradford, to preach in our church, by withdrawing his services as honorary church auditor and producer of the annual scout show (Rev. Bradford was a Methodist minister, who was a British-Israelite and Unionist MP).

All through my childhood, the church was the centre of my social as well as religious life. I was lucky that, although our minister had many shortcomings, he was deeply concerned about issues of social justice, which he called 'the currency of love in society'. Favourite topics for his sermons included Martin Luther King, Mother Theresa and Helen Keller, which had a big impact on me as a child. However, he never once alluded to the existence of a radical tradition within Presbyterianism, which values freedom of thought and expression, social justice and democracy and a suspicion of all forms of human authority.

It was only relatively recently that I stumbled on the names of Presbyterians I had never previously heard of, who were prepared to radically stand against injustice and oppression, and I wanted to know more. As I researched, I discovered a wide range of progressive Presbyterians. As I investigated further I made another stunning discovery – that the school I went to was established by a group of, what were considered to be, very dangerous Presbyterian radicals who had been involved in the United Irishmen. In its early days the school was embroiled for many years in a series of controversies with both the church and the state– something that was never mentioned to me the whole time that I was at school. Nor was it mentioned by my father or grandfather who had been at the same school.

It is clear that the most famous and best-researched radical Presbyterians were those involved in the 1798 rebellion. What fascinated me was to know whether their involvement was some strange kind of aberration, or whether their involvement was just one manifestation of a wider tradition, based on some fundamental principles, that has manifested itself in different forms over the last four hundred years, up to and including the present day. This study is an attempt to answer that question through research into the lives of individuals who can be described as progressive in various different ways.

In political discussions about Northern Ireland you very often hear the expression 'the Protestant tradition'. It has always made me feel very uncomfortable, because I knew that it was not a tradition that represented me, so I was either traditionless, or there was more than one Protestant tradition. And if there was more than one Protestant, or Presbyterian, tradition, what exactly was the less familiar one?

Most faiths have a way of celebrating, and being inspired by, members of the faith who have done exceptional things, shown outstanding courage, or compassion. It is a way of passing on what is good about a faith from generation to generation and motivating others to try to follow in their footsteps. We Presbyterians are different, however. We seem to have a fundamental forgetfulness when it comes to the past. We do not celebrate those who have done great things, or try to learn from, or be inspired by, their example. And I think we do need some inspiration.

The image of Irish Presbyterians, both at home and abroad, is probably not a very flattering one, being seen as personally rather dour and politically, as well as socially conservative. It is probably true that some aspects of this image are well deserved, but the purpose of this book is to highlight a very different Presbyterian tradition, that has at least as much call for our attention as the conservative one.

Unfortunately so little credence is given to their being a progressive Presbyterian tradition in Ireland that each time I let slip that I was endeavouring to write this book, the normal response that I received was 'well that won't take too long to read!'

Where the traditional image suggests authoritarian political conservatism, the alternative one is democratic, liberal or radical and strongly anti-authoritarian. Where the traditional one is defiantly British and unionist, the alternative one is prepared to acknowledge and celebrate its Irish and Ulster identity and culture. Where the traditional image is anti-Catholic, the alternative one is ecumenical, celebrating diversity, and promoting understanding and unity. Where the traditional image is one of strict adherence, above all else, to traditional belief systems, the alternative one stresses the values of love, social justice, freedom and equality in our relationships and in how society is organised.

However, there is a danger of further reinforcing stereotypes, even caricatures, which is not the intention of this book. Actually the research to create these profiles has highlighted the diversity of those individuals whose actions could be described as progressive. Those who could be described as progressive in politics, or social issues, or culture, were not necessarily progressive in other areas of life. For example, there were many orthodox 'old light' ministers involved in the 1798 rebellion and many evangelicals were strong supporters of the tenant right movement of the nineteenth century. It may be more useful, therefore to see it as a continuum of progressiveness. Many of the individual's views also changed over time. While the profile may highlight the most progressive period of someone's life, it may not always have been that way.

The word 'progressive' is used in public discourse in various different contexts. In the sense that it is used here, it is most often used in relation to politics and social policy. It can be defined as 'favouring or implementing rapid progress or social reform' (*Concise Oxford Dictionary*); 'favouring or advocating progress, change, improvement, or reform, as opposed to wishing to maintain things as they are'; or 'making progress towards better conditions; employing or advocating more enlightened or liberal ideas, new or experimental methods' (Dictionary.com). However, these definitions may not apply so well in the cultural field where some of the individuals profiled here were particularly engaged in trying to preserve the Irish language, myths and culture, when, for some at the time, to be progressive, was to abandon the Irish language and culture in favour of the English language and a more British culture and share in the economic engine of imperial expansion and trade.

Context

The context for the dissenters included in this book has changed enormously over the four centuries, from the early seventeenth to the late twentieth century. Many of the early Presbyterian settlers in Ulster, as supporters of the Solemn League and Covenant of 1643, were escaping political exclusion, religious and civil persecution in Scotland by the Confessional State, made up of the unified religious, civic and political authorities, under the monarch. Many of them also faced economic ruin in Scotland. They were not wealthy landowners, but usually poor tenant farmers. When they settled in Ulster, they quickly found that they faced further political and religious discrimination by the Irish establishment, which was controlled by the minority Episcopal Church, which was keen to maintain the Confessional State in Ireland. Economically, for many of them, their situation was as bad, or worse, than they, or their forebears, had experienced in Scotland, being forced to pay tithes to the Episcopal Church, other taxes from which they did not benefit, and high rents to harsh, sometimes absent, landlords.

The original Presbyterian ministers were initially welcomed by the Episcopal Church because they helped fill vacancies in their pulpits caused by a shortage of ministers. Then the Episcopal Church decided to enforce greater conformity and informed these dissenting ministers that their services were no longer required. They were, therefore, ejected from their churches and forced out of their livings. Their status as ministers was no longer legally recognised. Their preaching and the conduct of marriage ceremonies were made illegal, which had serious consequences for the children of couples they had married, when the parents died.

Presbyterians, horrified by the execution of the king, did not fare any better under Oliver Cromwell, because of their refusal to swear the 'Engagement' oath of loyalty to the Commonwealth. The restoration of the monarchy again resulted in disappointment as the new king reneged on a promise of toleration towards Presbyterians.

The Enlightenment that developed in Scotland between *c.* 1750 and 1770 played a crucial part in encouraging people to think for themselves and not to simply accept the word of those in authority; and in promoting tolerance, so that people could put their ideas into the public domain without fear of punishment from those in political or religious authority. Ulsterman, Frances Hutcheson, Chair of Moral Philosophy in Glasgow, is considered to be the father of the Scottish Enlightenment. Because Presbyterians, particularly those wishing to enter the ministry, were unable to attend university in Ireland (the only university in Ireland at that time, Trinity College in Dublin, only admitted Episcopalians) most of them went to Glasgow and were strongly influenced by these enlightenment ideas.

The penal laws and Test Act of the eighteenth century further alienated the Presbyterians of Ireland who were removed from all public office in the courts, army, and local and national government. Marriages by Presbyterian ministers were not considered to be legal, with major consequences for the children of those marriages and for inheritance.

In light of this context, in relation to the establishment of Presbyterianism in Ireland, it is hardly surprising that during the seventeenth and eighteen centuries a large number of Presbyterians were radical, anti-authoritarian agitators for political, legal, economic and religious reform, who had little respect for English rule in Ireland or the Episcopal controlled Irish parliament in Dublin. Others may simply have been keen to see the Presbyterian form of church organisation, highlighted in the Solemn League and Covenant established in the three kingdoms of Ireland, England and Scotland.

The radicalism this oppression bred eventually culminated in the 1798 rebellion. Of the original twelve members of the Society of United Irishmen in Belfast, ten of them were Presbyterian.

Nor is it also surprising that large numbers of Presbyterians emigrated to

America throughout the eighteenth century and many fought against the British in the campaign for American Independence. A substantial number of these Scots-Irish made a major mark on American politics. Six of the signatories to the Declaration of Independence were Ulster Presbyterians.

The French Revolution also had a major impact on the Presbyterians of Ireland, showing that the people could get rid of the political and religious authorities which were oppressing the people and herald in an era of religious and political freedom. For some Irish Presbyterians, the overthrow of the power the Catholic Church in France had particular significance for Ireland. The approaching millennium also gave the period a particular poignancy.

During the nineteenth century, after the failure of the 1798 rebellion and the passing of the Act of Union, the prospects for radical political change were reduced. But many Presbyterians were at the forefront of the vociferous tenant right campaign in Ulster; in the promotion of non-denominational education; and support for a liberal political agenda, including electoral reform and separation of church and state. Three events in the nineteenth century, however, were to have a profound impact on Presbyterians in Ireland.

The long-running debate about whether ministers and church elders should be required to sign up to the Westminster Confession of Faith and a specific Trinitarian theology was typified by major debates between conservative Henry Cooke and liberal Unitarian Henry Montgomery. The debate resulted in a split in the church, with the creation of, what became, the non-subscribing Presbyterian Church. This split has haunted many in the Presbyterian Church ever since, preventing real debate on theological issues, lest it would result in a further split between progressives and conservatives. For some, however, the split had a more positive impact, leading the way to the merger with the Seceders to form the General Assembly in 1840 and a spiritual revival.

The Great Revival of 1859, influenced by a religious revival in the United States two years earlier, strongly challenged traditional patterns of religious life. It began in Kells and Connor near Ballymena, with a wave of religious conversions, often accompanied by physical prostrations, and spread across Ulster in all the Protestant denominations. The revival provided many with a strong sense of assurance of personal salvation. Some Presbyterian churches lost members to other churches, such as Baptists and the Brethren, who were more enthusiastically conversionists and focused more on the baptism of believers. Although there were concerns about the impact of mass hysteria and the influence of uneducated preachers, most Presbyterians saw it as a 'year of grace'.

The third big event in the latter part of the nineteenth century was Gladstone's conversion to Home Rule for Ireland. Many Presbyterians in this period were liberal in their political and social outlook and were supporters of Gladstone's progressive political agenda for the United Kingdom and were shocked by Gladstone's change of heart. Two major factors powerfully influenced their reaction to the Home Rule proposals. As they saw it, the economy of the north of Ireland had boomed under union with Britain, while the economy of the south had remained largely rural and undeveloped. A conservative and authoritarian Catholic church, with bishops appointed by Rome, strongly influenced by ultramontanism, had also increased its influence over many aspects of life in Ireland. The memory of being excluded by a Dublin government controlled by a conservative hierarchical church meant that most Presbyterians found the prospect of Home Rule unpalatable. The prospect of breaking the link with Britain pushed the Ulster liberals into an alliance with the conservatives to oppose Home Rule.

For the first time the political allegiances of the vast majority of liberal Presbyterians were aligned with those of conservative Presbyterians and other Protestant churches. The creation, for the first time, of a common Protestant/unionist/loyalist political position in clear opposition to that of a common Catholic/nationalist/republican perspective would create a conflict that was to resonate throughout the twentieth century. It would also effectively stifle the progressive anti-authoritarian voices that remained. The compromise of the partition of Ireland and the creation of a Protestant state in the north and a Catholic state in the south, ensured eighty years of mutual hostility between the states and recurrent conflict and violence within the states.

Although it is perfectly consistent with the accusations that were often thrown at Presbyterian leaders of the tenant right campaign, one of the surprises arising from the research for this book was the important role dissenters played in the twentieth century in the development of socialism and the trade union movement in Ireland, from Christian Socialist ministers such as Harold Rylett, Albert McElroy and Arthur Agnew, to working class trade unionists such as Alexander Bowman, Jack Beattie, Victor Halley, Bonar Thompson, Billy McMullen, Harry Midgley, Jack MacGougan, and J. Harold Binks.

The second half of the twentieth century also began to see the re-emergence of the progressive Presbyterian dissenting tradition by those who were not happy to be confined within a Protestant/unionist/loyalist camp defined by its antipathy to the Catholic Church, the Republic of Ireland and Irish culture in general. Many of these were prepared to take risks to try and bridge the divide that had been created, to promote ecumenism, to work for peace and reconciliation through dialogue between churches and communities and build a society that could be shared between all the religious and political traditions in Ireland. The paramilitary ceasefires in the 1990s and the creation of the Good Friday Agreement and a power-sharing government for Northern Ireland, bringing those at the extremes into the centre, has at last created the potential for real reconciliation to take place and the potential to build a society, based on equality, justice and peace, in which those highlighted in this book could be justly proud.

One of the interesting revelations in writing these profiles has been uncovering a very strong cultural strand within Presbyterianism. The common view has been that Presbyterians are good at things like engineering and chemistry, building ships, inventing things and testing scientific theories, but not writing poetry or prose. 'This culture has not produced many poets, authors or artists' (Dunlop 1995). The research for this book refutes this utterly. Progressive Irish Presbyterians have a fine tradition in poetry from William Drennan and William Hamilton Drummond, through the 'weaver poets', like James Campbell, Thomas Beggs, David Herbison, Robert Huddleston, Samuel Thompson and James Orr, to Rose Maud Young, W.R. Rodgers and Robert Greacan. It has also produced fine playwrights, from Thomas Carnduff to Gerald MacNamara (Harry Morrow), Rutherford Mayne and John Boyd; and novelists, such as John Gamble, James Reynolds, Wesley Guard Lyttle, Samuel Keightley, Samuel Angus, Helen Waddell and Sam Hanna Bell.

Common Themes

Reflecting on the selection of brief biographies included in the book, it is interesting to consider what the individuals have in common. They do not all have the same views on the major political and theological issues. The book includes those who are theologically orthodox and those who are more liberal in their theological thinking. It includes those who have taken different positions on major political issues, like Home Rule. It is also clear that the thinking of many of the individuals has actually changed over a period of time during their lives. With this diversity, is it possible to identify some key themes or principles, which have been important in the lives of these dissenters?

Some principles may emanate from the form of church government considered to be important to the Presbyterian tradition. Presbyterian churches elect their elders who sit in a committee, the Kirk session, which is responsible for the governance of that individual church. The decision to call a minister to the church is made by the Kirk session, on the recommendation of a calling committee that the session appoints. At the level of the Presbyterian Church as a whole, decisions are made annually at a General Assembly of all ministers and representative elders. This can frustrate the desire for swift decision-making, but it is democratic. The

Presbyterian Moderator is elected annually at the General Assembly and is a first amongst equals. He (all have been male so far) does not have any significant decision-making power as Moderator, but is the ambassador and representative of the church for that year.

The commitment to democratic structures in the church also tends to extend to a commitment to democratic structures in the political governance of society. Many of the individuals highlighted in this book have been involved in trying to make government and society more democratic through parliamentary reform. With a commitment to democracy, comes a commitment to human rights – civil and religious liberties. These include the right to free speech; the right to equal treatment under the law; the right to vote and have equal representation; and the right to practise your own religion freely. Many of the individuals profiled in this book have been champions of civil and religious liberties.

Many of the individuals have been deeply committed to trying to bring about progressive change in society. They were not happy to just try to live pious lives, or to sit back and complain about the state of the world, but did something to change it, whether it was working for political reform, standing up for civil and religious rights, or trying to do something to meet the needs of the poor or excluded.

Many have been particularly concerned for the underdog – those groups and individuals who because of poverty or oppression do not have a voice in society, or the opportunity to fulfil their potential. Many of the dissenters in this book have been prepared to try to be a voice for the voiceless, and to do something to actually help them. For some this was through the labour movement, for example, or through forms of philanthropy or other kinds of social action.

Education is also a recurring theme in the lives of many progressive dissenters. Right from the earliest days, Presbyterian ministers were required to have a university degree before they could become ministers of the Presbyterian Church in Ireland (this was in the days when a university degree was a very rare commodity), and that university education was only available in Scotland. This meant that ministers often became the intellectual leaders of the period, eloquently giving moral and intellectual guidance through speeches, sermons, books and pamphlets. For some this intellectual leadership was in relation to the major political or social issues of the day. For others it was theological leadership – helping others to reflect on theological matters. They were also committed to the education of others, particularly those whom society did not consider requiring of an education, such as the poor, or women. Many took a lead in the establishment of Sunday schools, academies and other educational institutions, as well as libraries and reading societies. Others were actually involved as teachers, tutors, school managers or governors themselves.

It is not insignificant that many of the dissenters in the book were educated outside of Northern Ireland or had experience of working outside of Northern Ireland. The experience of being educated by the leaders of the Scottish Enlightenment (including Ulsterman Rev. Francis Hutcheson), or of experiencing a much broader range of world views helped these dissenters to broaden their intellectual perspectives and understanding of the world. Events elsewhere in the world, from the American War of Independence and the French Revolution to the experience of Liberation Theology in South America helped inspire many of our dissenters. It also helped reduce the suspicion of other religious denominations and often of other faiths, as they got to know and understand those from very different backgrounds and views.

In a country known for its religious and political conflict and violence and in a church that is renowned for splits within itself and disagreements with other denominations, many of the individuals represented here showed exemplary leadership in building the unity of people, regardless of their religious beliefs. They promoted tolerance and reconciliation, working to create understanding between denominations and different parts of Ireland, while maintaining a strong sense of their own faith.

Many of them were also cultural pioneers building and promoting an authentic non-denominational Irish culture through poetry, prose or music. Some also helped develop a distinctive inclusive northern culture. Some were key advocates of the revival of the Irish language.

It is hard to find a single definition that describes the wide range of types of individuals and issues reflected in these prophetic voices, but it does suggest that there needs to be great caution in making any assumptions about the 'Protestant Tradition', because it is very clear that there are many different traditions even within those who have an affiliation with the Presbyterian Church in Ireland, let alone the wider group of Protestant churches. There is much in these dissenting non-conformist traditions that we can be proud of and many people we can use as role models in thinking about how each of us can give authentic expression to our faith. Making this discovery has been deeply enriching for me, I hope it will also be for you.

One of my regrets in writing this book is that I was unable to create a gender balance in the profiles. Most of the profiles are of men. Until the second half of the twentieth century little attention was given to the role of women and they were generally excluded from many aspects of public life, with some very honourable exceptions. It has not been possible to adequately counteract this imbalance. Because of the excellent work on the Fasti and History of Congregations, there is a ready source of biographical information about ministers of the church, so there is also probably something of an imbalance in favour of ministers. Biographical research on church members, even church elders, is usually much more difficult, except in the case of prominent individuals.

As well as trying to indicate in this introduction what this book is, it is also important to say what it is not. It is not one of those books that have been written to celebrate the human achievements of the individuals described in it. There are many excellent books, which do that for the famous citizens of Ireland, Ulster and Belfast. I have drawn heavily on them, with gratitude for their work, but my purpose is very different from theirs. Nor is this book an attempt to suggest any kind of superiority for Presbyterians over other denominations. I do not feel any sense of superiority at all and the research for this book has highlighted many individuals from other denominations who have taken their own risks to promote freedom and social justice. Books about these other individuals and traditions I will leave for someone else to write.

By including particular individuals in this book, I also do not wish to suggest that other Presbyterians are any less important. I am particularly conscious of the fact that there is simply more information available about some individuals than others. Some of them were very proactive in getting their writings published; some wrote memoirs; some were copious letter-writers and the recipients were diligent in keeping the letters; some have been the subject of biographies; some have been the focus of the attention of very able and committed historians. It is probably true to say that for every person I have included in this book, there are many more that deserve to be included but the information is not available, or I have not found it. I apologise for any serious oversights, as I am for any errors that I am, inevitably, guilty of, despite my best endeavours.

The book is in the form of a collection of short biographies. However, rather than being placed in alphabetical order, they are in chronological order by birth-date. This means that the text should flow better historically, with a better grasp of the person in their historical context. Progressive Presbyterians born in one era, were very often intertwined with the lives of other forward-looking Presbyterians of the time. Using chronological order, hopefully, helps to make the connections more obvious. For those looking to locate a particular person, an alphabetical index is included at the back.

A brief historic timeline is included to help fill in some of the historical events that provide the backdrop, and in some cases the foreground of the lives of these radical dissenters.

Sources: Bardon 1992; Beckett 1981; Brooke 1994; Campbell 1991; Haire (ed.) 1981; Hamilton 1992; Herlihy 1996 and 1997; Holmes 1985; Holmes 2000; Kilroy 1994; Lyons 1973; McBride 2009; Moody and Martin 1967; Patterson 1980; Reid and Killen 1867 Vols I–III; Stewart 1977; Thomson 2001.

BIOGRAPHIES OF DISSENTERS
IN CHRONOLOGICAL ORDER

John Livingstone
1603–72

John Livingstone was born on 21 June 1603, the son and grandson of Presbyterian ministers. He was also the great-great-grandson of Lord Livingstone, guardian of Mary Queen of Scots. He was educated at Stirling, Scotland and in 1617 went to the University of Glasgow where he learnt Logic and Metaphysics from Robert Blair, who would become a Presbyterian minister in Bangor, County Down. He graduated in 1621. He developed an expertise in both modern and ancient languages. The congregation of Torphichen were keen that he would become their minister, but his nonconformity to Episcopal rituals made him unacceptable to Archbishop Spottiswoode of St Andrews. For the next two years he acted as chaplain to the Earl of Wigtown.

One of his first sermons was preached in Shotts in North Lanarkshire, Scotland in June 1630. Shortly afterwards he received an invitation from Lord Clandeboye to come to Ulster and be the minister of the church in Killinchy. He accepted and, as was required at that time, was ordained by Episcopalian Bishop Andrew Knox of Raphoe. However, within a year he was suspended for nonconformity by Bishop Echlin and deposed along with Blair on 4 May 1632 and spent most of the next two years preaching in Scotland or in secret in Ireland. For most of his ministry he was persecuted by the authorities controlled by the Episcopal Church. He often travelled to Antrim to support the church there. On one of these journeys he met a young lady, Miss Fleming, the niece of Robert Blair's first wife, whom he married in Edinburgh in June 1635.

He was eventually deposed by the newly consecrated Bishop Leslie in November 1635 and sentenced to excommunication. Livingstone, however, continued to preach in secret, at risk of severe punishment. In September 1636 he was part of the group of 150 Presbyterians who sailed from Carrickfergus on the *Eagle Wing* which, because of the very bad weather, had eventually, almost 2 months after they left, to return to Ulster, instead of reaching their planned destination in the American colonies.

Learning that there was a warrant for his arrest in Ireland for his secret preaching activities, he returned to Scotland and from July 1638 he was Presbyterian minister in Stranraer, Scotland, but regularly visited Ulster, helping to establish the Irish Presbyterian Church. Many Ulster Presbyterians also travelled over to his church in Stranraer for communion and baptisms.

In 1640 there was a complaint made against Livingstone and others to the General Assembly of Scotland, for encouraging secret gatherings for prayer and worship. The Killinchy congregation called Livingstone to return there but the Synod of Merse and Teviotdale refused permission.

After the rebellion of 1641 when many Presbyterians were killed by native Irish who had been dispossessed of their lands by the plantation, the west coast of Scotland was 'flooded' with refugees from Ulster.

When Charles II was restored to the throne in 1660, Livingstone refused to take the Oath of Allegiance and was again persecuted for his dissenting faith and banished from the kingdom altogether, having to go to Rotterdam, where he died on 9 May 1672.

Sources: Hamilton 1992; Holmes 1985; Witherow 1858.

John Hart
1617–87

John Hart was born in Scotland in 1617 and educated at St Andrews University where he gained his MA in 1637. He was ordained at Crail, Fife, not far from St Andrews in Scotland in 1643 and was married the following year. He then moved to northern Ireland and was installed as minister of Drumbo Church near Belfast in 1646, where he stayed for four years. He was then called to Dunkeld, Perthshire, where after two years he was deposed for nonconformity to the Established Church. The following year he was installed in Hamilton, South Lanarkshire in Scotland, where he remained for three years before returning to Ulster to become minister of Taughboyne church in Monreagh, County Donegal. On the petition of the congregation there, he was granted a salary from the Protectorate.

In 1658, Hart wrote to Henry Cromwell on behalf of the Presbyterian congregation in Raphoe, County Donegal to complain about Episcopalians ('prelaticall pairtie') disrupting deacons when they were collecting for the poor at the church door, assaulting the elders of the church, and being bound over at the assizes for exercising discipline. Hart also complained that he was being victimised for reporting scandalous and inadequate ministers in the Diocese of Derry. Hart did, however, successfully persuade the government to pay a salary to a Presbyterian minister Rev. Semple, who had been imprisoned by the bishops for six years for nonconformity, to preach in Strabane.

In the 1660s, after the 'Restoration', the Episcopal authorities again tried to enforce conformity with the practices of the Established Church. Hart refused to conform and was accused by Bishop Robert Leslie of Raphoe and Derry of holding illegal services, ('conventicles'). The Bishop ordered his arrest for holding these secret services and illegally baptising children. Hart, however, could not be located and was found guilty *in absentia*. Orders for his arrest were issued.

Hart was implicated by attorney, Philip Alden, of being involved in 'Blood's Plot', named after Captain Blood, a former army officer and small landowner. The real leader was probably Blood's brother-in-law, Rev.

William Lecky (see profile), a Presbyterian minister. They attempted to seize Dublin Castle and the Lord Lieutenant, but failed. Blood escaped and later tried to steal the Crown Jewels from the Tower of London, but Lecky was caught. This further convinced the authorities of the seditious nature of Presbyterians and all the remaining ministers were arrested. Only Lecky was found guilty and hanged. The rest were released and ordered to leave Ireland. After 'Blood's Plot' was over, Hart confessed that Rev. Lecky had had discussions with him about the planned rising.

In 1664, Hart publicly preached to 500 people in Taughboyne, County Donegal, for which he was summonsed to appear in court. He was then arrested for ignoring his summons. He was imprisoned on a writ *de excommunicato capiendo*. The Bishop of Down and Connor admonished Hart and his fellow ministers to sign the Oath of Supremacy, which they refused to do. They were jailed and left in prison for four years. They were eventually freed in 1670.

After the Galloway rebellion in Scotland, the Bishop of Derry wanted Hart and other dissenting ministers transferred from Lifford prison to a distant place because he said that in Lifford and Strabane they seduced the people 'under the pretence of being prisoners of the Lord', fermenting 'seditious doctrine amongst the people'. He also wanted the troublemakers to post bond that they would never come to Derry again, or anywhere else that the Lord Lieutenant might specify.

In 1675, Hart called a special meeting of the reformed Presbytery in order to help get some Presbyterian ministers out of Scotland.

In 1679 a group of Presbyterian ministers did eventually agree to sign a specially worded statement 'professing loyalty to Charles' and

> to obey his lawful commands & wherein we cannot in conscience, actively obey his Majesties Lawes, yet peaceably to submit to his Majesties undoubted Authority over us, exhorting the people among whom we labour to beware of all seditious disturbances.

In 1681 the Laggan Presbytery, including Hart, planned a public fast. Unfortunately for Hart, only the King was permitted to proclaim a fast day. For this crime he again went to prison on the orders of the Bishop of Raphoe. Hart died in 1687.

Sources: Greaves 1997.

James Gordon
c. 1620–*c.* 1685

James Gordon was born around 1620, the eldest son of Alexander Gordon of Salterhill in Morayshire, Scotland. He was educated at Kings College,

Aberdeen between 1641 and 1645. He was then ordained in Comber, County Down in 1646. He received a salary from the state and was also a private tutor to Dowager Viscountess Montgomery. His living provided him with a dwelling house and six acres of land, as well as his £100 annual salary and £50 expenses.

In 1661, however, along with most other Presbyterian ministers he was deposed from his position for nonconformity to the Established Church, losing his church and his income. This suppression radicalised Gordon and some other Presbyterian ministers who were then implicated in an attempted uprising, known as 'Blood's Plot'. This reinforced the Established Church hierarchy's views on the seditious nature of Presbyterianism. Bishop Jeremy Taylor wrote to Ormond the Lord Lieutenant and told him,

> As long as those ministers are permitted amongst us there shall be a perpetual seminary of schism and discontent ... they are looked on as earnest and zealous parties against the government.

As part of the campaign to try and destroy Presbyterianism, four ministers in the west of Ulster were arrested by the Church of Ireland bishop and were jailed for four years. The penalty for administering the Lord's Supper was a fine of up to £100.

Gordon was arrested for alleged involvement in 'Blood's Plot' and imprisoned in Carlingford, but released on the intercession of Lord Mount Alexander. The establishment remained very suspicious of him. They were annoyed by the efforts of Gordon and others to persuade those who had succumbed to pressure to conform to the Established Church to return to Presbyterianism. He was one of twelve Presbyterian ministers that the Bishop planned to formally excommunicate in 1664.

In 1679, Gordon, with other ministers drew up their own statement of qualified loyalty to King Charles, which still did not satisfy Ormond. He died around 1685.

Sources: Holmes 1985; MacConnell 1951.

Patrick Adair
1624–94

Patrick Adair was born in Greenock, Scotland in 1624. He was the third son of Rev. John Adair of Glenoch in Galloway, Scotland and the nephew of both mid-Antrim landlord Sir Robert Adair, who had come over as part of the plantation, and Rev. William Adair. As a twelve or thirteen year old boy, he was present in Edinburgh High Church (St Gile's) on 23 July 1637 when Presbyterian Janet Geddes threw a stool at the Dean, who was introducing Archbishop Laud's new Service-book. He studied in St Andrews University and graduated with an MA in 1642. In 1646 he was ordained and installed in the newly formed Cairncastle congregation, County Antrim, the year of the completion of the Westminster Confession of Faith.

The prospects for Presbyterianism in 1641 were bleak – while there were Scottish settlers with Presbyterian sympathies and some Presbyterian ministers and members operating in Church of Ireland parishes, there was no official Presbyterian Church and there seemed little prospect of creating one. Some of the original ministers in Ulster, like Blair and Livingstone, had been forced to return to Scotland. However the arrival of Munro's army in 1642 with Presbyterian chaplains resulted in a boost to the prospects for Presbyterianism in Ireland.

In 1643 the English House of Commons, at war with the king, held out the prospect of a uniform Presbyterian Church over all three kingdoms and an assembly of learned divines was summoned to Westminster to agree a common form of church government, doctrine and worship, from the wide diversity of practice around the three kingdoms. This was no mean task and they deliberated for at least five years before agreeing a Confession of Faith, Larger and Shorter Catechisms, a Directory for Public Worship and the Form of Church Government in 1646.

To gain Scottish support against the king, the English Parliament signed a Solemn League and Covenant with Scotland, which pledged both the extirpation of Popery and Prelacy. The Covenant was also administered in Ulster in 1644. From this point on the influence of Presbyterians with Parliament waned.

When Charles I was beheaded, Adair, as a leading Presbyterian acting on behalf of the church, refused to accept the 'Engagement Oath' of the Commonwealth of Cromwell. Those who refused to commit to this oath of loyalty either escaped to Scotland or were arrested and were replaced with Baptist or Independent ministers. Adair was one of only six Presbyterian ministers left remaining in Ulster and was one of a group of Presbyterians praying for the re-establishment of the monarchy under Charles II, who had promised to support the establishment of Presbyterianism. The few remaining ministers 'changing their apparel to the habit of their countrymen they frequently travelled in their own parishes and sometimes in other places, taking what opportunities they could to preach in the fields or in barns and glens, and were seldom in their own homes'.

Adair had an unproductive meeting with General Fleetwood in Dublin in 1652. When he returned home he could not find shelter because of his religion and had to hide amongst the rocks near Cairncastle. He continued to lobby in Dublin for tithes and salaries for Presbyterian ministers. In 1661 the Irish Lords Justices forbade meetings of 'Papists, Presbyterians, Independents, Anabaptists and other fanatical persons as unlawful assemblies'. Presbyterian ministers who had occupied Episcopal parishes during the interregnum, unless they conformed (of which seven or eight did), were no longer to be considered as ministers and were expelled. Many ministers continued their ministry in secret, often holding worship in the open, or other private locations, keeping away from the attention of magistrates. Members of the congregations had to continue paying tithes to a church of which they were not members.

However, with the restoration of the monarchy, the Established Church spent little time in evicting the dissenting ministers and, in the words of Adair, 'there came a black cloud over this poor church'. When the Bishop of Derry returned from exile after the restoration of the monarchy he was warned by Lord Charlemont that he faced serious difficulties particularly in the north of Ireland 'abounding with all sorts of licentious persons but those whom we esteem most dangerous are the Presbyterian factions'.

The suppression of Presbyterianism continued. Ministers were prosecuted for ministering to their own congregations. Presbyterian funerals and marriages were declared illegal by the Established Church, making the children illegitimate. Adair and others continued to lobby Ormond for 'liberty of conscience and to preach the gospel' under the king's protection, but to no avail.

Adair continued a secret ministry, 'taking what opportunities they could to preach in the fields or in barns and glens'. His home was raided by soldiers who took away papers which were highly critical of the current regime. This might have resulted in serious trouble for Adair if a courageous maidservant had not removed the incriminating papers from a soldier's bag when they stayed overnight near Larne.

In 1663 he was arrested on suspicion of being involved in 'Blood's Plot' and was detained in prison in Dublin for three months. He was discharged after the intervention of Lord Massereene (Sir John Clotworthy) with a temporary indulgence on condition of living peaceably.

In 1668 a meetinghouse was built for Adair in Cairncastle. In 1672 Charles II, involved in the second Dutch war, issued a *Declaration of Indulgence*, which enabled dissenting ministers to obtain licences to preach.

In 1674 Adair was appointed as minister of the First (and only) Presbyterian Church in Belfast in North Street, despite the disapproval of Lord and Lady Donegall, who owned most of Belfast.

The insurrection and defeat of the Scottish Covenanters at Bothwell Brig in June 1679 resulted in a renewed clampdown on Presbyterians in Ireland. Presbyterian meetinghouses were closed. They were forbidden to assemble for public worship. The monthly meetings of ministers had to be held secretly under the cover of darkness.

In 1687 the King issued his *Declaration of Liberty of Conscience*, permitting every citizen to profess any religion that he pleased. Presbyterian ministers were thus able to return openly to their congregations.

In 1689 Adair led a deputation of Presbyterians to see William III (William of Orange), who approved an increased *regium donum*, to the Presbyterian Church to pay their ministers, many of whom were in a very poor economic position, suffering great hardship.

Adair married three times. First to Margaret Cunningham, the daughter of Rev. Robert Cunningham of Holywood, County Down; the second to his cousin, Jean, who was daughter of Sir Robert Adair of Ballymena; and after she died, to Elizabeth Anderson (née Martin). He had four sons, two of whom became ministers, and a daughter. He not only played a crucial role in enabling the Presbyterian Church to even exist in the face of concerted suppression, but was also the first historian chronicling the early development of the Presbyterian Church in Ireland in his unfinished 'True narrative of the rise and progress of the Presbyterian government in the North of Ireland'.

He died in 1693/4. The exact date and place of burial in Belfast are unknown.

Sources: Bradbury 2002; Brook 1994; Herlihy 1997; Holmes 1985; Holmes 2000; Hume 1998; Kilroy 1994; Nelson 1985; O Saothrai 1983; Stewart 1993; Witherow 1858.

William Lecky
?–1663

William Lecky was the son of Rev. Robert Lecky, minister of Abbey Tristenagh, County Westmeath. In 1654 he went to Trinity College Dublin. He was ordained in Dunboyne near Dublin and in 1657 moved to a parish in County Westmeath where he received tithes, a common practice in the early days of the Presbyterian Church in Ireland, before it had its own meetinghouses.

In May 1661 the Houses of Parliament passed a declaration requiring all persons to conform to the Established Church, making being Presbyterian illegal. Many Presbyterian ministers who had operated in Episcopal parishes were expelled from their livings. In 1661 Lecky was deposed from the parish for refusing to conform to Episcopal practice, such as use of the *Book of Common Prayer*. In February 1663 a petition was circulated in Ulster for presentation to the House of Commons complaining of the persecution and excommunication of Presbyterians. A delegation of Presbyterian ministers were rebuffed when they sought the extension of Charles II's *Declaration of Indulgence* to Ireland.

In 1662, Lecky, by then the former minister of Dunboyne, had gone with

Colonel Blood to Ulster to gather support in their plans to attack the government. They met initially with Revs John Greg and Andrew Stewart to discuss 'the usurpation of the bishops, the tyranny of the courts, the increase in popery, and misgovernment in every affair'. Greg and Stewart however declined to become actively involved in Lecky's plans. Lecky and Blood had more success in Laggan and Armagh where they successfully recruited Revs McCormack and Crookshanks.

In April or early May the government received intelligence that there was a plot by Presbyterian ministers, army officers, and MPs to seize Dublin Castle and other strategic points around the country, in order, amongst other things, to restore 'the liberty of conscience proper to everyone of us as a Christian' and the restoration of lands held in 1659. The Government's first reaction was to round up the conspirators, since 'if a fire be kindled none knew how far it might burn'. However on reflection they decided that acting too early would result in having insufficient evidence against the conspirators. And it was clear that the government planned to make an example of them. This strategy almost misfired when the date of the plot was brought forward. However on the night before the coup the conspirators realised that they had been rumbled and decided to disperse, in the hope of being able to reassemble at some later date. However they were captured before they could get away and 24 of them, including Lecky, were arrested, although at least ten escaped.

The trials of Lecky and three others began in July. One of the crown witnesses against Lecky was 'a most handsome woman, who with very great soberness … informed the court that she was with Mrs Lecky … when the troops came to search for her husband and that Mrs Lecky expressed fear that the attack on Dublin Castle had been discovered'. Mrs Lecky was confident that her husband would be pardoned due to having contacts in high places, but all four were condemned to death. Lecky made various attempts to avoid his fate by variously trying to escape and feigning madness, which did manage to delay his execution. He was offered a reprieve if he conformed to the rites of the Established Church, but refused. He was executed at Oxmorton Green, Dublin in 1663. The plot, erroneously, became known as 'Blood's Plot' after Colonel Blood, the relative of Lecky, who was believed to have been involved.

Three weeks later the Government decided to take drastic action against these rebellious Presbyterian ministers, and instructed the bishops to round up those involved, or those with disloyal tendencies. This led to the wholesale detention of more than seventy nonconformist ministers, particularly in Ulster. The Government considered deporting the ministers but in the end decided that they had no choice but to release them. However they did try to separate the Presbyterian clergy from their congregations by offering a form of amnesty for the laity, by offering not to prosecute members of congregations who had contravened the law of uniformity of common prayer and church attendance, which was designed to suppress nonconformists, before 24 December.

Sources: Beckett 1966; Herlihy 1997; MacConnell 1951.

Andrew McCormack (also spelled McCormick)
?–1666

McCormack was born in Scotland and became a tailor. He then decided to train for the ministry and he and his family experienced great hardship to enable him to do so. He came to Ireland with Michael Bruce. He was ordained in 1656 and installed as the first Presbyterian minister in Magherally, near Banbridge, County Down, where he was in receipt of a salary from the Established Church. Along with the others he was deposed in 1661 for nonconformity to the Episcopal Church. Rather than keeping quiet, in the hope of being tolerated by the authorities, he, along with Revs John Crookshanks and Michael Bruce, preached openly against the persecution of the Presbyterian Church at large open-air 'conventicles'.

He was recruited into 'Blood's Plot' by Rev. William Lecky in December 1662 and was accused of recruiting conspirators in Ulster, but is believed to have become disenchanted when it became clear that assassinations were included in the plans. At least five other Presbyterian ministers were fully aware of the plot and did not report it to the authorities. Two of these allegedly met on the morning of the uprising to ask for God's blessing on the plans. Dozens of Presbyterian ministers were later arrested. McCormack was implicated by attorney, Philip Alden, to whom Lecky had shown a letter about the plot. It was alleged that McCormack had assured the plotters that they would get the support of 20,000 Ulster-Scots in the North, who were ready to join the revolt, which included plans to kill the king and Ormond.

McCormack found a safe haven in one of Lord Massereene's estates and a collection was organised to enable him to purchase a pardon. Bishop Leslie offered to release the Presbyterian ringleaders in his diocese, including McCormack, if they promised not to hold conventicles (secret open air services) or disobey the law. They refused. McCormack then fled to Scotland and fought with the Scottish Covenanters at Rullion Green in the Battle of Pentland in 1666 and was killed by government troops. His body was not recovered.

Sources: Greaves 1997; Kilroy 1994.

Thomas Kennedy
1625–1716

Thomas Kennedy was born in 1625 in Ayrshire, Scotland, son of Colonel Gilbert Kennedy of Ardmillan, Ayrshire, the elder brother of Gilbert Kennedy of Dundonald and nephew of John sixth Earl of Cassalis. He graduated from Glasgow University in 1843. He was appointed a chaplain to Munro's Army, which defeated Owen Roe O'Neill's army at Benburb in 1646. He was formally licensed by the Presbytery of Stranraer in Scotland on 3 December 1651. He was a minister in Leswalt, near Stranraer, Wigtownshire Scotland from 1654 until he was deprived of his ministry by Act of Parliament and then order of Privy Council. He initially did not obey and on 24 February 1663 was ordered to have moved within a month. Prior to that he was ordained in Donoughmore (also spelled Donaghmore) or Dungannon, in Ulster then installed as minister in the Episcopalian Church in Donoughmore (Carland).

In December 1662 there was a plot against the Government in Dublin involving Rev. William Lecky with his brother-in-law, Col. Thomas Blood. There had certainly been discussions with other Presbyterian ministers, although it is not clear the extent that the other ministers approved or participated in the plot. Various ministers were excommunicated by the Episcopal Church and imprisoned. Along with these Presbyterian ministers, who at that time preached in Episcopalian churches, Kennedy was deposed and lost his position and livings. However, he continued preaching from a log cabin, for which he was imprisoned in Dungannon for several years, even being denied visits from his wife, who continued to bring food and fresh clothing to the prison each day, which was kept by his jailers.

On release he went to Derry and unfortunately found himself besieged in the town by the Jacobite forces under James. After it had ended he fled to Scotland, taking up a ministerial position in Inner High Kirk, St Mungo's, Glasgow – south quarter. Before long however, he returned to Carland in 1693 and helped build a new church on the site of the old one.

In 1697 he was elected moderator of the Synod of Ulster. He died in 1716, aged 89. Two of his sons also became Presbyterian ministers.

Sources: Hamilton 1992; Scott 1915.

John Crookshanks
1626–66

John Crookshanks was probably born in 1626, the son of Rev. John Crookshanks, a Covenanter minister of Redgorton, Perthshire, Scotland until he was deprived of his ministerial position for nonconformity. John jr was educated at Edinburgh University and was then Regent there. He was ordained at Raphoe, Convoy in Ulster around 1657, where he received a state salary of £100 per year, until he was deposed for nonconformity along with many others in 1661. He continued to preach in secret, often against episcopacy, which made him a figure of particular suspicion for the authorities.

He was believed to be involved in 'Blood's Plot', against the establishment in Dublin Castle, led by Rev. William Lecky, with several other Presbyterian ministers. After conferring with other leading dissenters in Ulster, he decided for his own safety that it would be better for him to flee, first to Rochelle in France and then to Scotland.

In Scotland, he fought with the Scottish Covenanters, supported by ejected Scottish and Ulster Presbyterian ministers, in the rebellion in Galloway, which spread east to Edinburgh. Crookshanks recruited men from Donegal to support the rebellion, reinforcing concerns that there would be a simultaneous rising in Ireland. He was killed, aged forty, in 1666 at Rullion Green in the Battle of Pentland. In spite of the fact he was dead, the authorities insisted on trying him at the court in Edinburgh. He was found guilty *in absentia* of 'treasonable crimes' for being involved in armed rebellion. Although he was already dead, his punishment was execution and, more significantly for his family, his lands were confiscated for 'his Majesty's use'.

Sources: Greaves 1997; Scott 1915.

Henry Livingstone
1630–97

Henry Livingstone was the nephew of John Livingstone of Killinchy, one of the most prominent Scottish Presbyterians to come to Ireland. He became the Presbyterian minister of Drumbo, near Belfast, operating in an Episcopal parish and receiving financial support through the tithe system. Like the others in this position he was deposed in 1661. In 1663 he was involved in discussions with Rev. Lecky and Colonel Blood about their planned rising and, although he declined to become actively involved, it appears that he did suggest others who might be sympathetic to whom they might talk. 'Blood's Plot' confirmed the view of the establishment that Presbyterians were not to be trusted as they threatened the stability of the kingdom.

Bishop of Down, Jeremy Taylor, who particularly resented the efforts being made by the dissenting ministers to persuade those who had, under pressure, conformed to the rites of the Episcopal Church, considered Livingstone to be the most dangerous of all the dissenting ministers, 'the most perverse & bitter enemy we have to the Lawes'.

In 1664 Bishop Roger Boyle of Down and Connor summoned twelve of the Scottish Presbyterian ministers preaching in Ulster, including Livingstone in an attempt to excommunicate them through the courts. However, they did not receive the summons and had to be summonsed a second time. Archbishop James Margetson of Dublin used his influence to delay and then drop the case. Livingstone died in 1697, aged 67.

Sources: Greaves 1997.

John Greg (also spelled Greig or Gregg)
?–1670

John Greg was the son of Rev. James Greg. He was educated in Glasgow University where he gained his MA in 1638. He was licensed to preach in Ayr, Scotland on 8 May 1644 and was ordained in First Carrickfergus, County Antrim, possibly the first Presbyterian Church in Ireland, in 1646. He was installed three years later as minister of Old (First) Newtownards Presbyterian Church.

In 1650 he refused to take the Oath of Engagement and escaped to Scotland where he served as a minister for the next three years.

In 1654 he was added to the 'civil list' by which ministers in former Church of Ireland parishes were paid an annual salary of £100. However, on hearing that Greg had been appointed as a minister under the Episcopalian authority in Carrickfergus church, the town's governor, Thomas Cooper, a Baptist, protested to Henry Cromwell that no Scottish clergyman should be allowed into Ireland unless his loyalty to the Government was assured and that no Scot should be allowed to live in Carrickfergus, or various other particular parts of Ulster, for security reasons.

In 1659, after Oliver Cromwell's death, Henry Cromwell asked Greg to preach in places where only Catholics, High Prelates (Anglicans) and Anabaptists lived, which he did along with Rev. Gabriel Cornwall (see profile).

With the restoration of the monarchy the conflict between dissenters and the Episcopal Church began once more. Greg and others tried to find evidence to accuse Bishop Jeremy Taylor of unorthodoxy, even searching through copies of his books. Greg was also involved in trying to persuade those who did conform to the Established Church to return to Presbyterianism, to the great annoyance of the Bishop, who, in 1661, had Greg deposed with other Presbyterian ministers. Greg continued to preach and minister privately to his congregation, without any official salary.

Greg was one of the ministers that Lecky and Colonel Blood met to try and involve him in their plans for an uprising. Greg refused to sign a pledge of support, but was later investigated concerning the plot. In 1663 he was jailed in Carlingford Castle by the Bishop of Raphoe. In 1664 there was a public collection in support of him. The Bishop summonsed Greg and others to his court in order to excommunicate them. The defendants did not turn up and claimed they did not receive the summons and were summonsed a second time. Various Presbyterian congregations continued to provide support for Greg in prison. Greg died in 1670 before the issue could reach a conclusion.

Sources: Greaves 1997; Holmes 1985.

Thomas Gowan
1631–83

Thomas Gowan was born in Caldermuir in Scotland in 1631. He was educated in Edinburgh, receiving his MA in 1655. He was ordained as a Presbyterian minister in Donnagh, Glasslough, Glennan, County Monaghan in 1658. Although he was deposed as a minister in 1661 for refusing to conform to the rites of the Established Church, and lost his salary, he continued to minister in Glennan until 1666, when he became a supply minister to Connor, County Antrim. In 1672 he was installed as minister of Antrim Presbyterian Church, where he established the first Presbyterian classical school in Ireland – a school of philosophy and divinity. He was joined by John Howe the celebrated English Presbyterian, who was Lord Massereene's chaplain and author of *Living Temple* and *Delighting in God*. This was important in providing education and training for Presbyterians who were interested in going into the ministry and achieved wide recognition amongst the Presbyterian community in 1674.
In 1710, Gowan answered an attack on Presbyterianism from the Rev. Campbell, a County Down Episcopal rector, who sent a challenge to the whole Presbyterian Synod.

In 1673, leave was given by the bishop, for Gowan, who did not have his own meetinghouse, to preach to his Presbyterian congregation in the Episcopal parish church in Antrim. This created a serious dilemma for the nonconformists: If they agreed to hold their services in an Episcopal church, they were worried that they could be trapped into using the *Book of Common Prayer*, but if they did not, they would be faced with having no church services. A precedent had already been set when an English Presbyterian had been allowed to preach in the parish church in Antrim on Sunday afternoons. Attempts to have the local gentry build a meetinghouse for them failed and some Presbyterians did attend the Presbyterian worship in the parish church. Some chose to meet in an illegal meetinghouse in a thatched cottage. Gowan threatened to return to Scotland unless a meetinghouse was built and the people built one themselves in 1676, by which time the situation had improved for Presbyterian ministers, who were by then receiving the *regium donum* grant.

In 1681 he published 'Ars Sciendi' which gives advice on the method of educating young people. Gowan died on 15 September 1683 and is buried in Antrim. His son, Rev. Thomas Gowan became minister of Drumbo.

Sources: Duddy (ed.) 2004; Hamilton 1992; Holmes 1985; Kilroy 1994; McIvor 1969; Witherow 1858.

Jeremiah O'Quinn (There are various different spellings of his name) –1657

Jeremiah O'Quinn was born in Templepatrick into an Irish speaking Catholic family and was converted to Presbyterianism. Although he was older than the usual student, he was taught by Mr Upton, a member of the local landed family. He then went to Glasgow University and was awarded an MA in 1644. He was licensed to preach by Armoy Presbytery, County Antrim in 1644 and ordained at Billy (which was also called Ballintoy, or Dunluce, but is now called Bushmills).

In 1646, Berresford Ellis suggests, O'Quinn had become an independent minister and acted as a messenger to try and set up a meeting between the independent ministers, including Anabaptists, and the Presbyterian ministers. The Rev. Kennedy of Templepatrick, O'Quinn's home town was in hiding, and the people in the area would not reveal his whereabouts. A meeting was eventually agreed in 1652, which turned into a public debate between Anabaptist Weeks and Presbyterian minister Patrick Adair, in which, it seems, the Presbyterians acquitted themselves well, encouraging some Ulster ministers to return from Scotland.

In 1649 O'Quinn was required to read out in public the 'Representation' – a denunciation of the recent execution of King Charles I by the Cromwellians, but he, along with Rev. James Ker, refused, to the embarrassment of their colleagues who were politically monarchists. O'Quinn and Ker were sentenced to silence for the following three years until they admitted their errors and submitted to the authority of Presbytery.

The following year all Presbyterian ministers were required to sign an Oath of Allegiance to Cromwell's new Commonwealth regime. When they refused, the majority of ministers were arrested. Only O'Quinn and five others remained at liberty, operating under cover in secret locations.

In November 1651, because he was a fluent Irish speaker, O'Quinn was asked by Cromwell's Commissioners in Ireland to preach in Irish in

Dublin, Limerick and Kilkenny. In 1654 he also went to preach to the people in counties Kildare, Clare and Connacht.

Despite preaching at the request of Cromwell's Commissioners, in 1655 he was ordered to be transported to Connacht and Clare. His formal transportation was delayed a year while he was actually preaching in Connacht and Clare. It is not surprising that Charles Fleetwood described O'Quinn as 'somewat bitter against the interest of England'.

O'Quinn managed to avoid permanent transportation and eventually returned to the Billy congregation in County Antrim, where he remained until he died in 1657.

Sources: Blaney 1996; Holmes 2000; Newman 1993.

Gabriel Cornwall
Died c. 1690

Gabriel Cornwall was a member of a Scottish family which, following the plantation, owned extensive lands in the Dungannon area. He was a fluent Irish speaker who was educated at St Andrews University in Scotland. His parents, John and Grace Cornwall, made representations that their son might go to Ireland to preach. This was approved in 1653 and two years later (1655) he was ordained in Ballywillan, County Antrim. He lived in Maddybenny farm in Portrush.

Like the other Presbyterian ministers, he preached in the local Episcopal parish church and received a £100 annual salary (stipend) from the Protectorate. Because of his fluency in Irish he undertook preaching tours around Ireland, particularly a three-month tour to Connacht. In 1659, at Henry Cromwell's request, Cornwall went with Rev. John Greg (see profile) to preach in places where only Catholics, High Prelates (Anglicans) and Anabaptists lived.

With the Restoration of the monarchy and Episcopal Church in 1660, the establishment turned against having Presbyterian ministers preaching in Episcopal Churches and in 1661 Cornwall was deposed from his church and his livings. Like other dissenting ministers who refused to conform he suffered hardship and suppression, but continued to minister to his congregations in Ballywillan and Billy, near Bushmills.

He died in 1690. He had two sons (William and Josias) who also became ministers and one (Samuel) who became a doctor. William preached against the system of high rents charged by landlords and the tithes demanded by the Established Church. He felt so strongly about the injustices visited on Irish tenants that in 1718 he emigrated to New Hampshire in America with members of his congregation. However, he returned four years later and became the minister of St Johnston in County Donegal, until his death in

1735. His other son Josias was ordained by the presbytery of Monaghan in Cavanleck (Aghalurcher/Fivemiletown) in 1704, but was deposed in 1738 for gross misconduct and although restored to the ministry, never held a charge again.

Sources: Blaney 1996; Holmes 2000; Julia E. Mullin, *The Presbytery of Coleraine* (1979) and *The Kirk of Ballywillan since the Scottish Settlement* (1961).

John McBride
1650–1718

John McBride (sometimes spelled McBryde) was born in Ulster in 1650 and named after his father. He was educated in Glasgow, gaining his MA in 1673. He was ordained a Presbyterian minister in Clare, County Armagh in 1680, but left Ireland during the troubles of 1688 and became minister in Brogue near Kirkcudbright in Scotland from 1689 to 1694. He was installed minister of First Belfast congregation in 1694, shortly before it moved from North Street to a new meetinghouse in Rosemary Street. In 1697 he was elected moderator of the General Synod of Ulster and became involved in a pamphlet war between Joseph Boyse (see profile) and the representatives of the Established Church, the Bishop of Dromore and Rev. Edward Synge, who attacked 'dissenting Protestants'. Two years later McBride became a trustee of the *regium donum* grant.

In 1702 he wrote a pamphlet, *A vindication of marriage as solemnised by Presbyterians in the North of Ireland,* to try and gain recognition for Presbyterian marriages, which were regularly attacked by the Established Church. Bishops challenged the right of the Presbyterian Church to solemnise marriages because they considered them to be illegal and 'clandestine' and not done in accordance with the *Book of Common Prayer* and by an Established Church rector. They could see that if Presbyterian marriages were recognised then the ordination of Presbyterian ministers would *de facto* be as well. This refusal to recognise Presbyterian marriages had significant implications for couples who had to confess, in ecclesiastical courts, to 'fornication', and more so for their children who were declared illegitimate and for any inheritance, if the children were legally considered illegitimate. McBride pointed out that: Presbyterian ministers had been solemnising marriages for eighty years; that Roman Catholics and Quakers were not prosecuted for celebrating marriages; and that nonconformist marriages were permitted in other countries, such as Spain, France and Italy. He argued that Presbyterian marriages were not clandestine, but were openly proclaimed on three consecutive Sundays in the church prior to the wedding, had full parental consent, and were normally celebrated publicly in the meetinghouse. The legal situation did not change until 1738.

He refused to take the Oath of Abjuration in 1703, because he considered that it involved an unacceptable recognition of the status quo of church and state, and, when a warrant was issued for his arrest, he escaped to Scotland. The Irish House of Commons recommended that he be deprived of his *regium donum* salary. When he returned in 1705, a warrant for his arrest was issued. As a result he slept overnight in the fields near Ballymacarrett and again escaped to Scotland via Donaghadee. For the next three years (1705–09), being unable to return to Ireland, he acted as supply minister in Blackfriars, Glasgow. He declined the post of Professor of Divinity at Glasgow University.

In 1706 James Kirkpatrick was appointed to First Belfast as McBride's assistant. When McBride's warrant was quashed in 1708, he returned to Belfast with his congregation, divided into First and Second Presbyterian congregations in Belfast, with Kirkpatrick as the minister of Second congregation. In 1711 another warrant for his arrest was issued and he again had to flee to Scotland. In 1713, when he returned to Belfast, aged 62, in response to published attacks from Dr William Tyndal, the Rector of Belfast, McBride published an attempt to demonstrate how Presbyterians could reconcile loyalty to the monarch with opposition, even armed opposition to authority, entitled '*A sample of Jet-Black Prelatic Calumny*'. He argued that: 'We are only obliged to obey the highest human powers on condition they do not command what is contrary to the declared will of the Supreme Divine Power. Nor is our subjection due but upon condition of protection.'

McBride acknowledged that Presbyterians are obliged to respect the legally constituted authorities, but had difficulty hiding his contempt for them, 'Lest we should be suspected of disloyalty, in rejecting the testimony of crowned heads, though they be dead and rotten, all due respect shall be paid to them.'

McBride spoke out against the Sacramental Test introduced in 1704 to prevent Catholics and nonconformists from holding public, judicial or military office and their removal from offices, such as those in Belfast and Derry Corporations, which they already held. Presbyterians were either forced to conform to the Established Church or have no place in public life. He pointed out the hypocrisy of being forced to partake in worship in which they did not believe. The Sacramental Test was only repealed in 1780.

McBride died in 1718 and was succeeded in First Belfast by Rev. Samuel Haliday (see profile). McBride's son, Robert also became a Presbyterian minister in Ballymoney.

Sources: Brooke 1994; Herlihy 1997; Holmes 1985; Kilroy 1994; Nelson 1985; Newman 1993; Stewart 1993; Witherow 1858.

James Bruce
1660/1–1730

James Bruce was born in County Down in 1660/1, the eldest son of Rev. Michael Bruce, the minister of Killinchy who was ejected from his position by the Anglican Bishop Jeremy Taylor, soon after his son James was born. He was educated at Edinburgh University gaining an MA in 1678 and was ordained as a Presbyterian minister by Down Presbytery in Killyleagh. When the Jacobite forces were sweeping north in 1689, defeating the Protestants in Dromore and Killyleagh, Bruce sought refuge in Scotland, but returned after the Williamite victory in 1691.

He established his own 'philosophical school' in Killyleagh, County Down, which was eventually closed down by the political and religious hierarchy. Its most famous pupil was Ulster-born Francis Hutcheson, who became the Professor of Moral Philosophy at Glasgow University and a leader of the Scottish Enlightenment.

Although he subscribed to the Westminster Confession of Faith himself, Bruce was opposed to banning non-subscribers from fellowship. This resulted in Down Presbytery being divided between Bangor and Killyleagh. Bruce became the minister of Killyleagh.

Bruce died in 1730, aged seventy. Three sons and three daughters survived him. His son William (see profile) became a publisher-bookseller; Patrick became minister in Drumbo, Renfrewshire and Killyleagh; and Michael became minister in Holywood, County Down and was the first secretary of the Non-Subscribing Presbytery of Antrim and a prominent member of the Belfast Society.

Sources: Newman 1993; Stewart 1993.

Joseph Boyse
1660–1728

Joseph Boyse was born in Leeds, England in 1660 and came from an English, rather than a Scottish, Presbyterian background. His father was a puritan who lived for many years in the New England colonies, but returned on the setting up of the Commonwealth. Around 1680 he became chaplain to the Countess of Donegal.

After a short period as minister of a small English congregation in Amsterdam, he became a Presbyterian minister of Wood Street church in Dublin, which was not part of the Synod of Ulster and, in fact, co-operated closely with independent churches in the south of Ireland in a 'Southern Association'.

When Presbyterians were attacked in a 1694 pastoral letter by the Bishop of Derry, William King, entitled *A discourse concerning the inventions of men in the worship of God,* Boyse, outraged at being labelled as 'partial or half-subjects' made a robust defence of the position of Presbyterians, in *Remarks on a late discourse.*

He was opposed to the compulsory subscription to the Westminster Confession of Faith. He accused some of the subscribers of encouraging a factious spirit among the 'most ignorant and injudicious of their people', but hoped that 'moderate subscribers' might succeeded in 'averting an open rift'.

The Lords spiritual and temporal were appalled at the granting of the *regium donum* grant to Presbyterian ministers, believing it was used to further expand their influence, and tried to have it withdrawn. They claimed that Presbyterians have,

> Returned us evil for good; our forbearance hath only increased their rage and obstinacy, and by our own lenity the Northern Presbyterians have been encouraged to seek out and enlarge their borders. And, not content with the enjoyment of the free exercise of their religious worship in places where they had settled Meetings, have assumed a Power to send out Missionaries into several places of this kingdom where they have had no call, nor any congregation.

The authorities directed that a book by Joseph Boyse, *Reflecting on the Legislature and the Episcopal Order,* should be burned by the public hangman.

The Established Church was eventually successful in persuading Queen Anne to withdraw the *regium donum* grant to Presbyterian ministers, but within a year she was succeeded by George I who reinstated it, and four years later it was significantly increased. Persecution by the Established Church continued, however, with attempted prosecutions against ministers and Presbyteries for unlawful assembly.

Boyse was theologically orthodox, supporting the expulsion of his assistant minister in Wood Street church in Dublin, Thomas Emlin, for his unorthodox views (see profile). He was however opposed to the requirement to subscribe to the Westminster Confession of Faith. He believed that human tests of faith that went beyond scripture were putting man-made formula ahead of God's.

When the non-subscribers of the Presbytery of Antrim were eventually expelled from the Presbyterian Synod, by the votes of the elders (even though the majority of ministers opposed their expulsion), who tended to be less well educated than their ministers, Boyse complained of the 'dead weight of the ruling elders'.

Boyse also played an important role in the development of Presbyterian worship. It is hard, now, to imagine that there was a period when singing hymns to accompaniment was seen as dangerously radical (as opposed to unaccompanied psalms), but that was the situation in the eighteenth century. Boyse played a vital role in writing, collecting and promoting sacramental hymns, based on biblical texts to be sung in church. So successful was his first volume of hymns that he produced a second volume in 1701. He described hymn-singing as having, 'A genuine tendency to engage their attention, to quicken their devout affections, to raise and vent their spiritual joys and give them some relish of the inward pleasures of serious religion.'

Boyse died in 1728. He was eventually succeeded in Wood Street, Dublin by the more theologically radical John Abernethy. His son, Samuel Boyse who was a friend of Samuel Johnson, wrote for the *Dublin Weekly Journal* and became a famous poet.

Sources: Brooke 1994; Brown 1980; Herlihy 1997; Herlihy 1998; Holmes 1985; Holmes 2000; Kilroy 1994; McBride 1998; Stewart 1993; Witherow 1858.

Thomas Emlin (also sometimes spelled Emlyn)
1663–1741

Thomas Emlin was born in Stamford, Lincolnshire, England in 1663, the son of shopkeeper, Sylvester Emlyn and his third wife, Mildred (née Dering). He was therefore from the English, rather than Scottish, Presbyterian tradition. He was educated at a boarding school in Lincolnshire under two ejected dissenting ministers and then transferred to the Academy of Thomas Doolittle in Islington, London.

In 1683, he followed Boyse as the chaplain to the Countess of Donegal in England and in this capacity watched the execution of the Whig 'patriot' Lord Russell. He then accompanied the Countess to Belfast in 1684, where he became friendly with Claudius Gilbert who had been Presbyterian, but had conformed to the Established Church. Emlin and Gilbert regularly attended each other's churches and Emlin had a licence to preach from the Church of Ireland bishop and officiated for Gilbert in the parish church, leading to suspicions that Emlin too had conformed.

Earlier, in 1688, Boyse had asked him to join him at Wood Street but he was unable to at that time. Instead he returned to England, where he became chaplain to a Presbyterian Lord of the Admiralty, Sir Robert Rich of Beccles in Suffolk. Despite having read Dr Sherlock's *Vindication of the orthodox doctrine of the Trinity*, Emlin was influenced by the thinking of William Manning, a Socinian, who believed that Jesus was not of an equal status with God. Emlin became convinced that, 'God the father of Jesus Christ is alone the supreme being and superier in excellence and authority to his son ... who derives all from him.'

In May 1691, he accepted a second call from Wood Street church in

Dublin and was a minister there for the next eleven years without disclosing any unorthodox views he might have had. He was considered to be of great ability and an eminent preacher. With Boyse and others of different backgrounds they developed a programme for the training of new ministers.

In 1702, however, Dr Duncan Cumyng, a member of the congregation, told Boyse that he had doubts about Emlin's orthodoxy, because of his failure to ever mention the concept of the Trinity in sermons or prayers. Emlin was questioned and made it clear that he did not believe that Christ was equal to God and called into question the doctrine of the Trinity.

Although Boyse, while theologically orthodox, was a leading supporter of non-subscription to the Westminster Confession of Faith, he was concerned about Emlin's unorthodoxy in relation to the divinity of Christ. Emlin was eventually removed from his ministry by the other Dublin Presbyterian ministers, on the instigation of Boyse, because of his unorthodox 'Arian' views, particularly rejecting the concept of the Trinity.

Following his dismissal (although he had already offered to resign), Emlin was given permission to go to London on the strict instructions that he was not allowed to preach there. He clearly resented the way he had been treated and the authoritarian attitude of the Presbytery that he accused of acting like the Pope.

Boyse and Emlin continued the argument about the nature of the Trinity by pamphlet. As a result of one of these pamphlets, and to Boyse's dismay, Emlin, on a visit to Dublin to settle his affairs, was charged and convicted of blasphemy in 1703, by a court including the archbishops of Armagh and Dublin and five bishops. He was forced to walk round the forecourt with a placard around his neck proclaiming his offence and imprisoned for two years and fined £1,000, disowned by his friends and fellow clergy. On his release in 1705 he returned to England and was involved in further theological controversy.

He became minister of a small congregation there and continued to argue for liberty of conscience and belief, 'Might not I, who had been brought up in a diligent study of the scriptures and admitted to be a teacher of others, justly expect the liberty of declaring what I judged to be the doctrine of the gospel though rejected by others not more fallible than myself.'

Emlyn's conviction also had consequences in the north of Ireland where it gave ammunition to the orthodox subscribers to demand that all ministers be required to sign the Westminster Confession of Faith.

Emlin had married Esther Bury, a widow, daughter of a wealthy Jewish merchant and member of his Wood Street congregation, in 1694. He died in London in 1741. Unitarianism, and other forms of criticism of the doctrine of the Trinity, remained illegal until 1813.

Sources: Brooke 1994; Herlihy 1998; Holmes 1985; Kilroy 1994; McBride 1998; Stewart 1993; Witherow 1858.

John Toland
1670–1722

Toland's origins are shrouded in mystery. However, from what is known it seems that he was born into an Irish-speaking Catholic family near Clonmany in Inishowen in County Donegal. He worked as a shepherd boy until the age of thirteen. He got a scholarship to study at Redcastle School in Derry. At the age of fifteen he became a Presbyterian (some authorities think it was later, when he was at Glasgow University) and in 1688 managed to avoid the Siege of Derry by going to Glasgow University to study theology, along with many other Presbyterians and said that he 'had tried all sorts and found the Presbyterian religion to be the best'. From there he went on to study at Edinburgh University and Leyden (Leiden) in the Netherlands (1692–4), where he studied under the famous classical and biblical scholar, Bernhard Spanheim. He developed a reputation for being a free thinker.

Having moved to Oxford to use the library and then on to London, in 1696 he published *Christianity not Mysterious*, in which he criticised the church authorities for asking the people to adore what they do not understand. In contrast Toland argued that, 'there is nothing in the Gospel contrary to reason ... and that no Christian Doctrine can be properly called a Mystery'. The publication of the book was responsible for the creation of the Irish School of Philosophy and sparked enormous controversy with the idea that we should concern ourselves only with what we can know with our rational mind. Although, in the preface, he suggests that 'the use of reason is not so dangerous in Religion as it is commonly represented ... I contradict anything but Scripture or Reason', the book was denounced from pulpits across Ireland and burned by the common hangman. One of the Irish MPs suggested that Toland should be burnt along with it. Having returned to Ireland after its publication and received such a fanatically negative response to the book, in danger of being arrested, he spent much of the next decade on the continent, including being sent by William of Orange to explain the Act of Settlement (which he brought with him) to William's heir, Sophia, Electress of Hanover. He also got to know the philosopher Leibnitz and met Irish Franciscan monks in Prague.

In his early writings, Toland took a deist approach in which God builds an intelligent design into the universe, which then functions without the further requirement for miraculous divine intervention. In his later writings, however, he describes himself as a pantheist (the first person in the English language to do so) i.e. one who believes that the universe and the divine are the same.

Toland was a prolific writer, writing books and pamphlets in support of civil and religious toleration; advocating that the first Christians should be viewed as 'Jewish Christians'. This was a respected perspective in the second half of the twentieth century, but a highly controversial, not to say, heretical one in the early eighteenth century.

He also maintained a specific interest in Gaelic language and culture, viewing Irish Christianity before the tenth century as a golden age of an ideal Christianity, which was debased when it was appropriated by the establishment. He wrote a history of the Druids and a Breton/Latin/Irish dictionary. He published and edited works by notable Commonwealth republicans, John Milton, Edmund Ludlow, James Harrington and Algernon Sidney.

As well as being seen as the founder of the Irish School of philosophy he can also be seen as a key figure in the Enlightenment, along with Voltaire, Kant, Spinoza and Locke, in which, for the first time, reason replaced church theology and authority as the arbiter of everything.

Sources: Campion 1999; Campion 2003; Fouke 2008; Toland 1751.

James Kirkpatrick
1676–1743/4

James Kirkpatrick was probably born in Scotland in 1676. He was the son of Rev. Hugh Kirkpatrick who was a Presbyterian minister in Lurgan, Ballymoney and Templepatrick in Ireland and Old Cumnock in Scotland. James graduated in theology from the University of Glasgow where his fellow students included John Abernethy and John Simson (who as a professor in the University would be accused of heresy) and moved to Templepatrick, County Antrim, where he served as minister from 1699 to 1706. In 1706 he was appointed to be the assistant to Rev. John McBride in Belfast. The church expanded to such an extent that a Second church was built in Rosemary Street and Kirkpatrick became its minister. In 1712 he was elected Moderator of the Presbyterian Church (an annual appointment).

Kirkpatrick was a leading member of the Belfast Society, with Abernethy (see profile), who had studied with him in Glasgow under Prof. Simson. The Society was established for dissenting ministers, elders and students for the ministry to discuss ideas, including liberal theological ideas. Although an orthodox Trinitarian, Kirkpatrick was one of a group of ministers who tried to persuade the church that it should not require its ministers to subscribe to the Westminster Confession of Faith. He wrote a pamphlet in defence of non-subscription, which was published under the name of one of his elders, Dr Victor Ferguson and became known as *Ferguson's Vindication*.

He wrote various other publications, including *A historical essay on the loyalty of Presbyterians in Great Britain from the reformation to this present year 1713,* which outlined the sacrifices made by Presbyterians in Ireland and the persecutions they had received in reward and attempted in detail to justify Presbyterian loyalty to the king, while retaining the right to oppose his laws and the Established Church. He argued for the importance of individual conscience. He made it clear that loyalty was not synonymous with conformity to the Established Church, 'If we once believe that their consciences truly dictated to them the points wherein they differed from the Established Church, they could not (without manifest contempt of the authority of God) forbear to put their principles in practice.'

For Kirkpatrick, Presbyterianism encourages individual self-reliance in opposition to authority in church and state, 'The ecclesiastical constitution of presbytery ... lays such foundations for the liberty of the individual in church matters, that it naturally creates in the people an aversion from all tyranny and oppression in the state also.'

By 1725 the tide had turned against the non-subscribers who were separated from the Belfast Synod into a Presbytery of Antrim, although there was no particular geographical connection with Antrim. Kirkpatrick, who had substantial support from the wealthy and educated urban classes, complained,

> Nothing is more common amongst poor Country-people and amongst all who are ignorant of the state of the controversy, than to vent their jealousies against the Non-subscribers, and to say plainly that there must be something at the bottom of their Non-subscribing more than what has come to light; and by this means, all the ministers who have subscribed are teaz'd for their charity and Christian Forbearance toward their dear Brethren.

As well as a minister, Kirkpatrick was also a qualified doctor, a profession that he practiced in his later years.

He wrote several works outlining his theological position, including, *A Vindication of the Presbyterian Ministers in the North of Ireland,* which indicates how broad his views of religious liberty were, and *A Defence of Christian Liberty.* He died in 1743/4 in Dublin.

Sources: Bradbury 2002; Brooke 1994; Duddy (ed.) 2004; Herlihy 1998; Holmes 1985; Kilroy 1994; McBride 1998; McBride 1998–2000; Stewart 1993; Witherow 1858.

James McGregor
1677–1729

James McGregor was probably born in 1677, son of Colonel David McGregor near Magilligan Point in the parish of Tamlaghtard in northwest

County Londonderry. He is said to have been in Derry during the siege. Like most young men who wished to train for the Presbyterian ministry he studied in Glasgow University, returning to Ulster in 1701. He was ordained as a minister on 25 June 1701 in Aghadowey, on the banks of the Lower Bann in east County Londonderry. In 1704 the government imposed the Sacramental Test Act that excluded Presbyterians and other dissenters from all public and civic offices. Presbyterians were required to pay tithes to the Episcopal Church and Presbyterian marriages were not legally recognised which had significant implications for the status of the children and the administering of legacies.

In 1705 the Aghadowey church was enlarged or replaced. And in 1706 McGregor married Marion Cargill of Aghadowey with whom he had ten children. In 1710 he was commissioned by Synod to preach in Ulster Irish (close to Scots Gaelic) to other congregations in Derry, Antrim and Tyrone.

In 1717 crop failures had sent prices soaring, rents went up sharply and smallpox and livestock diseases were endemic. McGregor, whose ministerial salary was three years in arrears, and several other ministers, decided to emigrate with their congregations to America, to 'avoid oppression and cruel bondage, to shun persecution and designed ruin ... to have the opportunity of worshipping God according to the dictates of conscience'.

In the summer of 1718 eight hundred to a thousand Ulster immigrants, including McGregor, arrived in Boston to a hostile reception. However, in October he was successful in getting a grant of land from the Governor, on the frontier of Casco Bay, Maine. He initially settled near Boston at Dracut, while many others moved to Maine where they shivered and starved before moving to Nutfield in the Upper Merrimack Valley. The following April McGregor joined them in Nutfield and became their minister. However the area they were living in was in dispute and they were regularly harassed both legally and violently and McGregor had to petition the Governor. In June 1722 they were granted land for a town, which they eventually named Londonderry, but the area continued to be in dispute between New Hampshire and Massachusetts. On 5 March 1729 McGregor died.

Sources: Dickson 1966; Miller *et al* 2003.

John Abernethy
1680–1740

John Abernethy was born in Brigh, near Stewartstown, County Tyrone in 1680 and lived for some time in Ballymena, County Antrim and Coleraine, County Londonderry. His father, of the same name, was minister of Brigh Presbyterian Church and then Moneymore, County Londonderry. He had been appointed, with Patrick Adair, to congratulate William of Orange on his victory and assure him of Presbyterian loyalty. While he was away, civil disorder broke out in Ireland and so his son, John, was sent to board with relatives in Ballymena. During the Williamite War, he had to flee, without his mother, into the care of his maternal grandfather in Scotland. His siblings perished in the Siege of Derry.

John Abernethy was a fluent Irish speaker. He went to Glasgow University to do an MA and then studied theology in Edinburgh and was ordained and installed as minister in Antrim in 1703. He was called to Dublin to succeed Emlin (see profile), as assistant to Joseph Boyse (see profile), when Emlin was convicted of blasphemy, but, so that he could stay near his sick father, the Synod of Ulster allowed him to return to Antrim, where he would succeed his father. When he was called to Dublin again in 1717, he initially went there for three months but, against Synod's wishes, returned to Antrim. This caused controversy, but reinforced in Abernethy the importance of liberty of conscience.

In 1703 he married Susannah Jordan from Antrim, who died nine years later, leaving him to bring up one son and three daughters. He eventually remarried in Dublin. He was elected moderator of the General Synod in 1715.

He was strongly opposed to the 'Test Act' which required candidates for public office to have received the sacraments of the Episcopal Church. He contended that the secular authorities existed to protect the life, liberty and property of the subject and could not interfere with religious convictions unless they threatened the state. He crossed swords with Jonathon Swift about the Test Act and described it as a 'manifest infringement of our natural Rights and Liberty'. The Test Act remained until 1780.

Abernethy was a friend of Francis Hutcheson, the Ulster Presbyterian minister and Scottish enlightenment philosopher. Abernethy was one of the founders of the Belfast Society which shared books, sermons and ideas, including, what would become known as 'new light' theology, emphasising the primacy of sincerity, the rational basis of belief, individual conscience and capacity for moral improvement. At the meetings each member shared anything of particularly interest that they had been reading since the last meeting and two members were delegated to explore interpretations of particular Bible texts for the following meeting.

In 1719 he published a sermon on the theme of the text from Romans XIV 5 'Let every man be fully persuaded in his own mind'. In which he made a strong plea for the rights of individual conscience, arguing that Christian doctrines could never be imposed by ecclesiastical authority, but only accepted by personal conviction. He considered that reason is our 'greatest excellency' and it is the Christian's duty to examine all the evidence carefully and dispassionately and to accept and act on it only on the basis of his own private conscientious conviction.

The Rev. John Malcolm accused Abernethy of pretending to 'give new light to the world, by putting personal persuasion in the room of church government and discipline'. From henceforth the protagonists in the argument about subscription to the Westminster Confession of Faith became known as 'new lights' (against subscription) and 'old lights' (for subscription). The advocates of the new light did not consider that they were unorthodox, or were introducing new ideas, but rather that they were going back to the basics of the Bible and the New Testament church. They argued that it was the advocates of the old light that wanted to add an additional requirement in the form of subscription to the Westminster Confession.

In 1720, aware of a similar damaging dispute in Salters' Hall amongst dissenters in England, the Synod found a compromise in the form of the Pacific Act which stated that 'if any person called upon to subscribe shall scruple any phrase 'or phrases in the confession, he shall have leave to use his own expressions, which the Presbytery shall accept of, providing they judge such a person sound in the faith'. In 1725, however, the church was restructured in response to the subscription rift, with non-subscribing churches being brought together as the Presbytery of Antrim.

Abernethy's sermons made an important contribution to theological thinking in promoting 'practical Christianity'. Rather than the Calvinist emphasis on faith alone, Abernethy stressed the crucial importance of virtue and ethical behaviour, ' … God dealeth with men according to their moral conduct, and doth distinguish them by his favour, any otherwise than in proportion to the virtue and goodness which is in their dispositions and behaviour.'

Ninety families eventually left Abernethy's congregation in Antrim over the controversy and in 1730 he moved to be minister in Wood Street church in Dublin. He died suddenly in 1740, the year of the black frost.

Sources: Brooke 1994; Campbell 1991; Holmes 1985; Holmes 2000; McBride 1998; McBride 1998–2000; Newman 1993; O'Brien and Roebuck 1993; Stewart 1993; Witherow 1858 and 1879.

James Fleming
?–1730

James Fleming was ordained in 1704 by Armagh Presbytery and was installed as minister of First Lurgan Presbyterian Church, which was financially very weak and needed support from the Belfast and Monaghan sub-Synods to be able to pay their minister.

In 1708 two hundred Presbyterians in Drogheda petitioned the Synod to send supply preachers until a permanent minister could be called. Fleming was duly sent to preach on two Sundays, as part of this arrangement. But on the Monday morning following the first service, the Episcopal Dean Cox had him brought back to Drogheda and put in front of the mayor, who warned him not to come back. According to Hamilton in his *History of the Presbyterian Church*, Fleming returned the following Sunday and was duly arrested and charged with 'riot and unlawful assembly'. He only escaped being put in the stocks by members of the congregation who paid his fine. Then, on travelling home after the church service, he was charged with travelling on the Lord's Day.

The next minister that was sent to cover the following Sunday in Drogheda, Rev. William Biggar, minister of Bangor, who as minister of Limerick had previously been arrested by the mayor for preaching in Galway, on the suggestion of the Dean and sentenced to 3 months in jail. The authorities refused to release him unless he promised to make no further efforts to organise a congregation in Drogheda, which he refused to do. His case was brought before the Lords Justices (all members of the Established Church), but the prosecution was quashed and he was released having spent six weeks in jail. In 1711 Rev. Hugh Henry was called to Drogheda as the minister and remained there for 33 years.

The trial of Fleming was then transferred to the Court of Queen's Bench. The Lord Lieutenant however, stopped the case, as he stated, because 'the Queen was determined that Dissenters should not be persecuted or molested in the exercise of their worship'.

James Connolly, in *The Re-Conquest of Ireland*, used this and other examples of religious persecutions of Presbyterians in Ulster to illustrate how the Battle of the Boyne did not result in the introduction of civil and religious freedom, but further oppression of the working class.

In 1718, under Fleming's charge a meetinghouse was built in Lurgan, although the church remained financially very weak. The following year he was called by First Belfast congregation. His Lurgan congregation pleaded with him to stay. Even the Established Church landlord, Brownlow, wrote to the moderator of Synod to persuade him to allow their minister to stay with them, and eventually the Synod decided that he should remain in Lurgan

He died in 1730 while still minister of First Lurgan. Two years later his widow was still appealing to have the arrears in his stipend paid over, which is an indication of the poor financial position of the congregation while he was minister.

Sources: Barkley 1959; Connolly 1934; Hamilton 1992; Irwin 1890; MacConnell 1951; Reid 1834.

Robert Higginbotham
c. 1682–1770

Robert Higginbotham was born in County Antrim around 1682. In 1707 he graduated from Glasgow University and was ordained in Coleraine in December 1710. As he was a native Irish speaker, he was sent out as a missionary to Irish Catholics, for which he was paid 20 shillings a week.

In 1714 he was found guilty of failing to keep his promise to marry Martha Woods. His defence was that his father would not approve the marriage. Despite the attempts of Synod, his father remained unmoved. Under pressure from Synod, he married her without his father's approval. In 1717 he went to preach in Athlone and Dublin and two years later went to preach in Gaelic in Dublin.

When the debate arose about whether ministers should be required to subscribe to the Westminster Confession of Faith, in 1725 Higginbotham wrote a pamphlet in favour of non-subscription and was reprimanded by Synod. In response he withdrew his First Coleraine congregation from the Synod and joined the Non-Subscribing Antrim Presbytery. Two years later however, the congregation, with Higginbotham still as the minister was re-admitted to the Synod. Higginbotham was admonished to live at peace with former members who had left the congregation over the controversy.

In 1747 Higginbotham was elected moderator of the General Synod. He was irritated by attacks on the Church by Calvinist Seceder, John Swanson, and challenged him to a public debate, which took place in Ballyrashane, County Antrim in 1747. Higginbotham died in 1770, aged 88.

Sources: Blaney 1996; Hamilton 1992; Kirkpatrick 2007; Witherow 1858.

Samuel Haliday (also sometimes spelled Halliday)
1685–1739

Samuel Haliday was born in Omagh, County Tyrone in 1685, the son of a Presbyterian minister, of the same name. Samuel jr was educated in Glasgow where he obtained an MA and, more unusually, went on to study theology in Leyden in the Netherlands He was licensed to preach in Rotterdam and then ordained a Presbyterian minister in 1708 in Geneva, which, although being the place where Calvin had lived and worked, had developed broader 'terms of communion' which 'were not narrowed by any human impositions'. He became an army chaplain and served during Marlborough's campaign in Flanders. In his first two decades, therefore, Haliday accumulated considerable international experience. In 1718, he, with Joseph Boyse and Richard Choppin, secured an increase in the Government grant, the *regium donum,* which helped increase his popularity.

He was called to First Belfast in 1719, after having lived in London for some years, where he was present at the Salters Hall theological debates, along with a Rev. Samuel Dunlop, who developed the view that Haliday had unorthodox Arian views and was an enemy of all church government. Dunlop shared this with his colleagues back in Ireland, but was rebuked by Synod, who found that Haliday had demonstrated his innocence.

When he was installed in the First Presbyterian Church in Rosemary Street, Belfast in 1721, Synod had already passed the Pacific Act, which gave considerable latitude to those who refused to subscribe fully to the Westminster Confession of Faith. Haliday, however, refused to subscribe in any way to the Westminster Confession of Faith, or make any gesture towards subscription, as allowed under the Pacific Act. He gave his own statement instead,

> I sincerely believe the scriptures of the Old and New Testaments to be the only rule of revealed religion, as sufficient test of orthodoxy or soundness in the Faith, and to settle all the terms of ministerial and Christian communion, to which nothing may be added by any synod, assembly or council whatsoever; and I find all the essential articles of the Christian doctrine to be contained in the Westminster Confession of Faith; which articles I receive upon the sole authority of the Holy Scriptures.

As his statement did not make clear how much of the Westminster Confession he actually accepted, four members of the Presbytery objected to his installation. However, it proceeded and his refusal was accepted by the majority as a matter of conscience. He defended his statement by saying:

> My refusal to declare any adherence to the assent I gave to the Westminster Confession of Faith when I was licensed does not proceed from my disbelief of the important truths contained in it, the contrary of which I have often by word and writing declared ... but my scruples are against the submitting of human tests of divine truths, especially in a great number of extra-essential points without the knowledge and belief of which men may be entitled to the favour of God and the hopes of eternal life and ... to Christian and ministerial communion in the church ...

Some of Haliday's congregation were not happy however, and sought permission to erect a new church. Despite being urged to find an accommodation with Haliday, no accommodation was forthcoming and a third church in Rosemary Street, Belfast was built, funded from collections in Scotland, where the dispute had spilled over. There followed some unseemly wrangling about church property – 'cloaks, palls, flagons and cups'.

The most conservative members of the synod also decided to voluntarily demonstrate their commitment to the Westminster Confession, cleverly exposing those who refused to subscribe and opening them to the suspicion of heresy. To maintain peace within the church synod, in 1725, Synod decided to group the non-subscribing congregations under one presbytery, the Presbytery of Antrim.

Haliday died in 1739. He is buried in the graveyard beside St George's Church, High Street, Belfast. His son, Alexander Haliday became one of the foremost doctors in Belfast, President of the Belfast Library and Society for Promoting Knowledge (Linen Hall Library); physician to the Charitable Society; and a poet and playwright.

Sources: Boylan 1998; Brooke 1994; Holmes 1985; McBride 1998; Newman 1993; Stewart 1993; Strain 1970; Witherow 1858.

Thomas Nevin
1686–1744

Thomas Nevin was born in 1686, the son of Robert Nevin of Kilwinning, Ayrshire and grandson of Rev. Hugh Nevin, Vicar of Donaghadee from 1634 to 1652. Like many Presbyterians he was educated at Glasgow University. He was licensed to preach by Down Presbytery in 1709 and became minister of Downpatrick in 1711 where he remained for 33 years. Under his leadership they built a new church in the Flying Horse area of the town.

Nevin was a member of the Belfast Society that discussed intellectual and theological ideas. He refused, along with Abernethy, Haliday and Kirkpatrick, to subscribe to the Westminster Confession of Faith and supported the non-subscribers case by writing pamphlets. The Presbyterian Synod eventually voted, by a small majority, to separate the non-subscribers into the Presbytery of Antrim, on the votes of the church elders.

Nevin was accused of being an Arian by a Mr Echlin of Bangor, County Down and Nevin took an action against his accuser. A Captain Hannyington of Moneyrea and two others swore affidavits that they had heard Nevin say it was 'no blasphemy to say that Christ is not God'. In a letter Nevin said that he had stated that it was not blasphemy for Jews to deny the messiah and should not be punished for it. Joseph Boyse stated that he had heard Nevin preach against Arianism. The Church Synod asked him to declare his belief in the Deity of our saviour, which he refused to do on the basis of his non-subscription principles. He was excluded from the communion of the General Synod in 1724, but kept his status and income as a minister.

Unfortunately the church was not the only body that had an interest in his views. He was accused at Downpatrick assizes of expressing Unitarian (as opposed to Trinitarian) views, which at that time was still considered a serious crime. There were various Episcopal ministers present at the hearing and the judge asked each of them to explain what Arianism is. They each refused to do so. Although there was a young Presbyterian minister in court who was able to give a satisfactory explanation of Arianism the judge dismissed the charge as 'unmeaning, senseless and undefined'. Two years later Nevin joined the Presbytery of Antrim with many other non-subscribers.

He died in 1744. His son was Rev. William Nevin who succeeded him in Downpatrick, and who, in turn, was succeeded by his son, also called William.

Sources: MacConnell 1951; McBride 1998; Witherow 1858.

Michael Bruce
1686–1735

Michael Bruce was born in Edinburgh in 1686. His father, Rev. James Bruce (see profile), was one of the founders of a philosophy school in Killyleagh, County Down. His grandfather, Michael Bruce, was also a minister, born in Edinburgh in 1634, who spawned a dynasty that played a crucial role in the main events of the Presbyterian Church in Ireland over the next two centuries. He (Michael Bruce senior) moved from Scotland, with his family, to Killinchy, County Down in 1657. His younger brother was William Bruce, who became a radical publisher and bookseller in Dublin (see profile below).

Michael Bruce jr was educated in Edinburgh and was licensed as a Presbyterian minister by Down Presbytery in 1708, subscribing to the Westminster Confession of Faith. He was ordained in Holywood, County Down in 1711.

Bruce lectured in Belfast and is thought to have written *Narratives of Seven Synods*, an account of the first subscription controversy within the Presbyterian Church in Ireland. He was a member of the Belfast Society, which the nineteenth church historian described as 'a seed-plot of error, from which erroneous principles were carried out and disseminated over the church'.

Bruce was a friend of Abernethy (see profile) and Haliday (see profile) of the 'new light' wing of the church. He was also a cousin and friend of Francis Hutcheson (see profile), the enlightenment Professor of Moral Philosophy at Glasgow University. Bruce was the most prominent of a group of young ministers who accused their own church of lukewarmness after the failure of the church to agitate against the re-establishment of the Episcopal Church in the 1660s.

When the non-subscribers were separated from the Presbytery of Belfast into the Presbytery of Antrim, Michael Bruce and his congregation withdrew from the General Synod and he became the first secretary of the Antrim presbytery.

He retired in 1731 and died in 1735. He is buried in Holywood. Some of his sermons survive, including 'Six dreadful alarms' and 'Rattling of the dry bones'. His son, Samuel Bruce also became a minister. The Bruce family was to provide prominent Presbyterian ministers for generations to come.

Sources: Brooke 1994; Holmes 1985; Kilroy 1994; Newman 1993; Stewart 1993.

Alexander McCracken (also spelled McCrackan)
1668–1730

Alexander McCracken was probably born in 1668, a native of Scotland. He trained as a minister and was licensed to preach in 1684. In 1686 he received a call from Duneane and Grange, County Antrim, which he was reluctant to accept. The Presbytery pressed him to 'supply the church as frequently as possible'. McCracken still rejected the call. In 1687, when he was called to First Lisburn, County Antrim, four dissenters objected to the call on theological grounds, although what those were is not clear. The Antrim Presbytery's investigation found no evidence of unorthodoxy. The four dissenters withdrew their objection and McCracken was installed in Lisburn in 1688.

When the Government passed the Oath of Abjuration in 1703, requiring all 'preachers and teachers of separate congregations' to give their allegiance to the King and abjure any claims to the throne of the Pretender, McCracken, along with John McBride, refused to sign, on the basis that they believed it meant that they were obliged to recognise the existing church establishment as well as the state, which was currently denying Presbyterians their rights and religious liberty. They were also concerned about swearing that the Pretender was not the son of James II, when he could be. As a result of their refusal, the authorities agreed to remove the *regium donum* grant from them, although there is no specific evidence that this was actually carried out.

In 1700, the Belfast Presbytery and Synod of Ulster mediated between McCracken's Lisburn church and two members of the congregation, Robert Stewart and his father, for allegedly casting aspersions about McCracken. As a result, the Stewarts were excluded from communion.

In 1704 the judges in Carrickfergus ordered the grand jury of Antrim to present to the court those (called 'non-jurors') who failed to swear the Oath of Abjuration. However, this does not seem to have happened. Later in the year the Sheriff of Antrim offered a huge reward of £500 for information against McCracken. No-one seems to have taken up the offer, as McCracken was still acting as minister in Lisburn and attended the General Synod that year. By the time of the Synod in the following year, although McBride had gone into exile, McCracken was present and gave assurances of his loyalty to the Queen and Protestant interest. In 1707 the church was burnt down as the result of a fire that destroyed much of Lisburn.

Things seemed settled for several years, then in 1710 there were more threats against McCracken for his failure to swear the oath, led by three particular justices of the peace. In 1711 two Episcopal magistrates issued warrants for his arrest, along with McBride of Belfast and Riddel of Glenavy. He was arrested by the police, but when passing the house of the Bishop of Down and Connor he asked to speak to the bishop. This was granted and McCracken went in the front door and escaped out the back door. He fled to Scotland and took refuge in Castle Kennedy in Galloway. He then went to London and argued his case with the Duke of Ormond, the Earl of Oxford and other leading figures.

The following year it seems likely that the *regium donum* grant was suspended from all ministers who had failed to swear the Oath of Abjuration. In the 1712 Synod both McCracken and McBride were absent because of their exile. The Synod urged all those who had not signed the oath to do so swiftly. In 1713 McCracken and McBride decided to return to Ireland, regardless of the consequences, and McCracken was arrested and jailed in Carrickfergus and remained in jail until 1716, when he was released. He died in 1730.

Sources: Greaves 1997; Kilroy 1994; MacConnell 1951; Witherow 1879.

Francis Hutcheson
1694–1746

Francis Hutcheson was born in Drumalig near Saintfield, County Down in 1694. His grandfather was Rev. Alexander Hutcheson, from Ayrshire, Scotland, who had come over to Ireland to be puritan minister of Saintfield, based in the parish church, in 1657. Following the Restoration of the Monarchy he was evicted from the parish and the Established Church, but was eventually installed as the Presbyterian minister of Saintfield, County Down. Theologically orthodox, he was a 'man of good sense and excellent moral character, but of a modest and retiring nature', and was then Presbyterian minister in Downpatrick, County Down and then Armagh.

Francis was the second of the three sons of Rev. John Hutcheson and his first wife, Miss Trail. He was educated at John Hamilton's School in the Old Meeting House in Saintfield and James McAlpine's Academy in Killyleagh, County Down.

He went to study at Glasgow University where he received his MA and trained to be a Presbyterian minister, under the influence of the Professor of Divinity, John Simson, who challenged some of the harsher aspects of Calvinist theology, emphasising the beneficence and compassion of God. Simson did not believe that only Christians would be saved and questioned the doctrine of the Trinity, for which he was charged with heresy and forced out of his professorship. Hutcheson was also influenced by the lectures on Isaac Newton by the Professor of Moral Philosophy, Gershom Carmichael.

Hutcheson returned to Ireland in 1716 and was licensed as a probationer in 1719. His developing radical views are illustrated by the story of him preaching in his father's church as a young licentiate. One of the congregation spoke to his father afterwards and said,

> Your silly son, Frank, has fashed a' the congregation with his idle cackle. For he has been babblin' this 'oor aboot a good a benevolent God, and that the sauls of the heathen themselves will gang tae heaven if they follow the licht o' their ain consciences. Not a word does the daft boy ken, speer nor say about the gude auld comfortable doctrines of election, reprobation, original sin and faith.

Hutcheson was called as minister to a church in Magherally, County Down, but before he could take up the call he was invited to open his own academy in Dublin. There were several attempts made to prosecute him for teaching without an Episcopal license. He also published *Inquiry into the original ideas on beauty and virtue,* in support of the views of Shaftsbury that benevolence was a natural human instinct and later *The passions and affections.* On the strength of these very successful publications he was under pressure to conform to the Established Church and he made it clear that the form of church government was not 'determined in the Gospels'. Despite the career advantages it might have given him, he chose to remain Presbyterian.

In 1725 he married Mary Wilson, but over the next few years, his father and six of his seven children died. In 1729 he was offered the post of Professor of Moral Philosophy at Glasgow University, which he accepted, and innovatively began lecturing in English rather than Latin. He was an extremely popular and respected lecturer, becoming known as the father of the Scottish School of Philosophy, which was hugely influential around the world, as the Scottish Enlightenment. One of his pupils was Adam Smith. David Hume was also one of his colleagues.

The Scottish Enlightenment fundamentally reshaped thinking. It was no longer God at the centre of enquiry and learning, but human beings themselves. The Enlightenment, for the first time, presented human beings as the product of history and of their environment. The founders of the Scottish Enlightenment argued that human beings, including their moral character, are constantly evolving and developing, not in a chaotic arbitrary way, but in accordance with discernible principles. Thus the founders of the Scottish Enlightenment transformed every branch of learning and are also the true founders of social sciences. It is not surprising that the *Encyclopaedia Britannica* was first published in Edinburgh in 1768.

Hutcheson's work was particularly involved in a refutation of the theories of the philosopher, Thomas Hobbes, who believed that human beings are essentially selfish and depraved, requiring to be controlled by godly discipline – if you are a follower of Calvin, or by an authoritarian state – if you are a follower of Hobbes. Hutcheson believed that every human being, carrying with them the image of God's infinite goodness, has within them the ability to learn to be virtuous and be helpful to others. In our highest state, self-interest and altruism merge, in an 'invariable constant impulse towards one's own perfection and happiness of the highest kind' and 'towards the happiness of others'. To Hutcheson, Christianity was primarily a moral message, to inspire and uplift, rather than provoke fear and terror. He also believed strongly in the ideal of political and personal liberty and the right of resistance against oppression and slavery – decades before there was any organised abolitionist movement.

Although he was required to subscribe to the Westminster Confession of Faith twice and did so, he promoted a form of utilitarianism and coined the phrase 'the greatest happiness of the greatest number' long before Jeremy Bentham and John Stuart Mill, the exponents of the Utilitarian school.

On Sunday evenings he delivered talks on Christianity to students from across the University, exerting what conservative church historian Thomas Witherow called his 'evil influence'. He managed to avoid charges of heresy by his natural tact and diplomacy and an effective understanding of university politics. He assisted poor students and permitted them to attend his lectures free. His *System of Moral Philosophy*, of which he had sent early drafts to John Abernethy, William Drennan and William Bruce (the publisher), was published in 1755, after his father's death.

Not only was Hutcheson a crucial figure in the Scottish Enlightenment, which was to be influential around the world, but also his influence on the Presbyterian Church in Ireland was huge because 322 of the 350 Irish Presbyterian Ministers between 1720 and 1775 were educated in Glasgow. Hutcheson died there of a fever on his birthday in 1746, aged 52.

Sources: Boylan 1998; Broadie 2001; Duddy (ed.) 2004; Erskine and Lucy 1997; Holmes 1985; Holmes and Knox 1990; McBride 1998; McIvor 1969; Newman 1993; Stewart 1993; Witherow 1858.

Alexander Craighead
c. 1700–66

Alexander Craighead was born in Donegal town around 1700, the son of the Rev. Thomas Craighead, minister of First Donegal Presbyterian Church, who was originally from Scotland. This congregation was formerly called Raneeny. It was receiving supplies of ministers from the Laggan Presbytery as early as 1672. In March 1674 William Henry was ordained to the combined charge of Donegal and Belleek and Greystown and three years later was sent on supply to the people of Connacht, but was arrested by the order of the Bishop of Killalla and spent eighteen months in jail in Dublin.

In March 1698 the Donegal congregation presented a call to Thomas Craighead, Alexander's father, and promised to advance half a year's salary towards defraying the charge of transporting his family from Scotland. His father was ordained on the 6 July 1698. However, his name disappears from the Synod's records with no explanation, but it is known that he emigrated to America with his family, arriving in Boston in October 1714 and was there until 1739.

Alexander followed in his father's footsteps and was ordained and installed as the first regular minister of the Middle Octora church in Pennsylvania in 1735. After a couple of ministerial positions, including Windy Cove, Augusta County, Virginia, he was called to Mecklenburg County, North Carolina, where there were many Scots-Irish families. He was the minister of both Rocky River church and Sugaw Creek Presbyterian Church.

As an evangelical promoter of revival and 'the Great Awakening', in January 1742 Craighead led his congregation in renewing the old Scottish Covenants and he published *Renewal of the Covenants, National and Solemn League.*

Craighead was also a vocal critic of King George III and the Church of England. He considered the rights of man as sacred as that of kings. He often preached to his flock about threats to their independence. In 1743 he preached a powerful sermon on this theme, which came to be seen as an important precursor to the Declaration of Independence. Unfortunately the British authorities in the colonies took a dim view of what he said and he was arrested and charged with treason. However he managed to avoid being sent to jail and continued to be a fiery spokesman for the people of Mecklenburg and their desire to overthrow the yoke of the British. He is considered to be the father of the Mecklenburg Declaration, which foreshadowed the Declaration of Independence, even though the Mecklenburg Declaration was not signed until nine years after his death in 1766.

He is buried in the oldest burial ground in Sugaw Creek Presbyterian Church, Charlotte, North Carolina.

Sources: Sons and Daughters of Donegal (Ulster-Scots Agency); *Presbyterianism in Nashville: A Compilation of Historic Data*, William States Jacob, (1904); *A History of Charlotte and Mechlenburg County*, Dan L. Morrill (Source: www.danandmary.com/historyofcharlotteabs.htm); *A History of Sugaw Creek Presbyterian Church, Mechlenburg Presbytery*, Neill Roderick McGeachy, Rock Hill S.C.; 'Renewal of Covenants Middle Octarara', Alexander Craighead, Pennsylvania 11 November 1743 (Source: www.truecovenantor.com); 'A Discourse concerning the covenants containing the substance of two sermons January 10 and 17 1741', Alexander Craighead, Philadelphia (Source: www.truecovenantor.com); 'The reasons of Mr Alexander Craighead's receding from the present judicatures of this churh together with its constitution', Alexander Craighead (Source: www.truecovenantor.com).

Alexander Colville
1700–77

Alexander Colville was born in 1700 in Newtownards, County Down, the son of Rev. Alexander Colville of Dromore, who was a member of the Belfast Society. Alexander jr was educated at Edinburgh and Glasgow and trained for the ministry and licensed to preach. Following the death of his father, he was called as Presbyterian minister to Dromore congregation, County Down in 1725, but was refused ordination by the Presbytery of Armagh, because of his refusal to sign the Westminster Confession of Faith. He then went to London and was ordained in Rev. Dr. Calamy's Church, by ten English Presbyterian ministers. When the Presbytery of Armagh still refused to accept him, Calamy threatened to use his influence to have their *regium donum* grant cut off. Colville refused to appear before the Presbytery of Armagh or recognise their right to hear the dispute. Joseph Boyse (see profile) made representations to the Lord Lieutenant that the actions of the subscribers were unjust and tyrannical and obtained a declaration that his majesty, the King, was displeased at the divisions amongst the Ulster Presbyterians. Despite this, the Synod of 1725 suspended Colville for three months as a minister, giving the Presbytery of Armagh the power to decide what should happen after that.

Colville was eventually ordained by the Non-Subscribing Presbytery of Dublin and took up his father's position as minister of Dromore in 1725. Some of his congregation objected and called a new minister, although the majority of the congregation wished Colville to remain. He and the congregation eventually joined the Non-Subscribing Presbytery of Antrim in 1730.

He preached a sermon at the funeral of Thomas Nevin (see profile) who had been subjected to a heresy trial and published an attack on the Calvinist Seceders and, returning to the subscription issue, published a defence of Rev. John Cameron (see profile) against an attack from Benjamin McDowell.

When Rev. Cameron was moderator of the General Synod in 1759, Colville led a delegation from the non-subscribers to try and bring about reconciliation between the subscribers and non-subscribers, but was unsuccessful. He died of apoplexy (a stroke) in 1777.

Sources: Brooke 1994; McBride 1998; Newman 1993.

William Bruce
1702–55

This William Bruce was the youngest son of the ten children of the Presbyterian minister in Killyleagh, James Bruce (see profile), one of the founders of the Killyleagh Philosophy School, and his wife Margaret (née Traill). William Bruce became a publisher and Dublin bookseller (not to be confused with Rev. William Bruce who was initially a friend of William Drennan and theologically liberal, but moved politically to the right), or of Rev. William's son, also called William (who caused controversy when appointed a professor at the Belfast Academical Institution, because he was believed, like his father, to have Arian views).

This William Bruce was a cousin and friend of Francis Hutcheson, the enlightenment Professor of Moral Philosophy in Glasgow, who had a major impact on the many Irish Presbyterians educated at the University, including the Presbyterian ministers who trained for the ministry there. When John Smith, who had studied in Glasgow with Bruce, but had been expelled, took on Bruce as a partner in his publishing firm, the first book they published was Hutcheson's *An inquiry into the Original of our Ideas of Beauty and Virtue,* as well as Hutcheson's later books. Hutcheson also sent Bruce the first draft of his *System of Moral Philosophy.*

In 1731, Bruce and Rev. John Abernethy orchestrated a campaign against the Sacramental Test, which excluded Presbyterians from public, judicial and military office, but the campaign had little impact on the Irish Parliament controlled by the Anglican aristocracy. Bruce realised that 'only the threat of a revolution would dislodge the alliance of clergy and gentry'.

In 1738 he retired from bookselling and became tutor to the son of Hugh Henry a Dublin banker, who had been MP for County Antrim. In the 1740s Bruce was an elder in the church of his cousin Samuel Bruce in Wood Street, Dublin. In 1743 he was responsible for proposing the establishment of a fund for the relief of the families of deceased clergymen. This suggestion united the two wings of the church, subscribing and non-subscribing; by this stage separated into two separate presbyteries. The fund was finally approved in 1750. Bruce died unmarried in 1755 and was buried in Hutcheson's tomb.

Sources: McBride 1998; Stewart 1993.

Archibald McClean (also sometimes spelled MacLaine or McLaine)
1703–1740

Archibald McClean was born in Scotland in 1703 to the Rev. Alexander McClean of Kilmaglass, who had been a minister in both Argyll and Bute, Scottish Gaelic-speaking areas of Scotland. In 1699 when the Dublin Presbyterians wanted to undertake a preaching tour in Ulster they asked the Synod to provide an Irish-speaking minister, which they did in the shape of Rev. Archibald McClean sr. His son, Archibald Mclean jr was ordained in 1720 as the first minister of First Banbridge, which had originally been part of Magherally congregation, before controversially being separated into Seapark and Banbridge. He remained as minister there for the following twenty years.

He was a founding member of the Belfast Charitable Society, which provided crucial relief to the poor of Belfast. He was the first minister to be prosecuted by the ecclesiastical courts of the Established Church for celebrating marriages in the form laid down by the Presbyterian Church. This attack on Presbyterian marriages caused much anger amongst the dissenter community. The celebration of marriages had become a very sensitive issue and in 1740 at least two Episcopal ministers were hanged for not celebrating marriages in the accordance with the rules of the Established Church.

McClean died in 1740 while still minister of First Banbridge. All three of his sons became ministers.

Sources: Blaney 1996; Kelly 2001; MacConnell 1951; Witherow 1879.

Francis Allison (Also spelled Alison)
1705–79

Francis Allison was born in Leck, near Letterkenny, County Donegal in 1705, the son of Robert Allison, a Presbyterian weaver. He went to school in Raphoe and then studied at Edinburgh University where he graduated with a Masters of Arts degree. He then decided to study for the Presbyterian Ministry in Glasgow where he was taught by the radical Ulster philosopher Francis Hutcheson, a leader of the Scottish Enlightenment.

In 1735, at the age of thirty, he emigrated to the United States and became a tutor in the home of Samuel Dickinson, father of John Dickinson, known as the 'penman of the Revolution'. In 1737 Allison became minister of the Presbyterian Church in New London, Pennsylvania. Disturbed by the lack of educational institutions he started a free school in his own home in Pennsylvania's New London. At the school he passed on Hutcheson's utilitarian philosophy and political ideology that a citizen was not required to be subject to oppressive laws: 'The end of all civil power is the public happiness and any power not conducive to this is unjust and the people who gave it may justly abolish it'.

His students included several important young people who had emigrated from Ulster who would become important figures in the independence movement, such as Thomas Kean, Charles Thomson (see profile), James Smith, George Read and Hugh Williamson. Smith, Thomson and Read were all signatories to the Declaration of Independence. The University of Delaware traces its origins to this school. In 1744 the Synod of Philadelphia chose the school to train its ministers, and it was agreed that the school would come under the control of Synod. This arrangement continued until 1758, when responsibility for training ministers transferred to Princeton.

During the Revolutionary War years he regularly preached his radical nonconformist and anti-authoritarian message to the Continental Congress. He campaigned against Pennsylvania's petition to become a royal colony and the potential loss of Penn's Charter of Liberties, which had attracted Presbyterians there in the first place, and won a temporary victory. He also lobbied against new British taxes. When it was proposed that a hierarchy of Church of England bishops be appointed in the colonies, Alison wrote *The Centinel,* a collection of 19 essays against the creation of such an Episcopal structure. Alison created an ecumenical alliance with the Congregational Church.

In 1752 he took up a post at the new Academy of Philadelphia, handing over the school to Alexander McDowell. In 1755 he became vice-provost and professor of moral philosophy. He was awarded honorary degrees by Princeton, Yale and the University of Glasgow.

He supported the American cause in the revolution against the British but died in 1779, before American success. Benjamin Franklin said he was a man of 'great ingenuity and learning, a catholic divine', a description which would probably have caused him some amusement.

Sources: Fitzpatrick 1989; Green 1969; Kennedy 2001; Miller *et al* 2003.

James Adair
c. 1709–c. 83

James Adair was born in County Antrim around 1709 and had emigrated to America by 1735, probably through the port of Charleston, South Carolina. He began trading with the Cherokee and Catawba Indians, developing a relationship of trust. In 1744 he established himself with the Chickasaws around the headwaters of the Yasoo River in Mississippi. In the later part of this period he regularly visited the Choctaws to ensure a positive attitude towards the British and to counteract the influence of the French. He came into conflict with James Glen the Royal Governor of South Carolina, which, Adair said, eventually resulted in his financial ruin.

In 1751 he moved to the area now known as Laurens County and resumed trading with the Cherokees until 1759. From 1761 to 1768 he was again trading with the Chickasaws, when he wrote a book about the Native Americans, *A Star in the West*, which was published in 1816. It is respected for its detailed description of the history, customs, religion and vocabularies of the tribes he knew. His theory that they were descended from the lost tribe of Israel, while gaining some support at the time, has long since been discredited. He recognised the Chickasaws' 'love of the land, constancy in hatred and friendship, sagacity, alertness and consummate intrepidity'. Adair died around 1783.

Sources: *Dictionary of American Biography* 1930; Kennedy 2001.

Matthew Thornton
1714–1803

Matthew Thornton was born in 1714 in the Bann valley of northern Ireland. His ancestors had been English dissenters who were forced to move to Scotland to escape persecution and then to Ulster to escape further persecution in Scotland. In August 1718, at the age of four he emigrated with his parents to America, along with 120 other Presbyterian families from the Coleraine, Ballymoney, Aghadowey, Macosquin area. They arrived in Boston and settled first in Brunswick, Maine, overlooking Maquoit Bay, and then, having been attacked by a band of Native Americans, in Worcester, Massachusetts. There he studied in Worcester Academy. Due to the intolerance shown towards the Scots-Irish in the English puritan town of Worcester, they moved again to the neighbouring town of Pelham.

In New Hampshire, Thornton graduated as a doctor from Leicester College and, from 1740, practiced very successfully in a local town called Londonderry, named by Ulster Presbyterian settlers. In 1760 he married Hannah Jack and had five children.

He became involved in radical politics, supporting the American cause against the British, denouncing the 'unconstitutional and tyrannical acts of the British Parliament' in general and the Stamp Act in particular. His career was described as 'a chronicle of revolutionary progress in that part of New England'. He drafted New Hampshire's plan of government after dissolution of the Royal government. He was the first president of the New Hampshire House of Representatives and was elected to the Continental Congress in time to be a signatory to the Declaration of Independence. He was elected the first speaker of the House of Representatives following the adoption of the January 1776 Constitution. From 1776 to 1782 he served as Chief Justice in the superior court of New Hampshire. In 1779 he returned to Exeter, New Hampshire and settled on a farm there. He also owned a ferry on the Merrimack River, which is still known as Thornton's ferry. From 1784 to 1787, despite his age, he served on the New Hampshire State Senate and was also a State Councillor in 1785 and 1786.

In 1786 his wife died followed by his son the following year. He survived until 24 June 1803 when he died while visiting his daughter in Newburyport, Massachusetts. He is buried in Thornton Cemetery in Merrimack, New Hampshire. His grave is inscribed 'An Honest Man'. The town of Thornton, New Hampshire is named after him.

Sources: Kennedy 1998; Kennedy 2001; McReynolds 2009.

George Taylor
1716–81

George Taylor, the son of a clergyman, was born in 1716 in County Antrim. In his late teens he studied medicine in Ulster, but in 1736, when he was in his 20s, he emigrated to America, as an indentured servant, not having enough money to pay for the crossing himself. He settled in Chester County, which was dominated by the Presbyterian Scots-Irish. He became an ironworker and then a clerk at Warwick Furnace and Coventry Forge under a Mr Savage the ironmaster and eventually married his widow, Anne. He was a captain in Benjamin Franklin's militia which was commissioned to protect the frontier from violence, and gained a reputation as a radical who supported the ordinary citizen, such as farmers and labourers.

As a moderate radical, he opposed British rule in the American colonies and the idea of Royal government. He was elected to the Pennsylvania Provincial Assembly. When the British government introduced direct taxation on the colonists, through the Stamp Act, Taylor helped draft a robust response from the Assembly. In 1775 he was elected Colonel of Bucks County Assembly and appointed a delegate to the Continental Congress, to replace a delegate who refused to support the cause of independence. Between 1775 and 1778 he was very involved in the production of ordinance and ammunition with which to fight the British, first of all leasing Durham Furnace in Pennsylvania and then a forge in Greenwich, New Jersey

In 1776 he was a delegate to the second Continental Congress, replacing a delegate who had refused to sign the Declaration, and briefly served on the Supreme Council of Pennsylvania. As a representative of Pennsylvania he signed the Declaration of Independence from the British. He also participated in negotiations with the Susquehanna Indians. He died on 23 February 1781, aged 65. He is buried in Easton cemetery in Pennsylvania.

Sources: *Biography of George Taylor* by Rev. Charles A. Goodrich; Kennedy 2001; McReynolds 2009.

James Smith
c. 1713–1806

James Smith, second son of John Smith, a farmer, was born in Ulster around 1713. When he was about 10 his family emigrated to America, where his uncles already lived. They settled in Pennsylvania and he studied at Francis Allison's New London School, where he was influenced by Francis Hutcheson's radical political philosophy. He went on to study law in his brother George's office and at the University of Delaware. After being admitted to the bar he practiced in Shippensburg and then near York, supplementing his income as a land surveyor. However, he found that he was unable to break into respectable circles in Philadelphia dominated by English and Quaker merchants. Aged forty, he married Eleanor Armor from Newcastle, Delaware, who was twenty years his junior. He owned and ran iron manufacturing works on Coduras Creek.

He was radicalised by the Boston Tea Party when the British closed the port as a punishment. In 1774 he was a delegate from York County to a meeting of all Pennsylvania counties about what action to take. He submitted a paper on the constitutional power of Britain over the American colonies in which he urged a boycott of British goods and the establishment of a general congress of the 13 colonies. He raised a militia against the British in York, Pennsylvania in 1775 and was appointed captain and then colonel.

Having promoted the idea of a congress of the thirteen colonies he was appointed to the provincial convention in Philadelphia in 1775, elected to the Continental Congress in 1775 and appointed to the State Constitutional Convention in 1776, and signed the Declaration of Independence in July 1776. On retiring from Congress in 1778 he became a high court judge.

He was re-elected to Congress in 1785, but declined to serve because of his age. He was suspicious of federalism because of the concentration of power at the centre and opposed the Federalist constitution of 1787. He died on 11 July 1806, aged 85, and is buried in York First Presbyterian Church, Pennsylvania.

Sources: Fitzpatrick 1989; Kennedy 2001; McReynolds 2009.

Thomas Reid (also spelled Reade)
1720–1814

Thomas Reid was born in 1720 near Ballyrashane, County Antrim and licensed to preach by Route Presbytery in 1749. He was then ordained in 1756 and became minister of Old Presbyterian Church Glenarm, County Antrim, after the previous minister died in a drowning accident off Glenarm Bridge.

By 1771, the level of anger amongst the tenantry, who were mainly dissenters, against the oppression of the landlords had reached an extreme level. The tenants had to pay tithes to the Established Church and cess taxes to pay for roads and bridges. At the end of the leases they had been granted, the landlords were setting new rents at unaffordable levels. Those who could not pay their rents were evicted. Tenants who lost their land often did not receive any recognition of the increase in its value because of improvements made by the tenant, which was supposed to be the case under the 'Ulster Custom'. Many emigrated to America. Some of those who stayed decided to take more direct action and formed the 'Hearts of Steel' to attack the hated landlords, burn their houses and maim or kill their cattle.

Presbyterian clergy, like Reid, who was moderator of the Presbytery of Templepatrick, had to decide how to respond to this violence. They were clearly sympathetic to the terrible plight that their parishioners faced and lamented,

> the heavy oppression that too many are under, from the excessive price of lands, and the unfriendly practice of many, who contribute to that oppression by proposing for their neighbours' possessions; by which means they are too often deprived of the improvements made by their forefathers and themselves.

But Reid and other Presbyterian ministers could not condone the,

> many daring outrages of a most pernicious nature [that] have been lately committed, in the night … in several parts of this County, by some evil-minded persons, to the evident disquiet of society, and the notorious violation of the rights and properties of individuals, such as maiming and killing cattle, burning houses, destroying hay and oats, and extorting money and arms from the quiet and peaceable subjects, vowing, with the most execrable oath, the destruction of their lives and properties in case of a refusal.

He had to plead with his rebellious Presbyterian flock to desist from violence, both for their own sakes and for the reputation of Presbyterianism. However, until the land question and the other oppressions, which put such an enormous burden on tenants of smallholdings, were finally dealt with over the following one hundred and forty years, the rebellious Presbyterian spirit would frequently re-emerge, with different levels of support from particular Presbyterian ministers. Reid was elected moderator of the General Synod in 1782. He retired because of ill health in 1792, but lived another 22 years. He died in 1814.

Sources: Bigger 1910; MacConnell 1951.

John Cameron
1724–99

John Cameron was born in 1724 near Edinburgh in Scotland. He was apprenticed to an Edinburgh bookseller and then studied at Edinburgh University where he gained an MA.

He was originally a member of the Calvinist Reformed Presbyterian Church, known as 'Covenanters'. He became an 'outdoor preacher' and was sent on an itinerant mission from Scotland to Ireland and eventually became the Presbyterian minister of Dunluce, County Antrim, as one of two 'mountain men', as they were nicknamed in Ireland.

In 1785 he wrote an eschatological tract, but did not get it published, 'owing to the disturbed state of the country and to some political statements and allusions in the book, which were judged to be unseasonal'.

Having started out as a very orthodox Reformed minister, Cameron became a supporter of the 'new light' theological ideas, publishing several theological works, including *The Catholic Christian Defended, The Skeleton covered in Flesh: Doctrines of Orthodoxy*, and *Catholic Christian; or True Religion sought and found by Theophilus and Philander*. When his orthodoxy was challenged by Rev. Benjamin McDowell, the minister of Ballykelly, Cameron responded robustly, explicitly repudiating man-made creeds. If orthodoxy is the holding of religious opinions 'true and right in themselves, and perfectly agreeable to Scripture', then the test of a person's orthodoxy can only be the 'approbation of an infallible judge'. He also wrote a prose epic in nine books, *The Messiah*.

He advocated full inter-communion between all Christian denominations, including the Roman Catholic Church.

He was elected moderator of the General Synod of the church in 1768 and encouraged dialogue with the breakaway Non-Subscribing Presbytery of Antrim. He died in Park, Ballymagarry in County Londonderry in 1799, aged 75, and is buried in Dunluce. His son, William, was a member of the Birmingham congregation of the famous English Unitarian dissenter and supporter of the American rebels, Joseph Priestley.

Sources: Andrews 2006; Brooke 1994; McBride 1998.

David Manson
1726–92

David Manson was born in Cairncastle, County Antrim in 1726, the son of John Manson and Agnes (née Jamison). He was a sickly child, due to rheumatic fever, and received no formal schooling, except what he learnt from his mother, until he began attending the school of Rev. Robert White in Larne. There he thrived to the point of being qualified to become a teacher himself, teaching his own pupils in Drain's Bog in Cairncastle, tutoring Squire Shaw's children in Ballygally Castle, and tutoring sailors in navigation in Liverpool for a while.

He had initially worked as a farmer's boy, but moved to Belfast and became a successful brewer. But he had developed a love of education and in 1755 started an evening school in Belfast in his house in Clugston's Entry teaching English grammar, spelling and reading. He also offered a night school offering to teach other schoolmasters for free and opened a day school and, then in 1760, a boarding school, by which time he had three assistants. He developed very innovative teaching methods, based on encouraging success rather punishing failure, creating a hierarchy of success. He taught entirely 'without the discipline of the rod'. To make learning fun in his 'play school' he created playing cards for the children each with elementary lessons in reading, spelling and arithmetic. He published several school books, including an English dictionary, a pronunciation dictionary, a spelling book and a primer.

The school was so successful it moved to larger premises in High Street and eight years later to even larger premises in Donegall Street. He bought land half-a-mile away and created a bowling green on it for his pupils, where he also built a cottage for his father and brother, named Lilliput. His pupils included the children of prominent Presbyterian merchant families, such as the Joy family and Mary Ann McCracken (see profile). In 1779 he was granted the Freedom of the Borough for his educational work. In May 1782 he again moved his school nearer to the centre of town, at the corner of Donegall Street and Waring Street.

He wrote a book of advice to hand-loom weavers as to how to improve their lot by combining it with appropriate farming methods. He was also something of an inventor. He created a new kind of two-handed spinning-wheel, which set twenty spindles in motion; a 'machine of the velocipede or bicycle type'; and a 'flying machine', by which people could 'raise themselves above the tops of the houses'. Unfortunately, no evidence remains of this later invention, or how it worked.

He died in 1792. He was honoured with a torchlight funeral and buried in the old parish churchyard at the foot of High Street.

Sources: McNeill 1960; Newman 1993.

William Martin
1729?–1806/7

William Martin, eldest son of Reformed Presbyterian David Martin, was probably born on 16 May 1729 in Ballyspallen, near Ballykelly, County Londonderry. He was educated in Dumfries and Glasgow, Scotland and on 2 July 1757 was ordained at the Vow near Rasharkin, County Antrim, to become the first minister of the Reformed Presbyterian Church to be ordained in Ireland. Based in Kellswater, near Ballymoney, County Antrim, he had responsibilities for Reformed Presbyterians throughout Antrim and Down, including Cullybackey, Leymore, Cloughmills, Dervock, Londonderry and Vow. These were difficult times for him personally, with both his first and second wives dying. They were also challenging times, economically and politically, for Presbyterians, regardless of their particular theology. Political, religious and economic control was in the hands of the minority Established Church. After a sustained period of rent rises and evictions of tenants, Martin declared that 'enough is enough', 'anyone who knows anything about the Ulster countryside realises that the rents are so high that the land does not bring in enough to pay them. Many of us are beggared and in time all would be.'

He felt he could not stand idly by and watch his congregation being devastated by poverty and the inevitable violence against such oppression. He and his congregation pooled their resources and chartered five ships to take them to the American colonies, where they would be able to 'obtain free land and live free men'.

The ships sailed from Larne, Belfast and Newry on 4 October 1772, containing over 1,000 people from 467 families. With contrary winds they did not arrive until 2 December, when they landed in Charleston, South Carolina. By this time, on-board the *Lord Dunluce*, the ship which William Martin had sailed in, ten adults and several children had died of smallpox, so the ship was quarantined for 15 days. Another of the ships was quarantined for seven weeks. Martin and the other families settled in lands which were made available free to encourage Europeans to settle there, alongside other Calvinist Seceder Presbyterians from north Antrim. Most settled in Rocky Creek and worshiped in the meeting house there, which they called the Catholic Church, because it combined various Calvinist Presbyterian traditions in one church. Later they established a meeting house of their own.

When the revolutionary war broke out, Martin reminded his congregation of the treatment they had received under British rule in Ireland and denounced British colonial rule in America. He warned that the British would drive them off their land and they should not stand idly by, 'there is a time to pray and a time to fight and the time to fight had come'.

As a result the congregation sent two companies of militiamen to join the revolutionary army. The British heard of the actions of this dangerous minister and burnt the church down and Martin was brought before Lord Charles Cornwallis and jailed for six months. When he was released he lived in the strong dissenting community in Mecklenburg, where presumably he felt safer, but returned to his congregation in Chester County after the British surrender at Yorktown.

In 1785 he was dismissed by the Catholic congregation for intemperance, but remained with his own congregation at Rocky Mountain Road. He died after a fall from his horse in 1806/7.

Sources: Kennedy 1997; Kennedy 2001; Stephenson 1970.

Charles Thomson (sometimes spelled Thompson)
1729–1824

Charles Thomson was born, one of six children, on 29 November 1729 in Gorteade, Upperlands near Maghera, County Londonderry, beside Lough Neagh. His father, John Thomson, was a farmer and linen weaver. The family were members of Maghera Presbyterian Church. When Charles was still a child, his mother, Mary (née Houston), died in childbirth, and with the promise of a better life, the family emigrated to America, but his father died on the ship within sight of Delaware and he and his five brothers (William, Alexander, Matthew and John) and one sister, called Mary after their mother, became orphans.

At the age of ten he was put in the care of a blacksmith. However, when he overheard the blacksmith and his wife talking about having him indentured as an apprentice, he ran away. It is not clear how he met the kind and wealthy lady who supported him to attend Francis Allison's Thunder Hill, New London School in Chester County, where he was influenced by Allison's teaching of Francis Hutcheson's radical political and philosophical ideas. He eventually graduated as a teacher in Greek and Latin from Philadelphia Academy, where he taught until, aged 31, he decided to turn his hand to business.

In 1757 he was selected by the Delaware Indians as their secretary in the negotiations, which led to the Treaty of Easton. For his fairness and integrity he was given the name '*Wegh-Wu-Haw-Mo-Land*' by the Indians – meaning the man who speaks the truth.

When the news arrived in Philadelphia in May 1774 that the British planned to close the port of Boston, Thomson, along with fellow Ulster-Scot, Joseph Reed and Quaker Thomas Mifflin called a mass protest meeting which decided to work with other colonies to oppose this action by the British.

His first wife died, like his mother, in childbirth and he married Hannah Harrison. Despite his poor start in America, he entered business and became a merchant and a politician and proved a very able committeeman, espousing the revolutionary cause.

From 1774 he served as secretary to the Continental Congress for the following fifteen turbulent years to 1789. When it was a personally dangerous thing to do, he, along with Ulsterman, John Hancock, signed the first official Declaration of Independence from the British, adopted by Congress on 4 July 1776. When it seemed a safe thing to do, many others later signed. He was close to, and probably the second most important politician after, George Washington, who Thomson was asked to approach in his Virginia home to become the first President of the United States. Thomson is also reputed to have brought Benjamin Franklin round to the cause of independence.

Thomson designed the Great Seal of the United States and became known as 'the venerable patriot', having been virtually the prime minister of the United States until George Washington's appointment as President.

Thomson spent most of his time in retirement translating the Old and New Testaments of the Bible. He died on 16 August 1824, at the age of 95.

Sources: Fitzpatrick 1989; Kennedy 1997; Kennedy 1998; Kennedy 2001.

James Crombie
1730–90

James Crombie was born in Scotland on 6 December 1730, eldest son of James Crombie, a Perthshire stonemason and Mary (née Johnstone). He studied at the University of St Andrews and received his MA degree in 1752. He was licensed to preach by the Presbytery of Strathbogie on 8 June 1757 and became the parish schoolmaster. He was ordained in Lhanbryd in Scotland in September 1760.

He became a tutor to the Earl of Moray's family and then, with the approval of the Presbytery, although not of his own congregation, returned to studying, this time at Glasgow University, but was censured by the church for not returning to his parish. In 1769 Crombie was recommended by Prof. Leechman of Glasgow University and accepted a call to the Non-Subscribing First Presbyterian Church, Rosemary Street, Belfast, as a colleague to Rev. James Mackey. In 1774, he married Elizabeth Simpson and had four sons and a daughter.

In 1775, Crombie was a signatory to a petition to the King to 'sheath in mercy the sword of the civil war' so that the lucrative trade with America, from which Ulster benefited significantly, might be resumed. When the First Belfast Volunteers were formed to protect Ireland from invasion,

Crombie was one of the members, supporting drilling on Sundays. He even sometimes preached in his uniform. He published a sermon in 1779 entitled, *On the experience and ability of volunteer associations for national defence and security in the present critical situation in Belfast,* arguing that,

'Free states of ancient times owed their greatness to their native citizens in arms, and to them were indebted for their deliverance from the hostile attempts of foreign enemies.'

Crombie was awarded a Doctorate in Divinity from the University of St Andrews in 1783. Very committed to education, he established a school, Belfast Academy, (beside where St Anne's Cathedral is today) where he became the first principal and teacher of classics, philosophy and history (as well as continuing to be a full-time minister). He had initially planned that it would provide both school and college education, particularly for those wanting to enter the ministry, but early on it lost its college status. It later moved to the Cliftonville Road in North Belfast and achieved the designation 'Royal'.

Crombie was also one of the founders and first committee members of the Belfast Charitable Society, which established the Belfast Poor House and Hospital and he was named in the legislation setting it up in 1774. In 1782 it was decided that Crombie and others should go through the streets to try and reduce the number of beggars found on the street and in the same year he was deputised to thank William Drennan for introducing his innovative inoculation scheme to the Poor House and Hospital. He died on 1 March 1790 and was succeeded in Royal Belfast Academy by William Bruce.

Sources: Bradbury 2002; McBride 1998; Nelson 1985; Stewart 1993; Witherow 1858.

Rev. James, Samuel and Andrew Bryson
James *c.* 1730–96
Andrew 1779–97
Samuel 1776–1853

James Bryson's grandfather, John Bryson (1685–1788) came from Irish-speaking Donegal. James was born in Holywood, County Down and was educated by notable Irish scholars the Lynches of Loughinisland. In 1762 he was licensed to preach by Armagh Presbytery and then ordained a Presbyterian minister in 1763, subscribing in an ambiguous manner to the Westminster Confession of Faith. He then became minister of First Lisburn from 1763 to 1774, where he was involved in the establishment of a new meetinghouse. He held 'new light' liberal theological views and was called to Second Belfast in Rosemary Street, Belfast where he stayed for nineteen years from 1773 to 1792. When he retired, he, along with botanist John Templeton, prepared a catalogue of the books in the library of the Belfast

Society for Promoting Knowledge (which became the Linen Hall Library).

When the Volunteers were formed as a home guard against invasion, James Bryson became the chairman and chaplain of Belfast First Volunteer Company.

He then moved to Cliftonville Church in North Belfast in 1792, where there was a dispute with some members of his congregation. As a result he and a section of the congregation moved and formed a new Fourth congregation in Donegall Street, Belfast where he was minister until he died in 1796. He was known as a liberal and often used a catch phrase, 'All the children of God are our brethren'. He had two sons, Samuel and Andrew, who were also Irish speakers.

Samuel was born in Holywood, County Down in 1778. He studied medicine in Edinburgh, qualifying as a surgeon and apothecary. He served as a surgeon in the 32nd Regiment and later opened his own apothecary shop in High Street, Belfast. He became a well-known physician and was a key individual in the nineteenth-century revival of the Irish language and one of the financial subscribers to Rev. William Neilson's *Introduction to the Irish language* and O'Reilly's *Irish Dictionary*. He was a major subscriber to the Belfast Charitable Society and the Belfast Harp Society, in which he helped draw up their rules. He is most notable as a collector of important manuscripts in Irish and for his skills as an Irish scholar, translator and copyist. He died in 1853. Bryson Street in East Belfast and Cluan Place are both named after him.

Andrew was born in Belfast in 1776 and educated at Glasgow University where he graduated with an MA in 1782. He was licensed to preach by Bangor Presbytery. He was ordained in 1786 when he became the minister of Ballymascanlon Presbyterian Church, Dundalk from 1786 to 1795, where he frequently preached in Irish. Politically, it was said that

> He exercised an ardent and earnest ministry during a time of strenuous political struggle in Ireland. In the year 1782 he joined with his flock in boldly asserting the independence of the then Irish Legislature, and at the same time proclaimed their joy at the relaxation of the Penal Laws affecting their Roman Catholic fellow subjects.

With the establishment of the Belfast Harp Society in 1791, Andrew Bryson became a prominent member and was asked to translate for the harpers from the Irish language at the early meetings, but was unable to attend the Belfast Harp Festival. He retired in 1795/6 and died in 1797, a year after his father.

Sources: Blaney 1996; Killen 1990; Ó Snodaigh 1995; Witherow 1879.

George Bryan
1731–91

George Bryan was born into a Presbyterian family in Dublin in 1731. At the age of 21 he emigrated to Philadelphia to join a business partnership arranged by his father. When the partnership soon ended he became a successful retailer, importer and exporter. He married Elizabeth Smith in 1757 and had ten children.

During the late 1750s and early 60s he tried to mediate the dispute that had developed in the Presbyterian Church over the revival known as the Great Awakening. After Britain passed the Stamp Act in 1765 he took an active political role in the American opposition to the British. Along with other merchants he signed the Non-Importation Agreement, which probably led to his bankruptcy in 1771.

In 1775 he was a key mover with Thomas Paine in the anti-slavery campaign and campaigned hard for the Pennsylvania Assembly bill (the Emancipation Act), which would have not only restricted slavery but eventually abolished it, calling it 'The opprobrium of America'. Bryan was known as a lover of books and had a particular interest in the history of the resistance to slavery. However he was opposed by the slave owners and merchants and the bill was eventually watered down. The children of slaves were forced to remain slaves until the age of 28, when the majority would already have died. And there was no deadline agreed for the eventual abolition of slavery. At this time there were around 500,000 slaves in 13 states of north America, including 6,000 in Pennsylvania.

He was elected a member of the Supreme Executive Council of Pennsylvania representing Philadelphia from March 1977 to October 1779 when he became Vice-President of Pennsylvania. In May 1778 he became acting President, following the death of the former President Thomas Wharton, although failed to be elected President after the 7 month acting-up period was over, but remained as vice-President until October 1779. In April 1780 he became a judge of the Pennsylvania Supreme Court. He died on 27 January 1791.

Sources: Fitzpatrick 1989.

Arthur Kyle
1733–1808

Arthur Kyle was born in 1733, the fifth son of Samuel Kyle of Camnish, County Londonderry. He was educated at Glasgow University and licensed to preach by Derry Presbytery in 1759. He was ordained in First Coleraine on 23 September 1761. In 1770 he married Martha Wood, the daughter of James Wood and the grand-daughter of two Presbyterian ministers, Robert

Higginbotham (Kyle's 'new light' predecessor as minister in Coleraine) and Alexander Wood.

In 1797 he was involved, with the other eight clergymen in Coleraine in establishing a Charitable Association for the Relief of the Sick Poor. The founding document gives the background to this initiative:

> It is melancholy truth that however deplorable the state of street-beggars may appear, they are not in general the most necessitous. Back-streets and lanes exhibit spectacles much more affecting. There the wretched inhabitants are often found languishing under adversity, poverty and sickness, many of whom were once respectable members of society, but are now reduced by sickness, and by an honest shame withheld from seeking relief, often forgotten by their relations or having none who can assist them, destitute of friends; and to complete their misery, perhaps without the comforts of true religion which affords the great consolation in the day of distress. How pitiable then their situation must be.

> These being incontestable facts, a few of the friends of suffering humanity have for the present formed themselves into a society, each contributing monthly according to his ability; which institution they lay before and beg assistance of the charitable public.

> It is well known that the inhabitants of Coleraine and its vicinity have on all occasions, when applied to, manifested themselves the friends of the friendless. But never did poverty and distress call with so loud a voice as at this day.

The inter-denominational nature of this society was reinforced by the rules which stated that, 'the visitors do diligently and impartially seek for those who stand in the greatest need of help, but no enquiry is to be made concerning their church or religious opinions.'

He retired in 1799 and died in Laurel Hill, Coleraine on 11 August 1808. He was succeeded in Coleraine by Rev. Matthew Culbert.

Sources: *Aspects of Social History* (1969) HMSO.

William Campbell
c. 1727–1805

William Campbell was born around 1727, the son of Robert Campbell of Newry. He was educated at Glasgow University in 1744 and was licensed as a minister by Armagh Presbytery in 1750 and became tutor to the Bagwell family in Clonmel from 1751 to 1758. He then spent seven years in France where he was arrested for not 'adoring the host' i.e. not kneeling when the host was being carried in the streets. He returned to Ireland and was ordained by the Non-Subscribing Presbytery of Antrim in 1759 and installed in First Armagh, a member of the General Synod, in 1764, succeeding Rev. John Maxwell.

He married his cousin, Jane, daughter of Robert Carlile of Newry and they had eleven children. He was elected moderator of the Synod of Ulster in 1773.

When the American War of Independence took place, he reflected the feelings of Presbyterians in Ireland when he said that Presbyterians believed that the Americans were fighting on their behalf and that the liberties of the Empire at large depended on the result. He described the pride of Ulster Presbyterians when they heard that their friends and relatives had become the 'flower of Washington's army', fighting 'tyranny and arbitrary power'. He acknowledged that in the Presbyterian view, the war was 'unjust, cruel and detestable' and 'to have offered up prayers for success to the English arms, would have been a prostitution of character, a solemn mockery of things divine, approaching perhaps blasphemy', which clearly set Presbyterians at odds with the Established Church, as well as the government, who were clearly disturbed at these expressions of disloyalty. Reports of disloyalty in the north of Ireland were so common that dissenters were advised by their friends in the Irish parliament to clear their name.

Campbell was a non-subscriber in the Synod of Ulster and in 1773 almost managed to persuade the Synod of Ulster to repeal the rule that ministers were required to subscribe to the Westminster Confession of Faith before being ordained. In 1773 he also proposed a scheme for the establishment of a university in the north of Ireland, but it floundered due to the opposition of Henry Grattan.

In his *Vindication of the Principles and Character of the Presbyterians of Ireland* in 1787 he objected that the established clergy had too much power under the constitution and made it clear that he would also object to so much power being exercised by Presbyterian clergy.

In 1788 there was an election to appoint the person to represent the Synod of Ulster in the negotiations over the *regium donum*. Campbell was one of the two candidates, but was defeated by Rev. Robert Black. Deeply disappointed by this outcome, in 1789 he accepted a call to Clonmel Presbyterian Church, where the Bagwell family lived.

When the Volunteers corps was created to defend Ireland against foreign invasion, as the English troops had been withdrawn to fight in the war, Campbell, as Moderator of the Synod of Ulster, became chaplain of the Earl of Charlemont's Volunteer regiment. He was very enthusiastic about the impact of the Volunteer movement, saying that:

> The Kingdom of Ireland was better governed under the reign of the VOLUNTEERS than it had been under the reign of any of its Kings since its fatal connection with England ... It was no longer an abject province that stooped under the tyranny of a foreign oppressor, but stepped forth boldly, at once, in the vigour of manhood; and with a correct, steady pace assumed a rank among the nations of Europe, distinguished by magnanimity, by fortitude, generosity, and disinterestedness.

As an agent for the Presbyterian Synod, Campbell produced an assessment of the strength of Presbyterianism in the Synod of Ulster, which he calculated as 432,000 people in 180 congregations, plus 46 seceding congregations.

As a leading member of the Volunteers in Armagh, he noted how the mixing of Anglicans and dissenters, and marching to one church one week and the other the next week, reduced the prejudice of Anglicans towards the dissenters.

In 1796, with the draconian powers of the Insurrection Act, the government in Dublin decided to suppress the reform movement in an even more brutal way. Hundreds of northern Presbyterians were arrested for 'political' offences. As Campbell recorded, 'Fathers and sons were murdered, or torn from their families, put to torture, or sent into banishment, without even the form of a trial – their houses burnt; their properties destroyed and their wives and children left destitute.'

In his manuscript 'Sketches of the History of Presbyterians in Ireland', which was never published, Campbell became a vital historical and ecclesiastical chronicler of the period. Having gradually lost his sight, he died in 1805.

Sources: Brooke 1994; Holmes 2000; McBride 1998; Witherow 1879.

James Harper
1738–1802

James Harper, the youngest son of James Harper, a farmer in Mallusk County Antrim, was born in 1738. He was educated in Glasgow and the Associate Divinity Hall (Burgher) in Kinross, Scotland. He was licensed to preach by Down Burgher Presbytery and ordained in 1771 at Knockloughrim Church, County Londonderry. He was elected moderator of the Burgher Synod in 1784.

He was sympathetic to the cause of the United Irishmen and in 1798 was arrested and charged with high treason for his part in the rising. At his trial fellow Burgher minister, Adam Boyle of Boveedy, gave testimony against him. However, there was insufficient evidence to convict him and he was acquitted. He emigrated to America, soon after, along with many other supporters of the United Irishmen's cause. From America he wrote to the Burgher Synod accusing Rev. Boyle of perjury and persecution. The Knockloughrim congregation prepared a paper supporting his case. The minutes of the court martial were read out at Synod. Boyle was acquitted of perjury and persecution, but found guilty of unfriendly and unfeeling behaviour, including pursuing Harper for the debts of his son, while his father was very worried about his son's fate, due to his involvement in the rebellion. The Knockloughrim congregation rejected the finding of Synod and withdrew from the Burgher Synod and joined the Anti-Burghers.

In America, Harper supplied the pulpits of Abingdon, Beaver Creek, Silver Springs and Forks of Holestone Virginia from 1799 until his death on 15 September 1802, aged 64.

Sources: Baillie and Kirkpatrick 2005; Stewart 1950.

John Sherard
1738–1829

John Sherard was the first son of weaver Abraham Sherard of Coleraine. He was educated in Glasgow University and licensed by Route Presbytery in 1766. He was ordained in Tullylish, County Down and became their minister in 1774.

He was an opponent of the proposal that the *regium donum* grant should be paid at three different levels, according to the size of the congregation and to the Lord Lieutenant's veto on who did and did not get the grant. In his pamphlet, *A few observations on the nature and tendency of the changes lately proposed to be made in the constitution of the protestant Dissenting church*, published in 1803, he said,

> Must not everyone see that these changes go to dethrone the true king and head of his church, to give up that liberty whereby he has made his followers free, to overturn the constitution of the Presbyterian Church, and to substitute in its place a completely human establishment.

In 1811 some of the members of his congregation asked Synod to replace him. After an attempt by the Synod at reconciliation, they agreed to the request. Whether the dispute was due to the fact that it was considered that he 'celebrated marriages irregularly' because marriage conducted by Presbyterian ministers, particularly a mixed marriage, was still a very contentious legal issue during this period; his support for radical politics; or some other reason, is not clear.

It is believed that he was involved in the 1798 rebellion, but was not charged. He retired in 1811 and died in 1829.

Sources: Brooke 1994; McBride 1998.

Samuel Barber
1738–1811

Samuel Barber was born in 1738 in Killead, County Antrim, the youngest son of a farmer, John Barber and his wife Sarah. He entered Glasgow University in 1757 and gained an MA in 1759. He was licensed in Larne by the Presbytery of Templepatrick on 28 August 1761 and ordained the minister of Rathfriland, County Down by the Presbytery of Dromore on 3 May 1763, subscribing to the Westminster Confession of Faith in an orthodox manner. In 1771 he married the daughter of Rev. Andrew Kennedy of Mourne.

The influence of the Scottish Enlightenment and the revolutionary movements of the second half of the eighteenth century can be seen in his conviction that 'before Science sooner or later all tyranny will fall' and his increasing support for 'new light' theological ideas.

He was deeply conscious of the hostility of the Established Church towards Presbyterians and in 1787 wrote two polemic pamphlets in response to one from the Bishop of Cloyne about the *Present State of the Church of Ireland*. In the pamphlets Barber argued for the separation of church and state and strongly against the tithe system whereby the people of Ireland, regardless of their denomination, had to pay for the Established Church which ministered to only an eighth of the population. He suggested that if there had to be an Established Church it should be the church of the majority i.e. the Catholic Church.

> How will they be surprised to find on consulting history, that they ... planted, civilised and improved the province of Ulster, and while they were doing so forged their own chains, which in time became so firmly riveted, that to get rid of them they were obliged in great numbers to abandon their very country, they had made a comfortable habitation ... They assisted in conquering the Roman catholicks and were reduced to the same servitude.

In 1782 he supported the passing of a resolution in favour of religious liberty at the Presbyterian Synod.

He was a captain (from 1779), and then colonel (from 1782), of the Rathfriland Volunteers. He wrote the rules for the Corp, which excluded the use of corporal punishment. In a speech to the Castlewellan Rangers and Rathfriland Volunteers, he attacked the hated Sacramental Test, which excluded Presbyterians from public, judicial and military offices, cautioning his men against sectarian animosity, and said that it was necessary to address the following question:

> Why should we arm to support a Government and nation who treat us as aliens, declare us incapable of the meanest Post in the State army or revenue and say in the most express terms we ought not, must not, be trusted; ought we to support those Governors who even last session rejected a Bill sent from the parliament of Ireland for our own relief and preferred the Roman Catholicks to us. What reward did our ancestors receive who defended the Kingdom for William and expended their all in the cause?

In the contentious election in 1783 in County Down, Barber actively supported the then more progressive Robert Stewart of Mount Stewart over Lord Kilwarlin of the Hill family, who was so annoyed that he burst into Barber's meetinghouse one Sunday to denounce him. In 1787 John Wesley the Methodist preacher preached in Barber's meetinghouse in Rathfriland, describing Barber as a princely personage.

Although he was considered to have Arian views on the Trinity, in 1790/1 Barber was elected the Presbyterian Moderator for the year. In 1791 he supported the launch of the radical *Northern Star* newspaper of the United Irishmen and in the following year he was reaching out to the Catholic Defenders to support the reform movement. He formed a company of National Guards on the model of the French. He also suggested that his brethren should look west to America where every man worshipped God as his conscience dictated.

Around 1797 he was imprisoned for two years for the outspokenness of his political opinions and suspicion of involvement in planning the rebellion, but no evidence was brought as to his actual involvement, which took place the following year. At his court martial Barber insisted that 'I have always preached peace, goodwill and obedience to the laws and the following circumstances, that when the rebellion broke out in the County of Down, not one man in my congregation joined in it is proof that I did not preach in vain.'

He died in 1811 in Rathfriland, County Down.

Sources: Baillie 1981; Campbell 1991; McBride 1998; McBride 1998–2000; Newman 1993; Seery *et al* 2000; Stewart 1993; Witherow 1879.

Benjamin McDowell
1739–1824

Benjamin McDowell was born on Christmas day 1739 in Elizabethtown, New Jersey, the fifth son of Ephraim McDowell and brought up in Connor, County Antrim. He was educated at Princeton and Glasgow Universities and licensed to preach by Glasgow Presbytery in 1765 and ordained on 2 September 1766 to become the minister of Ballykelly Presbyterian Church, succeeding Rev. John Neilson who appears to have been 'new light' theologically. The congregation moved from the Derry Presbytery to the Route Presbytery at this stage, although eventually returned to the Derry Presbytery. In 1770 McDowell wrote a pamphlet in support of subscription to the Westminster Confession of Faith, entitled *Regaining Subscriptions to well composed summaries of Christian Doctrine as tests of Orthodoxy.*

Presbyterians strongly resented their exclusion from public life by the Episcopal church and civic authorities and having to pay a tithe to the state church. However, as tithe payers they were entitled to vote in the parish vestries, so in areas where Presbyterians were a majority they often managed to disrupt the work of these vestries. As a result the Irish parliament passed a law excluding Presbyterians from voting in the vestries. Opposition to this law, on the grounds that it further excluded Presbyterians and other independents from local decision-making, was led by McDowell who published a series of resolutions for consideration of the freeholders of the parish of Tamlaghtfinlagan who agreed them at a meeting in the Ballykelly meetinghouse County Londonderry. They were published on 9 June 1774 in the *Freeman's Journal,* as follows:

> Resolved that the late act of parliament by which dissenters are precluded voting at vestries, is unconstitutional, unjust, highly injurious to a very respectable part of His Majesty's Protestant subjects and calculated to sow the seeds of dissention and increase emigration to America.

> Resolved, that our present representatives, the Right Hon. Thomas Conolly and the Right Hon. Edward Cary, in consenting to it have betrayed their trust and justly forfeited our future confidence.

> Resolved therefore, unless they use their utmost influence to have it repealed at the meeting of next session of parliament, it is our determined purpose upon the ensuing election to oppose them to the utmost of our power, and to co-operate with our independent brethren in the County to bring in as our future representatives, men who we hope will pay a greater regard to the good of the public in general and of their constituents in particular.

Later in 1774 John Richardson of Walworth was put forward as a candidate in the 1776 election. Thomas Connolly then decided to go on the offensive and conducted an investigation into the resolutions, getting his agents to interview the signatories, many of whom felt forced to say that they had never subscribed to the resolutions. McDowell, however, acknowledged the contents of the resolutions and 'gloried in it in the presence of the Right Hon. Thomas Conolly, McCausland Esq. and Richard King'. Conolly eventually realised that he needed to compromise with the dissenters, many of whom were his own tenants. Conolly therefore put forward a bill to annul the hated clause, which prevented dissenters from voting at parish vestries. It was passed in the spring of 1776. John Richardson withdrew from the election and Conolly and Carey were again duly elected.

McDowell was called to St Mary's Abbey (Rutland Square) Dublin in 1778, just after the church had been rebuilt on the same site. He was succeeded at Ballykelly by Rev. Robert Rentoul of Lurgan who was installed there on 3 October 1779. The congregation then chose to call it Mary's Abbey. McDowell became the first minister in the new church in 1778 and stayed for 46 years. It is said that previously the congregation had dwindled away to six families and a few individuals but 'able preaching and faithful work' soon revived the dying cause. In 1786 he was elected Moderator of the General Assembly. By 1818, the congregation had two thousand members. Mr McDowell obtained, as his co-pastor, Mr James Horner, who was ordained on 4 November 1791. Both ministers were the recipients of DDs, as was also Mr James Carlile, (licensed Paisley), a non-subscriber, who was ordained as Dr McDowell's assistant on the 4 May 1813.

McDowell was somewhat of a controversialist – and from him came a notable book on *The Nature of the Presbyterian Form of Church Government*.

At a meeting of Synod in 1781 the divisive issue of subscription to the Westminster Confession of Faith was again raised. McDowell, the leader of the orthodox party, had a private conference with Dr Campbell of the non-subscribers and agreed a mechanism for allowing the existing state of play to remain i.e. subscription would be the official policy of Synod, but it would remain the responsibility of the Presbyteries, many of whom did not require subscription, to decide as to how this would be carried out. This, therefore, averted a crisis in the church.

McDowell married in 1794 the daughter of E.P. Carroll of Newtown, County Carlow and they had at least one son and one daughter. He retired in 1813 and died on 13 September 1824.

Sources: Crawford and Trainor 1969; Latimer 1893; Holmes 2000.

Thomas McCabe
1740–1820

Thomas McCabe was probably born in 1740 in Lurgan, County Armagh, son of Patrick McCabe. He became a watchmaker in North Street, Belfast and was also involved in cotton manufacturing with the Joy family and Henry Joy McCracken. McCabe even invented a revolutionary new loom for the industry. In 1762 he moved from Lisburn to Belfast.

In 1775 he was signatory to a petition to the king to end the war with America so that trade, which was important to Ulster, could be restored. He became famous for shaming Waddell Cunningham and some of the other Belfast merchants into abandoning their plans for getting involved in the lucrative slave trade, by writing in Cunningham's business subscription book, 'May God eternally damn the soul of the man who subscribes the first guinea'. As a result Wolfe Tone referred to McCabe as 'The Irish Slave'. He also supported Henry Joy McCracken's Sunday School, to improve the education of the poor as well as Manson's Lancastrian School in Frederick Street.

McCabe was involved in the first meetings of the United Irishmen, probably from April 1791, at which they (McCabe, Samuel Neilson, John Robb, Alexander Lowry and Henry Joy McCracken) resolved to,

> form ourselves into an association to unite all Irishmen to pledge ourselves to our country, and by that cordial union maintain that balance of patriotism so essential for the restoration and preservation of our liberty, and the revival of our trade.

McCabe, Sam McTier, William Sinclair and Thomas Russell met in October to establish the Society of United Irishmen, to which Wolfe Tone was an invited guest. Two days later the secret committee, including McCabe, met with various other United Irishmen, all Presbyterians, including Samuel Neilson (see profile), William McCleary, William and Robert Simms (see profile), Henry Haslett, William Tenant (see profile), John Campbell and Gilbert McIlveen.

The McCabe house and farm, 'the Vicinage', at Cross Loanings on the Antrim Road, up Buttle's Loney behind the Poor House, was a regular meeting house for Belfast United Irishmen and was attacked by Dragoons in March 1793. His shop was wrecked by drunken soldiers and all the windows smashed. He decided to keep the windows the way the soldiers had left them as a reminder to all who saw them of the damage the soldiers had done. McCabe was involved in procuring arms for the United Irishmen, including cannon that had belonged to the Volunteers. By 1797, having neglected his business affairs, McCabe was facing financial difficulties and moved back to Lurgan. There is no record of whether he was actively involved in the rebellion or not.

Thomas McCabe died in 1820. The Vicinage was sold in 1833 to the Catholic church and St Malachy's School is now on the site. His younger son William Putnam McCabe (see profile) was also actively involved with the United Irishmen, working to organise the rebellion in the south of Ireland. His older son, Thomas, had two children, Jane and Thomas who became a doctor.

Sources: Beckett 1983; Bradbury 2002; Campbell 1991; McBride 1998; McCabe 1997; O'Byrne 1990; O Cathain 2007; Stewart 1993.

William Crawford (also spelled Craford)
1739–1801

William Thomas Crawford was born in Crumlin, County Antrim, in 1739, the fifth generation of Ulster Presbyterian ministers in his family. His father was Rev. Thomas Crawford of Crumlin. Although his brothers became physicians, William Crawford chose to enter the ministry and was educated at Glasgow University where he gained an MA in 1763. He trained for the ministry and was later awarded a Doctorate in Divinity in 1784. He was licensed in the Armagh Presbytery in 1765 and was installed in Strabane church in 1766. He developed a reputation as a prominent 'new light' minister. In 1783 he was involved in discussions with James Stewart the County Tyrone MP, sympathetic to Presbyterians, about a potential increase in the *regium donum* grant to Presbyterian ministers.

Like many other Presbyterian ministers, who had previously been debarred from military involvement, he joined the Volunteer movement and exchanged the 'rusty black' for the 'glowing scarlet', as the chaplain in James Stewart's Tyrone Regiment of Volunteers. He was then involved in setting up a second Volunteer Corp in Strabane, which was not under the control of James Stewart, the agent of the Earl of Abercorn. Crawford became its commander and United Irishman, James Orr, its secretary. It pushed for reform of parliament.

Crawford was a member of the standing committee of the Volunteer movement which organised the Dungannon Convention of February 1782 and was involved in the resolutions put forward that day, particularly the resolution on toleration for Catholics. He was elected to the provincial volunteer committee to co-ordinate efforts to achieve the volunteer demands.

In 1783 he expressed strong support for radical political reform:

> The representations of the people in the great national senate is, in many instances, arbitrary, partial and inadequate. So long as a

majority of the commons is composed of members of boroughs, which compared with the nation at large are insignificant, and where a few individuals devoted to the selfish and impervious will of a still smaller number of absolute grandees, have the sole power of election, a spirit of venality must pervade the political system. To extirpate this radical evil, to procure such an addition to the commons as will render them the real and more equal representatives of the people, to establish a mode of election which would place the freehold tenantry, upon such occasions beyond the cognizance and the power of landlords who usurp a most unrighteous dominion over their liberty and the dictates of their conscience, are objects which should engage the spirited and persevering efforts of every friend to the true interest of his country. If they were obtained, and our parliament still more limited in its duration, we might flatter ourselves with the hope of enjoying not only external but internal freedom. We might hope that as the parliament of England have relinquished all claim of legislative authority over us, her ministers and our own would cease to corrupt our representatives.

In 1784 the Synod of Ulster was greatly concerned with the lack of education for young people and the following year appointed Crawford to set up and run an academy, teaching logic, mathematics, moral philosophy and later, natural philosophy and a course of experiments. With Presbyterian students debarred from Trinity College Dublin, so they had to go to Glasgow if they wished to obtain a university education, Crawford was involved in an attempt to found a Presbyterian University in Cookstown, which failed to get off the ground when Lord Fitzwilliam was recalled.

He published his *Volunteer Sermons* and a two-volume *History of Ireland*, in which, amongst other things, he discussed Catholic grievances. The 'benevolent reader' he anticipated, would be horrified by the 'inhuman treatment to which the natives were exposed from the rapacity of the English adventurers', the imposition of the Reformation on Ireland, and the hardships endured for their beliefs.

In his *History of Ireland* Crawford recounts the rise of the White Boys and Hearts of Steel who, suffering from poverty and oppression, engaged in acts of destruction and violence around the countryside. He argued that,

Is it not very astonishing that during the course of these disturbances which continued until very lately, government neither set on foot an enquiry to investigate their cause, or took any pains to remove it? A gibbit will cut off a few individuals who disturb the peace of society. Of such eveils as that mentioned above, it is but a temporary palliative. Men borne down by oppression, so long as their sufferings remain, can neither be contented with their state, or amenable to the law.

Although his brother, Alexander, most certainly was an active United Irishman for which he was jailed in 1797, Crawford does not seem to have been actively involved in the 1798 rebellion. He later moved to Holywood Old Church, County Down where he died on 4 January 1800.

Dr John Gamble described Dr Crawford as 'a most virtuous and excellent man ... respected to a degree that no one has ever been since; nor was this respect confined to those of his own persuasion, but extended to all religions and all descriptions of people'.

Sources: Brown 2013; Hazlett 2002; McBride 1998; McIvor 1969; Newman 1993.

Martha McTier
1742–1837

Martha 'Matty' McTier was born in 1742, the daughter of Rev. Thomas Drennan, minister of First Belfast Presbyterian Church, Rosemary Street and his wife Ann Drennan (née Lennox), who was half his age when they married. Martha was one of eleven children, of whom only three survived infancy. One of her siblings was her younger brother, William Drennan (see profile), one of the founders of the United Irishmen. When her brother moved to Edinburgh to study medicine in 1773, they began a correspondence which would last, with only a few breaks, for more than 40 years. During this time, after Edinburgh, he lived in Newry, Dublin and England, while she continued to live in or close to Belfast.

The Drennan-McTier letters now survive virtually intact, and were officially published in 1999. They provide a fascinating insight into late eighteenth and early nineteenth century politics, society and art, the United Irishmen and the growth of Belfast. They also demonstrate the role that Martha McTier played in, not only chronicling this period in Belfast's history, but, acting as support and advisor, even critic, of her brother, William Drennan.

In 1773, the same year her brother went to Edinburgh, Martha married Samuel McTier, a chandler by trade, who was a widower with an 11 year old daughter, Margaret. In 1781 McTier went bankrupt through a combination of bad luck and poor judgment and had to move in with Martha's mother Ann and sister Nancy, neither of whom seemed to particularly like Samuel. As a result of their misfortune, Martha's health suffered, eventually experiencing a breakdown, at which point her letters to her brother ceased for several years.

Things improved for the McTeirs when, in 1785, Samuel was employed as the Ballast Master to the new Harbour Commission in Belfast, and then set up as a notary public. This employment, and a loan from William, enabled them to purchase a site and build a small farmhouse just outside Belfast, which they christened Cabin Hill.

In 1789 William Drennan took over the medical practice of Dr James Moody in Dublin and developed a friendship with Thomas Addis Emmet. In 1791 he sent a paper to Sam McTier, which he circulated, proposing the establishment of a brotherhood for political reform amongst the Volunteers. In October that year, Sam McTier and others met Wolf Tone in Belfast. Samuel was appointed President of the First Belfast Society of United Irishmen and their home became a centre for United Irish activity. Martha shared the views of her husband and brother on political reform and Catholic Emancipation and was angered by the criticism of her brother's United Irishmen's oath, by her old friend, William Bruce. She recognised that there was going to be trouble ahead.

In 1792, the Government commissioned John Pollock to gather information on William Drennan in order to be able to prosecute him, as they had done with Archibald Hamilton Rowan. Pollock met with Drennan and asked him to work as a writer for the government, which Drennan refused. Martha engaged in an exchange of correspondence with Pollock criticising his actions. In June 1794, William Drennan was put on trial for sedition and convicted of publishing the *Address to the Volunteers*, but acquitted of writing it.

In 1793 as the French Revolution resulted in increasing executions, Martha became less enthusiastic about the revolution.

Martha and Sam's Cabin Hill home had regular visits from United Irish leaders, including Thomas Russell, whom she came to regard as another brother.

Samuel McTier died suddenly in 1795, during a holiday with Martha's cousin, Hamilton Young, in Scotland. Unfortunately her husband had left no will, so instead of receiving life interest on his property she found she was only entitled to one-third of it. She was therefore forced to move in with Margaret McTier, Sam's 34 year old daughter, and live in reduced circumstances.

William Drennan prophesied, correctly, that Ireland was going to drift 'from what may be called Civil Anarchy to Civil War'. It began with a military crackdown in Belfast, and Martha McTier describes General Lake's swoop on the northern United Irish leaders:

> Since 10 o'clock this morning Belfast has been under military government; a troop of horse is before my door, a guard on Haslet's, which is near us, one at Church Lane, the Long Bridge, and every

avenue to the town. Haslet is taken; Neilson and Russell have been walking the streets till about an hour ago when, the Library having been broken up and a search being made for them, they delivered themselves up. ... They are taken up for high treason. I hope there will be no irons. Neilson will be easily killed, though he looks bluff. Russell I feel for as if a younger, rasher Brother, tho' during years of intimacy I never heard a worse sentiment than his Book contained, and to those he has been consistent.

Belfast was under martial law and Martha McTier, in a letter written on St Patrick's Day, 1797, analysed the feelings of the community over whom General Lake was driving his iron harrow:

Every day produces something which a few years ago would have created amazement ... Murders and assassinations are dreadful subjects, but common here, and the natural consequence of what I often witness – men torn from their friends and Country, and put on board a tender without trial or anyone here at least knowing for what. The higher officers ... do not seem to relish the searching business, in which some of the Church magistrates go beyond them. The country people ... give them old rusty guns. Several good ones are sent in since General Lake's proclamation, and I believe many found hid in ditches.

I have one which ... shall never, if I can help it, be raised against the people. It was bought and used for a far different purpose. Like an Idiot I registered it, at a time when fools bluster'd and ten pound frightened me. If they come for it I will not falsify, but they shall never get Sam McTier's gun. I was right when I told you half-way business would not do in Belfast ... You seem to think I ought to fly. Why, I have not one fear. 'Tis only the Rich are alarmed, or the guilty. I am neither ...

I have reason to believe other strong measures are hatching, and will be enforced whenever the Town goes out of the peace ...

Preceding the Rising of '98, Martha McTier provided her brother with important intelligence on political developments in Belfast, including the arrests of key United Irishmen, many of whom were friends. However, she discovered that her letters were being opened in the post, and she began inserting in her letters, which were now focused almost entirely on domestic affairs, a series of pointed jibes at the postmaster who did General Lake's dirty work. But she realised, and stressed on her brother, the importance of discretion.

The most objectionable part of the military occupation was the practice of billeting soldiers in private houses. On one occasion Drennan, having protested against a demand for lodgings by two soldiers, had a squabble with the notorious magistrate, Swan, who 'began to abuse me, not very like a magistrate, calling me rebel, traitor, that my life was indulged to me by the Government that he would go and send 50 soldiers to the house.' Martha McTier had the gift of taking things more philosophically. 'My mother,' she tells her brother,

> had four soldiers for two or three nights. She, like you, argues the affair, and never mends the matter. My Pride always prevents anything but compliance, and I am never ill-treated. I cannot bear intercourse with these sort of gentry. Those who do their duty do right. Those who go beyond are only gratified by your complaints.

Martha McTier provides a picture of life in Belfast during those June days that witnessed the failure of the rebellion in Down and Antrim:

> Sunday afternoon eight soldiers, a woman and child were sent to me, and by Major Fox on horse-back desired to make their quarters good. I opened the door myself, and they immediately rushed into the parlour. I told them and the Sergeant my situation. He pressed me to bed them, which I offered to do if he insisted on it, but that I and my family must leave the house. He behaved well the instant they were well treated. I gave them good Ale, though they pray'd for water, being just off their march from Newton, where they had been fighting all day. I pitied them much. Two were wounded. They took a shilling apiece, and we parted with civility on all sides.

In a letter congratulating her brother on the birth of his son Tom, written shortly before the Union Bill became law, Martha McTier expressed her aspiration for the future:

> I know that your son, if he lives, must see better times; but I wish him educated in them no worse than his Father. Oh! till that time let Irishmen remain sulky, grave, prudent, and watchful, not subdued into tame servility, poverty and contempt, not satisfied till time blunts their chains and feelings, but ardent to seize the possible moment of national revenge, never to lose hope of it till obtained, and then in proud and glorious safety – scorn it.

The suppression of the 1798 Rising was followed by the abolition of the Irish parliament and the establishment of the Union, which Martha opposed as 'this degrading union'. After the Union was passed in 1801 she became weary of politics, 'the hope of my heart ... is no more' having for thirty years 'clung to free and rising Ireland, to justice tempered with mercy

... to a virtuous triumph for her and liberty's defenders'.

In 1803 young Tom came and stayed with Martha in Belfast. Initially the visit was to be for a couple of months but turned into a couple of years. This is likely to have provided a comfort for Martha following the execution of her friend Thomas Russell.

In 1807 on the death of Martha Young, both William Drennan and Martha McTier received significant legacies which eased their respective financial difficulties. Drennan moved back to Belfast, but tragically in 1812, Tom died, aged eleven, leaving only four surviving children.

Martha McTier was very well read and often corresponded with her brother on literary subjects. Amongst others, she read Edward Gibbon, Edmund Burke, David Hume, William Congreve, William Godwin, Henry Fielding, Maria Edgeworth, Elizabeth Hamilton, and Mary Wollstonecraft, whom she also encouraged her brother to read. On reading Tom Paine's *Rights of man* in 1792 she commented 'Truth seems to dart from him in such plain and poignant terms, that he or even she who runs may read'. She was familiar with the writings of abolitionist Anna Maria Falconbridge and was horrified by her account of colonisation of Sierra Leone.

On Boswell she wrote, 'What a fascinating book is Boswell's *Life of Johnson*' after devouring the volumes straight from the press, 'and how improved is the present stile of biography.' Her brother's enthusiasm rivalled her own. 'It is,' he replied, 'the first work of the kind since the days of Plutarch.'

She admired various French writers: novelist Marie-Madeleine, poet Prosper Jolyot de Crébillon, and philosophers Jean Jacques Rousseau, Constantin François de Chassebœuf, Comte de Volney, Charles-Louis de Secondat, Baron de La Brède et de Montesquieu, and Jacques-Henri Bernardin de Saint Pierre, who were submitted to her shrewd and searching criticism.

Her brother invariably sent his own writings to her, and she never allowed her pride in him to blunt the edge of her comments. She suggested alterations of both content and style. Although his sister was very supportive and encouraging, she could also be critical. In response to her brother's complaints of ill-treatment, she replied:

> I hate croakers and, above all, affected ones. You panted for fame. You got it. You were read, praised, admired, prosecuted, cleared, and abused. What would you have more? Could you suppose that in this career you would not make enemies, that you would not be painted in dirty colours? Even here I think you have escaped wonderfully, and I would rather suppose you were nettled that your abilities have not drawn forth some more dignified switching than silly paragraphs in a newspaper.

Martha McTier was committed to real education and knowledge of public affairs for the uneducated working class. As far back as 1795 she wrote:

> So much have I gained by newspapers, and so ardently have I seen them sought for and enjoyed by the lower orders, that I intend to institute for their good a gratis newsroom with fire and candles, a scheme which you may laugh at, but if followed in country towns might have a wonderful effect.

More than a century before anyone else had divined the possibilities of a general strike, the closing of the Belfast shops and warehouses on the day that the Earl of Fitzwilliam left Dublin after his dismissal as Lord Lieutenant, led Martha McTier to foreshadow the possibilities of a general strike as a political instrument:

> Were this to be the case all over the kingdom it would be a curious situation. Would not the People find themselves easily and freely got up in a Mass? Might not important matter start into their heads, and rush into their hands? Might not they waive ceremony with Lord Moyra, and take it into their head to protect the country themselves and save him that trouble? … Might not the Capitol, the Castle, be surprised? But this, I suppose, is all the fears of a weak woman.

Martha McTier died in 1837.

Sources: Agnew 1999; Kennedy 2004.

John (father), Richard and John (sons) Caldwell
John sr 1742–1803
John jr 1769–1850
Richard c. 1780–1812

John Caldwell jr was born on 3 May 1769, the eldest son of John Caldwell sr, a farmer, miller and linen manufacturer, and Elizabeth (née Calderwood) who died around 1796. John Caldwell sr led a company of Volunteers in the local area and had ensured that Catholics were admitted to the company, although he did not join the United Irishmen. They lived on Harmony Hill estate near Ballymoney, leased from Lord Antrim. John Caldwell jr was educated in Ballymoney and Derry before being sent to board in Bromley, Middlesex, England. Like his headmaster he was enthused by the successes of the American Revolution.

In February 1784 John Caldwell jr went to Belfast to work for merchant Samuel Brown and within a few years became Brown's business partner and a clerk in the Northern bank founded by Brown. In 1793 Caldwell went into the shipping business on his own and developed his contacts in America.

He became an early member of the Belfast Branch of the United Irishmen. He was elected a colonel in the rebel force and organised lotteries in County Down to help finance the United Irishmen. In May 1798, just before the rising broke out, he was arrested in Dublin

Two days after the Battle of Antrim, the army burnt the Caldwell family home and mill to the ground, giving the remaining members of the household five minutes to get out of the house.

After eight weeks, John Caldwell jr was brought to Belfast, where he passed the heads of comrades who had been decapitated, and was charged with treason. He was then moved, with many of his United Irish comrades, including Thomas Ledlie Birch, to the overcrowded and unsanitary Postlethwaite prison ship, which was anchored in Belfast Lough. Successful petitioning resulted in Caldwell being allowed to go to America, which he did in May 1799. After the ship in which they sailed had been twice battered by storms and had to return to Ireland, he chartered a ship, flying an American flag, and, after being nearly arrested by a French ship, took hundreds of Ulster radicals to Jefferson's America, where he became part of the American Society of United Irishmen and the Hibernian Provident Society with similar aims in relation to Ireland. He also campaigned against the Federalists in America. His father followed in July 1799 and rented a farm for them in Long Island and later bought Salisbury Mills in Blooming Grove near Newburgh in Orange County.

In 1803 his father died and the same year John jr married Ann Higinbotham (who died in 1818) and had two daughters.

Richard Caldwell, the younger son of John Caldwell sr, at the age of seventeen, was a general during the rising in 1798. He rallied a large contingent of men at Ballymoney, armed with guns, pikes, pitchforks and scythes tied to sticks and marched them to Ballymena where they joined the United Irish forces that had captured the town. He tried to ensure that no civilians were harmed. After the Battle of Antrim and realising that the rebellion was clearly lost, Richard Caldwell crossed the Glens of Antrim to get to Cushendall, from where he sailed to Scotland. However, before he could find a passage to America, he was arrested and brought back to Ireland. He was tried for treason at a court martial in Coleraine, found guilty and sentenced to hanging. Lord Castlereagh was petitioned by Richard Parks, Richard Caldwell's brother-in-law and John Caldwell sr petitioned Lord Cornwallis. These efforts eventually paid off and the sentence was lifted on condition that he lived for the rest of his life in America. Soon the whole family had moved from Ballymoney to New York. He and his brother John opened a business trading in Water Street.

In 1812 Richard Caldwell signed up for the New York Militia and became a captain. He took part in the march to Canada, but suffering from dysentery and the effects of a storm on Lake Champlain he died of exposure.

By 1834 the Caldwell businesses had failed and John Caldwell jr withdrew from business altogether. Friends got him a job as collector of arrears taxes. He retired in 1839 and died on 17 May 1850, at the age of 82, having completed a memoir.

Sources: McBride 1998; Wilson 1998; Wilson and Spencer 2006.

John Arnold
Died 1801

John Arnold was born near Magherally, County Down. He and his family attended Ballynahinch Presbyterian Church. In common with many of those interested in the ministry he was educated in Scotland (presumably Glasgow University). He was licensed to preach by Belfast Presbytery in 1768 and ordained in First Ballybay on 18 December 1782, becoming the fourth minister of the congregation. Under his ministry a new church was built in 1786. It was renovated and enlarged in 1889. The manse was built in 1894.

Arnold was a member of the United Irishmen and because of his involvement with the rebel cause, and presumably to avoid arrest during the military clampdown, he moved to America in April 1797. When his belongings were sold at auction at Old Flush Crossroads a seal of the United Irishmen was found in a secret drawer of his desk.

On 12 July 1798 his Ballybay congregation passed a motion of loyalty to King George and the principles of "our most excellent constitution"'. After great disputes in the Ballybay congregation, Mr James Morell was ordained there in August 1799, despite various attempts by some members of the congregation to prevent him being installed as minister, including locking him out of the church, which was only overturned by the actions of a troop of dragoons.

Arnold died in America, less than five years after emigrating, on 26 December 1801. Some of his children returned to the Ballybay area.

Sources: MacConnell 1951.

Robert Steele
Died 1810

Robert Steele was born in Ballykelly, County Londonderry. He was licensed to preach by Route Presbytery in 1788 and ordained in Scriggan (Dungiven) in November 1790, succeeding the first minister, Rev. John Adams (grandfather of the Rev. D.D. Boyle (see profile).

Seventeen years earlier, a disagreement over the settlement of Rev. Patton in nearby Boveva led to the formation of Scriggan congregation in 1773.

Steele was a strong supporter of the United Irishmen and in 1798 it was reported to the Synod that 'Mr. Steel had pleaded guilty to a charge of treason and rebellion before a court-martial', As a result his name was erased from the list of Presbytery ministers.

Steele decided that discretion was the better part of valour and, before sentence was carried out, sailed to America where he became the first minister of a great church, First Pittsburgh in 1803. He died in America in 1810.

Sources: MacConnell 1951; McBride 1998.

James Davidson
Died 1813

James Davidson was the second son of John Davidson, a farmer from near Bellaghy, County Londonderry. He was educated at Glasgow University, gaining an MA in 1780. He was licensed to preach by Ballymena Presbytery in 1783 and ordained in Aughnacloy on 10 July 1787, succeeding Rev. Hugh Mulligan. He married Ann Jackson in 1790.

Davidson was an active supporter of the United Irishmen and was named by the 'Liberty men' in County Tyrone to be their representative in the parliament that they planned would be established following the hoped for success of the 1798 rebellion. However, there does not appear to be any evidence that he was actively involved in the rebellion and was not prosecuted after the rising was put down.

He was suspended from the ministry in June and July 1811 (reason unclear), resigned as a minister on 19 August 1811 and died eighteen months later on 3 February 1813. He was succeeded in Aughnacloy by Rev. John Anderson of Dungannon.

Sources: McBride 1998.

Robert Scott
Died 1813

Robert Scott was the son of James W. Scott, a farmer in Balteagh, County Londonderry. He was educated at Glasgow University in 1754 where he trained for the ministry. He was licensed to preach by Route Presbytery and ordained on 28 June 1762 to become the minister of the united congregations of Duneane and Grange, County Antrim (which had been without a minister for ten years). The previous minister of Duneane, Rev. Henderson, had joined the Non-Subscribing Presbytery of Antrim in 1725/6 and was one of the last survivors of the Belfast Society.

Scott was involved with the United Irishmen and in 1798 was court-martialled on the charge of high treason, although he was eventually acquitted. He is described in the *Fasti* as 'non-evangelical', so we can assume that, like Henderson, he was 'new light' theologically.

He retired in 1808 and died at Ivybrook, Toome, on 17 April 1813. On Scott becoming infirm, the congregation called a very different kind of minister in arch-Tory Rev. Henry Cooke who was installed as the minister of Duneane and Grange.

Sources: *Northern Whig* 26 July 1827; Porter 1871; Swords 1997.

Thomas Stewart
Died 1816

Thomas Stewart was the sixth son of Archibald Stewart of County Down. He was educated at Glasgow University in 1757. Having trained for the ministry he was licensed by Bangor Presbytery in 1761 and ordained in First Cootehill, County Cavan on 22 April 1766, becoming the second minister of Cootehill, succeeding Rev. Andrew Dean who died there in April 1760.

He actively supported the United Irishmen and, with his daughter, was involved in swearing in members to the secret oath of the United Irishmen in a house which was described as being as 'public as a whiskey house'. So successful were they that almost everyone in the town of Cootehill were members.

It is very likely that Thomas Stewart, if not his daughter, was present at the Battle of Rebel Hill near Bailieborough, County Cavan in 1798. However, he does not appear to have suffered for his involvement in the ill-fated rising and remained as minister for over 40 years. In 1808 Rev. John Johnston was ordained as his assistant and successor. Stewart died on 10 December 1816.

Sources: McBride 1998.

William Findley
1741–1821

William Findley was born around 1741 in Ulster. At the age of approximately 22, he emigrated to Pennsylvania in 1763. He first settled in Cumberland County where he married and started a family. In the American Revolution he opposed the English, joining the Cumberland County Committee of Observation and the local militia, the Seventh Battalion of the Cumberland County Associators, as a private, rising to the rank of captain.

In 1783 he moved with his family to Westmoreland County in Pennsylvania, where we was very soon elected to the Council of Censors to discuss the 1776 radical constitution. He then served on four general Assemblies and the Supreme Executive Council. As an anti-federalist, he opposed the ratification of the federal constitution and was one of the leaders of the Convention that wrote the new constitution for Pennsylvania in 1789. He served in the second to the fifth Congress and then after two years in the Pennsylvania State Senate he served again in the eighth to the fourteenth Congress.

He challenged George Washington's authoritarian Treasurer Secretary, Alexander Hamilton's use of the expression 'the lower orders', saying 'we had not thought of a Distinction of orders in Society'.

In 1811 as the oldest Congressman he was designated as the 'Father of the House'. He died at home on 5 April 1821 and is buried in Latrobe, Pennsylvania.

Sources: *Biographical Directory of the United States Congress*; Fitzpatrick 1989.

William Staveley (sometimes spelled Stevelly or Stavely)
1743–1825

William Staveley was born in Ferniskey near Kells, County Antrim in 1743. He was the only son of Aaron Staveley, who owned a small lease-holding in the townland and was originally Episcopalian but converted to the Covenanter Presbyterian faith. His mother was the daughter of a Presbyterian minister. He had two sisters.

He was educated at a classical school in Antrim, staying in lodgings during the week. He then went to Glasgow University. He was licensed as a Reformed Presbyterian minister in 1769 and was ordained in Conlig in North Down in 1772. Gradually the scope of his responsibility expanded as far as Newry and Ballybay and Knockbracken near Belfast where a church was built in 1776. The same year he married Mary McDonald of Irishtown near Antrim.

With the death of the other Reformed Presbyterian ministers, Staveley became the sole remaining one in Ireland. Over the next quarter of a century he was responsible for the building of at least nine other covenanting churches. He was theologically evangelical and orthodox and an impressive orator. However, as a staunch supporter of the Solemn League and Covenant of 1643, he was an opponent of the civil and religious authorities based on the minority Episcopal church, as well as the Catholic church. Samuel Ferguson reported that one of his sermons was considered to be so seditious that a member of Staveley's congregation protested so violently that he later died of apoplexy.

When Thomas Paine published his *Age of Reason*, Staveley published a reply, defended the Christian faith, in a book entitled *Appeal to Light* in which he criticised Paine's views, while recognising him as a 'friend of the liberties of men, and a pointed opposer of despots'.

With the withdrawal of soldiers from Ireland to fight the American colonists, Staveley participated in the Volunteer home defence movement, becoming captain of the Drumbracken Volunteers and contributed to the *Northern Star*, the mouthpiece of the United Irishmen in Ulster.

Although he always denied that he was a United Irishman, there is evidence that he took the United Irish oath, initiated others and gave financial support to the United Irishmen. He was arrested during a church service in June 1797 for storing arms in his Knockbracken meetinghouse but was released after two months in jail.

In October 1797 he accompanied William Orr (who lived beside Staveley's wife's farm) to his execution, sharing the outrage of the Presbyterian community at Orr's fate.

He was re-arrested after the Battle of Ballynahinch and the soldiers took his furniture and burnt his house. He was imprisoned on board a prison-ship for several months from June 1798, for preaching seditious doctrines. He was offered a pardon if he agreed to exile, which he refused. He was later released. He was censured by Presbytery and unable to return as minister of Knockbracken.

In 1800 he accepted a call from a County Antrim congregation, comprising mainly Kellswater and Cullybackey. When the congregation was split into two districts he accepted a call from Kellswater. He was considered the father of the newly created Reformed Presbyterian Synod and became moderator. He died, while still an active minister – aged 82 – in 1825. His wife outlived him by another 23 years.

Sources: Allen 2004; Brooke 1994; Campbell 1991; Erskine and Gordon 1997; McBride 1998; Stewart 1995.

John Craig
1744–94

John Craig was born in Ballynahinch in 1744 and educated in Glasgow. He trained for the Burgher Seceder minister at the Associate Divinity Hall in Glasgow. A man of independent turn of mind he was considered by the strict Calvinist Burgher Seceders to be doctrinally suspect as a student, but eventually satisfied both his Presbytery and Synod and was restored.

He was licensed by Down (Burgher) Presbytery in May 1763 and ordained later the same year in Coronary Seceder (Burgher) Presbyterian Church. This was another of the congregations branching off from First Bailieborough church in County Cavan.

Craig was respected enough to be elected Moderator of the Burgher Synod in 1782. However, because of his involvement with the United Irishmen and the government clampdown on the movement, in 1793 he was forced to flee to America. One of his congregation was hanged for his involvement in the rebellion. Other rebel leaders, such as Bob Kelly, emigrated with Rev. Craig.

In America Craig became minister of Big Spring United Presbyterian Church, Newville, Cumberland County, Pennsylvania. He died there the following year, on the 14 or 17 May 1794. He was survived by his wife, Grizzell, and their daughter Mary.

Sources: Baillie and Kirkpatrick 2005; Stewart 1950.

William Steel Dickson
1744–1824

William Steel Dickson was born in Carnmoney, County Antrim on 25 September 1744, the son of John Dickson, a farmer in Ballycraigy, County Antrim, and his wife Jane (née Steel). He was educated at Ballycraigy School, with its 'almost useless routine' and then by Rev. Robert White, the minister of Templepatrick Presbyterian Church. He then went to Glasgow University, where one of his tutors was Adam Smith, and which later awarded him a Doctorate in Divinity in 1783. He was licensed to preach in 1767 and ordained in 1771, when he was then called to be minister of the Ballyhalbert and Portaferry Presbyterian churches in County Down.

Dickson was not content with faith as personal piety and developed what he called 'scripture politics' – the application of the Christian faith in the life and politics of society. He was a vocal supporter of the American colonists against the British and condemned the American war as 'unnatural, impolitic and unprincipled'. In a publication of his sermons, he argued for the necessity of reform and emancipation in Ireland on the basis of Christianity, backed by Scripture. He was very clear that the need for reform and emancipation was due because,

> Never were partiality and injustice more conspicuous on earth than they had been in the land of our nativity ... Not a small part, but three-fourths of its inhabitants, the great body of the people, have been reduced to the most abject and humiliating servitude, excluded from every office, honour or trust and emolument of the state.

When the War of Independence broke out in America Dickson said in a sermon that 'There is scarcely a Protestant family of the middle classes amongst us who does not reckon kindred with the inhabitants of the extensive continent'. In 1783 Dickson provided support to Robert Stewart over the more conservative Hill family in the general election. At one point he delivered forty voters to Stewart's door in Downpatrick, after marching on horseback through the town.

In 1793, on the passing of the Catholic Relief Act, which removed most of the onerous legal restrictions they had faced over the previous two centuries, Dickson as Moderator of the Synod of Ulster (an annually elected position) congratulated 'their Roman Catholic countrymen on their being restored to the privileges of the constitution' and expressed the hope that they would now cultivate and maintain the principles of civil and religious liberty which would 'prove to the world that the liberality of protestants has been neither ill-timed or unsafe'. The Synod also reaffirmed its opinion that 'a reform in the representation in the Commons house of parliament, is essentially necessary to the protection of the constitution', but assuring the Lord Lieutenant that they approved only of constitutional means to achieve reform 'rejecting with abhorrence every idea of popular tumult or foreign aid'.

He was a leading supporter, with the rank of captain, of the Volunteer movement. At Volunteer Assemblies he supported the revolution in France and the right of both Catholics and dissenters to vote (some others took a more cautious line on the enfranchisement of Catholics).

He also took the United Irishmen secret oath and attended at least one of their meetings (later he said he could not remember attending any others). The brutal suppression of the reform movement, of which Dickson was a leading spokesman, made him more determined than ever to stand up against injustice and oppression.

On the eve of the 1798 rising he was imprisoned in Fort George in Scotland until 1802, although no evidence was put forward against him. It was believed that he was the Adjutant General of County Down, replacing Thomas Russell. His arrest delayed the uprising in Down by two days, by which time the Antrim rising had already been put down.

After being released, Dickson returned to Belfast without a congregation or significant income. Dr Black, who controlled the *regium donum,* prevented him becoming the minister of Donegore. In 1802, he was called to a small new congregation in Keady, County Armagh where he was minister for 13 years, although he was denied the *regium donum* grant. He wrote a vindication of his position, *Narrative,* published in 1812, which angered many in the establishment and the church. He retired in 1815 and returned to Belfast, living in very humble circumstances, and died in poverty in 1824. Very few people attended his funeral where Rev. W.D.H. McEwan gave the oration. Many years later Francis Joseph Bigger paid for a gravestone to be placed over his pauper's grave in Clifton Street Old Graveyard.

Sources: Bardon 1992; Brooke 1994; Campbell 1991; Dunlop 1993; Holmes 1985; Holmes 2000; Latimer 1897; McBride 1998; Newman 1993; Seery *et al* 2000; Stewart 1993.

John Dunlap
1746/7–1812

John Dunlap was born in Strabane in 1746/7. When he was still a boy he moved to Philadelphia to live with his uncle, William Dunlap, a printer, publisher and bookseller, who married a relation of Benjamin Franklin and through his influence was appointed as postmaster of Philadelphia. John Dunlap followed in his uncle's footsteps into the publishing and printing business.

In 1766 William Dunlap felt a calling for the ministry and went to England for his theological training and handed the running of his business over to his nephew. In 1773 John Dunlap married Elizabeth Ellison (née Hayes) from Liverpool.

John Dunlap founded the *Pennsylvania Packet* in 1771, which eventually, in 1784, became a daily newspaper – the first in North America.

He became the official printer to Congress and first printed the Declaration of Independence, written by lawyer and planter Thomas Jefferson, at the request of John Hancock, of Ulster descent, when on 4 July 1776 twelve of the colonies agreed to declare the new states as a free and independent nation.

It is not known precisely how many copies of the original Declaration of Independence, which became known as the Dunlap Broadsides, were actually printed, although it is believed it may have been two hundred. By 1989 only 24 copies were known to still be in existence, until a flea market shopper found one inside a framed painting bought for four dollars. After authentication by Sotheby's it was purchased at auction by Norman Lear and David Heyden for $8.14 million dollars. Of the other copies, 21 are owned by universities.

The *Pennsylvania Packet* was also the first newspaper to publish the Constitution of the United States, which had been printed by Dunlap's firm.

In 1789 Dunlap wrote to his brother-in-law in Strabane, 'The young men of Ireland who wish to be free and happy should leave it and come here as quick as possible. There is no place in the world where a man meets so rich a reward for good conduct and industry as in America.'

He was a founder and officer of the First Troop of Philadelphia Cavalry, which became the bodyguard of George Washington during the battles of Trenton and Princeton. He personally donated $20,000 to help supply clothing and provisions to the army during a critical point in the war. He died on 27 November 1812.

Sources: *Dictionary of American Biography* 1930; Goff 1976; Kennedy 1998; Kennedy 2001.

Archibald Hamilton Rowan
1751–1834

Archibald Hamilton Rowan was born in 1751 in his grandfather's house in Rathbone Place, London. He was educated at Westminster School and Queen's College, Cambridge. He married in Paris in 1781 and settled in Rathcoffey, County Kildare in 1784. He later moved to Killyleagh, County Down. He travelled extensively in England, Holland and, particularly, France where he lived for eleven years from 1773 and became influenced by Rousseau and other French philosophers. He also met Thomas Jefferson and Andrew Jackson in the American colony of Virginia. In 1784 he returned to his estate and joined the Volunteers to defend Ireland against invasion.

He became publicly celebrated as a champion of the underdog when he took up the case of a poor Dublin girl, Mary Neal, who had been abducted and put to work in a brothel, patronised by Lord Carhampton, a prominent ascendancy figure. He also supported the cause of the silk weavers of Dublin when times were hard during a trade depression, something they never forgot and welcomed him when he returned to Ireland after his exile.

He was a founder member of the Northern Whig Club and in 1790, influenced by Wolf Tone, became a founder member of the Society of United Irishmen with William Drennan (see profile) and the secretary of the Dublin Society, which called on the citizen soldiers, called the First National Battalion, formed out of the Volunteers, to stand to arms when forbidden to do so by the Privy Council. The battalion backed down to the contempt of their Belfast counterparts.

In 1793, Rowan went to visit the Scottish republican Thomas Muir, when he was put on trial during the wave of reaction to the execution of Louis XVI in France.

With the outbreak of the war with France, the political atmosphere changed considerably. What looked like a radical reform movement in 1792 was viewed by the authorities as treasonable sedition in 1794. Hamilton Rowan was charged in 1794 with delivering seditious addresses to Volunteer companies and distributing seditious libel, in the form of a manifesto drafted by Drennan, which began with the words, 'Citizen Soldiers'. He was defended, in a famous speech, by John Philpot Curran, who also defended Wolf Tone, but was sentenced to two years imprisonment. After trying to provide France with information on the civil and military forces in Ireland, which would have been a capital offence if he had been prosecuted for that crime, he was lucky to be sentenced to imprisonment. He then escaped and fled to France, where he became friendly with Mary Wollstonecraft, and later travelled to Germany. His experiences of seeing the reign of terror in France prevented him joining others from Ireland in supporting the Revolution.

He was eventually pardoned in 1803 and settled on his estate in Killyleagh, County Down (and which is still the family estate). He continued to be a strong supporter of electoral reform and Catholic emancipation. He was a Unitarian theologically.

His son Sidney Hamilton Rowan was as conservative politically and theologically as his father was radical. He was a great friend and supporter of Henry Cooke, upon whom he had a profound influence. Archibald Hamilton Rowan died in 1834.

Sources: Boylan 1998; Campbell 1991; Holmes 1985; Holmes 2000; Stewart 1993.

James Porter
1752/3–98

James Porter was born in Tamna Wood near Ballindrait, County Donegal in 1752/3. He was the son of a farmer and scotch-miller. He initially became a schoolmaster at Dromore, County Down in 1773. In 1780 he married and moved to Drogheda and decided to enter the Presbyterian ministry. He studied at Glasgow University and was licensed to preach in 1786. A year later he became a minister of Greyabbey church in County Down, having to supplement his income, like many Presbyterian ministers, by farming.

He was an open supporter of parliamentary reform and Catholic emancipation. He joined the Volunteers, but took no active part in them or in the United Irishmen and refused to swear their secret oath. In 1794 he wrote regularly for the *Northern Star* under the pseudonym of Sydney, attacking 'the blood-thirsty, supercilious and unprincipled ascendancy'. Two years later he also started writing hugely popular satirical pieces for the *Northern Star* under the title of 'Billy Bluff and Squire Firebrand', which made fun of the local landed gentry, their Episcopal clergy and informers. His satirical view of the political state of Ireland included the following,

> O what a happy country we had before men turned their thoughts to thinking! Catholics thought of nothing but just getting leave to live, and working for their meat; Presbyterians thought of nothing but wrangling about religion and grumbling about their Tythes; and Protestants thought of nothing but doing and saying what their betters bid them ... O how times are changed, and all for the worse!

The powerful Lord Londonderry of Mount Stewart, who was the butt of Porter's satire cannot have been pleased to read, 'Did you ever see mushrooms in a dunghill? Then you have seen what our new race of lords and earls resemble. They have rotten roots, flimsy stems and spungy heads.'

In an ironic sermon delivered and published in 1797 he preached on the obligatory fast-day topic decreed by the government of giving thanks for the great storm that prevented the French landing in Ireland.

On the outbreak of the rebellion, he was arrested, condemned and hanged on the false word of an informer, in full view of his meetinghouse and home. It is believed that his satirical pieces had so angered the local gentry, particularly Lord Londonderry, that the rebellion was a great excuse to get rid of him. His son believed that, while his father was a United Irishman, he had been opposed to the rebellion taking place when it did because of the lack of planning and resources.

Sources: Boylan 1998; Campbell 1991; Holmes 1985; Holmes 2000; Latimer 1897; McBride 1998.

William Drennan
1754–1820

William Drennan was born in May 1754 at the manse of the First Presbyterian Church, Rosemary Street, Belfast, where his father, Rev. Thomas Drennan (1696–1768) was minister. Thomas Drennan, a friend of Francis Hutcheson, the liberal philosopher and theologian who was a leader of the Scottish Enlightenment, held strong liberal views on religion and politics, believing in the right of private judgement as the precondition of public and private virtue. Thomas Drennan's influence earned him an entry in the *Dictionary of Irish Philosophers*.

Rather than follow in his father's footsteps as a minister, William Drennan studied for an MA in Glasgow University and medicine in Edinburgh and qualified as a doctor. While in Edinburgh he rejoiced in the success of the American colonists, but kept his views to himself, except for his letters home.

He practiced as a gynaecologist briefly in Belfast and became involved in the Volunteer movement (the Blue Company) and Volunteer politics, before moving to Newry. He was one of the pioneers of inoculation against smallpox and promoting the washing of hands to prevent the spread of disease. In June 1783 he was struck down with typhus which nearly killed him, taking five weeks to recover.

The Volunteer movement began to change in 1784, with Dublin and Belfast companies opening their ranks to people of all religious persuasions. Drennan was involved in establishing the Newry Volunteers with involvement from all denominations.

In 1784 and 1785, he wrote a series of 'Letters of Orellana', which were published in the *Belfast Newsletter*, outlining a programme of political reform, providing a similar function to Thomas Paine in America. He described the ascendancy as 'rooted moral and national evil ... the peculiar curse of this country' and the land system as 'at best a mitigated feudality, and at worst, the connexion of planter and slave'.

Drennan moved to Dublin in 1789, where he developed his medical practice and was inspired by the French Revolution and the fall of the Bastille, which was celebrated by dissenters, although not by Catholics, in Ireland.

He became involved with Tone and Russell, in the establishment of the Dublin Society of United Irishmen in 1791, having proposed the formation of such a society five years earlier, and became its chairman. Having seen the apparent success of revolutions in America and France, he wrote to his then friend, Rev. William Bruce, who succeeded his father as minister of the family church, First Belfast, saying: 'Reform to be anything must be revolution. I think that revolutions are not to be dreaded as such terrible extremes.'

In 1792 Drennan organised a boycott of sugar and rum in order to prevent the extension of the slave trade to Ireland.

While he was working in Dublin at the time and involved in developing the Society of United Irishmen there, it was Drennan who wrote the United Irishmen's original prospectus and test or oath. In 1794, he was tried for sedition on 10 counts, as a result of injudicious contacts with a French spy, but was acquitted. He was allowed to go to America, but worked his way back to France where he encouraged the French government to sanction an invasion. However, he had no active participation in the rebellion and was disappointed by the response of the north to the rebellion which had cooled due to the French enthusiasm for the guillotine and war with its neighbours, including the Protestant cantons of Switzerland.

He was actively opposed to the Act of Union, which followed the failure of the 1798 rebellion, and founded the *Belfast Monthly Magazine* in opposition to the government.

In 1800 he gave up medicine, returned to live in Cabin Hill in Belfast and married a wealthy Englishwoman, Sarah Swanwick. He was determined that education should be non-denominational and with botanist John Templeton and John Hancock, founded the Belfast Academical Institution (known as 'Inst') in College Square East, Belfast.

Drennan was also a poet, writer and supporter of the literary movement and was founder and editor of *The Belfast Magazine*. It was Drennan who first coined the phrase, 'the Emerald Isle', in his poem, 'When Erin first Rose'.

Drennan had four sons and a daughter. He died in 1820. He left a request that his coffin be carried by six poor Protestants and six poor Catholics (to be paid a guinea each), with a priest and a dissenting minister to officiate.

It is Drennan's extensive correspondence with his sister Martha McTier that has provided very useful evidence for historians of attitudes and events of the time.

Sources: Bardon 1992; Boylan 1998; Bradbury 2002; Brooke 1994 Campbell 1991; Duddy (ed.) 2004; Erskine and Gordon 1997; Holmes 1985; Holmes 2000; McBride 1998; Newman 1993; Seery *et al* 2000; Stewart 1993.

Sinclair Kelburn (sometimes spelled Kelburne)
1754–1802

Sinclair Kelburn was born in Dublin in 1754. His father was Rev. Ebenezer Kelburn, a Dublin Presbyterian minister. Sinclair Kelburn was educated at Trinity College Dublin, which was usually preserved for members of the Established Church. He then went to Edinburgh University to study medicine and theology. He was orthodox theologically and was licensed to preach by Dublin Presbytery in 1778 and ordained as a Presbyterian minister of Third Belfast in Rosemary Street in 1780. In 1782 he backed resolutions for religious liberty, following the decision to allow the Irish parliament to make its own laws.

He was a strong supporter of the Volunteer movement. He even preached in his uniform with his musket leaning against the pulpit door, although he strongly disapproved of drilling on Sundays. He participated in the three-day Volunteer Convention of 1784 in the Exchange Rooms in Dublin. He was appointed to make the case for equal representation in parliament, but their request was rejected.

He was a supporter of Catholic Emancipation and parliamentary reform and between 1785 and 1791 was very involved in the reform movement. He was a member of the Jacobin Club of Belfast and a participant in discussions that led to the establishment of the United Irishmen. Kelburn was admired greatly by Wolfe Tone who saw him as a fervent democrat. In 1792, he chaired a crucial meeting in Belfast at which the issue of Catholic Emancipation was hotly debated. Some, including William Bruce, voted for gradual emancipation, but Kelburn and others successfully argued for immediate emancipation. The principal Catholics of Belfast were dining together in Belfast ten weeks later and proposed various toasts including one to 'Mr Kelburn'.

The petition for Catholic Emancipation was rejected by the Irish parliament. Sir Boyle Roche, seeking to have the petition disposed of by 'tossing it over the bar and kicking it into the lobby', referred to Belfast people as 'a turbulent disorderly set of people, whom no King can govern or no God please'.

In 1793 the elective franchise was given to Catholics but they were still excluded from being elected as members of parliament and other public and judicial offices.

Kelburn was also involved in philanthropic work, preaching a charity sermon to raise money for the Belfast Poor House and Infirmary.

In April 1797 he was arrested and taken to Carrickfergus jail and then imprisoned in Kilmainham Gaol in Dublin for his alleged links with the United Irishmen. His congregation wrote to the Lord Lieutenant, pleading his innocence and seeking his immediate release. During his imprisonment he developed paralysis, losing the use of his limbs. He was released without trial after six months. He attended Henry Joy McCracken when he was in Kilmainham Gaol and before his execution in Belfast in July 1798. The following year, however, with his deteriorating physical and mental health, which was starting to have an impact on the church, he was asked to resign by his congregation, which he duly did. He only lived another two-and-a-half years and died in October 1799. He is buried in the graveyard in Castlereagh Presbyterian Church. He published various works, including some of his sermons.

Sources: Armstrong 2001; Brooke 1994; Campbell 1991; Holmes 1985; Holmes 2000; McBride 1998; Newman 1993; Seery *et al* 2000; Stewart 1993.

Thomas Ledlie Birch
1754–1808

Thomas Birch was born in County Down in 1754, the sixth and youngest son of farmer and merchant, John Birch of Gilford, County Down. Thomas Birch was educated in Glasgow University and received an MA in 1772. A member of the theologically orthodox Presbytery of Belfast he was licensed to preach by Dromore Presbytery in 1775 and ordained as a Presbyterian minister in Saintfield in 1776. He married Isabella Ledlie, a relative from County Tyrone in 1783.

He was an ardent supporter of the American cause in the War of Independence against the British (many relatives of Irish Presbyterians were involved in the fight for independence and freedom from the British) and wrote an address expressing joy that America had thrown off the yoke of slavery, which the Yankee Club of Stewartstown sent to George Washington.

When the Volunteers were created to protect Ireland from invasion, after the army had been withdrawn to fight in the war, he joined the Volunteers and became chaplain to the Saintfield Light Infantry. He called his manse 'Liberty Hall'.

With the need to secure the loyalty of the Irish dissenters, who were now armed in protection of the country, the Government passed a series of acts of parliament to remove the hated Sacramental Test which had prevented Presbyterians, gaining public, judicial or military office. The new legislation also confirmed the validity of Presbyterian marriages.

The first opportunity for Presbyterians to demonstrate their new political confidence came in 1783 when a general election was called. Birch, Steel Dickson and other Presbyterians strongly backed Robert Stewart, who was then still a Presbyterian with liberal sympathies. Stewart's opponents who backed the more conservative landed gentry candidate ridiculed Birch as 'blabbering Birch', a name that his enemies would long remember. Stewart failed to get elected and began the long climb up the aristocratic pole. He conformed to the Established Church and eventually became a very powerful and conservative landed aristocrat, Lord Londonderry, father of Lord Castlereagh.

In 1785 Birch was so annoyed with the attitude of the government that he resigned his share of the *regium donum* grant, to which Presbyterian ministers were entitled and repudiated the whole concept of state support for religion. In response to a pamphlet from the Bishop of Cloyne in 1787 he wrote two pamphlets attacking the role of the Established Church, which held a monopoly on political and ecclesiastical power in Ireland.

Birch was a regular contributor to the *Northern Star*, the mouthpiece of the reform movement in the north. He was a strong supporter of Catholic Emancipation and became the leading promoter of the United Irishmen, often called the 'Liberty men', in Saintfield, County Down. The original declaration of all the United Irishmen Societies, passed by the Saintfield Society and echoed by his congregation the following day, was:

> In the present great era of reform, when unjust governments are falling
> in every quarter of Europe … when all government is acknowledged
> to originate from the people, and to be so far only obligatory as it
> protects their rights and promotes their welfare; we think it our duty,
> as Irishmen, to come forward and state what we feel to be our heavy
> grievance, and what we know to be its effectual remedy.

In a major debate at a Volunteer Assembly in 1792, Birch had strongly
opposed Henry Joy's amendment to the motion supporting immediate
Catholic Emancipation. He, like most Presbyterians, supported the
American colonists against the British and held celebrations in Saintfield
for the French revolution in 1792. The revolutions in America and France
and the approaching end of the century, combined with an apocalyptic
theology, gave a sense of destiny to those involved in radical politics. As
Birch said in a sermon to the Synod:

> We must think that the final overthrow of the Beast, or opposing
> power, is almost at the door; and especially as we may observe in a
> certain contest the seemingly literal accomplishment of the Battle of
> Armaggedon, in which the Beast and its adherents are to be cut off,
> as a prelude to the peaceful reign of 1,000 years.

In 1793, the Volunteers, which had become increasingly radical and vocal
for reform, were supplanted by the government-controlled militia. The
Catholic Relief Act was passed to try to keep the Catholic population
detached from the reform movement.

When the Presbyterian Synod was drawing up an address to the newly
appointed Lord Lieutenant in 1795, Birch objected that the letter
contained no mention of the fact that England was at war with France and
the address did not 'expressly recognise a desire for peace'. In 1795 he
preached a sermon to three Freemason Lodges which included the
following plea:

> Let it be your study … to cultivate peace, to unite the virtuous of
> every profession into one brotherhood, to protect and support the
> widow and fatherless, to supply the needy, and thus help forward
> the empire of peace, which seemingly (according to scripture
> prophecy) is about to be established. When wars shall cease, and
> swords shall be beat into ploughshares, and spears into pruning
> hooks: Nation shall not lift sword against Nation, neither shall they
> learn war no more!

At the Synod in 1793 he acknowledged the impact of enlightenment thinking, 'Let us consider that we live in a very advanced and enlightened period of the world, when ignorance and superstition are falling like lightening from heaven, and knowledge is making very rapid strides.'

He preached that it is the duty of ministers to bear public testimony against, and to endeavour to reform, the corruptions of the state. He described royalty as 'butchers and scourgers of the human race'.

Birch was charged with publicly saying positive things about a French invasion, but was acquitted, as his chief accuser clearly held a long-standing grudge against him. He was later court-martialled at Lisburn, County Antrim, in June 1798 for his involvement with the United Irishmen, and with encouraging the rebels who were going into battle against the army, in particular. He defended himself very ably and was acquitted having agreed to emigrate to America (his brother, a captain in the Newtownards Yeomanry used his influence to enable him to avoid a much more severe sentence).

Like many others towards the end of the eighteenth century, Birch was a millenarian, believing that the scriptures show that Christ would shortly return again. He published many sermons, including one entitled, *The obligation upon Christians and especially ministers, to be exemplary in their lives; particularly at this important period, when the prophecies are seemingly about to be fulfilled in the fall of the antichrist.* It was published towards the end of the eighteenth century when the French Revolution looked likely to see the overthrow of the Catholic church.

On his arrival in America he published an address to the people of England on *The causes of the rebellion in Ireland.* It highlighted the grievances of the people of Ireland since 1782, when the Irish Parliament had been granted the right to pass its own laws, but the system for electing members of parliament remained in the hands of the Ascendancy gentry, all members of the Church of Ireland. He outlined the attempts to subdue the reform movement militarily, but asked whether the king really wanted to, 'rule a depopulated, a desolated, and a discontented country' and whether

> the slaughter of a hundred thousand of the people of Ireland reconcile the survivors to that system of mal-government which they have risen to oppose? Will the faction which has provoked this scene of slaughter, become more popular by the carnage they have occasioned?

He pleaded with Englishmen to 'save four millions of people from the insulting tyranny of Ministers who have abused their powers, and instead of the mild genius of the British Constitution, have governed by the galling despotism of a military mob!'

Birch died in 1808 after ten years in America.

Sources: Brooke 1994; Campbell 1991; Holmes 1985; Holmes 2000; Hume 1998; McBride 1998; Newman 1993; Seery *et al* 2000; Stewart 1993; Witherow 1879.

Thomas Smith
1755–1832

Thomas Smith was born on 20 March 1755, the second son of John Smith, a farmer of Brigh, near Cookstown, County Tyrone. He was educated at Glasgow and trained for the Seceder (Burgher) ministry at the Associate Divinity Hall in Haddington, east of Edinburgh in 1776. He was licensed by Derry (Burgher) Presbytery in March 1776 and ordained three years later in Randalstown and Ahoghill (Brookside), County Antrim on 12 October 1779, succeeding Rev. William Holmes.

As an active supporter of the United Irishmen he was implicated in the 1798 rebellion and fled to America in 1799.

On 8 April 1801 he was installed as minister of Tuscarora, Philadelphia. When his church was united with another church he became the minister of McCoysville United Presbyterian Church of Tuscarora and Fermanagh on 12 February 1806. He lived on a farm in Spruce Hill, Juniata, Pensylvania. His son William died in 1823. Rev. Thomas Smith served the church for 26 years until his death on 12 February 1832.

Sources: Baillie and Kirkpatrick 2005; Stewart 1950.

John Glendy
1755–1832

John Glendy was born at Faughanvale near Maghera, County Londonderry on 24 June 1755, the son of Samuel Glendy, a farmer. He was educated in Glasgow University and was licensed to preach in Maghera in 1777 by the Presbytery of Derry. He was ordained as the Presbyterian minister of Maghera by the Route Presbytery in 1778. He and his wife, Elizabeth Cresswell lived on a 10–12 acre farm near the village.

He helped build a new Presbyterian meeting house in Maghera, where he remained for twenty years. Ironically, it was Glendy who baptised Henry Cooke, who was to become the leading political and theological leader of the conservative 'old lights' in the Presbyterian Church. In 1795 Glendy was called to Garvagh Presbyterian Church, County Londonderry.

Between 1792 and 1794, during the revival of the Volunteer movement, Glendy preached regularly on the theological justification for the reform movement. In 1792, for example, he preached to a meeting of Volunteers to mark the victories of the French armies. He preached to them on the Rights of Man to a meeting of radicals in Cookstown who passed resolutions in favour of complete radical reform of the House of Commons, speedy abolition of all civil and political distinctions on account of religious opinion and the right of private judgement in religious matters.

Having allegedly been involved in the 1798 rebellion, his home and church were destroyed and he was arrested on the order of Lord Castlereagh, although no evidence seems to have been presented against him. He was allowed to flee, dressed as a woman, and emigrated to America, on a barely seaworthy boat that almost sank. In America he preached in Staunton and Bethel in Augusta County, Virginia and met President Jefferson who invited him to preach in Washington. He became the first minister of the Second Presbyterian Church, a Commodore to the United States Navy, and eventually, Chaplain to the House of Representatives. In 1815 he was appointed as Chaplain of the Senate.

Failing health forced him to retire in 1832. He moved to Philadelphia where he died on 4 October 1832. He was buried beside his wife in Baltimore.

Sources: Campbell 1991; Holmes 1985; McBride 1998; Newman 1993; Sorrells 2002; Witherow 1879.

Hugh Crawford
1757–1819

Hugh Crawford was born near Ballymena, County Antrim in 1757. He moved to Belfast where he set up a shop in North Street. He moved into the linen trade and then into other commodities. He was able to invest in other businesses, including cordage and sail-cloth, a flour mill in Crumlin, and later sugar refining. He became a member of the Belfast Chamber of Commerce.

He was a member of the orthodox Presbyterian Third congregation, whose minister, Sinclair Kelburn (see profile) and many members of the congregation, including Henry Joy McCracken, were deeply involved in radical politics. He had been involved in the Volunteers, which were established to defend Ireland in the event of invasion, and supported their move to press for political reforms. When the Volunteers were proscribed, Crawford joined a cell of the United Irishmen, which had been started by bookseller and stationer John Hughes. It is not known what role he played in the rebellion itself, but he was very lucky not to be arrested and jailed, particularly when John Hughes turned informer.

In February 1800 he joined with most of the merchants of the town to protest against legislative Union with Britain, 'an Experiment of so alarming and desperate a measure ... '.

Despite his radical involvement he continued to thrive financially. He bought a new house at Orangefield, which was then in the country. He was so successful that in 1807 he was able to commission the building of a 400 ton ship from William Ritchie's shipyard. The following year he became a foundation partner in the Belfast Bank.

Crawford died on 15 November 1819 and was buried in Knockbreda Cemetery Belfast. He was survived by his wife Elizabeth (1759–1823) and at least one daughter and various sons.

Sources: Chambers 1985; O'Regan 2011.

Adam Hill
1757–1827

Adam Hill was born near Randalstown, County Antrim in 1757 and was educated in Scotland, presumably at the Glasgow University, where he would have trained for the ministry. He was 'new light' theologically and licensed by Route Presbytery in 1782. He was ordained in preparation to go to America in 1783. However, he apparently decided not to go to America and was installed as minister of Ballynure, County Antrim on 16 August 1785, connected to the Non-Subscribing Presbytery of Antrim. The fact that he married the daughter of a local minister the following year may give an indication of why he decided to stay in Ireland rather than emigrate.

He was a United Irishman and in 14 October 1797 it was Hill, rather than his own minister, that William Orr requested to accompany him to the scaffold from Carrickfergus jail as his chaplain. Orr became a martyr for the cause of the United Irishman, and 'Remember Orr' became their rallying cry.

Hill was accused of taking part in the rebellion and being at Donegore Hill, the main rallying point for the army of thousands of rebels in County Antrim on 7 June 1798. He was found 'partly guilty' and sentenced to a year's imprisonment. He apparently managed to avoid the death sentence on the evidence of a soldier, who was a Presbyterian, who refused to identify him at the battle.

Hill's congregation stood by him and he remained minister of Ballynure. He eventually retired in 1826 and died the following year at Bankhead Hill, Westerkirk, Dumfrieshire Scotland on 21 July 1827. He is interred at Ballynure.

Source: *Northern Whig* 26 July 1827; Swords 1997.

John Campbell White
1757–1847

John Campbell White was born in 1757. He trained as a physician and practiced as a doctor in Belfast.

He was one of the original members of the Society of United Irishmen and a member of its mainly Presbyterian Provincial Executive, including Henry Joy McCracken, William Tennent, Samuel Neilson and the Simms brothers. The Executive was responsible for the network of the secret oath-bound units organised into a hierarchical structure of baronial, county, provincial and national committees. Various existing Volunteer companies, masonic lodges, reading societies and defender cells were subsumed within this structure.

At a town meeting on 28 January 1792, called to draw up a petition in support of Catholic Emancipation, Dr White was on the side of those who favoured immediate emancipation as a natural right, against those, including William Bruce, Dr Haliday, Henry Joy and Waddell Cunningham, who favoured a much more cautious approach. Campbell White also played a leading role in the establishment of elementary education for poor children in Belfast.

In 1798, after the rebellion failed, he fled to America to escape arrest and eventually became a successful Baltimore doctor. He also founded White and Sons distillery.

He had two sons: John Campbell White, who became cashier of the Baltimore branch of the Second Bank of the United States and became a trustee in 1821; and Henry White (1794–1882).

Sources: McBride 1998; John Campbell White papers – Maryland Historical Society.

Henry Haslett (also spelled Hazlett)
1758–1806

Henry Haslett was born in Clooney Close, Limavady, County Londonderry in 1758. His name appears on an early role of the Belfast Volunteers in March 1778, which notes that he was an 'uncertain attender, mostly abroad', which suggests he was involved in the import/export business. By 1783 he was certainly involved with other members of the family in a successful woollen drapery business in Rosemary Lane, Belfast. By the early 1790s his business interests widened to include shipping and Whitbread's porter, becoming a key member of a shipping syndicate known as the 'New Traders' who commissioned a number of ships from William Ritchie's yard in Belfast, with names like, *Shamrock*, *Hibernia* and *Saint Patrick*. He also became Secretary of Belfast's first insurance company, Belfast General.

Haslett was a captain in the Volunteers, established to defend Ireland against invasion, and supported their call for political reform.

Haslett was radical politically and was one of the founders of the Belfast Society of United Irishmen on 14 October 1791 in Crown Entry, off High Street, Belfast, with Robert and William Simms, William Sinclair, Sam McTier, Thomas McCabe, William McCleery, Samuel Neilson, William Tennent, John Campbell, Gilbert McIlveen, Wolf Tone and Thomas Russell.

He was one of the twelve proprietors of the *Northern Star* newspaper, the mouthpiece of the United Irishmen. The first number of the *Northern Star* appeared on the 04 January 1792. It was published twice a-week. In June 1794 Haslett and the other proprietors were prosecuted for 'mischievous, seditious and flagitious' libel and found guilty. It was finally suppressed, and the offices destroyed, by the militia in 1797.

On 16 September 1796 he was arrested, along with eight other prominent radicals from Belfast and Lisburn, charged with high treason and held in Kilmainham Gaol, Dublin for fourteen months. During this period, two of his children died, as did his 23 year old sister who was nursing one of Haslett's children, while in Dublin to visit Haslett in jail. The graveside oration in Knockbreda Belfast was by fellow United Irishman Rev. William Steel Dickson.

After the rebellion was over, Haslett returned to concentrate on commercial life and was a member of the council of the Belfast Chamber of Commerce in 1802 and 1804, involved particularly in issues concerning Lagan navigation and port charges where he ended up in dispute with other leading businessmen.

Haslett married Jane Gaw, probably the daughter of Patrick Gaw, a wealthy Belfast merchant. He died on 4 December 1806, aged forty-eight. His brother, William, who was also initially involved in the radical political scene in Belfast, slipped off to America.

Sources: Chambers 1983; Dickson 1997; Killen 1997.

James Campbell
1758–1818

James Campbell was born in 1758 in the parish of Cairncastle, County Antrim. He learnt his trade as a weaver and moved to Ballynure, where he worked in several places adjacent, as a journeyman. He married and settled in Ballynure village where he and his wife had seven children. He later moved to the townland of Ballybracken. He joined the United Irishmen and, when he was arrested, all his papers were seized, including his poems and songs. When he was released his papers were not returned to him. He was so poor he was struck off the tithe roll of the Established Church. In *Adieu to Tithe* he expressed his resentment of the requirement of Presbyterians to pay tithes to the established Church and of the role of the Episcopal Church in general,

> The Church and the state have been long linked secure,
> We keep the crowd dark and the state keeps them poor ...
> From the fruits of your fields ne'er replenish their bowls
> Till ye see how their labour has nourished your souls.

John Fullarton said of James Campbell of Ballynure, as he was known, that he had a 'hostility to the upper ranks', including the clergy and that he 'owed no gratitude to the wealthy men of the world'. As Campbell wrote, 'Who make the rich? The answer's sure, it must be the industrious poor … '. He also wrote *An inscription for the Tombstone of Thomas Paine*.

He wrote a poem, 'The Rejected Yeoman', after his friend and fellow poet, James Orr, was not accepted by the Yeomanry, when Napoleon appeared to be a threat. He then wrote another one, 'Dirge Written at the Grave of Orr' after Orr's death. He also wrote more humorous pieces such as 'The Epicure's Address to Bacon' and love poems like 'The Devotion and Molly Hume'.

He died in 1818 and had a large Masonic funeral. His *Posthumous Works* were edited and published in 1820 by Samuel Corry of Ballyclare two years after his death in order to generate money for his widow and children.

Sources: Ferguson 2008; Hewitt 2004.

James McKinney
1759–1803

James McKinney was born on 16 November 1759 in Cookstown, County Tyrone. Like many young men destined for the ministry he studied at the University of Glasgow, graduating in 1778. He continued his academic studies in both theology and medicine and was licensed by the Reformed Presbyterian Church on 19 May 1783. He was then installed as the minister of Kirkhills, Dervock in County Antrim. In 1784 he married Mary Mitchell of County Londonderry.

He became involved with the United Irishmen and after preaching a radical sermon on 'The Rights of God' was indicted for treason. When soldiers came to arrest him they found that he was away from the house. He then decided to sail to America, where his four brothers (Samuel, also a minister; Archibald, a doctor; John, who was one of the framers of the constitution of Tennessee, and Robert, who settled near Pittsburgh) had already emigrated, arriving in 1793.

In America he ministered to a scattered group of Reformed Presbyterian societies from Vermont to the Carolinas and in May 1798 formed a Reformed Presbytery with Rev. William Gibson. McKinney's political radicalism influenced his attitude to politics in America, in general, and his attitude to the new constitution, in particular, which he considered trampled underfoot the rights of man and decried the reign of Christ as King over the nations.

Under McKinney, therefore, a remnant of the church maintained its position of dissent from the government, but shifted the basis of the dissent from the Solemn League and Covenant and the Revolutionary Settlement to the secular nature of the new American constitution. This marked a new intellectual beginning for the church and was the answer to the question of the relationship of the Scottish church to the United States that satisfied the remnant of the people who opposed the secular nature of the constitution.

McKinney also called for the liberty of African slaves and bore an early and persistent testimony against the evils of slavery. He formed a committee, which travelled round the scattered Reformed Presbyterian communities to inform them of the resolution of the Reformed Presbytery against the sin of slavery.

McKinney died in August 1803, having become the minister of Brick Church, Rocky Creek, Chester County in South Carolina a few months earlier.

Source: Broomall Reformed Presbyterian Church website (broomallrpc.org/index.php/articles/the-history-of-the-broomall-pa-congregation-of-the-rpcna); Glasgow, William Melancthon (1888) *History of the Reformed Presbyterian Church in America*.

Oliver Bond
c. 1761–98

Oliver Cromwell Bond was born around 1761 in St Johnstown, County Donegal, the son of a dissenting minister. He became a successful woollen merchant, setting up his business north of the Liffey at 54 Pill Lane, Dublin in 1782, while he lived in Bridge Street, south of the river. In 1791, he married Eleanor Jackson, the daughter of fellow radical, Henry Jackson, who was owner of an iron foundry in Pill Lane, an officer in the Volunteers and member of Dublin Corporation.

In November 1791 the Dublin Society of the United Irishmen was formed in that city. The office-bearer roles rotated, with Bond serving as secretary. The nature of his business meant that Bond regularly travelled all round Ireland, which not only gave him the opportunity to do business, but also to encourage people to join, and swear the oath of, the United Irishmen.

Radicals from the north, such as William Tennent and Samuel Neilson often lodged with Bond whenever they were in Dublin.

In the autumn of 1792 Bond, along with Hamilton Rowan and Henry Jackson set up a new Volunteer company which they provocatively called the National Guard in imitation of the French revolutionary national guard. The following year, Louis XVI was executed in Paris in January and England declared war on revolutionary France. As a result, in May 1794, the government decided that they needed to suppress political radicalism in Ireland, including the Dublin Society. With Hamilton Rowan and Wolfe Tone in exile, the leadership of the Dublin Society of the United Irishmen fell to Oliver Bond and Henry Jackson.

When the reforming Lord Fitzwilliam was appointed Lord Lieutenant by William Pitt in 1794, there was hope that at last the government may introduce political reform, including Catholic Emancipation. His withdrawal a very short time later, in February 1795, to be replaced by Lord Camden, a descendent of Judge Jeffries, the 'Hanging Judge' of the 'Bloody Assizes', was the last straw for the United Irishmen. When Camden suspended *habeas corpus* and introduced the Insurrection Act, the United Irishmen went underground. Bond, Jackson and the other members of the United Irish committee in Dublin toasted the hope that the same fate would befall Lord Camden as befell his ancestor's victims.

In 1796 when Wolfe Tone was in France trying to persuade the French to invade and the French fleet was being prepared in Brest, General Hoche, via Colonel Shee, told Tone that he wanted last minute information on the situation in Ireland and Tone suggested sending Bernard MacSheehy. Tone gave MacSheehy Oliver Bond as the key contact for information in the United Irishmen. However, by the time MacSheehy returned to France, having successfully completed his mission, the fleet had already set sail. Later, when Arthur O'Connor returned from negotiating with General Hoche in 1797, it was to Bond and Jackson and the other members of the Pill Lane group of conspirators that he went to in Dublin to report progress. However, with heavy storms, the French fleet did not manage to land. Bond was also corresponding with United Irish leader, Rev. William Steel Dickson, in County Down.

As preparations for the rebellion were taking shape, Bond issued promissory notes to the poor, payable after the revolution, to encourage their support and create a vested interest in the outcome.

Due to the presence of spies, the activities of the United Irishmen in Dublin were well known to the government. On 12 March 1798, the police surrounded Bond's house in Bridge Street where fourteen members of the Leinster Directory of the United Irishmen were meeting. They were arrested and their documents seized.

Bond stood trial on 23 July 1798, on the evidence of informer Thomas Reynolds. Bond was defended by Philpot Curran. Armed soldiers continuously interrupted Curran in court and threatened to do him violence. Curran told them 'you may assassinate, but you shall not intimidate me'. After 19 hours, Bond was found guilty and sentenced to hang, be disembowelled and beheaded.

In order to save Bond's life, Arthur O'Connor and other rebel leaders made a deal with the government, that they would make a full statement about their own involvement in the rebellion. This enabled Bond to get a full pardon, on the condition that he left the country. This leniency was clearly too much for some of the loyalists. On the day that he was reprieved, Bond's dead body was found outside his cell. The authorities claimed that he died of natural causes, although he had been in very good health. Despite the anger of the other rebel leaders, they made no official complaint, to ensure that his wife would be able to inherit Bond's estate.

Ten years after Bond's death, his wife had a stone erected over her husband's grave at St Michin's churchyard at the west end of Pill Lane.

In 1809 Eleanor Bond emigrated to America with her father, Henry Jackson, first going to Pennsylvania and then Baltimore, Maryland. Henry Jackson died in 1817.

Sources: Curtin 1998; Whelan 2010.

Henry Henry
1760–1840

Henry Henry was born in 1760, the second son of Matthew Henry a farmer from Dunboe, near Coleraine. He was educated in Glasgow in 1779 and licensed by Route Presbytery in 1788. He was ordained in First Garvagh Presbyterian Church on 13 May 1788, but within a few months was called to Connor in the Presbytery of Ballymena and was installed there on 9 December.

In the troubled times of the 1790s many people were attracted to the black and white orthodox doctrines of the Reformed Presbyterians. Henry, although quite orthodox himself, was disturbed by this and asked 'Why are the covenanting ministers so much followed by the multitude?' He published a critique of the Reformed Presbyterians in a question and answer format, *Address to the People of Connor*, in the name of his sexton, Sanders Donald.

Henry was suspected of involvement in the 1798 rebellion, was arrested and imprisoned that year, but was released.

Lord Castlereagh had been advised by Alexander Knox that the period after the rebellion was a favourable moment,

> For forming a salutary connection between the Government and the Presbyterian body of Ulster than may again arrive. The republicanism of that part of Ireland is checked and repressed by the cruelties of Roman Catholics in the late rebellion and by the despotism of Bonaparte. They are therefore in a humour for acquiescing in the views of government beyond which they ever were or (should the opportunity be missed) may be hereafter.

In 1803, therefore, when the government introduced an increase in the *regium donum* grant, it was decided to give it at different amounts to different ministers. Henry warned that Castlereagh's attempt to make the Presbyterian Synod a tool of the state must be resisted, asking,

> What are the great principles of our dissent? Are they not – the rights of private judgement? – the liberty of conscience, in opposition to all human authority, in matters of religion? The acknowledgement of CHRIST alone as head of his church? – And the sufficiency of the word of GOD as the rule of faith and practice

Although there was considerable opposition from many in the church, including William Drennan, to the classification of the greatly increased *regium donum* government grant paid to Presbyterian ministers into different levels, Henry Henry was the only Presbyterian minister to hold out. Originally it had been paid equally across all ministers. It was now to be paid at three different levels, according to the size of the congregation, to provide greater control of Presbyterian ministers by the state. Receiving payment also required the taking of an Oath of Allegiance. Henry's opposition did not seem to dent his popularity and he was elected moderator of General Synod in 1807.

Henry was one of the founders of the Belfast Academical Institution, which is significant, because of the accusations that the Academical Institution was a hotbed of unorthodox Arian theological views, while Henry was from a very orthodox theological tradition. In 1813 he was one of the ministers who supported Rev. Steel Dickson (see profile) against the conservative Rev. Robert Black, at the Presbyterian Synod in support of the Belfast Academical Institution. He retired in 1829 and died on 11 November 1840.

Sources: Brooke 1994; Campbell 1991; Holmes 1985; McBride 1998; Witherow 1879.

William, Robert and John Tennent
William: 1760–1832
Robert: 1765–1837
John jr: 1772–1813

William, Robert and John Tennent were sons of Rev. John Tennent sr from Scotland who was educated in Edinburgh and Abernethy Anti-Burgher Theological Hall. He was licensed by Edinburgh Anti-Burgher Presbytery and ordained in Carnabouy, Derrykeighan and Roseyards, County Antrim on 16 May 1751. He was one of the first Scottish Anti-Burgher ministers to settle in Ulster and a member of the tiny Associate Presbytery of Primitive Seceders, who were Calvinist in theology. However, he supported the United Irishmen's paper, the *Northern Star,* in its early days. He died in 1808.

William Tennent was born in 1760. He was employed as a junior manager in the New Sugar House in Waring Street, Belfast, eventually becoming a partner. He also developed other business interests, including insurance, becoming a shipbroker with the Belfast Insurance Company and banking, becoming senior partner in the Commercial Bank. This success enabled him to purchase various properties in Belfast.

He was one of the small group of wealthy Presbyterians who met with Wolfe Tone to found the Society of United Irishmen in October 1791. He was also one of the original subscribers to the *Northern Star* paper, which became the mouthpiece of the reform movement in Ulster, producing its first paper in January 1792. He is believed to have been a member of the Belfast Directory of the United Irishmen in the lead up to the rebellion and was arrested soon afterwards and jailed in Fort George in Scotland until 1802. However, this did not prevent him eventually being appointed to various public bodies, including the Spring Water Commissioners and the Police Commissioners.

William had 'new light' theological views and was one of the founders ('managers') of the Belfast Academical Institution. He was a lifelong supporter of the Linen Hall Library. He died in 1832.

Robert Tennent was born in 1765 and became a doctor. Unlike his brother William, Robert had very orthodox theological views. He was working as a ship's surgeon when the Table Bay mutiny took place, but was out of the country during the 1798 rebellion. In 1813 he planned a public meeting to discuss the nature of Orangism, which had played such a negative role in promoting sectarianism and preventing democratic reforms. Rev. Edward May, son-in-law of the Marquis of Donegall who owned most of the land in Belfast, attempted to prevent the meeting and it seems that Dr Tennent and Rev. May came to blows. Tennent was arrested and imprisoned. He later sued, unsuccessfully, for unlawful imprisonment.

Dr Robert was one of the founders of the Belfast Academical Institution and on the board of visitors. He chaired a St Patrick's Day dinner of the joint Boards of the Belfast Academical Institution at which allegedly disloyal toasts were drunk by the radical founders of the Institution, which resulted in serious problems for the school from its conservative detractors in government and Synod, including the loss of their annual government grant of £1,500. At the dinner he highlighted proposals for the establishment of a new society: a 'centre of union to those who love their country' to 'promote the eternal principle of equal, impartial justice'. He argued that, 'were this standard once erected in our land and the people but convinced that it were so – how soon would all our lamentable dissensions vanish and the Irish character be again displayed in all its native beauty and excellence.'

Dr Robert was to play a key role in most of the progressive developments in Belfast until his death in 1837. He was a founding member of the Belfast House of Industry, which provided work for the poor. They were supplied with materials and implements with which to make goods, which were then sold in the House of Industry's shop. The running of the House required a significant time commitment by the members of the committee. The House of Industry closed with the passing of the Poor Law Act.

In 1808 he was one of the subscribers to establish the Irish Harp Society and was appointed treasurer. In 1811 he joined the committee of the Society for Promoting Knowledge (later the Linen Hall Library) becoming vice-president in 1824 and president in 1828. In 1813 he was on the committee of the Friends of Civil and Religious Liberty and of Internal Peace and Accord, chaired by William Drennan, which drew up a petition against the Orange Order. He also played an important role in providing clean water to the citizens of Belfast as a member of the Pipe Water Committee of the Belfast Charitable Society and both he and William were two of the nine Spring Water Commissioners appointed in 1817.

Dr Robert's son, Robert James, was also politically progressive and a leader of the Friends of Civil and Religious Liberty which campaigned for Catholic Emancipation, playing a key role in the creation of the Protestant declaration in favour of emancipation. He stood for parliament, with William Sharman Crawford, but failed to win a seat because he refused to declare his views on a repeal of the Act of Union. Robert James was also on the board of the Belfast Academical Institution.

The third son, John Tennent jr, was born in 1772. He became involved in the United Irishmen, fled to France and died in the service of Napoleon, aged 41.

Sources: Brooke 1994; Campbell 1991; Hall 2011; Holmes 1985; McBride 1998; Newman 1993.

Robert and William Simms
Robert 1761–1843
William 1763–1843

Robert and William Simms were both merchants who owned a paper mill in Ballyclare, County Antrim, a flourmill in Crumlin, County Antrim and a tan yard in North Street, Belfast. They were also both members of the orthodox Third Presbyterian Church in Rosemary Street, Belfast.

Robert Simms was baptised in Belfast in 1761, the fifth child of seven of Robert Simms, a merchant and tanner, and his wife Elizabeth (née Stephenson). He was signatory to a petition to bring about an end to the War of Independence with America in order to restore the valuable trade with America, and was a key participant with other leading Belfast citizens to support 'Roman Catholic suffrage'.

William Simms was baptised in 1763, the sixth child in the family. He became a proprietor of the *Northern Star*, the mouthpiece of the reform movement and the United Irishmen often used his house for meetings.

The brothers were both charged with publishing a seditious address in the *Northern Star* in 1794 but were acquitted. When the paper was finally suppressed and the presses destroyed the Simms brothers were the two remaining proprietors.

Both Robert and William were founders of the Belfast Society of United Irishmen and members of the Northern Executive (Robert was the secretary). At McArt's Fort on Cavehill, the two brothers, with McCracken, Tone, Russell and several others swore an oath to, 'never to desist in our efforts until we had subverted the authority of England over our country and asserted her independence'.

William was the first National Secretary of the United Irishmen and Robert was appointed to the National Executive in 1796. He was arrested in February 1797 and was in jail until June when he was released from Newgate Prison. He became the commander in chief of the United Irish forces in Antrim, but he and twenty of his twenty-two colonels in Antrim refused to act at the appointed time without a French invasion in support of the rebellion, resigning at the last minute, causing a crucial delay in the rebellion.

In 1797, both Robert and William were arrested in Belfast with Samuel Neilson and Thomas Russell and imprisoned with William Drennan and the Tennent brothers, but were released to be two of the few United Irish leaders who were free at the time of the rebellion.

Thomas Emmet wrote to his old friend Robert Simms in 1805 to warn him against the French, saying that any French expeditionary force would establish a satellite government in Ireland propped up by the Catholic establishment.

After the 1798 rebellion both brothers were key players in the educational and cultural development of Belfast. They were involved in the founding of the non-denominational Belfast Academical Institution with William Drennan and others, and the founding of the Belfast Literary Society, also with Drennan, which was a forerunner of the Gaelic League. They were also founders of the Irish Harp Society in 1808. Both Robert and William Simms died in 1843.

Sources: Bardon 1992; Brooke 1994; Campbell 1991; Holmes 1985; McBride 1998; Stewart 1993.

Samuel Neilson
1761–1803

Samuel Neilson was born in Ballyroney, County Down in 1761 and educated in the local school. He was the third son of the Presbyterian minister of Ballyroney, Rev. Alexander Neilson. At sixteen he was apprenticed to his elder brother, a woollen-draper. He then set up his own successful business, trading in wool, silk and linen in Waring Street, Belfast. In 1785 he married Anne Bryson, daughter of a local merchant, and in due course had five children.

Having made his fortune he was able to engage in various non-commercial ventures: becoming treasurer of the Belfast Charitable Society, which ran the Poor House; journalism, which he loved; and also getting involved in politics. He acted as electoral agent for the Liberal Robert Stewart (later the right-wing Viscount Castlereagh), joined the Northern Whig Club and the Belfast Volunteer Company.

He became friendly with Henry Joy McCracken, Wolf Tone and others, with whom he formed the Society of United Irishmen. He signed the manifesto drafted by Tone which called for 'the radical reform of parliament', a 'cordial union among all the people of Ireland', the 'abolition of bigotry in religion and politics', and 'the equal distribution of the rights of man through all sects and denominations of Irishmen'.

In 1792, Neilson founded the *Northern Star* newspaper to promote the United Irishmen's ideals in the North, contributing more than a quarter of the capital, and became its editor. Jemmy Hope described it as the 'moral force of Ulster', which 'sowed the seeds of truth over the land, and the opposition of the enemy only caused its roots to strike deeper in the soil, and they are now springing up in all directions', and which 'works on the opponents of truth like a consuming worm'. The success of the paper was an annoyance to the Government and its proprietors were tried twice for sedition, although acquitted both times. Under more draconian legislation, the press was destroyed by the military and Neilson arrested and jailed.

Neilson was the leader of the Dissenters, with Drennan, when they and hundreds of Volunteers, led by the Light Dragoons, marched through Belfast on 14 July 1792, not, as was customary, to celebrate King William's victory at the Battle of the Boyne, but to celebrate the storming of the Bastille in Paris. He supported immediate Catholic Emancipation at the great debate that followed the march. Toasts that day included to 'the sovereignty of the people', 'Tom Paine', 'The rights of man', 'the French army', and 'the abolition of the slave trade'. He was also involved in developing contacts with the Catholic Defenders, although felt that they were an 'undisciplined rabble'. Wolf Tone described him as 'an honest, a brave and a worthy fellow … a good Irishman, a good republican'.

The success of the French army in Europe, gave the British and Irish parliaments grave cause for concern, particularly with the strength of the reform movement supporting the French Revolution. They were determined to ruthlessly stamp out the United Irish movement and the Insurrection Act gave the Lord Lieutenant and the courts draconian powers including execution of those swearing secret oaths.

Those involved in the reform movement were angered by the withdrawal of the progressive Lord Lieutenant, Fitzwilliam, who had been committed to the removal of the Penal Laws. Pitt had effectively abandoned the fate of Ireland to a small group of Anglican landed gentry who controlled parliament, the judiciary, military and the land. Neilson was one of the small group of comrades who, in May 1795, on Cave Hill, swore to 'never desist in our efforts until we had subverted the authority of England in our country and asserted her independence'.

As a result of what was written in the *Northern Star* newspaper Neilson was prosecuted a number of times, including for treason in September 1796 and was jailed in Dublin. In a gesture of solidarity, his supporters came out in large numbers and harvested his crop of potatoes, which would have been ruined. As a result of his imprisonment, his health suffered and he was released on the condition that he abstained from 'treasonable conspiracy', which he ignored and became involved in preparing for the rebellion. So many Catholic priests came to see him to discuss Catholic emancipation that one of the bedrooms in their house was nicknamed the 'priest's bedroom'.

He was on the Northern Executive of the United Irishmen and then, when most of the members of the Dublin-based Directory (National Executive) were arrested, he was a key player in the Society in Dublin in the period leading up to the rebellion. In speaking before a secret committee of the House of Commons, enquiring into the rebellion, Neilson told the committee that 'When discussion is utterly at an end I know of no means of resisting tyranny but by arms'.

In participating in an attempt to rescue Edward Fitzgerald, Neilson was wounded, arrested and indicted for high treason. He agreed to banishment, but was held in Fort George in Scotland from 1799 to 1802 before he was deported to Holland. After secret return visits to Dublin and Belfast he emigrated to America, where he died in Poughkeepsie, just as he was about to launch an evening paper in New York in 1803. His son, W.B. Neilson was a founder of the Belfast Academical Institution.

Sources: Bardon 1992; Boylan 1998; Campbell 1991; Erskine and Gordon 1997; Holmes 1985; Latimer 1897; McBride 1998; O'Byrne 1990; Seery *et al* 2000; Stewart 1993.

Joesph Cuthbert
Born 1762

Joseph Cuthbert was born in 1762 and became a master tailor in Belfast. He joined the United Irishmen and played an important role in developing an alliance with the Catholic Defender movement. Cuthbert worked closely with Henry Joy McCracken, two Catholic lawyers and a wealthy Catholic linen merchant to try and prosecute magistrates who encouraged or condoned Protestant attacks on Catholics.

The United Irishmen were very conscious of the crucial role of the military in Ireland once the rebellion broke out and the need to convince individual soldiers in the militia and yeomanry to side with the rebels. Cuthbert played a key role in this. As a result, in April 1793 he was arrested for enticing soldiers from their loyal allegiance and distributing seditious and treasonable handbills. He was sentenced to one year in jail. To set an example to any soldiers who might think of defecting, General Whyte had him stand in the pillory for the edification of his troops who marched past.

Cuthbert, however, does not seem to have learnt his lesson and in July 1796 turned up in a coach and four, with his wife and Catholic solicitor, Daniel Shanaghan, to the military camp at Blaris, Lisburn, handing out money to the soldiers to persuade them to defect to the United Irishmen. The under-secretary of the Castle warned the government that 650 soldiers had already signed up with both the Defenders and United Irishmen and 1,600 had signed up with the United Irishmen alone. Cuthbert was arrested, on the information of the infamous spy Belle Martin, jailed in Dublin and committed for trial in Carrickfergus. The trial collapsed when the chief witness for the prosecution, Belle Martin, disappeared. The last edition of the United Irishman's newspaper, the *Northern Star*, in 1797, included the following advertisement which had been inserted by Cuthbert:

> Joseph Cuthbert, tailor and ladies' habit-maker, (now confined in Kilmainham Jail, on a charge of high treason), solicits the continuance of his numerous friends and customers to his house, as the business is now conducted by a skilful foreman. He hopes the unmerited persecution he has suffered, on his being acquitted by a jury of his country, to be immediately detained upon a new warrant, that the usual liberality of Belfast will be now be exerted in his favour. He requests those indebted to him to pay Mrs. Cuthbert.

Cuthbert was transferred to a jail in Fort George Scotland, where he was imprisoned with George Cumming, Rev. William Steel Dickson, William Tennent, Samuel Neilson (see profiles) and other rebel leaders. When he returned from Scotland, a Charles Brett of Belfast put up a reward of '£22 for the killing of Joseph Cuthbert and associates'. Cuthbert, along with his wife and niece, Nancy Park, emigrated to America, via Hamburg, Germany. The date of Cuthbert's death is unknown.

Source: Curtin 1998; O'Regan 2010; Whelan 2010.

Whitley Stokes
1763–1845

Whitley Stokes was born into an Episcopal Church family in Waterford in 1763, son of Rev. Gabriel Stokes and Susan (née Boswell), and grandson of Gabriel Stokes, Deputy-Surveyor of Ireland. Whitley left the Church of Ireland and became a Presbyterian.

He was educated in Waterford and Trinity College Dublin, where he graduated in 1793 in Medicine. While a student he became a member of a political club founded by Wolfe Tone. In 1792 he joined the Dublin Society of the United Irishmen. In July that year he travelled to Belfast with Wolfe Tone to celebrate the fall of the Bastille with the Volunteers. Tone called Stokes 'The Keeper of the College Lions' and suggested that if Ireland became independent Stokes would make a good 'head of a system of national education'. As a result of his nationalist views, in April 1798, he was summoned before Lord Clare, and admitted to having previously been a member of the United Irishmen. He was suspended from his teaching post for three years.

He was eventually able to return to teaching and in 1805 became a senior fellow; in 1816 he became a lecturer in natural history; and in 1830 became Regius Professor of Physic in Trinity College Dublin.

In addition to his prominent medical career, Stokes was the first person for a hundred years to translate parts of the New Testament into Irish, starting with the 'Gospel of Luke' and 'Acts of the Apostles' in 1799. In 1806 he published the four gospels and 'Acts of the Apostles' in Irish in four volumes. In 1810, he wrote a pamphlet on the importance of publishing the Scriptures in Irish. He also produced estimates of the number of Irish speakers in each county of Ulster and Leinster. In 1814 he published, at his own expense, an English-Irish dictionary.

Stokes died on 13 April 1845. His son (1804–1878), of the same name also became Regius Professor of Physics at the University of Dublin. His grandson (1830–1909), also of the same name, became a famous Celtic scholar.

Sources: Blaney 1996; Elliott 1989; Stewart 1878.

Robert Acheson
1763–1824

Robert Acheson was born in Clough, County Antrim in 1763, son of James Acheson. His initial ambition was to be a doctor and he went to study medicine in Edinburgh. When he returned from Scotland, he practised medicine for a while in Coleraine, County Londonderry, where he married his cousin, Elizabeth Smith. He discovered that he had an alternative vocation to become a Presbyterian minister. He was licensed to preach by Templepatrick Presbytery and came to Glenarm on the east coast of County Antrim, as assistant and successor to his uncle, Rev. Thomas Reid and was ordained in 1792. He lived in Cairncastle and ran a school there. However he had 'new light' theological views which did not always go down well with the local orthodox Presbyterians.

Acheson also held strong political views and like many others became involved in the United Irishmen. He drilled men for the rebel army in the fields behind Glenarm. In the Sunday before the rising he preached a stirring sermon in Glenarm meeting house on Luke 12:4, 'Be not afraid of them that kill the body'.

On the Thursday morning, when the rebels began to gather at a rallying point close to Acheson's farm, behind Glenarm Castle on Bellair Hill, the local yeomanry and a small detachment of Tay Fencibles were aware of their plans and decided to try and nip the rebellion in the bud by a pre-emptive strike. They managed to capture Acheson and two other leaders and occupied the Castle and the best defensive positions. The rebels then captured some loyalists and threatened to shoot them unless Acheson was released, along with two other Glenarm men held captive. Two negotiators (one of whom, a Catholic priest, turned out to be a Government spy) managed to arrange an exchange of prisoners and Acheson was released. The Fencibles holding him may have been less keen to release this minister if they had known that he would immediately put on full regimental uniform – green jacket faced with yellow, white breeches, black hose and silver-buckled shoes – and take command of the rebel base at Bellair Hill. He was cheered enthusiastically by the 2,000 men.

In the light of the morning, the defeat of the rebels at Antrim and the potentially terrible fate that awaited the rebels on Bellair Hill, had made Acheson rethink and so he negotiated terms for the surrender of the rebels. It was agreed that the rebels would lay down their arms and in return they would be forgiven 'without any reservation'. Acheson had to try to persuade the rebels on the hill of the benefits of the deal. They did eventually surrender. Despite the terms of the deal, Acheson was court martialled and conducted his own defence, but in the end was acquitted, thanks to Colonel Leslie, the President of the court and nephew of Rev. Thomas

Reid.

Reid felt that Acheson should not return to his congregation in Glenarm and he eventually accepted a call to Donegall Street Presbyterian Church in Belfast (Fourth Belfast) on 20 June 1799 to Donegall Street, Belfast, (which later moved to Cliftonville in north Belfast). Its first two ministers were Rev. James Kirkpatrick (see profile) and Rev. Gilbert Kennedy. During the ministry of Rev. James Bryson (see profile) a dispute within the congregation led him to form a new congregation in Donegall Street in 1791. Robert Acheson succeeded Bryson on 20 August 1799. He ministered in Donegall Street until his death on 21 February 1824, and was succeeded by Rev. George Bellis, who was in turn succeeded by Rev. Isaac Nelson (see profile).

Source: McBride 1998; Nelson 1985; Stewart 1995.

Walter Graham (also called Watty Grimes)
c. 1763–98

Walter Graham was born around 1763 in the townland of Crewe, or Creeve, near Maghera in County Londonderry. His father, James Graham, was a farmer and an elder and clerk of the Kirk session of his local Presbyterian Church of which Rev. John Glendy (see profile) was the minister (who emigrated to America after the rebellion). When Rev. Glendy preached a sermon celebrating the success of the French Revolution, 'the signal interposition of heaven on behalf of the French Nation and Universal Right of Conscience, with rational Enthusiasm', the Session of the congregation inserted a vote of thanks to their minister in the paper of the United Irishmen, *The Northern Star.*

By 1793 Walter Graham, as well as being a successful farmer, owned several looms and, like his father, was an elder in the church and accompanied Rev. Glendy as a representative of the Presbytery of Route to a meeting of General Synod in Lurgan.

He became a colonel in the National Guard, which was formed out of the Volunteer movement on the model of the revolutionary French National Guard. He became a United Irishman and was arrested and taken to Moneymore, for recruiting 200 people into the cause, by getting them to swear the secret oath. He was probably released on bail and appeared before the Spring Assizes of 1797. He was either let off with a caution or bound to keep the peace, but either way, he was freed.

He became a leader of the rebels in Maghera and met with other local leaders from Maghera, Castledawson, Garvagh and Kilrea on 29 May 1798 to make final preparations for simultaneous risings with Toome and

Randalstown. They were to secure and disarm the local yeomanry and Orangemen and distract the army. They were then to meet up with the rebel force from Antrim, if they were required.

On 7 June the rising took place in Maghera, involving around five thousand men, five hundred of whom had firearms. The rest were armed with pitchforks, pikes and spades. Having taken the town they were informed that Bovevagh Cavalry under Captain Keyland was on its way to put down the rising. The rebels fled, leaving their leaders, including Graham to negotiate terms. The other two leaders, William McKeiver and William Harper, were able to escape and fled to America. Graham, however, was betrayed in Newtownlimavady and was captured by the military.

In the days following the attempted rising in Maghera, soldiers and yeomanry burnt everything in Maghera Presbyterian Church, except the Bible. They also court-martialled and hanged two of the rebels, Walter Graham and William Cuddy. There is a local tradition that Cuddy was revived and eventually smuggled to America. Graham, however, was beheaded. Rev. Henry Cooke reported that he saw soldiers burning Watty Graham's house.

Sources: Newman 1993; O Saothrai 1984.

Jemmy Hope
1764–1847

Jemmy Hope was born in 1764 in Templepatrick, County Antrim. His father, John Hope, a highlander and linen weaver, had left Scotland rather than give up his Covenanter faith. As a result he was a member of the Secession church of Rev. Isaac Patton in Lylehill.

Hope was not like many of the well-educated middle class Presbyterians involved in radical politics of the period. He was the son of a fugitive covenanter and had worked as a labourer. The only formal schooling he had was 15 weeks in a school by the age of 10. He then went to work. He was fortunate to be taught to read and write by some of the farmers he worked for, including: John Gibson, John Ritchy and William Bell, who read him Greek and Roman history after work. From this experience he said he 'could read a little in the Bible, though very imperfectly'.

Working on the land he came to believe that 'The Most High is lord of the soil; the cultivator is His tenant' and that landlords who abused this relationship caused misery. He worked as an apprentice linen weaver then as a journeyman, continuing his education at night classes. He married the daughter of his employer, Rose Mullen. He became a member of the Roughfort Corps of the Volunteers. It was this involvement in the

Volunteers that radicalised him politically. He described in his autobiography how 'his connection with politics began in the ranks of the Volunteers' and that they were 'the means of breaking the first link of the penal chain'. He recognised the oppression that was faced by the vast majority of the people of Ireland,

> As a people, we were excluded from any share in framing the laws by which we were governed. The higher ranks (in which there never was, nor never will be a majority of honest-principled men) usurped the exclusive exercise of the privilege, as well as many other rights, by force, fraud and fiction. By force the poor were subdued, and dispossessed of their interests in the soil; by fiction the titles of the spoilers were established; and by fraud on the productive industry of future generations, the usurpation was continued.

In 1795, believing that 'the condition of the labouring class was the fundamental question at issue between the rulers and the people', he joined the Society of the United Irishmen, and swore his oath on a Bible, although he made it clear that he disapproved of secret societies, preferring to state his position and act openly. His nickname amongst United Irishmen was 'Spartan' and his personal followers were known as 'The Spartan Band'.

Although he admitted to being a poor public speaker, the following year he went to Dublin to recruit others to the cause, working at this time as a cotton weaver. He narrowly managed to avoid being drowned by members of the Dublin Society, when, unknown to Hope, one of his comrades disclosed a secret entrusted to him.

Hope empathised with the position of those dissenters and Catholics in rural areas, like Armagh, who were oppressed by the landlords. He played a lead role in bringing the Catholic Defenders into the movement and reconciling them with their traditional enemies, the Peep O'Day Boys under the banner of the United Irishmen, reducing the sectarian tensions in Ulster. The cause of the United Irishmen was simply called 'The Union' and Hope played a key role in 'planting the Union' in towns all around Ulster. This strategy was very effective and,

> The influence of the union soon began to be felt at all public places, fairs, markets, and social meetings, extending to all the counties of Ulster, for no man of an enlightened mind had intercourse with Belfast, who did not return home determined on disseminating the principles of the union among his neighbours. Strife and quarrelling ceased in all public places, and even intoxication.

He recognised, however, with the great expansion of the reform movement, came both people who were less committed and also a large number of Government spies, who infiltrated the movement at every level.

Hope became a close friend of the leaders of the 1798 rebellion in the north who were forced 'by burning of houses, and the torturing of the peasantry, into resistance'. He was deeply disappointed when he realised that many of the wealthier 'men who unthinkingly staked more than was really in them' had refused to rise and were deserting the cause when it came to the crunch. Hope remained steadfast, however, and led a detachment of weavers and labourers in what became known as the 'Spartan band' in the Battle of Antrim. He believed that 'it would ill become one, who has pledged his life to his country, to shrink from death in any shape'. When defeated by General Nugent, he and McCracken tried to rally the fleeing insurgents, but to no avail and he then followed McCracken into hiding in the hills of Slemish and then Cave Hill.

After McCracken's capture, Hope fled to Dublin and opened a little haberdasher's shop in the Combe, where he was joined by his wife, Rose and their family, and maintained his radical political views, becoming involved in Thomas Russell and Robert Emmet's 1803 plans for an insurrection, but lived in constant fear of arrest and had to flee a number of times. He went with Thomas Russell, 'The man from God knows where', to the north to rally support for the rising, which Emmet was planning, but without success. When the rising was a fiasco, he was lucky to avoid the same fate as Emmet and Russell – to be captured and executed. Through both the 1798 and 1803 rebellions, he was one of the only leaders never to be arrested. He maintained his belief that it was the condition of the working class which was the fundamental question between rulers and the people and that it would be the labouring class – the labourers, the small tenant farmers and the underprivileged who would, in the long run, prove to be the incorruptible inheritors of the struggle for Irish freedom.

In 1806 after the political amnesty, Hope returned to Belfast and resumed work as a linen weaver and also wrote poetry. As late as the 1840s, when he was well into his seventies, despite misgivings about the nature of O'Connellism, he was chairing Repeal meetings, promoting the repeal of the Act of Union

His wife died in 1831. He died in Brown Square Belfast in 1847 aged 83 and was buried at Mallusk, County Antrim. He had four children who reached adulthood, three sons (Robert Emmet Hope, Henry Joy McCracken Hope and Luke Neil Hope) and a daughter who survived him.

Sources: Bardon 1992; Boylan 1998; Byrne and McMahon 1991; Campbell 1991; Holmes 2000; Hope 1972; Latimer 1897; McBride 1998; Newman 1993; O'Byrne 1990; Seery et al 2000.

John Smith (sometimes spelled Smyth)
1766–1821

John Smith was born in 1766, the eldest son of William Smith from near Moneymore, County Londonderry. He was educated in Glasgow University, graduating with an MA in 1785. He was licensed to preach by Tyrone Presbytery in 1786 and ordained in First Kilrea on 17 March 1794, succeeding Rev. Arthur McMahon as minister. He married Charlotte Galt of Moyagney.

Smith was accused of complicity in the 1798 rebellion and was imprisoned for a long period in Belfast, Carrickfergus Castle and Fort George in Scotland and was eventually charged with 'seditious practices'. He was released unconditionally after two years, but while he was in prison his farm in Lisnagrot, near Kilrea, had been taken from him and so he was left homeless and beggared on his return to his congregation, who accepted him back.

Later he was again arrested as a rioter and again sentenced to some month's imprisonment. Throughout his troubled life his congregation remained loyal to him. He was also involved in a dispute with a licentiate from the presbytery, who was apparently acting on the instigation of another party, with the aim of damaging Rev. Smith. Because of this dispute, in 1805 the Synod granted his request to be moved from Route to Ballymena Presbytery. Rev. William McMillan wrote, 'John Smith, a man of talents and celebrity he has been described as being of independent mind, great imprudence great misfortunes and somewhat secular in his pursuits, and in his day was regarded as a dangerous character.'

His wife died in July 1821, aged 29, and six weeks later Rev. Smith died on 7 September 1821. He was succeeded as minister on 12 April 1825 by Rev. Hugh Walker Rodgers.

Sources: Kernohan 1912; O'Crilly 1849; McBride 1998; McMillan, 'Presbyterian ministers and the Ulster rising' 1997.

Samuel Thomson
1766–1816

Samuel Thomson was born on 25 May 1766 on the slopes of Lyle's Hill at Carngaggy near Templepatrick, County Antrim and lived for fifty years in a small thatched cottage, he called 'Crambo Cave' – after a simple children's rhyming game. Although often described as one of the Ulster weaver poets, he was in fact a school-teacher running a small 'hedge' school from the cottage. He was close friends with many leading United Irishmen and other radical poets. He wrote poetry which, from 1792–7, was published in the radical newspaper of the United Irishmen, the *Northern Star*, often under a pseudonym. In 'To the Cuckoo' he showed his support for radical politics,

Sweet bird, exulting, sing aloud,
Thru' every green wood, glad and glen,
No more thou meet'st a quarrelling crowd
But TRUE UNITED IRISHMEN!

His last poem published by the *Northern Star* before it was closed down by the military, was a stinging satire about the gentry, entitled 'Epigram to a proud aristocrat'. After the failure of the rebellion and the execution of his friend, Rev. James Porter (see profile), who had also written scathing satires on the local gentry, his poetry no longer included direct references to the political situation. When 'To the Cuckoo' was republished in his second volume of poetry in 1799 (*New Poems on a variety of different subjects*), the verses about the United Irishmen were omitted. His later animal fables in Scots dialect contained more subtle political messages.

Although like many Presbyterian radicals he was probably inspired by Thomas Paine's *Rights of Man,* as a religious man, he was deeply unhappy with Paine's atheism and anti-religious stance expressed in *Age of Reason.*

Thomson was a huge admirer of Robbie Burns and in 1793 dedicated his first volume of poetry, *Poems on different subjects, partly in the Scottish Dialect*, to him. The following year he went and visited Burns in Dumfries, Scotland. Thomson was the first of the contemporary County Antrim poets to publish their work and played an important role in encouraging other local poets, including James Orr (see profile).

In 1806 he published his final collection of poems (*Simple poems on a few subjects*) under the patronage of Lord Templetown of Templepatrick, much to the consternation of some of his fellow poets, including James Orr. With six hundred subscribers, compared with three hundred for each of the previous volumes, his popularity had clearly increased over the years. The subscribers included almost a dozen Presbyterian ministers.

Thomson died in 1816, having seen a revival of Ulster-Scots folk poetry, and is buried in an unmarked grave.

Sources: Ferguson and Holmes 2008; Scott and Robinson 1992.

William Orr
1766–97

William Orr was born in Farranshane, near Shane's Castle, County Antrim in 1766, the eldest son of Samuel and Alice Orr. They were a prominent Presbyterian family, of Scottish origin, who owned a large farm and bleach green, for the bleaching of linen. He inherited land in Toome and Farranshane, County Antrim, where he settled with his wife, Isabella (née

Greer) after they married in 1788. He was known to be 'new light' theologically and to hold radical political views, occasionally contributing to the *Northern Star* newspaper.

He joined the United Irishmen and advocated a moderate position at meetings in Carrickfergus. In 1796, when he was still largely unknown, he was arrested for administering the United Irishmen's secret oath to two soldiers, Lindsay and Wheatley, of the Fifeshire Fencibles. This had been made a treasonable, and therefore capital offence under the Insurrection Act, which had recently been passed as part of the Government's attempts to put down the reform movement. When he was named as one of the people administering the oath he went into hiding, but returned to his parents' house when his father was ill and was caught by the military.

Unlike the other United Irish leaders who were taken to Dublin, Orr was jailed in Carrickfergus. His trial was postponed for a year, but when it did take place it only lasted one day. He was accused by the two soldiers, one of whom turned out to be a paid informer. Wheatley later admitted to two Presbyterian ministers, James Elder and Alexander Montgomery, to being a perjurer. Even Orr's own lawyer turned out to be in the pay of the government, who had clearly decided to make an example of Orr, as a warning to other would be reformers. Orr denied the charge, but was found guilty. The verdict caused great public consternation in Ireland and London and there were many appeals for leniency, including from Lady Londonderry, but to no avail. Although the jury had recommended leniency, Orr was hanged in October 1797, in 'Gallows Green' where the Woodburn River enters Belfast Lough, accompanied by Ballynure Presbyterian minister, Adam Hill and Reformed Presbyterian minister of Knockbracken, William Staveley. His final words were, 'I am no traitor. I die a persecuted man for a persecuted country ... I die in the true faith of a Presbyterian'. Attempts to resuscitate him failed. There was a wake with his body *en route* to Castle Upton Cemetery in Templepatrick, for which Rev. Hill was arrested.

Orr had become a martyr even before he was buried. Many cards, rings, bracelets and lockets were produced to commemorate his death and the watchword for United Irishmen for many years afterwards was 'Remember Orr'. William Drennan wrote a moving epitaph in the form of a poem, entitled 'The Wake of William Orr', which included the following memorable words, which link his political commitment to reform to his Presbyterian faith:

> Truth he spoke and acted truth
> Countrymen, Unite! He cried
> And died for what his Saviour died

Sources: Boylan 1998; Brooke 1994; Campbell 1991; Holmes 2000; McBride 1998; Nelson 1998–2000; Seery *et al* 2000.

Henry Joy McCracken
1767–98

Henry Joy McCracken, known as Harry to his family and friends, was born in High Street, Belfast, into a wealthy Presbyterian family in 1767. His father was a sea captain and also the owner of a large rope works. His mother was a member of the Joy family that owned the *Belfast Newsletter*. When he was old enough (aged 22), Harry was put in charge of a cotton mill the family owned, but was not a great success as a businessman and the mill failed in 1795.

Inspired by the French Revolution, McCracken became involved with other wealthy Presbyterians, in the establishment of the United Irishmen in Belfast to try and bring about reform to the corrupt and oppressive political system of the time. He strove, 'to forward a brotherhood of affection, an identity of interest, a communion of rights and an union of power among Irishmen of all religious persuasions'.

When it became clear that peaceful attempts to bring about reform were unsuccessful and with the brutal suppression of those with radical views, the United Irishmen went underground and developed their plans for rebellion. In 1795, on the Cave Hill, McCracken met Wolfe Tone and others and swore their allegiance to the United Irish cause. Tone, a member of the Church of Ireland, who had been in France to gain support, promised that help would be provided by France. McCracken recruited members of the United Irishmen from the Catholic Defenders in County Armagh and from as far as County Offaly

In 1796, McCracken was arrested and jailed in Kilmainham Gaol in Dublin for 13 months, until released on bail. When the 1798 rebellion took place, McCracken was the Commander of the Northern forces, at short notice, leading the attack on Antrim, with Jemmy Hope. The garrison had been quickly reinforced by the 22nd Dragoons. After the rebels were defeated, McCracken escaped the battlefield and hid out on Slemish Mountain and then a gamekeeper's cottage on the Cave Hill, near Belfast. The daughter of the gamekeeper had had a secret child by McCracken.

McCracken was eventually captured outside Carrickfergus by the yeomanry, trying to escape to America. He was court martialled at the Exchange in Waring Street Belfast, and held in the Donegall Arms Hotel in High Street. When he refused to inform on his fellow insurgents, including Robert Simms, who had severely damaged the rebellion in the north by resigning at the last minute, he was tried convicted and hanged on the corner of Cornmarket and High Street on 17 July 1798, one of twenty thousand to be killed during the rebellion. He was buried in the grounds of Corporation Church (St George's) in High Street.

Sources: Bardon 1992; Boylan 1998; Bradbury 2002; Byrne and McMahon 1991; Holmes 2000; Latimer 1897; McBride 1998; Stewart 1993.

James Bones
1767–1841

James Bones was born in 1767 in Duneane, near Randalstown, County Antrim to John Bones, a Presbyterian farmer, and his wife Elizabeth (née Scott). James also became a farmer at Ballygarvey, near Ballymena, County Antrim, and also worked as a linen bleacher. In 1790 he married Mary Adams, whose family were also in the linen business at Checker Hall (named after the fabric woven by her father, a pioneer of industrial linen weaving), near Cloughmills. After they married they moved to Ballyportery, near Ballymena and carried on their linen business and farm.

James and his brother Samuel, were passionate supporters of civil and religious liberty and were inspired by the French Revolution. They both joined the Society of United Irishmen when it was established. However, James' name appeared on a government list of suspected United Irishmen supplied by spies. Against his name was written 'Bad in every sense of the term'. However, he was not arrested prior to the rebellion, as many United Irishmen were. He was part of the rebel band to march into Ballymena on the morning of 8 June 1798 and attack the Market House, forcing the surrender of the loyalist forces. Unfortunately, on hearing the news that Henry Joy McCracken had been defeated at the Battle of Antrim and that government forces were on their way to Ballymena from Antrim, the rebels realised that their cause was hopeless and dispersed, trying to return to their homes without being caught. Both James and Samuel Bones were captured and arrested. Samuel was tried in the Court House in Broughshane and sentenced to 500 lashes from the cat of nine tails. James, however, managed to escape. The story is told that the guards were so moved by his beautiful wife, with their baby in her arms, coming to the prison in Ballymena, that they allowed him to escape. Following his escape he eventually managed to make his way to the island of Jamaica, where he was joined by his wife and child.

After two years the family returned to Ireland. In 1809, he eventually managed to obtain a lease on his old farm at Ballyportery. However, within a year the whole family had emigrated to the southern states of America via Savannah and lived in Cedar Grove. James and Mary had nine children altogether, who made successful lives for themselves in America. One of Bones' grandchildren, James, married Woodrow Wilson's aunt and the future president became a close family friend.

James Bones died on 17 December 1841 aged 74 and is buried in Summerville Cemetery, Augusta, Georgia.

Sources: Brown 1998; Dunlop 1993; 'The James Bones Family Circle', *Familia: Ulster Genealogical Review*, no. 14, 1998.

James Bryce
1767–1857

James Bryce was born in Airdrie in Lanarkshire in 1767, the son of John Bryce and Robina (née Allan). They were both descendants of Lanarkshire landowners who had lost their property in the previous century for adhering to their covenanting principles in religion. Bryce was educated at New Monkland parish school and Glasgow University, but left without graduating. He was licensed to preach in 1792 and was ordained minister of the Anti-Burgher Secession church of Wick, Caithness in Scotland in 1795.

In 1797 Bryce was accused of latitudinarianism (unorthodoxy) before the Calvinist General Associate Synod. He was accused of minimising the difference between his own and other denominations of Christians, condemning the extreme use of power by clergy and arguing that too much respect was shown to dogmatic creeds rather than the scriptures. He was suspended from the Synod for two years, although allowed to continue to preach. He decided to move to Ireland where he became minister of the Anti-Burgher church of Killaig in County Londonderry.

When it was proposed that the *regium donum* should be paid at different levels depending on the size of the congregation and on condition of ministers taking the oath of allegiance, with the Lord Lieutenant having an absolute veto on who should receive it, the Burgher and Anti-Burgher bodies in Ireland, who had never received the grant before, initially denounced these terms, but eventually accepted them. Only Bryce stood out against the proposed arrangements, arguing that they were dishonouring to Christ as the supreme head of the church and tended to enslave ministers and degrade their office. For his stance he suffered financially and to try and make ends meet taught classics in his own home. He did not receive support from his fellow ministers or the church in Scotland and eventually formed an Associate Presbytery of Ireland, which was ultimately united with the Scottish United Presbyterian Church.

Bryce died in 1857, aged 89, having been an active preacher right up to his death. His three sons all had very successful careers in education.

Sources: Hamilton 1992; Latimer 1893; *Oxford Dictionary of National Biography*; Stewart 1950.

Benjamin Mitchell
1768/9–1815

Benjamin Mitchel was born in Maghera, County Londonderry in late 1768 or early 1769 and was educated in Strabane, County Tyrone. Having decided to enter the ministry he was licensed to preach by Route Presbytery in 1796.

In the revolutionary 1790s, Mitchel was an active supporter of the United Irishmen, as a result of which, he was arrested in 1797, charged with treason and jailed in Derry, the year before the rebellion, for alleged involvement in illegal activities, but was eventually released.

Mitchell passed two trials with the Presbytery of Antrim, but in 1799, following the death of Rev. Alexander Marshall, he was called by First Ballymoney (known as the 'Big Meetinghouse' built in 1877) congregation in County Antrim, with the support of the vast majority of members, on an annual stipend of £80. As a result he returned to the Presbytery of Route, which included Ballymoney. However, because of his radical political views and involvement with the United Irishmen, he was disapproved of by many of those in the Route and some members of the congregation, including several magistrates who petitioned the Presbytery of Route against his settlement in First Ballymoney. Because of the Route's treatment of the congregation, in 1800 the congregation memorialised the Synod to remove them from the Presbytery of Route to the Presbytery of Ballymena. The Synod of Ulster unanimously agreed to the move.

Benjamin Mitchell was formally ordained in First Ballymoney by the Presbytery of Ballymena on 12 November 1800 and over the following decade the congregation seems to have flourished under his leadership and received a satisfactory visitation from Presbytery. However, as a result of ill health, exacerbated by continued conflict with some members of the congregation, he resigned on 9 May 1815, and died on 13 August 1815 aged only 46. He was buried in Lamb's Fold Quaker graveyard near Ballymoney. He was succeeded by Rev. Robert Park who was ordained in the church on 18 March 1817. In 1840 Ballymoney returned to the Presbytery of Route with the merger of the two synods.

Mitchell was survived by his wife, who died in 1851, and four children, including the eldest daughter Mary and youngest Elizabeth who lived until 1904. The Lord Chief Justice William Moore of Kilrea was a grandson of Mitchell's.

Sources: Eddies 'Book of Extracts'; Card Index of ministers in the Presbyterian Historical Society.

William Dunlop
1768–1821

William Dunlop was born in the Maine, Limavady, County Londonderry in 1768. He was educated in Strabane and the University of Glasgow. He was 'new light' i.e. non-evangelical theologically and licensed to preach by Strabane Presbytery in 1789. He was ordained in Badoney, near Gortin, County Tyrone on 15 March 1790.

It is not known whether he was a United Irishman or just had strong sympathy with their cause, but Rev. Classon Porter described how, the night before the rebel 'turn out' in 1798, Dunlop agreed to deliver some important papers for the United Irishmen. He dressed himself in a blue semi-military coat and, secreting the papers in a grouse bag, rode through a troop of Tipperary militia, adopting an 'air of official importance'. The sergeant in charge of the troop attempted to stop him but was over-ruled by the officer-in-command, who said, 'Sir, would you attempt to stop a Government express?' Dunlop was allowed to proceed with his secret documents. The military blue coat was preserved by his family in recognition of his 'courage and self-possession'. Dunlop, who was never arrested, also wrote at least one poem in support of the cause of the United Irishmen, which included the following stanza:

> Long had Hibernia's warlike sons in strife inglorious bled,
> And long from her discordant isle had injured freedom fled;
> At length her genius from above, descending stood confused,
> And thus in bold persuasive voice the listening realm addressed:
> Unite my warlike sons, and yet be free,
> Unite and from oppression's chains you'll gain your liberty.

A few months after the 1798 rebellion, he resigned from Badoney and was installed in First Strabane on 10 November 1798, succeeding Rev. William Crawford (see profile). He married Eliza Anderson of Archmount Strabane.

He was elected moderator of General Synod for the year 1810–11 and achieved fame for standing up to the Government agent and minister in Londonderry, Rev. Dr. Robert Black, who controlled the *Regium Donum*.

Dunlop resigned from his ministry on 21 February 1820 and died the following year on 24 November 1821.

Sources: Campbell 1902; Swords 1997.

George Cumming (also spelled Cuming)
Born *c.* 1768

George Cumming was born in Newry, County Down. He trained as an apothecary and physician. He moved to County Kildare where he joined the Leinster Directory of the United Irishmen. He was arrested in Dublin on 12 March 1798 as he was one of three Leinster representatives to attend a secret National Executive meeting in Bond's, after informer Thomas Reynolds had told the Government about the meeting. His position on the

National Executive was quickly given to respectable farmer Michael Reynolds. Cumming was imprisoned in Belfast and then, when there was suspicion that the group of United Irishmen were conspiring further, they were transferred to a jail in Fort George Scotland, with Rev. William Steel Dickson, William Tennent, Samuel Neilson (see profiles) and others, for three years.

Like other United Irishmen who had been imprisoned, rather than being immediately executed, he was released on the basis that he would emigrate to America and not return. In the autumn of 1802 he sailed for New York. When he arrived he stayed with John Caldwell, one of his United Irish colleagues. With Caldwell he joined Erin Masonic Lodge and the Friendly Sons of Saint Patrick. Cumming said to Caldwell that he 'lamented the unhappy divisions among the Irish republicans and feared the degradation of the Irish character in the city'. Three years after arriving in New York he put up fellow radical John Chambers when he, in turn, arrived in America.

Cumming quickly became actively involved in American politics on the side of the Republicans against the British and became a leading local Republican politician and office-holder. He was generally a supporter of deWitt Clinton, but supported James Madison over Clinton, because he disliked Clinton's Federalist supporters.

He was concerned about the worship of money in American society and welcomed the economic slump which followed the end of the Napoleonic wars on the grounds that less commerce would mean more liberty and would check the growth of an aristocracy of wealth.

In 1816 he was appointed City Inspector. In 1827 he chaired the meeting in Tammany Hall, which decided to erect a marble memorial in memory of Thomas Addis Emmet.

He was a member of Trinity Church in New York and, in an ecumenical gesture, gave a subscription to St Paul's in New York, for the building of a granite shaft.

Sources: Miller *et al* 2003; Wilson 1998; Wilson and Spencer 2006.

John Pinkerton
1768–1840

John Pinkerton was born in Glendermott, just outside Londonderry, in 1768. He trained for the ministry and was licensed by Derry Presbytery, but was actively involved in the 1798 rebellion and, as a result, was removed from the care of the Presbytery. After five years, enough time must have passed to allow him to be accepted back into the ministry in 1803. The following year he received a call to Limerick congregation and was formally ordained there in 1804, succeeding the retiring minister, Rev. Abraham

Torby Seawright.

During Pinkerton's ministry, to accommodate an expanding congregation and an influx of Scottish merchants, a new church was built in Upper Glenworth Street, Limerick in 1817.

Pinkerton retired in 1828 and died on 21 December 1840. He was succeeded in Limerick by Rev. Matthew Dickie who was called from Paisley, Scotland.

Sources: History of Congregations; Card index at the Presbyterian Historical Society Belfast.

Archibald Warwick
1769–98

Archibald Warwick was born in 1769, the grandchild of David and Margaret Warwick of Loughriescouse, County Down. He was licensed to preach the gospel by Belfast Presbytery in 1797, but had not yet been formally ordained as a Presbyterian minister.

Like many others he became involved in the United Irishmen and was given a position of leadership in the rising in the Ards, County Down. When the rebellion was put down, Warwick was arrested. At his trial he was accused by an excise officer, William Harvey, who had been taken prisoner by the rebels, of being with the rebels, on horseback with pistols and also of being at Inishargie, near Kircubbin on the Ards peninsula where Harvey said that Warwick reproached a rebel leader called Dalzell 'for leading his men too hastily, for that he would have them all slaughtered'. This clearly demonstrated Warwick's seniority in the rebel hierarchy.

Warwick was eventually court-martialled in Newtownards and hanged at Kircubbin, four months after the end of the rebellion, in the midst of a thunderstorm, with a heavy armed guard to prevent any attempt at rescue. He was accompanied during his execution by Scottish Presbyterian minister George Brydons. Warwick is buried in Movilla cemetery, beside the Old Abbey in Newtownards. Warwick's participation in the rising and hanging was immortalised in Florence Wilson's poem, 'The man from God knows where',

> I met McKee in the throng O' the street,
> Says he 'the grass has grown under our feet
> Since they hanged young Warwick here.

His son, of the same name, was licensed in Down and ordained as a minister on 8 October 1805 in Crieve, County Monaghan. In 1816 he had to 'request help in distress', from the Synod and died on 7 June 1817.

Sources: Allen 2004; O'Byrne 1990; Stewart 1995.

John Lowry
Died 1846

John Lowry was the son of Archibald Lowry of Donaghmore, County Down. He trained for the Burgher ministry at Associate Divinity Hall in Selkirk, under Prof. John Brown of Haddington. He was licensed by Down Presbytery on 3 April 1792 and ordained in the new church in Upper Clonaleese, County Tyrone in March 1794, following a major dispute about the building of a new church to replace the old one, resulting in a split in the Seceder congregations into Upper (Burgher) and Lower Clonaleese, which became anti-Burgher.

Rev. Lowry became a controversial figure for preaching from the pulpit in support of the United Irishmen, while the government was trying to suppress the movement and applying moral sanctions against those opposed to the 'Liberty men'. He preached against enrolment in the loyalist yeomanry and refused communion to a member of his congregation who was particularly active in suppressing the United Irishmen.

He was one of the founders of the inter-denominational Ulster Evangelical Society whose principles, according to the Burgher Synod, were inconsistent with the Secession 'Act and Testimony', and so he was censured by the Synod in 1798.

In 1802 he was in trouble again over a pamphlet, entitled *Halleluia*, favouring the use of hymns in worship (rather than only paraphrases and psalms), which caused further division within the church, including being libelled by his fellow minister, Rev. John Wilson of Lecumpher. Lowry was judged guilty but 'on admitting his error and professing sorrow, the Synod were satisfied with these evidences of contrition'. He wrote *On Christian Baptism* in 1812; *Able minister of the New Testament* in 1816; and *The Almanac Explained* in 1824. He was eventually suspended from the ministry in 1830, but after a humble submission to Synod in 1831 gained his restoration. He died on 18 April 1846 and was succeeded at Upper Clonaleese by Rev. Archibald Heron of Tipperary.

When, in 1906, the pulpits of both Upper and Lower Clonaneese congregations became vacant, the opportunity was taken to unite them again under one minister.

Rev. John Lowry's daughter, Florella Reid, married the Rev. Thomas Lowry of Glenhoy. John Lowry died in 1846.

Sources: Baillie and Kirkpatrick 2005; Curtin 1994; PCNI online History of Congregations; McBride 1998.

Robert Gowdy (also spelled Gowdie and Goudy)
Died 1798

Gowdy was the grandson of Rev. Robert Gowdy of Ballywalter and son of a prosperous Dunover farmer. He was licensed to preach but had not yet been ordained, but was believed to be supply minister of Dunover Presbyterian congregation, County Down.

He was accused of taking part in the attack by the United Irishmen on Portaferry, County Down and being in command at Inishargie, near Kircubbin in the Ards peninsula. He was also charged with being in contact with the overall Commander in County Down, Henry Munro, while he was at the camp in Saintfield and of bringing back a message to an Andrew Orr of Cunningburn.

At his trial Gowdy called Henry Joy McCracken's sister as an alibi. The sister of one of the rebel leaders, however, was not likely to impress the authorities. Apparent attempts by Rev. Hugh Montgomery to intercede on his behalf also failed because Colonel Atherton considered Montgomery also to be an enemy. Gowdy, in the shadow of the scaffold wrote a strong condemnation of Rev. Montgomery as a 'bloody Judas' who had betrayed him and the people and would one day meet a fate worse than Gowdy was about to face. But what Montgomery had done to deserve this is not clear.

He was court-martialled in Newtownards and hanged in 1798. Rev. Birch reported that on the gallows, Gowdy observed to 'Lord Londonderry and others that he would shortly argue the matter with them before a tribunal where there would be an impartial hearing'.

Sources: Allen 2004; Stewart 1995; Swords 1997.

James Reynolds
Died 1808

James Reynolds was from Cookstown in County Tyrone and trained as a physician. He was actively involved in the Volunteers and was a member of the Dublin Society of the United Irishmen. He also became the Grand Master of the Cookstown Masonic Lodge. In January 1793 he chaired a meeting of over forty Masonic lodges which passed various radical resolutions including,

> I solemnly promise and declare that I will by all rational means promote the universal emancipation and adequate representation of all the people of Ireland, and will not be satisfied until all these objects are unequivocally obtained.

He played a prominent role in the Dungannon Volunteer Convention of February 1782, which took place in Dungannon Presbyterian Church and at which a sermon was given by Rev. William Steel Dickson. Reynolds protested vehemently against criticisms of republican forms of government.

In March 1793 he was summoned before a secret committee of the Episcopal Church-dominated House of Lords to give an account of his activities. However he refused to be examined under oath as he said the House of Lords had no judicial power over him. As a consequence he was jailed for five months. When he was released he went to Dublin and became chairman of the Dublin Society of the United Irishmen.

In 1794 he was one of the United Irishmen who negotiated with the French to try and arrange matters so the rebellion would coincide with a French invasion. On hearing he was about to be arrested again he made his escape to America. On board the ship he did not exactly keep his political opinions secret as he hanged an effigy of George III from the yardarm and gave his shipmates rum to 'drink to the confusion of despots and the prosperity of liberty all the world over'.

Reynolds settled in Philadelphia along with many Ulster Presbyterians, quickly becoming embroiled in radical American politics. In August 1795 he met up with Wolfe Tone and Hamilton Rowan, who had recently come from France, in Philadelphia. Having persuaded a leading Republican editor to publish a story accusing the federalist Secretary of State, Timothy Pickering, of accepting bribes, in 1798, Reynolds found himself in court accused of libel. The following year he was involved in political agitation against the Alien and Sedition Acts and was prosecuted for seditious rioting.

Nor was he devoid of controversy in his medical career. He was a leading protagonist in one of the leading medical controversies of the day over the origin of yellow fever. As a result of this he was removed from the Philadelphia Board of Health. His removal in turn became a leading issue in the impeachment of the Governor of Pennsylvania, Ulsterman Thomas McKean.

Reynolds was also the first known writer to write a utopian novel, entitled *Equality*. He died in 1808.

Sources: Green 1969; McGuire, James and Quinn, James (2009) *Dictionary of Irish Biography*; O'Keefe, John (2013) 'Transatlantic Radicals, citizenship and Cultural Assimilation during the Adams Administration', paper presented to the American Studies Association Annual Meeting in the Renaissance Hotel Washington DC; Wilson, David (1998) *United Irishmen, United States: immigrant Radicals in the Early Republic*.

James Worrall
Died 1824

Worrall, unusually for a Presbyterian minister in Ulster, was a native of Limerick and a convert from the Church of Ireland. He had been educated at Trinity College, which was only open to members of Anglican church. After embracing Presbyterianism he moved north and became the tutor of the family of Mr Turnly of Rockport, County Down.

Worrall trained for the Presbyterian ministry and was called to Larne Old Presbyterian Church in 1796. He was theologically and politically radical and by 1798 had sworn the United Irishmen's oath. His congregation in Larne included many of the leading figures in the area, on both sides of the political conflict, including Dr George Casement who was on the jury which had sentenced William Orr. This made Casement a priority target when the rising in Larne started.

When the appointed leader of the rising in Larne fled to Scotland, having handed over evidence against the rebels to the government, it is likely that Worrall played a significant leadership role although he was of poor health, suffering from asthma. He was eventually arrested and put in jail. Dr Halliday interceded with Lord Castlereagh on his behalf, claiming his views were limited to emancipation and reform, not rebellion. He was, however, convicted and imprisoned, but remained the minister of Old Larne until 1807, when he became the minister of Clonmel, County Tipperary. He died in 1824.

Sources: McBride 1998; Stewart 1995.

Arthur McMahon (also spelled McMechan)
1755?–1815/6

Arthur McMahon was probably born in 1755, the son of Alexander McMahon, a farmer from Dunanelly in the parish of Inch, County Down. He was educated at Glasgow University where he received his MA in 1777 and then was a student for the ministry under the guidance of the Non-Subscribing Presbytery of Antrim. After he was licensed he became a tutor to the family of Lord Castlereagh. He joined Killyleagh Presbytery in 1786 and was ordained in First Kilrea Church, County Londonderry, part of the General Synod in 1789, where he stayed for five years. In 1794 he got married and also became the minister of Holywood Non-Subscribing Church in County Down.

In the build-up to the rebellion of 1798, McMahon became one of the United Irishmen's most trusted couriers. He was appointed a member of the

National Executive and one of the seven colonels for County Down to lead the rising. To avoid arrest he travelled from Bangor to Scotland. He then made links with sympathisers in England and France and worked closely with Father Quigley to try and organise United Englishmen in Liverpool, Manchester and London. In May 1798, on his behalf, his wife resigned his position as minister and three days later the Presbytery of Antrim declared the congregation of Holywood disannexed from their minister. In the September 1798 'fifty pounder' list (indicating the size of the reward – £50) published in the *Belfast Newsletter* McMahon's name was given as wanted. He was eventually 'proclaimed', which meant being publicly named and warned to be of good behaviour.

He eventually fled to France and in 1805 became an officer of the Irish Legion in the service of Napoleon and the French Republic. He served in Flushing from 1807 until he was arrested in 1809 and became a prisoner of war in England. In 1814 he was released and returned to France, serving once more in Napoleon's army. He is believed to have been killed at Waterloo in 1815/6.

Sources: Elliott 1989; Maguire 1970; notes provided by Rev. John Nelson; Swords 1997.

James Hull
Died 1833

James Foster Hull was the third son of Rev. James Hull, minister of Ballyvarnet in Rathgael, Bangor, County Down, a non-subscriber. James Hull jr was licensed to preach in 1796. Although not yet ordained, he was appointed as full-time supply minister to Donaghadee meetinghouse, but there was some difficulty with the appointment and Hull never actually took it up. In May 1798, however, he was one of a group of supply preachers who took the Sunday services in Donaghadee meetinghouse. This group included Revs Steel Dickson, James Porter and David Baillie Warden.

Hull was actively involved in the 1798 rebellion in County Down. He seems to have had a leadership role in the Ards and was identified at Movilla Cemetery prior to the attack on the town. Hull and Rev. James Townsend actively prevented looting by the rebels, rebuked those who had engaged in looting and, 'abused them as cowards and traitors to their cause, compelled them to re-assume their arms, and marched them to a hill called Scrabo, near Newtown'.

It seems to have been Hull, on horseback, armed with pistols and a sword, who was responsible for bringing six 3-pounder swivel guns up from Bangor on some common farm carts for use by the rebels.

Hull was arrested for his role in the rebellion, and it was initially believed that he had been executed, but was fortunate enough to be only 'proclaimed', which involved being publicly named and warned to be of good behaviour. However he decided to sail to America with many other rebels. In July 1799 he was appointed Episcopal rector of St Paul's in New Orleans, where Presbyterians were permitted to worship until they built their own church in 1809. Hull served as minister for only eighteen months, before becoming a lawyer and moving to Cambridge, South Carolina. He eventually returned to New Orleans and was ordained as an Episcopal priest, becoming the second rector of Christ Episcopal Church in 1814. He died in New Orleans in 1833.

Sources: Allen 2004.

James Orr
1770–1816

James Orr was born in 1770 near Ballycarry, County Antrim, the only child of James Orr sr, a weaver on land rented from the Red Hall estate. They attended Ballycarry Presbyterian meetinghouse. Although his parents appear to have had Calvinist 'old light' views, the young James Orr developed a 'new light' theology, inspired by the Enlightenment. He received little in the way of formal education and so largely educated himself, supplemented by membership of local reading societies and libraries. He became a weaver, like his father, and joined the United Irishmen, participating in the rising of 1798. With the failure of the rising he spent much of the second half of the year on the run from the authorities, with Henry Joy McCracken and others. He was eventually arrested and taken to Carrickfergus jail, although was eventually allowed to emigrate to America, where he had poems published. When the threat of arrest had died down he returned to Ireland and, with the threat of invasion by Napoleon, attempted to join the local yeomanry, but was rejected.

Orr was an accomplished poet in the Ulster-Scots tradition and was friends with other poets of the time, including Samuel Thomson, Thomas Beggs, John Dickey and Alexander McKenzie. His poem 'Donegore Hill' describes the hosting of the pikemen before marching on Antrim and criticises those rebels who failed to do their duty at the Battle of Antrim in 1798. In 'The Execution' he described the hanging of one of his fellow United Irishmen from a tree and in 'The Wanderer' describes the fate of those trying to avoid detection and arrest.

He published various individual poems in the United Irish newspaper, the *Northern Star* and the *Belfast Newsletter*. He only produced one collection of poems in his lifetime, entitled, *Poems on Various Subjects*, which was published in 1804, with the support of 470 subscribers. John

Hewitt praised his Ulster-Scots vernacular, his 'firmness of structure and consistency of language' in such poems as 'The Penitent' and 'The Irish Cottiers Death and Burial', although his best-known poem, 'the Irishman' is in Standard English, which begins,

> The savage loves his native shore,
> Though rude the soil and chill the air,
> Then well may Erin's sons adore
> Their isle, which Nature formed so fair …

After his death on 24 April 1816 his friends produced a second collection of his poetry called *The Posthumous Works of James Orr of Ballycarry: With a Sketch of his Life*. He requested that any profits would go to the poor. He is buried in Templecorran Churchyard.

Sources: Ferguson 2008; Hewitt 2004; Robinson 1992.

Thomas Alexander
1770–1851

Thomas Alexander was born on the 1 January 1770, the second son of Robert Alexander of Knockcair, Crumlin, County Antrim. He was educated at Glasgow University where he graduated in 1791, aged 21. He was 'new light' theologically and licensed to preach by the Presbytery of Templepatrick in 1792 and the following year was ordained at Cairncastle, County Antrim, where he became assistant and successor to his father-in-law, Rev. John Lewson. During the early part of his ministry Rev. Alexander ran a school in the town. He was an active member of the United Irishmen and attended a meeting of the Society in Larne just a few days before the rebellion, which agreed to send a deputation to the French Convention.

On the day the rebellion broke out in the area, (Thursday, 7 June 1798) Alexander said that he was visiting the house of his sister in Crumlin, who had just died, and, as they returned home the following day, he said he could see the flames above Templepatrick. As they reached Ballynure they saw people carrying furniture out of their houses to prevent them being destroyed by the soldiers. According to this story they did not get home to Cairncastle until the early hours of Saturday morning. There is another version of events, as one of his school pupils claimed to have seen him 'commanding a company of rebels and marching at their head'. Whatever the truth of the story, on the Sunday morning Alexander was preaching as usual in his church.

After the rebellion had been defeated, Alexander and the frail Rev. Lewson organised an escape network for United Irishmen who were fugitives from justice, with Mr Shaw of Ballygalley. The rebels would stay in one of their houses, until a boat could be arranged to take them to Scotland. One of those fleeing after the Battle of Antrim was a Bob Major. When a boat was arranged, Alexander and Shaw set out from shore with some Larne fishermen to look out for the rescue boat. However, the rescue boat had been captured by a revenue cutter and Alexander and Shaw were taken prisoner. Alexander was held for a fortnight in Carrickfergus market house. Bob Major eventually escaped to Norway and then Prussia. No further proceedings seem to have been taken against Alexander and he returned to his ministry at the church and married Lewson's daughter. Rev. Lewson died in 1802 and Alexander continued as minister until retiring in 1833.

When the Non-Subscribing Remonstrant Synod was created in 1830, Alexander led his congregation in joining the new Synod and they retained the church. His son also became a non-subscribing minister in Newry.

After Alexander retired he moved to London where he died on 26 May 1851.

Sources: McBride 1998; McMillen 1997.

John, Samuel and William Neilson (also spelled Nelson)
John: c.1770–1827
Samuel: died 1798
William: 1782–98

John, Samuel and William were three brothers who lived in the small, mainly Presbyterian, village of Ballycarry, near Larne in County Antrim, which contained many supporters of the United Irishmen. All three brothers took part in the 'Turn Oot' at the Battle of Antrim, in support of the rebellion on 7 June 1798. The youngest William, who was only 16 was appointed a messenger, to ride on horseback between the insurgents in Ballycarry and Islandmagee. After the defeat of the rebel forces in Antrim, all three were arrested and imprisoned in Carrickfergus jail. William was pressurised to give the names of other rebels, which he refused to do. He was court-martialled, found guilty, and hanged on a tree outside his widowed mother's house. He became known as the Ballycarry martyr.

Samuel was permitted to sail to America, but the ship was captured by the French en route, who treated them with kindness. Unfortunately, the English later recaptured the ship and sent it, with its passengers, to the West Indies. Before the ship arrived at its destination, Samuel died.

John, who is believed to have escaped from the authorities, successfully reached America. He became a US citizen in 1804 and was a very successful architect and a personal friend of Presidents Thomas Jefferson, for whom he built parts of the University of Virginia, and James Madison, for whom he built a house, Montpelier. Upper Bremo plantation is regarded as one of his greatest achievements. He remained friends with other United Irish exiles, such as James Butler, from the south-east of Ireland and was friends with Robert Emmet's nephew, John Patten Emmet, a professor at the University of Virginia.

John Neilson died in June 1827 having just received news of his daughter's death. At the time of his death, his wife, Mary was living in Loughmourne Carrickfergus, County Antrim. He is buried in Maplewood graveyard Charlottesville, Virginia, where a memorial was erected to a 'United Irishman, political exile, architect at Monticello and the University of Virginia.'

Sources: Hume 2005; *Dictionary of Ulster Biography*; *Dictionary of Irish Biography*.

Mary Ann McCracken
1770–1866

Mary Anne McCracken was born in High Street, Belfast on 8 July 1770, into a wealthy Presbyterian family, one of a family of seven children, three years after her brother, Henry Joy. Her father, John McCracken was a sea captain and also the owner of a large rope works. Her mother, Ann, was a member of the Joy family that owned the *Belfast Newsletter* and a linen firm. Mary Ann attended David Manson's progressive co-educational school, where she developed a love of mathematics and modern literature. She was inspired by reading Mary Wollstonecraft's *The Vindication of the Rights of Women* and believed that her era would 'produce some women of sufficient talents to inspire the rest with a genuine love of liberty'. To generate some income, she established a muslin business with her sister, Margaret.

She acted as a secretary to Edward Bunting, organist of Second congregation Belfast, a family friend who moved into the McCracken household, in order to record the Irish music of the past, which had been handed down orally, to ensure that it would not be lost. She also helped him organise a unique festival of Irish harpers.

She was strongly in favour of political reform and Catholic Emancipation and supported her three brothers who all became involved in the United Irishmen. When her brother Henry Joy, was captured and imprisoned by a Government determined to stamp out the reform movement, she, regardless of her own safety, travelled to visit him in jail in Dublin. After the failed rebellion of 1798 and Henry Joy was on the run, she scoured the countryside to try to find him, and eventually tracked him down to the gamekeeper's cottage on Cave Hill. She tried to help him escape to America, but he was recognised, imprisoned and sentenced to death. Despite all her efforts to obtain clemency for him, he was hanged. Afterwards she was to write a moving account of the execution. In 1803, she provided similar help to Thomas Russell, charged with being one of the leaders of the rebellion of 1803, but he too was executed.

With the Act of Union, which abolished the Irish Parliament, which had been controlled by the Anglican landed gentry and their clergy and had tried to violently suppress the political reform movement, it was clear that the momemtum of the revolutionary movement was largely at an end. Many of the revolutionaries emigrated to America, denied or renounced their previously held principles.

Mary Ann McCracken already had other responsibilities in bringing up the illegitimate daughter of her brother, Henry Joy, despite the objections of her family. However, she decided to use her commitment to her principles in other ways and became involved in a series of philanthropic and educational initiatives, particularly for the poor in Belfast. She was a tireless reformer who constantly pressed the governors of the Belfast Poorhouse for reforms, which would improve the lives of the residents. She established a training workshop for poor women to give them a skill with which they could earn money. She campaigned for the abolition of the use of boy chimney sweeps and against slavery and was involved in an association to help the victims of the Great Famine in the 1840s. She was one of those who greeted prison reformer, Elizabeth Fry to Belfast in 1827. She later became reconciled to the union with England and hoped that it might lead to reform in Ireland.

She died in Belfast, aged 96, on 26 July 1866.

Sources: Bardon 1992; Bradbury 2002; Byrne and McMahon 1991; Campbell 1991; Keogh and Furlong; McBride 1998; McNeill 1960; Stewart 1993.

James Burns
1772–1863

James Burns was born on 13 March 1772 in Ballynure near Templepatrick and baptised by Rev. Wright, the minister of Donegore, as the position of minister of Templepatrick was vacant, until the installation of John Abernethy (see profile) in 1774.

As a young man, Burns enlisted in the Royal Irish Artillery, but influenced by radical thinking decided to desert. He swore an oath to support the cause of parliamentary reform and equal representation of all the people of Ireland and became both a United Irishman and a Defender, organisations of which most young men in the village of Glynn were members.

He was at a meeting of United Irishmen in a barn in Ballycushion, which tried and acquitted William Glen on the charge of giving information to Lord Templeton. During the rebellion, Burns fought at the Battle of Antrim with Henry Joy McCracken and Jemmy Hope (see profiles). On fleeing from the battle, with Paul Douglas of Parkgate, armed with muskets, they were pursued by two cavalrymen, whom Burns and Douglas shot as they jumped a thick hedge and Burns and Douglas managed to escape. Burns, along with McCracken, Jemmy Hope and around 53 others hid out on Slemish mountain for 21 nights, until they were informed on by Sam Orr, the brother of martyr William Orr (of 'Remember Orr' fame).

The band split up and Burns went to Ballycastle, where he got a boat to the isle of Islay, and where he worked in a garden for eighteen months, calling himself James McCormick. He then returned to Templepatrick, but following an argument with some Templepatrick yeomen on Christmas night, he was informed on and arrested at Lyle's Hill. Rather than being charged with desertion from the army, he was charged with burning down a house at Tildarg, for which David Woods had already been hanged at Doagh. Burns, who told his story to Classon Porter many years later, denied having any involved in burning the house. He was imprisoned in Belfast, where Mary Anne McCracken sent him a half-sovereign.

After six weeks he was moved to Dublin and then New Geneva near Cork, where he stayed for five months, before agreeing to serve in the army with the 3rd Buffs regiment. He served with the regiment in various places including Plymouth and Jersey. He was discharged, after 14 months, in 1802 and returned to Templepatrick. Increasingly the men in Templepatrick became Orangemen and Burns felt he could not stay, so moved to Kilwaughter, where he worked as a weaver, as well as in Glynn and Island Magee. To avoid being forced back into the army, he moved again, this time to Groomsport, County Down. But he did not settle there and after another short period in Templepatrick, moved to Broadisland, where he lived and worked as a weaver for the next 19 years. He was married by Rev. Bankhead to a Molly Scott, and had a daughter, but separated from her on account of her temper, living as a virtuous 'grass widower' for the next 55 years and never got to see his grandchildren.

He lived for a while again in Scotland, but as before felt the need to return to Ireland, finally settling in Ballynure, County Antrim. He died in Larne Poorhouse in 1864, aged 92. He is buried in the Old Graveyard in Templecorran.

Sources: Porter 1976.

David Baillie Warden
1772–1845

Warden was born in 1772, the eldest son of Robert Warden (1729–99) and Elizabeth (née Baillie). He came from a long-established family in the townland of Ballycastle near Newtownards (not to be confused with the town of the same name on the north coast of Antrim). He was not a great success at school, where his teacher described him as a 'blockhead'. However he was to prove the teacher wrong and went on to Glasgow University where he studied medicine, theology and the arts, winning two prizes. He gained his MA in 1797 and the same year was licensed to preach by the Presbytery of Bangor in May 1797 and preached his first sermon in Belfast. He was initially a pupil of Rev. James Porter at Greyabbey (he kept notes of Porter's lectures on natural and experimental philosophy which he later sent to Porter's son). In the summer of 1798 he became a probationary supply minister in Killinchy as well as tutoring the children of the Hughes family, but was not yet formally ordained. In May 1798 he was one of a group of local ministers on a roster to fill in during the absence of the minister of Donaghadee.

His name appeared regularly in reports from the spy Nicholas Mageean as participating in meetings of the United Irishmen in early 1798 to plan the rising. After the rising he left an autobiographical 'Narrative' of the events of the summer of 1798, under the pseudonym of William Fox. He never confirmed his authorship, but later evidence (including the evidence of handwriting experts) confirms that it was indeed the work of this probationary minister. It is clear from this narrative that Warden had a leadership position in the rebel army in the Ards, probably with the rebels in Killinchy.

Although he was clearly a strong supporter of reform and the insurrection itself he recognised that 'the Insurrection commenced in confusion' and that the rebel forces were 'in no better order than a mere country mob'. Indeed on 3 June 1798, he read a message to a senior rebel leader in County Down, which said that, although 5,000 Catholic Defenders were ready, the colonels of United Irishmen in the County of Antrim were averse to action, but County Down was to put itself into a state of readiness. When the plan of action was approved, Warden went to get the colonel of a particular company of rebels to put his part of the plan into action.

The first stage in the rebel plan was to gather on Scrabo Hill. Warden describes his mortification of waiting there until one o'clock in the morning, but by which time no one had turned up and saw evidence that the garrison in the town of Newtownards knew of their plans. When sufficient rebels had eventually gathered they advanced on Newtownards.

When they heard the sound of musket fire they were ordered to advance at the double. They were then almost trampled on by rebels from the other rebel division in Ards who had thrown down their arms and were retreating at the double. Both divisions fled to the cemetery at the top of Movilla Hill and regrouped while the leaders instilled some discipline into their inexperienced insurgents. They then decided to march to Conlig, near Bangor, to meet other divisions and recruit others to join them. The garrison in Newtownards left overnight and when the rebels returned, on what became known as Pike Sunday, the rebels easily took the town. They then marched on to success at Saintfield and then to Ballynahinch and ultimate defeat.

Warden was imprisoned in the prison ship anchored in the Pool of Garmoyle in Belfast Lough, along with Steel Dickson, who was arrested before the rising. Dickson reports that the hours would have passed heavily 'had it not been for the lively, rational, and entertaining conversation of a Mr. David B. Warden'.

Warden had his licence to preach withdrawn by Bangor Presbytery, 'from motives of prudence', which infuriated Warden who wrote a stinging address to the Presbytery of Bangor, accusing them of, amongst other things, 'meanness, injustice and cruelty'. Unfortunately the ministers who would have naturally supported him were either dead or in prison.

In a display of loyalty to the crown and government, two weeks after the rebellion, almost a thousand inhabitants of the local area gathered in Warden's church in Killinchy to thank Major-General Nugent for his discrimination in only inflicting vengeance on those involved in the rebellion, affirmed their loyalty to the King and Constitution and proclaimed their unanimous distain for the men of Killinchy who had rebelled against the King.

Warden was forced to emigrate to America and travelled to New Bedford on the ironically named, *Harmony*, never to return. He decided to switch careers and trained as a medical doctor. Then, with another switch of career, he became a very successful diplomat, becoming US Consul at Paris, where he eventually settled for the rest of his life. In the negotiations between France, ruled by Napoleon Bonaparte and the United States in 1812, Warden would have no doubt met with Britain's chief negotiator, Lord Castlereagh, archenemy of the United Irishmen. Castlereagh would presumably have been taken aback to be negotiating with the son of one of his tenants, who had lived just over the wall of his estate and had been a leading rebel in the area. Warden died in Paris in 1845.

Sources: Allen 2004; Latimer 1897; Stewart 1995.

Samuel Brown Wylie
1773–1852

Samuel Wylie was born in Moylarg, County Antrim on 21 May 1773, the son of Adam Wylie, a farmer, and Margaret (née Brown). He received the basics of a classical education locally and then went to study in the University of Glasgow, from which he graduated in 1797 with a Masters of Arts. He was a member of the Calvinist Reformed Presbyterian tradition. Returning home he took a teaching position in Ballymena and began his training for the Reformed ministry. Being theologically conservative did not mean being politically conservative, but it did present a serious dilemma: he could take the Oath of Allegiance to the cause of the United Irishmen and risk being shot or hanged by the army, or flee the country. 'Unwilling either to pollute their consciences or become the victims of ruthless cruelty, they chose the last: exile from their dearly beloved country'.

In the end, half of the Reformed Presbyterian ministers in 1798 were implicated in the rebellion. Wylie's denial of involvement, like many others, should probably be taken with a pinch of salt.

In the autumn of 1797 he sailed for Philadelphia in the company of Rev. William Gibson of Ballymena and John Black a fellow probationary minister. In the following spring they met up with another radical who had had to flee to America, James McKinney, founder of Dervock Volunteers who had published a sermon which was denounced as treasonable. Together they formed the Reformed Presbytery of Philadelphia.

He first took a teaching position in Cheltenham and then the following year became an instructor in the grammar school part of Pennsylvanian University. Not that these exiled Ulster radicals were popular with everyone. William Cobbett denounced Wylie for his 'violent and daring' expressions. Cobbett had little time for the United Irish émigrés who had become teachers in Pennsylvania.

> These miscreants, not by their superior knowledge, but by their superior impudence, get admission into almost every country school that they fix their eyes upon ... when they were not indoctrinating their students with democratic ideology, they spent their days drinking and debauching.

Wylie studied theology in America and was formally recognised as a student by the newly formed Reformed Presbytery. He was licensed to preach by the Reformed Presbytery in June 1799. He and Alexander McCleod were considered for the role of minister by the united congregations of New York and Wallkill, which eventually voted in favour of McCleod. Wylie was ordained a year later in Ryegate, Vermont. He was appointed to a committee on slavery and one of his first tasks was to ride round ensuring that members of the Reformed Presbyterian Church were carrying out the edict of the church not to have slaves.

In 1802 he married Margaret Watson of Pittsburgh and had seven children, four of whom survived. In November 1803, after a visit to Europe, he became minister of the church they founded when they arrived in Pennsylvania and professor of the new theological seminary in Philadelphia in 1810. He was a professor there until 1817 and again from 1823 to 1828 and also a professor of Latin and Greek at the University of Pennsylvania from 1828 to 1845. He died on 13 October 1852.

Sources: *Dictionary of American Biography*; McBride 1998; Wilson 1998.

Alexander Lowry
1773–after 1823

Alexander Lowry was born 1773 at Dumballroney, Linen-hill, Ballyroney, between Rathfriland and Dromara in south County Down. He was a linen draper. When the Volunteer movement was established to defend the country against foreign invasion, Lowry was elected captain of Ballyroney Volunteers and staged a military review in Rathfriland on 19 October 1792.

He became a member of the United Irishmen and was actively involved with Catholic John Magennis of Balooly in trying to bring together the Presbyterian-dominated United Irishmen, who were strong in north Down and the mainly Catholic Defenders, who were stronger in south Down, to create a joint movement. In May 1797 Lowry was involved in supporting and advising United Irishmen who were prisoners on trial at the Armagh and Carrickfergus. In June 1797 Lowry and Magennis met a group of twelve to fourteen hundred Defenders and tried to persuade them to immediate action. A Dr Malcolmson urged caution, and to prevent any action being taken, informed on them to Lord Annesley, who sent in mounted fencibles from Dromore to disperse them.

With the introduction of martial law in 1797 and the imprisonment of many United Irishmen, Lowry and others were forced to flee the country. Maginnis's home was burnt down by Annesley's yeomen, with Magennis just avoiding capture. Lowry also escaped and managed to get to Norway where he eventually married Christina Zedlitz on 24 April 1802. He then went to America, but eventually returned to Ireland. He died sometime after 1823.

Sources: Robinson 1998; (www.freepages.genealogy.rootsweb.ancestry.com).

William Orr
1774–1860

This William Orr, not be confused with his cousin, William Orr, from the same area who was born in 1766 and executed in 1797 (see profile). This William Orr was born in Creavery near Kilbegs, County Antrim in 1774 (twelve years younger than his cousin), the son of James and Eliza Orr. He trained as a watchmaker in Dublin and returned to the area in 1797, the year his cousin was executed. On 7 June in 1798 he took part in the rising in Randalstown, when they beat and disarmed the military. Samuel Orr led part of the rebel army to destroy the bridge at Toome. When the army, led by Colonel Clavering, arrived to put down the rebels, he threatened to burn down Randalstown if they did not surrender. Three-quarters of the rebels submitted. Two hundred remained, and as the loyalist prisoners had not been released, Clavering fulfilled his threat and burnt the town. The remaining rebels marched off to Ballymena, some of whom, including Samuel Orr, joined Henry Joy McCracken on Slemish mountain. William went into hiding. The retribution on the Orr clan for suspected involvement in the rising was severe: the homes of Samuel Orr of Kilbegs, John Orr of the Folly, his son Samuel of Harp Hill, and the widow of William Orr of Farranshane and their six children were all burnt down. A £100 reward was offered for William, John and Samuel Orr who were all in hiding. In July 1798, John fled to America.

The evidence suggests that William Orr continued his involvement with the 'Liberty men', attending meetings of United Irishmen at night, taking arms from loyalists and punishing informers by flogging.

After William Orr was captured, potential witnesses were threatened and bribed to implicate him, but almost all refused to do so. He was charged with a long list of offences including treason and rebellion. Unfortunately, the year before he had had an argument with a James Mayse and accused him of stealing some of his clothes. During the trial Mayse claimed that he witnessed Orr's offences, including raiding houses for arms and masquerading as a Colonel Green. Orr argued that he was completely innocent of the charges and that the one witness was unreliable. He offered to go voluntarily to America. In the end he was sentenced to serve in the army of the King of Prussia.

He sailed in the prison ship, *William and James,* to New Geneva near Cork and then on, not to Prussia, but to Botany Bay in Australia on board the *Friendship.* After 166 days and 19 deaths they eventually arrived in Sydney. While he was in Australia his mother used whatever influence she could to lobby for a pardon for her son, which was eventually granted, on a conditional basis, by 1803. In 1805, Orr left Australia, but did not return to Ireland, rather he sailed to Calcutta in India, where he adopted the name

William Jamieson. The following year he left Calcutta and moved to Penang in what is now Malaysia, and remained there for the following fourteen years.

Eventually, in 1822 he decided to return home to Ireland and travelled home on the *Amity*. He had obviously done well enough for himself in the Far East as on arriving home he was able to buy a house at Newgrove near Broughshane, County Antrim, and nearly 70 acres of land. Now aged 50 he married Ellen Killen, the daughter of local man, John Killen. They had no children. William Orr died on 27 December 1860, aged 86. He is buried in Kirkinrola.

Sources: Foy 1999.

William Porter
1774–1843

William Porter was born in Cranny near Omagh, County Tyrone in 1774, the son of farmer and strict Calvinist, John Porter and his second wife, Jane (née Nixon). He received part of his education in jail when his teacher was arrested for debt, but was permitted to continue teaching in jail. He was then educated by Rev. Andrew Millar, the Presbyterian minister of Clogher, County Tyrone. In 1791 he went to Glasgow University, where he graduated in 1795 and then went to Edinburgh to study theology, where his father felt the teaching would be more orthodox than in Glasgow, the cradle of the Scottish Enlightenment.

In 1798 he was licensed to preach by the presbytery of Strabane. It seems that, unlike some other Presbyterian ministers and probationers, he was not involved with the United Irishmen and the 1798 rebellion, although he joined with Henry Montgomery to take up the case of Rev. William Steel Dickson, who, having been involved in 1798, was denied the *regium donum* grant, and ended his days in poverty and was buried in a pauper's grave.

In 1799 Porter was ordained and became minister of Limavady and remained there for the rest of his life. A month after being ordained he married Mary Scott, who died not long after the birth of their son John Scott (see profile). In 1811 he married Eliza Classon, a former governess of Archibald Hamilton Rowan (see profile).

Porter was appointed clerk of the Presbyterian General Synod in 1816 and admitted to a commission, that was set up to investigate allegations against the Belfast Academical Institution, that he was an Arian and, as a result, was attacked by Cooke in the 1827 Synod meeting in Strabane. He said that the reason for the attacks on him in relation to his Arianism, were actually due to his support for Catholic Emancipation. Synod debated what should be done with Porter who, even his enemies accepted, had discharged his duties with 'ability and fidelity'. It was finally agreed to express 'high disapprobation' of his religious views, but allow him to remain in his job as Clerk.

In 1829, in the debate over appointments to the Belfast Academical Institution, Porter, as the only declared non-subscriber remaining, presented the *Remonstrance* signed by 18 ministers which led to the withdrawal of the non-subscribing ministers and congregations to form the Remonstrant Synod.

Porter died in 1843. His sons, John Scott, Classon and James Nixon became non-subscribing Presbyterian ministers. His son William (see profile) became a lawyer and then Attorney General in the Cape Colony in Africa, where he developed a reputation for integrity in standing by his liberal principles of equality between blacks and whites. The youngest son, Francis followed William to the Cape.

Sources: Campbell 1991; Holmes 2000; McBride 1998; McCracken 1993; McCracken 2001; Newman 1993.

William Neilson (also spelled Nelson)
1774–1821

William Neilson was born in Kilmore, County Down in 1774, the fourth son of Rev. Moses Neilson of Castlederg, who came to minister in Rádemon near Crossgar, County Down, preaching in Irish. His Mother Catherine (née Welsh) was a direct descendent of John Knox.

In 1789, William Neilson went to Glasgow University and afterwards helped in his father's school. He was licensed by Armagh Presbytery and ordained a minister in Kilmore, Dundalk in 1796, where he preached in Irish. He opened an inter-denominational school there, which was attended by all denominations. Students from his school went on to Trinity College Dublin, Maynooth and the Scottish universities. He published a textbook of *Greek Exercises* and then in 1808 he published a substantial *Introduction to the Irish language,* in which he said,

> In this language are preserved the remarkable annals of our country ... It has been said, indeed that the use of this language should be abolished and the English prevail universally ... It is surely reasonable and desirable that every person should be able to hold converse with his countrymen as well as to taste and admire the beauties of one of the most expressive, philosophically accurate and polished languages that has ever existed.

The subscription list to fund the publication included Rev. William Steel Dickson. He followed up his *Introduction* with an educational text, the first of its kind, in the Irish language. He preached regularly in Irish and was once arrested in Rademon by the Yeomanry for doing so. In June 1813 there was a notice in the *Newry Telegraph* announcing his intention to preach in Irish in the local meetinghouse in a few days' time. The editor added a note underneath the notice to say that 'to those who are proficient in Irish or who have made some progress in learning that language, the discourse of the learned doctor will be a source of much gratification and improvement'.

Neilson became president of the Belfast Literary Society and published the earliest printed folk-tale in Irish. In 1819, he retired from the ministry and was appointed Professor of Hebrew and Oriental Languages at the Belfast Academical Institution and at the Old College Belfast. While he was at the Institution he established Irish classes. There had always been a tradition of Irish speaking within the church, but this was boosted when in 1835 the Presbyterian Synod of Ulster made it 'imperative on candidates for holy orders' to learn Irish.

In the first edition of the *Ulster Journal of Archaeology*, the editor wrote of the debt to those who have helped promote the Irish language and 'nor must we omit that of our townsman, Dr. Neilson, to whose exertions, at a critical moment, we are, perhaps, indebted for a renewed interest in the ancient language'.

His three brothers each also founded schools in their own areas. His brother Andrew was one of the non-subscribing ministers who withdrew into the Non-Subscribing Remonstrant Synod.

William Neilson was awarded membership of the Royal Academy of Ireland and an honorary doctorate from Glasgow University. He died in 1821, aged 47, when he had just heard that he had been appointed Professor of Greek at Glasgow University.

Sources: Blaney 1996; Ó Snodaigh 1995.

William Putnam McCabe
1776–1821

William McCabe was born around 1776 to Thomas McCabe (see profile), a Belfast watchmaker, who had been involved with Wolf Tone in forming the United Irishmen. William played an important role in the United Irish newspaper, the *Northern Star*. In April 1793 Thomas Russell wrote in his journal about a meeting with McCabe and Samuel Neilson in Belfast, in which he says that,

> The spirit of the north is high … burning with indignation against government. They say they have gone the greatest lengths [to] hold

out their hands to the nation to join them in the reform but they have refused … From all this they conclude the sense of the country is against them … they feel disgusted at the conduct of Ireland.

In 1794, the Attorney General filed a libel action against McCabe and several others for the *Northern Star's* seditious material. In 1796 he was involved in organising the United Irishmen in the south of Ireland.

He was arrested in May 1798, but managed to bluff his way out of jail and participated in the rebellion. After the rebels were defeated he escaped to England where he promoted the uprising there. He then moved to France, but found little support for Ireland's cause. After a failure in establishing a cotton factory in Rouen he left France in 1803 and lived in Scotland. In 1814, while on a visit to Ireland, he was arrested and escorted out of the country. He eventually received a pardon, on the grounds of permanent exile. He died in 1821.

Sources: Bradbury 2002; Campbell 1991; Killen 1997.

John Gamble
1777–1831

John Gamble was born in 1770 in Strabane, County Tyrone. He trained as a doctor in Edinburgh and became an army surgeon serving in Holland. He loved to travel and journeyed extensively around Ireland, which he recorded in a series of books, which were published between 1810 and 1819, including *A View of Society and Manners in the North of Ireland,* and *Sketches of Dublin and the North of Ireland.* He also travelled more widely around Europe. He wrote various historical novels, including *Northern Irish tales.*

He described his fellow Presbyterians as 'an active, intelligent, frugal, honest and thinking body of men'. He considered that 'A love of liberty, indeed, is an essential feature in the northern character'. He was disturbed by the extent of immigration and bitterly regretted that because of 'oppressions, exactions and hardships' 'so valuable a … people' should be 'leaving their country in thousands'. However, he observed the change that took place in those who did emigrate. While in Ireland 'they become the greatest enemies of its government and institutions' in America 'they become the most valuable citizens, and zealous supporters of a government, founded, as they deem it is, on their beloved Rights of Man'. 'They are not obliged to … bend the knee, to any stern Lord, arrogant Squire, proud Vicar, or … upstart Agent'.

In 'Orange Lilies and Bleach Greens', published as part of *A View of Society and Manners in the North of Ireland,* he recounts the story of a Presbyterian minister who signed a petition 'in favour of the Catholics'. The following Sunday he 'found his meetinghouse closed against him, nor is it yet opened'. He also described a conversation on the 12th of July with a little group who wanted to know his opinion on the Catholic Relief Bil:

> 'Never mind acts of parliament, my lads', said I, 'but live peaceably with your neighbours. I warrant you your fields will look as green, and your hedges smell as sweet this time next year, whether the bill passes or not'. 'Maybe so', said one of them; and 'maybe we wouldn't be long here to smell or look at them'.

He made little reply to this, because, as he said, he did not believe that anything would 'weaken … the rooted prejudices of their lives'.

Gamble died in 1831. His description of Strabane as being like 'Venice in miniature' is still remembered in his home town.

Sources: Craig 1992; Ferguson 2008.

William Hamilton Drummond
1778–1865

William Drummond was born in Larne, County Antrim in 1778, son of Dr William Drummond, a surgeon in the Royal Navy who died young, and Rose (née Hare). His brother, James Lawson Drummond, was founder and Head of the Medical School at Belfast Academical Institution. William Hamilton Drummond was educated at Belfast Academy under Drs Bruce and Crombie and went on to study at Glasgow University. Poverty prevented him completing his studies. However, he discovered a great gift for poetry and prose and wrote various publications, including *The Man of Age*, which described the poverty of the peasants in Ireland at that time, suggesting that Ireland was being misgoverned, which was the almost universal view of Presbyterians during this revolutionary period.

Although Drummond did not take part in the 1798 rebellion, he was in Larne when the rebellion occured and was stopped by a group of loyalists returning from battle, bent on revenge for the death of Lord O'Neill. They put a pistol to Drummond's head saying 'you young villain, it is you and the like of you brought this upon us, with your infernal poetry!' Fortunately he was saved by his companion who turned aside the soldier's gun.

Drummond was licensed by the Presbytery of Antrim in 1800, without having to subscribe to the Westminster Confession of Faith and became the minister of Second Belfast. He installed the first organ in a Presbyterian Church in the north of Ireland and composed a number of hymns himself. He was an active founding member of the Belfast Literary Society. In 1810 a Doctorate of Divinity was conferred on him by Aberdeen University. In

1815 he received a call from Strand Street congregation in Dublin, to work with Rev. Dr James Armstrong.

In 1827, he entered the theological controversy with the publication of various essays in support of Unitarianism, including, *The Doctrine of the Trinity, founded neither on Scripture, nor on Reason and Common Sense, but on Tradition and the Infallible Church.* This received a wide distribution in three editions in Britain and Ireland and at least one in America. It brought him into conflict with both Calvinists but also leading members in the Church of Ireland. With the success of this essay, he was asked to speak at various leading Unitarian forums in England and Scotland. He was opposed to the concept of original sin and was a strong believer of the place of reason in religion.

Far ahead of his time, Drummond believed that animals have rights and published a book on the subject in which he said that animals are 'not proper subjects of contempt or disregard, much less of inhumanity' and that 'man is cruel when he seizes animals, not for food but for pleasure; when he tortures before he kills; when he hunts or destroys for his amusement'.

In 1840, Drummond published an edited autobiography of the radical United Irishman, Archibald Hamilton Rowan. Drummond was elected a member of the Royal Irish Academy and was its librarian for many years.

Having suffered from a loss of memory and faculties for some time, he died in Dublin in 1865. One of his sons and one of his grandsons (1863–1945), of the same name (William Hamilton Drummond), went into the Unitarian ministry, in Edinburgh and Belfast respectively. His other son became principal of Manchester New College, a Unitarian theological college.

Sources: Baillie 1981; Blaney 1996; Hill *et al* 1998; Duddy (ed.) 2004.

Fletcher Blakely
1783–1862

Fletcher Blakely was born in 1783 in Ballyroney, County Down, the youngest son of Joseph Blakely a farmer. He was named after the local minister, Rev. William Fletcher, the minister of Ballyroney, who provided his early training. He was educated as a Presbyterian minister at Glasgow University and licensed by Dromore Presbytery in 1805. He was ordained by the Bangor Presbytery in Moneyrea, County Down in 1809.

Rev. Henry Montgomery (see profile) described Blakely as 'the first avowed humanitarian preacher in Ulster'. His ministry in Moneyrea was described as turning the town into 'a radiating centre of liberal thought and Unitarian doctrine in the North of Ireland' although another commentator described Moneyrea as the place 'where there is one God and no devil'. Blakely's brand of progressive thinking and advanced Unitarianism was more prevalent in the second half of the nineteenth century than the first. In 1821, when John Smethhurst was sent by the English Unitarians on a mission to Ulster, Blakely was the first to receive him. In 1830, along with other congregations that disapproved of subscription to the Westminster Confession of Faith, he and his congregation withdrew from the General Synod and formed the Remonstrant Synod.

He was strongly in favour of education and published various works including, *An explicit Avowal of Truth* (1853). He was joint editor of *Bible Christian* from 1830 to 1833.

He gave evidence in 1844 to the Devon Commission on the occupation of land in Ireland and in 1851 he wrote to the *Northern Whig* newspaper on the relation between landlord and tenant following the repeal of the Corn Laws:

> Matters are approaching a fearful crisis; and an hour should not be lost in enabling the industrious to see that they shall have, at least, a moderate return for their outlay ... landlords ... must bear a large share of the various evils which a continuation of the present unsettled relation between landlord and tenant will rapidly and largely increase ... compensation for permanent improvements would be a mutual benefit to landlord and tenant, and would, at the same time, serve the community by increasing the demand for labour, and thereby reducing the poor rates.

As a strong supporter of tenant right, he was a key participant in the first tenant right meeting in Ireland on 17 November 1835 and at many other meetings of tenant farmers, including in Comber (July 1845) and the Musical Hall in Belfast (March 1848). He published, *Letters on the Relation between Landlord and Tenant* (1951). He retired in 1857 but continued to preach until his successor was appointed. He died in Worcestershire in 1862. His son W. Joseph Blakely also became a Presbyterian minister in York Street, Belfast.

Sources: Haire 1981; Newman 1993.

John West
1784–1864

John West was born in 1784, the fourth son of Thomas West, a farmer in Tullyvallen, near Newtownhamilton. He was educated at Glasgow University from 1812, and trained for the Burgher ministry in the Theological Hall in Edinburgh in 1816. He was licensed to preach by

Markethill Presbytery on 27 March 1821, after only three sessions at the Theological Hall, rather than the usual four, and was ordained two years later on 9 September 1823 in Second Newtownhamilton, County Armagh, succeeding the Rev. Robert Clarke who moved to Perth, Scotland. Rev. West was to remain their minister for almost forty years and conducted an educational academy there for many years. In 1823 he married the sister of Rev. John Weir.

In 1843, when the government established the Devon Commission to investigate the relationship between landlords and tenants in Ireland, Rev. West gave evidence to the Commission, along with Rev. Daniel Gunn Brown. He expressed concern about the level of poverty, as 'the average price of wages is getting every year less', and the lack of jobs, 'in the neighbourhood a great many men willing to work, but what are not able to get employment.' To try and ameliorate the situation he recommended 'some security to encourage the tenant to improve, and that he should not lose what he had expended in improving the land or building houses; but that, when the lease dropped, the rent should not be raised.'

He retired from Second Newtownhamilton in 1862. He died on 21 November 1864, aged 80. His two sons, John Dobbin and Thomas both became ministers.

Sources: Devon Commission; Baillie and Kirkpatrick 2005.

James Carlile
1784–1854

James Carlile was born in 1784, the first son of James Carlile a merchant in Paisley, Scotland. He was educated in Paisley Grammar School and then Glasgow and Edinburgh Universities. He was licensed as a minister in Paisley and ordained in Mary's Abbey in Dublin on 4 May 1813, to become the assistant to Rev. Dr McDowell.

When a new educational system was proposed for Ireland on non-denominational grounds, whereby Protestant, Catholic and Dissenter children would be educated together and religious education would only be provided by the ministers of the relevant denominations on an equal footing, many in the Protestant churches were very unhappy about the access that this would give priests to school children. Carlile, however, recognised the proposed system could do much to heal divisions in Irish society. However, in January 1832, at a poorly attended meeting of Synod, he was the only person to speak in favour of the proposed system. The history of Ireland may have been different if this argument had won the day, but unfortunately it did not. Although a majority of Presbyterian ministers voted in favour, the majority of church elders attending Synod voted in support of Henry Cooke who was against the system, which he said would 'encourage Popery', as he was against the Whig government which introduced it.

Carlile accepted an appointment as one of six commissioners of National Education, who would administer the system: two Roman Catholic, two Church of Ireland and two Protestant Dissenters, and later became Resident Commissioner. However, relationships between the Board and the Presbyterian Church rapidly deteriorated.

Ministers who connected their schools with the new Board were often persecuted by their congregations. The Presbyterian Church began to set up its own schools and put pressure on the National Educational Board to fund them. In the end, the pressure paid off and the Board funded the first Presbyterian school near Broughshane, County Antrim, despite the fact that it clearly did not comply with the requirements of the new National Educational system. Leading Roman Catholics like Archbishop Machale of Tuam also wanted exclusively denominational schools. From that point on, the educational system became a largely denominational one.

Carlile, although an evangelical theologically, defended the principle of non-subscription to the Westminster Confession of Faith against Henry Cooke and in 'Jesus Christ, the Great God and our Saviour', made it clear that the doctrine of the Trinity is inferred, rather than being a result of direct biblical revelation.

In support of the Belfast Academical Institution, Carlile eloquently rejected the threats of Lord Castlereagh to the institution, in the following words,

> Who or what is this Lord Castlereagh, that he should send such a message to the Synod of Ulster? Is he a minister of this body? Is he an elder? What right has he to obtrude himself on our deliberations? I revere the government of my country. I pay it a willing obedience in matters civil ... but I protest against government dictating an opinion as to the measures we should adopt for the interests of religion. As long as I can raise my voice, I will raise it against the principle of admitting civil governors, as such, to be heard in our deliberations ... this day's decision will tell whether we deserve to rank as an upright, independent, conscientious body, with no other end in view than the glory of God and the welfare of his church, or whether we deserve that Lord Castlereagh should drive his chariet into the midst of us and tread us down as the offal of the streets.

During the Great Irish Famine, to alleviate the economic hardship and distress, during which his own sister died, Carlile did considerable relief work.

In 1840 he was called to the Presbyterian Church in Birr, County Offaly, as a missionary of his St Mary's Dublin congregation. He received a doctorate from Glasgow University in 1844. He was elected Moderator of the General Synod (an annual appointment by election) in 1845. In his sermon at the Assembly as moderator, he made a plea for the open discussion of religious differences, praising the Synod of Ulster because its constitution allowed ministers to differ.

He died in Dublin in 1854 and was buried in Birr. His son, Warrand Carlile became a Presbyterian minister and went as a missionary to Jamaica.

Sources: Brooke 1994; Holmes 1985; Holmes 2000.

William McEwen
1787–1828

William Dalzell Huey McEwan was born in 1787, the eldest son of Rev. George McEwen, Presbyterian minister of Killinchy. He was educated in Glasgow, receiving his MA in 1806 and was licensed to preach by the Belfast Presbytery in 1807. He was ordained in 1808 in Usher's Quay (Ormond Quay), Dublin, as a colleague of Rev. Hugh Moore.

He married Jane Maxwell, whose father Thomas Maxwell from Ballygraffan near Comber was implicated in the 1798 rising and put to death. In 1813 he was installed in First Killyleagh, County Down, of which Archibald Rowan Hamilton was a member of the congregation. He was initially believed to be evangelical in theology but became 'new light'. He invited John Smithurst, an English Socinian, who disputed the divinity of Jesus, to preach, when he was on a tour in Ireland.

When McEwan was called to Second Belfast Non-Subscribing Presbyterian congregation in Belfast in 1817, he was succeeded in Killyleagh by Henry Cooke, who would later become the leading arch-conservative in the Presbyterian Church in Ireland. McEwan remained at Second Belfast until his death.

He became a part-time Professor of Elocution at the Belfast Academical Institution and was accused, along with two others, of holding unorthodox theological views by Henry Cooke. While a lecturer at the Academical Institution, he gave volumes of the works of Unitarian, Dr Richard Price, as prizes to his pupils, which enraged the strictly orthodox Cooke. He was later secretary of the Academical Institution and, with John Barnett, spent much time in London lobbying MPs to have the Institution's annual grant restored, which was eventually achieved in 1828.

He acted as temporary editor of the *Northern Whig* for a while with the help of two young law students, R.J. and Emerson Tennent, members of the well-known Tennent family (see profile).

McEwan died in College Square, Belfast in 1828, at the relatively young age of 41 and was buried in Killinchy. He was survived by his wife, Jane, and six children.

Sources: Brooke 1994; McCreery 1875; notes provided by Rev. John Nelson.

Henry Montgomery
1788–1865

Henry Montgomery was born in Killead, County Antrim in 1788. He attended a Sunday School in Lylehill organised by the Secession congregation's first minister Rev. Isaac Patton, who had been Jemmy Hope's minister. He was only ten when the 1798 rebellion took place, but he had two brothers who participated and the family home was burnt by the Yeomanry, which Montgomery remembered well.

He was educated at Crumlin Academy and the University of Glasgow. In 1800 he was ordained as a Presbyterian minister in Dunmurry, County Antrim, near Belfast and remained a minister there until he died. He was licensed to preach in 1809 and ordained the following year.

In Synod in 1812 Montgomery defended the elderly Rev. William Steel Dickson (see profile), who had been a leading spokesman for reform and had been arrested as one of the leaders of the 1798 rebellion, who published a memoir, *A narrative of the Confinement and Exile of William Steel Dickson.* Montgomery also spoke in favour of each church paying its own minister and not having the *regium donum* financial support from the state.

In 1817 Montgomery became a part-time Head of English at the Belfast Academical Institution and defended the institution against attacks from Henry Cooke who described it as 'a seminary of Arianism'.

Montgomery was a strong opponent of the tithe system, whereby farmers and the agricultural classes, regardless of their religion, had to pay a tithe, which went to the Established Church. In giving evidence to two parliamentary committees investigating tithes, he made a wide-ranging attack on the financing of the Established Church and its role in society. He saw the tithe system as a way of taxing poor people for the benefit of the wealthy, causing misery and hardship for centuries.

There were tremendous clashes between Henry Cooke and Henry Montgomery in the General Synods of 1827–9. Montgomery was a cultivated man who believed strongly in doctrinal pluralism and non-subscription to the Westminster Confession of Faith.

Montgomery saw that it was by 'uniting evangelicalism with orangeism' and 'the countenance of the aristocracy with the applause of the multitude' that Cooke had acquired 'extra-ordinary popularity and influence' (Holmes 1985).

Montgomery insisted that statements of doctrine – creeds or confessions

– were unscriptural and unsatisfactory tests of Christian faith. He also held that enforcing a belief in the man-made unscriptural doctrine of the Trinity was making an opinion the test of faith.

Cooke, however, persuaded the Synod to affirm its own Trinitarian belief and to establish a theological examination committee to test the theological convictions and personal religious experience of future candidates for the ministry, thus ensuring that only orthodox and evangelical candidates would be accepted.

Montgomery and his supporters tried to have this decision overturned but to no avail. Although supported by forty ministers in the General Synod, he was forced to lead the accession of three presbyteries and seventeen congregations into a Remonstrant Synod which eventually became the Non-Subscribing Presbyterian Church. Further bitterness was caused by disputes over ownership of the properties and endowments of the churches which supported the non-subscription side in the dispute. Orthodox minorities in congregations claimed that they were the true heirs to the properties and endowments, thus leading to very serious and acrimonious disputes at congregational level, often resulting in legal action. The disputes were only resolved by the passing of the Dissenters Chapels Act which allowed the non-subscribing congregations to retain the properties, if anti-Trinitarian doctrines had been taught in them for 'a reasonable period'.

Some of the younger ministers in the Remonstrant Synod wanted to go further than Montgomery in their theological thinking. Montgomery was so concerned about the extent of some of this radical thinking amongst the non-subscribing ministers that he attempted to introduce a Code of Discipline, including three questions for new ministers, to curb this enthusiasm for rationalism. In the face of the opposition, Montgomery had to back down in the end because of difficulties with the legal interpretation of the questions.

Montgomery was strongly in favour of Catholic Emancipation, but opposed Daniel O'Connell and his campaign for the repeal of the Act of Union. In response to O'Connell, Montgomery stated that,

> The liberal dissenters of Ireland, from North and South, who to a man, had been the zealous advocates of Catholic emancipation, and who at present no less united in the great cause of rational and effectual Reform ... are the uncompromising friends of liberty, they are equally the determined enemies of anarchy and confusion.
> 'A letter to Daniel O'Connell' Henry Montgomery ,(1991 edition)

Montgomery was a powerful theologian and eloquent speaker. He remained a minister in Dunmurry for fifty years. He died in 1865.

Sources: Boyd 1999; Brooke 1994; Campbell 1991; Hickey and Doherty 2005; Holmes 2000; Holmes 1985; McBride 1998; Montgomery 1831; Newman 1993; Seery *et al* 2000; Wright 1996.

John Brown
1788–1873

John Brown was born in 1788, the second son of Samuel Brown, a farmer in Garvagh, County Londonderry. He was educated in Glasgow University where he received his MA in 1813. He was licensed to preach by Route Presbytery in 1813 and was ordained as Presbyterian minister of Aghadowey, County Londonderry, 14 December 1813, when his brother Rev. Solomon Brown preached the sermon. In 1820, his own sermon, *The importance of Learning to Society and the Christian Ministry* was published. In 1832 he was elected moderator of the General Synod and agitated for an equalisation of the *regium donum* grant. He was theologically orthodox and in 1835 supported unqualified subscription to the Westminster Confession of Faith. He received an honorary doctorate in 1839.

He was politically Liberal and was a leading critic of ultra-Tory Edward Litton MP for Coleraine from 1837 to 1842. Litton initiated a libel action against Brown to try and silence him. When Litton was appointed master of chancery, John Boyd stood as the Liberal candidate. Brown, a member of the newly formed Coleraine Church Defence Association, published a letter to Boyd seeking his assurance that he would not step aside for a government nominee or abandon the Presbyterian cause for office. Brown eventually agreed to support Boyd's candidature.

At the Presbyterian General Assembly of 1843, with still little representation of Presbyterians in the House of Commons at Westminster, which, in terms of Irish representation, was still dominated by the gentry, who were generally members of the Established Church, he moved a resolution recommending the adoption of measures for securing the more adequate representation of Presbyterian principles and interests in the legislature. This was opposed by Rev. Henry Cooke, who was trying to forge an alliance with the Anglican Ascendancy. When he was defeated on this issue, Cooke withdrew from the Assembly for several years. The following year, Brown was elected moderator of the General Assembly. He was a supporter of the creation of an independent Presbyterian college to train its ministers, which was achieved with the foundation of Magee College in Derry.

Brown supported the struggle for tenant right, which he defined as 'the interest a tenant should have in the capital he has expended in money and labour, in building houses and making improvements'. In his view 'recognition of the tenant-right prevents their country being overstocked with a class of paupers, and causes every man to feel that he has a stake in the hedge', but he acknowledged that some landlords, including the London Livery Companies, who were trying to impose English customs, were trying to avoid their responsibilities under the Ulster Custom, 'I must say with deep regret, that many efforts have been made to deprive the tenant of that right.'

He was actively involved in campaigning meetings of the tenant right campaign in County Antrim, as did many other Presbyterian ministers. He gave extensive evidence to the Devon Commission, set up in 1843 to consider the relationship between landlords and tenants in Ireland. Under examination he said that 'Small farmers live in a state of misery it is painful to contemplate ... [and] ... the most enterprising, industrious and virtuous part of the people are quitting the country'. He warned that if the situation continued for twelve years that 'there will rise up a miserable class of people prepared for any impropriety'. He recommended that tenants should be given long leases, that the benefits of taxes paid should be distributed fairly and the Grand Jury System should be completely reformed and become elected.

Brown, along with Dr McKnight (see profile), became an active Presbyterian supporter of Samuel McCurdy Greer who stood as a Liberal in elections in South Derry and was successfully elected at a by-election in 1857.

During his career, Brown published more than thirty pamphlets. Topics included support for education and the Belfast Academical Institution; oppression in Ireland, where, he says, 'the energies of her peasantry are paralyzed by the iron grasp of ruthless minions, her wealth squandered in the giddy circles of a haughty rival, and her population [compelled] to crouch to superiors in foreign lands, being literally hewers of wood and drawers of water'; sectarian violence; and marches and commemorations in Derry, which he argued, 'often lead to intemperance, and thus prepare for brawls and discord' where participants are 'injured physically and morally, and their social peace and harmony destroyed.' He observed that the first commemoration of the siege was celebrated by local Catholics, including the bishop.

Brown retired in 1872 and died a year later aged 85. His brother, Solomon, was a Presbyterian minister, as was his nephew, John. Solomon's son, Samuel, became the Mayor of Belfast.

Sources: Brooke 1994; Dowling 1999; Hall 2011; Wright 1996.

Thomas Beggs
1789–1847

Thomas Beggs was born in 1789 in Glenwherry, County Antrim. His father was a labourer and his mother was cousin of poet James Orr of Ballycarry (see profile). In 1794 his family moved to Whiteabbey, County

Antrim where he developed a love of the sea. He got a job on a coasting vessel, but after a shipwreck off Rathlin Island he returned home to work on the family's new smallholding in Ballyclare. When a position with a Belfast linen firm fell through in 1819 he undertook a walking tour of the north coast, which resulted in the poem 'Rathlin'.

He published poems in *The Banner of Ulster* and *Belfast Newsletter*. His first collection, *Miscellaneous Pieces in Verse* was published in 1819 by F.D. Finlay, editor of the *Northern Whig*, but, with 'want of liberal patronage' had to rely on the support of his family. He then published *The Rhyming Pedagogues* in 1821, which included an elegy to James Orr. In 1825 he was employed at a bleach works at Cottonmount, near Belfast and married. He published *The Momento* in 1818 and *Nights in a Garret*. After he moved to a new job in Ardoyne, Belfast he published a book of prose, in 1830 and *The Minstrel's Offering* in 1834. He found himself out of work again and his family moved in with his brother, but he still produced a second volume of *The Minstrel's Offering* in 1836. He returned to work in Cottonmount, where he lived in 'a neat cottage standing on the bank of a solitary stream surrounded by trees and cultivated fields'.

He died of typhus in July 1847 and is buried in Ballylinny near Ballyclare. *The Poetical Works of Thomas Beggs, Ballyclare* was published posthumously.

Sources: Ferguson 2008; Hewitt 2004.

William Brown
Died 1860

William Brown was the first son of Robert Brown a farmer near Cookstown, County Tyrone. He was educated at Glasgow University where he gained his MA in 1808. He was licensed by Tyrone Presbytery in 1810. He became the fourth minister of the Presbyterian congregation in Tobermore, County Londonderry, where he was ordained on 20 November 1810. He was the author of a treatise in support of electoral and land reform, *The Philosophy of Intimidation: Historical Sketches on the Elective Franchise, Its Defects and Remedies*. In the preface he describes the purpose of his pamphlet as follows:

> The design of this Work is to exhibit the cause of the feature incident to the social condition of Ireland that the tenant must vote as the landlord orders; and to point out the remedy for this painful state. The cause is – the dependant condition of the Irish tenant.
>
> The sure remedy would be such a modification of the feudal laws

bearing on land as would introduce free trade in land. Free trade in land would soon cause large portions of that property, now in hands of a few great proprietors, to flow into the hands of the many. These having what they could call their own, would soon think and act independently.

When feudalism became established in Ireland, that grim power addressed landlords and agents, saying – And the fear of you, and the dread of you, shall be upon every cottier tenant, and every tenant at will that moveth upon the earth; into your hand they are delivered, that you may use them on occasion of elections to advance the interests of your families and friends; into your hand they are delivered.

You in Ulster will recognise tenant-right. The recognition of that right will entitle you to the votes of your tenants. Having done them much good by recognising the tenant-right, you will draw them towards you with chords of love, and the bands of a man. Forget not to recognise tenant- right. The moment you break the compact the tenants will then be free to vote as they please. Viewing you as covenant-breakers and false, they will no longer on their shoulders carry you into Parliament; but will be longing for the opportunity to vote against you, and to return men good and true.

Whilst thus, by means of feudalism, the landlord in Ireland can control the tenant in the matter of his vote, it is pleasing to observe there are many landlords who do not avail themselves of their privilege, but allow their tenants to vote as they please. Instances of this nature, however, are the exceptions to the law of constraint which is the rule.

May the Lord grant unto our nobles more enlightened views of their duty as landlords, and to our Parliament wisdom to devise, and power to execute a measure calculated to restore to the electors of Ireland that free and unhindered exercise of the franchise, which is their birthright, but of which they have been hindered hitherto.

Brown had a reputation as a strong advocate of free thought and speech. He also wrote a pamphlet on the subject of Baptism. He was minister of Tobermore for 50 years and died on 19 April 1860. The vacancy was filled by Mr William Anderson.

Sources: Brown 1856; MacConnell, *Fasti* 1951.

Robert Gray
1792–1857

Robert Gray was born in Dungiven near Maghera in 1792, son of John Gray, a tenant farmer. He was educated at Glasgow University where he gained an MA in 1815. He was licensed by Tyrone Presbytery in 1817 and was ordained two years later in Scriggan near Derry on 21 December 1819 and was their minister for almost fourteen years. He was called by the congregation of Burt, County Donegal in 1833 and was installed as their minister on 15 October that year.

Gray was actively involved in the tenant right movement, attending an Ulster Tenant Right Association dinner in 1833. He also participated in various other tenant right meetings, including speaking at a campaigning meeting of the Ulster Tenant Right Association in Londonderry in the late 1840s. In the 1840s he gave evidence to the Devon Commission on the plight of tenants in Ireland. He was very aware that 'Small tenants are in difficult circumstances' and argued that,

> A man, whether he has a lease or not, has a right, or should be allowed to sell his interest in the land … [and] … Taking away what we call the tenant-right at the caprice of the agent, without giving any remuneration to the occupying tenant, which I think is a great source of distress and crime.

He recommended the establishment of,

> [a] law, giving the tenant an interest in his land for substantial improvements, that would entitle him to it …Tenants possessing land … should be allowed, at the end of their terms or leases, a fair remuneration for their building, draining, fencing, and so on … in proportion to the sum expended.

He also recommended that commissioners should establish the level of rents on the basis of the price of wheat, oats and barley every three years. Unfortunately the Devon Commission did not come out in favour of legalising tenant right.

Gray was also a supporter of the non-denominational National Education system and at a crucial meeting of Synod in 1834 spoke in favour of it, in opposition to the conservatives who wanted to retain church control of denominational schools.

He was clerk of the Derry Presbytery from 1844 to 1857. Gray died on 19 October 1857.

Sources: Nelson 2005.

James Haughton
1795–1873

James Haughton was born in Carlow on 5 May 1795, the son of Samuel Pearson Haughton, a lapsed member of the Society of Friends and Mary (née Pim). Soon after he was born his parents left the Society of Friends. At the age of twelve he was sent as a boarder to school in Ballitore, County Kildare, under Quaker James White. After three years he returned to Carlow to assist his stepbrothers in their business. In 1812 he went to Cork to learn more about business from an uncle. After five years he moved to Dublin to work for another uncle and set up a business first with his brother, John, in the corn and flour trade and then his brother William.

In 1834 he joined Strand Street congregation in Dublin, where Rev. William Hamilton Drummond and Rev. James S Armstrong were 'new light' ministers.

He was a staunch opponent of slavery. He regarded slave-owners as wilful criminals, 'the doers of the sum of all crimes and wickedness'. He attended the anti-slavery conventions of 1838 and 1840 and wrote a memoir of Thomas Clarkson the anti-slavery campaigner.

He campaigned vigorously against capital punishment. He was concerned about poverty and the misery of the poor and proposed an amendment to the poor law to provide paid work. During and after the Famine he raised money, with people from other denominations for victims of the Famine. He was a supporter of tenant right.

Haughton was a peace campaigner and held to the principle that 'all war is anti-Christian – that a Christian should not, under any circumstances, deprive his fellow-creature of life.' He wrote frequently about British misrule and injustice in India. In the period leading up to the Crimean War he campaigned vigorously to try and prevent a declaration of war.

He proposed a campaign to ban hunting, shooting, fishing and cruelty to domestic animals to the Society for the Prevention of Cruelty to Animals that Wilberforce had helped found.

He was a supporter of Catholic emancipation and the repeal of the Act of Union. He became a friend of Daniel O'Connell who he described as 'the friend of universal liberty, civil and religious', visiting him in prison after he was arrested. He encouraged those campaigning for repeal to use moral not physical force. 'That which is morally wrong cannot be politically right'. An opponent of all forms of prejudice, he wrote,

> What a miserable feeling this religious bigotry is! It alienates men who wold otherwise live in brotherly love, and all is done in the name of the blessed Being, who has left it upon record that, if we would be his disciples 'we must love one another'.

After the Young Irelanders split from O'Connell's Repeal Association, Haughton tried to mediate to achieve reconciliation between the two groups. He resigned from the Young Ireland convention when they sent a letter of thanks to US Vice-President George Mifflin Dallas, who was a slave-owner, but failed to condemn slavery in the letter.

Haughton campaigned to have a 'People's garden' created in Phoenix Park Dublin; free admission to the Botanical gardens; the establishment of the Dublin Mechanics Institute to provide education for the working classes; and reduced admission charges on Sunday to Dublin Zoo.

He was a supporter of parliamentary reform and an extension to the franchise, including to women. He became a vegetarian in 1846, becoming president of the British Vegetarian Society, as well as being actively involved in the inter-denominational temperance movement. He was a generous philanthropist giving to a range of liberal and progressive causes.

For his wide range of reforming campaigns, he and his fellow campaigners were nicknamed as the 'everythingarians' and for his involvement in the temperance movement he earned the nickname 'Son of a Water Drinker'.

He died in Dublin on 20 February 1873 in the house he had occupied for the previous forty years.

Sources: Delany 2007; Haughton 1877; Rowlands 1971.

William Kirk
1795–1870

William Kirk was born to Mr Hugh Kirk and Eliza (née Miller) in Larne, County Antrim in 1795 and educated at a local school. He followed in his father's footsteps and became a linen merchant and bleacher. He also acted as agent for one of the Belfast banks. He was a member of the local Presbyterian Church and then joined the church in Keady in south Armagh, when he moved there around 1820. With his expanding linen business in the area he built houses for his workers and set up a school in Darkley. He was a founder member of the Ulster Liberal Society. He married Miss Ann McKean, whose father, James, resided in Darkley House, in 1820. Her father was also involved with linen. In 1840 he became a magistrate in Armagh.

He was very conscious of the extent of emigration from Ireland to America during the nineteenth century and the importance of the money that those who emigrated were able to send home. As Kirk told a select committee, 'what you trample on in Ireland will sting you in America'.

Ulster Presbyterians realised that they were not going to be able to get tenant right effectively legalised without strong political representation at

Westminster. Existing representatives tended to be landlords or agents of landlords. In May 1852 in *A Plain Appeal to the Presbyterian Electors of Newry* Kirk stated that:

> The Presbyterian interest has been used in this borough as a political convenience, as our Church has unfortunately been throughout the Province. Your opponents are now surprised to find that the Presbyterians of Newry are likely for the future to attend to their own interests, and that they will now support an independent candidate, without reference to landlord influence or Clique Nomination.

Kirk subsequently won the Newry seat at Westminster in 1852. He decided against standing in the 1859 election, but in 1866 stood in Armagh but failed to win the seat. In the 1868 general election he was again proposed for the Newry seat with broad Catholic and Presbyterian support. In his nomination speech, Kirk focused on his support for the disestablishment of the Church of Ireland and his commitment to religious equality. Kirk won with substantial Catholic support, defeating the Conservative Lord Newry by seven votes.

He was a supporter of the proposed non-sectarian National Education system, opposed by conservative elements within the Presbyterian and other churches. At a Free Trade banquet in Belfast in October 1852 he gave a toast to the National Educational system, 'It is hopeless to abate the prejudices amongst the old, they should therefore, educate the young together, to promote union amongst all'.

He initially refused to align himself with any party, saying that he would 'support the government or the opposition, or an independent member who will propose and strive to carry out measures to benefit this neglected country', and throughout his career there is evidence that he did just that. In later years one of his supporters, a Mr McGeorge, said that he tended to 'support measures rather than men'.

He learned early on the unpleasant truth that a person's policies can undergo a startling change during the relatively short journey from one side of the House to the other: 'Have we not men in power proposing and carrying measures which they opposed in Opposition?' and used this to justify his stance when he attracted criticism for not giving his allegiance to a specific party. At the outset he had insisted, 'I will join no party which will not be a party to serve the people', and continued to hold this line: '... no matter whether the measures they propose are measures borrowed from the Whigs, or whether they originate with the Tories, if they are good measures, I should give them my support.'

It was not until 1865 that he openly declared his support for the Liberals.

His public championing of the Ulster Custom of tenant right, his pleas for religious toleration, his insistence that Presbyterians needed a voice in Parliament and his pro-disestablishment stance gave him credibility with both Catholics as well as his fellow-churchmen. The fact that much of his business was carried on via the port of Newry guaranteed him support from its citizens, enabling him to carry the seat in 1852 and again in 1868.

He was a man with a liberal and improving cast of mind, caught up in the great movements for electoral reform, constitutional progress, social improvement, and industrial expansion. This was the age of John Stuart Mill, the Great Exhibition, a growing middle class imbued with a sense of personal dignity and public duty. It was also a period which saw a great flowering in the arts.

His main interests lay in the areas of free trade, religious equality, national education, and tenant right. Arguably, the issue of free trade was one which would materially affect his own business, but the easing of trade restrictions would also improve the prosperity of the town, and he outlined a scheme to introduce cotton manufacture, arguing that Ulster was importing a fabric which it had the skills to make, as well as promoting initiatives to create jobs for women. He supported electoral reform and the move towards a secret ballot, in particular, in order to leave tenants free to vote for their preferred candidate without being forced to follow the lead of their landlord by declaring their vote in public; he was instrumental in getting the railway system from Newry extended and improving the harbour.

He spoke out for equality for all whatever their background, while remaining an active and devout Presbyterian, 'I am now, as I ever have been, the advocate of Civil and Religious Liberty. What I claim for myself I concede to others, as I cannot but feel that if my neighbour's liberty is infringed, my own is in danger.'

In the election campaign of 1859 the deep-seated opposition to his liberal views became clear. He had signaled his intention to seek re-election, but there followed a series of scathing attacks and criticisms, which resulted in him deciding to stand down. The newspapers carried colourful descriptions of the methods employed to influence the outcome of the election,

> ... the Tory party are becoming more unscrupulous and desperate. Not content with serving notices to quit on electors who are known . to be favourable to Mr. Kirk, it is said that they have actually resorted to the infamous practice of man-stealing. We have heard that, on Sabbath last, they actually violated the sanctities of the Lord's Day, by making a bold effort literally to run away with one of Mr. Kirk's voters ... Let (the voters) beware of every man of the Tory faction who approaches them with an oily tongue, and who appears to be in a particularly jovial temperament.

Whether he was motivated by disgust at the depths to which the opposition would sink, or the pragmatism that convinced him that he was unlikely to win, is not clear, but his interest in politics was apparently undiminished, for in 1865, now retired from business, he again entered the arena, this time as a candidate for Armagh while his son, William Millar Kirk, contested, but failed to carry, the Newry seat. It was during this campaign that he declared openly for the liberals, but he failed to win the seat, perhaps because the conservative influence was still uppermost in the borough, or because he had lost the support of some of his co-religionists. A letter from 'A True Blue Presbyterian' to the editor of the *Belfast Newsletter* in July of 1865 is openly critical of his actions and skeptical of his good intentions,

> What are Mr. Kirk's claims on the Armagh constituency? He cannot pretend that he has any on the Conservative portion of the electors … on what pretence has he come forward as a Presbyterian candidate? If it be on the ground that he is a Presbyterian, the writer admits it; but there the claim ends; for on questions most affecting the honor and interests of the Presbyterian Church, Mr. Kirk in and out of Parliament has sacrificed the one and the other.

The writer goes on to accuse Kirk of siding with the government against the General Assembly over the matter of Presbyterian chaplains, and of failing to support the Assembly's agitation for an increase in the *regium donum* support for the clergy. Kirk was aware as far back as 1859 that Presbyterian support was dwindling, and he had tried to rally them,

> I feel it very hard to blame any class in the community, but I must say that I have not received that support from the Presbyterians to which I think I am entitled. I have at all times supported their rights; and I do think it extraordinary that a body of men, who ought to be sturdily upholding their own principles, should be found supporting an Episcopalian, and allowing themselves to be dragged at the chariot-wheels of a party who despise them.

His final appearance on the political stage was in 1868, when, returning to the hustings at Newry, he successfully contested his old seat. It is certainly not without significance that it was entirely due to the Catholic vote that he achieved his majority. By then he was entering upon his twilight years and a period of failing health, though he continued to attend parliament, and there is nothing to suggest that he did not take an intelligent interest in the affairs of state for as long as he was able. He stubbornly maintained his support for a just settlement of the land question, which would not begin to happen until Gladstone's Land Acts of

1870 and 1881, as well as continuing to work for the advancement of the town of Newry, so he ended where he had begun, as a member for, and staunch supporter of, the town through which so much of the output from his flourishing manufacturing concerns in the Callan valley left on its way into the wider world.

Some years before his death, he purchased the Keady estate comprising about 11,000 acres. The town of Keady grew from a poor village into a place of considerable size, with a thriving population. He was a Justice of the Peace, a member of the Grand Jury of the County Armagh and was appointed a Deputy-Lieutenant of the County.

He made generous contributions to the Church and Manse Funds. He was one of the founders of the Presbyterian Orphan Society and chairman of the Bible and Colportage Society for Ireland. He was a trustee of, and donor to, the General Assembly's College at Belfast. He took a deep interest in the movement for increased support for Presbyterian ministers and was a strong advocate of the Sustentation Scheme adopted by the Assembly in lieu of the *regium donum*.

Kirk died on 18 December 1870 and was buried in Second Keady Graveyard. A public meeting was held in January 1871 to erect a fitting memorial, which was erected in Keady. William Kirk and Anne McKean had eight children, six of whom seemed to survive their father.

Sources: Hall 2011; Nelson 2005; South Armagh Genealogical Project; Thompson 2002; Walker 1989; Wright 1996.

John Coulter
1796–1877

John Coulter was born in 1796 and educated at Glasgow University where he gained an MA in 1815. He was licensed by Monaghan Presbytery in 1818 and ordained in Gilnahirk near Belfast on 22 March 1820. He married in 1833. He was a prominent evangelical and helped bring about the union with the Seceders to create the General Assembly of the Presbyterian Church in Ireland, of which he became Moderator in 1851/2.

He was actively involved in the tenant right movement. He spoke at a Tenant League meeting in Dublin in January 1851 and proclaimed, 'the great rallying cry' of 'Old Ireland-All Ireland' ... 'I go further and proclaim from this place 'Ireland for the Irish'. The same month, at Tenant League meetings in Downpatrick and Broughshane he said 'Irish landlordism had plundered the people and driven multitudes of the best Irishmen into exile'. He was frustrated by the landlord's control of who would become members of parliament. In 1851 he said that the landlord, 'kept the tenants under his grasp, and employed them as mere tools and utensils in doing his dirty work, and sending whatever speechless blockhead he pleased into the Imperial Parliament to assist in making laws still further to crush and degrade them.'

In 1852 following the defeat of tenant right candidates in the general election Coulter criticised the 'unjustifiable means, which had been employed to put down the supporters of Mr Crawford'. He was also incensed by attempts by the Established Church to maintain the situation where marriages conducted by Presbyterian ministers were considered illegal. He retired in 1860 and died 26 May 1877.

Sources: Nelson 2005.

James Thompson
1800–83

James Thompson was born in 1800, the first son of Calvinist James Thompson of Kilmarnock, Scotland. He was educated at Belfast Academical Institution and Glasgow University. He studied theology at the Associate (Burgher) Theological Hall and was licensed to preach by Glasgow (Old Burgher) Presbytery in 1830. He was then ordained in Ballynahinch Seceder church on 31 December 1830. He and his congregation then decided to join the General Assembly of the Presbyterian Church and became part of the Down Presbytery in 1837. Two years later he resigned from the Ballynahinch congregation and on 26 February 1840 became the minister of Magherally.

He was a strong supporter of the tenant right campaign. At a monster meeting in Shaenrod near Dromara, County Down, in 1849 he said he 'deplored the position of farmers' as a result of the potatoes famine and the poor prices for their produce. He accused landlords of 'throwing dust in the eyes of the tenant farmers'.

Although from a Calvinist Seceder background, he criticised the 1859 revival which he said appealed to the emotions, but neglected sound instruction and encouraged the growth of small sects.

He retired from Magherally in 1882 and was succeeded by Rev. John Dunwoodie Martin from Newry. He died the following year on 27 October 1883. Two of his sons became ministers: James Thompson of Bellturbet and John Gibson Thompson of Lissara.

Sources: McElroy (undated).

David Herbison
1800–80

David Herbison, the bard of Dunclug, was born in Mill Street, Ballymena in 1800, the son of a publican, who later purchased a farm at Laymore outside Ballymena. His father had stood bail for four United Irishmen and had forfeited eighty pounds as a consequence. He was blind for the first seven years of his life, before the sight in his left eye was restored, which enabled him to attend school for the following couple of years and then a writing school for several months. Around this time he heard some verses of poetry by Allan Ramsey and was so impressed he walked all the way to Belfast to buy a book of his verse, as well as one by Robert Burns.

He worked on the farm and then managed to get an apprenticeship as a handloom weaver in the textile industry, eventually becoming a representative for Belfast linen firm, Messrs Finlay Brothers. However, in 1827, he decided to emigrate to Canada with other members of his immediate family, but having almost reached his destination the vessel was shipwrecked on the St Lawrence River and his sister and her child were drowned. After this tragedy, he stayed with another brother who had already emigrated, but within a couple of months he decided to return to Ireland.

In 1830 he married and had the first of many poems published in the *Northern Whig* newspaper. Over a period of ten years the *Ballymena Observer* also published sixty pieces by Herbison. In the poems 'The Pauper's Lament', 'The Pauper's Death', and 'The Pauper's Burial' he denounced the process of industrialisation, which destroyed his profession of handloom weaving and created the inhuman operation of the poor law.

With the conflict between landlords and tenants during this period he wrote a song in favour of tenant right. Between 1848 and 1876 he had five collections of poetry published, with the support of many subscribers, including *Midnight Musing; or Thoughts from the Loom, The Snow Wreathe* and *Children of the Year*. This makes him the most prolific of the poets from Antrim and Down of the nineteenth century.

He died in 1880, aged eighty years old. In 1883 *The Select Works of David Herbison* were published.

Sources: Ferguson 2008; Hewitt 2004; Vance 1990.

Samuel Lyle
1801–68

Samuel Lyle was born in Tullyroan near Tobermore beside Lough Neagh. His father, Hugh Lyle, was a farmer, married to Anne (née McNeill). He was educated at Belfast Academical Institution where he received his General Certificate in 1824. He trained for the ministry and was licensed to preach by Tyrone Presbytery in 1826. He was called to Ballycastle Presbyterian Church while he was still studying and was ordained in Ballycastle on 4 March 1829 and became the first minister of the new congregation.

He was very actively involved in the tenant right campaign in the 1840s and 50s, particularly around north Antrim and County Londonderry. He participated in a series of tenant right meetings in Coleraine.

He retired in 1867 and was succeeded at Ballycastle by George McFarland from Omagh. Rev. Lyle died the following year on 26 August 1868. His brother William was minister of Dunboe church.

Sources: McElroy (undated).

William Ferguson
Died 1859

William Ferguson was born in Donegore, County Antrim. He was educated at Belfast Academical Institution where he gained his General Certificate in 1840. He was licensed to preach by Carrickfergus Presbytery in 1842 and ordained in Ballygawley on 24 September 1844, where he succeeded John Steel Dickson who had been called to Ballysillan in Belfast.

He was very involved in the tenant right movement. At a meeting of the Omagh Tenant League, which hosted an important deputation from the south of Ireland including, amongst other people, Gavin Duffy and a Catholic priest, Ferguson rejoiced that:

> they might meet together as brothers; for, after all, were they not brethren created by the same Almighty God, inhabitants of the same lovely but desolate land, bowed down beneath a common oppressive landlordism, and activated by one common burning zeal to free their country from impending ruin.

Ferguson died on 9 December 1859.

Sources: Nelson 2005.

James Buchan Rentoul
1801–86

James Buchan Rentoul was born on 16 November 1801, the son of Rev .James Rentoul the minister of Ray Seceder congregation in Donegal (1791–1822). James jr was educated at Belfast Academical Institution where he gained his General Certificate in 1823. He was licensed by Newtownlimavady Presbytery in 1823. He was then called to be the first minister of Kilkeel Seceder congregation, but declined. He was eventually ordained in Second Garvagh Seceder congregation in 1827. He married Sarah, daughter of Rev. William Wilson of Crossgar in 1839.

He opposed the union of the Seceder Presbyterians with the mainstream Presbyterian Church in 1840, but joined the year after with his congregation. He was clerk of Coleraine Presbytery 1866–85 and was awarded a Doctorate in Divinity by Jefferson University in 1872.

Along with his brother, Alexander, also a Seceder Presbyterian minister, he was very active within the tenant right campaign. At a tenant right meeting in Garvagh in 1848, having spoken about the economic distress of the tenantry, argued for the importance of legalising the Ulster Custom of tenant right, despite the fact that they,

> had but few representatives in parliament; that those whom they sent there represented the landlords but not the tenants. He knew that in respect to elections in times past, they had been slaves. He knew that they had been led to the hustings by their landlords to vote at their bidding without respect to their own judgement or conscience.

In 1850 at a meeting in Ballymoney he declared that with the exception of William Sharman Crawford, 'they had the landlords as a class against them'. He attacked the current system of representation:

> The house of Commons, which was for the most part composed of landlords or the nominees of landlords, is against the tenant farmer ... in order to remove that state of things, every Irish voter ... for their representation to pledge themselves to support the principles of the League.

His two brothers J.L. and Alex became ministers and his three sons and a son-in-law also became ministers. He retired 1885 and died 3 December 1886.

Sources: Nelson 2005.

Alexander Patterson
1801–47

Alexander Patterson was born in 1801, the son of Rev. Alexander Patterson, minister of Magherally. He was educated at Belfast Academical Institution where he gained his General certificate in 1822. He then trained for the ministry and was licensed by Dromore Presbytery in 1824. He was ordained in First Clontibret in the Presbytery of Monaghan on 3 July 1827, becoming their minister. Less than three years later he accepted a call on 6 April 1830 to the newly built Second Ballymena in Wellington Street (which became the Third Church in 1840, and moved to a new larger church in 1863 and became West Church). The same year as moving to Ballymena he married the daughter of Rev. James Goudy of Clontibret.

Rev. Patterson conducted a non-denominational, non-sectarian school in Ballymena under the National Commission for Irish Education. At a meeting of the General Synod in Londonderry in 1834, Henry Cooke proposed a motion condemning the National Education system, which Patterson voted against. However, his congregation had other ideas and passed a motion, themselves, opposing the National Education system, despite the role of their minister. In protest at his vote against Cooke, the congregation also approved a motion halving their minister's salary. The issue then went to Presbytery, which resolved that Patterson should give up his connection with the National Commission, which under pressure, he had already done. It also decided that in future Patterson should vote against the National Education system, which Patterson resolutely refused to do, as he considered that it would be a violation of his right to private conscience. For this he was tried by the joint Presbyteries of Conor and Ballymena. The charge against him was that he had disturbed the 'united harmony' of the faithful. He was found guilty and publicly censured, but only after the moderator of the church court was forced to use his casting vote. Patterson then appealed to the General Synod, which discussed the issue at their next annual meeting where the charge against him was overthrown by 133 votes to 42. A motion was then proposed that the agitators against Patterson should be suspended for twelve months, which was defeated by Henry Cooke and his supporters, but they were formally admonished.

He remained the minister in Ballymena for seventeen years, until dying of a fever in the summer on 17 May 1847. He was succeeded by his son, Alexander Blakely Patterson, who joined the Indian Civil Service.

Sources: Akenson 1970.

William Campbell
1804/5–76

William Campbell was born in 1804/5 and brought up in Killyleagh, County Down. He was educated at Belfast Academical Institution where he gained his General Certificate in 1825. He trained for the ministry and was licensed to preach by Dromore Presbytery in November 1827. He was ordained on 14 April 1829 in Islandmagee, County Antrim where he stayed minister for 47 years. He was clerk of Templepatrick Presbytery from 1837 to 1841 and of Carrickfergus Presbytery from 1841 to 1876.

Campbell gave evidence to the Devon Commission, which was set up in 1843 to examine landlord-tenant relationships in Ireland. He expressed concern about the actions of landlords in breaking leases and raising rents,

> The breaking of the leases has retarded improvement, and the people have felt disappointed and dispirited. There is a want of confidence in respect of the landlord. They have not confidence in the landlord since the leases have been broken. The effect generally, indeed is injurious to the prosperity of the place, and the prosperity of the tenantry; and it is a great hardship in reference to those who have purchased land in the faith that these leases would run out the full term. The leases were broken, the rent was raised, and those who purchased farms considered themselves exceedingly aggrieved.

He actively participated in various tenant right gatherings, including the major meeting in the Music Hall in Belfast in 1851, at which a tenant right deputation from Ulster reported back on their attempts to lobby key government figures at Westminster. Campbell died on 17 August 1876.

Sources: Devon Commission.

John Scott Porter
1801–80

John Scott Porter, son of the non-subscribing Presbyterian minister, Rev. William Porter (see profile), was born in Newtownlimavady, County Londonderry in 1801. He was educated at Artillery Lane, a local classical school run by two Presbyterian ministers, George Hay and William Moore, and then at the Belfast Academical Institution. He worked as a schoolteacher and edited the *Christian Observer*. He was licensed by Bangor Presbytery in 1825 and the following year was ordained as a Presbyterian minister. He spent the next six years as the minister of the Unitarian Chapel Lane congregation in London and ran a school with another minister, David Davidson.

Porter was a friend and supporter of Henry Montgomery and withdrew with him to form the Remonstrant Synod in 1829, which later joined with the Presbytery of Antrim. In 1831 he was called to First Belfast Church, Rosemary Street and took up residence in the manse at 16 College Square.

Porter was soon involved in controversy with Calvinists and Episcopalians in Belfast. In 1834 he engaged in a major debate with Daniel Bagot, later Dean of Dromore, with members of various different churches present. One observer expressed his admiration for the way Porter conducted himself during the debate,

The transparent honesty of his method, the scrupulous fairness with which he recognised the strong points of his adversary's position, the frankness he exhibited in facing and meeting instead of ignoring difficulties … Scott Porter's exemplary conduct of his case covered him with honour.

Porter was an enthusiast for National Education and felt that education should be non-denominational. He lamented the tendency to please a party by sacrificing a principle. In 1837 he became the secretary of Belfast Academical Institution and the following year was appointed, with Rev. Henry Montgomery, as Professor of Theology for the Remonstrant Synod to the Institution, resulting in a bitter attack from Henry Cooke and conflict within the Institution itself. Some professors were also unhappy about appointments by the Remonstrant Synod on equal terms with themselves, who were nominated by the much larger Synod of Ulster, which argued for the establishment of a dedicated Presbyterian College and eventually withdrew from the Institution's theological faculty.

Porter edited the *Christian Monitor* and *Bible Christian* and was a prolific theological writer. One of his best-known works was *Principles of Textual Criticism*. He was also on the management committee of the Unitarian Society for the Diffusion of Christian Knowledge. He accepted that some of the birth narrative stories in the Gospels are unhistorical.

In 1846 he was involved with Dr John Edgar and the Belfast Ladies Relief Association in raising money towards famine relief in Connacht. His wife was one of the founders of the Ladies Institute in 1867, dedicated to the development of a high standard of education for women. He also supported the preservation of the Irish language.

In 1861 he was the Secretary of the Literary Society, which met each month in the homes of the members to discuss literature, arts, science, history, antiquities and 'the present state of Ireland'. He died in Lennoxvale in south Belfast in 1880.

Sources: Brooke 1994; Davidson 2002; McCracken 1993; McCracken 2001; Newman 1993.

James McKnight (also spelled M'Knight and M'Neight)
1801–76

James McKnight was born near Rathfriland, County Down in 1801, son of a Presbyterian tenant farmer who could speak Irish and was reputed to be fond of singing Gaelic songs. Although interested in theology, having been converted by reading Jonathon Edwards, he decided not to be ordained as a minister. He was educated at Belfast Academical Institution and became an expert in various modern and ancient languages. In 1826 he was appointed Deputy Librarian of the Linen Hall Library in the absence of the Librarian. In 1827 he became editor of the *Belfast Newsletter*. He then went to Derry as editor of the more liberal *Londonderry Standard* and then to Belfast as the editor of the Presbyterian newspaper, *Banner of Ulster* before returning again to the *Standard*.

McKnight opposed Cooke over the National Education system and stated that, 'Our principles, as Presbyterians, are fundamentally opposed to all forms of secular coercion in matters of religion'

He also opposed Cooke's demand for compulsory subscription to the Westminster Confession of Faith in two pamphlets: *The Dens Theology Humbug* and *Persecution Sanctioned by the Westminster Confession of Faith*. In the 1830s and 40s McKnight also resisted Cooke's attempts to forge a closer alliance – A 'Protestant Union' – with the Established Church in Ireland, which was in close alliance with the landed aristocracy, in opposition to the Catholic Church.

McKnight was a strong supporter and spokesman for the tenant right movement, which was established to protect, articulate and promote the Ulster Custom of fair rents, fixity of tenure and free sale, which would provide compensation for any improvements to the tenant's property if it was sold. He considered that the tenant's claim on the land took priority over the landlord's and that property has its duties as well as its rights. In 1848 he was a leading spokesman at two major demonstrations in Ulster. He shared a platform with Sharman Crawford at an anti-landlord, anti-government rally in Ballybay, County Monaghan and with the Coleraine barrister and liberal politician, Samuel Greer, at a rally in Dungannon, County Tyrone.

In 1848 he published *The Ulster Tenants' Claim of Right*, stating that, 'our church is now in her natural position, namely, in that of a guardian and a witness on behalf of the poor man's rights, in opposition to the rich man's tyranny'. In 1852 he joined the Tenant League.

He was a tireless spokesman for reform, arguing that, 'Ireland is almost the only country in the world in which the bulk of the population are treated as alien on the soil of their birth'. He said that he was happy to support reformist policies 'in pursuit of the same patriotic object that of elevating the masses of the Irish people, without distinction, to the realised dignity of British citizens'. His reputation was so strong that he was invited over to England to give advice to the Prime Minister, Lord Russell.

Although some on the right of the Church were concerned about the violent rhetoric of the tenant right movement and felt that the ordered framework of society was being threatened, the 1850 General Assembly of the Presbyterian Church continued to support it.

McKnight died in 1876, having campaigned for tenant right and political reform for thirty years.

Sources: Bardon 1992; Brooke 1994; Campbell 1991; Holmes 1985; Holmes and Knox 1990; Newman 1993; Thompson 2002; Wright 1996.

John Downs (also spelled Downes)
1802–66

John Downs was born in 1802, the first son of John Downs of Falkirk, Scotland. He was educated at Glasgow University and then studied theology at the Associate (Burgher) Theological Hall. He was ordained in Second Boardmills Old Burgher Seceder Church in 1827 and joined the Old Seceder Synod. He was married twice: in 1833 to Mary Jamison and after she died to Martha Gilmore in 1842.

He was moderator of the Assembly of the Burgher Remonstrant Synod in 1840. In 1852 he and the congregation joined the General Assembly of the Presbyterian Church in Ireland, after the merger with the Seceders.

He was actively involved in the tenant right campaign and there are records of his participation in meetings of tenant farmers in Banbridge in 1850 and Newtownards in 1851. He criticised 'irresponsible landlordism over a defenceless tenantry' and called for landlords to make 'large abatements of rent'.

In 1855 he resigned from the Church in Boardmills following a call to become minister in Hobart, Tasmania. He later moved to Learmouth, Victoria and the Clunes. He died in Victoria Australia on 29 May 1866.

Sources: Nelson 2005.

William McClure
1802–74

William McClure was born in 1802, the son of a merchant of the same name and grandson of Rev. John Thompson of Carnmoney. He was educated in Edinburgh and the Belfast Academical Institution, where he received his General Certificate in 1820. He was licensed to preach in Ballymena in 1823 and ordained as assistant and successor to Rev. George Hay of First Derry in 1825.

In 1834 McClure was elected Moderator of the General Synod and in 1847 of the General Assembly, when the church was united with the Seceders.

At a huge meeting in Hillsborough in October 1834, Rev. Henry Cooke appealed, in his particular brand of Toryism and conservative

Protestantism, for tenants and landlords and all Protestants to combine to defeat the 'papist' threat. This speech was considered so offensive to Catholics and liberals, that McClure issued a statement to the press dissociating the Presbyterian Church from his remarks.

McClure was convenor of the Colonial Mission and went to the United States with Rev. William Gibson to assess the religious revival that was taking place there. In 1861 McClure presided over a meeting to establish a church for the expanding population in the Waterside in Derry.

In the 1868 general election, McClure provided significant support for the Liberal candidate, Richard Dowse QC, as did the Catholic Bishop of Derry, Francis Kelly, and was duly thanked by Dowse in his victory speech when he defeated the conservative Lord Hamilton. Lord Hamilton in his speech as the defeated candidate attacked Presbyterian ministers for their part in his defeat and said that they were 'likely soon to be taught a lesson which they will not easily forget'. A fellow Presbyterian minister records what happened the following Sunday in one of the Presbyterian churches where the minister had supported the liberal candidate:

> The Sunday following the election brought a dreadful experience. Our church was more than half deserted; the congregation, resenting the defeat of their hero, Lord Claud, against whom my father had voted, had decided to leave the church. This was a terrible blow to my mother and the family, as it meant a serious diminution in the slender stipend on which the manse was kept going.

He was deeply involved in the foundation of Magee College in Derry in 1865. McClure died in 1874. His brother was Sir Thomas McClure (see profile).

Sources: Campbell 1991; Walker 1989.

Robert James Tennent
1803–80

Robert James Tennent was the son of Dr Robert Tennent (see profile) and nephew of William Tennent (see profile). Robert jr was on the governing body of the Belfast Academical Institution, which Lord Castlereagh saw as a 'deep laid scheme again to bring the Presbyterian Synod within the ranks of democracy'. He trained as a lawyer and while still a student helped in the editing of the liberal paper the *Northern Whig*, while they were looking for a new editor to replace one whose views were considered to be too conservative.

In the 1820s, he was a member of philosopher John Stewart Mill's London Debating Society and became interested in political economy and the socialist ideas of Robert Owen. He went with his cousin, James Emerson Tennent to help liberate the Greeks from the Turks. The two were later to become political opponents as Emerson Tennent became more and more conservative.

He married Eliza McCracken, Henry Joy McCracken's niece, in 1830 and had three sons and four daughters.

The 1832 Reform Act permitted Presbyterians, for the first time, to stand for election on their own terms. Tennent stood as a candidate along with William Sharman Crawford, but were defeated by the Marquis of Donegall's candidate, supported by the now Conservative James Emerson Tennent, who was also a supporter of the theology of Rev. Henry Cooke. Robert Tennent was defeated partly because of his refusal to declare his position on the Repeal of the Act of Union.

In 1847, A Fund for the Temporal Relief of the Suffering Poor of Ireland was established to be operated by the Episcopal clergy. This concerned the members of the General Relief Fund and Tennent wrote to the new Temporal Relief Fund asking for united action between the churches to bring relief to Ireland without distinction of sect or party, but the Established Church clergy refused to co-operate.

Tennent died in 1880.

Sources: Beckett 2003; Brooke 1994; Davidson 2002; Holmes 1985.

Hugh Moore
1804–93

Hugh Moore was born in 1804, the youngest son of Samuel Moore, a farmer of Craigantlet, Newtownards. He was educated at the Classical and Mercantile school in Newtownards under Rev. James Purse and Rev. David Davison before going to the Belfast Academical Institution, where he studied under Dr William B. Neilson (see profile). He then went to Glasgow University in 1821, where he gained an MA in 1823.

He was licensed by the Presbytery of Antrim in 1827 and was ordained in Newtownards, succeeding the Rev. Osborne, an unpopular loyalist who had been recommended to the congregation by Rev. Dr Robert Black, whom William Drennan called 'the Tory finance minister of the Synod of Ulster'. The previous minister, Rev. John McIwaine, on the other hand, had been perceived to be sympathetic to the United Irishmen.

Moore was concerned that the number of inmates in the workhouse in Newtownards had doubled between October 1846 and January of the following year and again between January and July 1847 and was a key member of a deputation requesting the establishment of an 'outdoor relief' scheme to be established. Although forbidden by the Poor Law of 1838, such schemes had been developed in various parts of Ireland. The deputation met with the workhouse guardians to state,

> ... that distress to an alarming extent now exists in the two electoral divisions of Newtownards, that the inmates at present in the workhouse considerably exceed the number it was originally built to accommodate, that in our opinion it would tend considerably to lessen the distress so generally prevalent, as well as diminish the number of applicants for admission, if one meal in the day could be given in the workhouse to persons who would be recommended by the wardens or otherwise approved of by the guardians, the expense of such relief to be charged to the said electoral divisions.

The request of the deputation was passed on to the Poor Law Commissioners by the guardians, who were, themselves, becoming increasingly concerned about overcrowding in the workhouse, and had developed plans for expansion.

Moore was also an active supporter of the tenant right campaign to protect and extend the rights under the Ulster Custom of fair rents, fixed tenure and free sale. He participated in tenant right meetings including in Upper Castlereagh in 1850. When the landlords called for protectionism, Moore denounced it as 'an artful device on the part of the landlord intent to stifle the cry for a reduction of rents'.

He provided support to the tenants on Lord Londonderry's County Down estate, and as a town commissioner since 1844, angered his lordship by asking the visiting Lord Lieutenant to help secure compensation for improvements the tenants had made to their farms.

Moore wrote, but never published a 'History of the Newtownards Church'. He retired in 1888 and died in 1893.

Sources: Hall 2011; Kinealy 1997; McElroy (undated); notes provided by Rev. John Nelson.

Samuel Davidson
1806–99

Samuel Davidson was born in Kellswater, County Antrim in 1806, son of Abraham Davidson and Margaret Mewha. He was educated at the village school, then a school in Ballymena, to which he walked the six miles there and back every day. He then went to the Belfast Academical Institution in 1824 where he gained first place in Greek and Latin. His studies were interrupted by periods of teaching in Londonderry and Liverpool, so, although he won first prize in Hebrew and a silver medal in Classics, he did not complete his studies until 1832. In 1833 he was licensed to preach by

Ballymena Presbytery. He was an evangelical at this stage in his life and subscribed to the Westminster Confession of Faith, although with exceptions, and spoke at a Twelfth Orange demonstration in Kellswater. Of this period he said that his 'mind was in traditional fetters'. But with an exceptional intellect, his thinking was to develop and broaden considerably.

After a period of supply preaching, in 1835 he was appointed as the first Professor of Biblical Criticism at Royal Belfast Academical Institution. He also became editor of the *Orthodox Presbyterian*, published by the General Synod in their battle against Unitarianism.

In 1839, he published his *Lectures on Biblical Criticism*, an emerging discipline, particularly in Germany, which was to throw much light on the understanding of the Bible. He was becoming increasingly dissatisfied with narrow attitudes in Ireland and the witch-hunt against liberalism and intellectual rigour which was being carried out by Rev. Henry Cooke and others in the Synod, which he described as 'alien to the gospel of peace'. He said that,

> The country, alas, is still rent with party divisions. Catholicism and Protestantism clash bitterly with one another. Races are antagonistic. Presbyterians are as much opposed to Roman Catholics as ever, having reached little breadth of view or of charity. And their preachers repeat the old Calvinist dogmas, the people liking to hear them.

He was a supporter of the movement to repeal the Act of Union and eventually decided to move to England two years later (1842), having completed his monumental work, *Sacred Hermeneutics Developed and Applied*, which demonstrated his unrivalled knowledge of contemporary German biblical scholarship. Between 1848 and 1851 he published three volumes of his *Introduction to the New Testament*.

He lectured on theology at a Lancashire Independent College in Manchester, developing his interpretations of German theology, but as he became increasingly radical he was forced to resign due to, what were considered to be, his unorthodox views, arising from his work on the Old Testament, particularly the authorship of the first books of the Old Testament, the Pentateuch, which would now be accepted as the traditionally accepted view. After retiring he published three volumes of *An Introduction to the Old Testament*.

He was considered to be one of the leading pioneers of English biblical criticism and sat on the body that produced the Revised Version of the Old Testament. The Old Testament Chair in London is called the Samuel Davidson Chair in his honour. He died in 1899.

Sources: Davidson 1899; Dunlop 1998–2000; Newman 1993.

John Rentoul
1806–69

John Lawrence Rentoul was born into a large Presbyterian ministerial dynasty. He was the fourth son of Rev. James Rentoul (1791–1822) of Ray Secession Church. John Rentoul was educated at Belfast Academical Institution, receiving his General Certificate in 1829. He was licensed by Donegal Presbytery in 1833 and was ordained and became the minister of Second Ballycopeland, County Down in the same year. In 1834 he married Dorcas (née Carmichael), with whom he had 3 sons and 6 daughters.

He resigned in 1837 to become minister of the Secession church in Ballymoney, which became Trinity Church. He disapproved of the union of the Secession church with the Presbyterian General Synod to form the Presbyterian Church in Ireland, but joined the General Assembly in 1841. He was clerk of Route Presbytery from 1864 to 1869.

He developed a reputation as an agitator on social issues, in particular campaigning in support of tenant right and the upholding of the Ulster Custom. In May 1848 he actively participated in an Ulster Tenant Right Association meeting in Dungannon. In 1850 at a meeting in Rev. Munnis' meetinghouse in Dervock he urged the necessity of returning to Parliament their own, 'tenant right representatives'. In 1851 he was an active participant as a speaker in a major tenant right demonstration, which took place in the Music Hall in Belfast. In support of the Irish Tenant League of North and South, he said that he 'trusted that orange and green would ever combine, and that no hand would render them asunder. But he also reminded the tenant farmers that they in turn had responsibilities towards labourers and their families'.

He was very clear that his involvement in the tenant right campaign was on the basis of his faith and that 'religion required him not only to love his neighbour but to feed the hungry, to clothe the naked, to visit the widow and the fatherless in their affliction and it required him to do good to all men without distinction'.

In January 1852 he said that neither Lord Russell nor the English people 'are disposed to put Irishmen on an equality with the British nation. They must be taught that Irish people are determined to have their rights'.

He had two brothers who were ministers and his two sons, James and John Lawrence, also became ministers, the latter developing a reputation for being unorthodox theologically. Rentoul died in 1869.

Sources: Campbell 1991; Latimer 1893; McElroy (undated); Stewart 1950.

Thomas McClure
1806–93

Thomas McClure was born in 1806, son of William McClure and Elie, daughter of Rev. J. Thompson. Both his grandfather and great-grandfather were Presbyterian ministers. He was educated at Belfast Academical Institution. He and his siblings were devout Presbyterians who held prayer meetings and Sunday school in the laundry of the house. His brother was the Rev. William McClure (see profile). Thomas McClure became a successful tea and general merchant, which enabled him to buy an estate at Belmont.

He was politically a Liberal and stood for election to Westminster, but was defeated. In 1857, during the debates on the long overdue disestablishment of the Church of Ireland and the need for legislation on tenant right, McClure was elected to Belfast Corporation. In 1868 he and Orangeman William Johnston of Ballykilbeg, who also supported land reform, defeated Conservatives Charles Lanyon, the architect, and John Mulholland, later Lord Dunleath to become a Westminster MP. McClure had significant Catholic support as well as from the Orange Order, although members of the Order who voted for McClure were soon expelled. There were bonfires and celebrations in Ballymoney, Dervock and Stranocum in County Antrim for the victorious McClure. The Tories tried to have the election of McClure overturned on the grounds of corrupt practice, but were unsuccessful.

In the 1874 general election, McClure, the sitting MP, and John Rea were reselected as the Liberal candidates. His opponents made much of the fact that two of McClure's five nominators were Catholics. McClure and Rea were heavily defeated by Tory, J.P. Corry, and Orangeman, William Johnson.

In 1878, on the death of Prof. Richard Smyth, MP for County Londonderry, McClure was selected to fight the seat for the Liberals, against the conservative landlord, S.M. Alexander. In his address McClure stated that he would support measures to enable tenants to gain the full benefits of the Land Act and would advocate land purchase by tenants. He made clear his support for the Liberals, who he said, had given religious equality, freedom for voters through the secret ballot, and security for farmers. He also criticised the Conservatives' foreign policy. At McClure's meetings Presbyterian ministers were well in evidence. He also received the support, if somewhat reluctantly, of the Ulster Home Rule Association. McClure secured 2,479 against Alexander's 1,878. McClure was again successful in the 1880 general election, but by 1885, he decided that it was time for someone else to carry the flag for the Liberals in County Londonderry.

He supported the disestablishment of the Church of Ireland. He was made a baronet by Gladstone in 1874 in recognition of his political support, although McClure withdrew this support after Gladstone decided to support Home Rule for Ireland.

McClure lived with his eccentric sister, Betty and gave £1,000 to build Belmont Presbyterian Church, where he was to be an elder for the next thirty years and an adjoining school. He was a trustee and the first treasurer of the Presbyterian Assembly's College.

He was on the committee for town relief in 1847 and 1858 and became first president of Belfast YMCA. When he died in 1893 he bequeathed nearly his whole estate for charitable and religious purposes.

Sources: Bardon 1992; Brett 1978; Davidson 2002; Stenton and Lee; Thompson 2002; Walker 1989; Wright 1996.

John McNaughton (also spelled MacNaughtan)
1807/8–84

John McNaughton was born in Greenock Scotland in 1807/8, the son of Donald McNaughton, a merchant. Having trained for the ministry, he was licensed to preach by the Presbytery of Paisley on 4 August 1830. He was ordained in 1831 in Scots Church (Crown Court Chapel) in London. He then moved to High Kirk in Paisley, Scotland. In 1837 he accepted a call from St Paul's Chapel, Edinburgh but was refused permission to become the minister there. In 1841 he married Jessie Buchanon and in 1843 became a Church of Scotland minister. He was then invited to become minister of Rosemary Street Presbyterian Church in Belfast, but initially refused. Rev. Henry Cooke tried to prevent the church from making a further call to him. The Presbyterian Supreme Court vindicated the right of the congregation to call McNaughton if they so wished. McNaughton took up his ministry in Belfast in 1849.

McNaughton, a leading liberal, took a lead, through a peace committee, in responding to the sectarian rioting and destruction that took place in Belfast in 1864, acting as a mediator between rival factions. He worked hard to reverse the expulsions of minority communities in predominantly Protestant and Catholic districts and from their place of work. He said that these expulsions must be 'put down at all hazards and all costs'. He secured a deal in the shipyard, with the support of the owner, Harland, that prevented the Catholic painters from being expelled by the shipyard workers.

McNaughton also played a prominent role in trying to persuade the Presbyterian Church to support the establishment of a 'united secular national educational system', with separate religious instruction, against the opposition of the Roman Catholic and Anglican churches and many within his own church. He also strongly advocated the full disestablishment and disendowment of the Church of Ireland and the setting of all the churches on an equal footing. He favoured the position that no churches would receive state support, including the *regium donum*.

In 1865 when agitation started for the establishment of a Catholic University, McNaughton was concerned that this would mean that Catholic students would leave Queen's College Belfast to go to the new university. When Magee Presbyterian College applied for affiliate status with Queen's University of Ireland, the nature of the debate changed and the advocates of a Catholic university sought to give the new university similar status. The major debate at the following Presbyterian Assembly confirmed the Presbyterian commitment to non-sectarian non-denominational education. In 1870 the Powis Commission enquiring into education in Ireland, recommended that Catholic demands for denominational education funded by the state should be conceded. McNaughton organised a National Educational League to try and defend the principle of non-sectarian education.

In 1868, McNaughton supported the tactical pairing of candidates for parliament in order to defeat the Tories. This strategy resulted in the election of Liberal Thomas McClure along with independent Orangeman William Johnston. He continued to denounce both party processions, which Johnston had been strongly in favour of (resulting in a jail sentence), and denominational education as threats to civil society.

McNaughton was one of the supporters of the use of musical instruments in church music. Prior to the mid-eighteenth century psalms, paraphrases and hymns were sung unaccompanied, led by a precentor, who provided a starting note in an appropriate key. The introduction of instruments such as a harmonium was initially very controversial and led to a long-running dispute, which was eventually won by McNaughton and the other members of the 'liberty' party. He was elected Moderator of the General Assembly in 1861. After his first wife died he married Matilda Hanna Suffern in 1868. McNaughton died in 1884.

Sources: Hall 2011; Holmes and Knox 1990; Scott 1915; Wright 1996.

Daniel Gunn Brown
1808–92

Daniel Gunn Brown was born on 5 January 1808 in Moy, County Tyrone. His father, William Brown, was a Congregational minister in Belfast and Moy. Rev. Hugh Kirkpatrick, Ballymoney, was his great-great-grandfather. He was educated in Armagh before going to Belfast Academical Institution.

He decided to follow in his father's footsteps and train for the ministry and went to the University of Edinburgh to study theology. Unusually, he also studied in Dublin. In 1831 he was licensed by Armagh Presbytery. On 5 March 1833 Brown was ordained and became the minister of First Creggan and Newtownhamilton in the Presbytery of Armagh, following two ministers who had been dismissed for misconduct. In 1835 the two congregations were separated and Brown chose to remain with Newtownhamilton.

The first thing that Brown did as the new minister was to visit all the members of the congregation. What is unusual is that he took notes of these visits, which survive today. In the notes he highlights many of the problems they face of poverty, disease, overcrowding, and the high infant mortality.

When the Devon Commission was established in 1843 by the government to examine the relationship between landlord and tenant in Ireland, Brown gave evidence to the commission, giving witness to the poverty in the country, 'For the last two years ... I have scarcely seen meal or meat; and it is evident from the deterioration in their dress ... that they are rapidly getting worse'. He also made it clear that suffering and hardship were evils that could be avoided. He was very aware of the desire amongst the poor to find paid employment, 'There is a universal desire on the part of the people in that locality to work if they can get it'.

During the Great Famine he was involved in distributing food to those who were starving after the failure of the potato crops. He also became involved in the tenant right campaign, despite criticism from some quarters. He consistently condemned those who used violence to further the cause, but argued that it was important to look at why some people felt it was necessary to resort to violence. At a select committee to examine the anti-landlord violence that had been taking place in Armagh he refuted allegations that it was politically or religiously motivated.

He was a speaker at the mass meeting of the Ulster Tenant Right Association, held in Dungannon on 25 May 1848, along with other Presbyterian ministers and Catholic priests. He chaired a meeting of the League of North and South in Armagh, resisting attempts by Orangemen to break it up and chaired a soiree of the representatives of the League of North and South in Derry.

Although he supported Henry Cooke against Arianism, he was opposed to Cooke's efforts to bring about a much closer relationship between the Presbyterian Church and the Established Church, which was strongly opposed to the tenant right movement and political reform, 'why should ministers in the Synod of Ulster be so forgetful of their principles, or so ready to sacrifice them at the shrine of the world's expediency'. He went on to accuse those who sought closer links of courting 'the purple and gold and fine linen of Babylon'. He sometimes wrote under the pseudonym of John

Knox jr and under this name published *The First and Second Blast of the Trumpet against the monstrous union of Presbytery and Prelacy*. Even more controversially, he came out in support of Gladstone's Home Rule Bill.

When the Chair of Moral Philosophy at Assembly's College became vacant, Brown was encouraged to apply by his friends, but was rejected, presumably because of his outspoken views and independence of mind.

He resigned from Newtownhamilton in November 1870. He was clerk of Ballybay Presbytery from 1853 to 1875. He retired in 1888 and died on 24 May 1892. He is buried in Creggan graveyard in south Armagh.

Sources: South Armagh Genealogy Project.

Robert MacAdam
1808–95

Robert Shipboy MacAdam was born in 1808 in High Street Belfast, two doors from Bridge Street and close to Rosemary Street. He was the son of James MacAdam, a hardware merchant, and his wife Jane (née Shipboy). He was educated at the Belfast Academical Institution from 1818, when he was 10 years old. He became a member of the Non-Subscribing First Presbyterian Church in Rosemary Street, Belfast. After he left school he was apprenticed to his father's hardware business at 36 High Street, Belfast. However, when he was only 13 his father died.

At the age of 13 he was present when the Belfast Natural History and Philosophical Society was formed in 1821. He was a member and co-secretary of the Ulster Gaelic Society, when it was founded in 1828. While making visits around Ireland for his father's firm, he developed a fluency in the Irish language, which he was probably taught by William B. Neilson while at the Belfast Academical Institution. He was eventually fluent in over a dozen languages.

He began to collect folk tales and proverbs in Irish while on his travels. He also collected Gaelic manuscripts, including many ancient Irish texts and translated many texts from Irish. In 1835 he wrote an *Irish grammar* for use in language classes at the Academical Institution and was involved in the establishment of Irish schools. A substantial Irish-English dictionary that he produced with over 1,100 entries was never published.

In 1838 he began a retail business in Townsend Street, Belfast with his brother James. In 1844 they sold their shop, and two years later their house, to start the Soho foundry in Townsend Street, producing a wide range of iron products, including turbines for the booming engineering and manufacturing sector in Belfast.

In 1852 he and his brother James were leading organisers and promoters of an exhibition of Irish antiquities for the conference of the British

Association for the Advancement of Science, in the Belfast Museum, of which he was a founder. This led to the formation of the *Ulster Journal of Archaeology*, of which he was the editor for the first nine years. The journal made a crucial contribution to the preservation of Irish culture and language. For many years he was the Hon. Secretary of the Belfast Academical Institution.

He was an enthusiast of traditional Irish music and wrote many tunes, himself, on his flute. He was a member of the Harmonic and Harp societies and owned the skull of Turlough O'Carolan, the great Irish harpist.

In 1861 his brother, James died, leaving his diary that he had kept for much of his life. As Robert McAdam became more elderly, the business went into serious decline. By the time he retired he was in serious debt and was forced to sell much of his library and contents of his house, 18 College Square East. Eventually his friends made an appeal to create an annuity to allow him to live in reasonable comfort until he died.

He died in 1895 leaving an incredible legacy of achievements including the collection and preservation of a large number of ancient manuscripts. He is buried in Knockbreda cemetery

Sources: Blaney 1996.

Julius McCullagh (also spelled McCullough)
1808–66

Julius McCullagh was born in 1808, the son of Rev. James McCullagh, minister of First Newtownards. He was educated at Belfast Academical Institution, where he received his General Certificate in 1829. He trained for the ministry and was licensed to preach by Belfast Presbytery in 1833 and was ordained the following year in First Newtownards on 28 August 1834. In 1838 he married the daughter of Rev. Hugh Woods, minister of Bangor Presbyterian congregation.

He was very committed to the tenant right campaign, speaking at various meetings of tenant farmers, especially in County Down. In January 1850 in Newtownards he spoke of the growing economic distress of the farmers of the district and the need for rent abatements from the landowners. After the major three-day conference of the League of North and South in Dublin in 1850, which brought together representatives of tenant right associations from across Ireland, representatives of the League organised and spoke at campaigning meetings all over Ireland, some of which were very large indeed. At one of these, Rev. McCullagh, in considering the wealthy land-owners in Ireland, cited the admonition of Luther to the German aristocracy,

> Ye princes, ye men of power, you lavish in fine clothes, fine castles, fine eating and drinking, the peasants hard-won produce, and what you must do first and foremost is, to put a stop to all this vain luxury of yours, to close up the holes through which this money runs, so that you may leave some little part in the peasants' pocket.

McCullagh was elected a town commissioner in Newtownards in 1849. When the Lord Lieutenant, Earl of Clarendon visited Newtownards in 1850, the town commissioners, to the great annoyance of the local squire, Lord Londonderry, asked him to use his influence to 'secure to the tenant full compensation for all his improvements'. An angry exchange of letters turned into open hostility in the newspapers.

He also spoke at a tenant right meeting in Belfast the following year. In 1851 he told a tenant right meeting in Armagh that, 'they as united Irishmen should press their claims home upon the government'. In Saintfield in March 1852 he spoke at an electioneering meeting and accused the Established Church of 'propping up irresponsible and tyrannical Landlordism in Ireland'.

Many leaders of the tenant right movement were convinced that Lord Russell and the government introduced the Ecclesiastical Titles Bill, which was designed to prevent the Catholic hierarchy being re-established in England, to damage the tenant right campaign in Ireland, or in McCullagh's words of February 1851, to, 'afresh old grudges and differences – to divide a people now happily uniting'.

In 30 January 1852 McCullagh, dubbed 'Rev. Julius Caesar' by the landlord press, denounced landlordism, saying it was,

> high time that the people should be madder aware of the nature of irresponsibility and tyrannical landlordism, and that it should not be propped up, as hitherto it had been, by the clergy of the established Church ... The Apostle says, he that does not work should not eat. Landlordism and its apologetic divines, say that he who does work should not eat, and that the idle improvident, and extravagant upper classes, like the locusts that came up on Judea are to eat up every green thing.

He remained at First Newtownards congregation until he retired. He died on 7 December 1866 and is interred in Movilla Cemetery, Newtownards.

Sources: Duffy 1896; Hall 2011; Nelson 2005.

Samuel Browne (sometimes spelled Brown)
1808/9–90

Samuel Browne was born in 1808/9, the son of the Rev. Solomon Brown, Presbyterian minister in Castledawson, older brother of Rev. John Brown DD of Aghadowey (see profile). Samuel trained as a doctor and was licensed by the King and Queen's College of Physicians of Ireland and joined the Royal Navy as an assistant surgeon. In 1841 his rank was reduced after he was court-martialled for knocking down the captain.

He returned to Belfast and secured an appointment in the Belfast General Dispensary for the Cure of Children and the Eye. As Ulster's first eye specialist, he then set up the Belfast Ophthalmic Institution and Children's Dispensary in Mill Street (now Castle Street) in 1845. He specialised in eye and ear conditions, while Andrew G. Malcolm (see profile) treated the sick children. In 1873 Brown joined the staff of the Hospital for Sick Children as well as being consulting surgeon in the General Hospital and Samaritan Hospital in Belfast, inspector to the paupers coming in from Scotland, and first surgeon in the Belfast Ophthalmic Hospital.

Along with Malcolm, he had a strong interest in public health and was appointed one of six officers of health in Belfast with responsibility for sanitary matters. He became part-time Medical Officer of Health and then for many years Chief Medical Officer for Belfast. In 1870 he was elected Mayor of Belfast. Browne died in 1890. His son, Sir John (Jack) Walton Browne also became a surgeon.

Sources: Calwell 1973; Craig, D.H. 1973/4.

Isaac Nelson
1809–88

Isaac Nelson was born in Belfast in 1809, the son of a grocer in Barrack Street Belfast and was educated locally. He served as a classics teacher in Belfast Academical Institution before entering the ministry. He was licensed to preach by Belfast Presbytery and then ordained as a Presbyterian minister in Comber, County Down in 1838. He was called to Donegall Street (later called Cliftonville), Belfast in 1842, where he remained for the next 38 years.

Although theologically orthodox and a member of the Evangelical Alliance, he wrote a less than enthusiastic account of the revival movement of 1859 called *The Year of Delusion,* in response to William Gibson's *Year of Grace.* He was particularly concerned that the revival, rather than demonstrating true religion, would ultimately damage it by what he saw as an epidemic of mass hysteria and superstition – a 'huge juggle, a giant imposture, having really no more to do with Christianity than the phenomenon of electro-biology'. He was also concerned about the number of uneducated lay preachers who were questionable in terms of both theology and taste.

Nelson was also concerned about the language used to describe the church's involvement in primarily Catholic communities. He argued that terms like 'Mission to Catholics' and 'popery' were gratuitously offensive and reflected a 'blasphemous claim of doctrinal superiority'. He was also an opponent of slavery and published a lecture on the American Civil War and slavery.

In 1864 there was severe rioting in Belfast, witnessed by Nelson, who stated that,

> The mobs in my neighbourhood not only hunted poor Roman Catholic neighbours out of their houses, but I had to go and beseech them to grant so many hours to these poor people to take their furniture out ... I could have sat down and wept when a poor little girl came with a pet canary bird in a cage, when the poor people had been driven from the houses, the children in one direction and the father and mother in another.

He was a supporter of Home Rule and Parnell and became the chairman of the Belfast Home Rule Association, publishing *The Present Importance of Irish History*. When Judge Keogh made offensive anti-Catholic remarks in a judgement about the validity of the election of Captain Nolan in 1872, Nelson declared that the judge 'had done more to bind the hearts of the Roman Catholic people of Galway to their spiritual counsellors than has been done by any single act of any single party for the last half century'.

With increasing dissatisfaction with the limited impact of the 1870 Land Act, a key tenant right conference was held in Belfast in January 1871, with over 30 tenant right organisations represented. Nelson represented the Belfast Home Rule Association. The conference repeated demands for the full implementation of the '3 Fs' of the Ulster Custom.

With the support of Parnell, Nelson eventually became a Home Rule MP for Mayo from 1880 to 1885, having been defeated in Leitrim. He became President of the Protestant Home Rule Association in Belfast. At a Land League meeting in Maghera he said that 'no man could be a friend of Ireland without being an enemy of English rulers'.

He died in Belfast in 1888, aged 76 and is buried in Shankill graveyard. The Nelson Memorial congregation was established on 12 May 1896 from his sister's legacy.

Sources: Bardon 1992; Campbell 1991; Hamilton 1992; Holmes 1985; Moody 1981; Newman 1993; Wright 1996.

Alexander Porter Goudy
1809–58

Alexander Porter (A.P.) Goudy was born in 1809 on the Ards Peninsula, the son of Rev. Andrew Goudy, the minister of Ballywalter congregation and the grandson, on his mother's side, of the ill-fated Rev. James Porter who wrote biting satires about the local gentry and vicar and was hanged between his church and manse at Greyabbey in 1798 on a trumped-up charge of robbing a mail train. Other relatives, both subscribers and non-subscribers, had served as ministers in the area. His family traced its ancestry to Scotland, and from there back to Norway.

He was educated at Belfast Academical Institution where he was a fellow student of Dr James McKnight, of Rathfriland, a leading liberal (see profile) who was later to become editor of the *Derry Standard* newspaper. Alexander Goudy was licensed to preach in December 1830 by the Bangor Presbytery, and on 20 September 1831 was ordained as the minister of Glastry, County Down, succeeding Rev. Sinclair, who had been minister for 50 years, following on from the ministries of United Irishmen, Rev. William Steel Dickson and James Sinclair. Goudy did not stay in Glastry long, however. He resigned on 1 May 1833 when called to First Strabane where he was installed on 20 March 1833 and remained the minister there until he died. He was succeeded at First Strabane by James Gibson, son of Rev. Prof. William Gibson of Assembly's College, author of *Year of Grace*.

In 1838, Goudy, and three other ministers, engaged in a pamphlet war with Episcopal curate Rev. Archibald Boyd in defending Presbyterianism and its form of government. He became an influential force in the General Assembly and its Moderator in 1857. He came to prominence in the public life of Ulster as well as in his own church assemblies, and many of his sermons and pamphlets on various subjects were widely read. He was a noted poet and writer of political satires.

Goudy played a leading part in the battle for justice to overthrow a law which made marriages illegal between members of the Established Church and the Presbyterian Church when conducted by a Presbyterian Minister. Fierce passions were aroused by the subject, and it was not until 1844 that freedom from the stigma came about.

Writing in 'The Presbyterian Churchman' in 1886, Dr Thomas Croskery described Dr Goudy as a very striking figure who was possessed of a rare vitality and vivacity and who was known for his powers of oratory. He said some of Dr Goudy's best speeches were structures of solid argument, flashing from pinnacle to foundation with points of wit,

> As a man with a hand in many controversies, he could not but excite many resentments, but there was a perceptible mellowing of spirit in the last years of his life, for his character was really as gentle as it was

strong, and won hearts to a loyalty that no lapse of time and no change of circumstances could shake.

Goudy was an ardent supporter of tenant rights, and helped to prepare and solidify the public opinion which led to changes in the law. Although he supported Henry Cooke on the issue of subscription he said that 'we do not hold his political opinion on very many subjects'.

Goudy died on 14 December 1858, and more than 100 ministers were present at his funeral. His body was brought by train from Dublin and was met by a huge crowd at Strabane station. He was buried in the old cemetery at Patrick Street, Strabane.

His son Alexander became a Judge in the Supreme Court of the State of Louisiana, and was a state senator. He helped frame the constitution of Louisiana. His grandson James later became attorney-general of Louisiana. Goudy's daughter Anna married George Herdman of Sion House and had one son Henry and 3 daughters.

Sources: Croskery 1887; Latimer 1893.

William Wilson
1809–57

William Wilson was born in Ballycloughan, Broughshane near Ballymena, County Antrim in 1809 and baptised by Rev. Robert Stewart of Broughshane, who was famous for both being called by the congregation to be their minister through a controversial Sunday poll and for engaging in a three-day debate with the local parish priest.

Wilson was the eldest of the eleven children of Samuel Wilson, a farmer and merchant, whose great-aunt had been drowned at the stake in Scotland for refusing to swear the Oath of Abjuration, and had himself been a United Irishman, fighting for the rebels in Ballymena in 1798. Three of his brothers emigrated to Australia and were successful sheep farmers, along with their cousins, the McCaugheys.

William Wilson married Sarah Speer in 1833, who was six years younger than him, and, having moved to Ballyearl in Carnmoney, County Antrim had four children, but she died at the age of 30. He remarried a Jane Nelson Smith, seventeen years his junior, in 1847.

Having experienced the impact of very poor harvests during the Irish Famine from 1845–52, followed by disease, he was a strong support of the rights of tenant farmers who were suffering badly at the hands of the landlords. He became secretary of the local tenant right association and urged others to form associations and campaign non-violently.

Although his parents had not encouraged his education or reading, in

1850 he wrote the 'Catechism of Tenant Right; being an attempt to set forth and defend the rights of tenant farmers, point out some of the grievances under which they labour, with remedies for their removal', in support of this position. It was published by the Presbyterian *Banner of Ulster*. In it he defined tenant right as: 'The full value of all unexhausted, improvements on the soil, whether inherited, purchased, or created by the labour or capital of the tenant-farmer.' In 47 questions and answers he provided a simple guide for tenant right associations to the key issues for tenant farmers, including responses to criticisms of the tenant right campaign. In relation to the legal security of tenant-farmers he stated that: 'The capital of this class (worth many millions sterling) may be said to be in a state of outlawry, left without any legal protestion to the mercy of another class (the landlords), who may appropriate, and, with perfect impunity, proceed to devour it at any moment.' In one of his answers he quotes from scripture to describe what will happen to 'those who take away the rights of those who toil, and who exact unrequited labour'.

In 1851 Wilson moved to Ballycloughan from Ballyearl. He died of stomach ulcers in March 1857, while his wife was pregnant with their child, which was born 9 or 10 weeks after he died. His wife then died a few months later.

Sources: Wilson 1850; handwritten memoir 'Sketch of the Wilson family' by David Wilson.

William Reid
1810–58

William Reid was born on 10 February 1810. He was educated at Divinity Hall (Burgher) in Scotland and licensed to preach by Upper Tyrone (Burgher) Presbytery and ordained by Scarva Burgher congregation. He was elected Moderator of the Seceder Synod in 1826/7. In 1827 he married the daughter of Joseph McAllister of Glascar.

He was a regular speaker on tenant right platforms. At a tenant right meeting in Banbridge in February 1851 he gave examples of landlord oppression in the area. The following year in the same town he proclaimed how 'Presbyterians and Presbyterian ministers have been champions for liberty and unerring truth'. He also referred back to the radical activities of Presbyterians in the previous century and the need for strong action to influence the government,

> Our Government never do justice to the subjects of our Gracious Queen until society is rent and torn by agitation. We have reason to lament that distinguished patriots have been sacrificed, because they

were in advance of national reform. Witness from '82 to '98. Be of one mind when you attend the hustings.

Reid died on 24 March 1858. His son William became a minister.

Sources: Baillie and Kirkpatrick 2005; Hall 2011; Nelson 2005.

Henry Robinson Mecredy (also spelled McCreedy)
1810–95

Henry Mecredy was born in 1810. He was educated at Belfast Academical Institution where he received his General Certificate in 1845. He trained for the ministry and was licensed to preach by Belfast Presbytery in 1845 and ordained in Killead, County Antrim on 15 March 1850, succeeding Rev. Joseph McKee. The same year he married the daughter of Rev. John Carson of Templepatrick congregation. After her death he remarried a widow, Mrs Ruddell (née Holmes). He remained the minister of the historic congregation of Killead until his retirement in 1890.

Even from the first year of his ordination he was very actively involved in the tenant right campaign. At a meeting in the Saintfield meetinghouse in 1850 he harked back to the radical days of 1798 and said that the oppression being carried out by landlords is now driving 'the bravest and loyalest [sic] of Hibernian's sons' from their native land. He was very supportive of the development of a League of North and South, which united the tenant right movement in Ulster with that of other parts of Ireland. When they planned to hold a major North-South conference in Dublin he said they 'did rejoice ... that they lived in a day when North and South could, on one great subject, unite together in a common platform [and] forget the differences of the past'.

He was a main platform speaker at a large tenant right campaign meeting in Banbridge, County Down, where sixteen Presbyterian ministers and one Catholic priest were on the stage. He participated in a tenant right meeting in Upper Castlereagh in 1850 and spoke at a gathering of tenant farmers in Newtownards, County Down in 1851, suggesting that the landlord Lord Edwin Hill 'could be far better employed about Hillsborough Castle than in Parliament'. In 1852, in a speech in Saintfield, he denounced the landlords standing at the election and said they were 'utterly opposed to the just claims of the tenant farmers'. He also participated in various other tenant right meetings and demonstrations.

When the Government threatened to withdraw the *regium donum* grant to Presbyterian ministers in order to reduce the radicalism of some of the more outspoken ministers, Mecredy was scathing about these threats and said the withdrawal of the grant would not prevent Presbyterian ministers from speaking out.

He retired in 1890 and died on 10 February 1895. He is buried in the graveyard in Killead. He was succeeded by Rev. William John Baird at Killead.

Sources: McElroy (undated).

Samuel McCurdy Greer
1809–80

Samuel Greer was born in Springvale near Castlerock, County Londonderry in 1809, the son of Rev. Thomas Greer, Presbyterian minister of Dunboe, County Londonderry. He was educated at Belfast Academy and then trained as a lawyer at Glasgow University. He was called to the bar in 1835. He campaigned for the reform of Coleraine Corporation and legally represented the town commissioners against former officers of the Corporation.

In 1842 Greer proposed the establishment of Church Defence Associations to campaign against the Established Church on discrimination against Presbyterian marriages, much to Henry Cooke's dismay. He successfully supported the Liberal candidate, John Boyd, for Coleraine, in the election of 1843.

He was a founding member of the Ulster Tenant Right Association and gave a speech in support of the position of tenant farmers at their second meeting in 1847 and spoke at a series of meetings around Ulster in support of tenant right. In 1848 he became secretary of the newly formed Coleraine Tenants' Association. He wrote to the *Impartial Reporter* in November 1848 in support of tenant farmers.

> For years the tenant farmer had a valuable freehold interest in his farm, for which he could at once have obtained a ready purchaser and a large price. He could not now obtain a farthing for it, or get a ready purchaser on any terms … the greater of the value of the tenant-right interest that existed has been swallowed up in the general depreciation of agricultural prices.

When Downhill Castle, owned by Tory landlord, Sir Harvey Bruce, was burnt down in a malicious fire, the grand jury tried to put the cost of rebuilding the castle on to the county cess (rates). Greer made a name for himself by conducting a successful legal campaign to prevent this happening.

He shared a platform with James McKnight at a big demonstration in

Dungannon in support of tenant right and was a member of a deputation to Westminster to make the case of the tenant farmers and the need to have rent controls during this very difficult economic period. On their return he spoke at various meetings to let the tenant farmers know what reaction they had received at parliament, including at a major meeting in the Music Hall in Belfast.

In 1850 he was a co-founder of the Tenant League with Gavan Duffy. He urged the legalisation of tenant right, arguing, in 1852, that landlords continued to oppose this because,

> they are anxious that the law should still confide to them the unjust and irresponsible power of seizing upon the tenant's interest at their pleasure, that they may be able to control and over-influence the tenants at elections, and on other suitable occasions, and thus may augment their own power and authority.

He told the tenants,

> you cannot suppose that your present so-called representatives, who were prepared a few years ago to lay the whole burthen [sic] of the poor-rate upon the shoulders of the tenantry, will labour very strenuously for the interests of the tenantry upon the present occasion.

There was clearly significant anti-landlord support for the tenant right movement and Greer stood in County Londonderry on a tenant right platform at the 1852 general election. He said 'if, then, we love liberty more than despotism we will vote against all supporters of the present Government'. Greer, however, along with the other tenant right candidates, was defeated. In 1857 he failed to win a seat for the Presbyterian Representation Society at a by-election earlier in the year. However, with the support of other Presbyterians like Rev. Dr John Brown, minister of Aghadowey and Dr James McKnight, he was eventually successful as a tenant right candidate in becoming MP for Derry City and County Londonderry at the general election later in 1857, defeating Sir Harvey Bruce, the Tory candidate. Even Orangemen supported Greer and at least forty of them were expelled from the Orange Order for doing so (secret ballots were not introduced until 1872).

Greer opposed attempts by Rev. Cooke and others to bring the Presbyterian Church into a close relation with the Church of Ireland, which was against tenant right, political reform and Presbyterian marriages. He was Recorder for Derry from 1870 to 1878 when he became a judge in Cavan and Leitrim.

He died in 1880. His brother, Thomas Greer (licensed Coleraine), was ordained in 1839, and had a long ministry in Anahilt, County Down which lasted till his death on 26 March 1886.

Sources: Campbell 1991; Duffy 1896; Latimer 1893; Nelson 2005; Newman 1993; Wright 1996.

Francis Davis
1810–85

Francis Davis was born in Cork in 1810 before moving to the north where he learned his trade as a muslin weaver in Hillsborough, County Down. He campaigned for Catholic Emancipation as a young man. He moved to Manchester for a short time but returned to Belfast in 1843, where he was moved by the preaching of Rev. John Radcliffe of Castledawson. In 1848 he began writing for the Young Ireland paper *The Nation*, for which he interviewed William Carleton.

In 1868 he went with Hugh Leslie Stewart and Henry McDonald Flecher to visit their fellow poet Robert Huddleston at Moneyreagh. In 1849 Davis published *Lispings of the Lagan*. In *A Song of Eighteen Hundred and Forty Eight* he wrote about the military fiasco of the Young Ireland revolt of 1848, criticising the timidity of his enslaved countrymen, 'Crawl on, ye worthless reptile race, Crawl on in tearless degredation'.

In 1852 he published *Miscellaneous Poems and Songs,* which demonstrated his desire to see the radical purpose of uniting the national identity of Irishmen revived, 'Our island has wakened to freedom again'; 'Twas only in slumber she thought of a chain!'.

He was also conscious of divisions between north and south and expressed hope for reconciliation in *My Southern Brother.* He started his own weekly magazine, *Francis Davis, the Belfast Man's Journal* but it did not survive long. He became a Catholic just before his death in 1885.

Sources: Hewitt 2004; Vance 1990.

John Rogers (also spelled Rodgers)
1811–86

John Rogers was born in Agivey near Garvagh, County Londonderry. He was educated at Belfast Academical Institution where he received his General Certificate in 1835. He was licensed to preach by the Presbytery of Coleraine in 1837 and ordained in Second Comber on 27 March 1939, becoming their first minister. He married in 1840.

He was deeply affected by the impact of the famine, which encouraged him to develop his views on the rights of tenants who suffered so badly during this period. He developed a reputation, along with Rev. William Dobbin, John Rutherford, David Bell, J.L. Rentoul of Ballymoney and J. Johnston of Tullylish (see profiles on each) of been agitators on social, as well as on religious issues and was actively involved in tenant right demonstrations and meetings between 1848 and 1870. In May 1848 he raised the issue of tenant right at a Loyalty meeting, with such effect that those present drove the estate management away from the meeting altogether. He said that these Loyalty meetings had been used to make the Government believe that 'the people think this was a land flowing with milk and honey'. He was involved in a tenant right meeting in Comber in 1849.

When the government sent an inspector to examine the condition of tenant farms, Rogers accused John Andrews, who had accompanied the inspector, of making sure the inspector saw only what Andrews wanted him to see. Andrews was so incensed by this accusation that he accused Rogers of libel. The issue went to the Presbyterian Church court, but when it was considered, the matter was dropped. Later he attacked Lords Londonderry and Hertford for refusing to reduce their rents in the face of economic ruin that some tenant farmers were experiencing.

In March 1850 Rogers was part of a deputation to Westminster to lobby on behalf of the tenant farmers and tenant right. On their return the deputation spoke at a series of tenant right meetings around Ireland to report on their meetings in Westminster, including at the Music Hall in Belfast. At one of these meetings Rogers publicly criticised Lord Castlereagh. In County Kerry he made his view very clear that,

> Presbyterian Ulster is not Orange. Presbyterianism is incompatable with, and destructive of, Orangeism. Orangism is Toryism, and the genius of Presbyterianism is utterly antagonistic to such a despotic creed. Orangism is intolerance, and Presbyterianism has ever been foremost to rebuke intolerance, and to vindicate and defend civil and religious liberty.

At a meeting in Enniscorthy, County Wexford he recalled the radical days of 1798, in which Wexford and Ulster were united by a common cause. At a later meeting representing the League of North and South he argued for the value of working together with those of a different religious outlook to help the tenant farmers,

> Does my Presbyterianism forbid me to be a patriot? ... Will the farmers of Ireland – because they may conscientiously differ on their religious opinions – look on one another with distrust, and jealousy,

and hatred, while landlords and the legislature, that differ in religion
as widely as we do, one combined heart and soul, to carry on against
you the old familiar work of robbery, extermination and death.

In 1851 he was involved with the Tenant League in Armagh, Ballymoney
and Annaghlone and the following year in Donaghadee.

After the famine he saw the 'fair valuation of the land indispensable'. He
argued that the role of the tenant right movement was to 'stop landlords
appropriating the property of the tenant'. In the Irish Tenant League he saw
a 'union of north and south in one glorious brotherhood for the
regeneration of their common country' for which he felt they should
'labour energetically and determinedly by legal and constitutional means'.

In 1850, in the House of Lords a Tory magnate, Lord Londonderry
launched a savage attack on the campaign for tenant right as 'socialism and
communism', saying that the Ulster Custom was not a legal right. He called
the Presbyterian ministers who called for reform as 'clerical agitators'.
Rogers replied that, 'I owe no apology to landlords. The church of which I
am a member has never been a sychophant or slave of power'. In 1851 he
was one of several tenant right leaders to participate in deputations to the
Lord Lieutenant in Dublin.

Rogers inevitably came into conflict with the conservative Presbyterian,
Rev. Henry Cooke, when Rogers proposed a motion at Belfast Synod to
back the tenant right campaign. Cooke accused him of preaching
communism, when Rogers said that 'the entire outlay of the tenant farmer
has gone periodically into the pockets of the landlord'. Rogers rebutted
Cooke's accusations by saying that 'Communism is on the other side. It
would seem to be forgotten by some members that the poor man has
property which should be as fully secured as that of the rich'. He went on
to win the vote on tenant right in the Belfast synod. In 1850 four out of
the five Synods voted in support of tenant right.

He also made known his opposition to the Orange Order, which he
stated bluntly,

> Presbyterianism is incompatible with, and destructive of,
> Orangeism and Orangeism is Toryism and the genius of
> Presbyterianism is utterly antagonistic to such a despotic creed.
> Orangeism is intolerance but Presbyterianism has ever been
> foremost in rebuking intolerance and to vindicate and defend civil
> and religious liberty.

The major difficulty facing the Tenant League was how to keep the
northern and southern parts of the movement together, when they differed
so strongly on the key issue of the Act of Union. The southern members

tended to be supporters of the repeal of the Act of Union and the northern members against. In the Limerick by-election the Tenant League put up a strong pro-repeal candidate. Rogers, while trying to offer the 'least possible offence', had indicated that he was not personally in favour of repeal, but was attacked by Daniel O'Connell's son, John, leader of the Old Repeal Party, for 'denouncing Repeal'.

In the 1864 riots and industrial unrest in Belfast, John Rogers went, with the conservative Rev. 'Roaring' Hugh Hanna, to find a resolution to the strike at Murphy's Mill, most of whose workers were Catholic.

Rogers was appointed Professor of Sacred Rhetoric and Catechistics at Assembly's College Belfast from 1869–86, in succession to Henry Cooke, during which time he received his doctorate from Edinburgh University. Unusually, he was elected twice as Moderator of the General Assembly in both 1863 and 1865. During this period, great efforts were made to achieve an increase in the *regium donum* grant, which was under attack from an 'unholy alliance of Anglican supremacists and English voluntaryists'. Rogers' earlier involvement in the Tenant League enabled him to get support from a significant number of southern MPs. In 1870 he supported Dr James McKnight in going to meet Gladstone to negotiate changes to the Land Act, to include a clearer definition of the Ulster Custom. He retired in 1886, aged seventy-five, and died later the same year.

Sources: Duffy 1896; Latimer 1893; McElroy (undated); Wright 1996.

John Radcliff (sometimes spelled Radcliffe)
1811–98

John Radcliff was born in 1811, the son of Robert Radcliffe of Castlewellan. He was educated at Belfast Academical Institution, where he received his General Certificate. He was licensed to preach by the Belfast Presbytery in 1839 and was ordained in Castledawson, County Londonderry in 1841. He married Jane Wilson in 1845. She died eleven years later in 1856.

In September 1848, he recounted how the famine had affected his congregation,

> In the year 1846 occurred the great failure of the potatos crop. For a number of years previous there had been evident symptoms of failure … There ensued a winter of the direst calamity. Hunger was visible in its [fainests?] aspects. The people, suddenly changed in their food, from potatoes to the Indian meal, were visited with a most wasting dysentery. To meet these things were established Relief Committees. They were composed of the resident magistracy, the clergy of the three denominations, Episcopalians, Roman Catholic

and Presbyterian ... It was a wearisome thing to spend days after days at these Relief Committees and to come into contact with the hideous picture of misery, which was then prevented. It was more sorrowful still to look out and see the hungry look of the multitudes and to mark that all joy seemed to disappear from the human face.

The figures for the number of people going to the workhouses between December 1846 and May 1847 showed a very substantial increase to more than 3,000. The spread of fever caused further alarm, as Radcliff recorded,

The winter which succeeded which was that of 1847 was a drearful one of fever. From January 1847 until January 1848 there died out of this congregation fifty-two persons, one every week. On two separate occasions I recorded three funerals meeting in the graveyard at the same time. On two other occasions I saw two coffins brought together in the same cart. I hope God in his providence will spare the country from such a disaster in future and myself from ever witnessing anything similar.

In 1848 Radcliff resigned from his congregation in Castledawson to go as a missionary to Jamaica in the West Indies. He died in 1898.

Sources: Kinealy 1997.

John Martin
1812–75

John Martin was born in Loughorne near Newry, County Down in 1812, the son of a liberal-minded Presbyterian minister. He was educated locally at Dr Henderson's School in Newry, where he met John Mitchel and then at Trinity College Dublin, where he studied medicine, but eventually gave it up. Having received money from an uncle's will, he decided to travel extensively around America and Europe. When he returned to Ireland he was radicalised by the famine and joined the Young Irelanders and the Repeal Association. When his friend John Mitchel was arrested and his paper, the *United Irishman* suppressed, Martin started his own paper, the *Irish Felon*, to continue the struggle. His views are well summarised in the following quotation,

The English Parliament and Government cannot do good to Ireland, even if they were supposed to be willing to try. No matter what laws they make or change or amend, by way of relief or boon to Ireland, while their rule remains, it acts like a poison or cancer on the body of the Irish community, deranged its vital functions, crushing its vital forces, destroying its health or soundness ... It is not revolution or changes in constitutional forms that Ireland needs, or that the Irish people desire. It is simply Ireland for the Irish; for the Irish of every creed and class – for tenants and landlords – for Catholics and Protestants – for rich and poor.

Martin was tried for the felony of treason, for his membership of the Irish Confederation, and sentenced to transportation to Tasmania for ten years, although he was pardoned after five and returned to Ireland in 1856. He organised the National League in 1864.

He was a supporter of tenant right during the 1850s and critical of the extremism of the Irish Republican Brotherhood, although he delivered the oration at the funeral of the Manchester Martyrs in 1867, for which he was again charged with sedition, but this time acquitted. He was also involved in efforts to protect and promote the Irish language.

He was elected as the Irish Parliamentary Party MP for Meath in 1871 and became secretary to the Home Rule League and a member of the Home Government Association. In his maiden speech he opposed the Government's Coercion Bill. He held his seat until his death in 1875, a few days after attending the funeral of his friend and colleague, John Mitchel. He was known as 'Honest' John Martin, for his lifelong integrity. His successor as MP for Meath was Charles Stewart Parnell.

Sources: Boylan 1998; Campbell 1991; Hickey and Doherty 2005; Newman 1993.

Joseph McDonnell
1813–70

Joseph McDonnell was born in 1813, son of John McDonnell of Myroe, County Londonderry. He was educated at Belfast Academical Institution where he received his General Certificate on 1 June 1845. He was licensed by Belfast Presbytery in 1846 and ordained in 1848 in Terrace Row (Third) Presbyterian Church, Coleraine, succeeding Rev. William Magill who moved to Trinity, Cork.

He was very involved in the tenant right movement, attending and speaking at various Ulster Tenant Right Association meetings and conferences between 1848 and 1855, including those in Dungannon, Coleraine and Derry. At these meetings, as well as sharing the platform with other Presbyterian ministers he was happy to sit on the stage beside sympathetic Catholic priests.

As a result of the influence of the 1859 revival his church had to be enlarged to accommodate the additional members of his congregation. He died on 17 November 1870. He was succeeded by Rev. Robert Beattie Wylie.

Sources: McElroy (undated).

Robert Huddleston
1814–87

Robert Huddleston was born in 1814 at Tullyhubart Road, Moneyreagh, County Down, in view of Scrabo. He was the son of James and Agnes Huddleston. His father was a farmer and gunsmith, who fitted wooden stocks to guns in a workshop beside the house, and after his early education in the Old Session House in Moneyreagh, his son, Robert, followed in his footsteps. His brother John died young in 1836.

He was politically liberal – his hero being Thomas Paine. He was also 'new light' theologically and a member of the local Non-Subscribing Presbyterian Church. Two of his local influences were non-subscribing ministers, Rev. Fletcher Blakely (see profile), about whom he wrote a poem, and Rev. Harold Rylett (see profile), who was very active both on social issues and politically.

Huddleston was a prodigious poet and contributed poems to the *Ulster Magazine* and in the 1840s produced two major collections of his poetry, *A Collection of Poems and Songs on Rural Subjects* (1844), which was supported by almost four hundred subscribers and *A Collection of Poems and Songs on Different Subjects* (1846). In 'Co. Down Steeplechase' he used a horse-racing analogy to describe the issue of the tenant right campaign and the demand to give legal backing to the Ulster Custom. In 'Those who revile the unfortunate' he wrote a poem asking for a greater sense of compassion, and another about the plight of an unmarried mother. He wrote about capital punishment, hare coursing, exploitation of tenants, clergy who put the letter of the law before the spirit, hypocracy and narrow-mindedness in all its forms. But he also wrote in praise of Comber Whiskey and the Lammas Fair, the latter which would become his best-known poem.

He did not marry until the death of his mother in 1861, when, on 26 February 1862, he was married by the non-subscribing Presbyterian minister Rev. John Jellie (see profile) to Margaret Jane Ellison, thirty years his junior. When he died, aged 73, on 15 February 1887, his wife survived him and lived until 1922. Two of their three children, James and Nancy, also survived him. His daughter, Mary had died in 1877 and he had expressed his grief in several poems.

He wrote his own epitaph, in which he described himself as 'the unlettered muse'. He is buried in Moneyreagh graveyard. He has been described as "one of the most accomplished and prolific of the Ulster-Scots poets in the nineteenth-century".

Sources: Hewitt 2004; Ferguson 2008; Gilpin 2009.

Matthew Macauley
1815–1907

Matthew Macauley was born in 1815 in Drumgooland between Banbridge and Castlewellan, County Down. He studied theology at Belfast Academical Institution for three years and, after a final year in Edinburgh, was licensed to preach in Rathfriland in 1847. He was ordained later the same year in McKelvey's Grove near Castleblayney in County Monaghan and became their first minister. However, the congregation was very poor and there was no meetinghouse or manse and so Macauley held services in a local barn. He was then called to Boveedy, County Londonderry, by a majority of one vote, over Rev. John Gilmore. However, the level of conflict within the new congregation, over the controversial practice of local hand weavers keeping some of the yarn they were given, in order to make a whole weft of their own, made being the minister untenable and he returned to McKelvey's Grove before even being formally installed in Boveedy.

In 1886 when the moderator called a special Assembly in order to deplore Gladstone's move towards Home Rule and specifically the creation of an Irish Assembly without safeguards for minority groups, Macauley was the only minister who attempted to oppose the motion, although his opposition was not formally recorded on that occasion. At the General Assembly three months later, it was recorded that Macauley warned the Assembly not to 'provoke jealousy, bitterness or strife in any part of the country'.

During this period, many Protestant home rulers were attacked or boycotted for their support for Home Rule. In Macauley's case, local Orangemen got up a petition against him, saying they would not enter his church or pay a farthing towards his stipend while he was still the minister, which was signed by 50 members of his congregation. The church at McKelvey's Grove was desecrated and he was physically attacked in front of his wife, by a 'gang of Orangemen'. Macauley was eventually forced to resign. This case received prominence in parliament.

Macauley was also a strong opponent of landlordism and supporter of the rights of tenants. He retired in 1886 and became an active Justice of the Peace. He died in 1907.

Sources: Latimer 1992; McCann 1972.

James Miller Killen
1815–79

James Killen was born in Ballymena, County Antrim in 1815, the son of a merchant. He was educated at Glasgow University where he gained an MA in 1838. He was licensed to preach in Ballymena in 1841 and was ordained two years later, on 9 May 1843, in First Comber, County Down, succeeding the controversial 'home ruler' Rev. Isaac Nelson, as their minister. Killen was awarded a Doctorate in Divinity by Jefferson University in America. He married in 1843, but his wife died and he remarried ten years later in 1853.

He was an active supporter of the tenant right campaign and was a platform speaker, along with other Presbyterian ministers and a Catholic priest, at the large tenant right meeting in Banbridge in 1849. He said that Ulster landlords in both Houses of Parliament were misleading public opinion on the real state of the north of Ireland and that in fact 'Ulster was on the edge of pauperism'. He went on to say that 'all those who had advocated the cause of the tenant farmers had been reviled by the landlords and their creatures, as levellers, Communists, Red Republicans, Socialists, confiscators or property and public robbers', but he warned landlords that the Presbyterian clergy, 'were rather troublesome antagonists, and they would do well not to provoke them'.

In February 1850 he said that 'tenant right in County Down was currently enjoyed at the sufferance of the landlord or his agent … a right such as the Czar of Russia would give to his serfs'. In March 1850 when the deputation on tenant right to parliament in London had returned to Ireland there was a major meeting held in the Music Hall in Belfast to report back on the response from the people they met. Killen was one of the platform speakers.

Killen, like many supporters of tenant right wanted to see stronger representation from liberal Presbyterians and in 1850 argued that getting tenant right enshrined in law would enable tenant voters to be independent of the conservative political control of their landlords and return MPs of their own choice.

He had two publications printed, *Our Friends in Heaven* and *Our Companions in Glory*. He died on 3 September 1879. He had two sons-in-law who became ministers, Rev. David Gordon of Conlig and Rev. William Wilson of Spa.

Sources: Nelson 2005.

John Mitchel
1815–75

John Mitchel was born at Camnish near Dungiven, County Londonderry in 1815. His father was, Rev. John Mitchel, a non-subscribing Presbyterian minister who had been a United Irishman and his mother was Mary (née Haslett) from Maghera. When his father was called to the church in Newry, after four years in Derry, they moved into the manse at Dromalane and John jr was educated in Dr Henderson's school, Newry, where he met John Martin, and at Trinity College Dublin.

In 1836, and then again in 1837, Mitchel eloped to England with his sixteen-year-old girlfriend, Jane Verner, and eventually married her. They had six children.

He considered various careers, including working for a while in his uncle's bank in Derry, but in 1840 he became apprenticed as a solicitor in Newry. He later settled in Banbridge where his outspoken views brought him into conflict with the Orange Order. As a lawyer he often defended Catholics against local Orangemen. There he also met Thomas Davis, whose place he took on the journal *The Nation*. He moved to Dublin, after Davis died in 1845, until he had a disagreement with Charles Gavin Duffy who refused to publish two of his more militant articles. In 1848 Mitchel founded the *United Irishman*.

He was a member of the Repeal Association (to repeal the Act of Union) and, under the influence of James Fintan Lawlor, joined the Young Ireland movement. He broke with Daniel O'Connell and became a member of the militant Irish Confederation and openly advocated sedition to 'the men of no property', as fifty years earlier they were inspired by events in France and contemplated revolution.

Mitchel advocated a militant policy to defend tenant farmers during the Great Famine, including not paying rent or rates, resisting eviction, ostracising all who did not co-operate, sabotaging railways and arming themselves. He believed that a complete break with England was required. He was tried for treason and felony and sentenced to transportation to Van Diemen's Land (Tasmania) for 14 years, where he initially lived with John Martin and where his family joined him in 1851. He escaped to America in 1853, where he published his *Jail journal or five years in British prisons*. He supported slavery and the South in the Civil War and two of his children were killed in the conflict. In 1865 he was arrested by the military authorities for his articles in the *Daily News* and spent five months in jail. In America he denounced the Fenian movement and home rulers.

When he eventually returned to Ireland in 1874 he was elected an MP in both 1874 and 1875 but was each time declared ineligible as an undischarged felon. He died during the second victory celebrations.

Amongst other works he edited the poems of James Clarence Mangan and Thomas Davis. He died in Dromalane, Newry, County Down in 1875 and was buried beside his parents.

Sources: Bardon 1992; Boylan 1998; Brooke 1994; Byrne and McMahon 1991; Campbell 1991; Dillon 1888; Hickey and Doherty 2005; Hume 1998; Newman 1993; Wallace 1999; Wright 1996.

William Dobbin
1816–1900

William Dobbin was born at Cappagh in Annaghlone, County Down in 1816. In 1830 the family moved to Cranfield, Randalstown, County Londonderry. He was educated at the Belfast Academical Institution, where he received his General Certificate in 1836. He was licensed by the Ballymena Presbytery in 1838 and ordained in Second Annaghlone Church in 1839. He was clerk of Banbridge Presbytery from 1849 to 1893 and then the Belfast Synod.

In the period following the Great Famine, the economic pressures on tenants were still considerable. Particularly under attack was the Ulster Custom – the '3 Fs', of fair rents, fixity of tenure and free sale. A campaign built up in both the north and south of Ireland. Dobbin became the secretary of the Banbridge Tenant Right Association.

The climax of this campaign came in the summer of 1850 with two big conferences, one in the north and one in the south. The Belfast conference was attended by 1,600 delegates. The Presbyterian Church was represented by Dobbin and Rev. David Bell of Ballybay. Dobbin's speech captured the mood of the conference:

> I rejoice that on this subject (of tenants' rights) there is now but one opinion in Ireland … Six million of Irishmen shall soon, in reference to this matter, be one united band. The policy of divide-and-conquer has had its day. The people fought and bled, and starved and died, and the landlords gained and revelled and rack rented and evicted, but our day of folly is drawing to a close. Affliction's sons are brothers in distress; and ere two months elapse, the North and South shall be banded together on this land question (tremendous cheering) – and from Ireland's united people a voice will soon go forth far too loud to be unheeded – too stern to be disregarded – proclaiming in the face of the empire, that feudal tyranny – a system that flesh and blood can no longer endure – poor, suffering, patient and loyal Ulster must at length be free.

Dobbin, along with a Catholic priest and an Episcopalian minister, was appointed as joint secretary to the movement. Dobbin's statements on tenant right, which made it clear the ministers' determination to be tenant advocates, so angered Tory magnate, Lord Londonderry that he launched a verbal attack on Dobbin, accusing him of incendiarism in Down and Antrim, using subversive language and stirring up tenants not to pay their lawful rents. He was also attacked from inside the church by Rev. Henry Cooke, who accused Dobbin of propagating communist doctrines and the worst practices of the French Revolution. He particularly condemned Dobbin for his contacts with the south of Ireland and supporting fraternity with Catholics.

Dobbin retired in 1890 and died in 1900.

Sources: Campbell 1991; Nelson 2005.

Charles Wilson
1817–93

Charles Wilson was born in 1817, son of United Irishman Samuel Wilson, and whose great-aunt, Margaret Wilson (the 'Wigtown martyr') had been drowned at the stake in Scotland for refusing to swear the Oath of Abjuration, and his wife Mary (née Smylie), and brought up in Ballycloughan near Broughshane, County Antrim. Despite the disapproval of his parents and minister, he emigrated to Australia in 1838, with his brother, when his father's investments in the Agricultural Bank turned out to be worthless as the result of a swindle. They had to walk over 600 miles to find suitable land. However the brothers eventually became the largest sheep farmers in Victoria, Australia owning 10,000 acres of land.

In Australia he became a lay preacher and provided free education for the children of all his workers. The family financed the rebuilding of the principal Presbyterian Church in Melbourne. He returned on visits to Ireland in 1856 and 1859 when he married Elizabeth Jane Leece from near Preston in England and had two children, Harold Charles and Frances Anne, who married Sir George Baden-Powell. They returned to Australia in 1869. After thirty years in Australia he retired from the business, which was continued by his brothers Samuel (who became Sir Samuel Wilson) and Alexander. He eventually decided to return to the northern hemisphere and moved to Cheltenham in England.

In February 1874, having had difficulty identifying a suitable candidate, a meeting of County Antrim tenant right deputies selected Wilson to stand in the general election, despite the fact that he was largely unknown. Wilson committed himself to stand on liberal and tenant right principles. It was, as Wilson suggested, a 'purely tenant-right contest'. Wilson's Presbyterianism and attacks on his conservative opponents for failing to support various burial bills since 1868, suggests that many of those who voted for him were supporting a traditional dissenter cause against their traditional enemy – the gentry and the Episcopal Church. Because of his time in Australia, Wilson was nicknamed by his opponents as a 'returned convict' and accused of being a 'vulgar, rich squatter of farmer origin and connection', and some questioned the value of a candidate who had never subscribed or contributed to the benevolent institutions of the area. It also seems that Wilson was not a great public speaker, but the liberals campaigned hard for their candidate in the short time available. One local Conservative, H. H. McNeile, commented on Wilson's campaign,

> I fancy he is about what you would expect – a vulgar, rich squatter of farmer origin and connection. It is said he is a poor performer, but he has very busy partisans, well organised through the tenant leagues and he has the sympathies of a vast number of the tenant class, who have only just had their appetites whetted by the land bill – and who believe that Wilson's return will go far to get them further important slices of their landlord's property

Wilson received considerable support from Presbyterian clergy. At one of his campaign meetings there were no less than seven Presbyterian ministers present, including J.B. Armour. In the end Wilson received over 4,000 votes but was defeated by the Conservatives, James Chaine and Lord Edward O'Neill, by only 133 votes, despite being virtually unknown, greatly improving the poor liberal by-election performance in 1869.

In 1876 Wilson was elected as president of both the Antrim Liberal Association, chairing its first meeting in Clarence Place Hall in Belfast on 7 June that year, and the Central Antrim Tenant Right Association and presiding over its first meeting.

In planning for the 1880 general election, the Antrim Central Tenant Right Association, representing farmers groups, sought the help of Lord Waveney, President of both the Ulster Liberal Society and the Central Tenant Association to ask him to persuade Charles Wilson to stand again. The leader of the Antrim Tenant Right Association, Samuel C. McElroy (see profile) believed that 'Wilson can carry the County, and the gain of even one seat would be of much value to the Liberal party'. Wilson eventually agreed to stand again and emphasised his support for fair rents, 'to be adjusted by arbitration', continuous occupation, and free sale. He pledged his support for equal treatment of all Irish farmers, the ultimate creation of peasant proprietorship and the right of local self-government throughout the United Kingdom, but he and tenant farmer, Samuel Black (see profile), were again narrowly defeated by the two Conservative candidates.

In January 1882, the Antrim Central Tenant Right Association again approached Wilson to stand as a Liberal in the general election. Wilson initially agreed, but by June had decided against standing again and effectively retired from politics. Wilson died in Cheltenham in 1893 aged 76.

Sources: McElroy (undated); Thompson 2002; Walker 1989; handwritten memoir of David Wilson.

David Bell
1818–90

David Bell was born in Mosside, County Antrim, probably in 1818, the son of Rev. Thomas Bell of Mosside, a native of the Ballybay area in County Monaghan. He was educated locally and then at Royal Belfast Academical Institution. After studying theology, he was licensed in Coleraine and then ordained in 1839 and became Secessionist Presbyterian minister of Derryvalley Presbyterian Church a mile from Ballybay. With his experience of the Famine in this rural area, he could not avoid the 'awful spectacles of poverty and wretchedness that the hearts of ministers were wrung with agony at witnessing them' and became actively involved in social issues.

He was a strong support of tenant right. At a tenant right meeting in 1848 he moved a motion, 'That no proprietor of land is justly entitled to a larger sum in the form of rent than the produce of the land would be worth in its natural state'.

He played a critical role in the establishment and development of the Tenant League, which was established to promote the fixity of tenure at fair rents. He was on the platform of the first Tenant Right meeting in Ballybay in 1848, with Rev. Hanson of Drumkeen and Rev. Parr of Corlea and a dozen Catholic priests and another in Carrickmacross in February the same year. He successfully defeated a landlord protectionist gathering in Monaghan. In May 1848 he spoke at a mass meeting of the Ulster Tenant Right Association in Dungannon.

He organised, and acted as secretary for a major meeting of the Tenant League, which was held in Ballybay, County Monaghan, in 1850, at which they expected 500 people and had to make arrangements for the 30,000 people that turned up. The meeting required great diplomacy because of the careful balance that was required between the Protestant and Catholic elements. Even the issue of where the speakers should stay overnight was one of great sensitivity. Staying at the York Hotel owned by Orangeman's Sam Grey's family was seen as important in maintaining local Protestant involvement, but offensive to local Catholics. In the end the speakers stayed in two different places, and to some it seemed that 'all the old animosities of the people were forgotten, buried in oblivion'. Bell and the Rev. Philip Brennan put forward the resolution to the assembled meeting,

> That in this locality every engine which earth and hell could set in motion has been mustered to prevent this meeting. Many have been kept away whose hearts are with us, who had not sufficient resolution to overcome the unlimited and ruthless powers of our merciless oppressors.

Bell was a northern member of the Tenant League who also went on deputations to southern Tenant League meetings. He was a staunch opponent of the Orange Order, which had been established by members of the Established Church. In a meeting in Kilkenny, he stated that 'Presbyterian Ulster is not Orange', 'No one therefore, but an ignorant and apostate Presbyterian could be an Orangeman … I will tell you who the Orangemen of the North are – landlords and agents in the one extreme – bailiffs and the rag-tag and bobtail of society in the other'. This did not do his popularity in Ulster any good, and potentially damaged the attempt to keep the Tenant League, north and south, together.

Bell was criticised for sharing Tenant League platforms with Catholics, many of whom were publicly in favour of Repeal of the Act of Union, which the *Belfast Newsletter* described as 'the stigma of an implied alliance with Popery and Repeal'. In response to this and Lord John Russell's letter to the Bishop of Durham describing the organisation of the Catholic hierarchy in England as 'aggression of the Pope upon our Protestantism' 'as insolent and insidious', Bell responded, 'Why should I object to Catholics, whose religion has been stigmatised and reprobated by Lord John Russell, repelling the insult and banding together in sustainment of civil and religious liberty.'

He was a member of the delegation in March 1850 that went to Westminster to plead the case of the tenant farmers and spoke at various meetings around Ulster to let the tenant farmers know the reaction they had received in parliament, including at a meeting in the Music Hall Belfast where he said,

> Let the people know the fate of their neighbours on the property of Mr Shirley of Carrickmacross where you could ascend a hill and count tens and fifties and hundreds of ruined homesteads whose blackened walls and silent desolation tell to God and man that the merciless destroyer has been there; where there are thirteen auxiliary workhouses and more sought for, as all are crammed in suffocation … In the name of justice, in the name of humanity, in the name of mercy, in the awful name of God, I call upon Lord John Russell; I call upon the Government; I call upon the Imperial Legislature to render the poor man's property as sacred as that of the rich.

Under pressure from the Tory members of his congregation, he was forced to resign as minister in 1853. Having despaired of constitutional methods of bringing about change, he met Jeremiah O'Donovan Rossa in Manchester and swore the oath of the Irish Republican Brotherhood (Fenian) movement. He edited the pro-Fenian *Irish Liberator* newspaper for a time in London, as well as promoting the IRB newspaper, *Irish People,* and, in 1864, generating support for the IRB in Scotland. He was appointed to their Executive in 1865. He promoted their cause in both England and in America, where he was sent for a year in 1864. When all the other members of the IRB Executive were arrested he was lucky to avoid capture in 1865, when he managed to escape to France and then America, where he founded the *Irish Republic* paper and where he eventually died in 1890, aged 72. He is buried in Flushing Meadow, New York.

Sources: Campbell 1991; Dowling 1999; McElroy (undated); Murnane and Murnane 1999; O Cathain 2007; Wright 1996.

Robert Black
1818–85

Robert Black was born in Shercock, east County Cavan in 1818. He was educated at Royal Belfast Academical Institution, receiving his General Certificate in 1841. He was licensed by Baileborough Presbytery in 1844. He was ordained in Ballycopeland, County Down on 10 June 1846, succeeding Rev. Samuel James Moore, in what were described as 'difficult times of famine and distress'. He was clerk of the Ards Presbytery 1856–60. He married in 1860.

Black was a strong supporter of the tenant right movement and attended the first meeting of the Tenant League of North and South in Dublin in 1850. At a meeting in Greyabbey, County Down in February 1851, he called for a 'union among Irishmen' and decried 'the absurdity of division among Irishmen'. That year he claimed that 'Nineteenth-twentieths of the farmers of Donaghadee had subscribed to the League – and that even in the districts where the insatiable leech of landlordism was drinking the lifeblood of the people – many had come forward with their 2d and their 3d'.

On 11 June 1860 he accepted a call to Dundalk, where he succeeded Rev. William McHinch. He was convenor of the Soldiers and Sailors Mission. He retired in 1879 and died on 15 April 1885.

Sources: Nelson 2005.

William McIlwaine (also spelled M'Ilwaine)
1818–1902

William McIlwaine was born on 8 July 1818, the youngest son of William McIlwaine a merchant of Ramelton in County Donegal. He was educated locally and then Glasgow University where he graduated with an MA (Glas) in 1837. He was licensed to preach by Letterkenny Presbytery, County Donegal in 1840. He turned down a call from a Belfast congregation and instead accepted the call to be ordained to the ministry in Aughnacloy by Clogher Presbytery on 14 February 1843. Rev. J. Steel Dickson preached at his ordination.

During the 1845–7 period of the Great Famine, McIlwaine was 'chiefly occupied with meetings of relief committees and organisations for alleviating the pressing necessities of the suffering around us'. He was secretary of an inter-denominational relief committee chaired by Archdeacon Stokes, which met two or three times a week and set up a soup kitchen, sold half price food subsidised by the Relief Committee and provided work for unemployed men cutting roads amongst other jobs. At times, McIlwaine said, he was 'planning work for over 150 men'. After the Famine, came the spread of disease and again McIlwaine and Stokes, were involved in raising money to establish a fever hospital in Aughnacloy, of which McIlwaine was secretary for 50 years. He was also secretary of the Jackson Almshouse.

He fundraised extensively to rebuild the church by 1850, after a brief period using the primitive Welseyan preaching house. In 1858 the church put in gas lighting. The following year 'The Great Revival' had taken hold around Ulster. Although McIlwaine felt that it, on balance, was a good thing, he also recognised that it 'was accompanied with unwanted results'.

McIlwaine was also a strong supporter of both primary and intermediate education. He established a Sunday school next to the church in 1853. In 1864, he established a Day School, for which he fundraised in Liverpool. The commitment to education left the church with significant debts, which he managed to pay off during a long fundraising trip to the United States and Canada in 1869/70. After the passing of the Intermediate Education Act of 1878, McIlwaine was involved in the establishment of an Intermediate school, initially in the old Methodist preaching house. In 1885 the commissioners of National Education provided a grant of £255 to replace the sub-standard school building. McIlwaine was also a key player in the establishment of a local library and reading room in 1853, to which, again, he was appointed secretary.

Politically McIlwaine was liberal and chaired a political meeting in March 1880 in Monaghan in support of one of his church elders and Sunday School superintendent, John Givan (see profile). The election was fought on the issue of land reform and Givan was eventually elected along with William Findlater (see profile).

In 1887 McIlwaine published an address he had made to the members of his congregation about the history of the area and the church. In 1889 a new church was built. McIlwaine retired on 2 August 1892 and in 1901 he followed the initial publication with *A retrospection and outlook* and the following year with *A recent chapter on our congregational history and a thought bearing on the century yet in its infancy.*

McIlwaine died on 13 October 1903 and was buried on 16 October in the graveyard in front of the church.

Sources: Barkley 1986; McGimpsey 1982; McIlwaine 1887, 1901 and 1902.

Andrew George Malcolm (sometimes spelled Malcom)
1818–56

Andrew Malcolm was born in Newry in 1818. He was the sixth child of Rev. Andrew George Malcom, who was a non-subscribing minister in Newry, and moderator of the General Synod in 1820. Unfortunately his father died of typhus fever when Andrew jr was only four years old. His mother was Eleanor (née Hunter) also from Newry.

The early and mid-nineteenth century was a period of great poverty and disease in Ireland. Sanitation and public health care were both virtually non-existent. His father, Andrew Malcolm (who used a different spelling of the surname), had been secretary of the Newry Board of Health which was only established to deal with the high levels of fever that had started to occur in the area.

In 1829, the family moved to York Street in north Belfast and became members of First Belfast Non-Subscribing congregation and were there when John Scott Porter was called as minister. Andrew Malcolm jr was educated at Royal Belfast Academical Institution, where he won prizes in Moral Philosophy and Rhetoric and Logic. So highly regarded was he, as a student, that he was appointed as an assistant by the Professor, the famous non-subscriber, Rev. Henry Montgomery. He then moved to Edinburgh to study medicine and received his medical certificate in 1842. He worked as a student in Frederick Street Fever Hospital in Belfast and wrote his thesis on *Pathology and Continuing Fever*, which won a gold medal. In the process he contracted fever himself, which he survived. After qualifying as a doctor he started his medical practice from his mother's house in York Street and was appointed to the voluntary position of District Medical Attendant to the poor in north Belfast with the charity, Belfast General Dispensary, where he was involved in visiting the homes of the poor in the area who were not capable of visiting the dispensary, as well as working out of the hospital. When the Dispensary was re-organised on a more professional basis, Malcolm was appointed to a salaried position of District Medical Attendant for the Dock District.

In 1845, he was appointed as an attending physician at the Fever Hospital. He also conducted children's eye clinics and argued for the establishment of a hospital for sick children and corresponded with Dr Charles West who set one up in London. In his work Malcolm put a great emphasis on the training and instruction of students.

Malcolm strongly advocated the use of the microscope – a long time before its importance was recognised by the Medical Council. He also gave annual lectures on diseases of the skin and became a lecturer on pathology at Queen's College, before there was a medical faculty.

From his experience with families in the area, Malcolm became concerned about the 'slave-labour of the working people' and the health of the large number of workers, from as young as ten, then employed in the unregulated textile mills. He wrote a paper in 1855 on 'The influence of factory life on the health of operatives'. He strongly supported the Ten Hour Act, which limited the number of daily hours worked to ten a day. He encouraged employers to facilitate the education of their workforce and establish reading clubs and music societies for their employees.

Malcolm was so concerned about the welfare of the poor that he founded, and became the first President of, the Belfast Working Classes Association for the promotion of general improvement. Their first annual meeting was held in the ironing room of a public washhouse where there was a banner which read, 'Labour – the only source of wealth'. The Association developed a popular reading room and in 1847 published its own magazine the *Belfast People's Magazine*, which Malcolm edited. It was a campaigning vehicle for Malcolm to try to bring about improvement in housing and sanitation, as well as moral and recreational improvements. He was clear that the 'education of the working classes has been for a long time too much neglected'. He also planned to support the involvement of the poor in the arts by establishing a school of design, when the government decided that it was such a good idea that they would take over the idea. The Association then opened a newsroom to make available local, national and international newspapers to those who could not otherwise afford them and a circulating library, so there would be books available to the poor.

Malcolm also organised a series of lectures through the Association on topics like *Education for Women, Sanitation, Adulteration of Food* (Malcolm himself), *The Social Position of the Working Classes* (Rev. William Johnston of Townsend Street – see profile) and *Practical Education* (Rev. Isaac Nelson – see profile).

Malcolm was an active member of the Belfast Social Enquiry Society which campaigned for the opening of a public park. He was also secretary of the Belfast Society for the amelioration of the condition of the working classes, founded in 1845, which decided that its priority was the provision of public baths and washing houses. Malcolm visited various similar initiatives in six English towns and was eventually successful in building a public baths and washing house between Townsend Street and Divis Street.

Unfortunately it quickly ran into financial trouble and Malcolm campaigned vigorously for it to be taken over by the town council. His lobbying included getting support from clergy from all denominations and the doctors of Belfast, but to no avail and the bathhouse closed.

When the Great Irish Famine hit in 1845, an outbreak of fever was not far behind. With the spread of disease, a Board of Health was established in Belfast and Malcolm became one of the officers of the Board to try and tackle the outbreak, although with such poor sanitation and housing there was only a limited amount they could do. A year later, as the epidemic subsided, the Board of Health was abolished despite objections from Malcolm, who saw the need for a permanent health body.

In 1847 he wrote a series of articles outlining the findings of sanitary inspections he conducted in what is now inner north Belfast. He was deeply concerned about the level of overcrowding, the poor ventilation and almost non-existent sanitary provision and the lack of clean water and the impact of these conditions on the health of families and the ever-present danger of disease. He dramatically said 'the churchyards have been fattened with the children of toil, and the poor-houses are thronged with their orphans'. Despite all his efforts he found general apathy regarding the need to tackle these social conditions for the poor. He continued with his lobbying and recommended to the town council improvements to drainage, ventilation, water to every house, street cleaning, public lavatories and the strict control of the building of new houses. In response the town council established the Belfast Sanitary Committee. In 1848 after a series of warnings from Malcolm, cholera arrived in Belfast and lasted for a year, with over 2,000 cases reported. With the ending of the cholera epidemic the town council closed down the Belfast Sanitary Committee.

Malcolm published a *History of the General Hospital and other Medical Institutions in Belfast*, in 1851, to generate funds for the hospital. In 1845 he had married and two years later had a son, who unfortunately died of meningitis. Malcolm died of heart disease in 1856, after moving to Dublin to access the best medical assistance available. He was later moved to Belfast for burial.

Sources: Bardon 1992; Calwell 1977; Malcolm 1851; Newman 1993.

William Johnston
1818–94

William Johnston was born at Crieve House near Ballybay, County Monaghan in 1818, the son of Rev. John Johnson of Tullylish and Frances (née Jackson). In 1827 the family moved to Banbridge, County Down. He was educated at a small private school locally and then, in 1834, with his brother, Jackson, at Belfast Academy, under Rev. Dr Bryce. In 1835, when he decided that he had a vocation for the ministry, he enrolled at the Royal Belfast Academical Institution.

In 1838 his mother died and two years later his brother, Jackson. He completed his studies for the ministry in Edinburgh. An orthodox evangelical theologically, he was licensed to preach by Dromore Presbytery in 1840, the year that the General Synod of Ulster and the Seceders formally joined together as a single church.

He was ordained in Berry Street, Belfast in 1842. In this poor inner city congregation, during the plague which followed the Famine in the 1840s, every day he would visit the hospitals and their overflow tents and sheds, ministering to the large numbers of sick and dying. This was despite the experience of his brother who had died of a contagious disease as a result of close contact with someone who was already ill with the disease. He did, in fact, get ill but managed to recover after several months of recuperation.

In 1847 he was installed as minister of Townsend Street church in Belfast, where he spent the rest of his ministry and where he developed his reputation as a preacher.

He was deeply concerned about the lack of education for the poor in Belfast and began establishing small schools. He ended up managing 16 national schools. He would rent a tenement and gut it completely, or persuade a local builder to build a modest school house. He would supply the desks and forms and appoint a teacher.

In the debate on National Education, Johnston was concerned about the power of landlordism and the Anglican Church and the position of minorities in rural areas who would have to send their children to primary schools run by other denominations. He was strongly opposed to denominationalism in education.

Johnston was concerned about the plight of children whose parents had died and so founded both the Presbyterian Orphan Society and the Society of Orphans of Ministers. He also founded the Sabbath School Society and the Aged and Infirm Ministers' Fund and was a popular preacher and educationalist. He was elected moderator of the General Assembly in 1872. He received a doctorate from Princeton in 1879. He married the daughter of Rev. James Porter of Drumlee. Johnston died in 1894.

Sources: Barkley 1986; Newman 1993; Prenter 1895; Wright 1996.

Thomas Miller (also spelled Millar)
1819–58

Thomas Miller was the son of Rev. Thomas Miller of Second Cookstown, County Tyrone. He was educated at Royal Belfast Academical Institution where he gained his General Certificate in 1841. He was licensed by Tyrone Presbytery in 1841 and ordained by the Home Mission on 24 May 1842. He resigned from the Home Mission in 1844 to become the minister of First Lurgan on 1 October 1844, following the Rev. Hamilton Dobbin.

He was a strong supporter of the tenant right campaign. At a meeting in Lurgan in March 1848 he advocated fixity of tenure and the right of the tenant to a 'permanent property in the soil'. He supported James McKnight's belief that during the plantation, landlords had only been give property on public trusteeships, and he advocated fixity of tenure and the right of the tenant to a permanent property on the soil. He was the founder of the *Lurgan Messenger*.

Miller was killed in a train accident in the Trent Valley near Nuneaton on 10 May 1858 aged 39.

Sources: Barkley 1986; Nelson 2005.

Nathaniel McAuley Brown
1820–1910

Nathaniel Brown was born at Burren, near Ballynahinch in 1820 and was educated at Royal Belfast Academical Institution. Following his studies he was ordained as a Presbyterian minister in Drumachose 1845 and became minister of Newtownlimavady.

Despite the huge growth in industrialisation around Belfast, the rural economy and land in particular continued to be a critical and emotive issue. In Ulster, the tenant farmers had traditionally enjoyed the right through custom to be reimbursed for improvements made to their holdings during their tenancy. The Ulster Custom had no basis in law only in custom and practice. It was not popular with Ulster landlords who began to disregard the custom, with the help of their lawyers who demonstrated the lack of any legal basis for the practice and argued that it contradicted the right of property.

In the 1840s the tenant right movement gathered momentum, demanding, what Brown, minister of Limavady, called the '3 Fs': fair rents, fixity of tenure (except for non-payment of rent) and free sale of the tenant's interest in the holding. Brown played a very influential part in the tenant right movement and often shared a platform with Catholic clergymen at land meetings.

When the National Tenant League was formed in 1850 the northern delegation was led by ten Presbyterian ministers and four Catholic priests.

In 1873 he made a very powerful speech in support of the Ulster Custom at a public demonstration in Ballymoney.

Brown was a founder of the Protestant Nationalist Party, which ultimately failed to persuade any significant number of Protestants to support Home Rule.

Brown was one of the key players, with A.P. Goudy (see profile), Henry Cooke's great rival; Dr John Brown (see profile) and others in trying to get an independent Presbyterian college established with an undergraduate as well as theological department, resulting in the foundation in 1865 of Magee College, Derry and Assembly's College Belfast.

He married in 1857, was moderator of the General Assembly in 1891/2 and died in 1910, aged ninety.

Sources: Barkley 1993; Campbell 1991; Hickey and Doherty 2005; Holmes 1985; Latimer 1893; McElroy (undated).

David Maginnis
1821–84

David Maginnis was born near Downpatrick, County Down in 1821. He was educated at Royal Belfast Academical Institution, where he received his theological training under non-subscribers Henry Montgomery and Scott Porter and received his General Certificate in 1839. He was licensed by Antrim Presbytery in 1842 and ordained by Bangor Presbytery in the Non-Subscribing York Street congregation in Belfast later that year.

Maginnis was one of a group of younger ministers who wanted to go further than Montgomery in his progressive theological thinking. He was accused of 'denying the personality of the devil, the pre-existence of Christ, and spoke of Jesus in the same way as Paul or Socrates'. Montgomery was so concerned about the extent of this radical thinking amongst the non-subscribing ministers that he attempted to introduce a Code of Discipline to curb this enthusiasm for rationalism. In the face of the opposition of Maginnis and others, as well as Unitarian journals such as *The London Enquirer*, Montgomery had to back down in the end because of difficulties with the legal interpretation of the questions.

In 1848 Maginnis edited the *Irish Truth Seeker*, in 1858 the *Beth-Berie Magazine* and *The Non Subscriber* from 1858 to 1861. He was elected Moderator of the Non-Subscribing Remonstrant Presbyterian Synod in 1851.

In 1861 he resigned from York Street and moved to Stourbridge in England where he was minister until his death in 1884.

Sources: Haire 1981; McMillen 1969; notes from Rev. John Nelson.

John Maxwell
1822–83

John Maxwell was born in 1 July 1822, the son of Lieutenant William H.M. Maxwell of the 72nd Highlanders. He was educated at Royal Belfast Academical Institution where he received his General Certificate in 1843. He was licensed by Omagh Presbytery in 1845 and ordained at Brigh Presbyterian Church near Stewartstown in County Tyrone, on 30 June 1846. He succeeded Rev. Samuel H. Elder who had died more than two years earlier.

At a tenant right meeting in Cookstown, County Tyrone in February 1848, very conscious of the suffering of the tenant farmers who made up most of his congregation, he attacked the laws as 'investing the landlord with an almost arbitrary and irresponsible power – a power which in a free country, should not be possessed by any man'. He also attacked landlords for 'withholding ... leases from the tenants'. He strongly supported the legalisation of tenant right, 'As the landlord furnishes the material to the wrought upon, while the tenant applies industry and capital, both are entitled to a proportionate share of the profits arising from the joint result.'

Maxwell died on 29 June 1883.

Sources: Barkley 1986; Nelson 2005.

Thomas Armstrong
1822–97

Thomas Armstrong was born in Monaghan in 1822, the son of John Armstrong. He was educated at Belfast Academical Institution and in 1837/8 studied the Irish language. In 1842 he received an Edinburgh General Certificate. He was licensed by the Monaghan Presbytery in 1844 and ordained in Ballina, County Mayo in 1846. He soon became aware of the terrible effects of the Famine on the people of Connacht and played a major role in trying to alleviate the suffering and distress he found. He was a very active member of the inter-denominational relief committee. He recounted his experiences in *My life in Connaught*. In particular he had been horrified at the ruthlessness of the policy of forced emigration and said:

> There would have been wisdom in this course if carried out with kindness and care. Provision should have been made for these humble people to enable them to emigrate with comfort to another land where their toil would be repaid by prosperity and comfort. But as a rule this is not done. Ensure families were turned out on the roadside without a shelter, sometimes even in the cold and rain of wintertime. 'The Crowbar Brigade' unroofed the houses and broke

down the walls, so that the poor creatures had nothing to protect them from the weather, even in the ruins of their own homes.

Armstrong struggled to establish a proper meetinghouse in Ballina. However, it officially opened in 1851. In 1868, he became Superintendent of the Connacht schools, where he remained for 27 years. In poor health he resigned in 1895 and died in 1897.

Sources: Barkley 1986; Blaney 1996.

John Shaw Brown
1822–87

John Shaw Brown was born in 1822. He became a linen manufacturer and a member of the local Presbyterian Church. In March 1880, Belfast Liberals elected him as their candidate for the general election. In his election address Brown called for compensation for industrial injuries and land reform.

He described himself as a liberal Presbyterian 'anxious for justice to all classes of countrymen'. He also declared that he backed free trade and opposed the Government's foreign policy. By this time the Belfast Liberal Association had collapsed, so a special liberal committee was formed to support Brown's campaign. Brown was ultimately defeated by the official Conservative candidates, two former MPs, J.P. Corry and William Ewart. Overall the 1880 general election marked the beginning both of the dominance of the Irish Parliamentary Party and Charles Stewart Parnell in Irish politics. The Irish Parliamentary Party won 62 of the 103 Irish parliamentary seats. Two later defected to the Liberals. Parnell was presumed to have had the support of 25 of the MPs. When the Parliamentary Party reassembled in Westminster Parnell was elected session chairman of the party in place of William Shaw.

In June 1884, Brown became President of the revived Belfast Liberal Association and the vice-president of the newly formed Ulster Reform Club, designed to improve the organisation of liberals in Belfast. He rejected the move towards an accommodation with the Conservatives against the Nationalists. In 1885 he chaired a meeting of the General Committee of the Ulster Reform Club to meet Prof. James Bryce MP for Tower Hamlets who was known to be a close colleague of Gladstone. It was at this meeting that Gladstone's liberal supporters in Ireland got their first inkling that Gladstone was seriously considering Home Rule for Ireland.

In 1885, Brown was selected by the County Down Tenant Farmers' Association as the Liberal candidate for the County Down seat in a

Westminster by-election. At a meeting of the National League, nationalists were encouraged to vote for Brown, although he was a supporter of the union. This time, Brown was only narrowly defeated by the Conservative Orange Grand Master, Lord Hill.

In 1885 Brown was again chosen as the County Down Liberal candidate for North Down, but, along with all the other Liberal candidates, was defeated, this time by the Conservative, Colonel Thomas Waring. Brown died two years later in 1887.

Sources: McKnight 1896; Walker 1989.

John Rea
1822–81

John Rea was born in West Street, Belfast in 1822. He studied law and became a solicitor. A prominent Young Irelander he was imprisoned in Kilmainham Gaol for nine months following his participation in the debacle of the 1848 Young Ireland 'rising' at Ballingarry in County Tipperary. As a solicitor he was involved in the case of the Roman Catholic victims of the Dolly's Brae incident of 1849, where Catholics where killed in fighting when Orangemen paraded through Catholic Dolly's Brae area.

In 1854 Rea instigated a lengthy legal action in the Court of Chancery in Dublin against the Belfast Corporation, the town clerk, the treasurer and 16 councillors for alleged misappropriation of funds. All the allegations were proved and those responsible for the corruption were fined £273,000. The town clerk and treasurer resigned. The fine eventually went to arbitration. The case was only resolved by the Belfast Award Act of 1864 implementing the compromise recommendations of the arbiters. Rea, who was deeply opposed to the compromise, had to be forcibly ejected from the House of Lords committee hearing.

In 1855 Rea was elected to the town council, where he was characteristically disruptive and was removed the following year, but returned to the council later.

In 1873 Rea tried but failed to get the nomination to stand as a Liberal in a by-election in Lisburn. The following year he unsuccessfully stood in Belfast for election to Westminster at the general election. Outside a polling station he was seized by a group of men and dropped into a heap of mud.

Rea also led the legal defence of the Land Leaguer, James Bryce Killen, who was in court with Michael Davitt in 1879. Rea was often imprisoned for contempt of court, being welcomed on release by torchlight processions. Rea joined the campaign to spread the Land League in Ulster. In 1880 he helped organise a meeting in Saintfield, County Down, with Michael

Davitt, J.G. Biggar and others, but the Orange Order was determined to stop them. In the end trouble was only prevented by the presence of 600 police. He eventually died in 1881 by shooting himself.

Sources: Boylan 1998; Holmes and Knox 1990; McElroy (undated); Moody 1981; Walker 1989.

John Kinnear
1823–1909

John Kinnear was born in Clonaneese, County Tyrone in 1824, the son of Rev. John Kinnear, minister of Lower Clonaneese, Donaghmore, County Tyrone. He was educated at the Royal Belfast Academical Institution and Glasgow University. He was licensed to preach in Dungannon, County Tyrone in 1847 and was ordained in Letterkenny, County Donegal on 27 December 1848, where he spent the rest of his life, publishing a number of his sermons.

He strongly supported the tenant right movement, which he believed was based on the 'principles of justice' and argued for the creation of a peasant proprietary as well as the more immediate object of the '3 Fs' of fair rents, fixity of tenure and right of free sale. In Omagh in 1850 he applauded 'the career of the League of North and South'. In 1881, the Land Bill was passed, despite Conservative opposition, giving tenants increased rights. Land courts were also established to settle contentious cases.

He was involved in politics and was elected a Liberal member of parliament for County Donegal from 1880 to 1885, defeating the Tory landlord, Lord Hamilton, during the Land War, thus becoming the first Presbyterian minister, with a congregation, to sit in parliament.

Kinnear was well read and was awarded a Doctorate in Divinity by Washington University in 1874. He was interested in history, especially of the church, and was a founder member of the Presbyterian Historical Society. Kinnear died on 8 July 1909 at the age of eighty-six.

Sources: Barkley 1986; Barkley 1993; Hickey and Doherty 2005; McElroy (undated); Newman 1993.

David Hanson
1824–65

David Hanson was born near Macosquin, County Londonderry in 1824. He was educated at the Royal Belfast Academical Institution where he received his General Certificate in 1843/4. He was licensed by Coleraine Presbytery in 1846 and ordained by the Presbytery of Ballybay in

Drumkeen, County Monaghan on 16 March 1847 to assist and then succeed Rev. Richard Ross. Seven years later he accepted a call by Fahan, County Donegal and was installed there on 12 September 1854, succeeding Rev. John Macky who went as a missionary to New Zealand.

Working in these rural communities with large numbers of struggling tenant farmers, faced with high rents, insecurity of tenure and poor harvests, Hanson became a strong supporter of, and advocate for, the tenant right movement. On 11 January 1848 he was on the platform of a tenant right meeting in Ballybay with various other ministers and Catholic priests. After speaking at one tenant right meeting in 1848 he was violently attacked.

He was then involved in planning a major Tenant League Demonstration in Ballybay, which took place on 1 October 1850, attended by Tenant League representatives from around the country.

In August 1860 he moved to a more urban congregation, becoming minister of York Street church in Belfast, which had opened in 1839. Hanson was only the second minister, the first being Rev. David Hamilton.

Hanson died of typhus fever, while still at York Street, on 8 January 1865, aged only 41 and is buried in Balmoral Cemetery, Belfast. He was succeeded by Rev. Hamilton's eldest son, Thomas.

He was survived by his wife, Ellen Houston, the daughter of Rev. Clarke Houston of Macosquin, and four sons, two of whom died within seven years, Clarke and Marcus, who both became Presbyterian ministers: David Hamilton Hanson of Ballygoney, County Tyrone, Gardenmore Larne and chaplain to the forces during the First World War; and George Hanson of First Ballymena who emigrated to Canada.

Sources: Barkley 1986; Gravestone Inscriptions, Belfast, Vol. 3; Murnane 1999.

William Findlater
1824–1906

William Findlater (known as Billy) was born in 1824, the son of William Findlater, a shipwright of Londonderry and nephew of a liberal Presbyterian brewer who built a new church in Dublin, and Sophia (née Huffington). When his father died in 1831, Billy's education was paid for by his uncle Alexander who was unmarried. He worked as an apprentice solicitor from 1840, with his fees paid for by his uncle. He eventually qualified as a solicitor in 1846, at the start of the Great Famine, which had a major influence on the development of his political views. He worked as a solicitor in various partnerships eventually trading as William Findlater and Co. He was also a member of the Dublin brewing firm, Findlater & Co. founded by his uncle Alexander. When Alexander died in 1871 Billy became the sole proprietor of the firm, which also employed his cousins and nephews, including various members of the Blood family who were descendants of the famous Colonel Blood, who had conspired with Rev. William Lecky to seize power in Dublin after the Restoration of 1660.

He married the daughter of John Wolfe one of his legal partners, but she died in 1877. The following year he married Marian Park and they had three children, Victor, Percy and Muriel.

He was active politically, particularly on the land issue and acted as agent for the successful Liberal candidate in South Londonderry in 1874. He was selected as a Liberal candidate for County Monaghan, with John Givan, in the general election of 1880, strongly supporting the position of tenant farmers. He was successfully elected the MP for the area and actively participated in debates in support of Gladstone's 1881 Land Act.

In a change in Liberal tactics in Monaghan, Findlater organised a massive meeting with T.A. Dickson (see profile) and a local parish priest, Canon Smollen, in support of the Ulster Custom of fair rents, fixity of tenure and free sale and tenant proprietary. It was recognised that tenant right, which was only established by custom and practice, not by law, had not provided sufficient protection against eviction or high rents. Findlater proposed 'a scheme somewhat on the lines of our Fixity of Tenure Bill, with such improvements as the more advanced views of land reformers might commend'. He campaigned for an extension of the 1881 Land Act to include leaseholders. He said that he had been elected to, 'fight the battle of the down-trodden tenants ... and endeavour to emancipate them from the unwanted bondage in the representatives of feudal landlordism held them shackled and confined.'

In 1882 he actively supported the Arrears Act, which provided loans to tenant farmers in debt and also spoke on the Poor Law. He was also active on housing issues and said he would like to see the workingman well housed in a comfortable dwelling, with good sanitary applications. He founded the Artisan Dwelling Company which was committed to the building of good quality low-cost housing.

In the 1885 general election, at a meeting of Liberal representatives for polling districts in the area, he was selected for South Londonderry, where he had been born and brought up, but was defeated in the end by the nationalist, T.M. Healy, and polled less votes than the Conservative. The 1885 election saw the collapse of the Liberal vote in Ulster, with constitutional politics coming to the fore ahead of issues such as the land question.

He was a founder member of the Ulster Reform Club and President of the Statistical and Social Enquiry Society of Ireland. He was chairman of the Solicitors' Benevolent Fund, a member of the Dublin Benevolent

Society of St Andrews, and actively involved for over thirty years in the Royal Hospitals for Incurables in Donnybrook.

Findlater retired in 1885 and in 1890 sold his interest in the brewing firm for £80,000. In 1896, having twice been elected the President of the Incorporated Law Society, and created a Findlater Fellowship in the Society, he was awarded a knighthood. He died in 1906 in Killiney, aged 82 and was buried in Mount Jerome.

Sources: Findlater 2001; McElroy (undated); McKnight 1896; Stenton and Lees 1976; Walker 1989.

John Jellie
1824–1918

Jellie was born in Moneyreagh in 1824 and educated at Royal Belfast Academical Institution. When he was ordained by the Presbytery of Bangor, there were objections to the form of the ordination and the dispute ended in the church court which found by 20 votes to 5 that the ordination had been 'unconstitutional, irregular and reprehensible'. The ordination was allowed to stand. He served as minister in the Non-Subscribing congregations of Glenarm (1852–55), Ravara (1855–59) and Moneyrea (1859–62).

In 1862, Jellie became the minister of the York Street congregation. Prior to his installation, the congregation asked whether it was the intention of the Presbytery to put the three questions contained in the new Remonstrant Synod Code of Practice to Rev. Maginnis' successor. When told that they would be put to the new minister, the congregation withdrew from the Remonstrant Synod of Ulster. Like Maginnis, Jellie was renowned for his radical theology. He remained at York Street for ten years to 1873. During this period a gallery was added to the church, which indicates that the congregation had increased significantly.

He was a strong supporter of the tenant right campaign. At a meeting in the Commercial Hotel, Belfast on 29 September 1876 he was elected to speak at a series of tenant right meetings and was later involved in a tenant right meeting in Waring Street Belfast in 1879.

In 1876 he accepted a call from Cairncastle Non-Subscribing congregation near Larne. Jellie stayed at Cairncastle until he retired from the ministry in 1880 and died on 28 November 1918.

Sources: Courtney 2008.

William Gardner Boyd
1825–89

William Boyd was born in 1825 in Finvoy, County Antrim. He was educated at Royal Belfast Academical Institution where he received his General Certificate in 1852. He was licensed in Magherafelt in 1852 and ordained in 1853 in Ramoan near Ballycastle, County Antrim, as the assistant and successor to Rev. John Simms. In 1856 a new church was built beside the school, which had been built in Ramoan in 1827.

Boyd was actively involved in the tenant right campaign in County Antrim and regularly participated in meetings and demonstrations in Ballycastle and Ballymoney. He attended the inaugural meeting of the Central Tenant Right Association in 1876 and represented the local Ballycastle Tenant Right Association at the 1877 Central Association annual meeting. In a consultation on the land question in Ballymoney in 1873 he put forward a motion demanding amendments to the very unsatisfactory 1870 Land Bill.

In January 1874 he attended a major north-south tenant right conference in Belfast on the land questions and express disappointment at the 1870 Land Bill. The resolutions adopted demanded the legal establishment of a fairly assessed rent, free sale, the right of continuous occupancy so long as the rent was paid, and the provision of loans to facilitate tenant purchase of land. Boyd died in 1889.

Sources: Barkley 1986; McElroy (undated).

Robert McGeagh (also spelled MacGeagh)
1825–91

Robert McGeagh was born in 1825, the son of John McGeagh and brother-in-law of Thomas Dickson MP (see profile). McGeagh became a merchant in Belfast.

In August 1868 a selection meeting of the Belfast Liberal Association nominated Thomas McClure (see profile) as the Liberal candidate and formed an election committee, including McGeagh, J.G. Biggar (see profile) and Thomas Sinclair (see profile). McClure was defeated.

It was in 1885, at a meeting of the General Committee of the newly formed liberal Ulster Reform Club, that McGeagh and others had their first indication that Gladstone was moving towards a policy of Home Rule for Ireland. In 1886 Thomas Dickson was defeated by the conservative J.P. Corry. McGeagh reviewed the state of liberal politics,

> the liberal party here has, for the time, disappeared as a factor in
> Ulster politics. While most of the leaders and the more intelligent

followers remain true to the party, the great masses of the rank and file, especially in rural districts, have gone over to the Tories; or rather forgotten old differences in face of what they consider the common danger, the masses of the two parties have amalgamated as Unionists, sinking for the moment all minor questions.

McGeagh was for a considerable period President of the Ulster Liberal Unionist Association. He died in 1891.

Sources: McKnight 1896; Walker 1989.

Samuel Finlay
1825–87

Samuel Finlay was born in 1825, son of William Knox Finlay a farmer of Kilcranny, Coleraine, County Londonderry. He was educated at Royal Belfast Academical Institution where he received his General Certificate in 1845. He was licensed to preach in Coleraine in 1846 and, following the death of Rev. Robert Love at the age of 36, was ordained in First Kilraughts, County Antrim on 12 March 1850, and became the minister of this historic congregation.

Finlay was very committed to the tenant right campaign in County Antrim and actively participated in tenant right meetings, especially in Ballymoney during the decade up to 1878. At one of the tenant right meetings in Ballymoney in 1869 a thousand farmers attended.

He attended the major North-South conference on the land question in 1874. He was also involved in the inaugural meeting of the Antrim Central Tenant Right Committee in 1876, along with at least sixteen other Presbyterian ministers. Samuel McElroy, the leader of the tenant right campaign in North Antrim said that 'Kilraughts men were the local bone and sinew of the movement'.

Finlay resigned from the ministry in 1885, aged sixty and died on 12 December 1887 after a three-year illness. His brother Henry Finlay was also a Presbyterian minister (Moneydig).

Sources: Barkley 1986; McElroy (undated).

Daniel Taylor
1825–89

Daniel Taylor was born in Coleraine, County Londonderry in 1825, the eldest son of Daniel Taylor of Coleraine and Eliza (née Denison). He was educated in Coleraine and became a director of Derry Central Railway Company, which some hoped would break the monopoly of the Northern

Counties Railway Company on traffic in Coleraine. He supported work to be carried out on Coleraine harbour to beat off competition from Portrush, but it ran into financial difficulties. He was chairman of the Coleraine Commissioners in 1864, 1865 and 1873.

With an increased franchise as a result of the Ballot Act, in 1874, six Presbyterians stood and were elected to Parliament, four of them liberals, including Daniel Taylor, who defeated conservative Sir Harvey Bruce. The *Coleraine Chronicle* expressed its delight because,

> Above all, he is a Presbyterian. By electing him Coleraine will confer an invaluable service on the Presbyterian Church. We complain of being hewers of wood and drawers of water. Why? Because we had not risen above political drudgery, because we have not prized our birthright. For a mess of conservative pottage it has ignominiously sold and it is a glorious sign that Presbyterians are beginning to adopt broad, independent principles and are espousing a candidature so highly fitted to blot out a reproach and rectify a wrong.

Taylor was described by Lord Beaconsfield as one of nine dangerous radical and revolutionary politicians. He had a flexible position on national education, supporting the establishment of a Catholic university. He was in favour of county boards to administer county affairs.

He was a strong supporter of Tenant Right and put forward two bills in 1879 and 1880 to meet the grievances of tenants over the 1870 Land Act, specifically, granting the right of free sale, removing the doubts about leaseholder tenants' rights, reversing the presumption of the rights of tenants from the landlord to the tenant. Neither received a second reading.

Taylor was defeated by Sir H.H. Bruce in the general election of 1880. He was one of the first vice-presidents of the Ulster Liberal Unionist Association when it was formed in 1886. The Association was made up of those who upheld the traditional liberal values of reform, equality and liberty, but opposed Gladstone's Home Rule policy and hosted Joseph Chamberlain in Coleraine when he came to Ireland in 1887 to oppose Gladstone's Home Rule proposals.

Taylor was a trustee of the Presbyterian Commutation Fund. He died in Coleraine 1889.

Sources: Holmes and Knox 1990; McKnight 1896; Stenton and Lees 1976; Wright 1996.

Richard Smyth
1826–78

Richard Smyth was born in Carnculagh near Dervock, County Antrim in 1826, the second son and fourth child of Hugh Smyth and Mary (née Wray). He was raised in the Dervock Presbyterian congregation. When he was still young, the family were evicted by their landlord from their home and land, both of which they had improved, and had to move to a poorer dwelling as a result of the caprice of the landlord. This left an indelible impression on him.

He was educated in the local Ganaby School, Ballymoney Grammar School and Glasgow University, where he obtained a BA, and after a three-year break, an MA. One of his essays was in support of Poor Law reform. He then went on to study in Bonn, Germany; Assembly's College Belfast; and Cambridge, England, where he was described as 'a brilliant, if not the most brilliant product of the London College'. He gained doctorates in Divinity and Law.

He was licensed to preach by Route Presbytery in 1853. He rejected a call from Carryduff congregation and decided instead to go to Hampstead in England. He was eventually installed as Presbyterian minister in Westport, County Mayo in 1855 and was then called to First Derry in 1857, where he remained for nine years. He was an evangelical who was involved in the 1859 revival. In 1865 he was appointed as Professor of Hebrew and later as Professor of Theology at the new Magee College, Derry. In 1869, aged only 43 he was elected as Moderator of the General Assembly and, unusually, was elected for a second term, due to his important role in negotiating the *regium donum*.

In the debates on the disestablishment of the Church of Ireland, Smyth argued that disestablishment was desirable but it did not mean that Presbyterian ministers should lose their *regium donum* grant. He argued for parity of esteem with the Anglican Church. His negotiations with Government resulted in the establishment of the Sustentation Fund, which became the Central Ministry Fund, replacing the *regium donum*.

In the debate on a national education system, Smyth, along with James McKnight, recognised the need to conciliate Catholic claims, although he also was a supporter of non-denominational education, where religious education would be provided separately.

He opposed the privatisation of reformatories for young people who had been in trouble with the law, arguing that no one should make a profit out of supervising offenders and that they should be made effectively accountable. He also did not want to see reformatories becoming segregated by becoming denominational.

Smyth was a strong supporter of Church Union between the reformed churches. He expressed the view that unfortunately for many people in Ireland 'their love of God was measured by their dislike of their neighbour'. He suggested that everyone was in favour of union as long as others joined their own side and accepted their opinions. Smyth's view, in contrast, was that 'there may be real unity among Christians without an absolute uniformity of opinion.'

He was politically a Liberal and in 1870 proposed the successful candidate Richard Dowse for the seat in Derry. Smyth, himself, became Liberal MP for County Londonderry, from 1874 to 1878, having been nominated by the County Londonderry Tenant Farmers' Association. When he took his seat he argued for the idea of a federalist United Kingdom, which included Ireland.

Having had such a negative experience of the rapaciousness of landlords when they are not controlled, he was a strong supporter of tenant right and argued for the extension of the Ulster Custom throughout Ireland. In 1875/6, he alone of the Northern Liberals supported the Bill put forward by Isaac Butt, leader of the Home Rule Party, designed to extend tenant right, inclusive of fixity of tenure at fair rents with the right of free sale over the whole of Ireland (as opposed to only in the north), and to remedy the defects of the 1870 Act, highlighted at the 1874 tenant right conference, and strongly supported by the Route Tenants' Defence Association (originally called the Route Tenant-Right Association). He put forward his own tenant right bills in 1875 and 1877 to improve on the 1870 legislation, but neither was given a second reading.

He was a strong advocate of temperance and was primarily responsible for the Sunday Closing Act. In a speech in the House he laid out what was then a very progressive position that 'drunkenness is a disease as much as a crime'. The bill was passed in 1878 – the year he died at the relatively young age of 52.

Sources: Barkley 1986; Barkley 1993; Holmes 2000; Newman 1993; Reid 2001–03; Walker 1989; Wright 1996.

Archibald Robinson
1826–1902

Archibald Robinson was born in Garvagh in 1826, the son of Dr Matthew Robinson of Feeny, County Londonderry. He was educated at Royal Belfast Academical Institution, where he received his General Certificate in 1846. He was licensed to preach by Glendermott in 1850 and ordained in First Broughshane, County Antrim in 1853, where he remained for 33 years.

In a debate in the Presbyterian General Assembly in June 1868, Robinson argued in favour of the disestablishment of the Anglican church of Ireland on the grounds of equity and justice. He openly stated that he sympathised with Catholics who found the establishment of the Church of Ireland, which represented only a small minority of the population, a legitimate grievance.

At least 67 Presbyterian ministers participated in tenant right campaign meetings, conferences and demonstrations in County Antrim alone. Of these, Robinson was one of the leading Tenant Right campaigners in the north of Ireland and participated in many conferences and meetings, including in Ballycastle, Ballymoney and Ballymena. He put forward a motion to express disappointment at the 1870 Land Bill and was a delegate to a major North-South National Tenants Rights conference organised by the Route Tenants' Defence Association (Ballymoney) in Belfast in January 1874. The resolutions adopted demanded the following throughout Ireland: the legal establishment of a fairly assessed rent, free sale, the right of continuous occupancy so long as the rent was paid, and the provision of loans to facilitate tenant purchase of land. Robinson supported these demands and expressed his support for Gladstone, who he described as 'an honest and conscientious man, who was convinced that injustice had been done to Ireland in the past'. However he came into conflict with Joseph G. Biggar who believed that change would only come by the use of force.

On 30 March 1882 he presided over a meeting of tenant farmers in Broughshane, County Antrim, pointing out how the policy adopted by the landlords all along had been at the root of past misgovernment of this country by Great Britain in matters connected with the land. He warned the landlords that their safest and best course was to accept the Land Act of 1881, and suggested that if they did not do so they might have difficulties to encounter perhaps greater than any they had yet experienced. Samuel Black (see profile) delivered an address on peasant proprietorship.

In the last two decades of the nineteenth century there was considerable disquiet amongst Presbyterians about the lack of public appointments being given to Presbyterians. McMinn, in *Presbyterianism and Politics,* has shown that in 1898 Presbyterians had less than 7% of public appointments in Ulster, compared to 29% for Catholics and 63% for the Church of Ireland. In the 1881 Presbyterian General Assembly, Robinson highlighted the situation in County Antrim where in a Presbyterian population of almost 123,000 there were only 12 Presbyterian magistrates, compared with 105 Church of Ireland Magistrates for a population of less than 46,000. There were even 5 Roman Catholic Magistrates for a population of less than 56,000.

In 1886 Robinson became Professor of Sacred Rhetoric and Catechetics at Assembly's College Belfast where he taught the art of good preaching to the trainee ministers. He opposed the introduction of hymns and pipe organs. He remained at Assembly's College until 1902 when he died.

Sources: Barkley 1986; Hall 2011; McElroy (undated); Thompson 2002; Wright 1996; *Northern Whig* 1 April 1882.

Henry McDonald Flecher
Born 1827

Henry McDonald Flecher was born in Ballinderry, County Antrim in 1827. He became a schoolmaster in Moneyreagh, County Down and wrote poetry which he had published in the *Northern Whig*, edited by F.D. Finlay. In 1859 he won second prize in the paper for poems celebrating the centenary of Robert Burns. The same year he had his first book published anonymously entitled, *Rhymes and Ravings of a County Antrim Lad.*

The historical poems and verses in support of Daniel O'Connell and Smith O'Brien show that he was politically a nationalist, which is presumably the reason he chose to have them published anonymously. He also wrote of the difficulties faced by many teachers in this period. As well as using Ulster-Scots vernacular he used many Irish words, foreshadowing the Irish literary revival thirty years later.

In 1866 he had his second volume, *Poems, Songs and Ballads*, published. It contained over two hundred pages of verse. Around this time he moved to Belfast to manage a mill for a short while, before emigrating to Texas, USA. In 1900 in published *Odin's Last Hour and Other Poems.* He was still living in Texas in 1909, so presumably died there.

Sources: Hewitt 2004.

Alexander Field
1828–1904

Alexander Field was born in Killyleagh, County Down in 1828. He was licensed to preach by Belfast Presbytery in 1854 and ordained three years later as minister of Dervock Presbyterian Church, succeeding Rev. Joseph Bellis, and where he remained for the rest of his ministry.

From 1869 onwards Field was an active supporter of the Route Tenants' Defence Association. He was evicted from his farm at Knockanbouy Dervock, County Antrim in 1876, along with two other tenants, which outraged supporters of the tenant right campaign. Field successfully brought a case against the landlord, Samuel Allen, for compensation under the 1870 Land Act and eventually received £885.

The success of the case lent significant support to the tenant right campaign for stronger legislation on fixity of tenure for those who paid their rent. Field himself became very actively involved in the tenant right campaign, attending the inaugural meeting of the Central Tenant Right Association in 1876. He died in 1904.

Sources: Barkley 1986; McElroy (undated); McMinn 1979; Nelson 1985.

Joseph Gillis Biggar
1828–90

Joseph Gillis Biggar was born in Belfast in 1828, son of Joseph Bigger of Mallusk and Isabella (née Houston) of Ballyreal. He was educated at Belfast Academy. As a teenager he fell off his horse and damaged his spine which left him with a permanent curvature. After his formal education he went to work in his father's provisions firm in Henry Street, Belfast, taking over running it in 1861. Biggar lived in Donegall Street, close to Royal Avenue.

He became involved in politics and was elected a member of the town council and Water Board. Although living in Donegall Street, Belfast, he was elected as a Home Rule member of parliament for Cavan in 1874, defeating Orangeman, Colonel Saunderson, and was an MP until his death in 1890.

Biggar was treasurer of the Land League and became member of the supreme council of the Irish Republican Brotherhood, but was expelled for refusing to abandon parliamentary activity.

With the extension of the franchise, the number of Nationalist MPs at Westminster increased significantly, giving them more political clout. Biggar was famous for obstructing parliamentary business in order to promote the cause of Home Rule. He once spoke for four hours on swine fever.

With a reputation for being outspoken and abrasive, with an accent that many MPs in the House of Commons could not understand, Biggar was not afraid to let people know his opinions.

Biggar eventually converted to Catholicism in order, as he said, to 'annoy his sister' and died in February 1890 in London and was buried in Belfast.

Sources: Bardon 1992; Boylan 1998; Bradbury 2002; Campbell 1991 ; Hickey and Doherty 2005; Newman 1993; O'Byrne 1990; Thompson 2002; Walker 1989; Wright 1996.

John Rutherford
1829–89

John Rutherford was born in 1829, the son and grandson of a Burgher Presbyterian minister, named, respectively, John (minister of Ballydown, near Banbridge, County Down from 1800 to 1846); and Samuel (minister of Newbliss and Drum 1770–1801). His father had been the first minister of Ballydown (Burgher) congregation, near Banbridge, County Down. John Rutherford (the son) was educated at Royal Belfast Academical Institution, gaining his General Certificate in 1845. The following year his father died. Like his father and grandfather he trained for the ministry and was licensed by Belfast Presbytery in 1848 and ordained the same year, when he succeeded his father at Ballydown, where he stayed for the following twenty-six years.

Tenant farmers had always been the backbone of the Presbyterian Church. They argued that the Ulster Custom should be established in law and extended universally across Ireland. The government and landlords remained deaf to these pleas and rents continued to rise and evictions increased. As a result the tenant right movement became more militant.

In late 1849, the tenants in the Kilmood estate on the inland shore of Strangford Lough in County Down petitioned the Marquis for a rent reduction, which he refused. There was public outrage at this decision, led by Rutherford and another Presbyterian minister, William Dobbin (see profile). At a tenant right meeting in Garvagh in December 1849 he explained that 'In espousing the cause of the tillers of the soil, he was espousing that of an oppressed and poverty-stricken people, and endeavouring … to … abolish … the white tenant slavery of the North of Ireland'. The following month he addressed a monster meeting in Shaenrod near Dromara and one in Banbridge, County Down in January 1850, with sixteen other Presbyterian ministers, one Catholic priest and 7,000 people. At the meeting he declared that, 'landlords had harassed, oppressed and deprived the tenants of their hard-earned property … They had submitted long to this system of spoliation but would they longer submit or would they rise in their might and demand their rights?'

He said that 'Ireland will never be a nation until the present feudal and irresponsible system of landlordism shall be completely reformed'. He argued that the Scottish settlers had brought the land from 'a state of primeval barreness to its present fertility' so they should pay no more than the original rent paid by their forefathers for the unimproved land. Landlordism, he said, had no justification in the Bible. In January 1852 Rutherford spoke in favour of emigration to Australia, 'to go to a free soil, where they would be rid of British rule and be no longer kept in a state of slavery and bondage'.

Rutherford was denounced by Henry Cooke as being a socialist and communist and by Lord Londonderry, who claimed to have a letter from him, which he described as imprudent and contemptible. Londonderry suggested that Presbyterians who held such anti-Ascendancy views should be arrested and that the *regium donum* grant should only be paid to ministers who were loyal to the crown. The letter was proved to be a fake.

Rutherford's tenant right speeches were even raised in parliament. However by the mid-1850s four out of five of the northern Presbyteries had declared unanimously, or nearly so, for tenant right. Rutherford resigned from the church in 1874, married the daughter of J. Hopkins from Shoeburyness, Essex and emigrated to the USA. He died in 1889.

Sources: Barkley 1986; Campbell 1991; Fitzpatrick 1989; Holmes 1985; Holmes and Knox 1990; Nelson 2005; Rutherford 1850; Wright 1996.

Samuel Black
1830–1910

Samuel Black was born in 1830 in Randalstown, County Antrim into a farming family and became a tenant farmer, himself, which he supplemented by working as a merchant.

He was a leading member of the campaign for tenant right in County Antrim, which worked to protect and extend the Ulster Custom. He actively participated in many meetings, demonstrations and conferences designed to further the aims of the campaign. At a convention on the land question in 1875, involving home rulers from the south and liberals from the north, Black proposed a motion which declared that the 1870 Land Act was inadequate to protect tenants from eviction, arbitrary increases in rent, appropriation of their property without compensation for their improvements and unrestricted right of sale. The motion was seconded by a young Charles Stewart Parnell and passed.

In 1879 Black was asked to stand in the general election by the Central Liberal Association. In his election address he made clear his support for the '3 Fs' of fixity of tenure, fair rents and free sale and that he would welcome the creation of a peasant proprietorship. He was supported by the local tenant associations, most Presbyterian ministers and some Catholic priests. In the end, Black was defeated by the Conservatives. *The Witness* said that it regretted the defeat of two liberal Presbyterians by two members of the Episcopal Church of Ireland, 'There is something rotten somewhere when a great Presbyterian County like Antrim goes on, from generation to generation, electing as its representatives men who belong to the church of the minority.'

In 1880, Black, alone of the Liberals, made a specific demand for a general reduction in rents, in addition to the general Liberal demands for legal recognition of the Ulster Custom and an extension of the facilities for tenant purchase.

In April 1882 he delivered an address on peasant proprietorship at a tenant farmers meeting in Broughshane, County Antrim in which he quoted statistics showing the success which had attended the establishment of systems of peasant proprietorship in other countries on the continent. He also urged, with much force, the necessity of doing away with primogeniture, entail, and settlement, and adopting a more simple form of conveyancing.

With the creation of the Ulster Reform Club to improve Liberal organisation, in 1884, Black was elected on to the committee. He chaired an important tenant right meeting in Central Hall Belfast to discuss the Land Act. He died in 1910.

Sources: McElroy (undated); McKnight 1896; *Northern Whig* 1 April 1882; Thompson 2002; Walker 1989.

Thomas Neilson Underwood
1830/1–76

Thomas Neilson Underwood was born in Strabane in 1830/1. He was a descendant of United Irishman Samuel Neilson on his mother's side. He became a lawyer and was elected secretary to the Strabane Tenant Right Association. He described the Tenant League as 'a true union of Irishmen. This was the green shamrock of Ireland, that had risen up from the desolation of the past'.

He said that Lord Russell's strategy was to, 'sow discord amongst the Irish people, and thereby break up the only truly political association formed in Ireland since the Volunteers grounded their arms, and the fatal Act of Union condemned your country to a base dependency on the will of another.'

In May 1852, he wrote an open letter to the 'Protestant Electors of Ulster', to try to persuade voters to defy the aristocratic bidding of their landlords. On the landed class he warned tenants, 'vote for them, and when the thing is done, do they care that the devil has you, or the emigrant ship, or the ditch side …'.

In 1856 there were attempts to avoid a highly acrimonious municipal election in Strabane by agreeing a list of candidates. At the nomination meeting, Neilson proposed a list of 21 candidates including eight Catholics. The chairman of the town commission, William Ramsey, however, produced an alternative list, with only two Catholics. As agreement could not be reached the election went ahead. In the end no Catholics were elected on to the commission.

Underwood went to London to train for the bar and observed the work of English freehold land societies and, as a result, developed a plan for owner-occupation for the tenants of Ireland, which was published in *The Nation* in 1857. The same year he was a key speaker at a large protest meeting in Kilmacrennan, County Donegal which was organised to protest against Lord Leitrim's treatment of his Donegal tenants.

In May 1859 he proposed a conference of all Irish Liberal MPs in order to create concerted action in parliament on tenant right.

In 1860, having completed his studies, he was accepted to the English Bar, but never practiced there. He made various attempts to be admitted to the Irish Bar, with the support of some influential benchers of the Queen's Inns, but was always outvoted.

He moved to Dublin and got heavily involved in the national petition campaign. At a big meeting in the Rotunda on 4 December 1860 he proposed one of the motions in favour of the national petition, advocating self-government for Ireland within the Empire, with Ireland and the other colonies having representation at Westminster.

In 1861, he organised activities in response to the clearance of the tenants from John George Adaire's Glenveigh estate. Having provided assistance to the destitute in Gweedore and Cloughaneely, County Donegal for some years, in 1861 he fostered weekly collections for the poor and destitute in the west of Ireland, known as 'St Patrick's pence'.

In the same year, writing under the pen-name of 'Celt', which he used when publishing his poetry, he put forward a proposal in the *Irishman* that St Patrick's Day should be celebrated in Ireland and Britain with banquets as it was in America. The idea got enthusiastic support and the Brotherhood of the Friendly Sons of St Patrick was formed, with ambitions to play an important role in promoting nationalist politics. It drew on the *ad hoc* framework of the national petition movement. On 9 March 1861 it adopted the name of 'National Brotherhood of St Patrick'. Underwood chaired the Dublin banquet in the Rotunda on 18 March 1861 and launched the Brotherhood. Speakers included John Martin. The green ribbon became the badge of the Society. Banquets were held in about six other places in Ireland and more in Britain, where local branches of the Brotherhood were formed. Underwood was President of the National Brotherhood for several years in the early 1860s.

He was involved in organising the funeral of rebel Terence Bellew McManus in 1861. In 1864 he was visited by well-known Fenian and founder of the Irish Republican Brotherhood (IRB), Jeremiah O'Donovan Rossa. When the IRB was routed the following year, Underwood was jailed, but because of lack of evidence of his active involvement, the removal of the Fenian threat, and his failing health, he was released after a few months. This experience did not stop him accepting the position of the Ulster representative on the IRB supreme council when it was re-established in 1967. Along with Charles Guilfoyle Doran, he wrote the constitution and rules of the new organisation.

Underwood had a play, *The Youthful Martyr – An Irish Drama* published in a London newspaper in June 1867.

In 1874 he was found guilty of contempt of court in the case of Mason and McCurdy, for failing to comply with a court order, for which he was jailed for four years in Omagh jail. His period in jail further damaged his health and he died at home in Main Street, Strabane, two months after his release, on 7 October 1876. He is buried in Glasnevin Cemetery, Dublin.

Sources: Comerford 1985; Campbell 1902; correspondence with Michael A. Harron; Nelson 2005.

James George Kirkpatrick
1831–96

James George Kirkpatrick was born in 1831, a native of Tullyallen, Ballylane, County Armagh, but was brought up in Newry. He was educated at Queen's College Belfast, where he gained a BA (RUI) in 1863; and Assembly's College Belfast.

He was licensed by Newry Presbytery in 1864 and ordained as a minister in Dunluce, County Antrim on 26 September 1865 and became their minister. A church hall was built in 1894, but fell down almost immediately and had to be rebuilt.

He was an enthusiastic supporter of the tenant right campaign and participated in various County Antrim tenant right campaign meetings and demonstrations, especially in Ballycastle and Ballymoney in the decade up to 1878 and attended the Ulster Conference in 1870.

He died in 1896 and bequeathed £8,000 for the building of a church in Belfast. It was committed to replacing Ormiston Church on the Upper Newtownards Road, Belfast. Kirkpatrick Memorial was completed in 1924.

Sources: Barkley 1986; McElroy (undated); Mullin 1995.

R.J.O. Moore
1832–1924

Robert John Orr Moore was born into a farming family in Ballinacannon, Ringsend, near Coleraine, on 1 April 1832. He was educated at St Andrews University, Scotland and Princeton University in the United States. He was licensed by Philadelphia OS Presbytery in 1867, but returned to Coleraine in the following year. He was ordained in Corvalley on 2 July 1869. Less than three years later he accepted a call to Third Garvagh and was installed on 12 March 1872. He remained there for over nine years until accepting a call from his (and his wife's) home congregation of Ringsend where he was installed on 13 July 1881.

During the early 1880s there was considerable tenant agitation. The number of evictions of tenant farmers had increased considerably. Moore chose to come down clearly on the side of the tenants. In a speech in Ringsend he felt the need to justify his decision,

> My answer to those who want to know why I took part with the tenants in this struggle is that I am a farmer's son myself, born and brought up on a farm; I love my neighbours and I an anxious to see justice done ... Besides, my people are almost all farmers, and their interests are my interests and I stand here at their request and at the request and entreaty of hundreds of tenant farmers of all denominations.

He retired in November 1911 and died on 4 July 1924, aged 92.

Sources: Barkley 1986; *Coleraine Constitution* 25 November 1982; Thompson 2001.

W.D. Andrews
1832–1924

William Drennan Andrews was born in Comber, County Down in 1832, son of John Andrews. He was educated at Royal Belfast Academical Institution and Trinity College Dublin, where he gained gold medals in Ethics and Logic. He became a barrister in 1855 and a QC in 1872.

In 1878, on the death of James Sharman Crawford the MP for County Down, Andrews suggested that Sharman Crawford's brother should stand for the seat. He was unwilling to stand, however, and Andrews was nominated by the tenant right associations and selected by a meeting of Liberals, chaired by Thomas McClure, to stand.

Andrews' campaign was organised by Hans McMordie and Edward Gardner. In his election address, Andrews highlighted his support for tenant right, and the proposed new Land Bill that had been put forward by Sharman Crawford, which would extend legal protection for the '3 Fs'. He also declared his support for reform of the Grand Jury. Andrew's Conservative opponent was Lord Castlereagh, son of Lord Londonderry, with a very significant family political history. Andrews was defeated and Lord Castlereagh, who had conducted a well-organised campaign, took the seat, with the significant support of many Catholic voters, who were keen on denominational education, which Castlereagh supported. Castlereagh's campaign was also helped by the Conservatives publishing their own Land Bill extending tenant right to leaseholders.

In 1882 Andrews was appointed a high court judge. He died in 1924.

Sources: Walker 1989; Wright 1996.

Margaret Byers
1832–1912

Margaret Byers was born in Rathfriland in 1832. At a young age she went to live in Stoke-on-Trent in England and went to school in Nottingham. She then became a teacher at the same school where she was influenced by a progressive headmistress, whose motto was 'women can do anything under God'.

In 1852 she married the Rev. John Byers and they both went to be missionaries in China. Tragically he died shortly after the birth of their baby, while they were returning from a mission to Shanghai – Margaret Byers was only 21. She returned to Ireland and began teaching in the Ladies Collegiate School in Cookstown, County Tyrone. She was very conscious that, while there was educational support for boys, there was little education available for girls, except by governesses, so in 1859 she opened her own Ladies Collegiate School in Wellington Place, Belfast. The school quickly expanded from its initial 35 pupils and had to move premises several times. It eventually moved to Lower Crescent in south Belfast, in a large Scrabo stone building which had been built by the Corry family, where it was to stay for the next 100 years and became known as Victoria College, after Queen Victoria.

Initially the authorities did not allow girls to sit the exams for higher education and so Byers lobbied the government until they agreed that they could and by 1890 the girls were obtaining up to, and including, degree level qualifications. She said that 'My aim was to provide for girls an education ... as thorough as that which is afforded to boys in the schools of the highest order'.

As well as being an educational pioneer, Byers was a social reformer and philanthropist, being the driving force behind various initiatives including helping to establish a Home for Destitute Girls and the Prison Gate Mission for women, which provided a home and employment for women coming out of prison. She became the first president of the Irish Women's Temperance Union and was active on the committee of the Ulster branch of the National Society for Women's Suffrage. She was an opponent of Home Rule.

Her son, John Byers became a prominent doctor and professor of midwifery at Queen's University Belfast. He was also twice president of the Belfast Literary Society and promoted Irish folklore, language and Belfast architecture. He wrote a pamphlet on *The Characteristics of the Ulsterman*.

Margaret Byers died on 21 February 1912. Her son Sir John died in 1920. They are both buried in Belfast City Cemetery.

Sources: Blaney 1996; Bradbury 2002; Hartley 2006; Holmes and Urquhart 1994; Jordan (undated); Luddy 1995; Newman 1993.

James Christopher Street
1832–1911

James Street was born in Nottingham on 18 January 1832, son of Christopher Street. He was ordained in Manchester in 1860 and for the next three years was a Manchester Superintendent Missionary. In 1863 he became the minister of a non-conformist church in Newcastle-upon-Tyne.

In 1871 he moved to the Non-Subscribing Second Belfast Presbyterian Church. He was involved in controversy even before he took up his position because of his pro-Congregationalist views, which meant that he believed the call should solely be made by the congregation of the Non-Subscribing Second Belfast Presbyterian Church, and not be endorsed by the Presbytery, made up of ministers. This eventually resulted in Second Belfast withdrawing from the Presbytery of Antrim and forming the Congregational Union with several other congregations.

Street was not only theologically progressive, but also committed to demonstrating his faith in practical action. Within months of his arrival in Belfast he set up a scheme for erecting schools alongside the church, where both Sunday schools and congregational meetings could be held. He also founded the Rosemary Street Mutual Improvement Association, the earliest of its kind in Belfast, which sought to improve the intellectual, social and moral advancement of its members, regardless of their religious denomination. Street was also involved in the development of the Royal Victoria Hospital and was made a life governor, along with other initiatives to help the poor in the city. He was also a supporter of tenant right and often spoke and preached on behalf of tenants.

In 1890 he returned to England to take up a post in Northampton, for a year and then in the Church of the Saviour in Birmingham. His last ministerial position was in Shrewsbury in 1895.

He retired in 1908 and died in 1911. His son Christopher James Street (1855–1931) also became a Unitarian minister.

Sources: Campbell 1991; notes provided by Rev. John Nelson.

Thomas Dickson
1833–1909

Thomas Alexander Dickson, born in 1833, was a factory owner and merchant in Dungannon, County Tyrone. He was politically a Liberal and wanted to correct the lack of representation of dissenters in parliament. In the 1868 election he collected pledges of support for the Liberal candidate, James Brown of Donaghmore, but with the moderator of the General Assembly, backing the conservative candidate, Brown was forced to withdraw.

With the introduction of secret ballots in 1872, Dickson stood as a Liberal against the conservative Colonel W.S. Knox in the 1874 general election. Dickson's main platform was the amendment of the 1870 Land Act. Dickson was successful and was elected as Liberal MP for Dungannon.

In the early 1880s, with the failure of crops, small farmers were, according to Dickson, 'in the deepest distress, bordering on starvation'. There were 20,000 people receiving poor law relief in Ulster. The land question was clearly the key issue in Irish politics. The establishment of the Land League split the reform movement between tenant right, supported by Dickson, demanding the '3 Fs' and the more radical Land League demanding the forcible expropriation of the land belonging to landlords. The Land Act of 1881 and its administration caused continued controversy and failed to fulfil the expectations of those looking for a resolution of the land question. Dickson played a leading role in highlighting its weaknesses.

Dickson was re-elected, with substantial Catholic support, at the general election of 1880. The election was challenged on the basis that a Dickson aide had bribed an elector to stay away for the day and the election was set aside, resulting in a by-election later in the year. This time Dickson's son, James Dickson, stood against, and successfully defeated, conservative Orangeman, Colonel Knox, with both Protestant and Catholic votes.

In 1881 there was yet another election in Tyrone when the sitting MP, Litton, was appointed commissioner to the new Land Court. Dickson and Colonel Knox were selected as candidates. Dickson, with substantial Catholic and Protestant support, narrowly defeated the Tory Knox, despite opposition to Dickson from Parnell as well as the Tories.

The following year the new Franchise Act massively increased the number of people entitled to vote. In addition to the outlawing of Corrupt Electoral Practices Act in 1883, the power of landlords to control the elections to parliament had been fundamentally undermined.

In 1885, Dickson tried to get appointed to the Land Court and issued a pamphlet outlining *An Irish policy for a liberal government*, which recommended the passing of a land purchase act and abandonment of the Coercion Acts, the comprehensive reform of local government, and substantial changes to the management of Irish affairs.

In 1885 he declared his intention to stand again in Tyrone, to the annoyance of the Conservatives and was eventually forced to withdraw, standing in mid-Antrim instead, where he was defeated by R.T. O'Neill, son of Lord O'Neill.

In 1885, Gladstone's conversion to Home Rule caused difficulties for liberals, like Dickson who was strongly opposed to the proposed alliance with the conservatives in order to ensure the defeat of nationalist candidates. Dickson stood in a by-election in Mid-Armagh in February 1886, supporting the compulsory sale of land, against Sir J.P. Corry, a

Conservative, and was decisively beaten. His brother-in-law concluded that, 'The Home Rule scare carried the election, and every other consideration will be regarded as of secondary importance in every protestant home-stead in Ulster until this bogey is laid.'

Dickson replaced E.T. Herdman as chairman of the Tyrone Liberal Association, when Herdman became involved in the northwest loyalist registration and electoral association. When it was clear that a majority of Liberals opposed Gladstone's Home Rule proposals a group of those in favour formed the Irish Protestant Home Rule Association, who became known as the Gladstonian Liberals, with the support of Dickson. In the 1886 general election, Dickson stood for a Scottish seat as a Gladstonian Liberal. The Home Rule proposals gave Randolph Churchill the opportunity to engage in political manoeuvring and play the 'Orange Card'. In rallies in Larne and Belfast he proclaimed 'Ulster will fight and Ulster will be right'.

When 600 Liberals met in Belfast in March 1886 there was clearly great division over the issue and it was agreed to take soundings from leading politicians in England. Dickson died in 1909.

Sources: Bardon 1992; Campbell 1991; Latimer 1893; Stenton and Lees 1976; Wright 1996.

Samuel Craig McElroy
1834–1914

McElroy was born in 1834, son of Daniel McElroy of Ballymoney. He initially became a house painter. He then largely educated himself which enabled him to become an auctioneer, valuer, shop owner and editor of the *Free Ballymoney Press*. He also contributed articles to the *Northern Whig*. He was an elder and choir member of Trinity congregation Ballymoney. He was a leading tenant right activist in Antrim establishing the first tenant right organisation, the Route Tenant-Right Association, (also referred to as Route Tenants' Defence Association)which was the direct result of the by-election in Antrim in 1869 which 'powerfully stimulated the agitation on the land question' and convinced many people that elections without land reform is useless. For McElroy 'the evil of the time was uncertainty of tenure, uncertainty of rent, and uncertainty of sale of tenant right'. The Ulster Custom which protected northern tenants more than their southern counterparts was only custom and practice and not a legal right. The failures of the 1870 Land Act, according to McElroy, 'brought rights more prominently to the footlights'. He was secretary of the first Ulster Land Committee for several years and of the Route Tenants' Defence Association for over thirty years to 1900.

From 1873 leasehold tenant right agitation became more strident. At a conference in Ballymoney all the tenant right groups recognised the importance of returning candidates who would strongly support tenant right reform in parliament. The day after this conference, according to McElroy, 'deputies from several tenant-right associations was held with reference to the parliamentary representation of County Antrim ... [and] arrangements were made for organising the County'. However, even then McElroy could see that 'it is evident that the Home Rule question is working irreparable mischief among the Liberals of Ulster' with liberals and conservatives tending to converge.

In 1876 the Antrim Central Tenant Right Association was formed of all the Antrim farmers' groups, with McElroy as its President. It was involved in trying to ensure a Liberal candidate who was strongly sympathetic to the tenant right cause, stood in Antrim in the general election. In the end Charles Wilson narrowly failed to get elected.

By 1885 with the conservative Lord Ashbourne's Land Purchase Act, the gap narrowed between conservative and liberals, which had existing when the liberals alone were lobbying for tenant right in the 1880s, until 'doubts are abroad whether there is any difference between conservatives and Liberals on the land question'. He tried to persuade the Liberals to adopt a more radical policy on tenant right, but without success. By this time nationalism had also become a major factor in Irish politics.

In the 1886 general election, McElroy, himself, secretary of both the Ulster Land Committee and Route Tenants' Defence Committee, was selected as a Gladstonian Liberal candidate in north Antrim. In an election where northern voters split into traditional unionist and nationalist camps, McElroy was soundly beaten by the conservative Edward MacNaghten.

McElroy was a defendant in a court case to protect the public right of way to the Giant's Causeway. He died on 13 September 1914. He was survived by his two daughters from his first marriage and his second wife, Martha.

Sources: McElroy (undated); Thompson 2002; Walker 1989; Wright 1996.

John Ferguson
1836–1906

John Ferguson was born in Belfast in 1836, the son of Leonard Ferguson, a Presbyterian provisions merchant, whose father had been a tenant farmer and United Irishman, and Charlotte (née Ferris) a member of the Church of Ireland. He went to school in Crumlin, probably in a school run by the non-subscribing Rev. Nathaniel Alexander. His father died when he was only eight years old. The family returned to Belfast and he was apprenticed to the stationery trade where he showed promise and continued his education through self-study. He then moved to Glasgow and worked as a traveller for the stationery and printing company of Cameron & Co. This proved to be a very successful move and in 1867 he was made a full partner and quickly built up the renamed printing and publishing enterprise Cameron and Ferguson. He became actively involved in the Church of Scotland and continued his self-education by reading very widely and attending public lectures. He was particularly inspired by Herbert Spencer, John Stuart Mill, William Gladstone and John Bright.

In 1862 he had married Mary Ochiltree from Markethill, County Armagh and they had four children, one of whom died in childhood.

Ferguson began to become involved in liberal, and increasingly radical, politics. He attended the inaugural meeting of the Reform League in London. In the mid-1870s he made contact with Isaac Butt, MP for Limerick, ascendancy Protestant who had been radicalised by the Great Famine, and also with some of the members of the Irish Republican Brotherhood while they were in Scotland, becoming actively involved in agrarian and Irish nationalist politics. He was one of the earliest champions in Scotland of Butt's new Home Rule movement, becoming its leader in Glasgow. He campaigned for an amnesty for the fifty or so alleged Fenians in jail, although eventually the Home Rulers and the Fenian IRB fell out. In 1873 Ferguson was elected to the executive of the Home Rule Confederation of Great Britain when it met in Manchester.

Ferguson became a close friend and colleague of Joseph Biggar and the Rev. Isaac Nelson and, although mainly based in Scotland, became very actively involved in Irish politics, particularly in support of Home Rule. Ferguson gave a lecture at the first meeting of the Home Rulers in 1874 and made it clear that he supported a form of Home Rule, but not complete separatism:

> All our interests point to union with England … But a large number
> of Irishmen require some reason for entering into union upon any
> terms with that nation which has been such a terrible destroyer in the
> past and is today proud and insulting in its demeanour towards us.

He argued that the authorities in England would be prepared to grant self-government and that geographically and commercially it made sense. Alternatively, he felt that separation would be likely to result in the imposition of export tariffs that would make it impossible for Ireland to become a manufacturing nation, 'in fact the trade of Belfast would be as completely destroyed by such a course as was the old woollen trade'.

In January 1878, along with Charles Stewart Parnell, Ferguson met Michael Davitt in Kingstown, when he was released from jail on a 'ticket of leave', having been imprisoned for an abortive raid on Chester Castle in 1867, and was involved with him in his campaign of land agitation. In

1880 Ferguson chaired a meeting of Land League branches and farmer's clubs from all over Ireland. This meeting resolved,

> Pending a ... final and satisfactory reform of the Irish land system, we call upon the tenant farmers ... to refuse to occupy any farm from which another is evicted for non-payment of unjust rent as the best check upon landlord wrong and as the best method of abolishing landlordism.

Between 1879 and 1881 he spoke at land reform meetings all over Ireland and Britain. He was one of only two Protestants elected to the central committee of the Irish National Land League, becoming its chairman. When Henry George came to Ireland to promote land nationalisation, Ferguson was one of his strongest supporters in Belfast. He had radical views on the taxation of land values and on land nationalisation, but was completely opposed to the use of any form of violence. Ferguson died in 1906.

Sources: Holmes and Knox 1990; McFarland 2003; Moody 1981; O Cathain 2007; Wright 1996.

Isabella Tod
1836–96

Isabella Maria Susan Tod was born in Edinburgh in May 1836, daughter of a Scottish father and Irish mother from Holywood, County Down. She was brought up in Belfast and educated privately, as was common for middle-class women of the time. She lived in Claremont Street, Belfast and later in College Park East, Belfast. She was a member of Elmwood Presbyterian Church for over thirty years.

She was a pioneer in promoting the rights of women in the north of Ireland. In 1867, she founded the Ladies Institute providing training courses for women and campaigned for women's education, petitioning Queen's College (later Queen's University) to allow girls to take university Honours courses and examinations. The University initially only agreed to let women take tests and award them certificates rather than degrees.

She initially campaigned on women's rights through writing articles for the *Dublin University Magazine* and the *Banner of Ulster* and other journals. She later became a leading Belfast suffragette, and was elected the secretary of the Northern Irish Branch of the National Society for Women's Suffrage, established in 1871. Her campaigning was rewarded by the introduction of votes for women in municipal elections in 1887.

With Caroline Norton, she lobbied for changes in the law in relation to women, which resulted in the introduction of the Married Women's Property Bill. She also campaigned against the Contagious Diseases Act, on behalf of prostitutes through the Ladies National Association. It was repealed in 1886.

She was a founder of the Unionist Women's Association and the Liberal Unionist Association and campaigned vigorously against Home Rule.

In 1900, James Dewar wrote about her, 'She was an eloquent and forcible speaker … and a potent leader for the benefit of her sex … From 1867 until near the time of her death in 1896 Miss Tod never knew what it was like to be without some public work.'

She never married and died in December 1896 and is buried in Balmoral Cemetery, Belfast.

Sources: Armour 2004; Bradbury 2002; Gravestone Inscriptions Series, Belfast, vol. 3; Holmes and Knox 1990; Holmes and Urquhart 1994; Luddy 1995; Newman 1993.

Andrew Porter
1837–1919

Andrew Marshal Porter was born in 1837 and was a Unitarian and non-subscribing Presbyterian, although his wife, Agnes, was a Scottish born Anglican. He became a lawyer and eventually a QC. In 1881 the Derry Liberal Union chose him as their candidate in the by-election caused by the sitting MP, Hugh Law being made Lord Chancellor of Ireland. Law had suggested Porter as a candidate, indicating that Porter was likely to become the next Attorney General, which turned out to be correct. In his election address, Porter indicated his support for Gladstone and the benefits of the 1881 Land Act. Porter was supported by Thomas A. Dickson (see profile) and many Presbyterian ministers. Porter was faced with both a conservative candidate, Sir Samuel Wilson and a nationalist Land League Candidate, Daniel Dempsey.

Just before the election, *The Times* published a letter by F.H. O'Donnell saying that he had been instructed by Parnell to go to Derry to tell the Catholics to vote for the conservative candidate, Samuel Wilson, in order to damage the liberals. Fortunately a sufficient number of Catholics decided to ignore this advice and voted Liberal, enabling Porter to be elected.

In 1883 Porter was appointed as Master of the Rolls. He was eventually knighted. In later life he and his wife lived with their unmarried daughter, Helen Violet in Clontarf West, Dublin. He died in 1919.

Sources: Stenton and Lees 1976; Thompson 2002; Walker 1989.

John Givan
1837–95

John Givan was born in 1837 into a Presbyterian family in Castlecaulfield, County Tyrone. He started as teacher in the local school and then became a legal clerk in a solicitor's office. He eventually became a successful solicitor in Aughnacloy, County Tyrone and was admitted to the bar in 1870. He was prominent in actions brought before the land courts in defence of the rights of tenants, including the first case under the 1870 Land Act in Monaghan. He later became a magistrate for County Tyrone and chairman of Aughnacloy Town Commissioners.

He was a member of Aughnacloy Presbyterian Church, of which Rev. William McIlwaine was the minister. He was elected a member of the Church Committee, and became Sunday School Superintendent and Church Elder. He provided the premises for a day school and personally paid two-thirds of the cost of the site.

He married Elizabeth (known as Eliza) Hopper of Crewe, County Tyrone. In January 1880, he, accompanied by his friend Thomas Dickson MP for Dungannon, addressed a meeting of Liberal electors in County Monaghan, where Eliza had connections, and expressed his willingness to contest the seat on tenant right principles. He also called to see the Catholic Bishop Donnelly, the local power-broker.

A month later, at a selection meeting held in the Catholic Church in Castleblaney, Givan was selected, along with Monaghan landlord, Sir W.T. Power, who later withdrew to be replaced by William Findlater (see profile). In their joint election address they stated that they were in favour of the '3 Fs', an opportunity for the tenant farmers 'to become the owners of their holdings by loans from the government, the abolition of distress for rent, and lastly the reform of the Grand Jury system, and its substitution by a number of boards elected by the cess payers'.

In March, Givan spoke at a large meeting in Monaghan town, chaired by the Presbyterian minister of Aughnacloy, Rev. McIlwaine (see profile) in support of his candidature and land reform. Givan was successfully elected along with Findlater, with both Catholic and Protestant support, defeating the Conservative Anglican landowners, Sir John Leslie and Swallis Evelyn Shirley.

In November of the same year, Givan spoke at a massive Land League meeting, where a wide range of speakers from a Catholic priest to an Orangeman supported the extension of rights to tenants including the '3 Fs' and tenant proprietorship. In defence of agitation, Givan said,

> If anyone tells me that agitation is based on lawlessness I will throw back the falsehood in his face, and tell him that agitation in its legitimate form has been caused by unjust laws – and in its

aggravated development I can trace it to the gilded chamber of the feudal lords – and to the treatment the Disturbance Bill received at their hands.

In 1883, Givan vacated his seat to become crown solicitor for counties Kildare and Meath. In his new role he was criticised by members of the Land League for supporting the Government against the League.

After his first wife died, Givan married Arminta Read, daughter of James M. Ross of Liscarney, County Monaghan. A couple of years before his death he returned to Martray, Ballygawley. Givan died in 1895, aged 57/8.

Sources: McGimpsey 1982; Stenton and Lees 1976; Walker 1989.

William Sinclair
1837–1900

William Pirrie Sinclair was born in Belfast in 1837, son of Presbyterians John Sinclair and Eliza (née Pirrie) of Conlig near Bangor, County Down. He was educated at Royal Belfast Academical Institution, Queen's College Belfast and Heidelberg University in Germany. He became a successful businessman in Liverpool. He was a church elder and a member of the Mersey Docks and Harbour Board. His family had been active supporters of the Presbyterian Church, giving generous donations for the building of the church in Conlig near Bangor, County Down, as well as for the Church and Manse Fund. The family also had long-established links with the Sinclair Seaman's Presbyterian Church.

In an Antrim by-election caused by the death of the sitting conservative MP, James Chaine, in one of the two old county seats before the redistribution of 1885, Sinclair was asked to stand in the election by the County Antrim Central Tenant Right Association, at a meeting in Liberal headquarters in Belfast. In his election address he declared his support for the extension of the Land Act to leaseholders, an important issue in County Antrim where most farmers were leaseholders, and land purchase, but there was not a lot to distinguish his position from that of the conservative Hon. R.T. O'Neill's, although O'Neill, the son of Lord O'Neill, was a strong supporter of free trade which was unpopular in Belfast. With T.A. Dickson's involvement in his campaign, Sinclair became more radical, coming out in opposition to Gladstone's Coercion laws. He was also helped by the Government coming out with a commitment to a new Land Purchase Bill. In the end, Sinclair was successful against O'Neill, polling 3,971 votes against O'Neill's 3,832.

Following the redistribution of seats and boundaries, and with the perceived ominous threat of Home Rule looming, Sinclair was selected by the Route Reform Association for the new divisional seat. John Pinkerton, a Unitarian and member of the Association was also proposed, but refused to allow his name to go forward. He eventually decided to stand as an independent and picked up a significant number of Catholic votes, splitting the vote and ensuring the defeat of Sinclair and the success of the conservative, Edward MacNaghten. In 1878 Sinclair stood successfully as a Liberal in Falkirk in Scotland and was an MP there for 15 years to 1893. He died in 1900.

Sources: McMinn 1981; Stenton and Lees 1976; Walker 1989.

Thomas Sinclair
1838–1914

Thomas Sinclair was born in Fisherwick Place in Belfast on 23 September 1838. He was the son of Thomas Sinclair, joint founder of J. & T. Sinclair trading company and a generous donor to the Presbyterian Church, building Conlig Church and the Seaman's Mission. The young Thomas Sinclair attended the Royal Belfast Academical Institution (Inst) and Queen's College (later Queen's University), where he received a BA, first class in Mathematics and a Gold Medal. He went on to gain an MA in English Literature.

Sinclair joined his father in the family merchandise firm, J. & T. Sinclair, along with his brother and became president of the Chamber of Commerce. He actively participated in the establishment of the Royal Victoria Hospital.

He was involved in the Presbyterian mission in Harding Street, Belfast and the establishment of a new Duncairn Presbyterian Church in north Belfast, where he took over the Sabbath school from his father. He lobbied the General Assembly over its fund to help needy members of Presbyterian congregations. He was actively involved in the Seaman's Friend Society and, with the other members of his family, saw through the building of the Sinclair Seaman's Church designed by Sir Charles Lanyon, who designed the main Queen's University building.

Sinclair was concerned about the land question and supported land reform to help local farmers.He was also very concerned with the issue of education and, along with Rev. John McNaughton, organised a National Education League to fight for non-denominational education against the Powis Commission which, in 1870, conceded to demands to allow education along denominational lines.

He was a founding member of the liberal Ulster Reform Club and first president of the Ulster Liberal Unionist Association, but Presbyterian memories of political and ecclesiastical oppression under an authoritarian hierarchical church were strong, and they were not keen to return to what they saw as a similar situation under the Catholic Church this time. Although he was not insensitive to the 'rights of the Irish people and the wants of Ireland', he, as a businessman, saw Home Rule as a disaster which would, 'Empty their mills, clear their rivers and shipyards, would stop their looms, would make the voice of their spindles silent and would cause a complete destruction of the industry that had made the province so prosperous.' He seconded a motion against Home Rule at the General Assembly in March 1886.

During the latter part of the nineteenth century, Sinclair was a strong supporter and fundraiser for the Sick Poor Society, providing the forerunners of the health visitor and the district nurse. He became president of the Charity Organisation Society in 1909 which provided financial support to the very poor.

He was married twice. His first wife, Mary died, but his second wife survived him. They had four sons and three daughters. He died at home on the Antrim Road, Belfast on 14 February 1914. He is buried in Belfast City Cemetery.

Sources: Bradbury 2002; Hartley 2006; Holmes 1985; Holmes 2000; Holmes and Knox 1990; Jordan 1992; Peatling 2006; Walker 1996; Wright 1996.

Henry Pringle
1838–1921

Henry Pringle was born in 1838, the third child of John and Mary Ann Pringle. The Pringle family had lived variously in Monaghan and Tyrone for many generations. Henry Pringle became a successful butter merchant, as well as farming a small-holding in Clones, County Monaghan, which gave him great empathy with the tenant farmers in the area. He played an important role in the Land Law reform movement.

In 1863 he married Matilda King, from County Tyrone, who was the same age as him. They had 10 children, of whom six survived. They lived at 9 Clonboy, Clones, County Monaghan. Of the nine dwellings in Clonboy, Pringle eventually owned seven of them. One of the remaining two was a small fever hospital.

Along with his brother, Robert from Castleblayney, Henry Pringle was politically Liberal. In the 1883 election in Monaghan, following John Givan's (see profile) resignation to become Crown Solicitor, he stood as a reluctant Liberal candidate. He had initially turned down the approach to stand, as had John Shaw Brown (see profile), J.H. Fay and landowners James B. Ross and David Ross, but under pressure, changed his mind.

The Ulster Land Committee endorsed Pringle as a strong supporter of land reform. Thomas Dickson, MP for County Tyrone, also actively supported Pringle's candidature.

In his election address Pringle referred to himself as an Independent Liberal, presumably to distance himself from Gladstone's claims that the 1881 Land Act was the final solution to the land issue and from the government's repressive coercion measures. He said that he wanted to see a peasant proprietorship, the cost of which should be entirely borne by the government. He supported changes to the 1881 Act to ensure no rent increases could be levied on tenant improvements and to ensure that the occupiers of town parks would be protected. He also supported abolishing the Grand Jury system, to be replaced with county boards elected by the people.

He fought the election against well-known nationalist, Tim Healy, the sitting MP for the borough of Wexford, who although very young, had introduced the Healy clause into the 1881 Land Act; and Conservative John Munro QC. In the previous election the Catholic clergy in the area had ensured Catholic support for the Liberal candidate, John Givan. This time they supported the nationalist candidate. Even some of the Presbyterian voters defected to Healy and Munro. In the end, Pringle only received 270 votes against 2,376 for Healy and 2,011 Munro.

Pringle died in 1921. Their son, Harold, became a surgeon and histology lecturer at Edinburgh University.

Sources: McGimpsey 1982; Thompson 2001.

James Bryce
1838–1922

James Bryce was born in Arthur Street, Belfast in 1838. His father was a schoolteacher and geologist, also called James Bryce, and his mother, Margaret (née Young), was the daughter of a Belfast merchant. He had a happy childhood spending a lot of time at his grandfather's home, Abbeyville, just outside Belfast. He was educated at Glasgow High School for a period, when his father went there to teach from 1846, and then in 1852 to Belfast Academy, where his uncle was principal. He then went to Glasgow University and Trinity College Dublin. This was followed by a scholarship to Oxford where he won many prizes and graduated with first class honours, completing his university education at Heidelberg in Germany. He practised at the bar for a period, before being appointed Regius Professor of Civil Law at Oxford in 1870.

He wrote a book in 1877 about his travels to Russia and Armenia, *Transcaucasia and Ararat* and in his support for Armenia became an opponent of Disraeli who backed the Turkish Empire.

Bryce joined the Liberal Party and was successfully elected MP for Tower Hamlets in east London in 1880. In February 1881 he raised a parliamentary question about the condition of Michael Davitt, whom he had met the previous December and had thought well of, and was now in jail. He advocated that Liberals should seek to win Catholic and Home Rule votes. In 1885 he went to talk to the General Committee of the newly created liberal Ulster Reform Club and suggested to them that they would need to go much further than reform of local government, which was the first indication to the Irish liberals that Gladstone was considering more radical changes for Ireland in the form of Home Rule.

He then became MP for South Aberdeen from 1885 to 1906 and with his Irish contacts kept Gladstone informed of Irish attitudes towards the land question and Gladstone's Home Rule proposals. He was a member of three cabinets, including Under-Secretary for Foreign Affairs under Gladstone, but was never prepared to give all his energies to politics, and was, therefore, perhaps not as successful as he could otherwise have been.

In 1888 he published a book, *The American Commonwealth* and in 1897 his *Impressions of South Africa* in which he criticised the Conservative's foreign policy.

In relation to Irish politics, he was convinced that Home Rule was inevitable and helped Gladstone prepare the Irish Home Rule Bill, wrote *Two Centuries of Irish History 1691–1870* and edited the *Handbook of Home Rule*. He became Chief Secretary for Ireland in 1905.

In 1907, he became ambassador to Washington. He was then made a Lord and with ex-President Taft of the USA, promoted the establishment of the League of Nations as well as continuing his writing. Bryce died in Sidmouth England in 1922.

Sources: Boylan 1998; Brett 1978; Byrne and McMahon 1991; Duddy (ed.) 2004; Hickey and Doherty 2005; McKnight 1896; Thompson 2002; Walker 1989.

James Mairs
1839–1927

James Septimus Mairs was born in 1839, the son of James Mairs of Crossgar, County Down. He was educated at James Bruce's classical school, Coleraine Academical Institution and Belfast Academy where he gained his General Certificate in 1863. He then went on to Queen's College Belfast and to Assembly's College to train for the Presbyterian ministry. He was licensed in Coleraine in 1865 and ordained in Dunloy on 30 March 1866.

Mairs was one of the leaders of the tenant right campaign in County Antrim attending local meetings and the Ulster Conference of tenant right associations in 1870. He was a regular contributor to newspapers on the land issue. At a tenant right meeting in 1892 Mairs proposed the following, 'We earnestly urge upon the farmers and labourers the necessity and importance of raising the land question above the strife of potential parties, and demand for it a supreme place in all electoral efforts for the social advancement of the country.'

Samuel McElroy of the North Antrim Tenants Defence Association and *Ballymoney Free Press* saw Mairs as one of the key people responsible for making north Antrim the centre of the tenant right movement. He was also a key member of the Ulster Land Committee. Prior to 1886, he was a Liberal politically and then a Liberal Unionist and finally a supporter of T.W. Russell (see profile). He lived with his unmarried daughter, Magritta Theodora and remained minister of Dunloy church until he retired on 27 May 1913. He died on 11 May 1927.

Sources: Barkley 1986; McElroy (undated); McMinn 1979.

Hugh Waddell
1840–1901

Born in Glenarm, County Antrim in October 1840, the son of the local Presbyterian minister of the same name, Hugh Waddell was educated at the local Irish National School, controlled and staffed by Catholics; Royal Belfast Academical Institution; Queen's College Belfast; and Assembly's College Belfast before being ordained as an Irish Presbyterian minister and missionary to China on 19 January 1869. Before departure he married Miss Jenny Martin of Katesbridge, County Down. He was forced to return to Ireland due to ill health in 1872 before serving in Cordova, Spain (1872–4) and then in Japan with the United Presbyterian Church of Scotland. In Japan he was also a lecturer for a time at the Imperial University. He later lectured in Old Testament History and Christian Literature at the Presbyterian run Tsukiji Theological School (now the Meiji Gakuin University).

Waddell along with three other missionaries, John Piper, David Thomson and George Cochrane, combined to translate the Bible into Japanese and in 1877 they published their translation of the Book of Genesis. His wife died of typhoid fever in 1892 and with the ten children to look after he returned home and married his cousin Martha Waddell and moved into Glandole, Cavehill Road, Belfast. He returned to Japan. In 1896 the Scottish Mission Board informed him that they no longer required his services in Japan, but under pressure relented and the family spent the next five years in Japan, returning to Belfast in 1900, when the Mission Board finally decided to close the mission he had founded in Tokyo. He died on 20 June 1901 in Belfast and was interred at Magherally.

His youngest child, daughter Helen Jane Waddell, born in Tokyo in 1889, was educated by Margaret Byers (see profile) at Victoria College and became a distinguished academic and author. Her books include *Lyrics from the Chinese* (1913); *The Wandering Scholars* (1927); *Medieval Latin Lyrics* (1929); *Manon Lescaut* (a translation 1931); *A Book of Medieval Latin for Schools* (1931); *Abbe Prevost* (1933); *Peter Abelard* (1933); *Beasts and Saints* (1934); *The Desert Fathers* (1936); and *Stories from Holy Writ* (1949).

His fourth son, Samuel Waddell, was born in 1878 and was brought up by relatives in Banbridge, County Down. He worked as an engineer for the Irish Land Commission redistributing land on the great estates in the west of Ireland. As a writer and actor he took the pen and stage name of Rutherford Mayne. He was the author of twelve plays: *The Turn of the Road* (1907); *The Drone* (1909); *The Troth* (1909); *Red Turf* (1911); *The Captain of the Host* (1911): *If!* (1913); *Evening* (1914); *Nell Gallina* (1916); *Industry* (1917); *A Prologue* (1925); *Peter* (1936); and *Bridge Head* (1939), based on his experiences with the Land Commission. He was a founder member of the Ulster Literary Theatre and its magazine, *Ulad*. He died in 1967.

Sources: Barkley 1986; Corrigan 1986; Killen 1997.

David Wilson
1840–94

David Wilson was born on 4 May 1840, the son of Ballymena merchant, John Wilson. He was educated at Royal Belfast Academical Institution, where he gained his General Certificate in 1840. He was licensed to preach in Ballymena, County Antrim on 2 July 1842 and ordained in Carnmoney, County Antrim on 31 January 1844, succeeding Rev. John Dill who died in 1841. However, he stayed in Carnmoney less than a year and was called to Limerick where he was installed on New Year's Eve 1844, succeeding Rev. Robert McCorkle. His congregation grew rapidly and he often conducted five services on a Sunday. A new congregation was formed in Ennis, County Clare. In 1862 he was awarded a Doctorate in Divinity from the USA. He was elected Moderator of the General Assembly two years in a row 1865–7.

In 1868 the government established a Commission, chaired by Lord Powis to examine primary education in Ireland and the practical working of the Board of National Education. Wilson was a member of the Commission but refused to sign the report and opposed its recommendations. His objections came to 44 pages. He was very unhappy that there was no attempt to improve the salaries of teachers or to make any provision for infirm or aged teachers to enable them to retire. He was particularly incensed by the evidence given by the Archbishop of Dublin, Dr Paul Cullen, to the Commission, when he said,

> Too high an education will make the poor oftentimes discontented and will unsuit them for following the plough, or for using the spade, or for hammering iron or for building walls. The poor ought to be educated with a view to the place they hold in society, in which it will be impossible for them to cultivate the higher branches of literature and science.

In response Wilson said,

> I stand up for the interest of all Ireland, the poorest as well as the rich of her children ... I would educate all together, whatever their creed. The National system of education ... is a system promotive of the educational interests of all religious denominations on a common platform.

Wilson died on 4 December 1894.

Sources: Barkley 1986; McIvor 1969.

George Raphael Buick
1841–1904

George Buick was born in 1841 the son of Rev. Frederick Buick of Ahoghill. He was educated at Queen's College Belfast and trained for the ministry at Assembly's College Belfast. He was licensed to preach in Ahoghill on 5 February 1866. He was ordained two years later on 1 February 1868 in Cullybackey, near Ballymena, County Antrim and succeeded the fifty-year ministry of Rev. Hugh Hamilton. Buick spent his entire ministry as minister of Cunningham Memorial in Cullybackey. He was elected moderator of the General Assembly in 1895.

Towards the end of the century Buick was a founding patron and vice-president of the Belfast Gaelic League, which was established to promote Gaelic culture and language and ran weekly Irish classes.

He is also believed to be the author of an anonymous biography of his father entitled, *Buick's Ahoghill*. Buick died in 1904 while on a visit to Damascus and was succeeded by Rev. William Corkey.

Sources: Barkley 1986; Blaney 1996.

Thomas (T.W.) Russell
1841–1920

Thomas Wallace Russell was born in Cupar, Fifeshire, Scotland in 1841, son of a Scottish stonemason, David Russell and his wife Isabella (née Wallace) and the grandson of an evicted crofter. He was educated in Madras Academy in Cupar. He moved to Ireland in 1859 and worked as a draper's assistant in Donaghmore, County Tyrone, eventually becoming a successful hotelier. He was active in the temperance movement, becoming secretary of the Dublin Temperance Association in 1864 and helped secure the passing of the Sale of Liquors on Sunday (Ireland) Act 1878. He then decided to go into politics.

During this period, tenant farmers were struggling with falling prices for their produce but rising rents from often absentee Anglican landlords. Russell became a leading supporter of tenant right and an opponent of the landlords' treatment of tenant farmers.

In 1885, he became a Liberal MP for Preston, Lancashire. In the 1886 general election, called after the defeat and resignation of Gladstone, under the new expanded franchise, opponents of the Tory Unionists did very well. Russell, a supporter of tenant right, was successful in the rural constituency of Tyrone South, where the land question was top of the political agenda, defeating the Irish Parliamentary candidate, William O'Brien. Russell held his seat until 1910.

Russell had a strong dislike for landlordism which he called 'barbarous and inhuman', and accused landlords of engaging in 'systematised and legalised robbery'. He said that 'in pretending to fight for the Union these men are simply fighting for their own interests – that rent not patriotism was their guiding motive'. In 1902 he outlined his position on the land system, and landlords, whom he described as 'callous and heartless tyrants', in particular:

> These landlords and this land-system were the creation of the English Government. England for purposes of its own planted these men in Ireland – planted the English land-system in that country. For centuries and throughout periods of great trouble these men acted as the garrison of England in a conquered country. They served England with devotion. In doing so they became a hated class in the country of adoption … They governed the Church, the Land, the Representation of the People in Parliament, the Government, the country were all in their hands. They were veritable lords. The tenants were helots and slaves.

Russell was a man of strong intelligence, vigorous energy and considerable eloquence, who gathered considerable support from unionist tenant farmers between 1900 and 1905, who called themselves Rusellites. One Russellite MP, James Wood, was also elected in East Down in 1902.

In 1903, Parliament passed the Land Act which lent money to tenants to buy their land from the landlords who were encouraged to sell entire estates. Further legislation was required to compel the landlords to sell. The result of these bills was that, eventually, the land question dropped off the political agenda in Ireland.

While initially opposing Home Rule, Russell changed his mind and supported it, losing his South Tyrone seat in 1910 as a consequence. However in the following year, 1911, he gained a seat in North Tyrone. The Russelites eventually joined with the Liberals.

Russell had no time for Unionists who clung to the outdated ascendancy and land system. He believed strongly that Christianity should not in any way be associated with landlordism. He believed that right-thinking people of all denominations should come together under the banner of social reform, regardless of precise theological beliefs. He opposed the Orange Order and supported the establishment of the Independent Orange Order.

He founded the New Land Movement in Ulster, advocating the compulsory purchase of land, (which was eventually introduced in 1909). He published *England and the Empire* in 1901 and *The Irish Land question up to date* in 1902.

He was appointed a baronet in 1917, but withdrew from public life after the death of his only son during the war. He died in 1920 in Terenure, County Dublin.

Sources: Bardon 1992; Bell 1987; Brooke 1994; Campbell 1991; Erskine and Gordon 1997; Hickey and Doherty 2005; Holmes and Knox 1990; Hume 1998; McMinn 1979.

James Brown Armour
1841–1928

James Armour was born in Lisboy near Ballymoney, County Antrim in 1841 into a Presbyterian farming family with about 60 acres of land. As a boy he observed the famine at first hand. He was educated at local Ganaby School, under Mr Warnock and followed him to Ballymoney Model School when it opened in 1854 (requiring a daily 7 mile walk); the Royal Belfast Academical Institution; and the Queen's Colleges in Belfast and Cork where he studied Classics, teaching part-time to support himself. His experience in the south of Ireland helped him to develop 'a fuller understanding' of his Catholic fellow countrymen. He wanted to become a lawyer, but gave in to his father and brother's wishes and trained for the ministry. He was ordained as a Presbyterian minister in Second Presbyterian Church, Ballymoney in 1869 and stayed there for the next 56 years. He founded the Intermediate school there and lectured in Classics at Magee College in Derry (1885–1908). Like many Presbyterian ministers of the period he was very concerned about land issues and the position of tenants, which most Presbyterians were. When the Rev. Field (see profile) was evicted by landowner Samuel Allen from his home in Knockenboy near Dervock, Armour spoke at a meeting of Dervock congregation in support of their minister. In 1885 he spoke at a public meeting in Kilraughts in support of the Liberal candidate W.P. Sinclair (see profile) who was eventually successful.

In 1883 he married a widow with two sons, Jennie Hamilton, whose great grand-father, Rev. William Stavely (see profile), had ministered to the United Irishman, William Orr (see profile) at his execution in 1797.

According to his son, in 1890 Armour was considered by some to be unfit to hold a chair in church history at Magee College in Derry because he had put a spire (an 'invention of the evil one') on to his church.

While initially opposed to Home Rule, he changed his mind and became a prominent member of the Ulster Liberal Association and supporter of Home Rule for Ireland. He described Home Rule as a 'Presbyterian principle'. He collected over 3,500 Presbyterian signatures in support of Gladstone's Home Rule policy. When the Presbyterian General Assembly in 1893 debated a motion condemning Home Rule, Armour spoke strongly against the motion and moved an amendment, seconded by Prof. J.B. Dougherty (see profile) and John Steen, an elder from Portstewart, which was defeated, by 821 to 43 votes, although with 165 abstentions.

Armour supported land reform and the tenant right movement. He also supported the proposed establishment of a National (Catholic) University, and the teaching of Celtic Studies, the Irish language and scholastic philosophy at Queen's University where he served on the Senate. In the 1892 election he supported a liberal home ruler.

In 1911, he scoffed at loyalist threats of violent resistance to Home Rule as a bad attack of *delirium tremens*. And when the threats did begin to materialise he described Carson as the 'greatest enemy of Protestantism in my opinion existing, inflaming men to violence.' He described the signing of the Ulster Covenant in 1912 as 'Protestant Fools' Day'.

Despite the large public controversy and ridicule he inspired, including being physically attacked on two occasions, he maintained his principles and while they did not always agree with him, his congregation remained loyal to him. At the General Assembly in 1912 he moved an amendment that politics should not be allowed to divide the church. This provoked a storm of protest, to which he replied, 'If you deny the right of private judgement and of free speech, how much of Protestantism do you have worth keeping? Nothing at all'.

In 1913 he helped organise a meeting in Ballymoney Town Hall, attended by 400–500 people, chaired by Presbyterian elder and tenant right campaigner, John McElderry, at which home rulers Roger Casement, Jack

White and Alice Stopford Green spoke. Armour blamed the northern Unionists for the 1916 rising because of their actions in gun-running and promoting the use of force against the Crown.

In the General Assembly of 1920, he spoke against the Government of Ireland Bill and partition, as divisive and anti-unionist, as tending to accentuate racial and religious hatreds and as ruinous to the commercial prosperity of Ireland. Again the Assembly voted against him.

He had three sons by Jennie Stavely Hamilton, who already had two sons before she was widowed. He retired in 1925 and, although having being diagnosed with a heart condition in 1908, he survived until he died of pneumonia in 1928. Several years after his death his son, W.S. Armour, editor of the *Northern Whig*, wrote a biography of his father, which J.R.B. McMinn suggests did much to build and perhaps overstate the reputation of Armour as a radical and Ballymoney as a hotbed of radical opinion. He also wrote *Facing the Irish Question* (1935) and *Ulster, Ireland, Britain: A Forgotten Trust* (1938).

Sources: Armour 1934; Bardon 1992; Barkley 1986; Boylan 1998; Brooke 1994; Byrne and McMahon 1991; Campbell 1991; Erskine and Gordon 1997; Hickey and Doherty 2005; Holmes 1985; Holmes 2000; Hume 1998; McMinn 1985; Newman 1993; Wallace 1999.

Wesley Guard Lyttle
1844–96

Wesley Guard Lyttle was born in 1844 in Newtownards, County Down. He worked as a clerk in a solicitor's office. At one time he was also a school teacher and a lecturer on Dr Corry's *Irish Diorama*. He learnt shorthand and became a journalist. He eventually gained the job of editor of the liberal *North Down Herald* and became its owner. When the paper moved from Newtownards to Bangor, the name *Bangor Gazette* was added to the end of the previous name.

He wrote a regular comic column called *Rabin's Readings* and was in popular demand as an entertainer telling humorous monologues in the local rural dialect. He wrote three novels, *Sons of the Sod,* about the plight of tenant farmers, *The Smugglers of Strangford Lough* and his most famous, *Betsy Gray, or Hearts of Down: A Tale of Ninety-Eight* published in 1896. This sympathetically told the story of a heroine of the United Irish rebellion. It is still debated as to whether the character was real or fictional, although the stories certainly contain much that is historically true about Rev. William Steel Dickson and William Warwick (both profiled) and the period around 1798. In 1968 *Betsey Gray* was reprinted with other stories which had been published in the *Mourne Observer*.

Sources: Ferguson 2008; Hewitt 2004; Lyttle 1968.

William Clements
1844–1919

William Clements was born in Sixmilecross, County Tyrone in 1844. He was educated in Queen's College Belfast, Assembly's College Belfast and Glasgow University. He was licensed to preach by Omagh Presbytery in 1866 and ordained in Tartaraghan, County Armagh in 1868. He was installed as a minister in Benburb, County Tyrone in 1876. He was deeply affected by the plight of the poor in Tartaraghan:

> Both weavers and labourers are daily becoming less equal to work and starvation is pictured in their countenance. Numbers are subsisting on less than one meal per diem and upon raw turnips and any herbs they can gather. Already one case of death from starvation has occurred ... and several have only just been preserved from it, while fever has attacked very many in the district. Within the last few days, parties of twenty to thirty famishing men have been traversing the County demanding assistance. In the absence of all public works of any kind, and when our poor houses are nearly filled, we hardly know where to turn.

Clements complained bitterly about the obduracy of local landlords and the 'evil effects of absenteeism':

> The largest estate is under the administration of the Lord Chancellor for debt with no help whatsoever being obtained from it for its starving tenantry. A large portion of the parish is bog, the property of absent proprietors and upon it are located a large number of most wretched tenants who are not assisted by the landlord.

He was clerk of the Omagh Presbytery from 1904 until his death in 1919.

Sources: Barkley 1986; Kinealy 1997.

Jonathan Simpson
1844–1900

Jonathan Simpson was born on 26 September 1844, the son of William Simpson, a farmer in Inishadoghal, Aghadowey, near Coleraine in the east of County Londonderry, where his minister was a Rev. John Brown (see profile). Simpson was educated at the Royal Belfast Academical Institution where he received his General Certificate in 1835. He trained for the ministry and was ordained on 12 August 1840 by the Mission Board to undertake mission work in Enniscorthy in County Wexford.

Records of the history of Presbyterian preaching in Enniscorthy are sketchy. However, Simpson, as well as Rev. Robert Knox of Linenhall Street Belfast, did go there as missionaries. It was not, however, until some 20 years later that a congregation began to emerge, initially at two Mission stations: Ballingall and Clonrocke and then at a central Station at Enniscorthy. In 1865, Dublin Presbytery formed them into a congregation and in the following year the church was built by Mr Patrick Kerr, an elder in Union Chapel, Dublin.

Early in the nineteenth century, Portrush, County Antrim began to develop into a prosperous town due to its new harbour and the popularity of sea bathing, and from 1836 services were be held in the town 'during the bathing season'. In 1841 Portrush formally became a congregation and was supplied by the Presbytery until Rev. Brown persuaded Simpson to accept the call to Portrush. He was installed there on 27 December 1842.

Considerable difficulty was encountered in building a church there and, at the time of the installation, services were still being held in the Methodist Church, as only three courses of masonry had been completed and work was at a standstill due to lack of money. Mr Simpson spent a year fundraising in America and collected £1,150 which enabled the church to be completed in 1844. Between 1845 and 1852 Ireland experienced the Great Famine. Simpson became very conscious of the plight of tenant farmers and the need for land reform. In 1848 he again visited America and collected over £600 to build a manse. A school house was later built in 1853.

Simpson also visited Scotland where he was warmly received by Rev. Dr John Kennedy, the famous Free Church leader. During the '59 Revival the church was so packed that it was decided to double its size; it was re-opened in 1861. In 1880 Simpson again visited America and, as a result, a teacher's house, schoolroom and lecture hall were completed free of debt.

Politically Simpson was a Liberal and a supporter of the rights of tenant farmers. When John Givan, whom he knew from Aughnacloy, decided to stand as the Liberal candidate in Monaghan in the general election of 1880, on a platform on tenant rights and political reform, Simpson was keen to support him. Despite the distance, Simpson (and Rev. McIlwaine (see profile) spoke in support of Givan's candidacy at political meetings in Ballybay, Emyvale and Monaghan town. He was duly elected along with William Findlater (see profile).

Simpson retired in 1890 and died on 22 December 1900 aged 84. His autobiography is entitled, *Annals of My Life*. He was succeeded in Portrush by Rev. Robert Montgomery.

Sources: Barkley 1986; McGimpsey 1982; Simpson.

William Dodd
1844–1930

William Huston Dodd was born in Rathfriland, County Down in 1844, the only son of Robert and Letty Dodd. He was educated at the Royal Belfast Academical Institution and Queen's College Belfast, where he became friends with J.B. Armour of Ballymoney (see profile). He qualified as a barrister and was called to the bar in 1873 becoming counsel to the Crown for Dublin City and the Post Office.

He was politically a liberal and from 1868 to 1874 was the secretary of the Ulster Liberal Society, trying to organise registration of voters in Antrim. When Christopher Palles, a Catholic Solicitor General, was selected as the Liberal candidate in the Derry by-election of 1872, Dodd and other Liberals greeted him on arrival in Derry. Unfortunately, due to some of his unpopular statements as Solicitor General and attacks by the Bishop of Down and Dromore, he was defeated. In the 1892 general election Dodd stood as the Liberal candidate for North Antrim, on the recommendation of a sub-committee which included Revs J.B. Armour and J.S. Mairs, but, despite the additional public support from two Dublin Presbyterian ministers, Revs J.D. Osborne and J.C. Johnston, Dodd was defeated. He was defeated again in South Derry in 1895.

In 1905 he stood again, this time in Tyrone North and was successful, just defeating the Unionist candidate. He had to resign his seat and give up politics when he was appointed to the bench as a judge in 1907. He was appointed commissioner for charitable donations and bequests in 1911 and a member of the Privy Council in 1913. Dodd later became a High Court judge. He died in 1930.

Sources: Campbell 1991; McMinn 1979; McMinn 1981; *Thom's Irish Who's Who* 1923.

James Houston
1844–1935

James Dickey Craig Houston was born in 1844 in Parkgate, Donegore, County Antrim. He was educated at Queen's College Belfast and Assembly's College. He was licensed to preach by the presbytery of Templepatrick in 1874. He was ordained in the same year in Hydebank, just outside Belfast, where he remained the minister until he retired in 1923. He was a supporter of the tenant right movement, participating in the inaugural meeting of the Antrim Central Tenant Right Committee in 1876.

In 1892 he wrote a letter to the *Daily News* announcing his conversion to Home Rule. He lost 30 members of his congregation as a result as, in his words, 'the indignation of some people against me could not have been greater'. In a major debate on Home Rule in the General Assembly in 1893,

Houston tried to persuade his colleagues to avoid a knee-jerk reaction and not to condemn an untried political arrangement:

> If by a Protestant home ruler is meant one whose aspirations after self-government for Ireland are as ardent, and whose belief in the potential advantages of such a legislative change is as sanguine, as are those of their nationalist compatriots, then I frankly admit that there are comparatively few protestant home rulers in the north, or, indeed, in any part of Ireland. On the other hand, if by the term protestant home ruler is simply meant a liberal-minded politician – one who is willing to acquiesce in a fairly reasonable legislative scheme for the better government of Ireland ... who is disposed to give the scheme ... a fair trial, and who refuses to condemn it as unworkable and absurd until after having been tried by the practical test of experience it has proved itself to be so – if such, I say, is a permissible definition of a protestant home ruler, then there is a large number of such people in Ulster, far more, I believe, than anti-home-ruler writers and speakers are disposed to admit.

In the same year he also wrote a pro-Home Rule pamphlet with Rev. J.B. Dougherty (see profile), '*Are Irish Protestants afraid of Home Rule?*'

Many of his sermons were published during his lifetime including *Anxiety and its antidote*, published in 1912. He died in 1935.

Sources: McCann 1972; McMinn 1979.

James Dougherty
1844–1934

James L. Brown Dougherty was born in Garvagh, County Down in 1844 and educated at Queen's College and Assembly's College Belfast. He obtained an MA from the Queen's University of Ireland in 1865. He was licensed to preach by Coleraine presbytery in 1867 and was ordained in St Andrew's in Nottingham. In Nottingham he met and married Mary Donaldson who died in 1887. In 1889 he married Eliza Todd from Dublin.

He was Professor of Logic, Belle Lettre and Rhetoric at Magee Presbyterian College in Derry from 1874 to 1895.

He was a strong supporter of non-denominational National Education and became a member of the Educational Endowments (Ireland) Commission in 1885 and Commissioner for National Education in 1890, until 1895.

In the 1892 general election, Prof. Dougherty stood as a Liberal in North Tyrone and was defeated by a member of Lord Abercorn's family, standing as a Conservative.

In the teeth of substantial Unionist opposition, Dougherty supported Gladstone's Home Rule Bill in 1893, along with Rev. J.B. Armour, at the Presbyterian Assembly of April 1893. He and the Rev. J.D.C. Houston published *Are Protestants afraid of Home Rule?* They were satisfied that the new Bill included sufficient safeguards for minority rights under an Irish parliament. However, the General Assembly voted to oppose Home Rule. By 1908 the *ne temere* decree of the Roman Catholic church, which was held responsible for a Belfast Roman Catholic's abandonment of his Presbyterian wife, aroused strong feelings in Ulster and reinforced opposition to Home Rule.

To the horror of unionists, Dougherty was appointed Under-Secretary to the Lord Lieutenant by John Morley in 1895. He was knighted in 1902 and became a privy councillor in 1910. Following his resignation as Under-Secretary he was elected Liberal Member of Parliament for Londonderry in 1914, until 1918. Dougherty died in London in 1934.

Sources: Campbell 1991; Holmes 1985; Newman 1993.

Hans McMordie
1845–1921

Hans McMordie was born on 15 March 1845, the son of Hans McMordie, a farmer in Rathfriland, County Down and Mary Todd (née Magarry). He trained as a lawyer and practiced as a solicitor in Belfast. He married Agnes Jane (née Straghan), sixteen years his junior, in 1890 and had five children, four girls (Maggie, Agnes Jane, Sarah and Annie) and one boy, who was named after his father, but died as a young adult. They lived in Mullafernagh, Magherally, County Down.

Hans McMordie Snr. was a leading player in the tenant rights movement, defending the rights of individual tenants facing eviction or increases in rent. Over ten years he made various speeches including to tenant right meetings. On 30 March 1882 in Broughshane, County Antrim he delivered an address explaining the nature and effect of the recent court decision by the Court of Appeal in the case of Adams versus Dunseath. He pointed out that the effect of the principles laid down by the majority of the judges, and stated that in some instances these were most unfavourable to the tenant. He also advocated the formation of tenants defence associations and that farmers should keep before them the end of becoming landlords of their own holdings.

Later in April 1882, in Saintfield, County Down, he highlighted the historical discrimination against tenant farmers, who 'never had, any advocates for them in Parliament to defend their property'. Tenant farmers received unfair treatment 'by judges who were themselves landlords, or who were landlord nominees, and always selected from the small and domineering minority who monopolised all the land of Ireland'. He said he could now see matters coming to a crisis and for a decade had looked forward, as the 'great assembly of tenant farmers in County Down gathered together, organised their forces, and drawing themselves closer and closer together, to the end that they might achieve their complete emancipation'. In his view, the 'great land question could never be settled until every man became the absolute possessor of the farm he tilled'.

McMordie died in 1921.

Sources: 1991 census; *Northern Whig*, 1 and 24 April 1882.

James Shaw
1845–1910

James Johnston (J.J.) Shaw was born in Kirkcubbin, County Down on 4 January 1845. He was educated at Belfast Academy and Queen's College Belfast (1861–6), where his studies included logic, metaphysics and political economy. In 1866, having gained his Master's degree, he went to Edinburgh to study for the Presbyterian ministry, but in 1869 was appointed Professor of Metaphysics and Ethics at Magee College in Derry, where he remained for the following nine years. A year earlier he was appointed Whately Professor of Political Economy in Trinity College Dublin, combining this with a legal practice.

In 1888 he wrote a political pamphlet, *Mr Gladstone's two Irish policies: 1868 and 1886.*

He was a close friend of J.B. Armour of Ballymoney (see profile). In 1887, and again in 1892, he stood unsuccessfully as a liberal at the general election for North Antrim. The liberal vote continued to decline following Gladstone's conversion to Home Rule.

Shaw became QC in 1889 and in 1891 was appointed a County Court judge and a Commissioner of Irish National Education. He was an admirer of the political philosophy of John Stuart Mill, seeing him as a defender of liberty and enemy of oppression and injustice and one of the great moral teachers of the era, although he had criticisms of Mill's utilitarianism. He had a favourable opinion of Mill's book on *The Subjugation of Women.*

When Sir Henry Maine raised doubts about the ability of ordinary people ('the masses') to conduct themselves wisely under democracy, Shaw responded by saying,

> It is enough to say ... that in the stage of social progress at which we
> have now arrived the masses of the people are at least as likely to

understand their own interests, and as likely to pursue them wisely, as any governor or class of governors who are neither selected by, nor responsible to, them.

Shaw died in 1910.

Sources: Duddy (ed.) 2004; Woods (ed.) 1910.

William Baxter
1845–1918

William James Baxter was born in 1845, the son of Samuel Baxter of Tattykeel near Cookstown, County Tyrone. They moved to Ballymoney, County Antrim. He was educated at Ballymena Academy and Carmichael College, Dublin. He married Mary Wallace, the second daughter of Rev. Robert Wallace of Coleraine in 1892 and they had three daughters. He was a pharmacist and wholesale merchant, becoming head of his own firm in Coleraine, W.J. Baxter. He was actively involved in local affairs and sat on Coleraine Urban Council and the Coleraine Harbour Board. He was elected President of Coleraine Agricultural and Industrial Association.

He was politically liberal and became president of Derry County and City Liberal Association. He was a speaker at a meeting in Ballymoney Town Hall in 1907, organised by the North Antrim Reform Association, which was being addressed by the new Chief Secretary Augustine Birrell. Baxter was rather taken aback to be faced with shouts of 'Armour', and, as a result, Rev. J.B. Armour (see profile), who was in the audience, was forced to address the meeting.

Baxter contested the North Antrim seat for the Liberals in the general election of January 1910, hoping to succeed R.G. Glendinning, whose Liberal success in 1906 had been a real boost for the Liberals of Antrim, although whose parliamentary performance was less impressive. In his campaign he was subjected to heckling from Unionists about the issue of Home Rule, which Baxter had ignored in his election speeches.

When the sub-postmaster in Ballintoy, a small harbour village on the Antrim coast, died, his daughter applied to take over as sub-postmaster. When the post was given to a Catholic publican there was uproar amongst Unionists who raised the issue in the House of Commons, alleging that the appointment was as the result of pressure from the local parish priest. This caused difficulties for Baxter's campaign in North Antrim. In the end he was narrowly defeated by the Conservative Unionist William Moore (also a Presbyterian). Baxter was a JP for County Londonderry and was knighted in 1907. He died in 1918 in Coleraine.

Sources: McMinn 1982; Young 1919.

John Pinkerton
1845–1908

John Pinkerton was born in Ballymoney, County Antrim in 1845, the son of a tenant farmer and linen merchant from near Seacon, Ballymoney. He was educated at the local McFadden's school and then helped his father with the farm and linen business. He was a Unitarian theologically. He became involved in the Ballymoney Agricultural Society, the Route Tenants' Defence Association, the Antrim Central Tenant-Right Association and the Land League. He was a leading player in the tenant right campaign from 1878 to 1888, organising, presiding at, or putting forward motions at tenant right meetings. He was also a member of the Coleraine Board of Guardians, where he constantly came into conflict with the Unionist landowner and Trinity College Provost, Anthony Traill.

Pinkerton strongly identified himself with the demands of Catholics in north Antrim and increasingly diverged from the views of the Route Tenants' Defence Association in support of the Land League, which he described as the best means of freeing the 'white slaves of Ireland'. This divergence was illustrated when Pinkerton organised a visit by Michael Davitt and John Ferguson (see profile) to Ballymoney in 1882. The Tenants' Association and most Liberals would have nothing to do with the well-attended meeting at which Pinkerton asserted,

> Landlordism is doomed; it may continue to drag out a miserable existence through curative potions administered by quack politicians, and strengthening plasters, in the shape of a land bill, applied to its rickety old back, but sooner or later it must go. Every day is making more apparent the fallacy of double ownership ... The present state of things is equally undesirable, for while the landlords and tenants are pulling each other's ears in the land courts, the lawyers are making away with the cream. The landlords should either sell out or buy out.

He denounced the inadequacies of the 1881 Land Act and the work of the Central Land Commission and the valuers. The meeting was followed by serious disturbances.

He became a JP in 1885 and stood as an independent 'representative of small farmers and labourers' against the liberal candidate W.P. Sinclair (see profile) in the general election of 1885, which split the vote and allowed the Conservative Edward McNaghten to win the seat.

Pinkerton initially supported a comprehensive measure of self-government for Ireland, but not total separation from Britain, but eventually fully embraced Home Rule, and was a founder member of the Protestant Home Rule Association and spoke regularly at Liberal meetings in England and Scotland advocating the cause of Home Rule.

He joined the Parnellite Party and was elected in Galway City in 1886 and held the seat for the following 14 years, although he split with Parnell after the O'Shea divorce scandal. He was noted for his attacks on the various Coercion Bills and a campaign against the London Livery companies which held land in County Londonderry. When the party was reunited in 1900 he was replaced as a candidate for Galway by a supporter of John Redmond. He was a close friend of the Methodist home ruler Jeremiah Jordan from Enniskillen.

After 1900 he returned to farming in Seacon, chairing the Ballymoney Petty Sessions Court, acting as a councillor on Ballymoney Rural District Council and playing an active role as a member of the Ballymoney Board of Guardians. He died in 1908 after developing a heart condition.

Sources: McMinn 1979; Nelson 1985.

James Bryce Killen
1845–1916

James Bryce Killen was born in Kells, County Antrim in 1842, the fourth son of Samuel Killen and Mabel (née Shaw). He was the cousin of the historian W.D. Killen. He was educated at one of the Queen's Colleges in Ireland, (probably Belfast or Cork), where he studied law, but also married into a Cork family. He then went on to study Logic, Metaphysics and Political Economy at Galway. He was called to the bar in 1869.

In 1869 Killen addressed the Queen's College Belfast Literary and Scientific Society on 'The Spirit of Irish History'. His conclusion was that England could not rule Ireland because it had no idea of the concept of nationality, and the fact of the union divided the two nations even more deeply. This resulted in a question being asked in the House of Commons from an Ulster Tory, R. Peel Dawson, inviting the authorities to prosecute him. However, no action was taken.

He became involved in the Home Rule movement and with Michael Davitt, founded the Land League in 1879. He was arrested the same year, with James Daley, for making a seditious speech at a land meeting at Gurteen, County Sligo. There were protest meetings in Dublin and elsewhere. The case was eventually abandoned and Killen released.

In Belfast he briefly edited the *Northern Star* and later worked as a journalist in Dublin. He was temporarily the editor of *United Ireland*. In 1881, Killen was again arrested on suspicion of inciting tenants to refuse to pay rent. Killen himself frequently appeared on behalf of defendants being prosecuted during the land war.

In 1882 Killen attended a lecture in Dublin by economist Henry George who advocated land nationalisation and again when George returned in 1884. In 1887 Killen joined the Social Democratic Federation formed by British radicals. The same year he presided over a mass meeting of the unemployed held on Harold's Cross Green in Dublin. Killen told the crowd of 3,000 that the land and all the instruments of production should belong to the community and a worker was justified in 'using any means whatever in order to get rid of the idle class that fattened upon his misery'. He also made clear that this mass meeting was not in opposition to the National League, the main nationalist organisation, but that he wanted to see something done for the people of the city as well as tenant farmers. A week later he spoke at a demonstration in Phoenix Park, which followed a march from the Custom House in Dublin. At a meeting of the Labour League in 1887 Killen spoke in support of the Social Democratic Foundation reinforcing divisions in the movement. Although outdoor demonstrations had come to an end, Killen continued to contribute to discussions about socialism, including at the Dublin Socialist Club.

Towards the end of the century he went to America and wrote pieces for nationalist newspapers in America and Ireland.

Killen was a good friend of the Presbyterian minister Rev. J.B. Armour of Ballymoney (see profile) who also supported Home Rule. Armour helped Killen when he fell on hard times. He died in poverty in a Dublin lodging house in 1916.

Sources: Holmes and Knox 1990; Lane 1997; Newman 1993.

Samuel Simms
1846–1938

Samuel Simms was born in Belfast in 1846, the son of Rev. Samuel Simms. Having decided to enter the church he went to New York and studied theology at Union Theological Seminary. He was ordained by Long Island Presbytery of the American Presbyterian Church in June 1887 and became minister of Yaphank congregation Long Island. He also worked with Albany City Mission in New York.

In July 1893 he was installed as minister of Bethany Presbyterian Church in Agnes Street off the Shankill Road in west Belfast. It had originally been an independent congregation, but came under the care of the General Assembly in 1892. He lived in Parkmount Villas in the Castleton area and then moved into a manse on the lower Oldpark Road, known then as Oldpark Crescent.

In July 1907 Simms wrote a letter to trade union leader Jim Larkin during the dock strike, which Larkin read out at a public meeting. The letter said, 'The insane actions of the coal merchants have brought the matter to a crisis. The battle is now between the classes and masses, and the masses will ultimately win. Not one pound of coal shall I purchase from the federated employers any longer.'

Simms remained in Bethany for forty years, during which time the congregation increased substantially from 45 to around 500. He was an ardent supporter of the temperance movement. After his wife died he lived with his sister who was single in 7 Oldpark Road, north Belfast. He retired in 1934 and died on 29 November 1938.

Rev. Simms had a son, who was named after him. Samuel Simms jr had a brilliant academic career and became a very successful doctor. But he is equally renowned for his interest in Irish history and culture. He founded *The Ulsterman* with Denis Ireland (see profile) and Gerald Morrow and wrote a wide range of articles and books, including on United Irishman, Rev. James O'Coigley. His slide presentation to the Belfast Natural History and Philosophical Society in 1933 on *Brief Sketches of some Forty Authors of Belfast Birth* is a fascinating study of key literary figures from Belfast, many of whom are now forgotten. Dr Simms jr died on 28 February 1967.

Sources: Gray 1985.

Annie Tully
Born 1851

Annie B. Tully was born in 1851. Her sister, Rosetta, was the teacher at Carnalbanagh primary school and from the age of eleven Annie acted as a teaching assistant at this small school. In 1872 when her sister was leaving the school Rosetta wrote to Lord Antrim, the patron of the school and asked that her younger sister Annie, who lived in Broughshane in County Antrim, be appointed as the school teacher. This appointment was approved and Annie Tully took over the running of the school. In 1880 the two sisters' mother died.

In 1894 Annie Tully agreed to marry Patrick Magill a Catholic from Upper Bucknaw near Ballymena. As was common at this time, she was expected to resign from her employment to devote herself to the service of her husband, the family household and any children that came along. Annie Tully, however, had other ideas. She wrote to Lord Antrim and asked for permission to stay on as teacher at the school. Two months later she wrote to the education manager, Lord Antrim's agent, McDonald, to again ask to remain in her post. In her letter she cited other situations where a teacher who married was permitted to stay on as teacher. These entreaties were unsuccessful and she felt that she had no choice but to resign, which she did at the end of April 1894, a couple of weeks after her marriage. She gave notice that she would be leaving at the end of July.

As the time got closer to her date of leaving, she became more incensed by her treatment and wrote rescinding her resignation. She made it clear that as there were plenty of precedents of teachers staying in post after marrying, the only reason that she was being made to resign was that she had married a Catholic. As the school had both Protestant and Catholic children, she argued that this made no sense and she would be 'unjustly treated' if she could not remain in the school. She received a reply the following day that she could not withdraw her resignation and the process to find her replacement had been started. Lord Antrim's agent then unsuccessfully tried to get the keys of the school from her, but she refused to hand them over. On 25 August she wrote again refusing either to resign or hand over the keys, and threatened to take legal action in order to remain in the school. Lord Antrim also took legal action and in September advertised for a replacement teacher. It was not until October that Annie Maguire (née Tully) was finally removed and replaced by Agnes M. Alexander as the teacher.

Sources: Earl of Antrim's papers at PRONI.

Harold Rylett
1851–1936

Harold Rylett was born in Horncastle, Lincolnshire, England on 4 February 1851 and became a Unitarian minister in 1877. He was called to the Non-Subscribing Presbyterian congregation in Moneyrea, County Down.

In the early 1870s in Britain he became an associate of Joseph Arch, an agricultural labourer who established the National Agricultural Labourer's Union and eventually became a Liberal MP.

Rylett was a leading member of the Land League and shared a Land League platform with Michael Davitt, J.G. Biggar, a Catholic priest and others in December 1880 to try to spread the Land League message in Ulster. It passed a resolution that 'the land question can only be definitely settled by making the cultivators of the soil proprietors'.

Rylett criticised the Orange Order for coming to the rescue of the landlords. Unfortunately, 600 policemen were required to protect the meeting from attack from the Orange Order. When Davitt was jailed for the third time and sent to Portland jail off the Dorset coast, Rylett applied to visit him but was turned down.

Rylett attended the inaugural conference of the Democratic Federation of British radicals in 1881 and invited those present to send delegates to see the tumult for themselves. He was one of the main organisers of the Land League in Ulster and attended thirteen meetings of the Central Land

League between February and October 1881 and presided over a Newry Land League conference.

In 1881, Rylett stood as a Land League candidate in Tyrone, supported by the Democratic Federation and Parnell. He declared himself opposed to the coercion policies of Gladstone's Liberal government. He was heavily defeated by the Liberal Thomas Dickson (see profile) who had publicly opposed the coercion measures. In November 1882 Rylett chaired a Land League meeting in County Londonderry which elected C.J. Dempsey, Catholic editor of the *Ulster Examiner*, as their candidate. In the election, however, he only received 58 votes.

Rylett was a supporter of the views of economist Henry George who advocated land nationalisation and came to Ireland in 1882, meeting Rylett in Belfast. In the 1890s Rylett returned to England and continued to support radical political change. He was a friend and supporter of leading Fabian Sidney Webb.

In 1904 he became minister of Tenterden, Kent. He retired from the ministry in 1929. He died on 9 August 1936 in Ballygowan, County Down.

Sources: Campbell 1991; Lane 1997; Walker 1989.

Alexander Bowman
1855–1924

Alexander Bowman was born in Dromara, a small village on the river Lagan in County Down, in 1855, the product of a mixed marriage. Although he was baptised as a Catholic he was brought up a Presbyterian and continued to attend a Presbyterian church as an adult. His father (his mother's second husband), William McKeown died when Alexander was ten and the family were forced to move to Belfast. Alexander (who adopted the surname of his mother's first husband) began work as a part-time machine boy (hackler) in a flax mill. When he was barely twenty years old he was part of a workers' deputation to the factory manager to discuss a work grievance. For his efforts Bowman was dismissed, but soon found a new flax dressing job in William Ewart & Sons' Crumlin Road factory. In 1880 he married Rose (née Ritchie) in Eglinton Presbyterian Church and moved to live in Crimea Street in the Shankhill area of Belfast.

He joined the Flax Dressers' Trade and Benevolent Union and became interested in politics initially supporting Gladstone and the Liberals. He was in favour of the nationalisation of land, the end of the landlord system, a reduction in working hours, improved welfare rights, and votes for women. In 1881 he helped to form the Belfast Trades Council and became a very active member of the Belfast Debating Society, where he refined his oratory skills. He was also involved in a campaign to try to persuade the Belfast Corporation to open a public library. Unfortunately the campaign was unsuccessful.

In 1882 he was delegated by the Belfast Trades Council to be their first ever representative at a British Trade Union Congress in Manchester. At the congress Bowman spoke in favour of an increase in factory inspectors; making the Employers Liability Act mandatory; and extending the municipal franchise in Ireland. He also criticised Irish magistrates for how they dealt with cases arising from the Irish Land War.

In 1884 he changed job and became a traveller for the clothing firm of Black & Co in Royal Avenue, Belfast. He also became secretary of the Irish Land Restoration Society, whose chairman was Congregational minister Rev. Bruce Wallace.

In 1885 he was very involved in the Liberal Party, despite some concerns about the conflict between his role in the Trades Council and his increasing political persona. In the same year he became the first working class man in Ireland to stand for parliament, when he stood for election in north Belfast against his old employer in the linen mill, Conservative, Sir William Ewart. Some of his political meetings were attacked by conservative protestors. He said he was fighting the election on working men's principles and that he had nothing to say about the union between Britain and Ireland although his manifesto suggested he would support maintaining the link. Bowman polled respectably but was well beaten by Ewart.

In supporting Gladstone's Home Rule proposals in 1886, Bowman came into conflict with some of his trade union colleagues, as well as from Unionists. He felt forced to resign his position with the Belfast Trades Council and helped launch the Protestant Home Rule association, along with Thomas Shillington, David Briggs and Thomas McClelland. He spoke at various meetings around the country in support of Home Rule, although declaring he was a loyal supporter of Queen Victoria and against separation. He was appointed as the paid secretary of the Protestant Home Rule Association. Anti-Home Rule feeling was running high in many parts of Ulster and there was sectarian rioting in Belfast. With Orange mobs regularly attacking his house, Bowman felt he had to move his family away from the Shankhill Road to Greenmount Street in north Belfast.

He was a character witness in court when one of his wife's relatives was charged with rioting. In court Bowman emphasised his heritage as a dissenter and his disgust at how Presbyterians were treated by the still-dominant Church of Ireland. Afterwards he wrote to the papers complaining at the requirement to kiss the Bible in making an oath in court and the fact that there were still no Presbyterian peers in the House of Lords and very few government appointments or offices in Ireland were held by Presbyterians.

Bowman became increasingly involved in the land question and the imposition of large rack-rents by landlords. He campaigned on the extent of consumption (TB) amongst the working population of Belfast. He was involved in the formation of the Belfast Peace Society to reduce international disputes through arbitration. He also supported meetings to promote the vote for women. On Home Rule he became a supporter of Parnell. When the Government introduced the Crime Bill, which contained draconian powers to suppress the National League, Bowman was a leading campaigner against it, often facing loyalist counter-demonstrations, including ones orchestrated by arch-conservative Presbyterian minister 'roaring' Hugh Hanna.

The National League was eventually banned under the legislation and two dozen nationalist MPs jailed and Bowman just managed to avoid arrest for speaking at National League rallies. The Irish Protestant Home Rule Association (IPHRA) developed a close relationship with the Young Ireland Society. Bowman was extremely popular in the nationalist community, although he continued to emphasise that Home Rule did not mean independence and separation.

Following the post-Home Rule Bill riots there was a House of Commons Select Committee enquiry at which Bowman gave evidence of the anti-Catholic attitudes of magistrates, suggesting the administration of the law should be put in the hands of paid professional magistrates.

Financial hardship forced him to move to Glasgow to take up a job with the Universal Automatic Machines Co. and received a generous going-away gift from the IPHRA, which enabled him to rent a cottage for his family. He was a speaker at the Henry George Institute and became its President. In an address on 'God's gift to man' he declared:

> ... the earth that God created for the children of men; the gift is universal and man's need for it as universal as the gift. Yet in spite of the evident intention of their infinite Father, millions of his children are deprived of any share in his bounty and are condemned to lives of ceaseless toil and misery ... private ownership of land ... is based, not upon right, but on force and fraud ... Restitution is thus a duty incumbent on every one of the heirs and successors ... failing the performance of this duty, taking back the land emerges as a right on the part of the people.

In 1890 he became President of the council of the newly formed umbrella organisation, the Scottish Land Restoration Federation. With Rose expecting their fifth child and Bowman being distracted from his paid employment by his political activities the family were again facing financial difficulties. He moved to London to take up a job with the Ulster Bacon Curing Co. and was eventually joined by his family. In London he spoke at rallies of the Marxist Social Democratic Federation, as did George Bernard Shaw, and stood for them in two local council elections. He became involved in the embryonic stages of the formation of the British Labour Party.

In 1897 he returned to Ireland as a committed socialist and the following year was elected to Belfast Corporation for Duncairn ward in North Belfast. In 1901 he was elected President of the Irish Trade Union Congress. In his powerful presidential address he called for the 'uniting of all sects, creeds and parties in the attempt to raise our common and beloved country to that material, moral and social position to which she is entitled'.

Again facing serious financial difficulties, Bowman decided, for the good of his family, to give up politics and the trade union movement and took a job with Belfast Corporation as the superintendent of Falls Municipal Baths, where he remained for the last 21 years of his life. He died, aged 70, in 1924.

Sources: Bowman 1997; Walker 1989.

John St Clair Boyd
1858–1918

John St Clair Boyd was born in Holywood, County Down on 9 December 1858. His family were unionist and members of Holywood Presbyterian Church and had been long associated with the Blackstaff linen mill. He was educated at Queen's College Belfast, Edinburgh and Paris and qualified as a doctor (Master of Surgery) and worked in the Birmingham and Midland Hospital for Women as a surgical assistant. In 1888 he returned to Ireland and worked as assistant surgeon in the Hospital for Sick Children in Belfast, then also became a gynaecologist at the Ulster Hospital for Children and Women. In 1891 he then became senior surgeon at the Samaritan Hospital.

He was a strong supporter of the Irish language and became the first President of the Belfast Gaelic League formed in 1895, personally paying the bills of the League. He was very concerned about the decline in 'such a beautiful and noble language'. He was a member of the Belfast Naturalists' Field Club, which initiated Irish language classes and which grew naturally into the Belfast branch of the Gaelic League. At the first AGM Boyd spoke of their surprise at the 'extent of spoken Irish in east Ulster'.

Boyd was on the committee which organised a musical festival (Feis Cheoil) in 1898 in Belfast, a follow-up to the first one which had been held in Dublin in 1897 and was president of the Dublin Pipers' Club. He regularly adjudicated at musical festivals. He died on 10 July 1918 aged fifty-nine. His grave in Belfast City Cemetery is marked by a Celtic cross with an inscription in Irish.

Sources: Blaney 1984; Blaney 1996; Hartley 2006; Newman 1993; Ó Snoaigh 1995.

Samuel Keightley
1859–1940

Samuel Robert Keightley was born in Belfast on 13 January 1859, the elder son of Samuel Keightley JP, merchant and member of Belfast Corporation. He studied classics and law at Queen's College Belfast.

He was a poet and novelist. He had already published a book of poetry, *A King's daughter and other poems,* before being called to the Irish Bar in 1883. He wrote several novels with the backdrop of Irish history, including *The Crimson Sign* about the Siege of Derry and *The Pikemen,* sympathetic to the 1798 rising, published in 1903.

He married Gertrude Emily Smith in 1892 and had two sons, Philip and Maurice and two daughters, Katherine and Patricia. After his first wife died in 1929, he married Anne Vowell in 1930.

He was politically a liberal and a supporter of Thomas Russell (see profile). He stood as an independent Unionist in South Antrim in 1903, where he was defeated by the Ulster Unionist party candidate, Charles Curtis Craig, the brother of James Craig, by 849 votes; and later won as a Liberal in South Derry in 1910. He later moved to Fort House, Lisburn and attended Railway Street Church.

He was knighted in 1912. In 1920 he published the letters from his son, Philip, who died in 1919 of pneumonia, written while he was serving in Ypres and the Somme, entitled *Under the Guns.*

Samuel Keightley died in 1940.

Sources: Princess Grace Irish Library: www.pgil-eirdata.org; www.lisburn.com.

Archibald McIlroy
1859–1915

Archibald McIlroy was born in 1859 on a farm near Ballyclare in County Antrim. He was educated at James Pyper's Mercantile Academy and the Royal Belfast Academical Institution. He was considering becoming a minister, but got a job with the Ulster Bank and married the daughter of Rev. Adam Montgomery of Ballycairn. He turned his hand to writing, becoming an internationally acclaimed novelist, publishing various books, including *When Lint was in the Bell, The Auld Meetin' House Green, By Lone Craig-Linnie Burn* and *the Humour of Druid's Island.* He also wrote for the Presbyterian newspaper, *The Witness.* He set up home in Drumbo and was appointed a JP and elected to Down District Council.

He was a strong supporter of liberal politics and the tenant right movement. In *When Lint was in the Bell* he has one his characters discuss 1798:

> We talked much of the Rebellion or 'turn-oot', taking pride in the part which some of our forefathers had played in it. Nothing could have made us so angry as hearing our ancestors jeered at and called 'pike men', or to be reminded that the gallant patriots had gone to battle provided with grindstones for the occasional sharpening of their spears. It was a base calumny and unworthy of credence – almost as insulting as to be told that the brave men had fired on the soldiers from the insides of houses and shops.

In May 1915 he was drowned, with 1,200 passengers, when the *Lusitania*, was torpedoed by a German submarine.

Sources: Hamilton 1992; McIlroy 1897.

Edgar Fripp
1861–1931

Edgar Innes Fripp was born in London in November 1861, the seventh son of George Arthur Fripp. He was educated at University College London, where he graduated with a BA degree. He then went on to study in Manchester College and then again in London. This must have included theological training as he became a minister in Mansfield in 1888. In 1891 he received a call from Second Belfast Non-Subscribing Presbyterian Church and was installed in Rosemary Street in December that year.

In 1900, Fripp returned to England and served as a minister in Mansfield, Clifton, Leicester and Altrincham. In 1921, aged 60 he returned to Second Belfast where he was formally installed by the Presbytery of Antrim and remained there until he retired three years later.

When Harry Midgley stood in the 1924 general election for the Northern Ireland Labour Party, on the programme and record of the British Labour Party, he received the backing of Fripp, Rev. Bruce Wallace (Congregationalist, Christian Socialist and member of the Protestant Home Rule Association, who published *Brotherhood* and the *Belfast Weekly Star* in support of land nationalisation) and Rev. Agnew (see profile). The election took place just before the announcement of the border commission, so tensions were high. Midgley polled very well, but was defeated by the sitting Unionist, Sir Robert Lynn.

Following his retirement he devoted himself to the study of Shakespeare. He died on 9 November 1931.

Sources: Haire 1981; notes provided by Rev. John Nelson; Walker 1985.

Elizabeth Bell
1863/4–1934

Elizabeth Bell was born to a Presbyterian family in Newry, County Armagh *c*. 1863. Her father was Joseph Bell, the clerk of the Newry Union. She had a brother and one sister who also qualified in medicine. She was the first woman in Ireland to qualify as a doctor and gynaecologist in *c*. 1893 and was a member of the British Medical Association and the Ulster Medical Society. She married fellow doctor Hugh Fisher from Belfast, who was eight years younger than her. They lived in 4 College Gardens, Belfast and two addresses in Great Victoria Street, Belfast. Their one son, Hugo was killed at Passchendaele in 1917.

Bell had a medical practice in Belfast, which mainly treated women and young children. She was an honorary physician to the maternity and baby home for homeless and unmarried mothers at Malone Place hospital. She also worked for Belfast Corporation as a medical officer for its 'Baby Club' welfare scheme. During the First World War, she travelled to Malta and worked as a doctor for the British Army in the temporary hospitals for injured Allied soldiers.

Bell was active in the suffrage movement and a friend and ally of Mrs Emily Pankhurst and Lady Balfour, both prominent feminist figures of the time. She became a prominent member of both the Irish Women's Suffrage Society (IWSS) and the militant Women's Social and Political Union (WSPU). In 1911 she was imprisoned in Holloway, with fellow Ulster suffragette, Margaret Robinson, for suffragette disturbances, involving stone-throwing at department stores, carried out in conjunction with the WSPU. In 1913 she confronted the 'conspiracy of silence' in the movement concerning social and moral issues, seeing the vote for women as crucial in ensuring these issues would be tackled. She also campaigned for more married women in the workplace and she also worked as a doctor for suffragettes who were imprisoned for their activities in Crumlin Road Prison in Belfast. When many women from Protestant/Unionist backgrounds left the suffrage movement to support the campaign against Home Rule, Elizabeth Bell maintained her commitment to the movement.

Following the betrayal of Sir Edward Carson who reneged on an initial pledge to support women's suffrage in any new Northern Ireland administration, Bell was actively involved in the militant campaign that followed, which included the burning down of unionist-owned buildings and male dominated recreational facilities. She later asserted that she always made sure that properties were empty before setting fire to them.

After the First World War ended, Bell worked on Belfast Corporation's Child Welfare Scheme and Belfast's Mother and Babies Hospital.

She died in Belfast on 9 July 1934. One of her obituary notices described her as a 'pioneer of the feminist movement in Ireland'.

Sources: Ryan and Ward 2007; Urquhart 2000.

Frank Bigger
1863–1926

Francis Joseph Bigger was born in Belfast in 1863 and educated at the Royal Belfast Academical Institution, founded by his grandfather, amongst others. He then studied for a period in Liverpool.

He initially practiced as a solicitor, but was much more interested in the arts and culture. He edited the *Ulster Journal of Archaeology* and became involved in the restoration of important heritage monuments and buildings, especially castles and churches. He believed in the value of culture as expressed in music (he was an uilleann piper) poetry and song, supporting and accompanying Herbert Hughes in his quest around north Donegal to locate and preserve traditional tunes and songs, the results of which were published as *Songs of Uladh*, financed by Bigger. This ensured the survival of tunes such as 'My Lagan Love' and 'Gartan Mother's Lullaby'. He provided financial support for a quarterly cultural and political journal, *Ulad*. He advocated learning the Irish language and joined the Gaelic League founded by Douglas Hyde and Eoin MacNeill, frequent visitors at the Bigger home. He had a strong interest in Irish theatre and founded the Ulster Literary Theatre in 1902.

His home on the Antrim Road in Belfast, which he called 'Firelight' was a centre of a literary and cultural renaissance, involving both Catholics and Protestants. Shane Leslie described him as having 'the soul of one of the Irishmen of 1798'. He was a friend of Roger Casement.

In 1909, he had a stone put on the grave of William Steel Dickson who had been a key spokesman for the reform movement of the later part of the eighteen century, but had died in poverty and been buried in a paupers grave in the Old Clifton Street cemetery.

In his book, *The Ulster Land War of 1770*, he described the terrible oppression faced by tenants, mainly Presbyterian in Ulster, in the eighteenth century and the violent response to cruel landlords by those who joined the secret agrarian society, the Hearts of Steel.

He edited *Ulster dialect – words and phrases* and wrote a pamphlet on *The Northern Leaders of '98*. He died in 1926.

Sources: Bardon 1992; Boylan 1998; Bradbury 2002; Campbell 1991; Hickey and Doherty 2005; Newman 1993.

Samuel Shannon Millin
1864–1947

Samuel Shannon Millin was born in Belfast in 1864, son of John Millin, a flaxseed and salt merchant. Samuel was educated at the Royal Belfast Academical Institution, which he soon left only to re-enrol two years later; and Queen's College, which followed a similar path, not graduating from his three year course, until eleven years later, in 1892. However by then he had decided to enter law as a profession. He qualified in 1894 and took chambers in Royal Avenue and joined the Northeast circuit. He published his first book, *A Digest of the Reported Decisions of the Superior Courts relating to Petty Sessions in Ireland.* With his father's death he adopted his mother's name, Shannon.

Like his grandfather, who had moved from May Street congregation after hearing Henry Cooke preach on 'Total Depravity', Millin was a member of the Second Belfast congregation and in 1900 wrote a detailed account of its history. His older brother, Adam, was secretary of the congregation for forty years. Millin married Ella Catherine (née Morton), daughter of Colonel David Morton of Sterling and lived in Helen's Bay in north Down. They had two children, Terence John, born 1903, who became a pioneering surgeon, and Betty, born 1905, who became a school headmistress. In 1907 the family moved to St Kevin's Park, Daltry Road, Dublin, where he attended the Unitarian Church in St Stephen's Green.

Millin was actively involved in the Belfast Social Enquiry Society. He became the unofficial historian of the Society and contributed regularly to its proceedings. In February 1909 he read a paper to the Society on 'The Duty of the State Towards the pauper Children of Ireland' advocating prevention of pauperism rather than the kind of relief provided by the poor laws. He urged the removal of all children (5,645 in March 1908) from the 'demoralising influence of the workhouse' and the establishment of a Department of Children run by women. In 1914 he presented a paper on 'Slums: A Sociological Retrospective of the City of Dublin' highlighting 'the present deplorable condition of the housing of the poor, with its attendant deplorable consequences'. Historically he argued that when the Established Church controlled the political, religious, social and legal affairs of Ireland the state of the areas around its numerous churches 'were a living lie to the fundamental principles of Christianity'. He argued that 'property has its duties as well as its rights' and proposed a change in the law to improve overcrowding and tackle unsanitary conditions.

The following year he presented a paper on 'Child Life as a National Asset' in which he tackled the issue of child labour. He applauded Daniel O'Connell for championing the interests of children. The rights of children were significantly improved by the Children's Act of 1908, but Millin pointed out that the 'filth of our slum dwellings' defeated the intentions of the Children's Act and created 'the slaughter of the innocents'. In contrast Millin said, 'every human life is of national importance. Even the child in rags'. He also criticised the 'baby farming of the Foundling hospitals and the overcrowded Belfast schools.

He also lectured on culture, including the famous Belfast Harp Festival and Edward Bunting and on poets including Rev. William Hamilton Drummond. In 1928 Millin moved to Maida Vale in England. In the 1930s he wrote a two-volume history of Belfast, called *Sidelights on Belfast History*. He died in Inwood, Roehampton, England in February 1947.

Sources: Froggatt 2004 and 2005; Millin 1900, 1932 and papers to the Statistical Society.

Elizabeth A.M. McCracken
c. 1865–1944

Elizabeth A.M. Priestley was born around 1865. In 1900, she married George McCracken a solicitor, five years older than her, originally from County Armagh, who often acted for many of the suffragettes who ended up in court. They lived at 80 Bryansburn Road, Bangor, County Down. They had three sons, the eldest, George Stanley, born around 1901; Maurice Lee, born around two years later and the youngest, James, born around 1905.

Using her literary pseudonym, L.A.M. Priestley, McCracken became a prominent writer. She had the books, *Love stories of some eminent women* published in 1906 and *The Feminine in Fiction* published by Unwin in 1918. The latter considers the relations between the sexes as described in the novels of both male and female novelists, including Charlotte Bronte, George Eliot, Thomas Hardy, H.G. Wells, Fiona MacLeod and Sarah Grand. She hails the 'coming of an entirely new order of heroine the politically free woman whose progression and influence in the realm of fiction it will be of the greatest interest to watch'. She chronicles a progression, 'from a passive creature with whom fortune played, willy-nilly, subordinate to the conventions of sex, a spectator at the game of life, the heroine has become a capable being, with power and opportunity to shape her own lot.'

McCracken was very active in the women's suffrage movement and a member of the Irish Women's Suffrage Society. In the 1911 census, McCracken wrote 'Unenfranchised' under 'Specific Illnesses' on her census form.

In April 1913, McCracken made clear her views on militancy in support of the suffrage movement: 'Let it once and for all be understood that women in adopting such methods are only following a sort of natural law in the political world, a law they neither initiated or approved – men have done both, as the whole history of reform proves.'

Two months later, she wrote an article for the *Irish Citizen* in which she argued that the women's suffrage campaign represented

> a great spiritual awakening, a real religious revival among the best and noblest-thinking women of the times, who perceive that religion and morals, the home, the child, the nation, and the race, are in a perilous state as long as women's subjugation and enslavement continue.

In 1913, McCracken was jubilant at the 'marriage of unionism and women's suffrage', when a Unionist official stated that plans were being drawn up to include the franchise for women in the establishment of a provisional government for Northern Ireland. The Irish Parliamentary Party made no such pledge for a Home Rule Parliament. Edward Carson had, of course, no intention of honouring this pledge, which he made clear in the spring of 1914, which resulted in McCracken criticising unionist women for failing to demand women's suffrage as a precondition for conducting political work. She and many others joined the more militant English-based WSPU, leading to the collapse of the IWSS. Five Unionist-owned buildings were burnt down and male recreational facilities were also attacked, including Knock Golf Club, Newtownards Racecourse, and Belfast Bowling and Tennis Club. Lisburn Cathedral was set on fire and there was a public protest during a service at St Anne's Cathedral Belfast. Thirteen suffragettes were arrested.

After the outbreak of the First World War, the women's suffrage movement faced even greater challenges in the context of the north of Ireland, with its divided political loyalties. In McCracken's words,

> When the first cannon-shot crashed through the peace of Europe, the world of Woman Suffrage was shaken to its depths. Its organisation, its funds, its raison d'être seemed threatened and unstable … Some suffragists became war partisans, some became peace partisans.

McCracken was involved in organising a visit by leading English suffragist, Sylvia Pankhurst, to meet representatives of various suffrage societies in her own home to help energise the suffrage movement and agree tactics during this difficult period.

In February 1914, the *Belfast Newsletter* refused to publish her article on 'Ulster and women' because they considered it too contentious. It was, however, published in the *Irish Citizen*. In it she denounced the hypocrisy of unionist women supporting the arming of the Ulster Volunteer Force, while opposing the violent actions against property of the suffragettes. She encouraged unionist women to abandon their role as 'subservient factotum'. She argued that only if 'a woman will work and will pay, and will pass no criticism', will she be considered to be 'a valuable and valued political asset'.

In 1918, when women over the age of 30 were granted the vote and the ability to stand for parliament by the Representation of the People and the Parliament (Qualification of Women) Acts, McCracken was very keen to see independent female candidates, untainted by party politics, standing: 'Unless we want the Lady Londonderrys, and the Sir Edward Carsons, and the Mr Dillons, to carry them off as tame pussy cats to purr in contented acquiescence to male guidance within the House ... meek, docile, but useful in assisting men's plans.' In this objective she was to be disappointed.

As well as women's political representation, she was particularly concerned about assaults on women and girls and the lack of protection or redress under the law, particularly because women could not become lawyers or sit on juries. In a lengthy article in the *Irish Citizen* in 1919, she argued that wife-beating was very common, but women, for the sake of the children and concern for their own financial position, tended to put up with the abuse and suffer in silence. When they did go to court they usually got little sympathy or support. At worst, the men, if they were found guilty, were usually just fined.

In 1920 McCracken published a series of articles in the English suffragette journal, *The Vote*. Collections of her articles in *Irish Citizen*, *First Causes* and *Shall Suffrage Cease* were published as popular pamphlets. McCracken died in 1944.

Sources: McCracken 1918; Ryan and Ward 2007; Urquhart 2000.

Rose Maud Young
1865–1947

Rose Young was born in Galgorm Castle, Ballymena, County Antrim in 1865, the daughter of the Hon. John Young, a liberal and an active supporter of tenant right and Grace Charlotte (née Savage). She was the eighth of thirteen children. The family were members of one of the Presbyterian churches in Ballymena, as were her ancestors.

She was encouraged to take an interest in the Irish language by Bishop William Reeves, and became friendly with other Protestant women interested in the language including Margaret Hutton, Ada McNeill and Margaret Dobbs. She lived for a while in Dublin and got to know various people in Irish language circles there, including Douglas Hyde. As she had a particular interest in poetry, she was encouraged to compile and edit a collection of Irish poetry and songs, the first volume of which she published in 1921, while she was living in Cushendun, County Antrim. She published the second volume in 1924. Again, the preface was by Douglas Hyde. The 58 poems included biographical notes on the poets and show evidence of extensive research. The third and last volume, sub-titled *Historic Poems, Religious Poems, the Lays of Ossian, the Three Sorrows of Storytelling and others* was published in 1930 and, this time, she provided English translations, mainly by herself, for all 53 poems.

Young was particularly interested in Rathlin Island and wrote an article on the surnames, place names and type of Irish spoken on the island and concluded that there was a very strong Scottish influence. Towards the end of her life she lived with Margaret Dobbs, also an Irish speaker, at Portagolan, Cushendun, where she died in 1947.

Sources: Blaney 1996.

Harry C. Morrow
1865–1938

Henry Cooke Morrow was born on 27 August 1865, one of eight sons of George Morrow, a successful painter and decorator in north Belfast. Young Henry (known as Harry) was named after the famous Tory Presbyterian minister, Henry Cooke.

As well as running the father's business after he died, the sons played a crucial role in the development of a distinctive Ulster Theatre tradition. No more so than Harry, who, using the pseudonym of Gerald MacNamara, was one of the first Ulster playwrights to satirise both the Orange and Green traditions. Brother Fred became the main director of the plays and Jack, who, in 1906/7 was a director of the newspaper of the Dungannon Clubs promoting the ideas of Wolfe Tone, became the stage manager and sometime actor.

The Ulster Literary Theatre had been set up in 1902 by Bulmer Hobson, a Quaker member of the Gaelic League, who described himself as a disciple of Wolfe Tone; and architect David Parkhill. They were impressed with the achievements of Yeat's Irish Literary Theatre in Dublin, but got little encouragement from Yeats whom they went to visit. Belfast audiences also seemed to be not overly impressed with the early productions of Yeat's *Cathleen Ní Houlihan* or A.E.'s *Deirdre*, based on Irish myths and folklore. So the founders decided they would write plays themselves.

In 1904 they founded a 'non-sectarian and non-political' literary review, *Ulad*, which received contributions from many well-known individuals, as well as rising stars, including Roger Casement, A.E., Joseph Campbell,

Padraic Colum, Alice Milligan and Forest Reid. Harry's brothers, George and Norman, regularly contributed satirical cartoons or sketches of members of the Ulster Theatre Company or characters from the plays. George also contributed regular satirical cartoons to *Punch*. Harry, as Gerald MacNamara, was a founding member and became one of the leading writers for the thirty years of the Ulster Theatre Company. He pioneered the use of theatre to explore the issue of sectarianism in Ireland.

Suzanne and the Sovereigns was co-written with David Parkhill, writing as Lewis Purcell, based on a burlesque, where Suzanne from Sandy Row in Protestant Belfast falls in love with Catholic James II and so William of Orange is asked to come and rescue her. It had originally been created by the Morrow brothers for performance in their Belfast business premises. It was performed in December 1907 in the Exhibition Hall Belfast and what could have resulted in a riot, by effective use of humour, became an outstanding success. It was revived in the Exhibition Hall in January 1909 and the following year in the Grand Opera House to continued acclaim.

The play *The Mist that Does be on the Bog* was a parody of Synge's use of peasant speech in *The Playboy of the Western World* and *The shadow of the Glen*. However, again, its effective use of humour prevented it causing too much offence when it was performed in November 1909 in the Abbey Theatre, Dublin.

Originally commissioned by the Gaelic League, but rejected by them because it did not show due deference to the heroes of Irish mythology, *Thompson in Tir-na-nOg*, is an Orangeman, replete with sash and bowler hat, who is killed when his gun blows up at a sham Battle of the Boyne re-enactment in Scarva, County Down. On being resurrected he finds himself in the Irish mythological land of eternal youth with the heroes of Irish mythology, where he has to explain Ulster politics to Cuchulainn and others. It was performed in 1912 in the Grand Opera House Belfast at the height of agitation against Home Rule. It was revived in 1923 in London's Scala Theatre.

In the years following the Easter Rising in Dublin, MacNamara (Harry C. Morrow) had six further plays performed: *The Throwbacks* in 1917 in both the Grand Opera House Belfast and the Gaiety Theatre, Dublin; *Sincerity* in 1918 in the Gaiety Theatre, Dublin; and four in the Grand Opera House, Belfast, *Fee, Faw, Fum* (1923), *No Surrender* (1928), *Who fears to Speak* (1929), and *Thompson on Terra Firma* (1934).

In 1972, writing about theatre in Ulster, Sam Hanna Bell lamented the fact that only one of his plays has ever been published in book form and that 'his genius has been unfairly diminished'. In his view:

> behind his writings is discernible a serious and informed political
> intelligence familiar with the intricacies and paradoxes or whatever

period of Irish history he has chosen as a backcloth to his satire. Indeed it is this exhaustive knowledge that kept his pilloried audiences suspended in a state of bewilderment and laughter.

Rutherford Mayne described him as:

one of the finest comic geniuses that the Irish dramatic revival has produced' and that 'he hated cruelty in any shape or form – or lack of thought for things beautiful; the cruelty of extremists who hammered on dogmas, or on drums, or on human beings is mercilessly satirised in all his plays.

In 1940 the Ulster Theatre came under the guidance of Harry Morrow's nephew, Gerald Morrow and the Theatre became a professional theatre company as the Ulster Group Theatre. Harry Morrow died on 11 January 1938, survived by his second wife Marion and three children.

Sources: Bell 1972; Campbell 1991; Foley 2003; McMahon 1999.

Richard Lyttle
1866–1905

Richard Lyttle was born in 1866, the son of a linen merchant in Dromore, County Down. He studied for the ministry in the Unitarian Theological College in Manchester. He became the minister of the Non-Subscribing Presbyterian Church in Moneyreagh, County Down, succeeding Rev. Harold Rylett (see profile). He played a key role in the Gaelic League, which had been founded in Dublin in 1893 by a northern Catholic and a southern Protestant, to promote Irish literature, poetry, music, and song. It was successful in remaining non-sectarian. He was also a member of the Belfast Naturalists' Field Club and organised classes in the Irish language in Moneyrea, creating an unusually large number of Irish speakers in the area.

Lyttle was very committed to promoting the rights of tenant farmers and agricultural labourers and became the secretary of the Farmers and Labourers Union. At a meeting of the Ulster Tenants Defence Association which he convened in Rosemary Street Lecture Hall Belfast on 2 February 1898, where he said that landlords have, 'robbed their tenants of unnumbered millions, and by their relentless extractions, driven the flower of the Irish peasantry to the wilds of America and Australia ... This is one of the most gigantic swindles ... persisted in through two centuries – that has ever cried aloud to heaven for redress.'

Lyttle was a loyal friend and supporter of Presbyterian minister and Home Ruler Rev. J.B. Armour (see profile). In 1894 Lyttle supported the proposed establishment of an Ulster Liberal and National Union. He believed that with an election pending and recent Presbyterian and Unitarian support for Home Rule and the activities of the Liberal Land Committee there was 'the bones of an organisation' with a potential membership target of 10,000. Lyttle recruited the support of J.B. Armour. Lyttle became one of the two initial joint secretaries of the Association.

In 1905, he supported the establishment of Dungannon Clubs all over Ulster and beyond, founded by Bulmer Hobson. These clubs sought to build an Ireland, not 'for the Catholic or Protestant, but an Ireland for every Irishman, irrespective of his creed or class, or rank or station'.

Hobson paid tribute to Lyttle,

> Lyttle was a true spiritual descendant of those Protestant clergy-men who worked and fought with the United Irishmen in 1798. In Down, as in Antrim, the memory of the United Irishmen had not died out, and many of the older generation of farmers, grandsons of men who had fought at Ballynahinch and Antrim, were deeply, if mostly secretly, in sympathy with nationalist feeling. Lyttle was the natural leader of these men. He had great charm of manner, combined with ability and energy of a high order. His courage and sincerity and his exceptional powers as a public speaker made him an outstanding figure.

Lyttle died in 1905, aged only 39.

Sources: Blaney 1996; Campbell 1991; Ó Snodaigh 1995.

James Wood
1867–1936

James Wood was born on 17 July 1867 in Clones, County Monaghan. His family moved to Fermanagh, where the family were evicted for refusing to vote for the conservative candidate supported by their landlord, and Belfast where he attended Mountpottinger National School in east Belfast. He was then apprenticed to the legal firm of H. & R.J. McMordie in Lombard Street, Belfast and qualified as a solicitor in 1893. He set up a legal partnership with John Moorehead, who later became Northern Ireland's first Crown Solicitor after partition. Wood lived and worked a farm at Mount Salem, Dundonald east of Belfast. He was a strong support of tenant right against landlordism, defending tenants facing eviction.

He was a political liberal and when J.A. Rentoul, the Unionist and Conservative MP for East Belfast resigned his safe seat to take up his appointment as a judge, Wood stood as an independent candidate against Colonel R.H. Wallace, of Myra Castle, a local landlord, for the Unionists. Woods nomination was seconded by Rev. W. Carse the Presbyterian minister of Magherahamlet. Meetings in support of each candidate were held around the constituency. T.W. Russell (see profile) spoke in support of Wood at a meeting in Denvir's Hotel in Downpatrick. However, as a result of orchestrated attacks by his opponents, another meeting in Ballynahinch broke up in disorder. The local *Down Recorder* supported Wallace and was hostile to Wood. The east Down Division of the United Irish League, however, called on all nationalist electors to vote for Wood. As a result, attempts were made to link Wood to Home Rule and the Catholic University issue, but Wood, who supported compulsory purchase, insisted that the election was about the single issue of a permanent and final settlement of the land issue.

At the election on 5 February 1902, Wood (with 3,576 votes) won with a majority of 147, with both Catholic and Presbyterian support, in what Carson called 'an unholy alliance of Catholics and Protestants'. After the result, Wood and T.W. Russell were carried shoulder high to the Down Hunt Arms Hotel where they addressed the crowd of supporters. Rev. Richard Lyttle (see profile) also spoke, advising people in Ireland against being led into strife and pointed to the peaceful example of Wood's campaign where Protestant and Catholic worked side-by-side. That night, bonfires were lit across the constituency. The victory boosted Russell's campaign for compulsory purchase. The following year the Conservatives' modest Wyndham Land Act was passed by parliament. Compulsory purchase was eventually introduced in 1925.

In the 1906 general election, the East Down Unionists selected James Craig (who became Northern Ireland's first Prime Minister) to stand against Wood for the Liberals. Woods lost to Craig by 670 votes. He contested the seat again as a Liberal in 1910, but lost by 974 votes. From 1906 onwards Wood continued to develop his practice as a solicitor particularly in the farming community. In 2006 he was presented with an address signed by 22 of his prominent constituents, highlighting his achievements:

> We are proud to reckon you among the great Land Reformers of your country. For without efforts such as yours thousands of Tenants, who are now happy owners of their farms, would have been ground to poverty under the old rack rents, or ejected from their holdings, and driven with their starving families into foreign lands like so many of their countrymen.

Wood died on 31 October 1936 at his home, Marino House, Holywood, County Down.

Sources: Farr 2008; Jackson 1987; Walker 1978.

Rosamund Praeger
1867–1954

Sophia Rosamund Praeger was born on 15 April 1867 in the Crescent, Holywood, County Down. She was the daughter of William (Willem Emilius) Praeger, a Dutch linen merchant who moved to Ireland in 1860 and Marie Praeger (née Patterson). A few months after she was born the family moved to the newly-built Woodburn House, Croft Road, Holywood. Rosamund had five brothers: William Emilius, Robert Lloyd (the famous naturalist), Hendrich John, Egmont Apjohn and Owen Maurice. When Rosamund was only fourteen her father died.

Immediately across the road from Woodburn House was the manse of Rev. Charles McElester, the minister of Holywood Non-Subscribing Presbyterian Church and the dissenting Praeger family became members of his congregation. Rosamund and her brothers attended Rev. McElester's day school in the church on the Shore Road and then in its new Lanyon-designed premises in High Street, Holywood. Rosamund later taught in the Sunday school.

Rosamund then attended Sullivan Upper School in Holywood followed by the Belfast School of Art. Aged seventeen she went to Slade School of Art at the University College London and at some point also studied in Paris. She returned home around 1890 and worked in a studio in Donegall Square West, Belfast and sought a niche in the market for illustrated children's books, her own and those by other authors, while also developing her skill in sculpture.

She developed a strong interest in Irish folklore and mythology and wrote articles on rhymes and riddles of County Down for the *Irish Folklore Journal.*

Her many works included a *Gaelic Tableaux* at a Feis Ceoil in Belfast; Fionnula, daughter of Lir; *Fainne An Lae* (Gaelic League); illustrations in *The Nationalist; Shan Van Vocht; The Islandman* (a Harland & Wolff shipyard worker); *Patric* on Slemish; *Patrick the slave boy; St Brigid of Kildare* (both as a plaque and a figure); *A commission to commemorate the 50th anniversary of the Gaelic League; Johnny the Jig;* and *The Philosopher.* She became best known for her figures of children.

She was elected an honorary fellow of the Royal Hibernian Academy and in 1941 and 1942 she was elected president of the Ulster Academy of Arts. In November 1952 she finally gave up her studio in Hibernian Street, Holywood and sold off her remaining stock.

She died in Rock Cottage on 17 April 1954, two days after her eighty-seventh birthday. The previous Sunday she had been seated at her usual pew in church. She was buried in the Priory Cemetery, under the family memorial she had sculpted, 'Hope and Memory'.

Having no children she left various charitable bequests to further her philanthropic interests, including NSPCC, RSPCA and the National Trust to establish a seaside park which could be enjoyed by children. She hoped that her studio would become a centre for art instruction and therapy for children, but this never came to pass. She also furthered the development of Holywood Working Man's Club in King Edward VII Memorial Hall, which she had been a founding promoter.

Sources: Auld 2006; Blaney 1999.

W.J. Stewart
1868–1946

William John Stewart was born into a Presbyterian family in 1868. He owned a successful building firm Stewart & Partners and lived with his family and older unmarried sister, Agnes Anne, in Crawfordsburn, County Down. He married Caroline Margaret, 7/8 years his junior, and had four children.

He was very interested in politics and joined the Unionist Party. He was opposed to partition favouring union between Great Britain and the whole of Ireland, with a federal system of government throughout the United Kingdom of Great Britain and Ireland. He campaigned on housing issues, unemployment insurance, shortening the working week, universal compulsory free education, equality of the sexes and temperance.

In 1918 he resigned from the Unionist Party and founded the Democratic Unionist Electors Association to stand in Belfast (Ormeau) as an Independent Unionist at the general election of 1918. Although he received 4,833 votes he was defeated by the Unionist candidate Thomas Moles who received 7,460. Stewart rejoined the Unionist Party. On 30 May 1929 he successfully contested the Westminster seat of Belfast South at the general election, for the Unionist Party, defeating Independent Unionist, Philip James Woods. Stewart retained his Westminster seat uncontested at the general elections of 1931 and 1935. However he continued to criticise the party on a range of social policy and financial issues.

In December 1936 he launched a wider attack on official unionism at the joint selection committee of South Belfast Parliamentary Unionist Association at the Café Royal and challenged the current Northern Ireland government. He was roundly criticised by a range of his Unionist colleagues. His manifesto stated that,

> The situation is getting fast out of hand, and we are developing into an autocracy worse even than Hitlerism. Hitler makes no pretence of being anything but a dictator, but here, under the guise of constitutionalism, all the worst evils of dictatorship are being introduced into our public life.

In April 1937 Stewart founded the Justice for Ulster Committee to work for change from within the Unionist Party. They proposed, amongst other things, limiting offices of government to eight years or two parliaments. In June Stewart formed the Progressive Unionist Association, with branches in Larne, Armagh and Lurgan and in August the Ulster Progressive Unionist party (UPUP). However, Stewart's refusal to resign from the Unionist Party caused a rift in the ranks of the UPUP.

At the beginning of 1938, a general election was called for the Northern Ireland parliament and Stewart declared that the party would fight the election on the issue of unemployment. However, his party was ill-prepared for an election and only managed to produce a manifesto two days before polling. It focused, as promised, on unemployment, as well as bringing Northern Ireland up to British standards in relation to housing and social services, which had been neglected by the Unionist government. It also supported the programme of the Farmer's Union. The UPUP stood 10 candidates, concentrating on Belfast and east of the Bann and captured 12.9% of the vote (30.8% of the votes in the constituencies in which they stood). However, with proportional representation having been abolished by the Unionist government in 1929, in order to try and maintain Unionist Party domination, the UPUP gained no seats. Stewart reflected after the election that it has been,

> my aim and object to help the working people to obtain a higher standard of living ... the Union ... is gradually bringing our province down mentally and physically until in a short time our people will be so disheartened that they will not care whether they are under Dublin or Westminster.

Stewart did not re-stand for the Westminster general election of 1945 and died in May 1946.

Source: Brown 1984; Walker 1992.

Robert Lindsay Crawford
1868–1945

Robert Lindsay Crawford was born in Lisburn, County Antrim in 1868, the son of James Crawford, who described his profession as a scripture reader, and Matilda (née Hastings). He was educated privately. He became a journalist, based in Dublin and founded the evangelical paper, *Irish Protestant*, which he edited between 1901 and 1906.

From 1905, he was Grand Master of the newly founded Independent Orange Order, which tried to bridge the sectarian divide in Ireland, and claimed by then to have 55 lodges. He described it as, 'strongly protestant, strongly democratic ... strongly Irish. It was teaching Irish Protestants that love of Ireland was not incompatible with love of empire ... .they stood broadly for toleration ... They had as Protestants trafficked too long in the shambles of sectarianism.'

In the Magheramorne Manifesto, an attempt to establish a political party out of the Independent Orange Order, Crawford attacked the Ulster Unionist Council and called on Orangemen to befriend their fellow countrymen, regardless of creed. The Manifesto included the following statements,

> The landlords have used Protestant Ulster for generations for their own selfish ends, and have made the Orange Institution a stepping stone to place and emoluments for themselves and their families ... On the willingness and ability of Irishmen in carrying out reasonable reforms in their own country will rest the claim to a more extended form of self-government ... .Unionism is likewise discredited. ... we consider it is high time that Irish Protestants should reconsider their position as Irish citizens and their attitude towards their Roman Catholic countrymen.

The manifesto was signed by Crawford, Thomas Sloan MP, Rev. D.D.. Boyle (see profile) and Richard Braithwaite.

Crawford became increasingly radical in his views, giving support to feminism, the Gaelic League and aspects of socialism, attacking all aspects of wealth and privilege, which was all too much for the directors of the *Irish Protestant* and he was sacked as editor. In 1906, he returned to Ulster from Dublin and edited the *Ulster Guardian*, organ of the Ulster Liberal Association, but was forced to resign for supporting Home Rule and for attacking poor working conditions in the linen industry.

In 1907 he supported the striking workers and, with Jim Larkin, spoke from the platform in Queen's Square, encouraging the strikers, 'stand firm, out of this movement will spring not only the strength of organised labour but also ... the unity of all Irishmen.'

His involvement in the manifesto led to his suspension and eventual expulsion from the Independent Orange Order in 1908. He became a supporter of Home Rule.

From 1910 to 1914 he lived in Canada working on the *Toronto Globe*. After the Great War he founded his own journal, the *Statesman* for Protestant supporters of Irish Independence. He retired from journalism in 1922 although he became a trade representative to New York for the Irish Free State and died in 1945.

Sources: Bardon 1992; Campbell 1991; Hickey and Doherty 2005; Hume 1998.

Annie Entrican
1869–1960

Anne Jane (known as Annie) Entrican was born in Dundalk, County Louth, the second daughter of Samuel Entrican, a Presbyterian commercial traveller and his wife, Anne Jane, both from Castlecaufield, County Tyrone. They lived at 17 (and later, 33) Botanic Avenue Belfast, close to Queen's University where she graduated with a music degree. Her father died in 1905, aged 74. Her brother was in attendance.

She became the secretary of the Society to Brighten Workhouse Life, and as a result of her work with the Society was co-opted on to the Belfast Board of Guardians with responsibility for the workhouses.

She was very active in the women's suffrage movement in Belfast, becoming a member of the Irish Women's Suffrage Society and regularly sold their newspaper on the streets of Belfast.

Although they were living at 49 Finaghy Park Central towards Lisburn, she died of cancer in 81 University Street, Belfast on 16 December 1960, aged 91.

Sources: Urquhart 2000.

F.W.S. O'Neill
1870–1952

Frederick William Scott O'Neill was born in Belfast on 26 August 1870, to a middle class family that lived in a three-storey home in Fitzroy Avenue, Belfast, close to Queen's University. From the age of 14, he attended the Royal Belfast Academical Institution, where he was head boy. In 1889 he went to study at Queen's University where took logic, metaphysics, and political economy, graduating in 1893 with an MA in Mental and Moral Science. He chose to become a minister and studied theology at Assembly's College Belfast.

After his ordination, he spent his first year as the first theological travelling secretary for the Christian Student Movement. In May 1895, he and four other young ministers sent a letter to the church's mission board, offering themselves to work as missionaries abroad, to India or China. He was chosen to join the church's mission in Manchuria, the northeast of China, and appointed a missionary on 30 August 1897. After an initial period of training and learning Mandarin, he was sent in 1899 to Faku, a small country town 100 kilometres north of the provincial capital of Shenyang, a small and backward town with no running water, electricity, postal service, railway or paved roads.

In 1900, an anti-foreign and anti-Christian movement, the Boxer Rebellion, swept through China, with the encouragement of the government. In Manchuria, they killed 332 Chinese Christians, but no missionaries; in all of China, they killed 133 Protestant missionaries and 48 of their children. Among the dead in Faku was an elder named Shu, who was betrayed by members of his own family who wanted to seize his property. He and his son were beheaded. O'Neill escaped death by fleeing to Harbin in north China, a journey of nine days that included being fired at by Boxer snipers. From Harbin, he took a ship to Vladivostok. There he caught typhoid fever and was fortunate to be cared for by a missionary doctor. After the rebellion, he returned to Faku and rebuilt the church and Christian community there. The PCI opened a major seminary and a medical college in Shenyang to serve the whole mission: the aim was to have a church, a school and a medical facility at each centre and the first church in Faku served as a school on week days.

In 1902, he asked his long-standing girlfriend, Annie Wilson, then in Ireland, to come to marry him: she made the long journey to Shanghai, where they married in October 1903. They had five sons, of whom two died young of diseases contracted in Faku and three grew to adulthood. In 1904 he had an article on 'The unjust Steward' published in the *Expository Times*.

Manchuria was the site of the Russo-Japanese war of 1904–05 and both armies set up camp in Faku and the O'Neills entertained officers of the two sides. O'Neill was chosen as the town's temporary mayor, in an effort to protect it from the foreign armies. He became friends with the Japanese commander, who sent him a ceremonial sword after his return home.

In October 1909, the congregation opened a new church with space for 500 and a women's hospital, led by an Irish Presbyterian missionary doctor named Isabel Mitchell. In 1911, a pneumonic plague swept through Manchuria, killing thousands. Faku was placed in quarantine: schools closed, normal business nearly came to an end and the streets were empty. A sense of terror pervaded the town.

In October 1914, an Irish Presbyterian minister in Belfast questioned O'Neill's theological orthodoxy and threatened a charge of heresy. However, he withdrew the motion in October 1915, in sympathy after the death of Frederick's son Dermot, aged 16 months.

In 1916, O'Neill's health deteriorated and, on medical advice, he spent months on a lake next to pinewoods on Vancouver Island, Canada.

In March 1917, Isabel Mitchell, principal doctor at the Faku hospital, died of diphtheria after more than 11 years' service; she was just 38. She was buried in Jilin, near the home of her sister who had married another Irish Presbyterian missionary. O'Neill wrote a 220-page book describing her life and achievements.

From October 1917 until January 1919, O'Neill and another Irish Presbyterian missionary accompanied members of the 100,000 Chinese Labour Corps who were transported to France and Belgium to help the

Allied war effort. The two were decorated by the Chinese government for their work. He returned to Faku in early 1919 and that year published *The Call of the East*, describing the work of the mission in Faku.

In the 1920s, Manchuria was relatively peaceful; the church grew and trained an increasing number of Chinese ministers. By 1925, when O'Neill published *The Quest for God in China* the Christian community of Faku had five Chinese ministers, with a kindergarten, a girls' and boys' school, a women's Bible training school and a women's hospital.

In 1928, with 14 prominent Chinese Christians and five other missionaries, O'Neill attended an International Missionary Conference on the Mount of Olives in Jerusalem.

In September 1931, the Japanese army occupied Manchuria and in 1932 installed the last Chinese emperor, Pu Yi, as head of their puppet state of Manchukuo. In the spring of 1932, O'Neill and other missionaries secretly provided evidence of Japanese war crimes to the visiting Lytton Commission. Conditions became increasingly chaotic. The Japanese army controlled the cities but there was no law and order in rural areas, where bandit gangs roamed freely. Christians and preachers were frequently kidnapped and held for ransom. A gang of bandits besieged Faku for three weeks; its inhabitants built a deep trench and a fence of electrified wire. O'Neill was chosen as an intermediary between the residents and a Japanese force that came to lift the siege.

In 1936, O'Neill returned home for one year to take up the post of Moderator of the General Assembly. In April 1937, along with the incoming Moderator Rev. R. Hanna and Rev. James Irwin (see profile), he engaged in discussions with de Valera about the proposed new Irish constitution and at the General Assembly in June praised de Valera, the goodwill of the Catholic majority, and the new constitution, which recognised all religious denominations existing in the country. This created much controversy in the media.

From 1935 onwards, the Japanese became increasingly strict, wanting to control every aspect of society. They followed missionaries around and opened their mail. They demanded a 'juridical person' on the governing body of all missionary work who would report to the government. Missionary school students and teachers were ordered to attend Shinto shrines. In October 1939, the church reluctantly decided to close its schools, with 200 teachers and 5,000 students.

After the Japanese attack on Pearl Harbour, Frederick and other missionaries were interned in Shenyang, in a club for the foreign business community. The men slept together in the largest room and some in the billiard room in the top flat of the Hong Kong and Shanghai Building. In June 1942, he and most of the others were sent to Japan and put on a ship bound for Mozambique, where they were exchanged for Japanese prisoners; he was repatriated to Ireland.

O'Neill retired in June 1945 and lived in Belfast until his death in October 1952. This is how the Presbyterian Herald described him:

> Scholarly, eloquent, a master of languages and utterly fearless, he penetrated to the most unlikely places and made himself equally at home with the men of all the faiths of the East ... His influence was great among men of many races and all walks of life ... Independent of judgement, enthusiastic, disarming in his friendliness and a man of great decision of character, he subordinated all to his calling and thus became an outstanding personality in the Church at home and abroad.

He left a wife and three grown-up sons: Denis, Terence and Desmond. Denis served as a senior civil servant in the Ministry of Transport in London: Terence was an engineer: and Desmond was a psychiatrist in London. His wife, Annie, died on November 24, 1956, in Belfast. She donated their house, 'Innisfree' in Stockman's Lane, to the Church as home for missionaries on furlough.

Sources: Barkley 1986; Keogh and McCarthy 2007; O'Neill 1919; O'Neill 1925; material kindly provided by F.W.S. O'Neill's grandson, Mark O'Neill.

David Boyle
1870–1938

David Dorrington Boyle was born in Dungiven, County Londonderry in 1870, son of Rev. Dorrington David Boyle, a farmer of Ballynacallion near Dungiven. He was educated at Limavady Intermediate School and Magee College, Derry, where he graduated in Arts in 1892. He was awarded a BA (Respondent) by Trinity College Dublin in 1913 and a MA in 1916. He was licensed to preach in Limavady in 1895 and then ordained in Third Ballymoney (which became St James' in 1908) on 26 January 1896, where he was to be minister for the next twelve years. In 1898 he married Martha Moore Craig from Ballymoney.

He was an outspoken supporter of land reform and a leading member of the Route Tenants' Defence Association and after 1901, the North Antrim Land Purchase Association. In November 1903 he was expelled from the County Antrim Grand Orange Lodge for attending meetings of the new Independent Orange Order. As a result, six Ballymoney lodges handed in their warrants and became lodges of the new Order. Boyle became the Grand Chaplain of the Independent Order, which, by 1905, had seventy-one lodges. The new order developed a working alliance with the North Antrim Land Purchase Association.

Boyle was a signatory to the Magheramorne Manifesto which was issued in 1905 by the Grand Master of the Independent Orange Order, Lindsay Crawford. The manifesto stated that,

> The landlords have used Protestant Ulster for generations for their own selfish ends, and have made the Orange Institution a stepping stone to place and emoluments for themselves and their families … On the willingness and ability of Irishmen in carrying out reasonable reforms in their own country will rest the claim to a more extended form of self-government … .Unionism is likewise discredited. … we consider it is high time that Irish Protestants should reconsider their position as Irish citizens and their attitude towards their Roman Catholic countrymen.

This brave attempt to bring new political thinking, instead of the traditional Protestant siege mentality, in the face of the extended franchise and the Home Rule proposals was ultimately unsuccessful, but reflects an important development in the history of the Orange institutions. He played a major role in the election of the liberal R.G. Glendinning for North Antrim in 1906 and continued to be associated with him through the North Antrim Reform Association.

Following the retirement of Rev. W. Wylie, he was called to Downshire Road Presbyterian Church, Newry in 1908, although he only remained there for two years, when he was called to McQuiston Memorial in Belfast. At McQuiston the church expanded, building additional halls and Boyle organised popular evening classes. In 1912 the church had 600 families.

Boyle was awarded an honorary doctorate in 1937 and died the following year.

Sources: Barkley 1987; McMinn 1979; McMinn 1982.

Dora Mellone
1872–?

Dora Mellone was born in England in 1872, the daughter of Rev. William Edward and Elizabeth Amelia Mellone, Non-Subscribing Presbyterian Unitarians, who lived in 9 Back Sea View in Warrenpoint, County Down. Her mother was 5 years older than her father and Dora was born when her mother was already into her 40s. Dora had a sibling who may have stayed in England when the Mellones moved to County Down. Dora was present when her mother died just before Christmas in 1909. Her father was a Unitarian minister who graduated from Manchester College, Oxford and graduated DSc. at Edinburgh in 1895 and London 1896. He had previously been Unitarian minister of Kidderminster in England from 1876 to 1880. Aged 61 he became the minister of the Non-Subscribing congregation of Warrenpoint in 1896. He eventually retired in 1910, aged 75, by which point the numbers in the congregation and church finances had significantly reduced and the congregation was put under joint charge with Newry. He died three years later on 30 June 1913, aged 77. Dora was present in Warrenpoint at the death of both her parents

Dora Mellone became a teacher and an activist in the women's suffrage movement. She became the secretary of the Warrenpoint and Newry Suffrage Society. In summer 1912 she despaired that the chief obstacle to progress was the 'indifference' of 'very many women', although she was also conscious that the movement also suffered from a lack of money.

In 1913 Mellone wrote an article for the *Non-Subscribing Presbyterian*, where she tackled the stereotyped image of the suffragist as 'an ill-dressed female, armed with hatchet or bag or stones, just emerging from prison, where she could not even submit quietly to the punishment she so richly deserved, but must plague long-suffering wardresses and doctors by adopting the hunger strike'. She suggests that people are increasingly asking what is at the heart of the movement – 'what is the inspiring force which drives some women to face physical suffering of no light kind, others to scorn delights and live laborious days in the hope of serving the cause of woman'. She goes on to argue that there is a strong connection between the suffrage movement and religion. She argues that the suffrage movement is:

> based on the ethical view of Christ, that men and women are human beings, and that every human being separately and equally is an end – an end in itself, and that in no case can it be made merely the means to another human being's end … On all alike the same moral law is binding: on all alike rests the same responsibility – to realise themselves as individual human beings.

She was proud of the movement's ability to transcend traditional divisions in religion and politics in Ireland. In the Irish woman's Suffrage Federation, she said, 'no-one ever asked another about her politics'. Representing the northern committee of the IWSF, she spoke in Hyde Park in London in 1913 and told the huge crowd that Irish suffrage societies were:

> Of all shades of political opinion, we have nationalists and unionists, orange and green, extremist and moderate. These women agreeing in nothing else agree on this one point … no one else has

ever done this; the IWSF is the only political organisation which has
ever held the north and south together ...

In August 1913, writing in *Irish Citizen* she said she was surprised, on
coming to England, at the level of ignorance about Ireland and the myths
that abounded.

With the outbreak of the First World War, Mellone became the Secretary
of the Suffrage Emergency Council, created by the Irish woman's Suffrage
Federation, in order to 'serve suffrage in a new way', because the 'nation was
in dire peril'. But it was a constant challenge to keep the suffrage movement
free from Irish constitutional politics during this volatile period. In order to
keep suffrage issues to the fore during the war, Margaret McCoubrey (see
profile) established a branch of the Irish Women's Franchise League, but
Mellone was unwilling to 'participate in anything that appeared to favour
national independence'.

Mellone wrote a preface to a pamphlet published in January 1919, by the
Irish Women's Suffrage and Local Government Association Reports of the
Irish Women's Suffrage and Local Government Association from 1896 to
1918.

Mellone was also an active temperance campaigner. By 1923 Mellone was
living in Booterstown Avenue, Blackrock, Dublin.

Sources: Bannerji, Majob and Whitehead 2001; Collins 2012; Morley and Walsh 1998;
Non-Subscribing Presbyterian no. 69, March 1913.

James Woodburn
1872–1957

James Barkley Woodburn was born on 12 March 1872, the son of Rev.
Matthew Woodburn, fourth minister of Ballywillan near Portrush, County
Antrim (licensed Garvagh, County Londonderry), who died on 28
November 1877, when James was only five years old. James was educated at
Queen's College Belfast; Edinburgh University; New College Edinburgh
and Assembly's College Belfast. He was licensed to preach in Magherafelt,
County Londonderry on 2 November 1897 and ordained in Rostrevor,
County Down on 2 January 1901. He married Ada Elizabeth Purvis on 19
January 1905. He resigned from Rostrevor on 3 November 1908, when he
received a call from Castlerock, County Londonderry. Woodburn succeeded
Rev. Samuel Waugh Chambers, at First Holywood, County Down, on 20
April 1916, when Chambers emigrated to America. Woodburn stayed in
Holywood for five years until he resigned on 14 December 1921 when he
was called to the congregation of Fitzroy Avenue, Belfast, on the resignation
of William Colquhon. He was installed there on 6 January 1922.

He was an historian of note and his 1914 book on *The Ulster Scot* is a classic on the subject. He was elected Moderator of the General Assembly for the year 1940/1. He was very disturbed by the terrible poverty that was uncovered in Belfast during the clear-up following the blitz in April 1941. He warned that 'if something is not done to remedy this rank inequality there will be a revolution after the war'.

Woodburn retired from active service on 31 October 1942 and died on 26 September 1957.

Sources: Barkley 1987; Cradden 1993.

Robert Hanna
1872–1947

Robert Kennedy Hanna was born on 8 October 1872, the son of George B. Hanna, a merchant from Kildrum, Kellswater, Ballymena, County Antrim. He was educated at Queen's College Galway and Assembly's College Belfast, gaining a BA (RUI) and MA (TCD). He was licensed to preach by Ballymena Presbytery on 18 May 1897 and ordained in 24 February 1898, becoming the minister of Whiteabbey congregation, County Antrim and living in Jordonstown, Monkstown. Later that year he also married Nora Sophia Pringle from Clones, County Monaghan. They had three daughters.

The *History of Congregations* suggests that he may have had serious qualms about people signing the Ulster Covenant of 1912 within his church building, and/or his liberal political outlook may have led him to be unhappy about the rejection of Home Rule by most Presbyterians in the north and that either or both reasons may have opened the way to him accepting a call to a southern ministry.

He was called to Adelaide Road congregation in Dublin and began his ministry there on 7 January 1914. The outbreak of the Rebellion on Easter Monday 1916, the serious interruption of services and normal church life during the troubles, and the subsequent partitioning of the country, with many Presbyterians going to live in the north, all led to a great loss in membership for Adelaide Road. In 1926 Hanna was elected Moderator of the General Assembly and awarded a DD from Glasgow University. He resigned from his charge on 4 February 1947 and died on 29 April 1947.

Sources: Barkley 1987.

Margaret Holland
1872–1950

Margaret Holland was born in south Belfast in 1872, the daughter of Elizabeth Holland. She wanted to become a doctor, but, although her father did not object to women being educated as long as they did not take jobs away from men, in the nineteenth century it was still considered important that women 'learned domestic arts and waited for a good husband' and so Holland abandoned this ambition.

She became involved in a range of charitable and missionary activities. She was an activist in the temperance movement; the working men's Sunday school attached to Rosemary Street Presbyterian Church; and in the distribution of food to the poor in east Belfast, especially during the depression of the 1920s.

After her mother died in 1921 she travelled to India to see the work of the Zenana Mission which trained local women for the medical profession and provided medical and educational welfare to Indian women and orphaned children, an experience she wrote in her book, *My Winter of Content.* She died in 1950.

Sources: Holland 1926; Newman 1993.

Alex Boyd
Died *c.* 1923

Alexander Boyd worshipped at Donegall Road Presbyterian Church. He succeeded Alexander Bowman (see profile) as trade's union organiser of the Municipal Employees' Association and became a member of Belfast Corporation. He was master of the Donegall Road Temperance Lodge and with Lindsay Crawford founded the Independent Orange Order to counteract the Orange Order's Toryism. In 1905 he became vice-President of the Trades Council.

In June 1907 Jim Larkin had organised the Belfast dockers into the National Union of Dock Labourers and had called them out on strike over a wage claim. 100,000 workers marched through the city. Coal workers followed suit. Even the police came out on strike for better pay and conditions. Protestants and Catholics supported the strikes and spoke together on platforms. Boyd responded to attempts by the employers to stir up sectarian conflict by making it clear that divide and rule 'would not be successful because men of all creeds are determined to stand together in fighting the common enemy who denied the right of workers to a fair wage.'

The employers brought in the troops to deal with the policemen's (RIC) strike. The coal dispute was settled in late July. The dockers were ultimately unsuccessful. There were serious riots in Belfast during which two people were killed. Boyd was critical of Larkin and the attempt to form an Irish Transport and General Workers Union in Belfast.

Boyd's stand on the strike lost him his St George's seat on Belfast Corporation. He regained it under Independent Labour in 1920 and was elected an alderman. He died not long afterwards during an operation.

Sources: Bowman 1997; Campbell 1991; Morgan 1987; Walker 1985.

James Irwin
1876–1954

James Alexander Hamilton Irwin was born in Banagher, County Londonderry in 1876. He was educated in Magee College, Derry graduating with a BA awarded by the Royal Universities of Ireland in 1900 and an MA with Honours in Philosophy in 1902. He then trained for the ministry and gained a Divinity degree in 1908. Following studies at University College Dublin, he was awarded a DPhil by the National University of Ireland in 1910. He was licensed in Glendermott, County Londonderry and ordained the same year in Killead, County Antrim, which he served for the next 13 years, as well as having a substantial farm, until he was declared bankrupt and resigned to take up the post of minister in St Thomas's Church of Scotland in Leith near Edinburgh in 1928.

He returned to Ireland in 1935 and was installed in Lucan and Summerhill, County Dublin. In 1937 his church was united with the church in Naas. The same year he represented the Presbyterian Church at the United Council of Christian Churches in Ireland. In 1948 he represented the Church at the Assembly of the newly formed World Council of Churches in Amsterdam. He also represented the church on the newly created British Council of Churches until his death in 1954.

Irwin was a supporter of the Irish republican movement in the 1930s and a personal friend and supporter of de Valera. Irwin shared political platforms with him in America to try and counteract the influence of a delegation sent by the Ulster Unionist Council, led by William J. Coote MP of South Tyrone and included six clergymen, including three Presbyterians, none of whom were actually officially sanctioned by the church. The delegation was sent to get support for the Unionist cause from Protestants in the USA. De Valera challenged Coote to a public debate, which Coote turned down, and de Valera offered to put a clause in the Irish Constitution granting full religious freedom to every citizen. He began appearing, with Irwin and Anglican minister Rev. J. Gratton Mythem, a descendent of Henry Grattan, before gatherings in Protestant churches. Irwin's message was that, in his experience, there was no sectarianism amongst Irish nationalists and that the Coote delegation did not represent the views of the majority of Ulster Protestants.

On his return to Ireland he was charged with sedition, and sentenced to six months imprisonment. He was released after six weeks, as a result of pressure from a group of North American Presbyterians who had met Irwin when he was in America. He was also asked to account to the General Assembly where he told his colleagues that he did not care if he was hanged outside Church House, but he would declare his views. The congregation was split over the politics of their minister, but he remained with them until he retired.

De Valera returned to power in 1932 and Irwin advised him on aspects of the 1937 Constitution. In 1939 he was appointed to the Fianna Fáil-led government's Commission on Vocational Organisation and served on it until 1943. He later joined the party and served on the National Executive, which regularly met in his manse, from 1945 until he died in 1954. He was approached to become the Fianna Fáil candidate for the Presidency of the Irish Free State in 1936, but declined, as he said he would not run against a Fine Gael candidate.

When Éire was declared a republic there was conflict within the church about holding church services to mark the establishment of the Republic. Irwin was the leader of the faction supporting the holding of a service.

Irwin was the convenor of the Presbyterian Church's Government Committee – the Church's spokesperson on political matters, along with the Clerk of the General Assembly. John Barkley said that Irwin did much to protect the standing and rights of the Presbyterian Church in Éire in a very disturbed and, at times, hostile environment.

He was nominated several times by his Presbytery for the position of Moderator of the General Assembly, but his unpopular political views ensured that he was never elected. In 1950 he was awarded an honorary DLitt by the National university of Ireland, of which de Valera was President.

He died in 1954. De Valera was a prominent mourner at his funeral. He is buried in Mount Jerome cemetery.

Sources: Barkley 1987; Barkley 1993; Cougan 1995; Mitchell 1995.

Thomas Johnstone
1876–1961

Thomas McGimpsey Johnstone was born in Newtownards in 1876. His ancestors, after coming to Ireland from Scotland, lived in Greyabbey, County Down. Johnstone was very conscious of the congregation's historic connection with Rev. James Porter who was hanged during the 1798 Rising, as a result of his satirical writing at the expense of the local aristocratic landlord and Episcopal vicar.

Aged fourteen, Johnstone was an office apprentice at George Walker's spinning mill in Newtownards. This gave him a real sense of what work was often like for most workers,

> It is deplorable to think that those who do all the hard, dirty, wet, cold work should have to put up with the worst wages, the worst homes, the worst food, the worst clothing and the worst prospects for their children. The whole thing is intolerable. A system which condemns scores of millions all over the world to poverty, and at the same time, for the artificial maintenance of prices, consigns vast and valuable stores of food to the incinerator, is a system which cannot too quickly disappear … The day is coming, and it cannot come too soon, when science and machinery will work not for company promoters and financiers, … but for the common good of all.

He then began studying in the evenings after a day's work. He was eventually able to get into Queen's College Belfast, funded by teaching shorthand at night. He received his BA in 1905. He then entered Assembly's College to train for the ministry. He was licensed to preach by Ards Presbytery in 1908 and the same year ordained at St James', Ballymoney. He was installed in Newington in north Belfast in 1910.

While acting as supply preacher in Great Victoria Street, Johnstone became involved in the Belfast dock strike. He was convinced of the justice of the dockers' cause and the integrity of their leader Jim Larkin,

> By this struggle I came to see that slavery is not really dead. That though the whipping-post and lash are no longer used against workers, other barbarous methods are occasionally resorted to, e.g. the lock-out or the refusal to negotiate settlements with men's leaders.

He was deeply concerned about the issue of unemployment and poverty as well as the treatment of those in work. He was convinced that economic arrangements 'must share justly and automatically with workers the wealth produced by their co-operative efforts'. He also was very conscious of how sectarian divisions could be heightened to defeat progressive measures, by using the fact that Larkin was a Roman Catholic, for example. The involvement of a Presbyterian minister brought strong criticism from the employer's side. Bloodied from this attack, in future, he tended to concentrate on other social and moral issues such as drink and gambling.

In 1927 he raised the issue of poverty and unemployment at a public meeting in Ballymoney accusing the government of adopting a 'leave-well-alone' policy towards the 25,000 unemployed. He also stated that:

> There were 48,000 struck off the unemployed register during the previous twelve months ... Many thousands of young people from 14–20 years who had never had a job ... already many suicides owing to unemployment, local asylums crowded from the same causes. Poverty has increased during the year by 100 per cent, and the Board of guardians have had to increase their meagre grants.

He was elected moderator of the General Assembly for 1934/5. When elected he summed up the contemporary sense of identity of Presbyterians in Ulster, 'If in one sense Ulstermen are Irishmen first and Britishers afterwards, in another sense they are Ulstermen first and Irishmen afterwards'.

In 1937 as Temperance Convenor of the Church he presented the report of the committee to the General Assembly and in doing so criticised the decision of a judge in granting a licence for a new public house, giving the legal grounds for such criticism. This resulted in the very unusual charge of contempt of court, for a case which had ended. He was convicted and fined, which on the principles of justice and free speech he refused to pay. The church called a special Assembly and gave him their unanimous backing. In the meantime an anonymous benefactor paid the fine.

In 1941 the Newington church and halls were destroyed in the blitz on Belfast, which also damaged the manse. Johnstone died in 1961 leaving an autobiography, *Vintage of Memory*. His brother and son also became Presbyterian ministers.

Sources: Barkley 1987; Holmes 1985.

Thomas Carnwath
1878–1954

Thomas Carnwath was born on 7 April 1878 in Strabane, County Tyrone, the son of Joseph Carnwath and his wife Mary (née Porterfield). He was one of a family of eight children. The Carnwaths came to Ulster from Lanarkshire, Scotland in the seventeenth century, and settled in Stoneypath four miles from Strabane and were members of Donagheady Presbyterian Church.

Carnwath was educated in Strabane and then Foyle College, Londonderry. He entered Queen's College Belfast in 1896, winning prizes and scholarships every year during his scientific and medical studies. In 1900 he graduated with a BA (hons) in chemistry and physiology and in 1903 with degrees in medicine, surgery and obstetrics. While undertaking further studies for a doctorate in public health and a special course in bacteriology, he worked as an anatomy demonstrator.

He undertook a major study in pollution in Belfast Lough, with Edmund Letts and others. In 1898 a Royal Commission was appointed to investigate the problems caused by dumping of large amounts of untreated sewage into rivers and estuaries. The commission sat for 16 years and produced nine detailed reports. Letts and Carnwath produced much of the evidence in relation to Belfast. They also studied the public health of the city of Belfast for the Local Government Board of Ireland. The main problems were related to sewage much of which was disposed of via a chute which discharged untreated sewage into Belfast Lough at night. By day, sewage from Harland and Wolf, which employed 10,000 men, was discharged directly into the Lagan. All this untreated effluent resulted in a vast increase in seaweed around the lough.

In 1906 Carnwath was awarded his Degree in Public Health from Cambridge University and travelled to Germany to study estuary pollution there. One of the three papers he published while in Germany was into the ground filtration system of dealing with sewage, which was used extensively in Germany and other parts of Europe. Carnwath's paper described the effects of using gravel or sand to assist in the filtration. He also examined the reasons for the increase in seaweed. His work contributed significantly to the introduction of the more advanced and sanitary methods of dealing with sewage in Belfast.

In 1907 Carnwath took up the first of a series of posts in England as assistant physician at the infectious diseases Hospital in Salford, Manchester, then assistant medical officer of health in Manchester, and in 1910 as medical inspector for His Majesty's Local Government Board and lecturer in Public Health at St Thomas's Hospital London. He served with the Royal Army Medical Corp during the First World War, including at Ypres, where he was praised for his courage and commitment to duty, eventually receiving the DSO. In January 1916 he was transferred to Salonika to set up field laboratories to deal with the problem of poisoned water supplies. There he fell seriously ill from dysentery and other diseases and at one point was given up for dead, but recovered after six months recuperation in Malta.

In 1919 the Ministry of Health was established in England following concern about the outbreaks of diseases as a result of soldiers returning from the war and the high death rate of infants at childbirth. Carnwath was appointed as a medical officer in the General Health and Epidemiology section in the ministry in its first year, eventually becoming senior medical officer in 1929, responsible for nutrition, food and drugs administration, and in 1935 he was appointed the deputy chief medical officer. He and the Chief Medical Officer played an important role in laying much of the groundwork for the promotion of preventative health and the eventual establishment of the National Health Service.

Carnwath's wife, Margaret Ethel (née McKee) suffered from severe arthritis and the long hours that Carnwath worked made life difficult, so in 1940 he chose to retire early and return to live in Whitehead, County Antrim in a house built by well-known suffragette and socialist, Charlotte Despard. However, retirement did not mean that he stopped working. In 1941 he undertook an investigation into the health of Belfast's population and its inadequate municipal health services. With an almost complete neglect of social housing between the wars by the Unionist controlled Belfast Corporation, in sharp contrast to developments in England, Carnwath reported on the worst working-class housing that he had seen,

> Damp, mouldering walls, many of them bulging, rickety stairs, broken floors, crumbling ceilings were common defects. Some of the 'houses' were mere hovels, with the people living in indescribable filth and squalor. Considering the accommodation, the rents seemed high. In a group of three of the worst houses, each sub-let to three tenants, and rents were 1/9d a week for a small attic which it was an adventure to approach.

In relation to Belfast's medical services, Carnwath reported:

> In its personal medical services, however, Belfast falls far short of what might reasonably be expected in a city of its size and importance and I believe the reason is that the Council is not quite certain what it is doing, whether it is worth doing, or whether they are the people to do it.

Carnwath also presented extensive evidence to the select committee of the government of Northern Ireland set up to consider the establishment of the National Health Service in Northern Ireland, following the developments in England.

Carnwath died on 2 April 1954. He was survived by his wife and two sons, Andrew and Douglas. A memorial service was held in the Presbyterian College chapel, conducted by his minister in Whitehead, Rev. W.F.S. Stewart.

Sources: Elwood 1982; Munck and Rolston 1987.

John Waddell
1878–1949

John Waddell was born in 1878, the third son of the Rev. John Waddell, minister of Newington in north Belfast (the brother of Rev. Hugh Waddell (see profile)). He had three brothers and three sisters. He was educated at

Belfast Royal Academy, Queen's College and Assembly's College Belfast. He was licensed to preach in Belfast in 1902, served a brief apprenticeship in First Derry and was ordained the same year in Bangor, County Down.

Waddell was politically liberal and supported progressive social reform. In 1912 he preached on the theme of *Christianity and Socialism* and instead of taking the traditional line that the two are diametrically opposed, outlined the Christian principles which should be used to judge any social issue. He said,

> Do not let us not push such questions aside, saying peevishly that the demand for better conditions, higher wages, reduced hours of labour and so forth, is merely an attempt, on the part of those who have not, to dispossess those who have. It lies deeper – it is an endeavour on the part of the oppressed to assert the rights of their personalities, and to claim a life other than that of machines. Is it too much to suggest to Christian people that men ought to reject all profit which involves a loss to others, and to find their happiness in the things which gain by being shared? ... I am sure the day is drawing near when some method of giving the workers a share of the profits of industrialism on a national basis ... The purpose of labour and of wealth production is to make the largest number of noble and happy human beings.

In the campaign to prevent the introduction of Home Rule, efforts were made to get as many people as possible to sign a Solemn League and Covenant to oppose Home Rule. All over Ulster places were set up where people could put their names to the League and Covenant. In many places churches were used for this purpose. In Bangor, Waddell refused to sign the Covenant himself or to join the Carson Volunteers. He objected to the use of church property for this political purpose and refused permission for them to use the Bangor church hall. This angered many members of his congregation. He was prevailed on to preach to a group of Unionist clubs, but in his sermon made clear his objection to the threat of violence contained in the Ulster Covenant to gain a political objective. This did not win him any new friends in the Unionist clubs and caused controversy in the press. The majority of his congregation, although opposed to his opinion in this matter, stood by him. Within a year, however, he decided to accept a call to the Presbyterian congregation of Egremont in Liverpool. The First World War began, so his new role involved providing considerable support to grieving families, many of whose loved-ones failed to return from the trenches.

He returned to Northern Ireland in 1920 and was installed as the minister of Fisherwick Church. He also became the convenor of the Home Mission. He was a supporter of greater unity between Christian churches.

In 1933 he unsuccessfully proposed, together with the Anglican Dean of Belfast, Rev. W.S. Kerr, that, 'Each church fully and freely recognises, as a basis for progress towards union, the validity, efficacy, and spiritual reality, of both ordination and sacraments, as administered in the other Church.'

Waddell, as Moderator of the General Assembly in 1936/7, thanked God for the new Irish constitution of 1937. He retired in 1945 and died four years later in 1949. H.C. Waddell wrote a biography of his brother.

Sources: *Bangor Spectator* 1912; Barkley 1987; Hamilton 1992; Holmes and Knox 1990; Waddell 1949.

Robert Lynd
1879–1949

Robert Wilson Lynd was born in north Belfast on 20 April 1879. He was the second of seven siblings. His father was a Presbyterian minister of the same name, who, although conservative theologically was liberal on social issues and preached frequently, in Berry Street and May Street Presbyterian churches in Belfast, against the wickedness of landlords, who, he said had 'sown the wind and reaped the whirlwind'. His grandfather was Rev. J.L. Rentoul of Ballymoney. He also had two great-grandfathers who were Presbyterian ministers, so the Calvinist influence on the family home was incredibly strong. He described Presbyterian Sundays as of,

> doubtful morality even to go for a walk on Sunday. Whistling on Sunday is suppressed as a sin, even if one whistles a psalm tune ... Boating is not permitted; going into a fruit-garden to pick gooseberries is immoral. There are even some subjects of conversation which you will do ill to broach on a Sunday in strict company.

He was educated at the Royal Belfast Academical Institution, which he said 'made no effort to dispel our ignorance of the history or natural history of our countryside', and Queen's College where he gained a pass degree BA in 1899, having focused more on other things than his studies – describing himself as 'indolent'.

As a student he became a socialist and formed the Belfast Socialist Society with three fellow students. He trained as a journalist with the *Northern Whig* and then in 1901, due to a lack of career opportunities, went to Manchester to work on the *Daily Dispatch*. He then moved to London working as a freelance journalist, sharing a studio with the Ulster artist Paul Henry. He joined the *Daily News,* which then became the *News Chronicle* and in 1912 became its literary editor. He was rejected for military service in the Great War.

His conversion to nationalism occurred at a performance by the Irish

National Literary Theatre of J.M. Synge's play *Riders to the* Sea in March 1904 at the Royalty Theatre and soon afterwards his writings were full of nationalist zeal.

He had met Sylvia Dryhurst at Gaelic League classes in Oxford Street, London and they married and had two children, Sigle and Maire. Sylvia became a novelist, critic and well-regarded poet. Their home in London became famous for its literary evenings, which involved many of the famous writers of the day, including James Joyce.

He wrote articles for the short-lived *Ulad*, the journal of the Ulster Literary Theatre and *The Republic*, the journal of the Dungannon Clubs. He blamed Rev. Henry Cooke, 'the evil genius of the North', as the 'killer' of Presbyterian liberalism and for destroying any nationalist feeling that the Presbyterians possessed.

He was a friend and supporter of Rev. J.B. Armour and was appalled that he was treated as a 'sinister legend ... a dangerous man, contentious and perverse ... a traitor ... a bitter and black-bearded agent of the enemy ... enemy Number One in his own church'.

At Irish classes he met and became friends with Roger Casement. Although Lynd was a strong supporter of non-violent Griffithism, he was active in trying to win a reprieve for Casement when he was found guilty of treason for gun-running in support of the 1916 Easter Rising.

Lynd was initially an internationalist and, in the Belfast Socialist Society, distanced himself from what he saw as sentimental nationalism, but increasingly came to see that imperialism which he described as 'surely the meanest and most dishonourable creed that ever deluded thousands of decent men and women', as well as capitalism which he said 'means the exploitation of the weak by the strong'. He was a member of the Belfast Dungannon Club, which produced a leaflet in support of Jim Larkin during the docker's strike of 1907 and invited him to give a talk on the labour movement. As a socialist and Irish nationalist, Lynd also wrote for *The Nation* and what became the *New Statesman*. His weekly essays, under the pen name YY, made his name and were published in book form each year.

He taught classes in the Irish language and supported the Gaelic League; edited some of the works of James Connolly, whom he admired greatly; as well as published a number of books including, *Home life in Ireland, Passion of Labour* (1920) and *Ireland a Nation* (1920).

He was a man of exceptional gifts – handsome and personally charming, loyal to his friends, deeply versed in Irish and English literature, shrewdly aware of the realities of contemporary politics and above all a gifted journalist and essayist. Lynd died of emphysema in London on 6 October 1949 and was buried in Belfast City Cemetery.

Sources: Bardon 1992; Boylan 1998; Byrne and McMahon 1991; Campbell 1991; Hartley 2006; Newman 1993; Robinson 2013.

Margaret McCoubrey
1880–1955

Margaret Mearns was born in Eldersey or Elderslie, near Glasgow in 1880. She left school, aged twelve, and went to work in a men's clothes shop in Glasgow, attending night classes to continue her education. In 1896 she qualified as a shorthand typist and eventually became the secretary of the managing director of the first telephone service in Scotland. She went on to teach in the Skerries Business Training College quickly rising to become deputy headmistress at the age of twenty-four. She met electrician John Taylor McCoubrey from Belfast and moved there in 1905, living in Candahar Street off the Ormeau Road. They had two children, a boy and a girl. In 1910 Margaret McCoubrey joined the Suffragette Movement and became an active militant. At the outbreak of the First World War she joined the Peace Movement and gave refuge to conscientious objectors from Great Britain avoiding conscription. She objected to the decision of WSPU to cease agitation on Women's Suffrage, and founded a branch of the Irish Women's Suffrage Society in Belfast. In August 1917 she single-handedly ran a month-long peace and suffrage campaign in Belfast, inspired by the thought that 'a woman looking down on a battlefield would not see dead Germans or dead Englishmen but so many mothers' sons.'

She became General Secretary of the Co-operative Guild and for six years, from 1910–16 was on the board of management of the Co-operative. She also taught economics at the Co-operative Society in the Education Department and contributed various articles to Co-operative journals. She wrote a history of the Co-operative Movement which she did not complete. She was a member of the Independent Labour Party (of which Sam Kyle was the Secretary) and in 1920 was elected a Labour Councillor for the Dock ward in inner city Belfast, one of very few women, along with Ida Boyd, to play a prominent role in the labour movement at that time.

In May 1926, McCoubrey had an article published in *The Labour Opposition*, Northern Ireland's first labour newspaper. In anticipation of the Annual Congress of the Co-operative Union, which was to meet in Belfast bringing together representatives of the co-operative movement from across the British Isles, McCoubrey argued for the importance of the co-operative movement from a socialist perspective, creating a 'peaceful revolution',

> There are socialists who think themselves above the consideration of what might be termed the bread and butter aspect of life. Marxian theory is to them more important than Pure Milk! There are also so-called socialists who support the multiple shop or any other shop offering a cut price, regardless of the conditions of labour or the destination of the profits of the concern. Out of the depths of an abysmal ignorance both types, upon occasion, grumble, grouse and

sneer at the Co-operative Movement. But the majority of socialists recognise that the Movement is a powerful organisation composed of working class people; that in the very nature of things its policy must lean towards industrial collectivism rather than individualism.

In 1933 she moved to Carnlough on the east Antrim coast, where she ran Drumalla House as a holiday home for members of the Belfast Girls Club Union. She died in 1955.

Sources: Morgan 1991; Munck and Rolston 1987; Newmann 1993; Urquhart 2002.

Blanche Bennett
1881/2–?

Blanche Emma Bennett was born in London in 1881/2. She married William Thomas Bennett, a Presbyterian wholesale confectioner from Belfast, who was considerably older than her. They lived in Evelyn Gardens, Belfast and had two children, Nora Mary and Blanche Ethel, who was born around 1900 and died in Purdysburn Hospital in 1970.

Blanche Snr. became active in the women's movement and became Secretary of the Belfast Branch of the Irish Woman's Suffrage Society. In October 1912 she denounced the unionist Covenant processions as 'a man's show entirely'. She lamented that unionist women had not also marched to demonstrate their place in public life.

In November 1912 Bennett celebrated the fact that the organisation had been:

> Able to fill the Ulster Hall (the largest hall in Ireland) three times, and the Belfast Opera House once, and more than once almost every other available hall in the city ... although hampered for want of funds and sufficient workers to meet the demand, nearly every large town in Ulster ... [had] been visited, in some cases more than once. In the country we found our audiences particularly sympathetic to our cause; we got patient hearings, and cordial invitations to come again.

During 1912–13 the IWSS held at least 47 open air meetings in Belfast. The IWSS and other groups spoke at street corners and held dinner hour meetings at factory and mill gates in Belfast to encourage working class women to get involved.

Sources: Urquhart 2000.

James Rutherford
1881–1942

James Spence Rutherford was born in College Green in Belfast in 1881, son of William Rutherford, a commercial traveller, and Lillian Watt (née Adams). After finishing his schooling he went to work in the Harland and Wolff shipyard in east Belfast and wanted to pursue a career in engineering. However when his mother died in 1903, he realised, at the age of 23 that his real calling was to the ministry. He studied at Assembly's College Belfast and then for a year in New College, Edinburgh. He was licensed to preach and became assistant minister at Newtownbreda, where he shared his accommodation with the Ulster novelist Forrest Reid. Twelve of his sermons there were published in 1914 under the title of *The Seriousness of Life*.

When the First World War broke out he served as a stretcher-bearer with the Royal Army Medical Corp. On returning home he served as a supply minister in Comber and was finally installed as minister in Warrenpoint in 1919. During his period there, he ordained the first two women to become elders in the Kirk session. In 1927 he was called to Kingstown Church in Dun Laoghaire, where he developed a good relationship with the local Catholic clergy and community. Shortly after the move to Dun Laoghaire, he published *The Truth of the Christian Faith,* which highlighted his desire to communicate the truth of the Christian faith as he saw it, simply and clearly. He was very aware of the defensiveness of the Church in Ireland,

> The mission of the Christian Church, however, is not a purely defensive one. It does not exist merely to fight against sinister forces, but to create an entirely new order of things, to break down not only the barriers which separate man from God, but those which separate man from man, to permeate all their relationships – political, economic and personal – with the spirit of Christ, to transform and Christianize the world of human affairs.

In 1931–4 he was a member of a joint commission between the Presbyterian Church in Ireland and the Church of Ireland set up to discuss the agreements and disagreements between the two churches but failed to reach any conclusions.

In 1938 he spoke at a Student Christian Movement conference and on the final day there were separate Eucharistic services in different rooms for different denominations and he was asked to lead the service for Presbyterians and Methodists. At the end of the service he stood at the entrance and noticed the students coming out of the Church of Ireland service. He suddenly felt that he had turned the Church's most solemn service in unity into a mockery. He was reduced to tears and vowed that he would never again agree to facilitate a multiplicity of such services at the one time and the one place.

He wrote part of a book to highlight his major concern for Christian unity, one which he had regularly given talks about, which was published after his death as *Christian Reunion in Ireland*. This book lays out his positive vision for unity. His view was that there should be the closest possible inner spiritual unity between the followers of Christ, but that unity should manifest itself outwardly,

> It is the will of Christ that his disciples should manifest their unity in Him to the world by their oneness in spirit, in faith, and in love. That unity cannot be made manifest so long as Christians are separated from one another by divisions which are largely hereditary and concerned with matters in no way essential to the faithful following of the divine Lord.

His vision was not only concerning unity between the Presbyterian Church and the Church of Ireland, which was a major debate at that time, and one in which Rutherford was positively involved, but one which over time could involve all Christian churches, including the Catholic Church, which he recognised as a 'genuine part of the world-wide, catholic Church of Christ' and Catholics as genuine Christians. He therefore strongly disapproved of trying to proselytise Catholics. He recognised that at that time in the Catholic Church's history, unity without surrender and absorption would not be possible. But he was very unhappy about the habit of 'dividing Christians into different parties, and attaching labels to them, and then assuming that no one can possibly wear more than one label'.

In 1937 he was a delegate at the World Conference on Faith and Order in Edinburgh.

During his final illness he lived in a small country farmhouse in Derryoge near Kilkeel and wrote movingly about the experience of illness in *Learning through suffering*, which was published after his death.

Rutherford died in 1942 after a prolonged period of illness. Two of his books were published after his death. He had been a man of devotion and action. A man committed to a vision of the future more in keeping with the true nature of the Christian gospel of love and forgiveness. He had four children, including Bill Rutherford discussed in his own profile below.

Sources: Ellis 1992; Rutherford 1942.

Hugh MacMillan
1884–1950

Hugh Walter Gaston MacMillan was born in Barnsley, Yorkshire in 1884. His father, Dr Hugh Wallace MacMillan was a Presbyterian, originally from Dundonald, County Down, but went to practise medicine in England for about twelve years during which time his son Hugh was born. In 1889 the family returned to Ireland and his father worked as a doctor on the Upper Newtownards Road until he died the following year in an accident.

Like his father, Hugh MacMillan trained as a medical student until his mother died in 1903 and he was left a substantial sum in her will, but which he would not be able to inherit for a further five years. From 1908 onwards he lived the life of a respectable, if eccentric, gentleman, with no apparent profession, in Ballysillan in north Belfast.

MacMillan had, however, developed a completely separate life as a writer, teacher and translator of the Irish language, and was known by the Irish name of Aoidhmin MacGreagoir. He may have learnt Irish from a native speaker, perhaps on Rathlin Island, when he was fostered after his father's death. We know that by 1900 he was in Belfast teaching Irish in Ballymacarrett and living with his mother and sister. In 1906 he published *Freamhacha na hEireann* (*Irish Roots*), which included a poem in Irish he had written and eight stories he had collected from different story-tellers on the Aran Islands. He followed this up in 1910 by a collection of stories in Irish from Rathlin, in which he showed a strong knowledge of the distinctive Scots form of Gaelic spoken there. In the following years he published various Irish poems and songs he collected in the Gaeltacht. He died in hospital in 1950.

Sources: Blaney 1996.

Charles Dickson
1886–1978

Charles Dickson was born in 1886 in Dromore, County Down, the son of John Mitchel Dickson, Unitarian linen merchant, and his wife Mary. They later moved to Holywood, County Down. His paternal grandmother, Matilda, was the sister of Young Irelander, John Mitchel (see profile). She lived until Charles was eleven years old.

He was educated locally and then at the Royal Belfast Academical Institution. In 1903 he went to the Belfast Medical School, where he became friends with William P. MacArthur and developed an interest in the Irish language, regularly visiting the Donegal Gaeltacht in order to become fluent in Irish. He and MacArthur founded the Queen's Gaelic Society and

Dickson became the first secretary and later, treasurer. He was a member of the Non-Subscribing Presbyterian Church.

He achieved a first class honours degree in medicine and worked as a house officer in the Royal Victoria Hospital for ten years and then carried out research in the Department of Pathology at Queen's, which earned him an MD. He then joined the civil service as Medical Officer with the National Health Insurance Commissioners, where he worked for over a decade, except for a period during the War with the Royal Army Medical Corps, earning the Military Cross for gallantry.

He was very interested in history and the 1798 rebellion in particular. In 1944 he published his first book on the rebellion, *Revolt in the North – Antrim and Down in 1798* and was to later write two others in 1955 and 1960. He also wrote *The Life of Michael Dwyer*. Dickson died in 1978.

Sources: Blaney 1996; Dickson 1944.

Jack Beattie
1886–1960

John Beattie, known as Jack, was born in east Belfast to a Presbyterian family on 14 April 1886. He was educated in Saunders Street and Dee Street local national schools. After leaving school he worked initially in a textile firm and the Belfast rope works. He then began an apprenticeship as a blacksmith in the Harland and Wolff shipyard in east Belfast. He became interested in trade union issues and was elected assistant secretary of the Associated Blacksmiths' and Ironworkers' Society. He served in the British Army during the Boer War, rising from a boy batman to a commission in the 8th Irish Hussars. After three years of service in the army he returned to the shipyard. He became assistant secretary of the Associated Blacksmiths' and Ironworkers' Society and in 1917/8 a delegate to the Belfast Labour Party. In 1918 he was appointed a full-time union official with responsibilities for the whole of Ireland, a position he retained until 1925. In the general strike in the shipyard over a forty-hour week, Beattie was a key representative of the striking workers.

Beattie became involved in labour politics and was a supporter of Irish Home Rule. In 1925 he was elected in east Belfast as the first MP for the Northern Ireland Labour Party to the Stormont parliament, with both Protestant and Catholic support. He was elected again in Pottinger in 1929, when his other labour colleagues all failed to gain election under the newly introduced first-past-the-post ballot. He held this seat in the 1938 general election, and remained an MP until 1949. He was a regular irritant to the Unionist government on their treatment of the Catholic minority and of the poor. In the depression of the 1930s he was a prominent spokesperson for the unemployed and those who depended on outdoor relief.

He was a fierce critic of the Poor Law system, arguing for direct cash payments, as was already the case in England. In 1924 in the Poor Law elections Beattie and William McMullen, with the support of the labour movement, were elected to the Board of Guardians and regularly 'raised a number of pertinent issues in an impertinent way'. When in 1925 he was elected to parliament as a Labour MP he spoke on the Poor Law issue in a debate on unemployment and regularly thereafter. In 1932 with evidence of poverty and unemployment and how badly the poor were treated in Northern Ireland compared with elsewhere in the UK, Beattie attempted to put down a motion in the house on unemployment and was immediately ruled out of order by the speaker. Beattie lifted the mace and threw it under the table which held the dispatch box. When it was returned to its cradle by the Sergeant at Arms, Beattie once again picked it up and attempted to throw it at the feet of James Craig, who was speaking at the time, but having been grabbed by various people, it fell well short. The police were called and Beattie was ordered out of the house.

In October 1932 there was a strike of 600 men on outdoor relief. The evening saw a demonstration of 60,000 supporters at the Custom House steps at which Beattie was one of the main platform speakers calling for an increase in the rate of relief. The next day 7,000 of the unemployed marched to the workhouse on the Lisburn Road, where the Guardians were meeting. That night and for the rest of the week there was serious rioting in Belfast, but not because of sectarianism. Food depots were established for the strikers in Belfast. By the end of the year the government were forced to give in and doubled the payments for outdoor relief and, in parliament, Beattie said that he was proud to be an agitator who had forced the government into doing its duty to feed the hungry, although he was not satisfied with crumbs off the table for the poor. Beattie was able to get the government to admit that the Master of the workhouse had been illegally taking money out of the pensions of the elderly residents of the workhouse.

Throughout the rest of the 1930s Beattie continued to fight for parity of treatment for the unemployed in Northern Ireland as pertained in Britain where the Poor Law was abolished and payments were made as of right by the local authorities.

In 1934 Beattie was appointed organiser of the Irish National Teachers' Organisation, based in Dublin. He resigned from this post in 1952.

When war broke out in 1939, Beattie, along with other socialist and nationalist opinion, was strongly opposed to conscription being introduced in Northern Ireland, reminding the government that he and others had defended Winston Churchill from physical attack when he came to Northern Ireland in support of Home Rule.

In the struggle in the Northern Ireland Labour Party over the party's position on the constitutional question, Beattie, a strong supporter of Home Rule, was expelled twice from the party in 1934 and 1944. He was elected to Westminster in 1943 and represented West Belfast from 1943 to 1950, when he lost his seat following a dispute within the West Belfast branch of the Independent Labour Party, and failed to regain it in a November by-election. He regained it in the following general election of 1951 by 25 votes, after a lengthy recount. In 1953 he tried to regain a seat in Stormont but came bottom of the poll, with a lost deposit. In the1955 general election, when the nomination of a Sinn Féin candidate reduced the support he had previously received from Catholic voters, Beattie got 16,050 votes, half of what he received in 1951, and was defeated by Jimmy Steele of Sinn Féin.

He died of cancer on 9 March 1960. He was survived by his second wife Violet (his first wife died in 1943) and his daughter. He is buried in Dundonald cemetery.

Sources: *Belfast Telegraph* 09 March 1960; Cradden 1993; Devlin 1981; Edwards 2009; Farrell 1980; McRedmond 1998; *Oxford Dictionary of National Biography;* Staunton 2001; Walker 1985.

Bonar Thompson
1888–1963

Bonar Thompson was born, possibly as John Bambridge, in Scolbow on the slopes of Carnearney mountain near Ballymena, County Antrim, on 16 December 1888, but precisely what his birth name was is not clear, because of disagreements about who his father was. He said that he was illegitimate and his father ignored him when he saw him. Thompson's own accounts of his life do not seem to always be accurate.

Thompson said that his parents were of Ulster peasantry and his father disowned him and his mother was unable to support him and moved to England, leaving the infant with an elderly aunt, Eliza Thompson. Aged seven he went to Ladyhill National School, although during the summer months he would work in the fields rather than attend school, under its disciplinarian schoolmaster. Even in the winter he often 'mitched' school.

His unmarried aunt was a strict God-fearing Presbyterian (probably reformed) of 'devastating piety', who had little knowledge of the world, but 'incredible certitude about the next'. Thompson felt he was forced to live under the 'dark shadow of Puritanism'. Sunday, in particular, was a 'holy terror' for the young Thompson, filled with 'the heavy monotony of droning religiosity', with two Sunday services and Sunday school in between. He had little time for the many evangelicals and revivalists, whom he dealt with by using ridicule, accusing them of being responsible for much insanity in the area. He was clearly influenced more positively by two Presbyterian ministers, Revs Thomas West and Samuel Moffett. He learnt about Irish history and other topics from his uncle, school teacher John Bonar Thompson.

When Thompson was thirteen his mother contacted him and invited him to join her in Manchester, so having never having been as far as Belfast, he said goodbye to his aunt and joined his mother in England, where he worked in a variety of shops, offices and workshops, before becoming a brakeman's assistant at the Great Central Railway. In his spare time he discovered Manchester Free Public Library and read extensively. He regularly attended the theatre. He also attended the public air forum at Stevenson Square in Manchester, listening to rebels and revolutionaries. At age seventeen he gave his public performance in Blexely Square in nearby Salford.

With increasing unemployment and poverty in the country, Thompson became involved in the Unemployed Movement campaigning on the right to employment and on benefits for the unemployed. During one protest Thompson smashed shop windows in Manchester and was arrested. At his trial he made a defiant speech against 'the apathy, inactivity and indifference of the Government towards Distress Committees [for the unemployed] and general poverty'. He was sentenced to Rochester Borstal for one year. In 1910 Thompson moved to London, where he survived by collecting money after his talks, selling pamphlets and cadging money. He was a member of the Independent Labour Party.

When the First World War broke out and Thompson was called up, he declared himself a conscientious objector, with these words:

> I have been a revolutionary Socialist for over ten years. I am anti-Nationalist, anti-Militarist, anti-Patriotic. I believe in the International Brotherhood of the Workers. I believe this War to be the outcome of the jealousy and the greed of the Capitalist Class. I have opposed it from the commencement and would suffer any penalty; prison, Torture, or Death, rather than lift a finger to help in its prosecution. Upon these grounds I claim total exemption under the provisions of the Military Service Act.

His pacifist cry was 'Half the misery of the world is caused by ignorance, the other half is caused by knowledge' He was jailed and served in a variety of work-camps, until he walked out and laid low until the end of the War. Having opposed the War, his services as a speaker were little in demand, so he earned a living selling home-made toothpaste and then a book on contraception, which proved more successful. In 1922 he wrote his first autobiographical publication, *An Agitator of the Underworld*, printed by

Openshaw Socialist Press in Manchester. He also wrote articles for the *The Worker,* the mouthpiece of the Clyde Workers' Committee.

He lived in Newcastle for three years and joined the local drama society, which inspired him to create 'Dramatic Recitals', including Shakespeare, Dickens and Oscar Wilde's *Ballad of Reading Gaol,* for performance at left-wing meetings. He returned to London in 1924 and began speaking about socialism at Hyde Park corner. Unhappy with his earlier autobiography, he wrote a second one, *Evangel of Unrest,* in 1926, which highlighted his political philosophy, 'There is one hope and one only, for the tortured peoples of Europe today. That hope is Socialism – Socialism alone will end the rule of wrong and bring the Kingdom of Man on Earth'.

After the General Strike he became increasingly disenchanted with politics in general, including his former colleagues on the left. He continued to entertain crowds at Hyde Park with his caustic commentary on the week's local and international events, but admitted

> I am the only living speaker who is unable to solve the world's problems, the only figure who has not visited Russia. I am neither right-wing, left-wing, centre or any other part of the political chicken. I have no policy, no programme, no plan, no message, no mission. If I knew how to abolish poverty, I would abolish my own.

In 1930 he launched a review called *The Black Hat,* which he edited, but it failed after eight editions. An attempt to resurrect it in 1947 also failed.

He took part in various radio shows and resurrected his dramatic recitals, which he put on in various theatres. He joined a travelling theatre company and performed in Bernard Shaw's *St Joan.*

In 1934 he wrote his final description of his life story, including details (although often unreliable) about his childhood, under the title of *Hyde Park Orator.*

Thompson died on 6 January 1963 and was cremated at Golders Green. In 1980 Michael Foot, who often listened to Thompson speak in the open air, gave over a chapter of his *Debts of Honour* to Bonar Thompson, as the 'Hyde Park Sceptic'. Foot said that 'He never did anyone any harm and did nameless, countless multitudes plenty of good'.

Sources: Foot 1980; Foy 1991.

William Harrison
1889–1951

William John Harrison was born in Belfast in 1889, son of Robert James Harrison, a commercial traveller, who died before William was born, and

Elizabeth (née Downey). His family were members of Ravenhill Road Presbyterian Church. After leaving school he went to Magee College in Derry and gained an Arts degree. He then went on to study theology in Princeton in the US and Assembly's College Belfast. He was licensed to preach by Belfast Presbytery in 1916 and was ordained very soon afterwards in First Ballyeaston, near Ballyclare, County Antrim during the First World War. He had a very successful ministry there, remaining with the congregation until he was called to Crumlin Road, Belfast in 1931. As a minister on the Crumlin Road he also became the Presbyterian chaplain to Crumlin Road Prison.

During the depression of the nineteen-thirties, Harrison frequently spoke out at the General Assembly about the poverty and unemployment of this difficult period, inspiring other young ministers, including the Rev. Ray Davey (see profile), who was also impressed with how he dealt with his disability, which affected the use of his arm.

He was actively involved in the Church's Social Services and State of Religion Committees as well as the Education Board of the Church and was moderator of the Synod of Belfast in 1940. In the air raids of 1941, Crumlin Road church was demolished. Much of his energy was then taken up in the process of rebuilding the church. Unfortunately he died before he saw this work achieve its completion. He died in 1951. He had four daughters and a son.

Sources: Davey (undated); obituary in the *Presbyterian Herald* 1951.

Joseph Johnson
1890–1972

Joe Johnson was born in Tomagh near Castlecaulfield, County Tyrone in 1890, son of John Johnson, a farmer of a 30-acre farm leased from Lord Charlemont. His father also supplemented his income by teaching in the local national school. As none of the children showed any interest in farming, the land was transferred to other tenants. Joe Johnson was educated at Dungannon Royal School and in 1906 went on to Trinity College Dublin, where he took a degree in Classics and Ancient History winning two gold medals. At university Johnson set up a co-operative which provided food for students at affordable prices.

In 1910 Johnson went to Lincoln College, Oxford to do a further degree in Humanities, specialising in history and archaeology. He graduated in 1912. On returning from Oxford he wrote a polemical book, *Civil War in Ulster* attacking Carson and the arming of the Orangemen. In 1914 he married schoolteacher Clara Wilson. The same year he successfully applied for an Albert Kahn Travelling Fellowship, which gave him the opportunity for extensive travel, visiting India, where his brother was in the civil service, China, Japan, France and the USA. The trip engendered a strong interest in him in the relatively new discipline of economics and particularly on what we would now call development economics.

After the 1916 Rising he acted as a special correspondent for the *London Times* reporting on the condition of the country following the rising and during the civil war, for the *Manchester Guardian*. In supporting Home Rule Johnson was in favour of dominion status for Ireland. He continued his involvement in the Trinity co-operative society and supported the Co-operative movement generally. In 1925 he wrote a book, *Groundwork of Economics*, based on the Barrington lectures on economics he delivered. In it he tried to popularise contemporary economic ideas and apply them to the struggling Co-operative movement. From 1922 to 1924 he was a member of the Agricultural Commission established by the Free State government on agricultural issues. In 1925 he was appointed as an economics lecturer by Trinity College. In the 1930s he engaged in a series of personal agricultural experiments and published a range of academic articles. In 1938 he was elected at the second attempt to the Irish Senate and ploughed a lonely furrow in defending the Protestant contribution to nation-building. In 1934 he published *Nemesis of Economic Nationalism*, critical of de Valera's economic policies. In this period Johnson became a founder member of the Irish Association, established to promote an all-Ireland perspective, eventually becoming president.

Johnson was returned to the Seanad in 1944. In the same year he opposed the Land Bill, on the grounds that it was unjust to confiscate land that had been confiscated 300 years earlier, as well as on the economic grounds that small farms were much less efficient, so larger landholdings needed to be kept together and there would not be the agricultural investment required if land tenure was insecure. In 1951 Johnson published *Irish Agriculture in Transition*. Having been maintained in the Seanad by de Valera, Johnson finally left in 1954.

Johnson died in 1972. His son, Roy, who was born in 1929, published a biographical book, *Century of Endeavour*, about his father's experiences in Ireland and his own development as a left wing activist and scientist.

Sources: Johnston 2003.

Ernest Davey
1890–1960

James Ernest Davey was born in Ballymena in 1890, the eldest of seven children of the Rev. Charles Davey, minister of Ballymena, St Enoch's Belfast and Fisherwick Belfast, and Margaret (née Beatty). He was educated

in Belfast at St Enoch's National School, Methodist College and Campbell
College, as a boarder. He then went to King's College, Cambridge in 1909,
where he gained several distinctions in classics and a fellowship in theology.
He graduated with a first class honours BA degree in 1912 and an MA in
1916. He then went on to Edinburgh University, where he gained a
theology degree. He was licensed in 1916 and became a fellow of King's
College that year. In 1917 he was appointed Professor of Church History
in Assembly's College Belfast. In 1922 he published *Our Faith in God* and
the following year, *The Changing Vesture of Faith*. In which he said,

> We live in an atmosphere of conflicting thought-currents which will
> torture and lacerate the man who is willing to seek truth and to
> bring to naught the powers of fear, suspicion and hate. Truth will
> cost ... We need men and women who will draw to themselves the
> virus of their day and generation, and who, in the strength of God,
> will neutralise it in their own souls.

Unfortunately Davey was to attract the attention of the McCarthy-like
witch-hunter Rev. James Hunter, of Knock Church in Belfast, who was
perpetually on the lookout for apparent heretics. He had failed in his
attempt to accuse the missionary, Rev. F.W.S. O'Neill of heresy and began
to look elsewhere. He was convinced he would find it in Assembly's
College. In 1926 he accused Davey, then Professor of Biblical Criticism at
the College, of heresy and in particular that in *The Changing Vesture of
Faith,* which included restatements of the great central Christian themes of
incarnation and atonement in a modern context, Davey had not only
changed the vesture, but the very essence of these fundamental theological
concepts, including the literal truth of the Bible and that he believed that
the concept of the Trinity was not set down in scripture.

Davey gave an erudite defence in front of Presbytery and the General
Assembly, in which he used the Westminster Confession of Faith to support
his argument that the Bible is a translation of a record of the word of God
and is, therefore, inspired by God, rather than the literal word of God. He
said that Jesus, himself, criticised parts of the Old Testament. He asked
whether that meant that some parts of the Bible are the word of God and
not others. In this way he argued for the importance of on-going biblical
scholarship. His impressive defence, which demonstrated his extensive
knowledge, intellect and essential orthodoxy, won him an acquittal, which
resulted in some of his critics leaving the church and forming their own
Irish Evangelical Church. James Hunter next set his sights on Prof. James
Haire, the Professor of Systematic Theology at the College, while others,
including some of his students, continued to treat Davey with contempt.
Although he was never a Presbyterian, Ian Paisley cited Davey's acquittal as

one of the reasons for the need for the Free Presbyterian Church.

From a twenty-first century perspective, the heresy trial of Davey can be understood, although not justified, in the context of the challenging development of new theological disciplines over the previous century, which were helping theologians to understand the Bible through, historical, literary, and linguistic criticism. People like Davey, despite being essentially traditional and orthodox in their approach were very influenced by the development of this thinking. But there have always been some in the church, who cannot accept any attempt to question who wrote different parts of the Bible, when and why. If it is the Word of God, surely, the argument goes, it is therefore above such analysis. Davey's acquittal, at least, was a sign that the church was not prepared to give in entirely to this fundamentalist perspective. However, it led to a period where, while major changes were taking place in theology, especially in Germany, America and Britain, most Presbyterians in Ireland, despite a history of engaging in fundamental theological debates, were unable to contribute significantly to some of, what some saw as, the most exciting developments in theology.

The seventeenth century Westminster Confession of Faith has therefore remained the basis of Presbyterian doctrine, which all Irish Presbyterian ministers and elders have to subscribe to, with all its uncharitable descriptions of the Pope and a Calvinist theology, which does not take into account any of the developments in religious thought and biblical, linguistic and historical criticism that has taken place over the following four centuries. In 1928 the General Assembly agreed a new form of words to define subscription to the Westminster Confession of Faith required of clergy and elders. It was to be understood as signifying 'a declaration of adherence' to 'the fundamental doctrines of the faith as set forth in the Westminster Confession' upon which the church is 'fully agreed'. Later attempts to get the General Assembly to address the short-comings in the Westminster Confession of Faith, by the creation of a Declaratory Act, have, to date, failed and the church has decided to simply keep its head down and try and avoid further public controversy. However, the General Assembly did later agree that subscribing to the Westminster Confession of Faith did not necessarily mean the subscribers agreed that the Pope is the 'Anti-Christ'.

In the 1930s Davey pioneered an inter-denominational club, with participants from all denominations as well as communists and others, which met in Frederick Street. He was concerned that Northern Ireland had become 'close to a one-party state', although some people at least recognised 'the civil rights of other parties'. He saw parallels between Northern Ireland and South Africa, Germany, and Russia, where the myth of inherent superiority results in the failure to recognise the humanity and rights of others. In his inaugural address as Moderator he also highlighted his concerns about racism.

Davey wrote a centenary history of the General Assembly and went on to become the principal of Assembly's College in 1942. He was a joint convenor of the Presbyterian Church's Inter-Church Committee from 1946 and was elected Moderator of the church in 1953. He was an active contributor to the Murlogh House Ecumenical Study Conferences between 1959 and 1962. He also pioneered the Churches Industrial Council, which had representatives from all the main Protestant churches as well as the Catholic Church. In 1958 it examined the problem of unemployment and set up a group with representation from a wide range of interests to see whether the Council could provide some leadership on the issue. Through this process they realised that there was a major problem in that the Unionist government in Stormont refused to recognise or engage in dialogue with the main trade union body, the Irish Council of Trade Unions, because its headquarters were in the Republic of Ireland. The Council mediated on this issue and with some flexibility from ICTU, the government in 1964 finally developed a direct relationship with the trade union body.

Ray Davey (a distant relative), who studied under him at Assembly's College, described Ernest Davey as 'one of the greatest men I ever met' and King's College, Cambridge in their annual report on the year of his death described him as 'probably the most distinguished scholar whom the Presbyterian Church in Ireland has every produced'. Ernest Davey died of cancer in 1960. He is buried in Belfast City Cemetery along with his father.

Sources: Barkley 1993; Fulton 1970; Hartley 2006; Holmes 1985; Holmes 2000.

Billy McMullen
1892–1982

William McMullen was born in north Belfast in 1892. He was employed in Harland and Wolff shipyard and became involved in trade union issues. He worked closely with James Connolly between 1911 and 1913 and became organiser of the Irish Transport and General Workers' Union in Belfast. He was the first chairman of the Belfast Branch of the Independent Labour Party (Ireland) and one of the leaders of the labour movement in Belfast who supported the approach of Connolly and David Campbell in promoting the creation of an all-Ireland labour movement rather than emphasising a strong attachment to the British labour movement, promoted, in particular, by two other key labour activists (who were incidentally both Presbyterians), William Walker and Harry Midgley (see profile below).

In 1925 McMullen was elected as a Northern Ireland Labour Party representative for West Belfast to the Northern Ireland Parliament at Stormont, along with Jack Beattie and Sam Kyle.

McMullen was a fierce critic of the Poor Law system and was determined to change it. In 1927 he and Jack Beattie were elected as Poor Law Guardians. They were constantly active on behalf of Belfast's poor, demanding that outdoor relief be paid in cash as was the case in Britain. In parliament they constantly criticised the Belfast Guardians for failing to fulfil their responsibilities to the poor.

In advance of the 1929 elections, the Unionist government abolished proportional representation for elections, in order to reduce the ability of smaller parties to get MPs elected. This was despite the fact that it had been part of the settlement when partition was agreed and was included in the Government of Ireland Act of 1920. Proportional representation was replaced by the first-past-the-post system which favoured the two big voting blocks, Unionist and Nationalist. McMullen stood against publican, Richard Byrne, who was also a slum landlord, but was supported by veteran nationalist, Joe Devlin. Having lost crucial votes on the previous election, as a result of the new voting system, McMullen was defeated.

He moved to Dublin in 1932 and became President of the Irish Transport and General Workers' Union. In 1933, when a strike in Belfast led by the railway workers against their employers over wage cuts, turned violent, McMullen led a torchlight procession of 5,000 trade union members from the Belfast City Hall to the Custom House steps.

As chairman of the Belfast Trades Council, McMullen had signed a call for the establishment of a Republican Congress and in September 1934 the Congress met in Rathmines Town Hall, Dublin, which he presided over. There were 186 delegates, thirty of whom were from the north. The Congress was to be a revolutionary organisation to unite Protestant and Catholic, north and south, in an attack on the capitalist system. It produced its own magazine. The same year he stood again for parliament in West Belfast against two other candidates including nationalist T.J. Campbell, who fought his campaign on clearly sectarian grounds, and Anti-Partition League and former Labour Party colleague Harry Diamond. McMullan came second.

In 1951 McMullen wrote an introduction to a biography of James Connelly by Desmond Ryan. McMullen died in 1982.

Sources: Campbell 1991; Cradden 1993; Devlin 1981; Walker 1985.

Harry Midgley
1892–1957

Henry Cassidy Midgley was born in Seaview Street north Belfast in 1892. When young Harry was still a child his mother, Elizabeth Midgley, remarried a William Young and moved to Glencollyer Street, Duncairn

Belfast. In the census of 1911 the parents described their religion as Brethren and Harry as a 'Gentile'. He was educated at Duncairn Gardens School until the age of twelve, when he followed his father (who died at a relatively young age) into the shipyard. Midgley became interested in labour politics and having met the Labour leader, Keir Hardy, joined the Independent Labour Party.

In the First World War Midgley joined the army and fought at the front in France. Out of this experience he published a small book of poems, *Thoughts from Flanders,* some of which reflected his religious beliefs. He was then appointed as an official of the Irish Linenlappers' and Warehouse Workers' Union. He became a key player in the Belfast Labour Party, which was created after the war. In 1921 he stood unsuccessfully for the Northern Ireland Parliament and for Westminster in 1923 and 1924. He was successful in being elected to Belfast Corporation for the Dock ward in 1925. He was secretary of the Northern Ireland Labour Party in 1923–5 and then in 1932–8. He was then chairman from 1938 to 1942. As leader of the Party he was elected to the Northern Ireland Parliament, for a five year term, in 1933 for the Dock ward.

While electioneering he stated that he was a member of Agnes Street Presbyterian Church, although he regularly attended the popular Rev. A.L. Agnew's (see profile) Non-Subscribing Presbyterian Church in York Street, which had a strong labour tradition.

Midgley maintained a strong interest in international affairs and was a prominent supporter of the Republican side in the Spanish Civil War. Unfortunately for Midgley the Catholic Church sided with the Nationalists/Royalists and Midgley lost Catholic support, and his seat in 1938, as a result. He was elected again in Willowfield in east Belfast in the by-election in 1941. The following year, however, having failed to persuade the Northern Ireland Labour Party to adopt a stance in favour of the union, he resigned and the pro-nationalist, Jack Beattie (see profile) became leader. Midgley then formed the Commonwealth Labour Party in December 1942.

During the Second World War he joined the Northern Ireland government, as Minister for Public Security and later Minister of Labour. Midgley resigned to fight and retain his seat in 1945. He joined the Unionist Party and eventually became Minister of Education, where he raised the school leaving age to fifteen and substantially increased the school building programme.

Having taken ill at an Ulster Teachers' Union conference, he died in 1957.

Sources: Devlin 1981; Walker 1985.

Denis Ireland
1894–1974

Denis Liddell Ireland was born in 17 Malone Park in south Belfast in 1894, the son of Adam L. Ireland, a linen merchant and manufacturer in Lurgan and Isabella (née McHinch). His father was well mannered, but also a perfectionist and subject to violent rages. Ireland remembered watching his father's hand-loom weavers in their stockinged feet. Clippings, emblems and mottos attached to each individual loom indicated what religion the weaver was.

He was educated at the Royal Belfast Academical Institution and then Queen's University where he studied medicine. His studies were interrupted by the First World War and he joined the reserve battalion as a subaltern and was sent to Derry and Donegal where he was transferred to the Royal Irish Fusiliers, serving in France and Macedonia. His brother served in the navy and was killed.

With many of his comrades being killed, Ireland was eventually promoted to the rank of Captain, but was invalided home, where he resumed his medical studies, but decided it was not the career for him. He was increasingly concerned about the stunted 'loom-fodder of the industrial system'. His medical training seemed of, 'little use when the dark satanic mills that made them what they are remain to grind the life out of them almost as effectively as the creeping barrages blew the lives … out of the cannon-fodder at the front.'

He worked for the family linen business, marketing the business to West End department stores and overseas, from a base in London. This gave him extensive opportunity for travel, including Paris, Strasburg, Munich, Salzburg, Budapest and America, as well as extensive travel around Ireland. He developed a particular interest in Russia, but never managed to actually get there. He also read extensively, both literature and history. He was particularly conscious of the difficulty for 'a son of the Ulster Protestant industrial ascendancy to orientate himself in relation to his country's history'. He considered that the 'present is … meaningless' without 'knowledge of the past'. But he was not impressed with the level of thinking coming from the youth in the south of Ireland and felt that:

> it is the Ulster Presbyterian who is the real juggler with metaphysical subtleties, the dreamer, and the potential liberator of Irish art and literature – potentially, that is, when he has abandoned … his present attitude of life-wasting negation … What is needed is a new artistic revolution, or rather renaissance, in the North, a renaissance which only requires Ulster artists and writers to stay at home instead of rushing to London.

He also became interested in politics. He attended a Liberal Party reception in London in 1929 and met Lloyd George, but was not impressed by 'this little Welsh opportunist' who 'let loose the Black and Tans in Ireland immediately after a war waged on behalf of democracy and the rights of small nations!' In Dublin he met de Valera and took an 'immediate and instinctive liking' to him. He found Dublin 'provincial', which he said was caused by the union with Britain. The ending of this provincialism required 'the return of the Irish, including the Northern Irish, as opposed to the pure Gaels, into the political life of Ireland'. He felt that 'Ulster Unionism … is founded on false premises, and that, since the foundation is rotten, the whole thing will one day collapse'.

He stopped working for the family business in 1930 to become a freelance writer and broadcaster, which he successfully did for nearly forty years. In 1936, his first book, *From an Irish Shore*, an autobiographical memoir and travelogue, was published. He reflected on the state of his itinerant life:

> That was what became of being an inarticulate poet. No wife … or cosy suburban bedroom, nothing but this eternal itch to keep moving and looking – as if moving and looking could satisfy a man at an age when he should be striking the earth with his heal and finding it solid and immovable beneath him.

He was elected to the Senate of the Irish Free State and became the first resident of Northern Ireland to be a member of the Oireachtas. He believed that his political views were in the true tradition of Presbyterianism. In *Red Brick City* he expounded the view that Presbyterians were the only true republicans in Ireland. He wrote a life of *Wolfe Tone, Patriot Adventurer; Six Counties in Search of a Nation* and two volumes of autobiography. He died in a nursing home in 1974.

Sources: Boylan 1998; Campbell 1991; Ireland 1936 and 1973; Newman 1993.

Arthur Agnew
1896–1977

Arthur Linden (A.L.) Agnew was born in 1896, the eldest son of William J. Agnew JP, of Quay House, Moira, County Down. When his parents died Arthur Agnew lived with his maternal grandparents, William and Elizabeth Weatherall and was educated at Moira National School, Lurgan College and Queen's University Belfast from 1914. His university education was interrupted by war service with the Royal Naval Air Force between 1916 and 1919. He then returned to his studies and received a BA degree in

1920. He spent a year at the Presbyterian Assembly's College to train for the ministry and completed his theological training by spending a further two years at Manchester College, Oxford.

Agnew was ordained in 1923 by the Presbytery of Antrim and installed in York Street Non-Subscribing Presbyterian Church. Belfast, where he encouraged various left wing groups to meet. Under his leadership membership of the congregation grew rapidly

He had a strong labour congregation and supported Harry Midgley (see profile), a socialist and labour activist when he stood for the Northern Ireland Labour Party in the 1924 general election, which took place under the long shadow of the Boundary Commission which was due to report shortly, and which hardened Unionist resolve not to 'give an inch'. Although he polled a creditable 21,122 votes he was defeated by the Unionist Sir Robert Lynn.

In 1925 Agnew wrote an article entitled 'Why I am a Socialist' in *The Labour Opposition* arguing that Christianity and Socialism were the same thing and that Christians should be 'concerned more with present day matters: Housing, education, wages and peace, than with the past doings of the Prince of Orange or the future policies of the Pope of Rome'. He arranged a visit to see the Soviet Union.

The church was bombed during the blitz on Belfast in the Second World War and the congregation moved to Second Belfast in Elmwood Avenue, where Agnew was formally installed in 1944. He was elected moderator of the Non-Subscribing Presbyterian Church for two periods from 1935 to 1937 and 1975 to 1976. Like his father he became a Justice of the Peace and was awarded an OBE. He died in 1977 while still minister of both congregations.

Sources: Boyd 1999; Courtney 2008; notes provided by Rev. John Nelson; Walker 1985.

George Gilmore
1898–1985

George Gilmore was born in Portadown in 1898 and brought up in Dublin. His father was a leading Dublin accountant. As a boy Gilmore was strongly influenced by the growing desire for national independence and joined na Fianna Éireann. He became the IRA leader of the South County Dublin Battalion from 1915 to 1926, participating in the Easter Rising of 1916 and was active throughout the War of Independence.

He took the Republican side in the Civil War and led a raid on Mountjoy prison in Dublin in 1926 which helped 19 republican prisoners to escape. He was arrested various times between 1919 and 1923 and even escaped from Mountjoy prison. He was arrested in 1926 and refused to wear prison clothing, demanding political status. He was released the following year. He was arrested again in 1931 and sentenced to five years, but was released the following year under the general amnesty. In 1932 he was wounded by the Garda in County Clare.

He was one of several individuals who were trying to move the IRA towards a more socialist position. At an Easter Commemoration in north Kerry he spoke of uprooting the capitalist system and building a new society in which the 'wealth-producing resources of Ireland are the property of the people of Ireland and not of the exploiting class'. He also responded to his critics saying:

> in answer to certain people who are suggesting that we are sullying the flag by introducing bread and butter politics and that we should keep our movement on a higher and more spiritual plane I say that the spiritual life of a nation is not a thing apart from its material welfare but that it can be compared to a blossom growing from its roots.

In 1934 he left the IRA and helped establish the left wing Republican Congress of socialist and republican groupings aiming to overthrow British Imperialism and set up a worker's republic. Gilmore wrote a pamphlet in which he traced the Congress back to Henry Joy McCracken in 1798, through the Young Irelanders of 1848, the Fenians of 1867 and the Easter Rising of 1916. This time the movement was to be led by representatives of the working class. He became joint honorary secretary, but it split over whether or not to fight elections. During the Spanish Civil War in the 1930s he organised support for the International Brigade on the Republican side against the fascists, including recruiting volunteers to fight. He died in Howth, County Dublin in 1985 aged 87.

Sources: Munck and Rolston 1987; Search's Web 'Guide to Irish History'; obituary in Geocities.

Dorothy Macardle
1889–1958

Dorothy Macardle was born in Dundalk in 1889, the daughter of Minnie Macardle, who described herself on her census form as a freethinker. Her family were the owners of the Macardle brewery in Dundalk. She was educated in Alexandra College, Dundalk and then University College Dublin, where she was radicalised by the extent of poverty in the city, and the desire of the people to control their own destiny. She then went to teach English in Alexandra College. She supported the Irish cultural movement of this period and joined the Gaelic League. Politically she was sympathetic to the republican cause and joined Cumann na mBan in 1917. The following year she was arrested by the British Army while teaching in a classroom.

When the republican movement split in 1921 over the Anglo-Irish Treaty, she sided with the Anti-Treaty republican side and in 1922 was arrested and imprisoned in Mountjoy and then Kilmainham gaols, under the new Irish Free State government. She wrote her experiences of being involved in the civil war in *Earthbound: Nine Stories of Ireland*, published in 1924. In the early 1920s she was involved with the White Cross organisation providing assistance to the jobless and homeless. She was arrested at a meeting of the Women Prisoners' Defence League in 1922 and imprisoned again in Kilmainham. As a result she was sacked from her teaching job. She participated in a hunger strike in the jail which ended in November 1923 and she and other prisoners were released in December. She related some of the stories told to her by republican prisoners in *Tragedies of Kerry.*

She then went to work as a journalist for the *Irish Press* at the League of Nations in Geneva while her close friend Eamon de Valera was Irish President, and developed as a writer and playwright, using the pseudonym of Margaret Callan. She also carried out research for what would become her most famous book *The Irish Republic*, which was the first complete political history of the seven year period from the 1916 rising to the end of the civil war in 1923, published in 1937, which has been through many editions. However, she was saddened by de Valera's betrayal of women when a clause in the proclamation of 1916 which guaranteed equal rights and opportunities 'without distinction of sex', was removed in the drafting of the new Irish constitution of 1937. She wrote to de Valera saying, 'As the constitution stands, I do not see how anyone holding advanced views on the rights of women can support it, and that is a tragic dilemma for those who have been loyal and ardent workers in the national cause.'

During the Second World War, Macardle, who was a confirmed anti-Fascist, disagreed with de Valera's policy of neutrality. She considered that 'Hitler's war should be everyone's war'. She went to work for the BBC in London and developed her fiction writing, but spent much of her spare time working with refugees from Nazism. During the late 1940s she travelled extensively in Europe and was particularly involved in the issue of refugee children. In 1949 a book about their experiences and needs, *Children of Europe*, was published.

In 1951 she became president of the Irish Association of Civil Liberties. Macardle died in 1958 and was accorded a state funeral, with de Valera giving the funeral oration.

Sources: Ellis 2006; *Irish Democrat* website.

Austin Fulton
1901–86

Austin Alfred Fulton was born in Clooney Road, Londonderry in 1901, the son of James Austin Fulton, a builder, and his wife Fanny. He was educated at Foyle College and Magee College, Derry, Trinity College Dublin, Princeton in the United States and Assembly's College Belfast. He obtained a first class honours degree in 1924 and a Bachelor of Divinity in 1927. He was licensed to preach in Derry in 1928, but decided to go as a missionary to Manchuria in China, rather than take up a position as a minister in Ireland. After more than a decade in China he went to work with the Bible Society in Canada in 1941. He wrote a history of the Presbyterian mission in China *Through Earthquake, Wind and Fire*. In 1945 he returned to Ireland and was installed as minister of St Enoch's in Belfast.

In 1961, Fulton attended the third General Assembly of the World Council of Churches and was a member of the WCC Central Committee for the following seven years. As outgoing moderator of the General Assembly in 1961 he called on Irish Presbyterians to 'draw closer to Roman Catholics in Christian charity, exploring ways of co-operating with them for the common good'. He also steered through a resolution on ecumenism, which headed off a much more negative approach from the church's backwoodsmen. Two years later the General Assembly stood in tribute to Pope John whose death was announced during the opening meeting of the Assembly. In 1965 the Assembly welcomed the Vatican Council's decree on ecumenism and passed a resolution of penitence for past uncharitableness towards Roman Catholics.

In 1970 he published a biography of 'J. Ernest Davey', who had been tried for heresy (see profile). In 1981, in a chapter in *Challenge and Conflict* Fulton discussed the undoubted tensions within Presbyterianism, from an historical perspective, particularly the tension between fear and faith.

Fulton was one of the former moderators of the Presbyterian Church who attended a funeral in a Catholic Church of a murdered Catholic man to show the solidarity of the Presbyterian Church against this act of sectarian violence. He died in 1986 aged 85.

Sources: Holmes 1985; Patterson 1997.

William Thompson
1902–62

William John Thompson was a man of prophetic vision and acute social conscience. He was born in Ballylinney, County Antrim in 1902, the son of Robert Bell Thompson, a farmer, and went to church with his family in Ballyclare Presbyterian Church. His mother died when he was still a child.

He was educated in Ballylinney Primary School, Ballyclare Intermediate School and Royal Belfast Academical Institution. He then attended Magee College in Derry and Trinity College Dublin, where he graduated in 1924. He finally took his theological training at Assembly's College Belfast, where he developed a friendship with Ernest Davey. He was licensed to preach by Carrickfergus Presbytery in 1926 and was ordained in 1928, becoming the minister of Connor Presbyterian Church, County Antrim.

He was very committed to the development of young people, particularly those who are most disadvantaged, and in the 1930s, when poverty and unemployment were at very high levels, began running camps in the country for unemployed young people.

After nine years at Connor he was called by College Square Church in Belfast and was installed there in 1937. He was greatly concerned about the position of many young people around the Sandy Row and Grosvenor Road area and started a city youth club for both boys and girls, turning the old manse into a youth centre.

He ran an inter-denominational group after the war, involving people from a wide range of denominations and backgrounds and was involved in the Churches Industrial Council, linking the church, both Protestant and Catholic, to industrialists and trade unionists.

He was concerned about the problem of homelessness and isolation amongst young people and opened the doors of his home to as many as he could. But realising the need was greater than he could address from his own home, he persuaded the General Assembly in 1943 to open a boys residential club, particularly to meet the needs of boys who had been in trouble with the law and boys serving apprenticeships in Belfast.

Thompson died suddenly in 1962. The original club was forced to close in 1973 due to financial difficulties and the political conflict of that period. In 1985 the church decided to open a home, in conjunction with the Probation Board for Northern Ireland, for young male offenders. The home, on the Antrim Road was appropriately named Thompson House, after the man who had founded the original club. The home is still in operation providing a valuable service to young offenders.

Sources: Barkley 1993; Holmes 1985; obituary of William John Thompson in the *Presbyterian Herald*; W.J. Thompson House brochure.

Tom Boyd
1903–91

Thomas William Boyd was born on the Woodstock Road in north west Belfast in April 1903, the son of William Boyd, a clerk, and Margaret Jane (née McCully). He was educated at Ravenscroft School, Belfast Technical

College and Queen's University. He became a pattern-maker by trade, working in the shipyard, and an active trade unionist, becoming an official of the United Patternmakers' Association and a member of the Northern Ireland district committee of the Confederation of Engineering and Shipbuilding Unions. He was also an active member of First Ballymacarrett Presbyterian Church in east Belfast.

He joined the Northern Ireland Labour Party (NILP) and in 1933 stood unsuccessfully for election to the Belfast Board of Governors of the Poor House. He then stood in the 1938 general election for Stormont, in the Belfast Victoria constituency. He was beaten into third place. In 1945 he stood unsuccessfully in the UK general election as a candidate in Belfast East, although gained 43.6% of the vote. He stood again in 1950, 1951 and 1955, polling credibly, but beaten each time by Unionist Alan McKibbin.

He stood in the general election for the Northern Ireland Parliament in 1949, when he was soundly beaten by Unionist Lord Glentoran in the Belfast Bloomfield constituency and in 1953 when he came close to capturing a seat in Belfast Pottinger. In 1958 the NILP made a significant breakthrough when Boyd and three others (Vivian Simpson, David Bleakley and Billy Boyd) were elected to the Stormont parliament. Tom Boyd was elected in Pottinger, a primarily Protestant constituency in East Belfast, where he defeated the sitting Unionist Samuel Rodgers. Boyd became the leader of the NILP. They all believed a new day had dawned for Labour and for Northern Ireland. However, Brian Faulkner as Unionist chief whip made it very clear to Boyd that no amendment on any subject that emanated from the Northern Ireland Labour Party would be accepted by the Unionist government. Due to the nationalist boycott of parliament, he was effectively the leader of the opposition until February 1960, when the boycott ended.

They were all returned again to Stormont in 1962. Boyd was, along with Sam Napier and Charles Brett, responsible for many of the party's key policy documents and put pressure on the Unionist government to undertake reforms. Boyd was a member of a small group that produced a joint NILP/NIC *Joint Memorandum on Citizen's Rights in Northern Ireland* in 1966, but the Unionists rejected it out of hand. The NILP policy document, *Electoral Reform Now* was to become one of the cornerstones of the civil rights movement. As pressure on Terence O'Neill from Paisley and others increased, Boyd, Napier and Charles Brett met with British Home Secretary, Roy Jenkins in November 1966 to make it clear that the implementation of reforms was crucial if an explosion was to be avoided and, with O'Neill drifting, the Labour government had to use whatever pressure was required to secure reforms. Also in 1966 Boyd called on the government to take action against the loyalist paramilitary UVF and UPV who were in the process of acquiring arms. Three days later three Catholic barmen were murdered in Malvern Street, Belfast.

He did not stand for re-election to the Northern Ireland parliament in 1969. He became co-convenor of the Social Services Committee of the Presbyterian Church in Ireland. He was appointed Deputy Lieutenant of Belfast in 1975.

Charles Brett described Boyd as 'relaxed and easy-going'. He died on 6 December 1991.

Sources: Brett 1978; Cradden 1993; Staunton 2001; Walker 1985.

Victor Halley
1904–66

Victor Halley was born in 1904 in Carew Street Belfast, the second son (and fourth child) of James Halley, a labourer, and Julia (née McCormick). The family then moved to 150 Parkgate Avenue, Belfast. He became an official of the Amalgamated Transport and General Workers Union (ATGWU), the largest trade union in Northern Ireland at that time.

He was a member of the Belfast Central Independent Labour Party in the early 1930s. He became a member of the Socialist Party of Northern Ireland, which was formed after the Independent Labour Party disaffiliated from the British Labour Party. Halley had been on the Provisional Council which was responsible for encouraging the Irish Labour Party to expand into the north. He became a member of the editorial board of their newspaper, the *Irish Democrat*. In 1949 he was also involved as a representative of the Irish Labour Party in trying to create a Unity Council representing the various different strands of nationalism in Northern Ireland

He stood for the Socialist Republican Party in Belfast Central ward in a Stormont by-election in August 1946, after Nationalist Thomas Joseph Campbell, was appointed a county court judge. He was defeated by Frank Hanna of the Northern Ireland Labour Party by 5,566 to 2,783 votes.

He was a member of the Belfast committee established to support the Spanish Republicans in the civil war against Franco, with Betty Sinclair, Jack MacGougan and others. He was actively involved in the Relief Fund, which sponsored a Scottish volunteer ambulance crew in Spain. They included two Northern Irish members of the Socialist party, one Protestant and one Catholic. Halley said that:

> They know that the struggle in Spain was not only the struggle of
> the Spanish workers but was the struggle of the working class the
> world over.

They went with the medical unit because by doing so they knew they were going to be of some service to those who were sick, to those who were wounded, and to those innocent victims of the Civil war into which the officer caste has plunged Spain. The Unit has taken more than 100 miles of bandages and many large boxes of anti-gas and anti-tetanus serums.

Halley was a member of the Belfast Commemoration Committee, based in Hawthorn Street, off the Springfield Road in west Belfast, established in 1948 to commemorate the 1798 rising. The committee produced a commemorative booklet of short stories, articles and ballads, called *Ninety Eight*. The introduction to the booklet made the link between the democratic republican ideals of Wolfe Tone and the contemporary situation in Northern Ireland very explicit. The committee also organised a rally to be held at a bomb-site off High Street, near where Henry Joy McCracken was hanged, but it was banned from the city centre by the Unionist Minister of Home Affairs, Edmund Warnock. It took place in west Belfast instead. The *Irish News* described Halley's role as follows,

Mr Victor Halley, a Presbyterian and member of the Commemoration Committee, said out of Wolf[e] Tone and his times had come a memory and a tradition of political behaviour that is ever-fresh in the hearts of freedom-loving Irishmen everywhere. The people who destroyed Tone in Ireland were those who feared the Protestant tradition of association with America, French Republicanism, freedom and democracy. Controlling by legal forms their corrupt and illegal coercion of freedom in Ireland, they killed the physical support for freedom. But powerful as they were, they could not kill ideas ... of Liberty, Equality and Fraternity ... To unite the whole people of Ireland – to abolish the memory of all past dissensions, and to substitute the common name of Irishman in place of the denominations of Protestant, Catholic and Dissenter – these were his means – these were the aims of the United Irishmen and these would be the aims of a United Ireland.

There was a procession a week later along the Falls Road to Corrigan Park, ending in a rally attended by 30,000 people, at which Halley was one of the main speakers.

In 1950 and 1951 Halley was Harry Diamond's chief lieutenant in the Irish Labour Party and sided with Diamond in an acrimonious dispute with fellow party member and MP Jack Beattie. Halley and Diamond were eventually expelled from the Belfast branch of the party. Halley died in 1966.

Sources: Collins 2004; Staunton 2001; International Women's day: Solidarity with Spain, 1936–9.

Sam Hanna Bell
1909–90

Samuel Hanna Bell was born in Tollcross, Glasgow on 16 October 1909. His father was James Hanna Bell, a Scotsman whose father, a mercantile clerk who became a newspaper editor and manager, was originally from Kilwaughter in County Antrim before moving to Scotland to look for work. His mother was Jane Bell (née McIlveen) from Raffrey near Crossgar in County Down. Sam Hanna Bell was baptised in 1909 in the Presbyterian Victoria United Free Church of Scotland in Glasgow. When he was only eight years old his father died, which had a profound emotional and economic impact on the family, which after three years moved back to Belfast to live in a house on a farm owned by his maternal grandparents, who were strict sabbatarian Presbyterians. His mother had to supplement her income by taking in lodgers and sewing. By the time Sam was twelve the family had moved to India Street in south Belfast.

When he was fourteen he had left All Saints Public Elementary School (his brothers went to Belfast Royal Academy) having achieved success in his Leaving Certificate, and worked at a series of jobs: a labourer, potato grader and salesman, lab technician, clerk in a woollen business, night watchman, toy salesman, railroad booking clerk and welfare officer. Through these brief occupations he developed his experience of working class life in the city and he became a socialist in his political outlook and became involved with the Labour Review and Left Book Club. During this period he had ambitions to be a painter and studied drawing at the College of Technology in Belfast, which gave him a lifelong interest in art.

In 1941 Bell gave a talk on 'Ulster Protestants', focusing particularly on the United Irishmen, at a meeting of the left-wing International Club. In 1946 Bell married kindergarten teacher Mildred Reside who the following year gave birth to their son Fergus. The family moved into Chrome Hill Cottage in Lambeg near Lisburn, County Antrim and soon after King's Road in east Belfast.

In 1943 he co-founded a literary journal, *Lagan,* with flatmates John Boyd, a playwright, who became its editor, and Bob Davidson, with the aim of developing an enriching a distinctive Ulster literary tradition, which avoided either a super-imposed English or sentimental Gaelic outlook.

Bell's first collection of short stories, *Summer Loanen,* was published by Mourne Press in 1943 and reviewed in the second edition of *Lagan.* In 1945 Bell was recruited to the post of Features Producer at the BBC by poet Louis MacNeice. He was to work at the BBC for almost twenty five years, where he, as a freethinker and socialist, engaged in the 'constructive subversion of the Unionist grip on the BBC', which at that stage employed no Catholic producers. In his time there, he wrote about forty radio scripts and commissioned and produced over two-hundred and fifty from other writers, such as W.R. Rodgers (see profile), John Boyd (see profile), Maurice Leitch, Michael J. Murphy, John D. Stewart, J.J. Campbell and Sam Thompson. Two of his most successful programmes, which he wrote himself, were *A Kist o' Whistles* about the debate that raged in the Presbyterian Church about the introduction of the organ or harmonium into worship (in writing this piece he took advice from Prof. John Barkley (see profile)), and *The Orangemen*. His own features included one on Jemmy Hope (see profile) a weaver and United Irishman and on Edward Bunting, who played an important role in preserving Irish traditional music. Bell, himself, played an important role in saving many Belfast street songs, collected by Sam Henry and Hugh Quinn, by including them in his programmes. He was influential in getting the BBC to broadcast two series of traditional folk music, *Listen Here a While to Me* and *Sing North, Sing South*, which Bell sometimes introduced and later in the 1960s two television series, *The Lilt of Music* and *Make Music*.

Bell had always had a particular interest in myths and folk customs and in 1950 was commissioned to write a book on Ulster customs which was eventually published in 1956 as *Erin's Orange Lily*.

As an indication of the respect Bell was held in, in 1950 he was asked to edit an anthology of *The Arts in Ulster*, which was published in 1951, the same year that Bell's first and most famous novel was published, *December Bride*, drawing on his childhood experiences living on a farm.

In 1961 Bell's second novel, *The Hollow Ball*, was published. Set in working-class Protestant lower Ormeau Road, Belfast in the 1930s, where unemployment was a major social problem, the hollow ball of the title is football, played by the main character. By the time this book was published, he had already started work on an historical novel set in the period of the 1798 Rising and its aftermath, which was originally to be called '*Dweller at the Ford*'. It was not completed until 1970 and was published as *A Man Flourishing*. It tells the story of James Gault, a student of divinity at Glasgow and a radical Presbyterian.

Bell's final novel, *Across the Narrow Sea*, set in the period of the plantation in the early years of the seventeenth century, was published by Blackstaff Press in 1987. His wife Mildred who had been suffering from ill health since 1972, died two years later in 1989. Bell died the following year on 9 February 1990. His funeral was in Knock Presbyterian, which he had regularly attended, and at his request donations in lieu of flowers were to go to the Simon Community, his favourite charity. In 1999 Sean McMahon wrote a biography of Sam Hanna Bell.

Sources: Bell 1972; Craig 1999; Craig 2006; McMahon 1999.

James Haire
1909–85

James Loughbridge Mitchell Haire was born in the Shankill area of Lurgan, County Armagh in 1909, the son of the Very Rev. Dr James Haire and his wife Charlotte Eleanor. His father, who also qualified as a medical doctor, was a Presbyterian minister and became the Chair of Systematic Theology at Assembly's College, and, as a result of the witch-hunt against liberals at the time within the church, a year before Ernest Davey's heresy trial, successfully submitted to an examination of his teaching by the College committee.

James jr (Jimmy) was born in 1909, educated at the Royal Belfast Academical Institution (1921–9), Worcester College, Oxford, New College, Edinburgh and Assembly's College Belfast. In 1935 he studied in Zurich, Switzerland over the summer and in 1936/7 studied in Basle, Switzerland under the famous theologian, Karl Barth.

He was ordained in 1940 and became assistant to Rev. Dr James Thompson of Great James Street, Londonderry. In 1940 he became minister of Maghera Church, County Londonderry. Four years later he succeeded his father as Professor of Systematic Theology at Assembly's College. David Lapsley, who was one of his students, described Haire as being popular with students, having 'great grace' and 'boundless energy'.

He went to the first Assembly of the British Council of Churches (BCC) when it was formed after the Second World War and represented the Church on the Council until 1957. He attended the initial Assembly of the World Council of Churches (WCC) in Amsterdam in 1948, the report of which was circulated to all churches seeking their support for the recommendations.

He again represented the Presbyterian Church at the WCC Faith and Order conference in Lund in Sweden in 1952, which agreed that the churches 'ought to act together in all matters except those in which deep differences of conviction compel them to act separately'. In 1954 he became the chairman of the BCC Faith and Order Department and was made vice-president in 1965.

In the 1960s Haire wrote a pamphlet *A United Church: Is it biblical?* as part of a series of ecumenical pamphlets published by the Irish Council of Churches, stating:

> Clearly separated Christians and separated Churches are called on by the Bible to aim at being one in Christ. They are called to make this unity as visible as possible, that men may see the power of God, reuniting people who by themselves tend to be deeply apart. True unity is thus something that has all the time to be striven for. The church is a pilgrim people on its way to perfect unity (Heb 13:14).

> Such unity may not be attained in this world, but all the time we
> have to seek for this unity – the unity which the spirit gives – and
> this unity for which we are to strive is clearly a visible unity.

Haire represented the Irish churches in the translation of New English
Bible, which was initiated in 1946 and not published until 1970. In 1968
he invited Michael Hurley SJ to give a lecture to Assembly's College
students on the Catholic doctrine of baptism, only to have to defend
himself at the following General Assembly. A motion of censure was
defeated.

He was elected moderator of the General Assembly in 1970, as his father
had been 31 years earlier. But by this time Vatican II had opened the way
for formal ecumenical dialogue between the main churches in Ireland,
which took place in Ballymascanlon, County Louth, between 1973 and
1978. The first conference in 1973 identified the key agenda items and
working groups were established to consider these issues. Haire was the co-
chair of the 'Church, Scripture and Authority' working group with
Archbishop Ryan, which reported to the meeting in 1975, outlining the
position of the churches on the key issues. They considered that the
meetings had 'not only helped towards a deeper understanding of our
positions, but have enabled us to become increasingly conscious of our
unity in Christ'.

In the 1977 Ballymascanlon meeting, Haire delivered a paper on *The
Theology of Christian Unity*, in which he described progress to date
recognising that a common faith had not yet been achieved, but they had
attained a sufficient common recognition of our common faith to enable us
to do certain things together, listen to each other, come together before
God in prayer and Bible study and work on practical problems such as
education, marriage and the political system in Northern Ireland. He also
outlined the six main areas of difference between the churches, including
the sacraments, the place of good works in salvation, the Virgin Mary,
marriage and papal infallibility.

His personal commitment to ecumenical dialogue included hosting
regular meetings of the '140 club', in his own house in 140 Malone Road
in south Belfast, which involved various Catholic clergy, including Des
Wilson, Denis Faul and Padraig Murphy. Haire was also a regular
contributor to Irish journals which were then beginning to discuss
ecumenical issues. In *The Furrow* in 1963, Haire praised Abbe Couturier
for initiating the Week of Prayer for Christian Unity which had been
adopted by most of the churches, including the Presbyterian.

In the debates on the Presbyterian Church's membership of the World
Council of Churches, Haire attempted to get the General Assembly to
withdraw its suspension of membership of the WCC but was unsuccessful.

Brian McConnell recounts a story about Haire, that one day he was walking along when he was stopped by a couple of scallywags who said 'Are you one of those modernisers'. Haire enquired as to what they meant by moderniser. 'One of them fellas as says we sprang from monkeys'.

Haire was a founding member of the Irish School of Ecumenics and regularly invited the Director of the School, Michael Hurley, to speak at Assembly's College. Bishop Cahal Daly (later Cardinal Daly) became a good friend of Haire's and he was regularly a visitor to the family home.

After retiring he taught comparative religions for the Open University, including in the prisons. He was elected moderator in 1970/1. He died in 1985, leaving five children. His son Rev. I. James M. Haire was a missionary in Indonesia from 1972 to 1984 and involved in the creation of the Uniting Church of Australia becoming its president in 2000/1 and now works in world development in Australia.

Sources: Baillie 1981; Patterson 1997.

William Thomson
1909–74

William George Millar Thomson was born in Glasgow in 1909 but moved to Larne where his family were members of First Larne Church. He was educated at Larne Grammar and then Queen's University Belfast where he gained a BA in 1930. He then went on to study for the ministry at Assembly's College. He was licensed by Carrickfergus Presbytery in 1933 and was assistant to the minister in Stormont in east Belfast. He was then ordained by Second Castlederg, County Tyrone in 1936, where he stayed for three years before becoming minister of First Ballymacarrett in 1939.

He was very involved in youth work with the Scouts, Boys Brigade and the Association of Boys Clubs. He was convenor of the Youth Committee of the Presbyterian Church and the government's Youth Committee. He had a very deep commitment to other social issues, including homelessness, mental health and learning disability and became convenor of the Board of Social Witness and chairman of the working committee on addiction.

He pioneered the work of the Samaritans in Northern Ireland, providing a crucial listening ear to those who were distressed or suicidal, and became full-time director in 1963.

Because of their commitment to social action and their similar names, Revs W.G.M. Thompson and W.J. Thompson (see profile) were nicknamed the 'Angel brothers'. He died in 1974 and was survived by his wife and son.

Sources: Barkley 1993; General Assembly Memorial Record 1974; Holmes 1985.

Bertie (W.R.) Rodgers
1909–69

William Robert Rodgers was born in east Belfast in 1909. His parents, Robert Skelly Rodgers and Jane Ferris (née McCarey) were strict Presbyterians. He was educated at Ballymacarrett Elementary School and Queen's University Belfast where he gained a BA degree in English. He then attended Assembly's College Belfast to train as a Presbyterian minister. He was ordained in 1935 and appointed minister of Cloveneden Church in Loughgall, County Armagh. In 1938, he began to write poetry. John Hewitt introduced him to the work of W.H. Auden, Dylan Thomas and others and he became a friend of Louis MacNeice. In 1941 he exploded on to the contemporary scene when his debut poetry collection, *Awake! and other poems* was published to critical and popular acclaim.

He had a good relationship with his congregation and his sermons were legendary, but his poetry increasingly demonstrated a move away from a narrow Calvinism to a more unorthodox life-affirming Christian ideology. Prior to the Second World War writers in Northern Ireland had made little attempt to describe the culture or character of Northern Ireland and its people. Rodgers, along with John Hewitt, Sam Hanna Bell and Louis MacNeice started to provide an alternative Protestant vision to the one portrayed by the government – one that recognised difference and dissention and one that recognised an all-Ireland perspective, as well as a distinctive Ulster one. In 1943, Rodgers published an article in the *New Statesman*, entitled, *Black North,* where he tried to describe some of the distinctive Ulster characteristics. In the article he also stated that 'the unionist government has not sought for better relations between Protestant and Catholic, but has … used ill relations in order to keep power'. Some of his congregation were less than pleased. Rodgers made it clear that there were two distinct groups in Northern Ireland, with a triple barrier between them:

> It is one of religion, of race, and of class, all coincide. It separates Catholic from Protestant, Gael from Scotch settler stock, poor from rich. It operates from birth to death … Men of one group go through life having as little to do as possible with men of the other group. Each segregates itself: In every Ulster town you will find a Catholic quarter, and always it is the poorer one.

In 1943 Rodgers took leave of absence and moved to Oxford to write and work for the BBC. In 1944 he returned to his congregation for a while, but in 1946, resigned and joined the Features Department of the BBC in London, having been recruited by Louis MacNeice. At the BBC he pioneered oral literary history. However, after publishing *Europa and the*

Bull and other poems, he wrote little poetry. In 1949 he and MacNeice were invited to compile a book on *The Character of Ireland,* but it was a project they never completed. In 1965, Rodgers wrote:

> Language is fundamental to society: words, spoken or written, are a unique means of communication. Because they can express concepts and ideas, and can precisely give us past, present and future tenses (as music, painting, sculpture cannot) they are the basis of social activity, the vehicle of our history.

He died of bowel cancer in 1969. Seamus Heaney read at his funeral in First Ballymacarrett Presbyterian Church. He was buried in Loughgall.

Sources: *Honest Ulsterman* no. 92, W.R. Rodgers Supplement; McIntosh 1999; *Oxford Dictionary of National Biography*; Stallworthy 1995.

John Barkley
1909–97

John Montieth Barkley was born in Belfast in October 1910, the son of Rev. Robert James Barkley and Mary Darcus (née Monteith). John Barkley says that he did not just grow up in Irish Presbyterianism, he 'was steeped in it, nursed and nurtured in it'. He spent his early childhood in Malin in Donegal where his father was minister. The family moved to Aughnacloy in 1917; Loanends, near Templepatrick in County Antrim in 1926; and finally Claremont in Derry, each time his father was installed in a new congregation. John was educated as a boarder at Campbell College and then Shaftsbury House School as a day-boy. He trained for the ministry at Magee College in Derry and then Assembly's College Belfast, where Ernest Davey was a professor. Barkley was disturbed by the attempt to have him convicted of heresy, which had taken place when Barkley was aged seventeen.

Barkley was licensed to preach in 1935 and was ordained the same year in Drumreagh, County Antrim. In 1939 he was called to Second Ballybay and Rockorry, County Monaghan. From 1947 on he became increasingly involved in a wide range of church committees, especially concerned with education and inter-church matters and represented the church at the World Presbyterian Alliance. This was a period of great personal growth, expanding his thinking.

In 1949 he was called to Cooke Centenary Church in Belfast. In 1951 he wrote a booklet on the basics of *Presbyterianism,* which he updated three times. In 1954 he was appointed Professor of Church History at Assembly's College. In 1976 he became Principal of the College.

In 1965 Barkley was actively involved in church unity discussions. When it was agreed to open talks with the Methodists and Congregationalists, Barkley expressed the hope that discussions would include the Non-Subscribing Presbytery of Antrim and Remonstrant Synod, which had been excluded from the General Synod. The response to this suggestion was described by Barkley as 'if looks could kill …'.

Barkley was a regular participant in the unofficial Glenstal and Greenhills ecumenical conferences which were the start of a serious dialogue between the churches, which laid an important foundation for the Ballymascanlon meetings in the 1970s. These initial dialogues produced what Barkley described as 'sincere, deep and meaningful relationships and understanding'.

At the 1973 Ballymascanlon ecumenical meeting Barkley delivered a paper on the contentious issues of *Baptism–Eucharist–Marriage*, in which he recognised the crucial difference made by Vatican II, which created the situation where everyone could recognise each other as fellow Christians. This had profound implications for inter-church relations and, in Barkley's opinion, should lead to 'the ending of all human estrangements in both Church and society based on differences of denomination, race or class'. A special working group was established on mixed marriages. In relation to these dialogues, Barkley felt that 'In the ecumenical movement the one essential thing is that every question is open for discussion and no church nor council of Churches has the right to veto a topic or problem'.

Writing in 1990, he said that 'it cannot be overemphasised that the people in the Churches must demand of their leaders that the Ballymascanlon Talks do not fail. It is equally essential that ecumenism speaks at the local level.' In 1979 he met the Pope during his visit to Ireland.

Barkley was strongly opposed to the Presbyterian Church's withdrawal from the World Council of Churches (WCC) over its Programme to Combat Racism, which was providing humanitarian aid to African liberation movements, and in 1980 moved an amendment to the withdrawal motion, seeking the ending of its suspension from the WCC, but the motion failed, and the Church withdrew. The Church also refused to join the new Council of Churches of Britain and Ireland.

Barkley retired in 1981, but continued to be active, preaching at Armagh St Patrick's Catholic Cathedral during the Week of Prayer for Christian Unity and at a conference organised by the SDLP on *Options for a New Ireland* and in 1988, having become a widower, married Carrie Barnett, a member of the Corrymeela Community, supporter of the Glenstal Conferences and Sunday school organiser.

In 1986 a small working party in which Barkley had been a key player produced an agreed ecumenical order of service for holy communion.

He died in 1997. Flann Campbell described Barkley as the 'philosophical heir to Armour of Ballymoney ... a thorn in the side of both church and state establishments over a period of fifty years' and Andrew Boyd, in his book on Cooke and Montgomery, described him as 'the last great Presbyterian liberal'.

Sources: Barkley 1993; Boyd 1999; Campbell 1991; Gallagher and Worral 1982; Holmes 2000.

Harold Binks
1911–86

Joseph Harold Binks was born in 1911 and having trained as an engineer, survived the crash of the British-built airship *R101* on 5 October 1930. He was very conscious of the poverty in Belfast during the 1930s, when large numbers of unemployed men drew unemployment benefit for six months and then transitional relief for a further six months, but after that 'as far as the state was concerned, he could live on grass'. He knew of many families with no carpet or lino, because they had been forced to sell them by the Poor Law guardians. He described one ingenious way of dealing with the problem of bad housing, low incomes and high rents,

> People organised themselves in cells, as they were called then. They used to come around and knock at the door, find out if people had paid their rent and how much. The rent book would be looked at and the woman be paid back because they had stopped the rent collector at the end of the street and relieved him of all the rent he had collected. The rent agent couldn't reclaim the money because it was marked paid in the rent book.

Working conditions in the 1930s were also very poor. He said in particular that 'the textile industry was an exploiting industry, 100%. The boss used to announce periodically that the first man to join a trade union would be immediately sacked. Very few were union organised'.

He became the Northern Ireland Secretary of the Clerical and Administrative Workers' Union and a member of the Northern Ireland Labour Party (NILP). At the 1942 NILP conference he demanded better pay for the armed forces.

At the 1945 Irish Trades Unions Congress (ITUC) he welcomed the formation of the Northern Ireland Committee of the ITUC, but thought it should be elected by the membership in the north, not appointed by the executive. He was appointed to the new Northern Ireland Committee. He also called for more housing at lower rents. At the Northern Ireland Committee conference in October 1948 he called on members of the movement not to accept government appointments unless they were nominated by the Northern Ireland Committee. He also complained about the attitude of the Unionist Minister for Labour, who did not want to see a united trade union/labour movement.

In 1948, along with Denis Ireland, Jack MacGougan and Victor Halley, he was a member of the Belfast Commemoration Committee, to commemorate the 1798 rising, based in Hawthorn Street off the Springfield Road in west Belfast. In 1949, at the Northern Ireland Committee meeting following the ITUC Congress, he announced his resignation from the Northern Ireland Labour Party and the Parliamentary Labour Party, however he seems to have remained a member.

In 1950 he was elected to the National Executive of the ITUC 1957 he was chair of the Irish Congress of Trades Unions and chaired their conference, at which he said in relation to, 'The task of organising our members to take political action to elect a government which shall represent our people … we are driven immediately to the conclusion that if the government will not act, we must act politically as well as industrially.'

He played an important role in uniting the trade union movement by merging the ITUC and CIU to become the Irish Congress of Trade Unions. He was awarded an MBE and retired in 1976. He died on 30 April 1986, aged 74.

Sources: Munck and Rolston 1987.

Donald Fraser
1911–93

Donald Fraser was born in Glasgow on 8 September 1911, the seventh child of Alexander and Jessie Fraser. He left school at the age of fourteen and worked on the railways. He eventually felt called to the ministry and, while continuing to work on the railways to support himself through university, eventually obtained an MA at Glasgow University and in 1938 was ordained at Balbeggie Free Church of Scotland in Perthshire and married Ellen Hart McAllister the following year, having three children over the following twelve years. In 1945 he accepted a call to Croftfoot congregation Glasgow.

In 1949 he moved to Ireland, having been appointed as Sabbath School Organiser of the Presbyterian Church in Ireland, working closely with Carrie Barnett (now Carrie Barkley) bringing new methods and approaches; training Sunday school teachers around the country and in the Belfast Bible College. He organised the World Conference of Sunday School leaders in Belfast in 1962.

In 1965 he was appointed the first Publications Officer of the

Presbyterian Church in Ireland, editing the *Presbyterian Herald* and dealing with the press during the increasingly turbulent environment in Northern Ireland as a result of the outbreak of violent civil conflict.

He was strongly committed to community relations and organised hundreds of cross-community summer holiday breaks for families from the Shankill Road and Markets areas of Belfast to Millport on the isle of Cumbrae. He was actively involved in the Churches Industrial Council, Churches Central Committee on Community Work, PACE (Protestant and Catholic Encounter) and Harmony Trust. Ahead of his time, he developed links with Protestant paramilitaries, particularly Andy Tyrie, as well as relationships with nationalists/republicans, as a result of which he was appointed to the Board of the Flax Trust in north Belfast.

From his working class upbringing in industrial Glasgow and his work on the railways, he had a strong interest in the trade union and labour movement and social, economic and political issues. He was a member of the Northern Ireland Labour Party, where he was involved with Billy (later Lord) Blease.

He was committed to a range of philanthropic causes, particularly in the field of disability, where he chaired a fundraising appeal for NICOD (now the Cedar Foundation). He was also on the national executive of the YMCA.

Throughout his life he continued to be proud of his Scottish roots and was actively involved in the St Andrew's and Burns' Societies.

He was awarded an honorary Doctorate in Divinity for his service to the church in 1976. He retired in 1981 and moved to Portstewart on the north Antrim coast. He died in hospital in Coleraine on 21 April 1993.

Sources: *Northern Constitution* 01 May 1993; entry in *Who's Who in Northern Ireland*; the address given at his funeral by Rev. Dr Jack Weir.

Jack Withers
1911–92

John Herbert Withers was born in Belfast in 1911, son of Robert Withers, a factory manager and Margaret (née Wilson). After obtaining a BA and BD he was licensed to preach by Belfast Presbytery in 1935 and ordained in St John's, Kenton in London in the following year. He was called to Portstewart and was installed there in 1940. Six years later he was called to Fisherwick in south Belfast, where he remained for the rest of his ministry.

In 1964, Withers, by then a well-known and respected preacher and broadcaster on radio and television, invited a Catholic priest, Hugh Murphy, to speak at his Sunday evening service. Unknown to Withers a neighbouring Methodist minister had decided to do the same. This was too much for Ian Paisley who organised protests against the Sunday evening talks. The Armagh Presbytery also unsuccessfully tried to get the Church to outlaw any religious meeting on church premises being addressed by a member of the Catholic Church.

When the Troubles broke out in October 1968, Withers was the Moderator of the General Assembly and said that, 'The first task was for the leaders of Church and State to call for calm, then fearlessly to analyse the causes of unrest and where justice was being denied to any section and driving it to despair.'

The next day he issued a joint statement with the other church leaders which reiterated the call for a 'period of calm to consider the implications of recent events and for prayers for the preservation of peace and goodwill.'

The following January, Withers announced that conversations were being sought with the Roman Catholic Church, 'Seeking to understand their dogmatic positions and equally to interpret to them our own Protestant evangelical theology'. The meeting took place at the end of the month which then established a standing joint consultative committee.

At the end of his tumultuous year as moderator, Withers reviewed the various church statements made during the year and emphasised Presbyterian support for just reforms and their willingness to acknowledge a share in the 'sins of apathy and discrimination'.

Withers retired in 1972 and died in 1992. Three volumes of his sermons were published during his lifetime.

Sources: Gallagher and Worral 1982; Patterson 1997.

John Boyd
1912–2002

John Boyd was born on 19 July 1912, the son of Robert Boyd a fireman on the railways and Jane (née Leeman). They lived in a kitchen house at 9 Baskin Street off Templemore Avenue in east Belfast and attended the local Presbyterian church, although later became members of the local Congregational church. When he was young the family moved to Bangor, County Down. His mother, however, did not like being away from her family, including her Orangeman father, and they soon returned to Ballymacarrett, moving into a parlour house at 46 Chatswoth Street. Aged five or six Boyd was sent to Ledley National School, which had a reputation for being rough, but his mother soon ensured that he was moved to Mountpottinger National School, beside the Presbyterian church.

His uncles William and Tom and his aunt Ida were all involved in the trade union and labour movement, and were socialist in outlook. Willie and Ida swapped houses with a Catholic family as a result of sectarian rioting in the area, which resulted in families in mixed areas feeling unsafe. Boyd learnt from his father about his mother's heavy drinking and the family moved to 9 Ranelagh Street in a quieter part of east Belfast.

Boyd won a scholarship to the Royal Belfast Academical Institution. It took him some time to feel that he fitted in. However, 'Inst' had some exceptional teachers and introduced John to new subjects. He was taught by the novelist Forrest Reid. Though Reid was from a very different background he and John shared a love of Irish literature. They struck up a friendship that lasted until Reid's death.

He loved languages and history but most of all he loved literature and the stage. He was fascinated by the theatre world. He was no actor, and just survived the teasing when he played Portia in a school play, with his rugby socks stuffed up his vest. He was even an extra in a play at the Opera House. He was taken to see Sybil Thorndike in *St Joan,* and the Abbey Players from Dublin perform O'Casey's *Juno and the Paycock*.

Boyd's uncle Willy and aunt Ida encouraged him to read the works of Marx, Engels and literature on the labour movement. Later in life Boyd was a delegate on a cultural exchange to the USSR with other writers, journalists and artists. The visit helped clarify his political ideas; he was a socialist but not a communist.

Boyd went on to Queen's University Belfast, gaining a BA and then an MA. Later he took an external degree at Trinity College Dublin, writing a thesis on Forrest Reid.

Following university, Boyd went into teaching. He married, found a modest house, and settled down to be a part-time writer; contributing anonymous articles to the *Irish Democrat*. After some years teaching in a primary school outside Lisburn, John was offered a post at Belfast Royal Academy grammar school. In subsequent years he also taught an Extra Mural class at Queen's University.

Sam Hanna Bell (see profile) persuaded him to edit a magazine called *The Lagan*. It only ran to four issues but it got him noticed and brought him into contact with new writers, including W.R. Rogers (see profile), Denis Johnson (see profile), John Hewitt, Michael McLaverty, Joseph Tomelty, Brian Friel, Louis McNiece and Tyrone Guthrie. Many of them became close friends.

In 1946, when Sam Hanna Bell was working at the BBC as a features writer and producer, he needed someone to organise a 'talks' section and he offered Boyd the job, which he accepted. However Boyd often felt constrained by the narrow parochialism of a purely Northern Ireland format and got into trouble for trying to break free of censorship and to liberalise the content of the talks. He went to work at BBC London for a short time, but chose to return to Belfast. In 1969 his play, *The Assassin*, was performed at the Gaiety Theatre, Dublin. It dealt with the struggle between the establishment and the younger generation in modern (1969) society. The Assassin is a young philosophy and politics student from a Belfast Catholic ghetto, who kills Rev. Colonel Luther A. Lamb (The Victim); a Bible salesman and head of his own Evangelical Party (with its army of thugs), which has just been successful at the elections. The martyrdom of Lamb sparks off a new round of trouble in Belfast.

Boyd eventually left the BBC in 1972 to concentrate on his writing and wrote a number of plays which were performed at the Lyric Theatre, including his most famous play *The Flats* (1971), which was the first play to deal with sectarian conflict since the start of the most recent period of violent civil conflict in Northern Ireland; *The Farm* (1972), dealing with disputes over the future of the family farm; *Guests* (1974), where the violence in Belfast intrudes dramatically on the lives of guests who have gathered on the anniversary of a widow's husband; *The Street* (1976), which is autobiographical, based on the street Boyd had been brought up in, and starred Liam Neeson; and *Facing North* (1978), in which a farm and factory owner's son's American girlfriend is abducted from the farm, but is released when she convinces her kidnappers that she is Catholic. The farm owner's home, Cromwell House, is under a compulsory purchase order to make way for a Catholic housing estate, and there is trouble at the factory when a worker hangs up a Union flag.

Other plays included a study of Oscar Wilde as *Speranza's Boy*, an adaptation of *Wuthering Heights*, and a joint translation of Ibsen's *Ghosts* made with Louis Muinzer; *The Flats* was filmed for RTÉ by Sheelah Richards in 1975. In 1992 the Lyric put on *Round the Big Clock*, a biography of the city of Belfast, centred around the Albert Clock, one of its famous landmarks. Characters from history appear as the shipbuilders, spinners, soldiers and sailors go about their daily business, until the clock stops in 1939.

Boyd edited the Lyric's magazine, *The Threshold* and later became Honorary Artistic Director at the theatre. In his later years, Boyd wrote two autobiographical books entitled *Out of My Class* and *The Middle of My Journey*. He died in 2002. A commemorative gathering was held at the Lyric Theatre, 23 February 2003.

Sources: Boyd 1985; Boyd 1990; Odling-Smee 2003.

Jack MacGougan (also spelled Magougan and McGougan)
1913–98

Jack MacGougan was born in Bloomfield Avenue in east Belfast in 1913, the son of John McGougan a pattern-maker and Mary (née Wilson). He was an accountant by profession and became a member of the CAWA trade union for clerical workers and then Irish Organiser of the National Union of Tailors & Garment Workers, eventually becoming general secretary. He was also actively involved in the TUC, becoming elected to the TUC General Council.

In the 1930s he became interested in politics and would go along to the public meetings at the Custom House steps on Sundays and listen to the speakers from the Independent Labour Party. In 1935 he was elected secretary of the Socialist Party of Northern Ireland, which was an integral part of the Northern Ireland Labour Party, formed by the local branches of the Independent Labour Party when it disaffiliated from the British Labour Party. The Socialist Party provided individual membership whereas the Northern Ireland Labour Party (NILP) was mainly trade union affiliates. He joined the editorial committee of the party's newspaper, the *Irish Democrat*. He also joined the Spanish Medical Aid Relief Fund, which financed a Scottish ambulance crew in Spain, which had two Northern Irish members, one Protestant and one Catholic.

MacGougan stood unsuccessfully for the secretaryship of the NILP in 1937, having been nominated by the Socialist Party (NI). Albert McElroy (see profile) became the secretary. In the surprise general election of 1938 MacGougan stood in the Belfast Old Park constituency for the Northern Ireland Labour Party (NILP). With his strong anti-partitionist stance he polled strongly amongst the Catholic voters, in the absence of a nationalist candidate.

In 1942 MacGougan became the vice-chairman of the NILP and two years later was elected chairman. The party pressed for one-man-one-vote in local elections and did well in the local elections of September 1946. He was involved in discussions with nationalists in the Anti-Partition League to avoid a split in the non-unionist vote, but these were unsuccessful. In 1949 he communicated the NILP's support for some sort of Unity Council or central co-ordinating authority of overall nationalist opinion.

In 1948 after having stood down as chairman of the NILP, he became the secretary. He was a member of the 1798 Belfast Commemoration Committee. The *Irish News* reports him as saying at a commemoration rally that, 'Wolfe Tone was the advocate of the new social forces that arose in all parts of the world during that period. And when they paid tribute to the United Irishmen let them remember that they had the closest fraternal links with the democratic forces in other countries.'

The rally was followed by an emotional parade up Cavehill to McArt's Fort and pledged themselves to the United Irishmen's' ideals of: Liberty, Equality, and Fraternity and the uniting of Catholic, Protestant and Dissenter. Several days later the Commemoration Committee planned to hold a commemoration ceilidh in the Ulster Hall, which was then banned by Unionist controlled Belfast Corporation. The Commemoration

Committee successfully challenged this decision in the courts on the grounds that it was discriminatory and the event went ahead.

In 1949 MacGougan left the NILP. He stood as an Irish Labour candidate for South Down in the UK general election of 1950. The Anti-Partition League decided not to oppose him, although they were, at best, lukewarm in their support. The Catholic clergy portrayed him as a communist. He gained 22,176 votes against 38,508 for the only other candidate, Unionist Captain Lawrence Orr.

In 1953 he stood for Irish Labour in the Belfast Falls constituency against two other anti-partition candidates and lost, polling only 1,361 votes. He became leader of the Irish Labour group on Belfast City Council, complaining about the lack of working class representation on the council. In 1956 he engaged in a public debate on *Labour and the Partition of Ireland*, with David Bleakley of the NILP in which MacGougan challenged the logic of partition and the failure of the NILP to effectively challenge discrimination. In 1959 he helped facilitate the merger of CIU and ICTU.

Paddy Devlin described MacGougan as his mentor in both the union movement and politics. MacGougan acted as his election agent when Devlin first stood successfully as an Irish Labour candidate for the Falls ward in a by-election for Belfast City Council. MacGougan retired to Milton Keynes, England and died on 14 December 1998.

Sources: Boyd 1999; Collins 2004; Cradden 1993; Devlin 1994; International Women's Day: Solidarity with Spain, 1936–9; MacGougan 1989; Staunton 2001; Walker 1985.

Ruby Purdy
1914– 2009

Ruby Matilda Eileen Heatherington was born on 20 September 1914, the daughter of George Heatherington. She was educated at Belmont School, close to home in east Belfast. When she was sixteen she started going out with William David Purdy, a motor mechanic, who was eight years older than her. He looked after the cars and vans in Maypole Dairy Company and then on the machines of Belfast Co-operative Dairy. David Purdy and Ruby's brother were both members of the Independent Labour Party in Belfast, which met in the old Labour Hall in York Street. Ruby would often attend public meetings at the Hall with her father and eldest brother.

Ruby's eldest brother went to hear the Rev. A.L. Agnew (see profile) preach on the theme of 'Christ or Nicholson', against a famous evangelical preacher, who Agnew had challenged to a debate. Her brother was so enthusiastic about Agnew that he persuaded his parents to attend York Street Church, instead of St Mark's Church of Ireland. Ruby attended morning and evening services in York Street, as well as the Sunday fellowship where a wide range of people were invited to speak resulted in some vigorous debates. The drama group in York Street would read the plays of Thomas Carnduff (see profile) who was also a member of the church before they would be put on at a theatre in Belfast. She would take part in church social activities, political debates and mock parliaments held in the church hall. In the 1930s she was involved in looking after anti-fascist refugees from the Spanish Civil War.

They were married by the Rev. Agnew in York Street Non-Subscribing Presbyterian Church on 21 October 1935 and moved into a shared house. In 1936 they moved into a new rented house in Torrens Avenue in north Belfast, until it was destroyed in the blitz and they were evacuated to Tullynore, Hillsborough in a house shared between nineteen people, including eight children. After the war they moved to the Holywood Road in east Belfast and as members of the Northern Ireland Labour Party, attended Labour Party meetings in Townsley Street and read the Labour paper, the *Daily Herald*. The Purdy's became friends of David Bleakley and his wife Winnie and actively canvassed for him as a candidate for the Northern Ireland Labour Party in Victoria Ward Belfast.

David Purdy organised fundraising events to raise money for a building fund to replace the rented Labour Hall in Townsley Street in east Belfast. He did not live to see the hall replaced. He died on 20 November 1965 and a week later David Bleakley lost his seat in Stormont. A community centre on the Holywood Road was named after him. Ruby Purdy moved to Orby Drive in east Belfast to live with a nephew and then into a flat in Kilbroney House on the Cregagh Road. The Bleakley's children lived with her for 4 or 5 months while their parents were working in Tanzania. She became an active member of the East Belfast Historical Society, contributing her reminiscences to a book on Belfast in the old days.

Ruby Purdy erected a plaque in All Souls Church, Elmwood Avenue, Belfast dedicated to her husband. She died on 29 September 2009 and her name was added to the plaque and her ashes scattered in the Memorial Garden beside the church where she had been a member of the Committee and Session, the Stipend Clerk and tireless organiser of church activities for many decades.

Sources: McFadden 1999; Steers 2009.

Brian McConnell
1914–2005

George Brian Greer McConnell was born in Armagh in 1914, the son of Rev. W.J. McConnell, who had been wounded during the First World War and was then minister of Markethill Presbyterian Church. He was initially educated by a private tutor, Elsie Edwards, and then at Mourne Grange. When his father was called to Stormont Church, the young McConnell moved to Campbell College, which had a strong Officer Cadet Force, which he described to his disapproving father as a 'war machine'. He gained a scholarship to Queen's University where he was awarded an honours degree in Philosophy. He then unusually decided that he would study theology, not in Scotland, but in Westminster College, Cambridge, which he enjoyed thoroughly and became interested in pacifism, joining the Peace Pledge Union. It was something of a disappointment to have to spend the third year of his theological studies in Assembly's College Belfast, although he found Ernest Davey to be particularly remarkable.

He was licensed to preach by Belfast Presbytery in 1939 and became assistant minister in Ekenhead, North Circular Road, Belfast. When the Second World War broke out in 1939 he preached against the war, which caused considerable controversy. He also continued to sell copies of *Peace News* in Royal Avenue. He then went to be an assistant minister in Abbey Church in Dublin. He was ordained in 1942 in Bray, County Wicklow, where he became assistant to Rev. Bob Crossett. He signed the Westminster Confession of Faith as required, despite his serious doubts about it and a continuing sense of disappointment that the Presbyterian Church in Ireland never followed the example of its sister churches which had developed new confessions.

During the War his brother was killed in the RAF. In 1945 McConnell was called to Donore in Dublin, where he remained for the rest of his ministry. In the same year he married Molly. His duties in Abbey included being Presbyterian chaplain to the South Dublin Union, which eventually became St James' Hospital; Mountjoy Prison; and Trinity College Dublin, as well as Catechist in St Andrew's School.

In 1952 McConnell was one of the leading organisers of *The Haven*, a home for elderly refugees in Dublin, initiated by the Irish Council of Churches. He was a founder of Koinonia house for overseas students in Harcourt Street. He was a founding member of the London-based board of what was then renamed as Christian Aid in 1958 and served until 1981. He remained a pacifist who was actively committed to the work of the Fellowship of Reconciliation

In the 1950s and 60s he was co-convenor of the Presbyterian Church's Committee on the Causes of War which eventually became the Committee on National and International Problems, with Ernest Davey as the, then, convenor. Following the war, one of the committee's reports was criticised for 'extra-ordinary tenderness towards Germany'. McConnell defended the report, talking movingly about the death of his brother, his father's role as a chaplain in the First World War and Christ's teachings on love of our enemies. In 1965 the committee asked the General Assembly to pass a motion seeking penitence for past uncharitableness towards Roman Catholics. It then produced a crucial report in 1966 on *Discrimination*, which acknowledged the problem of discrimination in Northern Ireland. The report led to the General Assembly, at which it was being discussed, being picketed by Ian Paisley.

He was a 'keen advocate of church unity and ecumenism' and contributed to many of the Glenstall ecumenical conferences. He became concerned that in more recent years the General Assembly had become 'increasingly anti-ecumenical … more like a narrow and frightened body hiding behind sectarian walls'.

After the UWC strike had brought down the Sunningdale Power-sharing government, McConnell (and Rev. Gordon Gray) proposed an amendment to a main resolution at the General Assembly. His amendment stated 'it is essential that there should be a sharing of responsibility and power between different sections of the community and that intimidation of every kind be utterly condemned'. The amendment was defeated by a slim majority. A revised watered-down amendment that 'co-operation between and acceptance of responsibility by different sections of the community who are prepared to act for the community's good and that intimidation of every kind be utterly condemned' was passed.

Under his leadership the Committee on National and International Problems produced reports on sexual ethics, which dealt with the issue of contraception and abortion. He was also courageous at challenging attitudes in the south towards Protestants and Unionists.

He retired in 1980, although he continued to act as supply minister in Lucan. Moving to Warrenpoint he joined the South Down Ecumenical Study Group. He also joined the Alliance Party. He wrote his autobiography, *Memoir of an unrepentant liberal*. He died in 2005.

Sources: Gallagher and Worral 1982; McConnell 2001.

Albert McElroy
1915–75

Albert Horatio McElroy was born in Glasgow on 14 February 1915, one of three boys of a traditional Presbyterian family that had emigrated from Ulster. He was educated in Jordanhill College in Glasgow, until his father took up a job as sub-postmaster in Toomebridge, County Antrim, when he transferred to Rainey Endowed School in Magherafelt. In 1933 he went to Trinity College Dublin to study French and English, where, together with Conor Cruise O'Brien, he set up the college Fabian Society and developed an interest in the ideals of the United Irishmen. He was secretary of the Northern Ireland Labour Party in 1937/8. He was also won over to non-subscribing Presbyterianism by Rev. Ernest Hicks.

During the war McElroy worked as a teacher and translator for the British Army and met Belfast school-teacher, Jan McDougal, whom he married in 1943. After the war he taught in Ballymoney Technical College and in 1945 stood, unsuccessfully, for the Northern Ireland Labour Party in Ards. Continuing to be inspired by the belief that those who 'led Ireland in 1798 ... derived their moral strength and integrity of character from their Presbyterian religion', he made the decision to go to Manchester College, Oxford to study theology.

Having achieved his Divinity degree, McElroy was ordained as a non-subscribing Presbyterian minister, and installed in a small congregation in Newtownards, County Down. He stood again unsuccessfully for the Northern Ireland Labour Party in the election in North Down in 1950 and 1951, being defeated by the Unionist candidate, Lieutenant-Colonel Sir Walter Dorling Smiles. He then became a founder and first chairman of the Ulster Liberal Association. During the following decades the Liberals built a solid base of support in Northern Ireland, getting Sheelagh Murnaghan elected, representing the party for Queen's University at Stormont. McElroy was heavily defeated in the 1964 general election, coming third place to the Unionist and Northern Ireland Labour Party candidates. He was defeated by Unionists Captain Bill Long in Ards in 1962 and Harry West in Enniskillen in 1965. He was nearly elected for the second Queen's University seat in 1966 (having failed to gain one of the four seats in 1958).

The start of the troubles quickly unravelled the support the Liberals had built up and its vote collapsed in the 1970 Westminster election and had no-one elected to the power-sharing Assembly, although he was a strong supporter of its establishment and effective co-operation with the Republic of Ireland. McElroy died of a heart attack at home in Newtownards on 13 March 1975.

Sources: Byrne and McMahon 1991; Walker 1992.

Donald Kennedy
1915–2000

Donald Moses Kennedy was born in Dublin in 1915. In 1937 he was awarded a first class honours degree in Modern History at Trinity College Dublin, where his father had been a fellow. He then studied theology in New College, Edinburgh, Strasburg and Assembly's College Belfast. He was licensed to preach by Dublin Presbytery in 1940 and became both the Presbyterian chaplain at Trinity College and Irish Secretary of the Student Christian Movement from 1940–42.

He had decided to go overseas as a missionary, although the war made the negotiations for this difficult. He served for a while with the YMCA in North Africa and was eventually ordained in 1942 to become a missionary to India. In 1944, he initially went to Gujarat and then, after two years, to be professor of history at Wilson College in Bombay, where he remained for 38 years. As one of the six members of the United Church of North India (initially containing the Presbyterians and the Congregationalists) negotiating team, he was a key figure in the discussions to create a united Christian church in India.

In the 1959 General Assembly debate on the merger in North India, over 100 members voted against the merger and in favour of an amendment which contained an implicit threat of financial sanctions if the merger went ahead. Kennedy was appalled by the attitudes of many in the mother church in Ireland who opposed the merger. He wrote a reply to one of the opponents in 1960 trying to explain the 'bitterness and hurt feelings' which the opponents had caused during the previous year's debate in the General Assembly. His letter concluded that 'We should put the needs of India, and of Christ's cause in India, first, giving only second place to the urge to use this opportunity to knock spots off Episcopalians or others in our homeland'.

In 1874 Kennedy eventually became the only non-Indian to be made a bishop in the Church of North India, a strong indication of the enormous respect in which he was held in India. He encouraged improved understanding between Christians and Hindus in India.

He retired in 1982 and became the editor of the *Irish Ecumenical News* for the Irish School of Ecumenics. He died in October 2000 and was survived by his wife Isobel (née Moses).

Sources: Ellis 1992; Memorial Record from the General Assembly 2001; Patterson 1997; Thompson 1990.

Ray Davey
1915–2012

Robert Raymond Davey was born in Dunmurry, on the outskirts of Belfast, during the First World War in 1915. His father, Robert Davey, was also a Presbyterian minister. He was educated at the Royal Belfast Academical Institution, where he demonstrated a particular skill at rugby and athletics. He went on to Queen's University Belfast where he became involved in the progressive Student Christian Movement, and then to Assembly's College Belfast to study theology, and served as an Assistant Minister in First Bangor. When the Second World War broke out Davey decided to join the YMCA and was sent as a field officer to North Africa, not to see Ireland again for five years. His experience of the creation of a makeshift form of a

Christian Community in the YMCA centre in Tobruk made a major impression on him as a young man just out of college. He was taken prisoner of war and was held in Italy and Germany, where he acted as chaplain. After the war he published a memoir of being a POW, *Don't fence me in* and, after he retired, published his *War Diaries*. His experience of being a prisoner of war and witnessing the saturation bombing of Dresden had a major impact on him and his developing thinking on peace and war.

After the war ended, he worked for seven months as assistant minister to Rev. David Dowling in McCracken Memorial in south Belfast, where he introduced various initiatives, especially in relation to the young people of the congregation. In 1946 he married Kathleen Burrows, whose father had come to Northern Ireland to fill the vacancy left by Rev. James Hunter's resignation from Dundela Presbyterian Church, Knock, Belfast after the acquittal of Ernest Davey, whom Hunter had accused of heresy.

Davey became the first full-time Presbyterian chaplain at the expanding Queen's University in a rapidly changing post-war world, and quickly established a sense of a supportive, but outward looking, Christian Community, rather than a traditional chaplaincy within the university. By 1962 a purpose-built Presbyterian centre, with some residential facilities was established, close to the university, which became the focus of new thinking about the future of Northern Ireland and the implications of the Christian Faith in the world.

In 1951, and again in subsequent years, Davey returned to Germany with a group of students to experience the impact that the war had on the German people.

Inspired by other Christian Communities, including Iona in Scotland, Taize in France and Agape in Italy, which he had visited with a group of Queen's students during his period as chaplain, Davey founded the Corrymeela Community in 1965 dedicated to reconciliation and 'healing the divisions in our broken society' (four years before the most recent outbreak of civic conflict and violence in Northern Ireland in 1969), with the words, 'We hope that Corrymeela will come to be known as the Open Village, open to all people of good will, who will meet each other, learn from each other and work together for the good of all.'

Starting as a Presbyterian initiative, the Corrymeela Community quickly broadened its base to include people from a wide range of Christian traditions. With the purchase and renovation of the residential centre at Ballycastle, through the help of a large number of enthusiastic volunteers, Corrymeela very soon came to public attention. The organisers of a cross-community conference, 'Community 1966', invited the Prime Minister of Northern Ireland, Terence O'Neill to be its main speaker. He asked the people of Northern Ireland to 'shed the burden of traditional grievances and ancient resentments', to 'work in a Christian spirit to create better opportunities for our children'.

The work of Davey and of Corrymeela took on a new impetus with the outbreak of violence in 1969 and developed an international reputation as a beacon of light in the otherwise dark and negative image of Irish Christianity at war with itself. The work of Corrymeela is well documented elsewhere, including in Davey's own writings, but he always had an ability to gather round him a group of enthusiastic young and not-so-young people who from their involvement in Corrymeela have themselves become involved in a huge range of peace-building, community development, youth work and other work to build a more just, inclusive and peaceful Northern Ireland.

In 1980, after the end of the first Republican hunger strike, which had a deeply polarising effect on Northern Ireland, Davey made history by speaking at Armagh Cathedral, at the invitation of Cardinal O'Fiaich.

Davey stood down as leader of Corrymeela in 1980, to be succeeded by the Rev. John Morrow (see profile), also of Ulster-Scottish Presbyterian stock, with Davey remaining actively involved as founder. He wrote several books including: *Take away this Hate* (Corrymeela Press 1985); *The Pollen of Peace* (Corrymeela Press, 1991); *A Channel of Peace: Story of the Corrymeela Community* (with John Cole, Zondervan, 1993).

He continued to provide inspiration to generations of young people and adults from all backgrounds to work for reconciliation, with his distinctively modest and unassuming leadership style that allowed others to identify and develop their own leadership qualities. This is attested to by the number of individuals interviewed for this book who referred to the inspiration of Ray Davey. He died after a long period of illness on 16 April 2012.

Sources: interview with Ray Davey; Davey 1985, 1991, 1993 and 2005.

Jim Boyd
1916–94

James Rowland Boyd was born in Islandbane, Killinchy, County Down in 1916, the son of a farmer, J.R. Boyd. He was educated at the Royal Belfast Academical Institution and Queen's University Belfast. From 1944 to 1949 he was Belfast secretary of the Student Christian Movement (SCM), which played a significant role in spreading new ideas about faith, politics and society after the upheaval of the Second World War which swept away many of the certainties of the pre-war world. He was then SCM schools secretary from 1944 to 1949.

He was licensed by Comber Presbytery in 1942 and in 1948 he was ordained and installed as assistant and successor to T.A.B. Smyth, minister of Great Victoria Street Church. In 1952 he attended the World Council of Churches 1952 Conference on Faith and Order at Lund, Sweden, which recommended that churches 'ought to act together in all matters except those in which deep differences of conviction compel them to act separately'. From 1953 he became the convenor of the Inter-Church Relations Committee.

In 1959, against much opposition, Boyd and Austin Fulton submitted a crucial positive resolution in support of the right of the Presbyterian Church in India to create a union with other Christian churches. In 1953 he became joint convenor of the Inter-Church Relations Committee, with Ernest Davey, and was actively involved in this role in the discussions to create a united Christian church in North India. In 1954 he attended the second World Council of Churches Committee in Evanston, Canada, sitting on the WCC Central Committee for the following seven years. He was also the Presbyterian representative on the British Council of Churches (BCC) from 1957 to 1962. In 1963 he was appointed the first Professor of Practical Theology at Assembly's College Belfast, where he helped students to think about such issues as caring for the mentally ill and about working conditions in industry.

In the very early days of the troubles, Boyd and other clergy met with Brian Faulkner, who was then a member of O'Neill's cabinet. Boyd urged Faulkner to end ratepayer franchise in local elections and concede the demands of the contemporary civil rights campaign, encapsulated in the slogan, 'One man – one vote'. He died in May 1994.

Sources: Gallagher and Worral 1982; Patterson 1997.

Jack Weir
1919–2000

Andrew John Weir was born in Manchuria in 1919, son of Presbyterian missionary Rev. Andrew Weir, who had been in Changchun, Manchuria since 1899 and Margaret (née Gillis), a missionary in Changchun for 12 years, whom Andrew Weir married after his first wife, Dr Eva (née Simms) died after only three and a half years of marriage.

In 1924 the family returned to Ireland for a visit and on their return to Manchuria, Jack went to school in the China Inland Mission School at Chefoo. In 1931 the family again returned to Ireland on a visit and Jack went to Cabin Hill Preparatory School and then Campbell College in Belfast, where he remained after his parents returned to China.

He went on to Queen's University where he graduated with a degree in Experimental Physics, followed by an MSC. He then studied theology in

New College, Edinburgh and completed his training for the ministry in Assembly's College. In his student days between the wars he became a member of the Peace Pledge Union. It is believed that the YMCA turned him down for service with them during the war because of his record as a pacifist.

After being ordained he worked as a missionary in China from 1944 to 1951. He initially worked for a year in 'Free China' engaging in the Student Christian Centre and relief work in the refugee National Northeastern University, then at Santai, Szechwan, before returning to Shenyang. By 1951 missionary work in China had become increasingly difficult for Westerners following the Moaist revolution of 1949 and he returned to Ireland and became minister of Trinity congregation, Letterkenny. In 1962 he was then appointed assistant clerk of the General Assembly and in 1964 the Secretary and Clerk to the General Assembly. He was involved in the ultimately unsuccessful discussions to bring about unity between the Protestant denominations in Ireland. In 1971 he was joint author of a working paper on *Bishop and Elder in a United Church*, which was circulated in each of the main Protestant denominations. In 1973 he presented a report summarising these efforts since 1920.

When concern arose about the World Council of Churches (WCC) Programme to Combat Racism, which was providing humanitarian support to various African liberation movements, Weir went to Canada with Methodist Eric Gallagher to discuss the programme with its chairman, Archbishop Scott. This and other discussions were ultimately unsuccessful in persuading the majority of Presbyterians that the Church should remain in the WCC.

In 1974, Weir was one of a courageous group of churchmen who arranged a meeting with the leaders of the IRA in Smyth's Hotel in Feakle, County Clare. For two and a half hours the church leaders tried to persuade the IRA to give up their campaign of violence. Weir made a strong humanitarian argument and highlighted the fact that the campaign would not achieve its objectives. The meeting was brought to an end on the receipt of information that the Irish Special Branch were on their way to arrest the IRA men at the meeting. The IRA promised to think about and respond to a draft paper the church leaders gave them. The IRA ultimately rejected the proposals but agreed a ceasefire over Christmas and the talks led to the government engaging in their own secret talks with the IRA. At Christmas church leaders launched a peace campaign with Weir as a key organiser, which involved full-page advertisements, broadcasts, car stickers and rallies, on the theme of 'Think, pray and talk peace'.

In 1979, when Pope John Paul II visited Ireland, the Catholic Church was keen to have an ecumenical dimension to the visit, but the then moderator was opposed to ecumenical activities and was unwilling to meet

Cardinal O'Fiaich let alone the Pope. It was Jack Weir who led a small delegation from the Church to meet the Pope in Drumcondra, just outside Dublin. Weir received a positive response to documents that he had given to the Pope through the Nuncio, and received a personally signed message from the Pope. Despite some criticism from within the Protestant churches, this meeting helped to kick-start the stalled Ballymascanlon dialogue.

He retired in 1985. In 1990 he and Cardinal Cahal Daly were awarded honorary degrees by Queen's University. In 1992 Weir was again involved in talks with various paramilitary groups and political parties, including Gerry Adams, in order to help bring about an end to violence. He developed Parkinson's disease, but against medical advice decided on one final visit to China which he undertook in 1996. He died in 2000.

Sources: Gallagher and Worral 1982; Patterson1997; notes of a lecture by Rev. Ivor Smith to the Presbyterian Historical Society 21 October 1999; Thompson 1990.

Robert Greacen
1920–2008

Robert Greacen was born in Derry on 24 October 1920 and his experiences as a young boy there informed much of his later poetry and prose. In *The Sash my father Wore* he said,

> The name of the city I was born in is disputed. At the time of my birth it was called Londonderry. Now the majority of its people call it Derry. If people in Ireland ask me where I was born I can, if wishing to be politic, say 'The Maiden City' or use the more recent coinage, 'Stroke City'.

> As a boy, from my aunts and mother I heard many a story of suffering endured by the defiant Protestant citizenry ... Derry for them – they said 'Derry' in conversation but used 'Londonderry' officially – meant Protestant Derry. History meant Protestant history.

In his poem, *Derry*, he reflected on the sectarian conflict in Northern Ireland in the 1970s, after he had moved away,

> As a child in Derry I heard the shots/And the cackle of burning timber/That signalled the ancient quarrel/Of Prod and Papist, that ritual feud/Lingering on in a lost province/Where memories of long-ago battles/Are as fresh as today's headline.

> Memories of Siege and horror, of Lundy,/The Apprentice Boys and the Boom/And God-knows what fag-ends of history/Making a

stirring tale for children/But light the fuse in the bitter heart./Tales of blood and sectarian thunder/Lead to a coarse and brutal logic/Where my side is whiter than white/And yours black as a crow's wing./Once more the thick urgent cries,/The pool of blood in the doorway, /The searing blaze of hate.

Yet I who have gone away/To safe and easy exile/Cannot just write them off/As simply ignorant thugs./I, too, am involved in their crimes.

His family moved to Belfast, where his father ran a local newsagent's on the Newtownards Road in east Belfast. He went to school in Methodist College Belfast, where he first discovered a gift for writing. He then went to Queen's University Belfast, where he developed his interest in left-wing politics and political poetry and co-edited a literary journal, *The Northman*, but never completed his arts degree. He then studied Social Studies at Trinity College Dublin, where he contributed to the literary journal *The Bell*. He married Patricia Hutchins, who shared his love of literature and they had a daughter.

In 1943 he published his first collection of poetry, *One Recent Evening*, which sold well. When his second collection, *The Undying Day* did less well he decided to try his luck in London, doing some freelance work and contributing poetry to literary journals.

As a poet, memoirist and a literary scholar, Greacen earned critical success and saw his work published in Ireland, England, Scotland, France and the United States. His *Collected Poems* won the *Irish Times* Poetry Prize in 1995. His other published poetry volumes include *The Bird* (1941), *A Garland for Captain Fox* (Dublin, The Gallery Press, 1975), *Young Mr Gibbon* (1979), *A Bright Mask* (Dublin, The Dedalus Press, 1985) and *Carnival at the River* (Dublin; Dedalus, 1991). His last book *Robert Greacen: New and Selected Poems* was published by Salmon Poetry in 2006.

He and his wife divorced in 1966, which resulted in seventeen years during which he wrote no poetry and in 1969 he published *Even Without Irene*, an autobiographical memoir. After counseling and other therapy he recovered to continue his poetry, creating the character of Captain Fox, as well as writing prose. For a while he taught English as a foreign language in London, before returning to Dublin to live. His work *Brief Encounters* (1991) is a memoir of literary life in London and in Dublin. He also authored critical work on the novelist C.P. Snow and the playwright Noel Coward, through the efforts of Muriel Spark.

He opposed nuclear weapons and was a member of CND. In the 1970s he joined the Peace People, started by Mairead Corrigan and Betty Williams.

In the poem *Church and Covenant*, from his collection, *Carnival at the River* he reflected on religion:

> The kitschy statues bleed./This theatre of God/Acts out a Latin poetry/A heretic can't translate./I think of pitch pine pews/A northern childhood knew./I wrestled with John Knox/Who ghostly in the aisles/Whispered 'thou shalt not'./

> I think of ancestors who lived/For Kirk and Covenant./They feared the anti-Christ,/The Roman man of sin,/Scorned English mitres too./Aware of thumbscrew rack,/They chose a martyr's stance./I lack their bigot pride, their certainty of Truth./I chose a slacker way,/An anxious tolerance.

Robert Greacan died on 15 April 2008.

Sources: Greacen 2006; Weaver 2006.

Bill Rutherford
1921–2007

William Harford Rutherford was born in Warrenpoint manse in 1921, the second of the four children of Rev. James Rutherford (see profile) and his mother Bertha. He was educated in the preparatory department of Kingstown Grammar in Dun Loaghaire, near Dublin, where his father had been installed in 1927 and then as a boarder to Campbell College, Belfast.

Academic success at school led, in 1941, to studying medicine at Trinity College Dublin, where he became involved in the Student Christian Movement (SCM) and moved into rooms with Rev. Donald Kennedy (see profile), who was chaplain to the Presbyterian students at Trinity. In 1942 he met his future wife, Ethne, a languages student at Queen's University Belfast, at an SCM conference in Friends' School Lisburn, County Antrim. In 1944 he did his houseman's year in Belfast City Hospital in order to be near Ethne. After he and Ethne were married, they felt called to go and work in the Foreign Missions in India and he was advised of the need to develop skills as a surgeon if he was to work as a doctor in India, so the Presbyterian Church paid him to study surgery in Edinburgh for a year.

In 1947, the year India became independent from Britain, he and Ethne went to India with the Presbyterian Church and learned Gujarati. He worked in Limadawala Hospital and remained in Anand for twenty years, where he made many Hindu and Jain friends, which convinced him that they were also showing the fruits of the spirit, although they were not Christian. This encouraged him to organise two 2-day inter-faith conferences, at the Broach Spiritual Life Centre, based in a former hospital, run by Hazel McClenaghan, where a series Christian and Hindu speakers, including Kaka Kalelkar, a close colleague of Ghandi, gave talks on key issues, followed by a first response from someone of the other religion and then opened for discussion.

He met many colleagues and followers of Mahatma Ghandi, who was murdered just 10 months after he and Ethne had arrived in India. He was deeply inspired by Ghandi's commitment to those who were considered to be of the lowest caste, whom he called Harijans, or People of God. He would go out of his way to meet and talk with those who had been friends and colleagues of Ghandi, like Kaka Kalelkar, who had also been a friend of Rabindranath Tagore, and had been campaigning for Indian independence even before Ghandi had returned to India from South Africa. Another such individual was Vinoba Bhave who was concerned for those who had no land or home and would walk from district to district and persuade landowners to treat him like one of their children and to give him a portion of their land, which he then divided up and gave to the poor and landless.

Bill and Ethne returned to Ireland in 1966 and he trained and worked as a surgeon at the Royal Victoria hospital in west Belfast where he was responsible for the Accident and Emergency Unit in the Royal, treating many of the victims of violence during the troubles which erupted in 1969, including leading Republican Gerry Adams when he was shot. His involvement in saving Gerry Adams' life meant that when he bravely went to participate in a forum in west Belfast and tried to help Republicans understand unionist thinking and feelings – he received an attentive reception.

He was a member of the Fitzroy congregation and their fellowship with Clonard monastery. When the fellowship went to Ballynafeigh Orange Hall to engage in dialogue with the Orange Lodge, Rutherford commented on the expression, 'Parity of esteem' that had achieved recent currency. He expressed the view that parity of esteem was too limited because it highlighted what one might feel deprived of, such as social and political entitlements. Instead, Rutherford suggested that it was important to concentrate on the Christian values of love and respect. He suggested we should use the expression 'generosity of esteem' instead.

Rutherford was a prominent member of the Corrymeela Community and was concerned that the various peace organisations were not working together for maximum impact. He therefore initiated a Peace Forum at which each peace organisation would be represented and be able to speak with one voice on the television or radio. The large and disparate nature of the peace organisations made it difficult for the Forum to be effective and it eventually folded.

He retired as a surgeon in 1986, but continued his reconciliation work and maintained close links with Gujarat, as well as caring for his wife who suffered from increasing ill health. She died in 1995.

His son, James is also a doctor and he and his wife, Sandra have been involved in reconciliation work through Fitzroy Church and she is a member of the committee which organises the Glenstall ecumenical conferences. Bill Rutherford died in 2007.

Sources: Smyth and Fay 2000; Thompson 1990; Wells 2005; biographical material provided to the author by his son James.

George Dallas
1922–98

George Gordon Dallas was born in Ballybay, County Monaghan in 1922, son of Alan and Florence Dallas, both teachers in the Presbyterian church school, where George and his brother Herbert were educated. However when an ability to speak Irish was made compulsory in the Republic of Ireland they moved to Dervock, County Antrim to take up teaching jobs there.

In 1938 Dallas contracted tuberculosis and spent three years in Foster Green Hospital in Belfast. With no antibiotics, he was treated by cutting pieces off each rib on the side of the diseased lung. As a result, for the rest of his life he had the use of only one lung and a lifelong interest in tuberculosis and, as antibiotics was introduced for the effective treatment of TB, other diseases of the chest and lungs. In 1941 he went to study medicine at Queen's University Belfast and worked as a doctor and eventually a consultant in most of the major hospitals in Northern Ireland.

Around 1940 Dallas and his family came into contact with the Oxford Group, which was established to promote a new social order based on the principles of the Sermon on the Mount. George was inspired by the group's thinking and considered becoming a medical missionary, but was ruled out because of his health.

He increasingly became disenchanted with the tendency in political debate and the media to lump all Protestants together, and was very conscious of the historical role of Irish dissenters, such as William Drennan, Francis Hutcheson and Rev. J.B. Armour.

He was a supporter of Northern Ireland Prime Minister, Terence O'Neill, and was despondent when he was forced to resign. He was also horrified by the political violence that took place from 1968 onwards and by the later collapse of the power-sharing Sunningdale Agreement.

Dallas wrote a short drama to be used to improve community relations, which was read in Belfast and Derry and generated interest from some Canadians who were also interested in conflict resolution. He made various visits to Canada and the USA to discuss Northern Ireland and the need for greater understanding and dialogue. On one of the trips to Canada he met his wife, Ruth (née Mathys), who was a teacher from Switzerland.

Dallas engaged in dialogue with a group of Anglican Trinity College Dublin graduates, who were his friends. They developed a wider understanding of Irish history and in 1977 published a statement to coincide with the Anglican General Synod, which highlighted the historic injustices of the Episcopal Church to Catholics and Presbyterians in Ireland.

Dallas became convinced of the need for Presbyterians to see themselves as fully Irish. In 1977, through a French Canadian, Laurent Gagnon, he began attending Bible study classes at Clonard monastery and was moved by the stories of discrimination and harassment told by some of the Catholics he met there.

In 1982 he wrote an article for *The Furrow*, entitled 'Is Irish unity possible?', in which he said,

> Irish unity will be possible when we learn to love and respect each other and, which may be more difficult, understand each other. Protestants need to understand the thought processes of those we have wronged. In a situation of continuing injustice peace will remain impossible unless we change our attitudes and behaviour. And we need to be willing to learn from those we thought could never teach us anything.

He also argued for more dialogue, not just between moderates on both sides, but between those with more extreme political views. In a related article for *The Tablet* in 1982 he asked 'Whither Northern Ireland Protestants?' whom he saw as facing an identity crisis, as a result of an ambiguous view of Britain and the need for them to embrace their Irishness.

He was involved, with Dr Roddy Evans and others, in establishing dialogue between Protestant and Catholic trade unionists, as a way of involving ordinary working class people in thinking about and discussing their differences and similarities and exploring ways forward in Northern Ireland. He also invited two Protestant paramilitary leaders, Andy Tyrie and John McMichael, to his home for a discussion with English Bishop, John Austin Baker.

In 1983 Dallas highlighted his views in a submission to the New Ireland Forum and was asked to go and talk to them in Dublin, which he did. He suggested that there was a need for repentance, particularly by the British and the need for forgiveness. He felt that for progress to be made the real dialogue needed to take place between the British and Irish Governments (which is precisely what happened, leading to the Downing Street Declaration between the two governments).

During the 1980s Dallas met Tom Hartley of Sinn Féin, a Belfast city counsellor and began to develop a dialogue, and then friendship, with him. This dialogue seems to have played an important role in Hartley's thinking which he expounded at the 1995 Ard Fheis, where he challenged the traditional view that northern Protestants would only change when they find themselves in a United Ireland,

> In other words we do not need to do anything about the northern Protestants until we get the Brits out. Such a view, in my opinion, makes the Protestants of the north a non-people, to such an extent that they are robbed of their power to be a crucial component of the Irish conflict and indeed to be a crucial component in the search for a just and lasting settlement on this island.

From this point on, the tone of many Sinn Féin statements in relation to northern Protestants showed a distinct shift which started to make the building of a peace settlement possible. Dallas, in an article for the republican newsletter, *IRIS*, reinforced the views expressed to the New Ireland Forum, but also challenged nationalists for their exclusion of those who are not Catholic, or do not see their total identity bound up with Irishness.

As well as becoming friends with Bishop John Austin Baker in England he became friends with Cardinal O'Fiaich in Armagh. Dallas died in 1998.

Sources: Dallas 1984; Evans 1999; Evans 2004; Wells 2005.

Alex Beattie
1923–2002

Alexander James Beattie was born in Dunmurry just outside Belfast. His family were members of the local Presbyterian congregation, where he would become an elder. Beattie chose a career in business, eventually becoming the accountant of a large group of Irish-based companies. However, he became increasingly disenchanted with the world of commerce and changed course to become a teacher in Lisburn Technical School, which did not require a teaching qualification. At the same time he became a part-time unqualified supply preacher. He then made a decision to become a full-time minister and returned to studying at Assembly's College to qualify as a minister. He was eventually licensed in south Belfast and the following year ordained in Townsend Street, Belfast where he was the assistant minister.

In August 1969, as violence erupted on the streets of Belfast, Beattie, as assistant minister in Townsend Street, was asked to go to Cupar Street, to act as a Protestant spokesman in dialogue with the local Catholic priests of

Clonard Monastery. He met with the Superior of the Monastery, Father McLaughlin, and they both undertook to organise meetings of local people of their respective religious communities and to appoint thirty stewards to keep the peace at a particular volatile intersection. Unfortunately as this meeting was taking place, Unionist MP John McQuade turned up and when informed of the peace pact between the priest and Beattie, McQuade immediately undermined it and said there was no need for it. That night saw the burning out of many Catholic houses in Bombay Street.

In 1971, Beattie became the minister of Newtownstewart and Gortin, County Tyrone and, two years later, Lisnabreen and Donaghadee Road in Bangor. During this period, with the expansion of the population in Bangor, a church extension congregation was established in Ballycrochan Road, which Beattie also ministered to, until in 1982 when it was well established enough in a new church building to have a minister of its own. Beattie chose to remain with the new church. In 1986 he moved to Moville, two years before he retired. He died in 2002.

Sources: Gallagher and Worrall 1982; Presbyterian Historical Society card index.

Desmond Mock
1923–2002

Desmond Edwin Kingston Mock was born in England in 1923. He lived near Hornchurch RAF station during the Battle of Britain and trained as a pilot, becoming a squadron leader and pilot instructor. He was posted as air attaché with the British Embassy in Vienna and then responsible for liaison with schools in the north west of England and Wales. Although brought up as a Methodist he was very influenced by two Presbyterian chaplains in the RAF and decided to train for the Presbyterian ministry.

He married an Irish Presbyterian girl while serving in Northern Ireland during the Second World War. He was licensed by Down presbytery in 1967 and was ordained six months later when he became assistant minister in Malone Church in south Belfast. In 1971 he accepted a call to be minister in Poyntzpass and Fourtowns, on the boundary line between County Armagh and County Down. In 1974 the two congregations of Greystones and Arklow, County Wicklow, were brought together and Mock was installed as the minister. In 1980 he was called to Macrory Memorial in Belfast.

He was very committed to community relations and was the founder of PACE – Protestant and Catholic Encounter, a group established in 1968 in response to the outbreak of conflict in Northern Ireland. He was particularly concerned about a violent Protestant backlash against the civil rights movement and wrote to the press suggesting that inter-denominational groups should be formed to meet together for discussion and prayer. He met with those who responded to his letter and they agreed that, if possible, groups should be set up across Northern Ireland, each with 50/50 Protestant/Catholic membership and joint Protestant and Catholic chairpersons. They agreed that the names of the organisation would be Protestant and Catholic Encounter (PACE) and the main aims were: to promote harmony and goodwill between communities; to demonstrate that there are many activities that people can take part in to work together for the common good; to work with those who desire the establishment of a social order based upon justice and charity, and enlivened by mutual respect and understanding.

The organisation was formally launched with a conference, *Understanding Each Other* in 1969. The first PACE groups were formed in Ballymoney, Holywood, Dunmurry and in and around Belfast. When the Community Relations Commission was set up, the organisation received a grant to employ a co-ordinator. At its height in 1975 there were 35 groups, with a total of around 2,000 members, organised into ten branches across Northern Ireland. Eventually the number of active groups declined and the organisation folded in 1995.

Mock retired in 1970 and moved to Newcastle, County Down. He died in 2002 and was survived by his wife and three daughters.

Sources: Barritt 1982; Presbyterian Historical Society card index.

Bill Jackson
1925–2006

William Moffatt Jackson was born in Sligo in 1925, the son of a Presbyterian minister, Rev. Cuthbertson Jackson, minister of Crescent Church in south Belfast, who in 1930 had got in to trouble with members of his congregation who were unhappy about his attendance at meetings of Moral Re-armament. In 1965, his father had been responsible for drafting a resolution put to the General Assembly, which said,

> The Assembly agreed to urge upon our own people humbly and frankly to acknowledge and to ask forgiveness for any attitudes and actions towards our Roman Catholic fellow-countrymen which have been unworthy of our calling as followers of Jesus Christ; and that the Assembly call upon our people to resolve to deal with all conflicts of interest, loyalties and beliefs always in the spirit of charity rather than suspicion and intolerance.

Bill Jackson was educated at Methodist College in south Belfast. During the Second World War he joined the Fleet Air Arm of the Royal Navy. After the war he went to Oxford University where he studied English. He completed his studies for the ministry at Assembly's College Belfast. He was licensed by Belfast Presbytery in 1953 and ordained the following year in Taughmonagh, a working class housing estate in south Belfast, becoming the fourth generation of the Jackson family to join the ministry.

In 1958 he went with his family to work with the synod of Livingstonia, Malawi (then called Nyasaland), to be the first Irish Presbyterian missionary there. He quickly learnt the local language, Kyangonde, and was soon able to preach in the language of the local people. This was a time of great upheaval in Africa as colonialism was giving way to African self-government. In the following year a state of emergency was declared in Malawi and his life was threatened. He stayed in Africa until 1969 when he returned to Ireland which was also going through a time of great upheaval.

He became minister of Townsend Street Church, Belfast and then in charge of the Shankhill Road Mission in west Belfast. When a member of the Townsend Street congregation was asked whether Jackson was a good preacher, the enquirer was told in no uncertain terms that 'Bill lives the Gospel'. At the Mission he was involved in providing practical support for the many disadvantaged families in the area and counselling individuals in distress. With Eric Lennon, he developed the work of the Mission with people with alcohol problems and also provided programmes for the children of the area, opening a house in Ballyhalbert, on the County Down coast.

In 1973 while preaching for Billy Moran (see profile) in Abbey Church, Dublin, Jackson met and became friends with Father Val McLoughlain SJ who became the organiser of Christian Life Communities and regularly visited and stayed with Jackson when he came north. In 1977 Jackson with some of his congregation attended an inter-denominational meeting of the Christian Life Communities of Belfast and Dublin in Dromalis Retreat House in Larne. The following year Father McLoughlain invited Jackson to participate in their annual conference in Clongowes near Dublin, which he did along with people from the Mission. They were very moved by the way they were received and the whole experience of the weekend. Following this experience, when they returned to Belfast they met with a group from each of the four main denominations in a room in Clonard Monastery every fortnight. Many of the discussions were deeply enriching and often challenging, particularly over the period of the hunger strikes, but they managed to accept, if not always overcome, their differences, in a spirit of Christ-centred love.

In 1981 Rev. Dennis Paterson led a *Come back to God* campaign in the Shankill Road Mission and encouraged the members of the congregation to commit themselves to the work of reconciliation, which many of them did. They shared their experience with the inter-denominational group in Clonard and in discussions over the next few months the group decided that they were being called to establish an inter-denominational Christian community on the Peace Line between the Shankill and Falls Roads, which they decided to call Cornerstone. By the end of 1982, with financial support from Sir Cyril Black, they were able to purchase two terraced properties on the Springfield Road in west Belfast. Jackson became co-leader of the Community with Sister Mary Grant. Jackson's commitment to reconciliation was not shared by all of those involved in the Shankill Road Mission and he encountered significant opposition, as well as receiving support.

He retired from the ministry in 1990 and moved to live in Harmony Hill near Lisburn, but remained actively involved with the Cornerstone Community.

He died in 2006. He is remembered as a very humble person, a man of prayer, someone who naturally created a feeling of reverence in his presence.

Sources: Jackson (undated); interview with members of the Cornerstone Community.

Billy Moran
1929–73

William Annesley Moran was born in Groomsport, County Down in 1929, son of William Moran from County Cavan, manager of the Royal Ulster Yacht Club in Bangor, County Down and Margaret (née Bryan), a teacher, originally born in Scotland, but brought up in Northern Ireland. He was educated at Royal Belfast Academical Institution and Queen's University, where he initially studied economics, but changed to arts, and graduated with a BA in Philosophy in 1953. Having decided to enter the ministry he was accepted as a student at Assembly's College Belfast and became a student assistant at Newtownbreda. He was licensed to preach in 1954 in his home church of Groomsport. He then continued his theological studies at New College, Edinburgh from 1954 to 1955. He completed his theological studies with a year at Assembly's College Belfast.

When John Barkley was appointed Professor of Church History in the College in 1954, the students, including Moran, 'kidnapped' him just prior to his expected appearance at the General Assembly. He was taken for a ride on a horse and cart around the centre of Belfast. The Moderator called for an apology from the students for insulting the house. Moran made the apology on behalf of the students.

He became assistant to Rev. David Dowling in McCracken Memorial in south Belfast from 1955 to 1957. In 1957 he was ordained in Convoy, County Donegal and became the first minister of the combined Convoy and Carnone congregation. During his time there, major structural improvements were made to the large barn-style Carnone church, which made it more suitable for the needs of the congregation. In 1958 he married Joyce Weatherup, who had been Assistant Dean to Ray Davey, the inspirational Presbyterian Dean of Residences at Queen's University Belfast and founder of the Corrymeela Community.

In 1961 Moran accepted a call to Abbey Church in central Dublin where he exercised an exceptional ministry. He was strongly committed to inter-church relations and worked closely with the Jesuits in responding to the terrible problem of inner city poverty in Dublin at that time.

When the well-known Findlater's grocery store (see the profile of William Findlater) in O'Connell Street closed in the late sixties, Moran was offered a large quantity of wooden crates from their cellars. Being a resourceful man he accepted the offer and then began to think what to do with them. Many people in those days lived in cold damp apartments in the immediate neighbourhood of Abbey Church and unemployment was rife. Moran decided to approach the Jesuits of St Francis Xaviour's Church in Upper Gardiner Street and the rector of St George's Church of Ireland to ask them to invite their members to join with those of Abbey so that they might chop up the boxes into sticks, bag them and then deliver them to needy families in the vicinity. Thus started the first ecumenical initiative between those three churches. The chopping and distribution of firewood continued in future years and expanded to include food hampers. Further involvement of Abbey in the community included co-operation with the Sisters of Charity in delivering meals on wheels and in helping at a senior citizens' club. This practical co-operation led to inter-church Bible study and many occasions of ecumenical worship in one or other of the three churches. This was the period when the influence of Vatican II was being strongly felt. It was an exciting experience for all involved and led to a strong bond between members of the three churches.

With the increase of visitors to Dublin from abroad, Moran took the opportunity to give them access on weekdays to a Presbyterian Church in the heart of the city. The church building was opened in the summer months and stewarded by members of the congregation. Dubliners also availed of the open door to enter 'Findlater's Church', which, until then, had been only a landmark to them. As a continuation of welcoming the stranger, coffee was served after Sunday morning worship in the hall beneath the church.

Moran was very committed to young people, expanding their horizons, recognising their talents and developing their skills. He attended conferences of the British Council of Churches (BCC) in Lausanne, Switzerland and in England. He led a delegation of 60 young people to a BCC conference in Leicester. He constantly challenged the members of the congregation to look outwards from the church to see what they could do in the world. He tried to break down barriers, build bridges and bring people of all denominations together. He and his wife Joyce were a crucial source of support for many northern students studying at Trinity College Dublin, some who, in turn, became Presbyterian ministers.

He died tragically young of leukaemia in 1973, leaving his wife, Joyce and three children, Paula, Peter and Judith. Because of the high esteem in which he was held by Catholics in the area, a Memorial Mass was celebrated in his memory, to which the members of Abbey were invited. In the ever-changing circumstances over the years Abbey Church has continued to build upon the outward looking stance pioneered by Moran.

Sources: Courtney 1990; interview with, and additional information from, Joyce Moran; interview with John Morrow.

Alec Watson
1927–2000

David Henry Alexander Watson was born in 1927 in his father, Rev. David Watson's manse in Donaghadee, County Down. His father died in 1950, which left the family without a home or significant income. Alec was educated at Regent's House, Newtownards, County Down; Magee College, Derry; Trinity College Dublin and St Andrews University, Scotland.

Watson was licensed by Ards Presbytery in 1953 and served as assistant minister in Dundee, Scotland, where he pioneered work with Pakistani and Indian students. He had also served as assistant minister in First Derry, First Bangor, and subsequently Cregagh Presbyterian Church in east Belfast, before he was ordained by the Presbytery of Dromore in the new church extension congregation of Lambeg and Seymour Hill near Lisburn, County Antrim. Initially the church had no premises and met in a local Orange hall and then in its own wooden building. The new permanent church was opened in 1959. He was minister there for 18 years.

He was deeply committed to issues of peace and reconciliation. In the 1960s, he was a founder member of the Corrymeela Community. As a pacifist he was a passionate supporter of CND and its campaign against nuclear weapons. He was also a founding member of PACE (Protestant and Catholic Encounter). In Lisburn, when he was minister nearby, he established *The Bridge*, a project designed to encourage reconciliation between Protestants and Catholics in the area. *The Bridge* also developed a range of initiatives to respond to community needs in the Lisburn area. He had a strong commitment to education and became chairman of the South Eastern Education and Library Board, as well as convener of the Youth Committee of the Presbyterian Church. He was also a founder member of the world development charity, War on Want Northern Ireland, when world development was a very new issue.

Watson had a reputation for treating everyone as a member of his family, calling them 'brother' and 'sister'. He was openly friendly with various Catholic priests, which was not popular in some quarters.

In 1975, Watson resigned and went to Scotland to be minister of Burns and Old Parish in Kilsyth, between Glasgow and Stirling, so that his Scottish wife could be nearer her elderly parents. In 1982 he moved to Anstruther in Scotland where he remained until he retired in 1993. He died in 2000. He was survived by his two brothers who are also both Presbyterian ministers, his wife, Jean and four children.

Sources: obituary by John Morrow; obituary in the *Presbyterian Herald*, July 2000; interview with his brother Rev. John Watson.

John Morrow
1931–2009

John Watson Morrow was born in 1931. He was brought up on the family dairy farm in north Down, becoming involved in the Boys' Brigade and later the Young Farmers' Club. He was educated at Campbell College and Queen's University where he gained a BSc, MAgr. and became involved in the progressive Student Christian Movement, which helped expand his world view. He also became involved in the Presbyterian Chaplaincy run by Ray Davey, where he met Rev. George McLeod of the Iona Community and was impressed with his ecumenical vision for the church and later went to Iona to experience it for himself.

He attended Assembly's College Belfast in 1955, but was disillusioned by the narrowness of thinking there and transferred to Edinburgh University, where he met his wife to be, Shirley (who qualified and practised as an orthodontist, but eventually decided to change career and run a playgroup for the children of women who were victims of domestic violence, as well as voluntary involvement with Corrymeela and the Simon Community NI).

John Morrow got further involved in the Iona Community, eventually becoming a member. Due to a lack of funds he had to do his third year of theological study at Assembly's College Belfast, which he found difficult, although he did appreciate the depth of knowledge of Ernest Davey (see profile), the Principal. He was licensed in 1958 and undertook a challenging two-year placement in the neglected Richmond Cragmillar area in Edinburgh under Rev. David Millar, a member of Iona.

He was ordained in Seymour Hill Church, Dunmurry near Belfast in 1960, and shared the ministry of Seymour Hill and Lambeg with Rev. Alec Watson (see profile). With increasing anti-Catholic tension fomented by Ian Paisley and his supporters in the area, Morrow wrote a letter to the *Belfast Telegraph* to highlight the activities of the Free Presbyterians, which he likened to fascists. The Free Presbyterians responded by distributing a leaflet throughout the area misquoting Morrow as saying 'Protestants are Fascists, Catholics are Christians'.

Believing that reconciliation was the central theme of the gospel, with the increasing openness to dialogue created by the Second Vatican Council, Morrow was one of a group of ecumenical clergy who participated with Rev. Jimmy Haire (see profile) and Father Michael Hurley in ecumenical dialogue in St Malachy's college and elsewhere. He also became one of the founders of the Corrymeela Community.

In 1967, just before the start of the troubles, he accepted an invitation to become overseas student chaplain at Glasgow University. In 1971 he returned to Ireland and became Presbyterian chaplain for the Dublin colleges, Trinity and UCD and founded an inter-denominational group to promote reconciliation, which was to be severely challenged in the days and weeks following Bloody Sunday in Derry. In 1976 he moved north to follow Ray Davey as Presbyterian chaplain at Queen's University Belfast. In the following year he and Shirley supported the efforts of the Peace People, who were initially housed in the attic rooms of Corrymeela House in Belfast, as well as continuing to be very actively involved in Corrymeela. In 1976 Morrow was awarded a PhD for his thesis on *The Theology of Peace and Peace-Making*.

He was actively involved in trying, unsuccessfully, to prevent the Presbyterian Church in Ireland withdrawing from the World Council of Churches over its Programme to Combat Racism. The church's anti-ecumenical stance was a source of 'deep sadness and pain' for him. He was an active member, and later chairman, of the Faith and Politics group that produced many pamphlets reflecting on key aspects of the situation in Ireland from a Christian perspective.

Three years later, in 1980, he followed Ray Davey to become the leader of the ecumenical Corrymeela Community. He became involved in an initiative to see how complaints against the police could be dealt with fairly and objectively and, as a result of contacts between those with a concern for human rights, the Committee on the Administration of Justice (CAJ) was formed. He became actively involved in the case of the 'UDR 4', with writer and broadcaster Robert Kee and then with Robin Wilson and Simon Lee in Initiative '92, in response to the lack of political progress. This resulted in a series of public hearings chaired by a Norwegian human rights lawyer, Torkel Opsahl. The *Opsahl Report* summarised many of the key points made during the hearings and outlined recommendations on moving forward.

In 1993 Morrow became a lecturer and Northern Ireland co-ordinator of the Irish School of Ecumenics, where he supported the development of the *Moving beyond Sectarianism* initiative. In 1995 he wrote a book, *Journey of*

Hope which outlined some of the key influences on Corrymeela's vision. He wrote a short book expressing his ecumenical vision and also had the opportunity to edit a book of lectures by Eberhard Bethge about his hero, Dietrich Bonhoeffer, the German theologian who was executed by the Nazis just before the end of the Second World War.

In his memoir, *On the Road of Reconciliation*, published in 2003, he outlined four key principles which he considered to be crucial: forgiveness, repentance, truth and justice. If any of these are absent, he says, you end up with what he calls 'cheap grace'. In 1996 Morrow was a founder member of the Northern Ireland Council on Christians and Jews.

He retired in 1997. In 2006 he was awarded an honorary doctorate by the University of Ulster for his contribution to inter-faith understanding. He died on 1 January 2009, having been predeceased by his wife, Shirley.

His brother Addie Morrow also played an important role in working for political reconciliation as a representative of the Alliance Party in the Northern Ireland Assembly and a Castlereagh councillor bravely challenging the Council over its 'Ulster says No' campaign following the Anglo-Irish Agreement in 1985.

Duncan Morrow, one of John Morrow's three sons trained as a political scientist and established Future Ways with Derrick Wilson, a former centre director of the Corrymeela Community, to explore the theory and practice of peace-building. In 1991 Duncan wrote *The Churches and Inter-Community Relations*. He then became the Chief Executive of the Community Relations Council, the statutory body responsible for promoting and co-ordinating good community relations in Northern Ireland until returning to academia in 2012.

Sources: Morrow 2003; interview with John Morrow.

Carlisle Patterson
1921–2001

Thomas Carlisle Patterson was born in 1921 and grew up in north Belfast. He was educated at Queen's University Belfast where he gained a first-class honours degree in Philosophy in 1943. He spent two years during the Second World War with the YMCA and in 1945 went to Assembly's College Belfast, where he gained his theology qualification. He was licensed to preach and ordained by Belfast Presbytery in 1947 and decided to go as a missionary to China, but events in China resulted in him being diverted to India where he was minister of Scots Church, Bombay and lectured in philosophy in Wilson College, Bombay.

He was employed by the Student Christian Movement (SCM), in the Midlands in England, where a lot of discussion was taking place on the place of faith in the world and the role of the church. In 1956 Patterson was ordained and installed in Conlig near Bangor, County Down, where he was branded by Ian Paisley as the 'Lundy of Conlig'. With the financial support of the member churches, the Irish Council of Churches, which did not include the Catholic Church, appointed Patterson as its first part-time organising secretary in 1958 – the first salaried ecumenical appointment in Ireland.

He was keen to get active backing for his work in the Council from the Anglican hierarchy and approached the conservative Bishop of Down and Dromore, Frederick Mitchell, amongst others, but did not get a positive response. The bishop then attended one of the international Anglican conferences at Lambeth, where he met people from the Anglican church from Africa and Latin America who really inspired him and shattered his self-contained and self-sufficient Irish Anglicanism. On his return he apologised to Patterson and organised a series of Murlough House conferences in Dundrum, which played an important role in inter-Protestant dialogue in Ireland. Ernest Davey (see profile) was a key speaker at the first of these conferences and made an important contribution to mutual understanding.

From 1958 to 1962 he enthusiastically helped organise these pioneering Murlogh Ecumenical Study Conferences. In 1959 he helped form the ecumenical Belfast Church's Industrial Council and the Social Responsibility sub-committee of the Irish Council of Churches. In 1960 he became one of the two convenors of the Presbyterian Church's Inter-Church Relations Board, which was already embroiled in the very contentious issue of the negotiated creation of a United Church of North India, which, for the first time, was to result in Presbyterian ministers becoming bishops in an Episcopal church. In 1961 he attended the World Council of Churches Assembly in New Delhi, India, which he found 'profoundly enriching'. However, by 1964 there were signs of opposition to the continued involvement of the Presbyterian Church in Ireland in the World Council of Churches, although as he argued that, 'membership involves no surrender of our true Reformed and Presbyterian witness, and moreover, that it presents a unique opportunity to make our witness effective where it may be heard, as an essential part of our evangelical witness in the world.'

In 1962 Patterson was called to the Crescent Church in Belfast and gave up his part-time role with the Irish Council of Churches, although not with the Inter-Church Relations Board or the broader ecumenical movement. In 1963 he was appointed secretary of the Congregational-Methodist-Presbyterian Negotiating Body to explore unity between these churches. These discussions were to prove controversial within the Presbyterian Church and ultimately unsuccessful. In 1964 the Inter-Church Relations Board submitted a positive statement on *Relations between Presbyterians and*

Roman Catholics to the General Assembly, in response to the recommendation of the Greystones Faith and Order conference to Protestant churches to 'consider in what ways we ought to respond in truth and love to our Roman Catholic brethren'. The Assembly in 1965 approved a statement, largely drafted by Rev. Cuthbertson Jackson, and presented by Patterson, which said:

> The Assembly agreed to urge upon our own people humbly and frankly to acknowledge and to ask forgiveness for any attitudes and actions towards our Roman Catholic fellow-countrymen which have been unworthy of our calling as followers of Jesus Christ; and that the Assembly call upon our people to resolve to deal with all conflicts of interest, loyalties and beliefs always in the spirit of charity rather than suspicion and intolerance.

Unfortunately, because of his strong ecumenical profile, the church twice rejected the recommendation of its nomination board to appoint Patterson to important administrative positions within the church. He represented the church at the WCC Assembly in Uppsala in 1968.

In the same year, when the troubles broke out in Northern Ireland in 1968, Patterson made a courageous statement about the causes of the conflict:

> We cannot evade the truth that for years we have known of various forms of social injustice and political discrimination within our community and that we have found it mentally more comforting, politically more acceptable and socially more convenient to acquiese in these things.

In 1970 he joined the staff of the Conference of British Missionary Societies in London, which he saw as the overseas mission arm of the British Council of Churches. In 1976 he was appointed as London-based Head of the Overseas Aid Department of Christian Aid which he had helped to establish in Ireland. He remained there until his retirement in 1987. In 1986 he was awarded an honorary doctorate in divinity.

He was very unhappy about the withdrawal of the Irish Presbyterian Church from ecumenical bodies, which he felt 'deprived it of valuable opportunities to make a distinctive contribution to the insights of our fellow-Christians across denominational and geographical boundaries, and in return to benefit from their experience'. In 1997 he wrote *Over the Hill* about the rise and fall of ecumenism in the Presbyterian Church. He sadly reflected that:

Doctrinal correctness has sometimes been valued at the expense of generosity of relationships and a willingness to accept and tolerate those who disagreed. Most seriously, a conviction about Reformed 'truths' has in many respects made the Irish Presbyterian Church conservative and even reactionary, reluctant to obey the injunction in the Church's Code that Christians are 'not ... to refuse light from any quarter'.

He died in April 2001 aged 79.

Sources: Gallagher and Worrall 1982; Patterson 1997.

Peter McLachlan
1936–99

Peter John McLachlan was born in Oxford in 1936, the son of the Rev. John McLachlan, a Unitarian minister and Joan (née Hall), a teacher. Both parents were themselves both children of the manse. Peter was educated at East Oxford Elementary School and gained scholarships to attend Magdalen College School and then Queen's College, Oxford, where he graduated with an MA in Classics (Greek, Latin, History and Philosophy).

He entered the civil service, moving to Northern Ireland, where his father had been installed as minister of the First Non-Subscribing Presbyterian Church in Rosemary Street, Belfast. Peter quickly rose through the ranks of the civil service to become an advisor on Northern Ireland to Prime Minister, Edward Heath. He was present during the Sunningdale talks to establish a power-sharing executive. He then decided to leave the civil service and become the administrator of the National Youth Orchestra (NYO), organising various tours around the world. He was also involved in various Unitarian initiatives, including the Foy Society, the International Religious Fellowship, the Hibbert Trust and the Board of *The Inquirer.*

After finishing with the NYO he worked as a parliamentary lobbyist in Westminster and then returned to Northern Ireland and became involved in politics, as an advisor to, and close supporter of, Brian Faulkner in support of power-sharing. In 1973 he was elected to the Assembly for the Ulster Unionist Party in South Antrim, but refused the offer of an executive post. The following year he stood in East Belfast at the general election for Faulkner's new party, the Unionist Party of Northern Ireland (UPNI) but, while gaining 27% of the vote, failed to get elected. In 1975 he stood again for UPNI for the Constitutional Convention in South Antrim, but again failed to get elected.

He was a key player in the major expansion of the voluntary housing movement in Northern Ireland following a crucial conference at Corrymeela in 1974 and served as chairman of the newly formed Northern

Ireland Federation of Housing Associations from 1977 and a member of the board of Belfast Improved Houses housing association (now Helm). He was a keen supporter of the integrated education movement.

In 1977 he joined the Peace People, founded the year before by Mairead Corrigan and Betty Williams and became chairman. He was then employed by them as Project Officer to manage the giving and monitoring of grants and loans. During a difficult period for the Peace People, relationships deteriorated and McLachlan resigned in 1980. The same year he became head of Bryson House, formerly the Belfast Voluntary Welfare Society and in this role pioneered a huge number of new initiatives, including Crossroads Care Attendant Scheme, Victim Support NI, the NI Conflict and Mediation Association, Lagan Watersports, Parents as Teachers, Belfast Hills Regional Park, Crescent Arts Centre, Shopmobility, Thanksgiving Square and the Northern Ireland Hospice. He was chair of the Prince's Trust in Northern Ireland.

McLachlan was a member of Corrymeela (and the Corrymeela Singers) and the Fellowship of Reconciliation. He was involved in initiatives to promote dialogue and community development in both Catholic and Protestant areas and, before it was considered an acceptable thing to do, engaged in discussions with grassroots loyalist groups to try and help them find a way of moving towards a society without weapons.

Although more of an innovator and man of action than a writer, he was the author of articles on *Teenage Experience in a Violent Society*; *Does Northern Ireland need Cross-Cultural Interpreters*; and *How Volunteers Help Victims*. In *Rainbows and Religion* he explored the different thought patterns of the Protestant and Catholic communities in Northern Ireland and their implications for reaching agreement. He reflected on the role of religion in making dialogue difficult, in particular, the different structures and approaches to leadership of the Presbyterian Church (democratic, open, egalitarian, prone to schism, provisional facilitative leadership) and the Catholic Church (hierarchical, authoritative, strong leadership) and how the differing approaches to decision-making in the churches tended to spill over into approaches to political dialogue. He argued for the creation of an inter-Church Commission to monitor major speeches and events and help in creating clearer understanding, without a loss of faith in the value of each tradition. He believed that, 'Only if this were in place can a political vision involving an accommodation between the two main resident communities in Ireland succeed and become reality, avoiding being broken and frustrated on the jagged rocks of misunderstanding.'

He also wrote the libretto for *A Requiem for those Who Die Young*, music by Toby Collins, which was first performed by the Accidental Theatre Company in Brighton in 1988. The profits went to the World Aids Day fund in Brighton.

He believed in experiencing the worship of different denominations and faiths, including the Society of Friends, where, in an exceptionally busy life, he could find time for quiet reflection. Having been diagnosed with cancer, he died in 1999 in the hospice he had helped to found, leaving two daughters, Heather and Fiona.

Sources: obituary of Peter McLachlan by Peter B. Godfrey; *Rainbows and Religion*; comments from his daughters, Heather and Fiona.

Donald Gillies
1909–96

Of all the profiles in this book, Donald Gillies is probably the one least likely to be viewed as progressive. However it is also a story of extraordinary personal change. He was born on 9 November 1909 in Ardrishaig, Argyllshire, Scotland and educated at Glasgow University where he graduated with an MA in 1932. He then studied theology at Trinity College, Glasgow and the Divinity Hall of Glasgow University. He was licensed to preach by the Presbytery of Inverary in 1936 and served as assistant in Cambusnathan Old Parish for almost seven years. He was eventually ordained in Barrow-in-Furness by the Presbytery of Liverpool in 1943.

In 1946 he moved to Ireland and was installed as minister of Agnes Street Presbyterian Church on 5 December that year. In 1971 he became the minister of Clifton Street Church in Belfast.

Gillies was a Unionist and in 1973 wrote a small book which was published by the Unionist Publicity Department, called *In Place of Truth: Ulster – victim of propaganda*, in which he describes, and attempts to refute, what he sees as propaganda about Northern Ireland, for example that the problems in Northern Ireland were caused by British imperialism, or partition, or fifty years of Unionist misrule, or internment. He considered that these myths were designed by the enemies of Ulster to break Ulster's historical link with Britain.

However, several years later he had reconsidered his views, including on the ecumenical movement and argued in favour of the retention of the Presbyterian Church's membership of the World Council of Churches. In 1980 he wrote a book explaining his theological thinking on the issue, entitled *Revolt from the Church*, in which he argued that the 'Protestant Church has obscured Christ by fundamentalism and confessionalism … setting ourselves up as judges of the hearts and consciences of others'. He felt, in reflecting on the scriptures, that 'we should show more consideration for the feelings and opinions of others'. He felt the issue so important that 'the unity of the church in Christ is at stake. The hope of reconciliation is at stake'.

He became a member of the Inter-Church Relations Board of the Church and eventually its chairman. He was also Convenor of the Inter-Church Relations Committee of the Belfast Synod as well as a Presbyterian representative on both the Irish and British Councils of Churches.

For his change of heart, Gillies was the target for particular abuse from Free Presbyterian followers of Rev. Ian Paisley, who were able to throw back at him what he had said in 1964 about ecumenism, saying he was 'condemned by his own mouth'. He was removed from his position as an officer in the Evangelical Protestant Society. When he, on an Orange Order platform on the Twelfth of July, expressed his sorrow at a fire at Holy Cross chapel in Ardoyne, north Belfast, he was subject to verbal abuse by the Saintfield District Lodge. The newspaper reporting was described by the Lodge as providing 'successful coverage' which achieved 'the goal of exposing the issues and promoting the existence of resistance to the ecumenical drift'.

On his death on 21 February 1996, Father Michael Hurley SJ wrote a letter to the *Presbyterian Herald* described how he and Gillies, despite deep initial differences, had developed a deep friendship through dialogue. He concluded that 'his life encourages all of us to be open to the spirit and ready for change so that the world may believe and be at peace'.

Gillies was survived by his wife and son.

Sources: Gillies, Donald (1973) *In Place of Truth*, Unionist Publicity Department; Gillies Donald (1980) *Revolt from the Church*; *The Revivalist* June 1975; LOL1310 Banner of the Cross – Orange Order Saintfield District website (lol1310.com/history); Michael Hurley 2003.

David Stevens
1948–2010

David Stevens was born in Holywood, County Down in 1948 and educated at Royal Belfast Academical Institution and Queen's University Belfast, where he met Presbyterian chaplain, Rev. Ray Davey and became involved in the newly established Corrymeela Community. He gained a science degree and then a PhD from Queen's. Rather than undertaking an academic career in research or lecturing, from 1973, he worked full-time for two years for Corrymeela. He then became General Secretary of the Irish Council of Churches from 1992 to 2003 and was actively involved in servicing the various inter-church, including Catholic/Protestant, structures and working groups. He worked closely with Fr Brian Lennon in the Inter-Church Faith and Politics Group which produced *Breaking Down the Enmity* in 1985 and *Understanding the Times* in 1986, following the signing of the Anglo-Irish Agreement. Over the following sixteen years he was a key member, often the main draftsperson, of the group as they produced a dozen further publications to help advance thinking on the situation in Northern Ireland from a faith perspective.

He was inspired by the work of a group of Dutch theologians and activists involved with groups from Northern Ireland, particularly Roel Kaptein who worked intensively and controversially with a number of Corrymeela members. In 1981 he initiated a 5-day conference in Holland bringing together the key players in education to promote co-operation on peace education.

In the late 1980s he became involved in the setting up of an inter-church working party on sectarianism, co-chaired by Mary McAleese (who would later become President of Ireland) and English Quaker, John Lampen. The Irish Inter-Church Committee was very nervous about publishing the controversial report, but did so in 1993, inspiring further work on sectarianism by the Irish School of Ecumenics. In 1992 he was one of the key instigators and initial trustees (with Carrie Barkley and representatives of the other main denominations) of the Churches Peace Education Programme. He was a regular contributor to *Corrymeela News*. In 1995 he contributed an article on forgiveness, entitled 'Liberty to Captives', in which he said,

> Forgiveness is not an issue for public policy. Nevertheless, it is something of vital existential importance. Its centrality can be located by asking three questions. How can we forgive those who have hurt us irreparably? How can those who have murdered forgive themselves or find forgiveness? How can those who have murdered and wounded, and those who have suffered the consequences of murder and woundedness, co-exist in the same land? Thus the issue of forgiveness is one of vital necessity so that people can live with themselves and with others.

In 1999 he put a considerable amount of work into planning the restructuring of the Irish Council of Churches and Irish Inter-Church Meeting, which were both his responsibility as General Secretary, into a single body. The proposals were accepted by all the churches except the Presbyterian Church. In 2000 he produced a thoughtful document on the proposal for a specific Bill of Rights for Northern Ireland.

In 2004 he became the leader of the Corrymeela Community. He was a member of the Northern Ireland Community Relations Council and the Faith and Politics Group. In 2004 he published a book, *The Land of Unlikeness – Explorations into Reconciliation*, in which he explores the meaning of reconciliation for societies in conflicted space. He was conscious that the word reconciliation can be used to 'slide away from issues of injustice and rightful disturbance', but wanted to reclaim the word from 'vacuity, false comfort and misuse'. He considered that reconciliation, amongst other things as,

> living together in difference; ... the inter-related dynamics of forgiveness, repentance, truth and justice; ... a set of attitudes and practices that are necessary for dealing with plurality, for fair interactions between members of different groups, for healing divisions and for finding common purposes'; and ... creating and sustaining conversation.

He recognised that reconciliation at a political level requires 'fair interactions between members of different groups; the overcoming of antagonistic divisions and the discovery and creation of common ground; and the presence of a society in which all citizens have a sense of belonging'. He also examined the concepts of forgiveness and dealing with the past, but recognised the challenges to reconciliation from the pressures for revenge and loyalty to the heroic sacrifices of the past.

In a paper to the Irish Social Studies Conference in 2004 on the religious changes to Irish society he concluded that religion was becoming more, rather than less, divisive.

The following year, in a paper on *The churches and Ten Years of the Peace Process*, he gave a typically thoughtful reflection on the role of the churches:

> Religion plays a profoundly ambiguous role in conflict situations. On the one hand, it can encourage hatred; anti-Catholicism is particularly potent in Northern Ireland, and has political consequences. Churches can reinforce community division and harden boundaries; Catholic views and rules on mixed marriage and the importance of church schools have had significant consequences in Northern Irish society. Religion can give divine sanctions to nationalisms, political positions and violence.
>
> On the other hand, religion can be a force for restraint ... Without the churches the situation would have been a lot worse; the preaching and living out of non-retaliation, forbearance and forgiveness have had real social consequences. The churches opposed those who espoused violence and the gods of nationalism. Churches working together have been a force for good ... The developing pattern of church leaders and others meeting together over the last thirty years in Northern Ireland, of clergy visiting victims of violence together, has been a significant social witness. Churches have been encouragers to politicians seeking political compromise. There have been individuals and groups working for peace and reconciliation. Contacts were established by church groups with paramilitary organisations; clergy and others acted as

go-betweens. The Irish Council of Churches, together with the Roman Catholic Church, have had a peace education programme working in schools, and so on. And, nevertheless, the picture is very mixed and deeply ambiguous ... Churches are part of the problem and struggle to be part of the solution.

The problem is that politics appears to dominate the churches more than vice-versa ... inhibiting churches in being agents of co-operation and raises profound questions about what is more important – religious commitment or political commitment. In theological terms, we are talking about the issue of idolatry. Churches tend to reflect people's fears, reflect community divisions, and reflect a community experience of violence and threat, rather than act as agents of change or transformers of conflict.

Stevens died after a short period of illness in 2010.

Sources: Hall 2005; Stevens 2004; Stevens 'The Churches and Ten Years of the Peace Process' in *Beyond Sectarianism* CRC; *The Irish Inter-Church Meeting – background and development*; interview with David Stevens.

Sources

Adair, Lynne and Murphy, Colin, *Untold stories – Protestants in the Republic of Ireland 1922–2002* (Liffey Press, 2002).

Agnew, Jean (ed.), *The Drennan-McTier Letters 1776–1820*, 3 vols (Women's History Project in association with the Irish Manuscripts Commission, 1999).

Akenson, Donald H., *The Irish Education Experiment* (Routledge & Kegan Paul, 1970).

Allen, Harry, *The Men of the Ards* (Ballyhay, 2004).

Allison, R.S., *The Seeds of Time – being a short history of the Belfast General and Royal Hospital 1850–1903* (Brough, Cox and Dunn, 1972).

Andrews, Stuart, *Irish Rebellion: Protestant Polemic 1798–1900* (Palgrave, 2006).

Armour W.S., *Armour of Ballymoney* (Duckworth, 1934).

Armour, Noel, 'Isabella Tod and Liberal Unionism in Ulster 1886–96' in Alan Hayes and Diane Urquhart (eds), *Irish Women's History*, (Irish Academic Press, 2004), pp 72–87.

Armstrong, Douglas, *Rev. Sinclare Kelburn 1754–1802* (Presbyterian Historical Society of Ireland, 2001).

Armytage, W.H.G., *Heavens Below: utopian experiments in England 1560–1960* (Routledge and Kegan Paul, 1961).

Auld, C., *Rosamund Praeger: the way that she went* (Spectator, 2006).

Baillie, W.D. and Kirkpatrick, L.S., *Fasti of Seceder Ministers Ordained or Installed in Ireland 1746–1948* (Presbyterian Historical Society of Ireland, 2005).

Baillie, W.D. et al, *A History of Congregations in the Presbyterian Church in Ireland 1610–1982* (Presbyterian Church in Ireland, 1982).

Baillie, W.D., *Conflict and Challenge* (Presbyterian Historical Society of Ireland, 1981).

Baillie, W.D., *Radicals and Revivals* (Presbyterian Historical Society of Ireland, 2006).

Bannerji, Himani, Majob, Shahrzad and Whitehead, Judith, *Of Property and Propriety: the role of gender and class in imperialism and nationalism* (University of Toronto Press, 2001).

Bardon, Jonathan, *A History of Ulster* (1st ed., Blackstaff Press, 1992).

Barkley, John M., *A Short History of the Presbyterian Church in Ireland* (Presbyterian Church of Ireland, 1959).

Barkley, John M., *Dissenter and Blackmouth* (White Row, 1993).

Barkley, John M., *Fasti of the General Assembly Presbyterian Church in Ireland* (Presbyterian Historical Society of Ireland, 1986).

Barkley, John M., *The Irish Council of Churches* (1983).

Barritt, Desmond, *Northern Ireland – A Problem to every Solution* (Northern Friends Peace Board, 1982).

Barton, Brian, *The Blitz: Belfast in the War Years* (Blackstaff Press, 1989).

Beckett, J.C., *Belfast: The Making of the City* (Appletree, 2003).

Beckett, J.C., *The Making of Modern Ireland* (Faber & Faber, 1966).

Bell, Sam Hanna, *The Theatre in Ulster* (Gill & Macmillan, 1972).

Bew, Paul and Gillespie, Gordon, *Northern Ireland: a chronology of the Troubles 1968–1999* (Gill & Macmillan, 1999).

Bigger, Francis Joseph, *The Land War of 1770* (Sealy, Bryers and Walker, 1910).

Blair, Adam, *Adam Blair 1718–1790* (hand-written autobiographical reflections in Church House, undated).

Blaney, Roger, 'Dr. John St Clair Boyd' in *Ulster Local Studies*, vol. 9, no. 18 (Federation for Ulster Local Studies, 1984).

Blaney, Roger, 'The Praeger family of Holywood' in *Familia: Ulster Genealogical Review*, no. 15 (Ulster Historical Foundation, 1999).

Blaney, Roger, *Presbyterians and the Irish Language* (Ulster Historical Foundation/Ultach Trust, 1996).

Blythe, Ernest, *Trasna na Boinne* (Sairseal agus Dill, 1957).

Bowman, Terence, *People's Champion: The Life of Alexander Bowman, Pioneer of Labour Politics in Ireland* (Ulster Historical Foundation, 1997).

Boyd, Andrew, *Fermenting Elements: the Labour colleges in Ireland 1924–1964* (Donaldson Archives Belfast, 1999).

Boyd, Andrew, *Montgomery and the Black Man: Religion and Politics in Nineteenth-century Ulster* (Columba Press, 2006).

Boyd, John, *Out of my class* (Blackstaff Press, 1985).

Boyd, John, *The middle of my journey* (Blackstaff Press, 1990).

Boyd, Robin H.S., *India and the Latin Captivity of the Church* (Cambridge University Press, 1974).

Boyd, Robin, *Ireland: Christianity discredited or pilgrim's progress?* (World Council of Churches, 1988).

Boylan, Henry, *Dictionary of Irish Biography* (3rd ed., Roberts Rhinehart, 1998).

Bradbury, John, *Celebrated Citizens of Belfast* (Appletree Press, 2002).

Brett, C.E.B., *Long Shadows Cast Before: Nine Lives in Ulster, 1625–1977* (John Bartholomew, 1978).

Broadie, Alexander, *The Scottish Enlightenment* (Birlinn, 2001).

Brooke, Peter, *Ulster Presbyterianism* (Athol Books, 1994).

Brown Katharine L., 'The James Bones Family Circle: A United Irishman's Southern American Heritage' in *Familia: Ulster Genealogical Review*, no. 14 (Ulster Historical Foundation, 1998).

Brown, A.W.G., *The Great Mr Boyse* (Presbyterian Historical Society of Ireland, 1980).

Brown, L.T., 'The Presbyteries of Cavan and Monaghan' (Ph.D. thesis, Queen's University Belfast, 1986).

Bryson, Andrew, *Andrew Bryson's Ordeal: An Epilogue to the 1798 Rebellion*, Michael Durey (ed.), (Cork University Press, 1998).

Byrne, Art and McMahon, Sean, *Great Northerners* (Poolbeg, 1991).

Calwell, H.G., *Andrew Malcolm of Belfast 1818–1856: physician and historian* (Brough, Cox and Dunn, 1977).

Calwell, H.G., *The Life and Times of a Voluntary Hospital: the History of the Royal Belfast Hospital for Sick Children 1873–1948* (Brough, Cox and Dunn, 1973).

Campbell, Flann, *The Dissenting Voice: Protestant Democracy in Ulster from Plantation to Partition* (Blackstaff Press, 1991).

Campbell, John, *A Short History of the Non-Subscribing Presbyterian Church in Ireland* (Belfast, 1914).

Chambers, George, *Faces of Change: The Belfast and Northern Ireland Chamber of Commerce and Industry 1783–1983* (Northern Ireland Chamber of Commerce and Industry, 1983).

Clarke, Richard, *The Royal Victoria Hospital, Belfast: A History, 1797–1997* (Blackstaff Press, 1997).

Clifford, Gerard and Arlow, William, *Northern Ireland – the Way Forward* (St Anne's Cathedral, 1983).

Colgan, Brendan, *Vere Foster: English Gentleman, Irish Champion 1819–1900* (Fountain Publishing 2001).

Collins, Lucy (ed.), *Poetry by Women in Ireland: a critical anthology 1870–1970* (Liverpool University Press, 2012).

Collins, Peter, *Who Fears to Speak of '98?: Commemoration and the continuing impact of the United Irishmen* (Ulster Historical Foundation, 2004).

Comerford, R.V., *The Fenians in Context: Irish Politics and Society, 1848–82* (Wolfhound Press, 1985).

Connolly, James, *The Re-Conquest of Ireland* (Irish Transport and General Workers' Union, 1934).

Coogan Tim Pat, *De Valera: Long Fellow, Long Shadow* (Arrow Books, 1995).

Cook, Tania, 'The Maplewood Progress July 2006' (Maplewood Presbyterian Church, 2006).

Cooke, Dennis, 'A Failed Romance? Irish Presbyterianism and the World Council of Churches' in *Ebb and Flow: Essays in Church History in Honour of R. Finlay G. Holmes*, W. Donald Patton (ed.), (Presbyterian Historical Society of Ireland, 2002).

Corrigan, D. Felicitas, *Helen Waddell: A Biography* (Gollancz, 1986).

Courtney, Anne and Brian, *The Story of Mary McCracken's Church* (Accourtney, 1994).

Cradden, Terry, *Trade Unionism, Socialism and Partition: The labour movement in Northern Ireland 1939–1953* (December Books, 1993).

Craig, D.H., 'A History of the Belfast City Hospital' Presidential address to the Ulster Medical Society in *Ulster Medical Journal*, vol. 43, no. 1 (Ulster Medical Society, 1973/4).

Craig, Patricia (ed.), *A Belfast Anthology* (Blackstaff Press, 1999).

Craig, Patricia (ed.), *The Rattle of the North – an anthology of Ulster prose* (Blackstaff Press, 1992).

Craighead, Alexander, 'Renewal of the Covenants, National and Solemn League; a Confession of Sins; and Engagements to Duties: and a Testimony; as they were carried out at Middle Octarara in Pen[n]sylvania, November 11, 1743', (B. Franklin, Philadelphia, 1743[?]), available online at: www.truecovenanter.com/covenants/octorara_covenant_renewal.html.

Craighead, Alexander, 'A Discourse concerning the Covenants: containing the substance of two sermons preached at Middle-Octarara, January 10 and 17, 1741, 2. Upon Joshua IX. 15.' (B. Franklin, Philadelphia, 1742), available online at: www.truecovenanter.com/covenants/craighead_discourse_on_covenants.html.

Craighead, Alexander, 'The reasons of Mr Alexander Craighead's receding from the present Judicatures of this Church, together with its Constitution' (B. Franklin, Philadelphia, 1743), available online at: www.truecovenanter.com/kirkgovt/creaghead_reasons_of_receding_1743.html.

Crawford, W.H. and Trainor, B., *Aspects of Irish Social History 1750–1800* (HMSO, 1969).

Croskery, Thomas and Witherow, Thomas, *Life of Rev. A.P.Goudy, D.D., 1809–1858: An Appreciation (1887) of a Theological Conservative and Political Liberal (Ascona)* (Moyola Books, 1994).

Cumiskey, Mary, 'Sir Thomas Jackson' in *Journal of the Creggan History Society*, no. 4 (Creggan History Society, 1990).

Curtin, Nancy, *The United Irishmen: Popular Politics in Ulster and Dublin, 1791–1798* (Clarendon, 1998).

Dallas, George, 'Wither Irish Presbyterianism?' in *The Challenge of Northern Ireland* (Furrow Trust, 1984).

Daly, Cahal and Worrall, Stanley, *Ballymascanlon – An Irish Venture in Inter-Church Dialogue* (Christian Journals Ltd, 1978).

Davey, Ray, *Take Away this Hate* (Corrymeela Press, 1970).

Davey, Ray, *The War Diaries* (Brehon Press, 2005).

Davidson, A.J. (ed.), *The Autobiography and Diary of Samuel Davidson LL.D., D.D.* (T. & T. Clark, 1899).

Davidson, Noel, *Who Cares? The story of Belfast City Mission* (Belfast City Mission, 2002).

Delany, Rory, 'James Haughton' *Oscailt Magazine* (Cork and Dublin Unitarian Churches, 2007).

Devlin, Paddy, *Straight Left: An Autobiography* (Blackstaff Press, 1994).

Devlin, Paddy, *Yes, We Have no Bananas: Outdoor Relief in Belfast, 1920–39* (Blackstaff Press, 1981).

Dickson, Charles, *Revolt in the North: Antrim and Down in 1798* (Constable, 1997).

Dickson, R.J., *Ulster Emigration to Colonial America 1718–1775* (Routledge and Kegan Paul, 1966).

Dictionary of National Biography, entry for 'John Gray (1816–75)' (Smith, Elder & Co., 1885–1900).

Dill, James Reid, *The Dill Worthies* (1888).

Dillon, William, *The Life of John Mitchel* (K. Paul, Trench & Co., 1888).

Directory of the Presbyterian Church in Ireland (Presbyterian Church in Ireland, 2007).

Dowling, Martin W., *Tenant Right and Agrarian Society in Ulster, 1600–1870* (Irish Academic Press, 1999).

Duddy, Thomas (ed.), *Dictionary of Irish Philosophers* (Thoemmes Press, 2004).

Duffy, Gavin, *League of North and South 1840–45* (Chapman & Hall, 1896).

Dunlop, Eull (ed.), 'S. Alex Blair's County Antrim Characters: "Portraits of the Past"' which first appeared in the *Ballymena Guardian*' in *Mid-Antrim Historical Group*, no. 19 (Ballymena, 1993).

Dunlop, Eull, 'Samuel Davidson (1806–98) and Kellswater' in the *Bulletin of the Presbyterian Historical Society in Ireland*, vol. 27 (Presbyterian Historical Society of Ireland, 1998–2000).

Dunlop, John, *A Precarious Belonging: Presbyterians and the Conflict in Ireland* (Blackstaff Press, 1995).

Elliott, Marianne, *Partners in Revolution: United Irishmen and France* (Yale University Press, 1989).

Elliott, Marianne, *Wolfe Tone: prophet of Irish Independence* (Yale University Press, 1989).

Ellis, Ian and Hurley, Michael (eds), *The Irish Inter-Church Meeting – Background and Development* (The Irish Inter-Church Meeting, 1998).

Ellis, Ian, *Vision and Reality: A Survey of Twentieth Century Irish Inter-Church Relations* (Institute of Irish Studies, Queen's University Belfast, 1992).

Ellis, Peter Beresford, 'De Valera's betrayal of women' in the *Irish Democrat* (Borehamwood, 2006).

Ellis, Peter Beresford, *Hell or Connaught: the Cromwellian Colonisation of Ireland 1652–1660* (Blackstaff Press, 1975)

Elwood, J.H., 'Thomas Carnwath' in *Ulster Medical Journal*, vol. 51, no. 2 (Ulster Medical Society, 1982), pp 98–109.

Erskine, John and Gordon, Lucy (eds), *Varieties of Scottishness: Exploring the Ulster-Scottishness Connection (Cultural Traditions in Northern Ireland)* (Institute of Irish Studies, Queen's University Belfast, 1997).

Evans, Roddy, *The Second Conversion of George Dallas* (published privately, 1999).

Farr, Berkley, 'James Wood: East Down's Liberal MP: The life and political career of James Wood, victor of the East Down by-election in February 1902' in *Journal of Liberal History*, no. 58, Spring 2008 (Liberal Democrat History Group, 2008).

Ferguson, Frank, *Ulster-Scots Writing: An Anthology* (Four Courts Press, 2008).

Fitzpatrick, Rory, *God's Frontiersmen – the Scots-Irish Epic* (Weidenfeld & Nicolson, 1989).

Flackes, W.D., *Northern Ireland – A political Directory 1968–1979* (Gill & Macmillan, 1980).

Foley, Imelda, *The Girls in the Big Picture* (Blackstaff Press, 2003).

Foot, Michael, *Debts of Honour* (Davis-Poynter, 1980).

Fouke, Daniel C., *Philosophy and Theology in a Burlesque Mode: John Toland and the Way of Paradox* (Prometheus Books, 2007).

Foy, R.H. (ed.), *Bonar Thompson – the old days at Carnearney* (Antrim & District Historical Society, 1991).

Foy, R.H., *Remembering all the Orrs: The Story of the Orr Families of Antrim and Their Involvement in the 1798 Rebellion* (Ulster Historical Foundation, 1999).

Froggatt, Peter, 'All-rounders and "equanimity" – Terence John Millin (1903–1980), Irish urological surgeon. A lecture to commemorate Professor Gary Love (1934–2001)' in *Ulster Medical Journal*, vol. 73, no. 2 (Ulster Medical Society, 2004).

Froggatt, Peter, 'Millin *pere et fils*: Samuel Shannon (1864–1947), local chronicler', paper read to the Belfast Literary Society on 5 December 2005.

Fulton Austin, *Biography of J. Ernest Davey* (Presbyterian Church in Ireland, 1970).

Gallagher, Eric and Worrall, Stanley, *Christians in Ulster 1968–1980* (Oxford University Press, 1982).

Gillies, Donald, *In Place of Truth* (Unionist Publicity Department, 1973).

Gillies, Donald, *Revolt from the Church* (Christian Journals Ltd., 1980).

Gilpin, Sanda, 'Lecture on Robert Huddleston' in Lyttle Hall, Moneyreagh, on 9 May 2009.

Goff, Frederick Richmond, *The John Dunlap Broadside: the First Printing of the Declaration of Independence* (Library of Congress, 1976).

Goodrich, Charles A., 'Biography of George Taylor' in Charles A. Goodrich, *Lives of the Signers of the Declaration of Independence* (William Reed & Co., 1856).

Gray, J. (ed.), *Life and Works of Thomas Carnduff* (Lagan Press, 1994).

Gray, John, *City in Revolt: James Larkin and the Belfast Dock Strike of 1907* (Blackstaff Press, 1985).

Greaves, Richard L., *God's Other Children: Protestant Nonconformists and the Emergence of Denominational Churches in Ireland, 1660–1700* (Stanford University Press, 1997).

Green E.R.R. (ed.), *Essays in Scotch-Irish History* (Ulster Historical Foundation, 1969).

Haire, J.L.M. (ed.), *Challenge and Conflict: Essays in Irish Presbyterian History and Doctrine* (Greystone Press, 1981).

Hall, Elaine, *A Celebration of the Churches Peace Education Programme 1978–2005* (Churches Peace Education Programme, 2005).

Hall, Gerald R., *Ulster Liberalism 1778–1876* (Four Courts Press, 2011).

Hall, Michael. (ed.), *Grassroots Leadership: Recollections by May Blood and Joe Camplisson*, vol. 1 (Island Publications, 2005).

Hamilton, Thomas, *History of Presbyterianism in Ireland* (Ambassador, 1992).

Harbison, John F., 'History of the Northern Ireland Labour Party 1891–1949' (unpublished thesis, Queen's University Belfast, 1966).

Harrison, Brian (ed.), *Oxford Dictionary of National Biography* (Oxford University Press, 2004).

Hartley, Tom, *Written in Stone: The history of Belfast City Cemetery* (Brehon, 2006).

Haughton, Samuel, *Memoir of James Haughton, with extracts from his letters* (1877; reprinted Nabu Press, 2010).

Hayton, D.W., 'Presbyterians and the Confessional State: The Sacramental test as an issue in Irish Politics 1704–1780' in the *Bulletin of the Presbyterian Historical Society*, vol. 26 (Presbyterian Historical Society of Ireland, 1997).

Heatley, Fred, *Henry Joy McCracken and his Times* (Belfast Wolfe Tone Society, 1967).

Herlihy, Kevin (ed.), *Propagating the Word of Irish Dissent, 1650–1800* (Four Courts Press, 1998).

Herlihy, Kevin, *The Politics of Irish Dissent 1650–1800* (Four Courts Press, 1997).

Herman, Arthur, *The Scottish Enlightenment: The Scots' Invention of the Modern World* (Fourth Estate, 2001).

Hewitt, John, *Rhyming Weavers: And Other Country Poets of Antrim and Down* (Blackstaff Press, 1974, new ed. 2004).

Hickey, D.J. and Doherty, J.E., *A New Dictionary of Irish History from 1800* (Gill & Macmillan, 2005).

Higgins, A.G., *A History of the Brotherhood Church* (The Brotherhood Church, 1982).

Hill, Myrtle, Turner, Brian and Dawson, Kenneth (eds), *1798: Rebellion in County Down* (Colourpoint Books, 1998).

Holland, Margaret, *My Winter of Content Under Indian Skies* (McCaw, Stevenson & Orr, 1926).

Holmes, Finlay, *Our Irish Presbyterian Heritage* (Presbyterian Church in Ireland, 1985).

Holmes, Finlay and Knox, R. Buick (eds), *General Assembly of the Presbyterian Church 18420–1990* (Presbyterian Historical Society of Ireland, 1990).

Holmes, Finlay, *The Presbyterian Church in Ireland: A Popular History* (Columba Press, 1999).

Holmes, Janice and Urquhart, Diane, *Coming into the Light: Work, Politics and Religion of Women in Ulster, 1840–1940* (Institute of Irish Studies, Queen's University Belfast, 1994).

Hope, Jemmy, *The Memoirs of Jemmy Hope: An autobiography of a working class United Irishman* (British and Irish Communist Party, 1972).

Hughes, A.J., *Robert Shipboy MacAdam: his life and Gaelic proverb collection* (Institute of Irish Studies, Queen's University Belfast, 1998).

Hume, David, '*To right some things that we thought wrong ...*': *The spirit of 1798 and Presbyterian radicalism in Ulster* (Ulster Society, 1998).

Hume, David, *Far from the Green Fields of Erin: Ulster Emigrants and Their Stories* (Colourpoint Books, 2005).

Ireland, Denis, *From the Irish Shore: Notes on My Life and Times* (Rich & Cowan Ltd, 1936).

Ireland, Denis, *From the Jungle of Belfast: Footnotes to History 1904–1972* (Blackstaff Press, 1973).

Irwin, C.H., *A History of Presbyterianism in Dublin and the South and West of Ireland* (1890, new ed. Forgotten Books, 2012).

Jackson, Alvin, 'Irish Unionism and the Russellite threat 1894–1906' in *Journal of Liberal History*, no. 33, Winter 2001–02, (Liberal Democrat History Group, 2002).

Jackson, Bill, *Send Us Friends* (privately published, undated).

Jacob, William States, *Presbyterianism in Nashville: A Compilation of Historic Data* (The Cumberland Press, 1904).

Jamieson, John, *The History of the Royal Belfast Academical Institution, 1810–1960* (RBAI, 1959).

Johnston, Roy H.W., *Century of Endeavour: A Biographical and Autobiographical View of the Twentieth Century in Ireland* (Lilliput Press, 2006).

Jordan, Alison, *Margaret Byers: pioneer of women's education and founder of Victoria College, Belfast* (Institute of Irish Studies, Queen's University Belfast, 1990).

Jordan, Alison, *Who Cared?: Charity in Victorian and Edwardian Belfast* (Institute of Irish Studies, Queen's University Belfast, 1992).

Joy, Henry, *Belfast Politics* (Athol Books, 1974).

Kelly, James, *Gallows speeches from eighteenth-century Ireland* (Four Courts Press, 2001).

Kennedy, Billy, *Heroes of the Scots-Irish in America* (Ambassador, 2001).

Kennedy, Billy, *The making of America* (Ambassador, 2001).

Kennedy, Billy, *The Scots-Irish in Pennsylvania & Kentucky* (Ambassador, 1998).

Kennedy, Billy, *The Scots-Irish in the Carolinas* (Ambassador, 1997).

Kennedy, Catriona, 'Womanish Epistles?: Martha McTier, female Epistolarity and late eighteenth century Irish radicalism' in *Women's History Review*, vol. 13, no. 4 (Routledge, 2004), pp 649–67.

Keogh, Daire and Furlong, Nicholas (eds), *The Women of 1798* (Four Courts Press, 1998).

Keogh, Dermot and McCarthy, Andrew, *The Making of the Irish Constitution, 1937* (Mercier Press, 2008).

Kernohan, J.W., *The Parishes of Kilrea and Tamlaght O'Crilly: a sketch of their history* (Coleraine, 1912).

Killen, John (ed.), *The Decade of the United Irishmen: Contemporary Accounts 1791–1801* (Blackstaff Press, 1997).

Killen, John, *A History of the Linen Hall Library, 1788–1988* (Linen Hall Library, 1990).

Killen, John, *Rutherford Mayne: Selected Plays* (Institute of Irish Studies, Queen's University Belfast, 1997).

Killen, W.D., *Memoir of John Edgar, D.D., L.L.D.: Professor of Systematic Theology for the General Assembly of the Presbyterian Church in Ireland* (C. Aitchison, 1867).

Kilroy, Phil, *Protestant Dissent and Controversy in Ireland 1660–1714* (Cork University Press, 1994).

Kinealy, Christine and Parkhill, Trevor (eds), *The Famine in Ulster* (Ulster Historical Foundation, 1997).

Kirkpatrick, Lawrence, *Presbyterians in Ireland: An Illustrated History* (Booklink, 2007).

Lane, Fintan, *The Origins of Modern Irish Socialism 1881–1896* (Cork University Press, 1997).

Latimer, W.T., *Ulster Biographies: Chiefly Relating to the Rebellion of 1798* (William Mullan, 1897).

Luddy, Maria, *Women and Philanthropy in Nineteenth-Century Ireland* (Cambridge University Press, 1995).

Lyttle, Richard, *Report of the Special Committee of the Ulster Tenants' Defence Association: On the Report of the Fry Commission on the Working of the Irish Land Acts; and Also, an Argument and Speech on the Ulster Custom Commission* (Ulster Tenants' Defence Association, 1898).

Lyttle, W.G., *Betsy Gray: Hearts of Down* (*Mourne Observer*, 1968).

MacConnell, James, *Fasti of the Irish Presbyterian Church, 1613–1840* (Presbyterian Historical Society of Ireland, 1951).

MacMillan, Rev. John, 'Account of the Life of Rev. D.G. Brown' (written *c.* 1930) in *Journal of the Creggan History Society* (Creggan History Society, 1990).

Magee, Hamilton, *Fifty Years in the Irish Mission* (Presbyterian Church in Ireland, 1890).

Maguire, W.A., 'Arthur McMahon: United Irishman and French Soldier' *Irish Sword*, no. ix (Military History Society of Ireland, 1970).

Malcolm A.G., *The Sanitary State of Belfast* (Belfast, 1852).

Malcolm, A.G., *History of the General Hospital and other Medical Institutions in Belfast* (W. & G. Agnew, 1851).

Mallie, Eamonn and McKittrick, David, *Endgame in Ireland* (Coronet Books, 2002).

Mayer, J. Eric, *A Song of Forgiveness: True stories of lives changed by the power of forgiveness* (Kingsway Publications, 1988).

McBride, Ian, *Scripture Politics: Ulster Presbyterians and Irish Radicalism in the Late Eighteenth Century* (Oxford University Press, 1998).

McBride, Ian, 'Presbyterians in the Penal Era' in *Bulletin of the Presbyterian Historical Society of Ireland*, no. 27, 1998–2000 (Presbyterian Historical Society of Ireland, 2000).

McBride, Ian, *Eighteenth Century Ireland: The Isle of Slaves (New Gill History of Ireland)* (Gill & Macmillan, 2009).

McCabe, John A., 'A United Irish Family: the McCabes of Belfast' in *Familia: Ulster Genealogical Review*, no. 13 (Ulster Historical Foundation, 1997).

McCann, P.J.O., 'Irish Protestant Home Rule Association and Nationalist Politics 1886–1893' (unpublished MA thesis, 1972).

McConnell, G.B.G., *Memoir of an Unrepentant Liberal* (G.B.G. McConnell, 2001).

McCracken, J.L., 'Liberalism under the Union: Three generations of an Irish Liberal family' in *Familia: Ulster Genealogical Review*, no. 17 (Ulster Historical Foundation, 2001).

McCracken, J.L., *New Light at the Cape of Good Hope: William Porter the Father of Cape Liberalism* (Ulster Historical Foundation, 1993).

McCreery, Rev. Alexander, *Presbyterian Ministers of Killyleagh* (Belfast, 1875).

McElroy, Samuel, *The Route Land Crusade* (Coleraine, undated).

McEvoy, Brendan, 'The United Irishmen in County Tyrone' *Seanchas Ardmhacha: Journal of the Armagh Diocesan Historical Society*, vol. 3, no. 2 (Cumann Seanchais Ard Mhacha/Armagh Diocesan Historical Society, 1959).

McFadden, Owen, *The Century Speaks: Ulster Voices* (Gill & Macmillan, 1999).

McFarland, E.W., *John Ferguson 1836–1906: Irish Issues in Scottish Politics* (Tuckwell Press, 2003).

McGeachy, Neill Roderick, *A History of Sugaw Creek Presbyterian Church, Mecklenburg Presbytery, Charlotte, North Carolina* (Rock Hill SC, 1954).

McGimpsey, Christopher, D., '"To raise the banner in the remote north"; politics in County Monaghan, 1868–1883' (unpublished Ph.D. thesis, University of Edinburgh, 1982).

McGougan, Jack, 'Letting Labour Lead: Jack McGougan and the Pursuit of unity, 1913–1958', *Saothar: Journal of the Irish Labour Historical Society*, no. 14 (Irish Labour Historical Society, 1989), pp 113–24.

McIlroy, Archibald, *When the Lint was in the Bell* (McCaw, Stevenson and Orr, 1897).

McIlwaine, William, 'A lecture by Rev. William M'Ilwaine, An addressed to the members of the congregation' (Aughnacloy, 1887).

McIlwaine, William, 'A recent chapter on our congregational history and a thought bearing on the century yet in its infancy' (1902).

McIlwaine, William, 'A retrospection and outlook' (1901).

McIntosh, Gillian, *The Force of Culture – Unionist Identities in Twentieth Century Ireland* (Cork University Press, 1999).

McIvor, John A., *Popular Education in the Irish Presbyterian Church* (Scepter Publishers Ltd., 1969).

McKay, Susan, *Northern Protestants – An unsettled People* (Blackstaff Press, 2005).

McKnight Thomas, *Ulster as it is* (Macmillan & Co., 1896).

McLachlan, Peter, 'Rainbows and Religion' in *A Journal for CR Trainers and Practitioners*, no. 8, Winter 1994/5 (NI Community Relations Council, 1994/5).

McMahon, Sean, *Sam Hanna Bell – a biography* (Blackstaff Press, 1999).

McMillan, William, 'The Subscription Controversy in Irish Presbyterianism from the Plantation of Ulster to the Present Day with Reference to its Political Implications in the Late Eighteenth Century' (unpublished MA thesis, Manchester University, 1953).

McMillan, William, 'Presbyterian Ministers and the Ulster Rising' in *Protestant, Catholic and Dissenter: The Clergy and 1798*, Liam Swords (ed.) (Columba Press, 1997), pp 81–117.

McMinn, J.R.B., 'Rev. James Brown Armour and Liberal Politics in North Antrim' (unpublished Ph.D. thesis, Queen's University Belfast, 1979).

McMinn, J.R.B., 'Presbyterianism and Politics in Ulster 1871–1906' in *Studia Hibernica*, no. 21 (St Patrick's College Drumcondra, 1981), pp 127–40.

McMinn, J.R.B., 'Liberalism in North Antrim 1900–14' in *Irish Historical Studies*, XXII, no. 89 (Irish Historical Studies, 1982), pp 17–29.

McMinn, J.R.B., *Against the Tide: J B Armour Irish Presbyterian and Home Ruler* (Public Record Office of Northern Ireland, 1985).

McNeill, Mary, *The Life and Times of Mary Ann McCracken, 1770–1866: A Belfast Panorama* (A. Figgis, 1960).

McNeill, Mary, *Vere Foster, 1819–1900: An Irish Benefactor* (David & Charles, 1971).

McRedmond, Louis, *Modern Irish Lives: A Dictionary of Twentieth-Century Biography* (Gill & Macmillan, 1998).

McSkimin, Samuel, *Annals of Ulster; or, Ireland fifty years ago* (1849).

Miller, Kerby A., Schrier, Arnold, Boling, Bruce D. and Doyle, David N., *Irish Immigrants in the Land of Canaan* (Oxford University Press, 2003).

Millin, S. Shannon, *A History of Second Congregation Belfast, 1708–1896* (Belfast, 1900).

Millin, S. Shannon, *Additional Highlights on Belfast History* (Belfast, 1938)

Millin, S. Shannon, papers to the Statistical Society: 'Our Society: its aims and achievements' in *Journal of the Statistical and Social Inquiry Society of Ireland*, vol. XIII, part XCVII (Statistical and Social Inquiry Society of Ireland, 1917–19); 'Slums: A Sociological Retrospective of the City of Dublin' in *Journal of the Statistical and Social Inquiry Society of Ireland*, vol. XIII, part XCIV (1913–1914); and 'Child Life as a National Asset' in *Journal of The Statistical and Social Inquiry Society of Ireland*, vol. xiii, part XCVI (1915–17).

Millin, S. Shannon, *Sidelights on Belfast History* (Belfast, 1932).

Mitchell, Arthur, *Revolutionary Government in Ireland* (Gill & Macmillan, 1995).

Montgomery, Henry, 'Letter to Daniel O'Connell', *A Belfast Magazine*, vol. 4, no. 1 (Belfast, 1831).

Montgomery, Henry, 'Outline of the History of Presbyterianism in Ireland' serialised in *The Non-Subscribing Presbyterian* (Belfast, 1925).

Moody, T.W., *Davitt and the Irish Revolution 1846–82* (Oxford University Press, 1981).

Morgan, Austen, *Labour and Partition: The Belfast Working Class 1905–23* (Pluto Press, 1991).

Morley, Louise and Walsh, Val., *Breaking Boundaries: Women in Higher Education* (Taylor and Francis, 1996).

Morrill, Dan, 'A History of Charlotte and Mecklenburg County' available online at: www.danandmary.com/historyofcharlotteabs.htm.

Morrow, John, *On the Road of Reconciliation: A Brief Memoir* (Columba Press, 2003).

Mullin, Julia E., *A History of Dunluce Presbyterian Church* (Dunluce Presbyterian Church, 1994).

Mullin, Julia E., *The Kirk of Ballywillin since the Scottish Settlement* (*Belfast Newsletter*, 1961).

Mullin, Julia E., *The Presbytery of Coleraine* (*Belfast Newsletter*, 1979).

Munck, R., Rolston, B., and Moore, G., *Belfast in the Thirties: an oral history* (Blackstaff Press, 1987).

Murnane, James H. and Murnane, Peadar, *At the Ford of the Birches: The History of Ballybay, Its People and Vicinity* (Murnane Brothers, 1999).

Nelson, John W., 'The Belfast Presbyterians 1670–1830: an analysis of their political and social interests' (unpublished Ph.D. thesis, Queen's University Belfast, 1986).

Nelson, John W., 'Remember Orr' in *Bulletin of the Presbyterian Historical Society in Ireland*, vol. 27 (Presbyterian Historical Society of Ireland, 1998–2000).

Nelson, Julie Louise, '"Violently Democratic and Anti-Conservative"? An analysis of Presbyterian "radicalism" in Ulster, *c.* 1800–1852' (unpublished Ph.D. thesis, Durham University, 2005).

Nesbitt, David, *Full Circle: A Story of Ballybay Presbyterians* (Cahans Publications, 1999).

Newman, Kate, *Dictionary of Ulster Biography* (Institute of Irish Studies, Queen's University Belfast, 1993).

Norwood, John, 'On the Working of the Sanitary Laws in Dublin, with uggestions for their Amendment' in *Journal of the Statistical and Social Inquiry Society of Ireland*, vol. VI, part XLIII (Dublin, 1872/1973), pp 230–42.

Ó Catháin, Máirtin Sean, *Irish Republicanism in Scotland 1858–1916: Fenians in Exile* (Irish Academic Press, 2007).

O Saothrai, Seamus, 'Patrick Adair – Minister of Cairncastle and Belfast, 1624–1694' (Glens of Antrim Historical Society, 1983) available online at: www.antrimhistory.net/patrick-adair-of-cairncastle.

O Saothrai, Seamus, 'Walter Graham of Maghera, United Irishman' in *Ulster Local Studies*, 9 (1984) and 13 (1991).

Ó Snodaigh, Padraig, *Hidden Ulster – Protestants and the Irish Language* (Lagan Press, 1995).

O'Brien, G., and Roebuck, P. (eds), *Nine Ulster Lives* (Ulster Historical Foundation, 1993).

O'Byrne, Cathal, *As I Roved Out: A Book of the North, Being a Series of Historical Sketches of Ulster and Old Belfast* (Blackstaff Press, 1982).

O'Neill, F.W.S., *The Call of the East: Sketches from the History of the Irish Mission to Manchuria 1869–1919* (James Clark, 1919).

O'Neill, F.W.S., *The Quest for God in China* (Allen & Unwin, 1925).

O'Regan, Raymond, *Hidden Belfast: A Secret History: Benevolence, Blackguards and Balloon Heads* (Mercier Press, 2010).

Oldfield, Sybil, *Women Humanitarians: Doers of the Word – a biographical dictionary of British women active between 1900 and 1950* (Continuum, 2001).

Oxford Dictionary of National Biography (Oxford University Press, 2004–05).

Patterson, Carlisle, *Over the Hill: Ecumenism in the Irish Presbyterian Church* (Ulster Services, 1997).

Patton, W. Donald, *Ebb and Flow: Essays in Church History in Honour of R. Finlay G. Holmes* (Presbyterian Historical Society of Ireland, 2002).

Peatling, G.K., 'Whatever happened to Presbyterian radicalism? The Ulster Presbyterian liberal press in the late nineteenth century' in Roger Swift and Christine Kinealy (eds), *Politics and power in Victorian Ireland* (Four Courts Press, 2006).

Pollak, Andy (ed.), *A Citizens' Inquiry: The Opshal Report on Northern Ireland* (Lilliput, 1993).

Porter, Classon Emmet, *Congregational memoirs of the Old Congregation of Larne and Kilwaughter* McIlrath R.H., and Nelson, J.W. (eds), (Larne, 1975).

Prenter, Samuel, *The Life and Labours of William Johnston D.D., Belfast* (Sabbath-School Society of the Presbyterian Church, 1895).

Reid, James Seaton, *The History of the Presbyterian Church in Ireland*, vols I, II & (with W.D. Killen) III (Presbyterian Church in Ireland, 1834–67).

Reid, Tom, 'Richard Smyth: Churchman, Theologian, Social Reformer' in *Bulletin of the Presbyterian Historical Society of Ireland*, vol. 28 (Presbyterian Historical Society of Ireland, 2001/03).

Richer, William, *Despair to Resurrection: First Lisburn Presbyterian Church 1688–1988* (First Lisburn Presbyterian Church, 1988).

Ross, David, *Ireland: History of a Nation* (Lagan Books, 2005).

Rowlands, Jean, 'James Haughton and Young Ireland Carloviana', *Journal of the Old Carlow Society* (Old Carlow Society, 1971).

Rutherford, James S., *Christian Reunion in Ireland* (Friends of Reunion, Irish Branch, 1942).

Rutherford, John, 'Ulster tenant farmers' property in the soil' speech at the Grand Tenant-Right Demonstration in Banbridge on 28 January 1850.

Scott, Ernest M., and Robinson, Philip, *The Country Rhymes of Samuel Thomson – the bard of Carngranny 1766–1816* (Pretani Press, 1992).

Scott, Hew, *Fasti Ecclesiæ Scoticanæ: the succession of ministers in the Church of Scotland from the reformation 1791–1872* (Edinburgh, 1915).

Seery, James, Holmes, Finlay and Stewart, A.T.Q., *Presbyterians, The United Irishmen and 1798* (Presbyterian Historical Society of Ireland, 2000).

Sinnerton, Henry, *David Ervine: Unchartered Waters* (Brandon, 2002).

Sloane, William Milligan (ed.), *The life of James McCosh: A Record Chiefly Autobiographical* (T. & T. Clarke, 1896).

Smyth, Denis, *Poet of the People: Thomas Carnduff 1886–1956 – a Belfast Man, a brief Story of His Life, Times and Literary Works* (Belfast, 1992).

Smyth, Geraldine, 'Peace Ten Years On – Where Are the Churches Now?' in *Beyond Sectarianism? The Churches and Ten Years of the Peace Process*, vol. 1 (Northern Ireland Community Relations Council, 2005).

Smyth, Marie & Fay, Marie-Therese, *Personal accounts from Northern Ireland's Troubles: public conflict, private loss* (Pluto Press, 2000).

Sorrells, Nancy, 'Fanning the flames of Revolution from the Presbyterian Pulpit: John Glendy, Irish and American Revolutionary' in *Familia: Ulster Genealogical Review*, no. 18 (Ulster Historical Foundation, 2002).

South, Heather, 'William Martin, Covenanter, Preacher and Revolutionary Patriot' in *Familia: Ulster Genealogical Review*, no. 18 (Ulster Historical Foundation, 2002).

Stallworthy, Jon, *Louis MacNeice* (Faber and Faber, 1995).

Staunton, Enda, *The Nationalists of Northern Ireland 1918–1973* (Columba Press, 2001).

Steers, David, 'Obituary of Mrs Ruby Purdy' in *The Non-Subscribing Presbyterian*, no. 1236 (November 2009).

Stenton, Michael and Lees, Stephen, *Who's Who of British Members of Parliament: a biographical dictionary of the House of Commons based on annual volumes of Dod's Parliamentary companion and other sources*, Michael Stenton (ed.) (Hassocks: Harvester Press, 1976).

Stephenson, Jean, *Scotch-Irish Migration to South Carolina, 1772: Rev. William Martin and his five shiploads of settlers* (Washington, 1971).

Stevens, David, 'The Churches and ten years of the Peace Process' *Beyond Sectarianism? The Churches and Ten Years of the Peace Process*, vol. 1 (Northern Ireland Community Relations Council, 2005).

Stevens, David, *The Land of Unlikeness: Explorations into Reconciliation* (Columba Press, 2004).

Stewart, A.T.Q., *A Deeper Silence: The Hidden Origins of the United Irishmen* (Faber and Faber, 1993).

Stewart, A.T.Q., *The Summer Soldiers: The 1798 Rebellion in Antrim and Down* (Blackstaff Press, 1995).

Stewart, C.W.V., 'Dr. William Stokes' in *A Compendium of Irish Biography* (Gill & Son, 1878), accessed 20 March 2013 from www.libraryireland.com/biography/DrWhitleyStokes.php.

Stewart, David, *A Short History of the Presbyterian Church in Ireland* (Sabbath School Society for Ireland, 1936).

Stewart, David, *Seceders in Ireland: With Annals of their Congregations* (Presbyterian Historical Society of Ireland, 1950).

Strain, R.W.M., *Belfast and its Charitable Society* (Oxford University Press, 1961).

Strain, R.W.M., 'Address to Ulster Medical Society on 3rd November 1970' in *Ulster Medical Journal*, vol. 40, no. 17 (Ulster Medical Society, 1970).

Swords, Liam (ed.), *Protestant, Catholic & Dissenter: The Clergy and 1798* (Columba Press, 1997).

Taggart, Norman W., *Conflict, Controversy and Co-operation: The Irish Council of Churches and 'the Troubles' 1968–1972* (Columba Press, 2004).

Taylor, Peter, *Loyalists* (Bloomsbury, 2000).

Thom, A., *Thom's Irish Who's Who* (A. Thom & Co., 1923).

Thompson, Frank, *The End of Liberal Ulster: Land Agitation and Land reform, 1868–86* (Ulster Historical Foundation, 2002).

Thompson, Jack (ed.), *Into All the World: A history of the overseas work of the Presbyterian Church in Ireland 1840/1990* (Overseas Board of the Presbyterian Church in Ireland, 1990).

Toland, John, *Christianity not Mysterious: Text, Associated Works and Critical Essays* (Lilliput Press, 1997).

Urquhart, Diane, '"An articulate and definite cry for freedom": the Ulster suffrage movement' in *Women's History Review*, vol. 1, no. 2 (Routledge, 2002).

Vance, Norman, *Irish Literature: a Social History – tradition, identity and difference* (Basil Blackwell, 1990).

Waddell, Harry C., *John Waddell* (*Belfast Newsletter*, 1949).

Walker, B.M. (ed.), *Parliamentary election results in Ireland 1918–92: Irish Elections to Parliaments and Parliamentary Assemblies at Westminster, Belfast, Dublin and Strasbourg* (Royal Irish Academy/Institute for Irish Studies, Queen's University Belfast, 1992).

Walker, B.M., *Ulster Politics: The Formative Years, 1868–86* (Ulster Historical Foundation and Institute of Irish Studies, Queen's University Belfast, 1989).

Walker, B.M. and McCreary, Alf, *Degrees of Excellence: the story of Queen's, Belfast, 1845–1995* (Institute of Irish Studies, Queen's University Belfast, 1994).

Walker, Graham, *The Politics of Frustration: Harry Midgley and the failure of Labour in Northern Ireland* (Manchester University Press, 1985).

Walker, Graham, 'Thomas Sinclair: Presbyterian Liberal Unionist' in Richard English and Graham Walker (eds), *Unionism in Modern Ireland: new perspectives on politics and culture* (Palgrave MacMillan, 1996).

Wallace, Martin, *Famous Irish Lives* (Appletree Press, 1999).

Webb, Alfred, *A Compendium of Irish Biography* (Gill & Son, 1878) (online version at BooksUlster.com).

Weller, Ken, *Don't be a Soldier!: The Radical Anti-War Movement in North London, 1914–18* (Journeyman Books, 1985).

Wells, Roland A., *Friendship towards Peace: The Journey of Ken Newell and Gerry Reynolds* (Columba Press, 2005).

Whelan, Fergus, *Dissent into Treason: Unitarians, Kingkillers and the Society of United Irishmen* (Brandon, 2010).

Who's Who in Northern Ireland (3rd ed., Inglewood Books, 2002).

Wilson, David A. and Spencer, Mark G. (eds), *Ulster Presbyterians in the Atlantic World: religion, politics and identity* (Four Courts Press, 2006).

Wilson, David A., *United Irishmen, United States: Immigrant Radicals in the Early Republic* (Cornell University Press, 1998).

Wilson, David, 'Sketch of the Wilson Family' (handwritten manuscript).

Wilson, William, *A catechism of tenant-right; being an attempt to set forth and defend the rights of tenant-farmers [in Ireland] ... By the Secretary of a Tenant-Right Association* (Belfast, 1850), (in the British Library).

Witherow, Rev. Thomas, *Historical Sketch of The Presbyterian Church in Ireland* (1858, new edition by Braid Books and Moyola Books, 1994).

Woods, Margaret G. (ed.), *Occasional papers by James Johnston Shaw* (Dublin, 1910).

Wright, Frank, *Two lands on one soil: Ulster politics before Home Rule* (Gill & Macmillan, 1996).

Young, Robert M., *Belfast and the Province of Ulster in the Twentieth Century* (W.T. Pike, 1909).

Websites

Biographical Directory of the United States Congress (http://bioguide.congress.gov/biosearch/biosearch.asp).

Broomall Reformed Presbyterian Church (www.broomallrpc.org).

Cahans Project Website (http://homepage.eircom.net/~denesbitt/menu.html).

Covenanted Reformed Presbyterian Church website (www.truecovenantor.com).

Donegal Presbyterian Church (www.donegalpresbyterianchurch.com).

Eddies Book of Extracts – Presbyterian Churches of Ballymoney, County Antrim (freepages.genealogy. rootsweb.ancestry.com/~econnolly/books/churchesofballymoney/firstchurch.html).

Geocities (website no longer available).

Hansard and Official Reports for the UK (www.TheyWorkForYou.com).

House of Lord website (www.parliament.uk/business/lords/).

Irish Democrat (www.irishdemocrat.co.uk).

St Mary's Church of Ireland Carrigaline (www.carrigalineparish.ie/index.php/ourparish/).

Searc's Web Guide to Irish History (www.searcs-web.com/hist.html).

South Armagh Genealogical Project (http://creggan.armagh.anglican.org/fifth.html).

Interviews
Author with John Dunlop.
Author with Rev. John Watson.
Author with David Lapsley.
Author with John Morrow.
Author telephone interview with Joyce Moran.

Correspondence
Correspondence with Heather and Fiona McLachlan.
Additional information provided on Rev. Billy Moran by his wife, Joyce Moran.
Notes on Non-Subscribing Presbyterian ministers provided by Rev. John Nelson.

Newspapers
Bangor Spectator.
Belfast Telegraph.
Coleraine Constitution.
Irish Democrat (website).
Northern Constitution.
Northern Whig.
Presbyterian Herald.

Television
RTÉ, *Would you Believe*, (broadcast March 2007).
UTV, *May Blood interview with Gerry Kelly*, (broadcast 26 April 2006).

Index of Biographies

Index of Congregations